lonely planet

Oman, UAE
& Arabian
Peninsula

D0860914

Kuwait
p94

Bahrain
p56

Oman
p130

Qatar
p237

United Arab
Emirates
p323

Saudi
Arabia
p272

Oman
p130

Yemen
p419

Jenny Walker, Jessica Lee, Jade Bremner,
Tharik Hussain, Josephine Quintero

Contents

PLAN YOUR TRIP

ON THE ROAD

GRAND MOSQUE, MUSCAT P140

GRAND PRIX, BAHRAIN P85

Contents

KHOR IN OMAN P130

ON THE ROAD

AL NOOR MOSQUE,
SHARJAH P355

FRANS SELLIES/GETTY IMAGES ©

Contents

BUR DUBAI SOUQ, DUBAI
P328

ABRAR SHARIF/SHUTTERSTOCK ©

WADI DARBAT, OMAN P213

Welcome to Oman, UAE & Arabian Peninsula

The spectacular emptiness of the Arabian landscape provides a blank canvas upon which is projected a riot of cultural, religious, intellectual and trading wonders.

The Desert

In describing his travels with the Bedouin across the Empty Quarter, 20th-century desert explorer Wilfred Thesiger acknowledged the power of the desert to leave an imprint on the imagination. This austere allure has attracted travellers to Arabia for centuries: Ibn Battuta, Marco Polo and TE Lawrence (Lawrence of Arabia) are among many famous explorers beguiled by the beauty and challenge of the barren landscapes. Thankfully, modern desert-goers no longer need risk life and limb to venture into the wilderness, as roads and camps make encounters with this inspiring landscape possible for all.

Urban Landscapes

When asked what they most like about their land of sand dunes, the Bedouin near Al Hashman in Oman reply that they enjoy coming to town. Town! This is the Arabia of the 21st century, built on oil and banking – sophisticated communities looking to the future and creating empires out of sand, or at least on land reclaimed from the sea. For those looking for a dynamic urban experience, the Gulf cities are the place to find it. With high incomes per capita, elegant towers, opulent hotels and eccentric malls, these cities offer the 'pleasure domes' of the modern world.

Legendary Hospitality

The essence of the Arabian Peninsula lies in its people: good-naturedly haggling in souqs, cursing on long journeys, sharing sweet tea on the edges of wild places. Unifying all is Islam, a way of life, the call to prayer carried on an inland breeze, a gentle hospitality extended towards strangers. This is what many travellers most remember of their visit here – the ancient tradition of sharing 'bread and salt' and of ensuring safe passage, albeit in a modern context. Visitors can expect friendly exchange as equally in supermarkets as in remote desert villages.

Cultural Riches

It's hard to think of Arabia without conjuring the Queen of Sheba and camel caravans bearing frankincense from Dhofar in Oman; dhows laden with pearls from Dilmun; the ruins of empire in Saudi Arabia's Madain Saleh. The caravans and dhows may be plying different trades these days, but the lexicon of *The Thousand and One Nights* that brought Scheherazade's exotic, vulnerable world to the West still helps define the Peninsula today. Visit a fort, barter in a souq or step into labyrinthine alleyways and you'll immediately discover the perennial magic of Arabia.

Why I Love the Arabian Peninsula

By Jenny Walker, Writer

Mention 'Arabia' and a host of familiar, media-weary images probably appear. I've spent half my life studying these images – of wilderness, wealth and war – in various academic pursuits. But there's so much more to the sophisticated culture of modern Arabia than is conjured by these stereotypes. I love the Peninsula because each day I encounter the complexity of Arabia in the dynamic, warm-hearted people who lie at the core of the region's enduring appeal. And of course the desert, with its life against the odds, has inevitably crept into my soul.

For more about our writers, see p512

Above: Prophet's Mosque, Medina (p293)

Oman, UAE & Arabian Peninsula

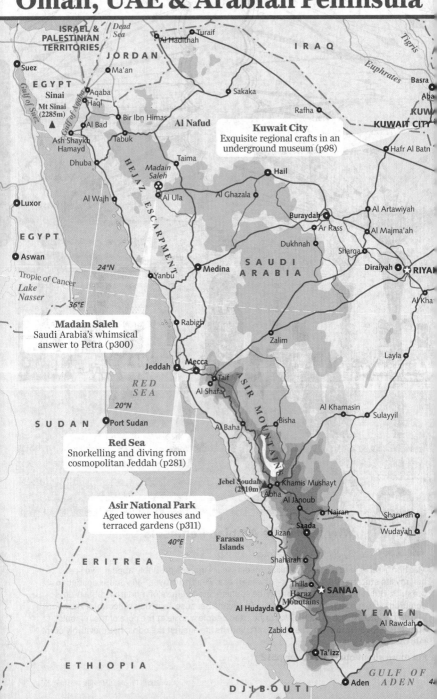

Kuwait City
Exquisite regional crafts in an underground museum (p98)

Madain Saleh
Saudi Arabia's whimsical answer to Petra (p300)

Red Sea
Snorkelling and diving from cosmopolitan Jeddah (p281)

Asir National Park
Aged tower houses and terraced gardens (p311)

⊕N 0 — 300 km
0 — 150 miles

Bahrain Fort
One of Arabia's
thousand forts (p81)

Dubai
Burj Khalifa: A modern-day
architectural icon (p327)

AFGHANISTAN

IRAN

PAKISTAN

● Shiraz

Sharjah
The region's densest
museum cluster (p354)

Doha
Restored old quarter abuzz
with new life (p239)

Mutrah Souq
Shop for frankincense in a
traditional bazaar (p135)

● Bandar-e Abbas

*Straight
of Hormuz*

Ras Al Jinz
Turtles returning to the
beach of their birth (p163)

riyah

● Jubail
Qatif ● ● Dammam
hahran ● ● ◉ MANAMA
Khobar BAHRAIN
QATAR ⊛ DOHA
lofuf ● ●
**Al Nasa
Oasis**
● Haradh

Ras Al
Khaimah
Ajman ●
Sharjah ●
Dubai ●

Musandam
Peninsula
● Dibba OMAN
● Fujairah

THE
GULF

⊛ ABU
DHABI

UNITED ARAB
EMIRATES

● Al Ain

Buraimi ● Sohar
●

Barka

*GULF OF
OMAN*

24°N

Tropic of Cancer

⊛ MUSCAT

Hajar Mountains
Jebel Akhdar
Jebel Shams ▲
Nizwa ●

Sur ● Ras Al
Hadd

Sharqiya

Sharqiya ● Al Ashkharah
Sands

⚓ Liwa

Khor Al Adaid
Off-road adventure around
an inland sea (p262)

SAUDI
ARABIA

Abu Dhabi
Graced by a magnificent
grand mosque (p370)

Hajar Mountains
Villages perched over the
vertical (p175)

The Empty
Quarter

Haima ●

● Duqm

*Gulf of
Masirah*

Masirah
Island

20°N

O M A N

*Suqrah
Bay*

● Shwaymiyah

Sharqiya Sands
Magical dunes fringed
with oases (p173)

*ARABIAN
SEA*

Kuria Muria
Islands

Dhofar ● Taqah
● ● Mirbat
Salalah
● Sarfait

16°N

adi
ramawt

Al Ghayda ● *Ghubbat
Al Qamar*
Ras Fartak

ELEVATION

2500m
2000m
1500m
1000m
500m
0

● Qusay'ir

Al Mukalla ●

ir 'Ali

Dhofar
Camels and cows graze on
green pastures (p206)

**Socotra Island
(Yemen)**

52°E

56°E

12°N

Arabian Peninsula's
Top 15

Sheikh Zayed Grand Mosque

1 In Arabia, the birthplace of Islam, faith is a living, breathing reality inextricably entwined in the daily lives of Peninsula inhabitants. Travellers will encounter it in the ubiquitous call to prayer, the warmth of welcome enshrined in the Muslim code of conduct and, for Muslim visitors, quintessentially in pilgrimage to the holy cities of Saudi Arabia. Visit magnificent Sheikh Zayed Grand Mosque (p373) in Abu Dhabi and see how faith is also expressed in masterpieces of architecture, carpet and landscape design.

Museum of Islamic Art

2 Vying with the Louvre Abu Dhabi as the best museum in the Middle East, Doha's Museum of Islamic Art (p241) narrowly wins with its priceless collection of hand-loomed carpets, ceramics and manuscripts, all of which help establish a broader cultural context for a visit to the region. Visitors may be surprised at the number of animal-themed items in the collection, dispelling the myth that Islamic art is only geometric in style and abstract in content. IM Pei's exciting contemporary building, in which the collection is housed, further dispels myths about Arabia's traditionalism.

MIKE FUCHSLOCHER/SHUTTERSTOCK ©

ZRIBIS/SHUTTERSTOCK ©

Burj Khalifa

3 Competitively slicing the sky, the audacious tower blocks that rise from the cities of the Gulf are a potent symbol of the region's ambitions. At 828m, Dubai's Burj Khalifa (p330) held the title of tallest building in the world for over a decade. Dine on top of this futuristic totem of steel and glass and escape the hurly-burly of the streets below: at this altitude, and lifted far above the ordinary cares of a routine day, you can quite literally have your head in the clouds.

Hajar Mountains

4 In contrast to its vast interior desert plains, the Peninsula also boasts some of the highest mountains and deepest wadis (dry riverbeds) in the Middle East. Camp near the summit of Oman's Hajar Mountains (p175) in winter for the exciting spectacle of hail thundering into the wadis below. Rain breaks on these mountains sporadically all year: watch how the precious water is channelled through ancient irrigation systems (known as *aflaj*) to bring life to plantations and a network of the nearby high-altitude villages. Below: Bilad Sayt (p183), Hajar Mountains

ESHEREZ/SHUTTERSTOCK ©

Madain Saleh – Saudi Arabia's Petra

5 They rise out of the gravel plains like lost camels, or sit crumbling to dust on mountain ridges, speaking of past greatness, prophets, kings and long-forgotten dynasties. Among the best preserved of these ruins of empire are the superb Nabataean ruins at Madain Saleh (p300). Smaller in number than similar rock-carved tombs in Jordan's Petra, the tombs here are just as impressive in terms of size and location. Sitting among these ruins on remote plains, it's easy to contemplate human frailty.

Sharjah

6 It may not generate the headlines of neighbouring Dubai or the sophisticated capital, Abu Dhabi, but Sharjah (p354) has quietly grown into the cultural hub of Arabia. In a celebration of local and indigenous heritage, Sharjah boasts the largest cluster of museums in the region with gems such as the Sharjah Heritage Museum among them. With the historic old quarter and chaotic alleyways undergoing major renovation in a project called 'Heart of Sharjah', the city offers a sense of ancient Arabia in the midst of the modern.

H. MARK WEIDMAN PHOTOGRAPHY / ALAMY STOCK PHOTO ©

Asir National Park

7 Many villages in Arabia survive on the spring water issuing from mountain wadis, often transported for many kilometres through irrigation channels. Plantation life along these channels offers the off-roader or hiker a fascinating glimpse into an ancient way of life. Asir National Park (p311) of Saudi Arabia, with its aged tower houses and green terraces, is one of the best places on the Peninsula to witness this traditional village life. The region is also one of Arabia's most spectacular, with an escarpment that tumbles thousands of feet to the Red Sea.

Mutrah Souq

8 They may not match the stock exchanges of New York, London or Tokyo in terms of dollars traded, but Arabia's souqs claim a far more ancient lineage. Get lost in Muscat's labyrinthine Mutrah Souq (p135), and participate in the brisk trade in frankincense or haggle-to-the-death of cloth merchants. The souq's covered alleyways cover commodities of monetary value (such as gold, diamonds and rubies), small-change items of sentimental value (such as baskets and beads) and memorable chats with shopkeepers. *Above right: embroidered items for sale in Mutrah Souq*

Souq Waqif

9 Many of Arabia's old town quarters have been restored in a bid to attract tourists. Crumbling mud-brick houses and old derelict bazaars have been brought back to life through new heritage guesthouses and local-cuisine restaurants. One of the best of these restoration projects is Souq Waqif (p239), in Doha, where you can buy anything from a shisha water pipe to a falcon. Teeming with life, particularly at night, the souq has become a popular social space with museums, art spaces and coffeehouses. *Opposite page top: Qatari man with hunting falcon at Souq Waqif*

Ras Al Jinz Turtle Reserve

10 Protecting an internationally important nesting site for the endangered green turtle, the Ras Al Jinz Turtle Reserve (p163) offers visitors a rare opportunity to watch these magnificent giants up close. Returning to lay eggs on the beach of their birth, green turtles are a common sight in the waters around Oman. The chance to see these extraordinary creatures and a number of playful cetaceans makes boats trips from any point along the shore of the eastern Arabian Peninsula a rewarding experience. Right: green turtle at Ras Al Jinz

NICOLA MESSANA PHOTOS/SHUTTERSTOCK ©

Bahrain Fort & Museum

11 Cresting a hilltop, guarding a coastline, walling a village or securing a dried-out riverbed, there is barely a town in Arabia without some kind of crumbling battlement. Oman has some of the best preserved of the Peninsula's forts in Bahla, Nizwa, Nakhal and Rustaq, but for a whole day out, Bahrain's fort (p81) with its museum, coffeehouse and night-time illuminations, is hard to beat. Learn to tell your forts (military only) from your castles (fortified residences) before exploring some of these mighty and magnificent buildings.

Red Sea Diving

12 Flanking the shores of Saudi Arabia, the crystal-clear waters of the Red Sea are home to epic dramas. In some of the world's finest diving sites, clown fish play the comedians in coral gardens fit for a Zeffirelli stage set, while sharks wait in the wings for heroic small fry. You don't need to dive for a balcony view: don a mask, snorkel and flippers and swim anywhere off the coast at Jeddah (p281), and you can't help but applaud the spectacle.
Bottom: Clownfish in the Red Sea

Sharqiya Sands

13 For centuries, Westerners have been attracted to the great desert wildernesses of Arabia, drawn by its limitlessness yet repelled by the void. Feel the desert's magnetic pull in Oman's Sharqiya Sands (p173), with tented camps and camel trips providing access to the magical dunes. Avoid the off-road playgrounds at the desert fringe and choose more sensitive hiking forays into its quiet centre – the habitat of highly adapted flora and fauna. Beware: the summer sands don't take prisoners, and the only stranger you're likely to meet between the dunes s yourself.

Dhofar, the Land of Frankincense

14 Gifted by wise men to babes (according to the Bible) and queens to kings (Queen Sheba to King Solomon), and harvested from the bark of ugly trees in the mist-swirling magic of summertime in Oman, frankincense is responsible for the history of Arabian empires. Catch its tantalising aroma in the house of a newborn, buy the curdled beads of amber-coloured sap in the souq or, better still, visit the living trees in Dhofar (p206) during the region's unique and remarkable July *khareef* (rainy season). Top right: Frankincense

Tareq Rajab Museum

15 Arabia's riches can be counted by more than the latest car or designer handbag. Gold twine in a dress cuff, a bead of carnelian threaded for a loved one, a basket woven with camel leather, words of wisdom entwined in a silver amulet – these are the riches of the region's ancient craft heritage. Find the most precious pieces collected under one roof in the enchanting underground Tareq Rajab Museum (p99) in Kuwait City. Musical instruments, jewellery and ancient manuscripts comprise a collection that mercifully escaped pillage during the Iraqi invasion.

Need to Know

For more information, see Survival Guide (p469)

Currency
Bahraini dinar (BD);
Kuwaiti dinar (KD)
Omani rial (OR); Qatari
riyal (QR); Saudi riyal
(SR); UAE dirham (Dhs);
Yemeni rial

Language
Arabic, English

Visas
Visas, required by all
visitors in all Peninsula
countries except Qatar,
are available for many
nationalities on arrival at
airports and most land
borders (except Saudi
Arabia and Oman).

Money
ATMs widely available;
credit cards accepted
by most hotels and city
restaurants.

Mobile Phones
Local SIM cards are
widely available in all
cities and most airports
across the region.

Time
Saudi Arabia, Kuwait,
Bahrain and Qatar are
three hours ahead of
GMT/UTC. The United
Arab Emirates and
Oman are four hours
ahead of GMT/UTC.

When to Go

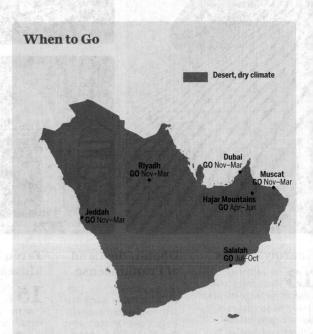

Desert, dry climate

Riyadh
GO Nov–Mar

Dubai
GO Nov–Mar

Muscat
GO Nov–Mar

Hajar Mountains
GO Apr–Jun

Jeddah
GO Nov–Mar

Salalah
GO Jul–Oct

High Season
(Nov–Mar)

➡ Perfect weather at
sea level with clear,
sunny days and cool
evenings.

➡ Shopping festivals
and sporting events
coincide with these
cooler months.

➡ Booking
accommodation is
necessary; expect
highest rates in
December.

Shoulder Season
(Jul–Oct)

➡ Good time to visit
southern Arabia with
light rains turning the
desert hills green.

➡ The *khareef*
(rainy season)
festival in southern
Oman attracts
many Gulf visitors,
leading to higher
accommodation
prices.

Low Season
(Apr–Jun)

➡ Extreme heat and
high humidity make
this a season to avoid
in most parts of
Arabia.

➡ Big discounts
often available for
accommodation.

➡ Best time to visit
mountain areas.

➡ June is harvest
time for fresh dates.

Useful Websites

Al Bab (www.al-bab.com) Links to dozens of news services, country profiles, travel sites and maps.

Al Jazeera (www.aljazeera.com/news/middleeast) Popular news- and views-oriented website.

Arabnet (www.arabnet.me) Useful Saudi-run encyclopedia of the Arab world.

InterNations (www.inter nations.org) Information service with networking opportunities exclusively for expats.

Lonely Planet (www.lonelyplanet.com) Destination information, hotel bookings, travel forum and photos.

Country Codes

Precede the following country codes with 00.

Bahrain	973
Kuwait	965
Oman	968
Qatar	974
Saudi Arabia	966
UAE	971

Exchange Rates

	US$1	UK£1	EUR €1
Bahrain (BD)	0.38	0.48	0.42
Kuwait (KD)	0.30	0.39	0.34
Oman (OR)	0.38	0.49	0.43
Qatar (QR)	3.64	4.63	4.06
Saudi Arabia (SR)	3.75	4.80	4.18
UAE (Dh)	3.67	4.67	4.09

For current exchange rates, see www.xe.com

Daily Costs

Budget: Less than US$150

➡ Shared room in budget guesthouse: US$100

➡ Street fare or self-catering at local markets: US$15

➡ Public transport and occasional taxi: US$25

➡ Entry costs: US$10

Midrange: US$150–500

➡ Double room in a midrange hotel: US$200

➡ Local-style dining in restaurants: US$30

➡ Car hire: US$100

➡ Entry costs/unguided activities: US$50

Top end: More than US$500

➡ Double room in five-star hotel or resort: US$300

➡ International-style buffet lunch/dinner: from US$50

➡ 4WD vehicle hire: US$200

➡ Entry costs/guided activities: US$100

Opening Hours

Opening times vary widely across the region and are erratic at best, all the more so during Ramadan and holidays. The weekend is Friday and Saturday in all countries except Saudi Arabia. The Saudi weekend is Thursday and Friday.

Banks 8am–noon or 1pm (closed Fridays)

Restaurants noon–midnight

Cafes 9am–midnight

Shops 10am–10pm (reduced hours Fridays)

Souqs 10am–1pm & 4–9pm (closed Friday mornings)

Arriving in the Arabian Peninsula

The main international airports are listed here. Airport taxis and hotel shuttles are the main methods of transport from airport to city centre.

Bahrain Airport (p93)

Kuwait Airport (p128)

Muscat Airport (p150), Oman

Hamad Airport (p271), Doha, Qatar

King Khalid Airport (p281); Riyadh, Saudi Arabia

Abu Dhabi Airport (p388), United Arab Emirates

Dubai International Airport (p349), United Arab Emirates

Etiquette

People are generally tolerant of social faux pas but it's best to be aware of some key aspects of etiquette:

Dress Dress modestly. See mosque etiquette p480.

Ramadan During Ramadan you must refrain from eating, drinking, smoking and chewing gum in public during daylight hours.

Left H\hand Avoid giving or touching with the left hand, which is reserved for personal hygiene.

Feet Don't show the soles of your feet to others, or walk in a house or mosque in shoes.

Shaking hands Be guided by local women as to whether they choose to shake hands with you.

Coffee Try to accept at least one cup of coffee if offered – it's considered impolite to refuse.

Manners Don't lose your temper, swear at anyone or refer to them (even in jest) as an animal (eg 'you old dog').

For info on **getting around**, see p484

PLAN YOUR TRIP NEED TO KNOW

What's New

Louvre Abu Dhabi

This fabulous new museum is famed not just for its world-class collection, but for its beautiful domed roof filtering a 'rain of light' inspired by palm trees. (p371)

Al Seef, Dubai

Stretching close to 2km along the Creek, Al Seef is a growing continuation of the historical Al Fahidi district, combining modern and heritage architecture. (p329)

Dubai Design District

This hub for creatives is luring visitors with its edgy architecture, contemporary restaurants, public art, galleries, and calendar of cultural events. (p334)

Misfat Al Abriyyin, Oman

An entire village has just discovered the value of tourism, helping to keep traditions alive in a region impacted by migration to town. (p185)

Al Baleed Resort, Salalah, Oman

This superb new luxury resort and spa, wedged between lagoon and oceanfront, is an example of understated refinement. (p210)

Mwasalat Bus Service, Oman

Formerly only accessible through taxi or car hire, key sights in Muscat are now connected to all cities by reliable public buses.

Qatar Blockade

Since June 2017, a Saudi-led coalition has isolated Qatar for alleged support for terrorism resulting in travel restrictions. (p483)

King Abdulaziz Center for World Culture, Dhahran

The stunning new 'Ithra' building looks like a space station on a foreign planet. Hosts opera, theatre and Saudi Arabia's only cinemas. (p307)

Al Shaheed Park

Kuwait's latest (and largest) urban park has jogging and walking paths covering more than 2km, botanical gardens, a lake, restaurants and two museums. (p104)

Jebel Jais

Thrill-seekers head to Ras Al Khaimah for the world's longest zip line and a via ferrata – found at the newly extended Jebel Jais. (p365)

Sheikh Faisal Bin Qassim Al Thani Museum

Offering the rare chance to cross the threshold of a rich sheikh's property; the personal belongings in this recently opened private museum include dhows and a whole Syrian house! (p260)

Third-Wave Coffee

Hip independent cafes with artisanal coffee are now to be found all over Kuwait City; try Mukha, a minimalist coffeehouse with many manual brews. (p116)

Mleiha Archaeological Site

This archaeological site, newly opened to the public, offers a day out among the remains of our ancestors, some of whom were touchingly buried with their horses and camels. (p359)

For more recommendations and reviews, see lonelyplanet.com/Destination

If You Like...

Desert Landscapes

If you thought 'desert' meant sand, think again. The Peninsula (in particular Oman, Saudi Arabia and the UAE) is full of diverse and spectacular landscapes that redefine the term.

Sharqiya Sands A fraction of the size of the Empty Quarter, these Omani dunes are just as beautiful and much more accessible. (p173)

Khor Al Adaid Qatar's inland sea, netted by high dunes, sparkling with shoals of silver sardines. (p262)

Wadi Darbat Camels and cows share abundant herbage in southern Oman's seasonal mists. (p213)

Jebel Shams Vertiginous glimpses into the Grand Canyon of Arabia from atop Oman's highest mountain. (p187)

Al Ula Saudi Arabia's magnificent wind-blown pillars of sandstone turn copper-coloured at sunset. (p299)

Liwa Oasis Date plantations punctuate the edge of the UAE's share of the Empty Quarter. (p394)

Mughsail Blowholes fling fish, seaweed and unsuspecting crabs into the air beneath Dhofar's dramatic undercliff. (p218)

Musandam Deeply incised Omani fjords with leaping dolphins and hidden villages. (p201)

Jebel Hafeet Drive to the top of this rocky spine to peer across to the Empty Quarter. (p390)

Empty Quarter Covering an area the size of France, the dunes of the Rub Al Khali conjure up your inner Bedouin. (p308)

Adventure

Travellers have been attracted to the Arabian Peninsula for centuries in search of adventure. Follow in the footsteps of Marco Polo, Richard Burton and Wilfred Thesiger in some of the region's best outdoor pursuits.

Yanbu The Red Sea offers one of the world's great underwater spectacles, accessible from this Saudi port. (p295)

Sharfat Al Alamayn Drive at high altitude through the Hajar Mountains and discover gears you didn't know you had. (p183)

Abha Go paragliding from Al Souda or rock climbing at Habalah in Saudi Arabia's dramatic Asir region. (p310)

Snake Gorge Plunge from pool to pool in one of Oman's most famous canyon adventures. (p183)

Masirah Island You won't wait long for a windy day off the western coast of Oman – perfect for kite-surfing. (p166)

Skydive Qatar Travel to earth (to the desert hinterland in Qatar specifically) at a speed of 200km per hour from a height of 4000m for the thrill of a lifetime. (p247)

Hatta Mountain Bike Trail One of only a few in the region, this trail offers more than 50km of rugged routes in the UAE. (p353)

Jebel Jais Flight Zip Line The longest zip line in the world takes thrill-seekers up to speeds of 150km per hour. (p366)

Museums

Museum of Islamic Art Doha's world-class museum is housed in an iconic IM Pei building. (p241)

Louvre Abu Dhabi This major collection includes pieces from the Paris Louvre, housed in a modern masterpiece of architecture. (p371)

Tareq Rajab Museum Stunning collection of regional crafts mercifully saved from the Gulf War devastation of Kuwait's National Museum. (p99)

Bahrain National Museum This excellent ethnographic museum in Manama proves there was indeed life before oil. (p59)

National Museum A full-scale reconstruction of a Nabataean tomb crowns Riyadh's world-class museum. (p276)

Bait Al Zubair Housed in a Muscat residence, this eclectic collection has become Oman's contemporary art hub. (p137)

Museum of the Frankincense Land Explores the supposed southern Arabian haunts of the legendary Queen of Sheba in Salalah. (p208)

Beit Al Quran Possibly the finest, most comprehensive collection of Islam's holiest book, the Quran, in the world. (p61)

Sharjah Heritage Area Museums, restored houses and souqs capture the tiny emirate's heyday. (p354)

Forts & Castles

While every country on the Arabian Peninsula has its own set of crenellations, the best forts and castles are found in eastern Arabia, keeping back trouble from the sea.

Jabreen Castle Unique painted ceilings distinguish this perfectly formed Omani castle. (p189)

Bahrain Fort Spectacular by night, Manama's fort looms over the sea. (p81)

Nakhal Fort Guarding what was once the regional capital, this fort appears to evolve from the rock. (p194)

Al Jahili Fort This Al Ain fort honours British desert veteran Wilfred Thesiger. (p390)

Fujairah Fort Part of a village reconstruction demonstrating the UAE has a history and not just a future. (p399)

Top: Boy with goat at Nizwa Souq (p176), Oman

Bottom: Yas Hotel (p381), United Arab Emirates

Bahla Fort This Unesco World Heritage Site dominates Oman's village of magic, potters and ancient walls. (p189)

Rustaq Fort Guarding the passes between desert plain and mountain interior. (p196)

Masmak Fortress Saudi Arabia's Ibn Saud made his daring raid here in 1902, marking the birth of a nation. (p276)

Architecture

Dubai, Abu Dhabi and Doha are putting the Arabian Peninsula on the map for innovative architecture. A few ancient wonders in Saudi Arabia and Oman show it has ever been thus.

Madain Saleh The Nabataean monuments of this 'petite Petra' lie in a wind-sculpted desert in Saudi Arabia. (p300)

Burj Khalifa At 828m, this downtown Dubai tower is officially 'megatall'. (p330)

Beit Sheikh Isa Bin Ali Al Khalifa Bahrain's best example of the air-conditioning wizardry of 18th- and 19th-century wind-tower architecture. (p76)

Sheikh Zayed Grand Mosque World-class masterpiece of modern mosque design in Abu Dhabi. (p373)

Kuwait Towers These iconic towers have come to symbolise more than just water in the desert. (p104)

Yas Hotel The only hotel in the world to straddle a Formula One racetrack. (p381)

Mutrah Corniche A picture-perfect sweep of balconied houses, mosques and forts in the heart of Oman's capital. (p136)

Al Balad Jeddah's old quarter, built of Red Sea coral and wood, is the jewel in the crown of Arabia's most famous pilgrim port. (p281)

Rija Alma Tower houses in this Saudi Arabian village cascade down the steep slopes of the Asir. (p311)

Wildlife

The Arabian Peninsula offers spectacular wildlife experiences. Watch turtles lay their eggs or track oryx across the plains, and you'll quickly realise that desert does not mean deserted.

Ras Al Jinz Watch record numbers of turtles return to the Omani beach of their birth. (p163)

Marina Bandar Al Rowdha Sail by dhow from Muscat to enjoy the company of acrobatic dolphins. (p139)

Damaniyat Islands Look out for whale sharks, the gentle giants of the Indian Ocean, in October. (p231)

Al Areen Wildlife Park & Reserve Watch the endangered 'unicorn of Arabia' at close quarters in Bahrain. (p84)

Wadi Darbat Meet the unlikely relative of the elephant when the desert turns green in summertime southern Oman. (p213)

Sir Bani Yas Island Spot gazelles among other indigenous inhabitants of Arabia in UAE's unique wildlife project. (p397)

Abu Dhabi Falcon Hospital Come eye to eye with hawks, which have worked with people for centuries. (p376)

Hawar Islands Sooty falcons, dugongs and the world's largest Socotra cormorant colony live around Bahrain's archipelago of desert islands. (p83)

Shopping

Browse the old, covered alleyways known as souqs for traditional crafts. Malls (their modern, air-conditioned equivalents) are mostly found in cities and offer entertainment for kids and shelter from the heat.

Souq Waqif Doha's tasteful reinvention of its Bedouin roots includes traditional coffeehouses. (p239)

Mutrah Souq Indian Ocean trade remains unchanged in Muscat's aged souq. (p135)

Dubai Mall This Emirates pleasure dome includes a walk-under aquarium. (p348)

Yas Mall Giving access to Ferrari World, this Abu Dhabi mall delivers burgers via roller coaster. (p387)

Nizwa Souq Famed for Omani silver daggers but also brisk trading in goats. (p176)

Jeddah Souq Saudi's gold souqs sell 22-carat jewellery by weight, not craftsmanship. (p286)

Souq Al Jamal You're welcome to browse rather than buy at this ancient camel market. (p277)

Bab Al Bahrain Pearls are still found in this gritty warren of shops. (p62)

Souq Marbarakia Heaped-high olives and dates, headdresses and perfumes in the heart of Kuwait City. (p99)

Month by Month

January

Bitterly cold in the mountains and at night on the desert plains, but gloriously warm and sunny everywhere else, this is the peak season for visiting the Arabian Peninsula. Expect the odd rain shower though!

🎆 Muscat Festival

The Omani capital comes alive with top-class acrobatic acts, international craft shopping and Omani heritage displays in venues across the city for a month around January and February. (p143)

🏃 Dubai Marathon

The Dubai Marathon (www.dubaimarathon.org) attracts thousands of runners with some of the highest prize money in international long-distance-running events.

☆ Qatar Open

This international tennis event (www.qatartennis.org) kick starts the Qatar sporting year and attracts the world's best players.

☆ Hail International Rally

This car rally (www.hailrally.com.sa) in the middle of Saudi Arabia draws crowds of spectators to watch international competitors in cars and trucks, and on motorbikes and quad bikes.

February

Still cool at night and warm in the day, but without the rush of New Year visitors, February is one of the best months to enjoy the bustle of the high season in the Gulf.

🛍 Shopping Festivals

Straddling January and February, the month-long Dubai Shopping Festival (p335) and the Hala Festival (p107) in Kuwait City offer big discounts in shops, as well as firework displays.

🎆 Janadriyah National Festival

Saudi Arabia's largest cultural event embraces the King's Cup camel race, falconry and traditional crafts. (p277)

🎆 Sharjah Light Festival

Celebrating arts and culture projected in lights, colours and music, this internationally acclaimed festival has been around for about a decade. (p357)

March

A flush of lime green clads the desert as spring brings an intense and brief flourish of flowers and butterflies before the onslaught of summer scares them away – along with the last of the tourists.

☆ Dubai World Cup

The horse race is worth US$10 million in prize money and is a major event on the UAE's social calendar. (p336)

☆ Emir's Sword Race

The Emir's Sword Race, held in Qatar, is one of the biggest international racing events of Arabian horses in the year. (p248)

Top: Royal Opera House Muscat (p149), Oman

Bottom: Performers at the Jenadriyah National Festival

and visitors must take care to avoid eating or drinking in public. Ramadan evenings, however, are marked by socialising and seasonal delicacies.

📅 Eid Al Fitr

Marking the end of the month of fasting, Eid Al Fitr (in May from 2020) is generally celebrated at home with the family, with increased traffic on the roads and higher prices for airfares.

June

With miserable heat and humidity, the only good thing to be said for June is that hotels offer discounts. Camping and 'glamping' in the mountains of Oman offer a respite from the heat.

July

Excessively hot in the desert, this is the season of the *khareef* (rainy period) in southern Oman. Regional visitors pour into the area to enjoy the relative cool. A good time to visit Saudi Arabia's Asir region, too.

👁 Turtle Nesting

Throughout the year, turtles return to the beaches of their birth to lay their eggs, but July is the peak season in Oman, when 100 green turtles lumber up the beach at Ras Al Jinz each night. (p163)

August

High season in the misty, green, bug-laden haven of southern Arabia, while the rest of the region pants in desiccating temperatures. A challenging, hot month for hajj (in July from 2021).

📅 Eid Al Adha

Families gather to eat the fatted calf and celebrate the return of pilgrims from Mecca and Medina.

🎆 Salalah Tourism Festival

Regional visitors flock to the festival ground in Salalah to picnic in the drizzle and enjoy a program of international entertainment and Omani cultural shows. (p209)

🍴 Buraydah Dates Festival

The world's largest date festival takes place at the world's largest date market, in Saudi Arabia, with lots of opportunities for sampling. (p306)

September

The cultural calendar in the region begins this month with opera houses reopening after the long, hot summer.

☆ Classical Music

The season opens with the Royal Opera House Muscat staging concerts, opera, ballet and jazz from internationally renowned companies. (p149)

October

A slight cooling in temperature at sea level, combined with a return to school and college locally, make this low season ideal for mountain visits before it gets too cold.

November

As the summer heat subsides, occasional rains help the wadis flow. Visitors begin to return to enjoy the reawakening of the Peninsula.

🏃 Oman Desert Marathon

International runners are faced with a tough challenge in the dunes of Oman's Sharqiya Sands as they head across the wilderness to the Indian Ocean. (p172)

☆ Abu Dhabi Grand Prix

Showcasing one of the most glamorous circuits in the world, the Formula One Abu Dhabi Grand Prix is now a highlight of the racing year. (p377)

December

The end of the year marks the peak tourist season for good reason – the sea is still warm, the air is crisp and clear, and evenings are warm enough for dining al fresco.

🎆 Dubai International Film Festival

Abu Dhabi and Doha host film festivals, but the Dubai International Film Festival (www.dubaifilmfest.com) is the star of the show. Running since 2004, it showcases cinematic excellence and casts a spotlight on Arab film.

☆ New Year

Although the Arab New Year falls on a different day each year, the region is never one to resist a party. Dubai offers some of the finest fireworks shows in the world to celebrate 31 December.

🏃 Mubadala World Tennis Championship

The most prestigious tennis tournament in the region is hosted in Abu Dhabi and attracts the world's best players. (p377)

Itineraries

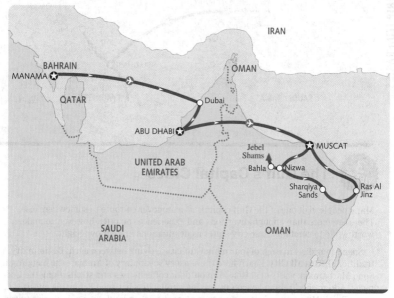

 Arabian Peninsula Highlights in a Hurry

Weaving between the sites of modern and ancient Arabia, this itinerary highlights the best Peninsula experiences feasible in the least amount of time. If focuses on three Gulf cities, then offers a relaxing contrast to the urban pace in the wilds of Oman.

Begin with two days in friendly **Manama**, with its pearl-trading souq and interesting museums. Visit Bahrain Fort to better understand how the whole Gulf region was intent on repelling attack from the sea.

Fly to **Dubai**, a city obsessed with the newest, biggest and best, for a two-day stop, including that totem of superlatives, Burj Khalifa. Spend a day in **Abu Dhabi**, the UAE's cultured capital, visiting Sheikh Zayed Grand Mosque – proof there's more to the Emirates than shopping.

For a complete contrast, fly from Abu Dhabi to **Muscat**. See how 40 years of 'renaissance' has created a modern nation underpinned by respect for heritage – evident during a four-day tour of **Nizwa** and **Bahla**. Allow three further days to forget history by hiking at **Jebel Shams**, camel riding across **Sharqiya Sands** and watching turtles return to the beach of their birth at **Ras Al Jinz** before returning to Muscat.

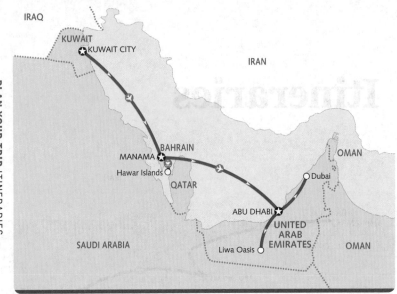

3 WEEKS The Gulf's Capital Cities

Many people visit one of the Gulf capitals as a stopover en route to somewhere else. There are more than enough diversions and experiences on offer, however, to make it worthwhile to combine these city-states as destinations in their own right.

Spend four days in each of four main Gulf cities, flying between each. Begin in dry, traditional **Kuwait City**. Learn here the sensory vocabulary of Arabia – the haggling in Souq Marbarakia, wafts of shisha from outdoor coffeehouses and strolls along the Corniche. Add to the Arabian lexicon by tracing similarities between Peninsula cultures at Tareq Rajab Museum and leave time to explore the urban landscape of high-rise towers – the quintessential symbols of Gulf modernity.

Oil is responsible for Arabia's rapid propulsion into the 21st century: see how in nearby Bahrain, home to the Oil Museum. Enjoy the glamour associated with black gold at the Formula One racing circuit. Pearls gave the Gulf its former livelihood: dive for a pearl off the Hawar Islands or buy a string at Gold City in **Manama** and see how the sea has retreated as land has been reclaimed.

Abu Dhabi, the cultural and political capital of United Arab Emirates, is another city reliant on reclaimed land – as becomes obvious on a walk along the beautiful Corniche. Punctuate your high-voltage city tour with an escape to **Liwa Oasis**, where life moves at the pace of a camel's stride.

If you miss the dynamism of the urban experience, then the best has been kept until last. Spend four days in and around **Dubai**, discovering what makes it the region's most internationally famous city. Cook with chefs, shop with sharks, view the city from the world's tallest tower and dine underwater in the Gulf's most can-do city.

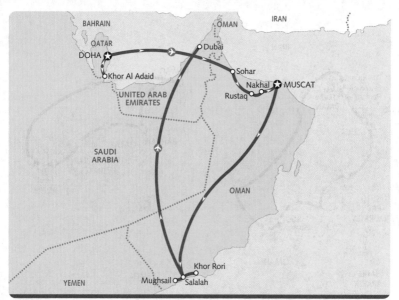

Top to Toe: Pan Peninsula in Four Weeks

They may share the same Peninsula (and a similar name), but arid urban Doha in the north and subtropical, rural Dhofar in the south are so different in character that they may as well belong to different continents.

In week one, fly into **Doha**, renowned for its commitment to hosting international sports, for a three-day visit to this energetic city with its spectacular modern skyline. Visit Souq Waqif and the magnificent Museum of Islamic Art for full cultural immersion and then leave human civilisation behind in a camping trip to timeless **Khor Al Adaid** in southern Qatar. Camp along the edge of the country's famous inland sea before returning to the city for a very different type of sundowner at a luxurious city bar.

Since a blockade was imposed on Qatar by some other Gulf states, a new route has opened up between Doha and **Sohar** in Oman. In week two, be one of the first to try the route out and begin a tour of the land of 1000 towers and fortifications at newly renovated Sohar Fort. Continue the fort theme by travelling to **Muscat** via **Rustaq** and **Nakhal**, boasting their own enormous forts, and end week two by spending a few days in Oman's hospitable capital.

Begin week three travelling to Dhofar, crossing the edge of the Empty Quarter on the flat and utterly featureless highway to Thumrait. The descent into Oman's southern capital **Salalah**, after 10 hours of stony-plain monotony, is sublime, especially during the rainy season when the desert turns green. End week four among frankincense trees near **Mughsail** and see where the precious resin was traded at Al Baleed and the ancient harbour of **Khor Rori**.

In week four, take another little-known air route between Salalah and **Dubai** to re-emphasise the contrast between top and toe of the Peninsula. A visit to the historic neighbourhood of Al Fahidi and the souqs of Deira will demonstrate that the connections between Arabian countries are greater than the elements that distinguish them.

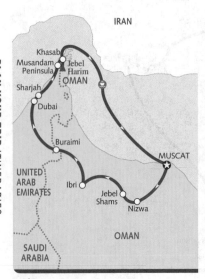

5 DAYS — Easy Escape from Dubai

If the intensity of Dubai begins to take its toll, a trip into the neighbouring emirates and Oman provides an enjoyable antidote. Oman's Musandam Peninsula makes a good weekend break, but with an extra day or two, a mini-tour of northern Oman is possible.

From **Dubai**, head north to **Sharjah**, a hub of heritage and Islamic arts. On day two, wind through the northern emirates to the Shams–Tibat border and enter Oman's fabled **Musandam Peninsula**. Enjoy the spectacular drive along the cliff-hugging road to **Khasab** and time your arrival for a dhow cruise in Musandam's celebrated *khors* (creeks).

Spend day three in a 4WD, exploring **Jebel Harim** and Rawdah Bowl with its 'House of Locks'. Return to Khasab and on day four take the ferry and bus to **Muscat**. Visit Mutrah Souq and Muscat's old quarter and on day five meander west to historic **Nizwa** and ascend **Jebel Shams**, the Peninsula's highest mountain. Return to UAE via the typical towns of **Ibri** and **Buraimi** on the UAE border.

1 WEEK — Easy Escape from Kuwait

Kuwait is a fascinating country to explore, but as a conservative, flat, dry state, hemmed in by travel-restricted neighbours, it doesn't offer many opportunities to let your hair down. For the complete antithesis of life in Kuwait City, take the following trip to Oman, UAE and Bahrain.

Fly to **Muscat** and enjoy the tolerant, cosmopolitan nature of the city. Spend a day at a beachside hotel and enjoy the novelty of a sea with waves, followed by sundowners and dancing in a nightclub. On day three be reminded of what mountains and orchards look like by hiking in clear fresh air, blissfully devoid of humidity, on **Jebel Akhdar**.

On day four, swap the desert wilderness for the urban wild side by flying to **Dubai** for extreme shopping, dining and partying. On day five, bring the temperature down a notch by flying to **Manama** for a fun but slightly less high-octane experience (unless of course the Grand Prix is in town), before buttoning up the collar for the journey back to **Kuwait City**.

Plan Your Trip
The Hajj

An experience of profound spiritual significance, the hajj – the pilgrimage to Mecca – is a lifetime's ambition for many Muslims. All able-bodied Muslims of sufficient means are expected to undertake the hajj at least once in their lives, as it is seen to be fulfilling one of the five key pillars of mainstream Islam. The hajj is an extraordinary spectacle, where millions of people from all over the world, rich and poor, able-bodied and otherwise, are unified by their state of ihram, which creates a sea of white as men donning two simple white cotton sheets, alongside women dressed equally simply, perform ancient rites over the course of five days, following in the footsteps of the prophets of the past.

The Hajj Experience
Before the Pilgrimage

Most pilgrims arrive in Saudi Arabia by air, landing at the hajj terminal of Jeddah's King Abdul Aziz International Airport (p286). Come prepared for the fact that more than two million pilgrims flood through this terminal – waiting times for buses to Mecca can last up to 12 long, hot and humid hours. Drinking water is provided, but bring snacks. You can buy food at the airport but inevitably queues will be long.

Before arriving in Mecca, local pilgrims stop at *miqats* (areas designated by the Prophet) to shower and change into their *ihram* outfit, which is the distinct two-piece, unstitched white cotton garment for men. International pilgrims landing at Jeddah airport will have already crossed this area and therefore be in a state of *ihram* already. Women are not permitted to wear the *niqab* or burka during the hajj. There is no gender segregation during rituals, as a sign that all pilgrims are equal.

An invocation in Arabic is performed – aloud, under one's breath or privately in one's head – at certain points on the way

What to Bring

Label everything and attach a coloured ribbon to your belongings to help identify them.

Clothing

➡ Two to three *ihram* outfits (for men, two cotton sheets; for women, a modest outfit), towels, indoor scarf (for women) and non-stitched comfortable sandals

Sleeping, Toiletries & Medical

➡ Pyjamas, pillow, toiletries (non-perfumed), hand sanitiser, sunscreen

➡ Medications, plasters, surgical/face mask (when in crowds)

Practical

➡ Travel belt, water-bottle carrier, umbrella, shoulder bag, camp stool

Spiritual

➡ Quran, pocket notebook and pen to record thoughts

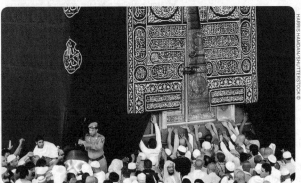

Top: Worshippers at Al Masjid al Haram (p289)

Bottom: The Holy Kaaba

to Mecca, depending on which direction pilgrims are coming from. This invocation is given as pilgrims reach the *miqat* near Mecca:

Here I am, oh God, at Your command! Here I am at Your command! You are without associate! Here I am at Your command! To You are all praise, grace and dominion! You are without associate!

The First Day

Arriving at Mecca's Grand Mosque, worshippers perform the *Tawaf Al Qudum* (*tawaf* of arrival). *Tawaf* is the act of circling counter-clockwise seven times around the Kaaba. Then comes the *saee,* which involves walking between the hills of Safa and Marwah (which are within the Grand Mosque grounds) seven times to simulate the desperate search for water by Hajar, the wife of the Prophet Ibrahim.

The next stop is the 'tent city' of Mina, a short distance from Mecca. It's a time for rest, reflection, reading the Quran and praying. Depending on the tour package, worshippers sleep in tents that accommodate up to 12 people each.

The Second Day

This is the most significant day of the hajj. The 'Day of Arafat' begins after sunrise, as worshippers leave Mina to travel to the Plain of Arafat. The time here is spent standing or sitting at the Mount of Mercy, asking God for forgiveness and making supplications. Some pilgrims rest in their tents. After sunset, everyone moves on to the Muzdalifah Plain to spend the whole night praying and collecting pebbles for the stoning ritual the next day.

The Third to Fifth Days

The third day begins shortly before sunrise in Mina, where worshippers once threw their pebbles at three *jamrah* (pillars) that represented the devil. In 2004, because of the many injuries caused by the fervour of the stone throwing, Saudi authorities replaced the pillars with long walls and stone basins designed to catch ricocheting rocks. The stoning can continue for three days and represents a rejection of Satan and an affirmation of Ibrahim's faith in God.

UMRAH: THE LITTLE HAJJ

Umrah is a shortened version of hajj in which rituals can be carried out within the vicinity of the Grand Mosque at any time of year (except during hajj itself), and at any time of day and night. Many pilgrims say umrah is a quiet, peaceful and contemplative experience.

The visa process is similar to applying for a hajj visa. Like the hajj visa, umrah visas are free, but they are only valid for 15 days; overstaying can have serious legal consequences. Applicants must make their booking through a Saudi-approved tour operator and provide the same required documentation as they would for hajj.

The stoning ritual is perhaps when pilgrims are most vulnerable to danger as worshippers crowd the Jamarat pedestrian bridge on their way to the pillars. Deadly stampedes have occurred here in the past, so it's important to pay close attention to instructions from guides and security personnel and to follow the multilingual signs along the route with care.

This is the first day of the three-day Eid Al Adha (feast of sacrifice), and pilgrims spend the remaining days carrying out these three rites after their first round of stoning. A sheep, cow or camel is sacrificed to show God a willingness to offer up something precious, and the meat is distributed to the poor. Men shave their heads, or trim their hair evenly, and women cut off a lock of their hair to bring them out of *ihram*. The final formal rite of hajj is the *Tawaf Al Ifadah/Ziyarah,* when pilgrims return to Mecca to circle the Kaaba again, pray at the Station of Ibrahim and perform another *saee*.

The Final Day

While the formal part of hajj is now over, many pilgrims choose to spend another day in Mina until sunset, to undertake more stoning and reflection; others return to Mecca. Before leaving Mecca and starting on their journeys back home, all pilgrims perform the 'farewell' *Tawaf Al Wada*.

Hajj Practicalities

With so many hajj pilgrims attending each year – some estimates put the number at 2.5 million or more – Saudi Arabia's Ministry of Hajj has streamlined the process to obtain a visa and perform the rituals. It's still complicated, but Muslims cannot be denied the right to perform the fifth pillar of Islam, regardless of whether they are Sunni or Shiite and regardless of their personal history.

Hajj Eligibility

The first step is to determine whether you are eligible to perform hajj. Muslims who have performed the ritual are not allowed to perform it again until five years have passed. An exception will be made for those acting as a *mahram* (guardian) to accompany a wife or family member who plans to go. All women under the age of 45 must be accompanied by a *mahram,* who must be a close male relative.

Visas & Tour Operators

The Saudi Ministry of Hajj website (www. haj.gov.sa) lists its requirements, which should be followed to the letter. The Ministry requires that all pilgrims go through one of the approved, licensed travel agencies (listed on the website) that operate tours for the hajj and umrah (the shorter pilgrimage outside of hajj season).

Travel-agency prices can be as low as SR6500 per person but can run as high as SR30,000 or more depending on the amenities offered. All tour companies offer meals, air-conditioned buses, transportation to Medina and side tours to significant religious sites. It is essential that you stick to the approved list of travel agencies.

These agencies handle everything, including obtaining a hajj visa (free and valid for 30 days) and permits, processing immunisation records (meningitis and hepatitis A and B are required jabs), and arranging accommodation and transportation. If the applicant is a convert to Islam, a letter from the applicant's mosque stating that he or she performed the *shahada* (statement of faith) must be produced.

Tour companies keep strict tabs on their clients once they arrive in Saudi Arabia. Pilgrims give up their passport for the duration of their stay and are issued with an identity card and wristband. It is important that pilgrims keep a copy of their passport (including all pages and visas), and travel documents with them at all times. Once in the Kingdom, travel for pilgrims is strictly limited to visiting Mecca and Medina and the cities and villages between the two cities.

Hajj Health & Safety

Hajj rituals can be difficult to perform for the very young and the very old. Depending on the time of year, temperatures can reach more than 40°C, and the crowds can be stifling.

Common sense and caution are the foundation of a safe trip. Eat and sleep when you can, drink plenty of fluids, wear a surgical/face mask – to protect against the small risk of MERS (coronavirus) – and sanitise your hands often.

Make sure you have the requisite immunisations, although heat exhaustion is the most common enemy of the pilgrim. If you feel sweating chills, nausea or dizziness, find shade and seek medical attention from one of the hundreds of emergency personnel stations throughout the pilgrimage route.

One of the greatest risks to pilgrims comes from the massive crowds and the danger of stampede. Always pay close attention to your surroundings and follow the instructions of officials; it's wise to keep to the outer limits of moving crowds wherever possible.

HAJJ CALENDAR

ISLAMIC CALENDAR	ESTIMATED EQUIVALENT IN WESTERN CALENDAR
8-12 Dhul Hijja 1440H	10-14 August 2019
8-12 Dhul Hijja 1441H	30 July-3 August 2020
8-12 Dhul Hijja 1442H	19-23 July 2021
8-12 Dhul Hijja 1443H	8-12 July 2022

Plan Your Trip
Expats

The days of being paid well for doing little are over, while the realities of extreme temperatures and different social norms remain. So why consider an expat life? Whether you're motivated by the ancient culture or the thrill of rapid change, you'll find it pays to anticipate the challenges before leaving home.

Everyday Life
Not So Different From Home

For many new arrivals in the region, the first few days on the Arabian Peninsula often come as a culture shock. The audible call to prayer five times a day, the extreme heat, the homogeneous clothing, the undisciplined driving and the ubiquitous aroma of shisha (water pipe used to smoke tobacco) combine to create an overwhelming sense of difference. This difference is further emphasised for many by the relatively barren desert landscape.

Give it a week, however, and the similarities start appearing and day-to-day life in Arabia appears not as 'foreign' as one had imagined. International-style clothing is worn in familiar-looking malls (albeit under an *abaya,* a full-length robe worn by women); favourite foods from many cultures, including the likes of Marmite, soy sauce and turmeric, are widely available in corner shops; schools cater expertly for the children of different expat communities; provision is made for non-Muslim worship; drinking water is safe; health centres are well funded; and most people speak English as a common language. The drinking of alcohol is tolerated in all countries except Kuwait and Saudi Arabia (and parts of the UAE), and you can even buy pork in some supermarkets.

Many expats enjoy the fact that living in any of the Peninsula countries means it is safe to leave houses and cars unlocked,

Key Differences

All Countries
Extreme summer heat. Weekend is built around Friday, the region's common day of prayer.

Bahrain
Extreme humidity in summer. Tiny land mass offers limited opportunities for free-time excursions. Pockets of political unrest. Tolerant of foreign customs and manners.

Kuwait
A dry state. Alcohol cannot be bought or consumed. Very little greenery. Tolerant of non-Muslim religious expression. Little to explore outside Kuwait City.

Oman
Slow pace of decision making. Tolerant of foreign customs and manners. Lives up to its moniker 'Beauty has an address'.

Qatar
Extreme humidity in summer. Quite conservative.

Saudi Arabia
A dry state. Highly conservative. Restricted movement outside city of residence. Non-Muslim religious expression restricted. Much to explore.

United Arab Emirates
Liberal exterior hides a conservative core.

ATLANTIDE PHOTOTRAVEL/GETTY IMAGES ©

Top: Boys play in a park with views to central Doha (p239), Qatar

Left: Bloomingdales in Dubai Mall (p348), United Arab Emirates

for children to play in the streets and talk to strangers, and that neighbours always have time for a chat. Times are changing in the big cities, but on the whole the friendly, safe and tolerant environment of all these countries is a major contributor to the quality of life. Even in Saudi Arabia, where public life is controlled by strict codes of conduct, expats generally enjoy a safe, relaxed and crime-free experience within their own compounds.

A Multicultural Experience

Expatriate populations outnumber national populations in all Gulf states. As such, the Arabian Peninsula is one of the most multicultural places on the planet. This is both a trial and a fantastic opportunity. The trial comes in learning to cope with another layer of cultural expectation. The opportunity comes in gaining an insight into richly different ways of life, expressed most noticeably through food, festivities and workplace practices.

Perhaps the most valuable aspect of the region's multicultural experience is learning from the resident Iraqis, Afghans and Palestinians that there are other perspectives on the politics of the region that are not often aired in the international media.

Gulf countries are finding their own ways of helping communities displaced as a result of war. This help has translated into cash handouts to the Syrian government, for example, but it also takes the uniquely local form of absorbing economic migration.

Regional asylum seekers are welcomed either as 'guests' or as professional or skilled employees on short-term contracts. In the absence of any formal recognition of the definition of refugee status, the emphasis is on providing temporary opportunities rather than embracing asylum seekers as fellow nationals. In other words, the expectation remains that one day these migrants will return home.

Climate

Without doubt, one of the biggest challenges of living on the Peninsula is learning to cope with the weather. If you're from a cold, wet and windy place, it is hard to imagine you would ever get bored of the endless blue skies. But in summer, the sky isn't blue; it's white with heat, and the extreme temperatures from April to October (which hover, on average, around 40°C and frequently rise above 45°C in the shade) require a complete life adjustment. Learning to live in the air-conditioned indoors for those months, to live life more slowly and find ways of exercising that don't involve going outside, is as difficult as coming to terms with winter in frozen climes. The upside is six months of benign winter warmth that bid friends and relatives to visit. Here are some key ways to beat the heat:

Embrace local timing Working hours across the region tend to favour mornings and late afternoons, either with a 7am-to-2pm regime, or a two-shift day from 7am to 7pm with a break between noon and 5pm.

Take a siesta If the job allows, follow local practice by eating your main meal at lunchtime and taking a nap in the heat of the day.

Drink plenty of water Expats often underestimate the amount of extra fluid intake they require in summer and become dehydrated and ill as a result.

Wear cotton clothing Excessive humidity in Gulf cities can make a temperature of 35°C feel more like 45°C and synthetic fibres stick to the skin, adding to the boil-in-the-bag effect. Avoid excessive use of sunscreen for the same reason and cover skin with cotton clothing instead.

Wear a hat and sunglasses It's no accident that local costume includes some form of head covering for all. You should also cover your neck and protect your eyes from glare (off white buildings and the sea especially). Avoid sitting in the summer sun altogether if you want to maintain supple, unwrinkled skin.

Exercise with caution Half the activity takes twice the effort in extreme heat so follow the locals by exercising just before dawn or at an air-conditioned gym. There's often a slight cooling of temperature at dusk before the night-time heat explodes.

Escape to higher ground Temperature reduces by around 5°C for every 1000m of altitude gained. A weekend break (or summer retreat to drizzling Dhofar in Oman) may just keep you sane for the rest of the week.

CULTURAL DOS AND DON'TS

Do

It is not always easy, especially in the big cities of the Gulf, to interact with the local people – and especially with the indigenous Arabs who are often outnumbered in their own countries by expat residents. Here are some simple ways to engage with the local culture.

Visit a heritage village Getting a feel for the region's Bedouin roots is a great way to understand differing concepts of time and hospitality. Visiting living heritage villages, especially during festivals and national days, provides insight into each country's rich song, dance, craft and cuisine inheritance.

Learn Arabic This is not necessary for survival, as English and other expat languages are so widely spoken, but just learning to read the street signs helps bring you closer to Arab culture.

Attend a wedding Invitations to these will surely be forthcoming and, for women especially, it's the quickest way to learn that Arab women are not the oppressed creatures portrayed in some international media.

Celebrate Eid, Diwali and Christmas Peninsula people love a party and are quick to give greetings at all religious festivals, not just those of Islam; joining them is the best way to understand the strong sense of community.

Play football Between acacia trees, on the sandy beaches or atop mountain passes, showing your interest in this regional obsession is the surest way to the Arab heart – for men and women!

Don't

Peninsula countries are, on the whole, very forgiving of the transgressions of foreigners (except in Saudi Arabia), but there is nothing to be gained by upsetting the citizens of your host country. To avoid giving offence or landing yourself in trouble with the authorities, don't do the following:

Wear revealing clothing Even in liberal Dubai, nothing causes more offence than exposing shoulders or thighs in shopping centres and other public spaces, or wearing tight and provocative clothing – that goes for men as well as women.

Show affection in public Avoid holding hands, kissing or hugging with members of the opposite sex.

Indulge in excessive drinking Public drunkenness is likely to get you deported or even imprisoned. In Saudi Arabia, where alcohol is strictly prohibited, the penalty is severe.

Drink and drive Even in countries tolerant of alcohol consumption, there is zero tolerance for drink driving.

Take drugs It's illegal in all countries on the Peninsula and can lead to death penalties.

Eat, drink or smoke in public during daylight hours in Ramadan Some countries also enforce a ban on gum chewing, singing and loud music.

Swear or use rude hand gestures In some Arab countries, this may not just be considered uncouth, it may also be illegal! It's also impolite to beckon with a finger or to use the left hand when touching, giving and eating.

Take photographs without permission This is the case when photographing people, particularly women. You should also avoid photographing anything military or 'strategic' (such as airports or bus stations).

Cohabit Despite the low risk of detection if you are discreet, it is illegal to live with a member of the opposite sex (or have a baby) unless you are married. In Saudi Arabia, men and women may not travel together (including by car) unless related.

The Law

In most Peninsula countries the law is based on Sharia law, which can lead to a wide interpretation of penalties for similar illegal activities from country to country – even from judge to judge – as there is no formal penal code.

Breaking the law on the Arabian Peninsula can have severe consequences, and embassies have very little jurisdiction (or inclination) to help foreign nationals in breach of local laws.

Some things that are legal in other countries, including public displays of affection, sex out of wedlock and consumption of alcohol, are illegal in some Peninsula countries and can carry a harsh sentence. Illegal acts across the region include taking drugs, public drunkenness, driving after drinking alcohol, lewd behaviour, adultery, cohabitation and homosexuality. Depending on the country you're in, breaking the law may lead to hefty fines (for traffic offences), jail (for causing accidental death), deportation (for cohabitation), public flogging (for adultery) or even a death sentence (for drug trafficking).

Note that penalties, and even what's considered illegal, can change frequently in some countries. As such, it is your responsibility to become acquainted with local laws before entering the country. Consult your HR manager and the embassy of the country in which you plan to work for guidance on legal matters before you take up employment.

Links to Legal Resources

Look for *Working in the Gulf* (Explorer Group, 2011) for a list of legal services by country. A helpful website, Gulf Law (www.gulf-law.com), gives a general introduction to Sharia and commercial law.

Working in the Region

Labour laws throughout the Gulf are extremely strict. It's illegal to seek work on a visit visa, and there are severe penalties for those caught working illegally. Although some travellers take the chance of applying for ad hoc work (in Dubai, for example), to remain within the law you should secure a position before arrival. Your 'sponsor' (usually your employer) acts as a kind of guarantor of your good conduct while you reside in the country and will help you obtain a visa.

Working and living conditions are usually of a high standard. Salaries (for the time being at least) carry the enormous advantage of incurring no personal taxation. It can be tricky, however, to change jobs if you decide you're not happy with the one you have. It can also be difficult to find long-term employment; many contracts are short term, renewable annually or every two years. While it's not necessary to speak Arabic (although it's an advantage), good spoken and written communication in English, the region's second language, is a prerequisite and many jobs require qualifications that would not be expected elsewhere.

Those offering professional skills in much-needed services, such as translating, nursing, engineering and teaching (particularly English), stand the best chance of gaining employment. Many administrative positions, on the other hand, are beginning to be filled by newly trained local professionals. Note that for English-language teaching, you will need at least a degree and teaching experience to be eligible for most job opportunities, but you don't necessarily need to be a native speaker.

International recruiting agencies headhunt for positions on the Peninsula. You can also enquire about job opportunities at cultural centres connected with your home country and through voluntary aid organisations.

Applying the Right Attitude

The working life of an expat, which often involves confronting fundamental differences in outlook, culture and education between colleagues, can be quite a challenge. It helps, therefore, to identify these differences from the beginning and then to celebrate the 'other', rather than seek to change it. The host nations, of the Gulf in particular, do this very well, accepting the expat for who they are and rarely attempting to influence their religious or social beliefs and customs. By the same token, it is important as an expat to learn to appreciate the Arab way of doing things and not assume that your own culture is always right.

PUTTING PEOPLE FIRST

Much of Arab life is underpinned by a sense of 'what will be, will be'. This fatalism stems from Islam and the belief that God determines fate – a belief reflected in the frequent conversational phrase, *inshallah,* which literally means 'if Allah wills it'. A belief in God's will threads through all aspects of life: it informs the response to a car accident, a soured business deal or the death of a loved one, and it leads to a culture where personal accountability and the culture of blame (both recognisable by those from a Western culture) have limited meaning.

For the expat who is unaware of this difference, there are many frustrations involved in social and business interactions. For example, when rushing towards a deadline (a movable concept across the region), it's not unusual to find colleagues have knocked off for a tea break. But then, from the Arab point of view, what can be more important than sharing time to discuss the day and swap family news? The deadline will be met if Allah wills it, so in the meantime take your rest and have a chat. More 'business' is conducted over a *chi libton* (cup of tea) than is ever concluded after a Powerpoint presentation, because in Peninsula society, people come first.

To enjoy, as well as to succeed in, living and working on the Arabian Peninsula, the expat has to learn to put people first (if this is an alien concept in their own culture). Any investment in good relations invariably pays unexpected dividends, smoothing the passage of daily life and opening up social and business opportunities.

The expat who listens to what people want, rather than guessing what they want, is more likely to make a genuinely valuable contribution to the emerging but complex countries of the region than those who rush in with solutions that are inappropriate to the context. Those who are determined their way is right often end up feeling defeated at the lack of application or implementation of their ideas or output.

Business Etiquette

People from the Arabian Peninsula have been eminent merchants for centuries, with global trade in copper, frankincense, pearls and, most recently, oil, running through their veins. Inevitably, they have developed highly refined customs and manners when it comes to commercial interaction, and they are always somewhat disdainful of their foreign counterparts, whose alacrity to get straight down to business shows, in their book, a lack of finesse in the fine arts of commerce.

Though urbane enough to tolerate the mores of their overseas counterparts, Arab business people are impressed with good manners. Observing the following courtesies, therefore, may just help seal the deal.

Clothing Wear a suit (with a tie for men) but avoid silk or linen, which either stick to the skin in the heat or crease badly; women should cover knees, cleavage and shoulders and avoid anything tight-fitting. Formal national dress, if it's your own (such as sari, *salwar kameez, kaftan*), are acceptable and often welcomed. Attempts at dressing local-style (in *dishdasha* or *abaya,* for example) are deemed ridiculous.

Timing Be on time for meetings, but be tolerant of late arrivals (an accepted part of local custom). Avoid meetings or telephone calls on a Friday, which is the day of prayer and rest; during afternoon siesta (except in the UAE and capital cities, where the practice is dying out), and in the holy month of Ramadan.

Greeting Shake hands readily with men, but wait for an Arab woman to proffer her hand first. Only use Arab greetings if you can master them, otherwise stick to formal English. Don't be surprised if people touch their heart after a greeting (as in Saudi Arabia), if kisses on the cheek are exchanged between men (as in the Gulf states), or noses are knocked or rubbed (as in areas of Oman) – equally, don't try to do the same.

Addressing Use Arab given names, as opposed to family names. Instead of Mr Al Wahabbi, it's Mr Mohammed. In the same way, expect to be called Mr or Ms plus your first name or initials (Mr John, Ms Geetha or Prof KPR, for example) and don't attempt to change this polite form to your family name. The correct formal address (or equivalent of Mr) is usually *asayid* (meaning sir) or *asayida* (meaning madam).

Preliminaries Exchange pleasantries about the weather and ask after health and family for several minutes before turning to the subject in hand. It's considered rude to go straight to the point. Men, however, should never enquire after another man's wife or daughters. Exchange business cards (which are a must) with your right hand (the left hand is reserved for ablutions).

Negotiating Bargaining is an important part of discovering value to the buyer weighed against worth to the vendor. The concept of a fixed price is a largely alien concept amid the highly social and personal interaction of reaching a deal in the Middle East. Build in, therefore, some room for negotiation – in all interactions, not just commercial ones.

Agreement Although some of the gentility of reaching agreement has vanished during recent economic tribulations, an Arab's word is his bond and, similarly, keeping your promise is considered a matter of honour.

Problem solving Keep smiling, keep your temper and avoid raising your voice. Confrontation, criticism, blaming and swearing are highly insulting in public as they involve loss of face for those concerned. Equally, making and forcing apology is best avoided. A quiet, sympathetic word in private is much more effective.

Socialising Before any kind of transaction – at the checkout in a supermarket, if the traffic police stop you, before a meeting begins, on the telephone between strangers – people greet each other thoroughly and preferably enquire after the other person's health. They often repeat these enquiries if there is a lull in the conversation. Never refuse a cup of tea or coffee as it may offend. Take your cue from the host and avoid asking for alcohol unless it is offered.

Conversing Avoid politics, sex and religion as topics of conversation (these tend to be favourite topics among locals); if you are drawn into such a discussion, keep your comments general, not personal. Also, avoid any comparisons of people with animals, even in jest, especially dogs (which are considered unclean by many Muslims) and donkeys (used as a common insult).

Closing The exchange of gifts is an important aspect of conducting business in the region. Well-crafted tokens representing an aspect of your home country are the normal currency of leave-taking – poorly made or obviously cheap, mass-made items will do more damage to your agenda than good.

Women in the Workplace

In the workplace, pay and opportunities for promotion are equal for both sexes (except in Saudi Arabia, where women are only employed in certain sectors). It is the norm in most Gulf countries for men and women to work side by side in an office or laboratory environment. Female professionals are respected for their qualifications and experience, and although it's often harder for local women to gain employment and promotion, this is not the case for foreign female professionals, who are accorded great respect in senior roles.

General advice regarding business etiquette is the same for men and women with one exception: women should take their cue from the other person when expecting to shake hands as some devoutly religious men will not touch a woman who is not a family member. Although disconcerting, this isn't intended to be insulting. If your handshake is refused, just touch your heart instead.

Expat Life for Children & Families

Arabs love the company of children and celebrate childhood often through large families and varying indulgences. As such, expat children are assured of a welcome. They may also find that they have more freedom than they have back home as parents feel safe in the knowledge that they are not going to be preyed upon in parks or offered drugs. Here's an 'ABC' of a few key family-related considerations that expats often enquire about before signing their contracts.

Activities There is little sophisticated child-oriented entertainment outside of the big cities, but a beach is never too far away, and there are often parks containing children's play areas (including swings and slides), even in small towns.

Birth and maternity leave Many expat women give birth in the region, and it presents no special difficulties in the main cities. There are prenatal and postnatal groups on hand to help. Maternity leave is enshrined in law in most Arab countries.

Childcare Nannies (usually from the Indian subcontinent or the Philippines) are one of the easily afforded perks of the region. Many parents opt for live-in home help, and villas often cater for this with the provision of maid's quarters. In some cities, babysitting services are available in malls.

Coffee mornings There are many groups, such as the Women's Guild in Oman (www.womensguild-oman.com), that act as a forum for non-working expat women. These groups are a lifeline for many new arrivals in the region, providing local knowledge about everything from schooling, home help and health care to voluntary work and leisure activities.

Dangers Illegal drug taking, although still a relatively minor problem, is on the increase among older teenagers. Reckless driving is prevalent in all the Peninsula countries and claims many young lives. Regional and national awareness campaigns are having some success in reducing these risks.

Education The standard of international schools on the Arabian Peninsula is excellent, offering similar curricula to schools back home, enabling a smooth transition into university or college outside the region.

Health care The extreme heat can be debilitating for children, particularly babies. Obstetric and paediatric units in hospitals and clinics are generally of a high standard and most scourges of childhood in hot climates (such as polio, malaria and typhoid) are under control.

Hotels and restaurants In top-end and some midrange hotels, young children can usually share their parents' room for no extra charge. Extra beds or cots are normally available. High chairs are often only available in top-end restaurants.

Infants Disposable nappies (diapers) are not always easy to come by outside large cities. Infant formula is widely available, however, as is bottled water.

Resources Expat Woman (www.expatwoman.com) or Mums Net (www.mumsnet.com) are useful forums for sharing advice and information on expat life in the Peninsula. For further advice on the dos and don'ts of taking the kids, see Lonely Planet's *Travel with Children*.

Special needs Catering for the needs of children with disabilities is highly challenging in the region as often locals attach stigma to physical and especially mental disability. Finding help or support for common childhood issues, such as dyslexia, ADD and anorexia, can be difficult and there are few concessions (handrails, ramps, Braille etc) made for those with physical disabilities.

Housing

Stories about wild parties on expat compounds where the residents never interact with people beyond the gates are thankfully largely a thing of the past. Company compounds do still exist in Saudi Arabia, but many expats in the Gulf are these days given an allowance and expected to find their own accommodation. Here is some general advice regarding housing:

➡ Rental accommodation can be found, usually unfurnished, through embassies, cultural centres and newspapers.

➡ Villas with gardens, apartments with a shared swimming pool or a residency within a self-sufficient and gated compound are the preferred expat residency options. Many hotels offer long-stay arrangements.

➡ Check that air-con, maintenance of shared areas and mains water are included in the rent.

➡ Shaded, off-road parking is highly desirable.

➡ Unless you are a fan of early mornings, you may prefer to avoid neighbouring a mosque where a wake-up call will occur well before sunrise.

➡ Check your employment contract covers temporary accommodation while you house hunt.

➡ Relocation consultants, as well as estate agents, can be found in most countries.

Health

Health care across the region is consistently of a high standard in major cities. In smaller and especially rural communities, health care may be confined to a visiting doctor at the local clinic. Health-care providers tend to be expats themselves, with many nurses from the Philippines and doctors from India.

Emergency treatment is often given free, but you shouldn't rely on this. Ambulance services are becoming more widely available, but sometimes a taxi is the best way to get to hospital in a hurry outside cities. Operations can be very expensive and many locals opt to have surgery in India or Thailand as they believe they will receive better care in those countries.

It's imperative to have health insurance for all the family. Carefully check the small print of any company-issued insurance, as it may well exclude dental and eye care; prenatal, delivery and maternity care; as well as pre-existing conditions.

Items uch as tampons and sanitary pads can be found in larger supermarkets, which tend to cater for expats, but these are not always available in more remote areas. Contraception is readily available, but abortion (other than on health grounds) is not readily supported. The term 'abortion' is often used interchangeably with 'miscarriage' among non-native English speakers in the region.

Red Tape

The countries of the Middle East seem to have a passion for bureaucracy and have large public sectors in place to administer it. For the expat, this entails various paperchases to ensure they have the correct permissions in place to work, own and drive a car, purchase alcohol and, in the case of Saudi Arabia, travel around the country. This isn't as daunting as it sounds as every company will have a fixer whose job it is to steer the employee over each bureaucratic hurdle. Note that for most countries in the region, you need to test negative for AIDS and tuberculosis before you gain a residency permit. This is treated as a routine and perfunctory part of the visa-obtaining process, so don't expect any pre- or post-test counselling.

You can speed up the obtaining of various permits by having at the ready a stock of passport-size photographs, some on plain white, and some on plain blue backgrounds; multiple copies of an abbreviated CV (two pages maximum); copies of your tertiary qualifications and the original certificates attested by your embassy.

Take a number on entering queuing stations, carry a book to read, be patient and stay friendly and polite, even when at your wit's end. When at length you get your residency card, driving licence or travel permit, check it's accurate (it's too late to change it once you've left the office) and carry it with you at all times – this is the law in most Peninsula countries.

Many countries will permit some nationalities to drive using a licence from home. Other nationalities must pass the local driving test. Check with your embassy or HR manager.

Transport

In general, except in the UAE, Doha and Muscat, which have good public transport systems, and in Saudi Arabia, where women have only just been granted permission to drive, it is really useful to have a car for getting to work and/or running family errands. Cities are spread out and offices, services and entertainments are far flung.

The Peninsula is a good place to buy a car, but note that you can't buy one without a residency permit. Most mainstream makes and models are available, and prices are low as there's no import duty (though VAT has been introduced in the UAE and Saudi Arabia, with the rest of the GCC due to follow). As when shopping for other items, bargaining is normal. A down payment of around 10% of the purchase price is usually expected if taking out a loan.

Because cars are cheap, they're also seen as disposable by the wealthy. There is a growing secondhand car market throughout the region. Note that change of ownership has to be completed with the local police. When buying a vehicle (or importing one), you usually have to register it with the police traffic department.

When secondhand car shopping, it's essential you ensure that the vehicle you're interested in purchasing has the following:

➡ an up-to-date test certificate

➡ a registration certificate (confirm that the engine and chassis numbers of the car match those on the certificate)

➡ a clean bill of health from a mechanic

➡ a clean record – fines outstanding on the car are usually transferred to the new owner.

Getting a Local Driving License

To obtain a local licence you'll need to have a residency visa, plus the following documents. For some expats, a driving test may be required:

➡ a valid foreigner's licence (and sometimes an IDP)

➡ a no-objection certificate (NOC) from your employer

➡ your accommodation rental contract

➡ photocopies of your passport

➡ passport-sized photos

NON-MUSLIM HOLIDAYS AS AN EXPAT

Non-Muslim holidays, such as Diwali and Onam, are recognised on the Arabian Peninsula, and Christmas is widely celebrated. In the malls and shopping centres there are lights and carols, mangers with babies and neon cribs, cards with angels and the three wise men, and Arab Muslims queuing to take the kids to see Santa. While it's common for locals to wish you a happy Christmas, the best response is 'thank you' rather than a return of the same greeting. In the UAE provision is often made for vacations to be taken at Christmas, but this is uncommon elsewhere in the region, and 25 December, as well as the days on which other non-Muslim religious festivals fall, are generally treated as normal working days.

New Year offers several opportunities for celebration as it falls on different days among different expat communities. The Arab New Year, which moves according to the lunar calendar, is often marked by a public holiday. The night of 31 December is an excuse for parties and fireworks (most spectacularly in Dubai), but 1 January is not necessarily a holiday. Chinese New Year is becoming an important cultural event.

➡ sometimes a certificate confirming your blood group

➡ some countries (such as Saudi Arabia) insist on Arabic translations of foreign documents.

Ramadan

The holy month of Ramadan is a time of spiritual contemplation for Muslims. For the expat it can be a time of heightened frustration as everyone works more slowly and drives more quickly.

Muslims fast from dawn to dusk during Ramadan. Foreigners are not expected to fast, but they should not smoke, drink or eat (including gum-chewing) in public during daylight hours in Ramadan. Business premises and hotels make provision for the non-fasting by erecting screens around dining areas.

Business hours tend to become more erratic and usually shorter, and many restaurants close for the whole period.

With this change of routine, and given the hardship of abstaining from water during the long, hot summer days, it's not surprising that tempers easily fray and the standard of driving deteriorates. Expats should make allowances by being extra vigilant on the roads and by being extra tolerant in all social interactions.

Further Reading

There are many informative books about the expat experience encompassing personal narratives and practical resources – these are readily available in capital-city bookshops and airports. The locally-published Explorer Guide series (www.askexplorer.com) is particularly useful. In addition, there are some excellent expat websites with discussion forums dispensing advice, sharing experiences and often organising local special interest groups and other social activities.

Internet Resources

A number of websites provide information and networking opportunities exclusively for expats:

British Expats (www.britishexpats.com)

Expat Arrivals (www.expatarrivals.com)

Expat Exchange (www.expatexchange.com)

Expat Forum (www.expatforum.com)

Living Abroad (www.livingabroad.com)

Plan Your Trip
Activities

The Peninsula offers many outdoor activities along the coast and in the desert interior. Largely gone are the days when these activities required survival and map-reading skills; there are now specialist agencies in each of the Peninsula countries making the great outdoors accessible.

Planning Your Trip

When to Go

Despite it being in one of the hottest regions of the world, the geography of the Arabian Peninsula is such that when camel riding in the Sharqiya sand dunes is out of bounds in the heat of mid-summer, diving and snorkelling are at their best in Musandam. That said, a trip to the region between May and October is not for the faint-hearted. The extreme heat and humidity at this time of year mean that any activity at sea level can be punishing, and picking the right time of day to hike or cycle can be a matter of consequence to your health.

As a rule of thumb, outdoor activities at sea level are best carried out between October and April, while mountain adventures are best from March to November, before freezing temperatures make camping and canyoning a challenge.

What to Take

A good pair of lightweight walking boots are essential for pretty much any land-based activity; sandals give less protection against burning sun, sharp stones, scorpions, snakes and shoreline hazards. Other than these, there's little need to bring much in the way of specialist equipment with you as all local tour operators provide this (including kite boards, fishing tackle and ropes for rock climbing).

Best Activities

Best Camel Trek
Sharqiya Sands, Oman; October to May

Best Diving & Snorkelling
Yanbu, Saudi Arabia; year-round

Best Dolphin Spotting
Musandam, Oman; year-round

Best Hiking & Biking
Misfat Al Abriyyin, Oman; October to May

Best Off-Road Routes
Hajar Mountains, Oman; October to May

Best Spa
Qasr Al Sarab Resort, Liwa Oasis, UAE; year-round

Best Water Sports
Yas Beach, Abu Dhabi, UAE; March to May and September to November

Best Outdoor Adventure
Hajar Mountains, Oman; March to December (but avoiding rainy days)

Equipment for wild camping and off-roading (for example, tents, cool boxes and sand ladders) can be bought inexpensively from many large supermarkets across the region.

Independent (as opposed to guided) activities require resourcefulness and some survival skills as the terrain is often remote and scarcely populated.

Getting Active

Camel Treks

The key places to head for four-legged treks in the dunes are Sharqiya Sands (p173) in Oman and Khor Al Adaid (p262) in Qatar. Almost all of the local desert camps can arrange treks of 30 minutes to an hour; for a multi-day trek, tour agencies in Salalah offer camel adventures in the Empty Quarter.

For a more authentic experience, choose a mounted rather than a walking guide through a company such a Oriental Nights Tours (p170) in Oman.

Off-Road Driving

The main outdoor activity in the region is off-road driving in the desert. All the countries in the region present endless opportunities for DIY routes (except Kuwait, which has a problem with stray ordnance) that weave through villages, along the bottom of wadis, up vertiginous mountain tracks and across sand dunes. Beware flash floods, soft sand and salt flat, and stay on tracks to protect the fragile desert ecology.

Pick up the locally published **Explorer Guides** when you're on the ground for off-road routes and their challenges.

Hiking & Cycling

Hiking is a highlight of the Peninsula, with Oman topping the list in terms of organisation and routes (pick up trail information from www.omantourism.gov.om). Allow one litre of water per person per hour, wear light-coloured clothing and stay out of wadis during and after rain.

Inspired by local long-distance cycling events such as Tour of Oman (www.tourofoman.om), cycling is becoming more popular. Contact Bike & Hike Oman (p176) for some route ideas.

DESERT DRIVING

The following tips may help if going off-road, but there's no substitute for experience. Many desert camps offer the chance to hire a 4WD and give some basic instructions. Some key things to be aware of before embarking on an off-road drive:

➡ Travel with another vehicle if you're heading for sandy areas so that you can pull each other out if you get stuck.

➡ Don't travel alone unless you can change a tyre (very heavy on 4WD vehicles).

➡ Use the services of a local guide if planning an extended dune trip – navigation is not as easy as it seems.

➡ Take a map and compass. A GPS and fully charged GSM phone are also helpful, but GPS is only useful for knowing exactly where you're lost (and not how to find the way out) and phones don't work in some mountainous or remote areas.

➡ Bring the equivalent of at least five litres of water per passenger per day and sufficient food to last several days. Dried dates are a good source of energy and keep well in high temperatures.

➡ Bring a tool kit with a tow rope, shovel, sand ladders, spanner, jack, wooden platform (on which to stand the jack), tyre inflator (and preferably a gauge) and jump leads. Also pack a first-aid kit.

➡ Tell someone where you're going.

Top: Qasr Al Sarab
Desert Resort (p396)
in Liwa Oasis, UAE

Right: A Bedouin and
his camels in Sharqiya
Sands (p173), Oman

ZEYNEP THOMAS/GETTY IMAGES ©

Climbing, Caving & Canyoning

The rocky Hajar Mountains in Oman and the UAE, and the Asir range in Saudi Arabia, offer opportunities for climbing on near-vertical limestone rock faces, as well as some sport bolted routes and via ferrata courses. Caving and canyoning (leaping from pool to pool through slot canyons) are also becoming better organised in these countries.

For specialist advice, contact Husaak Adventures (p142) in Muscat.

Water Sports

All seaboard cities have established water-sports centres offering swimming, jet skiing, water-skiing, kitesurfing, windsurfing, wakeboarding, stand-up paddleboarding, sailing and kayaking. Avoid south-eastern Arabia during the summer, when currents are ferocious and swimming is prohibited.

Organise activities through any of the seaboard five-star hotels and resorts, or through the marinas at Yas Beach (p375) in Abu Dhabi or Bandar Al Rowdha (p139) in Muscat.

Dhow Rides & Dolphin Spotting

One of the joys of being in the waters around Manama, Doha, Abu Dhabi, Dubai and Muscat is the chance to spot dolphins from the wooden deck of a traditional dhow. Go early in the morning for the best chance to see pods of dolphins in action.

Your best chance to combine a dhow and dolphin experience is from Musandam (p201). Most tour companies offer half- or whole-day trips, or turn up at the local marina and see what's heading out to sea!

Snorkelling & Diving

The Red Sea is one of the world's top diving destinations; the Arabian Sea offers easier access but has less coral. Both are wows in the water, but low-key experiences on land. Jeddah, Musandam, Muscat and Dhofar are the easiest places to organise an underwater adventure.

To see the kinds of experience on offer, contact Extra Divers (www.extradivers.com).

Fishing

Fishing has been an essential way of life on the Peninsula for centuries, and visitors can try their hand at catching yellow-fin tuna (weighing between 25kg and 60kg), sail fish, barracuda and shark from Manama, Doha, Abu Dhabi, Dubai and Muscat. Fishing licences are not needed on the Peninsula, but responsible catch-and-release fishing is encouraged.

In the UAE and Oman, you can book a trip with No Boundaries (p209). Alternatively, book through the local marina or negotiate an hourly rate directly with local fishers. Traditional fishing from a small boat is an option in Muscat.

Plan Your Trip
Family Travel

The Arabian Peninsula is very family-oriented and highly welcoming of visitors travelling with children. In fact, in a region where family is central to the notion of community, travelling with youngsters earns the respect of locals and often opens doors to unique local experiences. That is not to say it's easy travelling with kids and the very hot climate between May and October is something to be mindful of, particularly with very young children. The joys of open space and low crime rates, exciting nature-based adventures contrasted with sophisticated mall entertainment, make it a great destination for all age groups.

Bahrain

Bahrainis welcome visiting children, and a lively expat community means kids are never short of something to do. Look out for a handy booklet published biannually called *Fab Bahrain* (www.fabbahrain.com), available from bookshops, schools and **Seef Mall** (🖉77 911 111; www.seefmall.com.bh; Rd 2819, Seef; ☉10am-10pm Sat-Wed, to 11pm Thu & Fri; 🖱; 🚌41, A2, A2S, X2) in Manama. This free directory gives a full A–Z listing of what to do and where to go in Bahrain as a family, from the story-telling activities of 'Wriggly Readers' to waterskiing and wakeboarding. Also check out the 'Teens & Kids' section in *Bahrain this Month* magazine, which has heaps of information on fun activities, including lessons in hip-hop and salsa. Almost all tourist sites in Bahrain offer free or reduced admission for children, but few are pushchair friendly.

Kuwait

In many ways Kuwait is great for children. However, while there are plenty of family parking bays close to attractions and lifts

Best Regions for Kids

The Gulf Cities

The modern cities of the Gulf offer a high-tech toy-box for kids. With an indoor skating rink, ski slope, walk-through aquarium and various fun areas, the malls of Dubai are the champions of indoor, hot-weather diversion. All other capital cities include water parks, cinema complexes or playzones.

The Desert Interior

In the cooler months, there are numerous outdoor activities to interest older children and teens. The Hajar Mountains (shared by Oman and UAE) are a great destination to introduce youngsters to mountaineering, caving, canyoning and rock-climbing, while desert camps offer camel rides and buggy driving for kids.

The Coastal Fringe

The beaches of Arabia form more or less one giant sandpit and the often calm Gulf waters are a paddling pool of warm water for much of the year. Watersports for beginners are readily available across the region.

in shopping malls, Kuwait's streets are not pram-friendly. The sweltering heat can also be challenging for parents and kids.

In major shopping malls, mothers will find baby-changing facilities and breast-feeding rooms. Dads may find changing difficult as facilities are often attached to the womens toilets or to prayer rooms. Breastfeeding in public is possible if you are fully covered, but even then it is still a taboo in the Gulf.

Oman

Oman is a friendly and welcoming place for children. For younger kids, beach-combing, sandcastle building and paddling in shallow water make Oman a dream destination. That said, there are few specifically designed amenities for children, except for a park with swings in most town centres and fun zones in each city's main mall.

If you ask for an infant's 'cot', you will most likely get given a full-size adult mattress as this is the meaning of the word in the local use of English. Specific cots for children are less widely available, particularly outside Muscat, and if you ask for a child's bed in all but the top-end hotels, you'll most likely be given an adult-sized mattress.

High chairs are available in top-end restaurants and fast-food chains in Muscat. Kids are generally welcomed in the family section of all restaurants.

Safety seats for children under the age of four are now mandatory, although you wouldn't think it, given the number of

local kids who ride on the driver's lap or with their head out of the sunroof. Safety seats should be booked in advance with your car hire.

Nappy-changing facilities are available in hotels and malls in the big cities, but few (if any) amenities exist in the interior. Disposable nappies and milk formula can be bought in most supermarkets throughout the country.

Qatar

Qatar is a safe, easy-going, family-oriented country, and children are welcome and catered for in most places, especially malls, where there are changing facilities and activities.

Large resorts also have plenty of activities for young children, and sometimes kids clubs with daily schedules. At brunch (p252), some Doha hotels offer kids entertainers, face painting and other activities so parents can catch up with friends.

Doha is not a pedestrian-friendly place, and visitors with prams may struggle on the streets' uneven surfaces and big curbs. Nearly all public attractions have ample parking facilities, however, and the parks and Corniche are buggy-friendly.

Saudi Arabia

Although Saudis are family oriented, the country is not particularly friendly for travelling with children. There are almost no areas dedicated to baby changing, and

PRACTICALITIES

The region is overwhelmingly child-friendly, but not always child-oriented in terms of the facilities on offer. As a rule, the capital cities and main towns provide reasonably well for children, especially in modern malls, but small towns and villages have very few facilities beyond a park with swings. Here's a quick guide to what amenities are offered in the bigger cities.

Refer to Lonely Planet's *Travel with Children* for general details about travelling with children.

FACILITIES	BAHRAIN	KUWAIT	OMAN	QATAR	KSA	UAE
Pram-friendly pavements	No	No	No	No	No	Yes
Changing facilities	Yes	Yes	Yes	Yes	No	Yes
Reduced admission prices	Yes	Yes	Yes	Yes	Yes	Yes
Children's menus and high chairs	No	No	No	No	No	Yes
Child seats usually available in hire cars	Yes	No	Yes	Yes	No	Yes

most restaurants do not offer a children's menu, unless it is a fast-food joint. Also, in most places around the Kingdom, the pavements are not suited for pushchairs.

That is not to say Saudi Arabia is not a place for children – far from it. Children are welcome everywhere and many venues offer discounts for child entry. Almost every mall has a children's amusement or play area built into it, and increasingly waterfront paths up and down the country, such as Jeddah's Corniche (p281), are integrating more play parks and child-friendly features.

United Arab Emirates

It's easy to travel through the UAE with children. Many top-end hotels and some midrange ones have kids clubs, pools and playgrounds. There are plenty of beaches, parks, playgrounds and activity centres (many in shopping malls) to keep kids amused; many restaurants have children's menus and high chairs. Formula is readily available in pharmacies, and disposable nappies at grocery stores and supermarkets. Malls have excellent nappy-changing and baby-feeding facilities.

High kerbs on pavements can hinder pushchair use though pavements are sloped at traffic light intersections in city centres, and there are also pedestrian underpasses with ramps as well as stairs in built-up centres like downtown Abu Dhabi to aid with access.

Children's Highlights
Cooling Off

Wadi Adventure (p392) Al Ain's giant water park has rides and slides.

Aquaventure Waterpark (p334) Home to the world's longest water slide.

Yas Waterworld (p376) The pools and slides here are good for younger kids.

Lost Paradise of Dilmun Water Park (p84) Popular with the entire family.

Aqua Park (p107) Fridays are family days at this exciting water park.

Wahooo! (p66) Kids can learn to surf in indoor heated pools.

Hawana Water Park (p215) A surprise find in a remote location.

Indoor Fun & Learning

Ferrari World Abu Dhabi (p375) High-speed thrills in an enclosed theme park.

Green Planet (p332) The tropics brought indoors with sloths, toucans and a bat cave.

Warner Bros World Abu Dhabi (p375) Rides based on cartoon favourites.

Ithra (p307) Cinema and interactive workshops, including storytelling.

Children's Museum (p143) Muscat's low-key, high-interest learn-zone.

Scientific Center (p100) With an educational discovery zone.

Bounce (04 321 1300; www.bounce.ae; Bldg 32, 4B St, Al Quoz 1; 1hr session from Dhs85; 10am-10pm Sun-Wed, to midnight Thu, 9am-10pm Fri; Noor Bank, FGB) Indoor trampoline park in Dubai. Also in **Abu Dhabi** (04 3211 400; Marina Mall; 10am-10pm Sat-Wed, to midnight Thu & Fri).

The Zone (04 426 1413; www.atlantisthepalm.cm; Atlantis The Palm, Palm Jumeirah; Dhs50; 10.30am-6pm & 7-11pm; Palm Jumeirah, Atlantis Aquaventure) Teen-only space with movie lounge and DJ sets in Dubai.

Megapolis Entertainment Center (443 78444; http://megapolisqatar.com; Bldg B12, Andalucia Way, Medina Centrale, The Pearl; activities per hour from QR49, escape games per person from

TOP TIPS

➡ Across the region, restaurants have family sections where men and women can eat together with the kids.

➡ Even the tiniest hamlet tends to have a park with swings.

➡ Beware of the extreme heat in summer, which is difficult for very young children.

➡ Avoid ice cream outside big cities as power cuts often result in refreezing of frozen products.

QR100; ⊙10am-1am Sat-Wed, to 2am Thu, 1pm-2am Fri; ⊞) On The Pearl, in Doha, Qatar, with bowling and arcade games.

Mall Magic

Virtual Reality Park (☑04 448 8483; www.vrparkdubai.com; level 2, Dubai Mall; activities Dhs15-50; ⊙10am-10pm Sun-Wed, to midnight Thu-Sat; ⓜBurj Khalifa/Dubai Mall) Sightseeing in Dubai without stepping outside the mall.

Hub Zero (☑800 637 227; www.hubzerodubai.com/en; City Walk, Jumeirah 1; master/hacker/child pass Dhs160/195/95; ⊙2-10pm Sat-Wed, to midnight Thu & Fri; ⓅⓉ; ⓜBurj Khalifa/Dubai Mall) For gamers. It's great for older kids and teens.

Magic Planet (p129) At the Avenues with fairground attractions.

City Center Doha (p260) Ice rink in the desert? Every Gulf capital has one!

Gondolania (p259) Fairground-like games in Villaggio Mall.

Outdoor Activities

Marina Skate Park (p129) Kids burn off energy on a BMX or scooter.

Bahrain International Karting Circuit (p84) Smaller engines suited to younger drivers are available.

Jebel Jais Flight Zip Line (p366) UAE's ultimate adrenaline buzz for older teens.

Great Escapes for Kids

Husaak Adventures (p142) Family camping and canyoning in the Hajar Mountains.

Absolute Adventure (p335) The main Dibba hikes this company runs are suitable for active kids as young as eight.

Noukhada Adventure Company (p376) Family kayaking tours in Abu Dhabi's mangroves.

Kite Beach Centre (p364) Kitesurfing lessons plus kayak and SUP-board rental.

Challenging Adventure (p366) Family-focused kayaking around Ras Al Khaimah's mangroves.

Nature Encounters

Abu Dhabi Falcon Hospital (p376) Close-up encounters with birds of prey.

Al Ain Zoo (p392) A fantastic wildlife experience for kids of all ages.

Al Noor Island (p356) The butterfly house here will thrill younger kids.

Al Hefaiyah Mountain Conservation Centre (p405) Encounter the animals that inhabit the mountains of the Gulf.

Riyadh Zoo (p277) A host of exotic animals and birds visited by mini train.

Al Areen Wildlife Park & Reserve (p84) A chance to spot desert animals roaming in large enclosures.

Ras Al Jinz (p163) Even tots can help put baby turtles back in the water.

Royal Camel Farm (p92) Children can get up close and personal with Arabia's most famous animal.

Countries at a Glance

The term 'Arabian Peninsula' is so cohesive it's tempting to think the countries it comprises are alike. There are similarities of course – the heat, Bedouin roots, Islamic customs and the Arabic language – but the differences are just as pronounced. Head to the cities of the Gulf States to experience modern Arabia with fine museums, marble-clad malls, avant-garde restaurants and landscaped resorts. The interior, in contrast, offers a glimpse of the old Arabia with characterful souqs, remote villages, wild coastlines and ancient archaeological sites. At Arabia's desert core, the Empty Quarter is the magical landscape that lurks beyond 'the sown'.

Bahrain

Archaeology
Social Life
Culture

Honeycombed with burial mounds, ancient Bahrain was built on trade and entrepreneurialism remains key to its modern success. Sip coffee in fashionable Manama and rub shoulders with contemporary marketeers.

p56

Kuwait

Culture
Recent History
Shopping

From the Tareq Rajab museum to its landmark water towers, Kuwait's identity is preserved in diverse artistic treasures. While memories of war fade, this virtual city state has reinvented itself as a cultural hub.

p94

Oman

Landscapes
Wildlife
History

From the vertical heights of Jebel Shams to the horizontal desert plains, Oman is an adventurer's paradise. Hike through ancient villages, watch nesting turtles, or sail among dolphins for a glimpse of old Arabia.

p130

Qatar

Landscapes
Architecture
Culture

With the Gulf's most striking modern skyline, Doha's restless energy is magnetic. Currently shunned by some of its neighbours, Qatar focuses instead on the wider world with international sporting events frequently hosted here.

p237

Saudi Arabia

History
Landscapes
Islam

Looming large over the Peninsula, Saudi Arabia occupies most of the land mass and, as home to Mecca and Medina, lies at the heart of Islam. Conservative and difficult to access, it nonetheless confounds stereotypes.

p272

United Arab Emirates

Architecture
Urban Culture
Landscapes

Much admired for its urban vibe and modern architecture, the UAE is less known for its soulful hinterland. Don't miss camping forays into the Empty Quarter, rugged mountain drives and island retreats.

p323

Yemen

Inaccessible

Ravaged by tribal infighting and a proxy war between powerful neighbours, Yemen is trapped in conflict. As such, this dramatically beautiful country, with ancient tower houses and rabbit-warren souqs, is off limits to visitors.

p419

On the
Road

Bahrain بحرين

POP 1,491,600

Best Places to Eat

➡ Haji's Cafe 1950 (p68)

➡ Spicy Village (p83)

➡ Masso (p71)

➡ Rasoi by Vineet (p71)

➡ Banana Leaf (p68)

Best Places to Stay

➡ Fraser Suites Diplomatic Area (p67)

➡ Domain (p67)

➡ Palace Boutique Hotel (p67)

➡ Novotel Al Dana Resort (p68)

➡ Ritz-Carlton Bahrain Hotel & Spa (p68)

Why Go?

Like an oyster, Bahrain has a rough exterior that takes some prising open, but it's worth the effort. The storied location of the ancient Dilmun empire and home to the epicentre of the Gulf's pearling past, Bahrain has a history to reflect on with pride. Boasting its own Formula 1 Grand Prix, a growing art and foodie scene heavily cross-pollinated by Manama's huge expat population, and a wealth of activities enjoyed on the azure waters surrounding this collection of islands, Bahrain will appeal to travellers who seek an unpretentious, yet confident country bearing all the hallmarks of a modern, wealthy Gulf nation. This multilayered and multicultural destination is often overlooked by tourists, so you'll probably have the place all to yourself.

When to Go
Bahrain

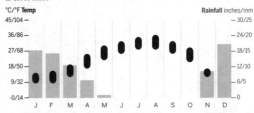

Oct–Mar Bask in the relative cool of a Gulf winter with daily blue skies.

Apr Join the fast lane during the Formula 1 Grand Prix.

May–Sep Extreme heat; better to visit another time.

Daily Costs

Bahrain is an expensive destination, and accommodation will eat up a big chunk of travellers' budgets. Bank on at least BD40 (about US$105) for a comfortable room, and note that some cheaper hotels double as brothels, especially in central Manama. Daily costs for midrange accommodation and dining land between BD50 and BD80 (about US$130 to US$215).

AT A GLANCE

Capital Manama

Country code ☏973

Currency Bahraini dinar (BD)

Emergency ☏999

Language Arabic, English

Mobile phones SIM cards widely available

Money ATMs are widespread; credit cards widely accepted

Population 1,491,600

Visas Available on arrival or online (www.evisa.gov.bh) for a fee

ITINERARIES

One Day

Bahrain's former capital Muharraq (p76) is a short hop across the water from Manama, making it easy to absorb the wonderful decaying reminders of old Bahrain before taking in the key highlights of the modern capital.

Start off wandering the narrow streets of historic Muharraq, where beautiful old residencies like Beit Sheikh Isa Bin Ali Al Khalifa (p76) whisk you back to a pre-oil innocence. Afterwards, cross the causeway and head into the Bahrain National Museum (p59) to get thoroughly educated on the nation's history and heritage.

After lunch, grab a taxi south to admire the majestic Al Fatih Mosque (p61). It's then a short hop to uber-chic Adliya, Manama's most creative neighbourhood. End your day in bustling Manama Souq (p62), where dining on Haji's (p68) traditional food will transport you back to a bygone Bahrain.

Three Days

Get up early in the hope of striking it rich on your prebooked pearl dive (p63) in the turquoise waters off Muharraq Island. Following lunch, head to the Unesco site of Bahrain Fort (p81) and then visit the Dilmun temple at Saar (p82).

Pick up the pace on day three at the Formula 1 Racetrack (p83), where you can reach speeds of 300km/h in a dragster (p84). For a more gentle afternoon, head to Al Areen Wildlife Park & Reserve (p84) and try to spot the creature historically mistaken for a unicorn. Stop at the Tree of Life (p84) at sunset to end your trip beside this ancient relic at its enchanting best.

Exchange Rates

The dinar is pegged to the US dollar and rarely fluctuates. For current exchange rates, see www.xe.com.

Australia	A$10	BD2.65
Canada	C$10	BD2.81
Euro zone	€10	BD4.24
Japan	¥1000	BD3.39
New Zealand	NZ$10	BD2.56
Saudi Arabia	SR10	BD1.01
UAE	Dhs10	BD1.03
UK	UK£10	BD4.90
USA	US$10	BD3.77

Resources

Bahrain Tourism (https://bahrain.com)

Lonely Planet (www.lonelyplanet.com/bahrain)

Time Out Bahrain (www.timeoutbahrain.com)

Essential Food & Drink

Machboos A casserole of rice with chicken, lamb or fish in a rich sauce.

Khanfaroosh Fried dough spiced with saffron and cardamom.

Tap water Not safe to drink; bottled water is widely available but be aware of your plastic impact.

Alcohol Available in top-end hotels and select licensed venues.

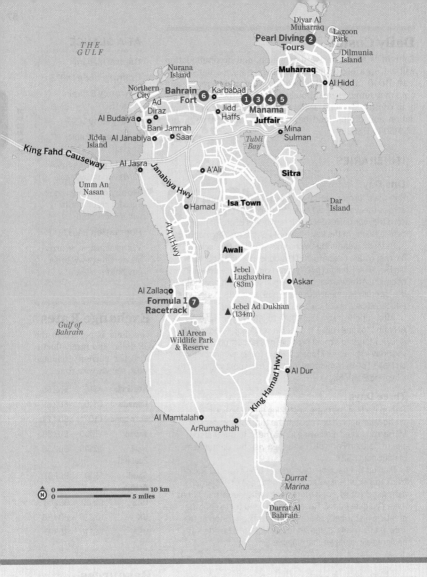

Bahrain Highlights

1 Manama Souq (p62)
Exploring the narrow streets and alleyways that possess all the energy and nostalgia of an ancient souq.

2 Pearl Diving Tours (p63)
Plunging into the azure waters like a seasoned pearl diver and seeking your fortune.

3 Haji's Cafe 1950 (p68)

Putting your feet up and enjoying street food with a 70-year heritage.

4 Bahrain National Museum (p59) Immersing yourself in this museum to understand Bahrain, past and present.

5 Bahrain National Theatre (p74) Enjoying world-class

performing arts in a world-class building.

6 Bahrain Fort (p81)
Admiring the 16th-century battlements atop the ancient Dilmun capital.

7 Formula 1 Racetrack (p83) Sampling life in the fast lane at Bahrain's annual glamour gig.

MANAMA'S GROWING GALLERY SCENE

More than any other Gulf city, Manama has a burgeoning arts scene. Its epicentre is the multicultural Adliya neighbourhood, formerly known for its nightlife. Adliya has added depth and a touch of the bohemian in recent years, with an explosion of cafes, fine restaurants and art galleries inhabiting converted Bahraini town houses.

La Fontaine Centre for Contemporary Art (Map p64; ☑ 17 230 123; https://lafontain eartcentre.net; Rd 639, Dhuwawdah; ☉ 10am-10.30pm Tue-Sun) **FREE** A stylish gallery that holds regular exhibits featuring contemporary artists from all over the world in a beautifully renovated 19th-century Bahraini town house.

Albareh Art Gallery (Map p64; ☑ 17 717 707; www.albareh.com; Bldg 38, Rd 3601, Area 336, Adliya; ☉ 10am-2pm & 4-8pm Sat-Thu; ☐ 43, 45) **FREE** Works by Middle Eastern and North African artists dominate this small Adliya gallery.

Manama Craft Centre (Craft Industries Development Centre; Map p64; ☑ 17 254 688; 263 Sheikh Isa Al Khebir Ave; ☉ 7am-2.15pm Sun-Thu; **P**) A variety of studios and workshops where locals have been trained to revive the island's traditional crafts, including palm-leaf paper making, pottery and ironwork, much of which is available for sale.

Arabesque Art Gallery (Map p60; ☑ 17 722 916; www.arabesque-gallery.com; Villa 182, Rd 3703, Block 337, Adliya; ☉ 9am-7pm Sat-Thu; ☐ 44) **FREE** This gallery exhibits the oils and watercolours of its owner, Wahab Al Koheji, who specialises in Gulf architecture. The gallery also contains rare antique maps and ancient lithographs of the Middle East.

MANAMA

المنامة

POP 335,610

Manama might lack the polish and outlandish commercialism seen in some Gulf capitals, but therein lies its charm. Yes, you'll find all the hallmarks of modern Arab prosperity here – vast air-conditioned shopping malls and daringly designed skyscrapers – but confidently nestled beside all that glass and glamour are delightful relics and reminders of the city's proud heritage as a busy port town. Historic sites are given equal footing with the brash, modern ones. This is most apparent in Manama's Souq, where the hustle and bustle still evokes an ancient bazaar, and the globally diverse local cuisine is slowly elevating the city into a foodie destination.

Manama's world-class National Museum, Beit Al Quran and avant-garde National Theatre represent the commitment of the city to not just preserve the past but actively celebrate it, creating a balance between the old and new rarely witnessed in this region.

◉ Sights

All of Manama's key sights fan out from Bab Al Bahrain (p62), including the narrow streets and alleys of the atmospheric Manama Souq (p62), where most tourists head first.

The more clinical diplomatic and financial areas to the west are home to many of the city's iconic modern buildings, including the award-winningly designed **World Trade Centre** (Map p64; ☑ 17 211 398; www. bahrainwtc.com; Isa Al Khebir Ave; **P**; ☐ 10, 41, 44, A1) and the sloping twin towers of the **Financial Harbour** (Map p64; ☑ 17 102 600; www. bfharbour.com; Block 346, Rd 4626, King Faisal Corniche). Beneath these, close to the causeway for Muharraq Island, are Manama's main cultural venues.

★ **Bahrain National Museum** MUSEUM
(Map p64; ☑ 17 298 777; www.culture.gov.bh; Al Fatih Hwy; BD0.5; ☉ 8am-8pm; **P**) Deservedly the country's most popular attraction, this is an outstanding introduction to Bahrain's history, with signage in English and Arabic. It's housed in a postmodern building on the waterfront, and the lower floor displays the archaeological finds of ancient Dilmun, the Hall of Graves and Bahrain's customs and traditions, where the south Asian impact on clothing is remarkably apparent. Upstairs, there are exhibits on the Tylos and Islamic periods, historic manuscripts and a delightful reproduction of a traditional souq.

The museum also has a temporary exhibition hall and an art gallery where displays periodically change. But arguably one of the most popular spaces, certainly with resident expat women, is the excellent museum cafe. Spacious, chic and comfortable, it has a

Bahrain

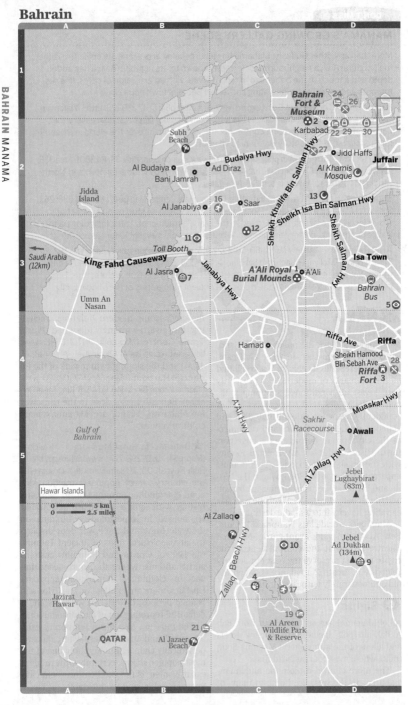

Bahrain Fort & Museum

24
26
Karbabad
2
22 29 30
27 Jidd Haffs
Juffair

Subh Beach

Al Budaiya
Ad Diraz
Bani Jamrah

Budaiya Hwy

Al Khamis Mosque

Jidda Island

16
Saar
Al Janabiya

13

Sheikh Khalifa Bin Salman Hwy

Sheikh Isa Bin Salman Hwy

11
12

← Saudi Arabia (12km)

Sheikh Salman Hwy

Isa Town

King Fahd Causeway
Toll Booth

Janabiya Hwy

Al Jasra
7

A'Ali Royal Burial Mounds
1
A'Ali

Bahrain Bus

5

Umm An Nasan

Riffa Ave
Riffa

Hamad

Sheikh Hamood Bin Sebah Ave
28
Riffa Fort
3

Muaskar Hwy

Gulf of Bahrain

A'Ali Hwy

Sakhir Racecourse

Awali

Al Zallaq Hwy

Jebel Lughaybirat (83m)
▲

Hawar Islands

0 ——— 5 km
0 ——— 2.5 miles

Al Zallaq

Zallaq Beach Hwy

10

Jebel Ad Dukhan (134m)
▲ 9

Jazirat Hawar

4
17

19
Al Areen Wildlife Park & Reserve

QATAR

21
Al Jazaer Beach

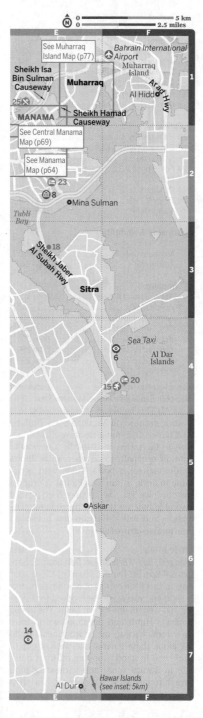

first-rate terrace looking across the bay to the stunning Bahrain National Theatre (p74). The museum is also where you buy tickets for the Qalat Bu Mahir Ferry (p93) to visit the Qalat Bu Mahir fort (p80) on Muharraq Island.

★ Al Fatih Mosque
MOSQUE

(Map p64; ☏17 727 773; Rd 2407, Juffair; ☺non-Muslims 9am-4pm Sun-Thu; P; ☐41) This is Bahrain's grand mosque, built as a grand statement in honour of the founder of modern Bahrain, Sheikh Ahmed Bin Muhammad Bin Khalifa, who was known as 'Al Fatih' (the conqueror). The mosque's foundation stone was laid by his direct descendant, the late emir Sheikh Isa Bin Salman Al Khalifa in 1983, exactly 200 years after Al Fatih liberated the nation from the Persians. Built at a cost of US$20 million, it is the most sumptuous mosque in the country.

Able to hold up to 7000 worshippers, Al Fatih has an air of majesty unmatched by other mosques in Bahrain and is the only one actively able to accommodate visitors. There are dedicated English- and Arabic-speaking guides on hand every day to give free guided tours. Simply turn up at the mosque office and request one. Those requiring tours in a different language or groups of 10 or more must phone ahead. Dress modestly.

★ Beit Al Quran
MUSEUM

(House of the Quran; Map p64; ☏17 290 101; Bldg 17, Rd 1901; ☺8.30am-1.30pm & 4-6pm Sat-Wed, 8.30am-1.30pm Thu; P; ☐41) **FREE** The finest collection of ancient Qurans in the region, this wonderful homage to Islam's holiest book displays Qurans from almost every century since the advent of Islam in 610, as well as some of the earliest translations into European languages. This includes the English translation by George Sale, published in London in the 18th century, a copy of which was bought by US founding father and president Thomas Jefferson.

Wrapped in carved Kufic script, the distinctive Beit Al Quran is a fine example of modern Bahraini architecture. As well as Qurans, it also houses manuscripts, woodcarvings and examples of Islamic calligraphy, and boasts a library that is home to works by the likes of ancient Persian poets Rumi and Omar Khayyam. The exhibits are well labelled in English and can be superficially perused within an hour. Phone ahead for a guided tour.

Bahrain

The main entrance and car park are at the back, on the southern side of the building. Visitors should dress conservatively.

A delightful little **mosque** is integrated within the Beit Al Quran complex and is open even when the museum isn't. Often overlooked, it has one of the most unusual features you are likely to see in a Bahraini mosque, a beautiful stained-glass dome. This sits above a mihrab (niche indicating the direction of Mecca) decorated with blue tiles that evokes Muslim Persia. The tiles in the courtyard have a similar effect, only they take you to Muslim Spain.

★**Manama Souq**　　　　MARKET
(Map p69; Bab Al Bahrain Ave; ☻9am-1pm & 4-9pm Sat-Thu, 4-9pm Fri; 🚍10, 12, 17, 18, 19, 41, 43, 44) Manama Souq is a warren of narrow streets and alleyways emanating south from Bab Al Bahrain. Here you can pick up everything from electronic goods and bargain t-shirts to spices and shisha pipes. But the real reason to visit is to wander through the bustling streets of a market that still evokes the atmosphere of an ancient souq.

Bab Al Bahrain　　　　MONUMENT
(Map p69; Bab Al Bahrain Ave, Manama Souq; 🚍10, 41, 44, A1) This handsome twin-arched gate is a fitting entrance to Manama Souq. Built by Sir Charles Dalrymple Belgrave, British adviser to the royals, in 1949, the 'Gateway to Bahrain' originally stood where huge dhows (traditional cargo boats) laden with goods came to dock, as this was Bahrain's original customs pier. The sea has since been pushed several kilometres north through land reclamation, and Bab Al Bahrain now houses an information centre (p92).

Little India　　　　AREA
(Map p69; Bab Al Bahrain Ave, Gold Souq; ☻8am-1pm & 4-8pm Sat-Thu, 8-11.30am Fri) Close your eyes in this little corner of Manama's historic souq and you would be forgiven for thinking you were in downtown Delhi. The lingua franca is Hindi, and the shop owners trace their roots back to the subcontinent. Walking along these narrow alleyways, a cup of *chai* (tea) in hand, stopping off for a quick bite in Swagat (p68) and witnessing *puja* (worship) inside the 200-year-old **Khrishna**

DON'T MISS

PEARLS IN BAHRAIN

Pearls are created when grit enters the shell of an oyster. The intrusive irritant is covered with a layer of mother-of-pearl, making it smooth and less irksome, and the longer the problem is nursed, the bigger the pearl gets. Large pearls have attracted huge sums of money throughout history, and though size counts, it's not everything. Other factors include the depth and quality of lustre, the perfection of shape, and the colour of the pearl, which can be as diverse as peach or iron.

Commercial pearling was halted with the pioneering of the 'cultured' pearl in Japan in the 1930s. Cultured pearls are created by artificially injecting a bead into the shell of an oyster. These farmed pearls are more uniform and develop quicker, but are not pure because they have a foreign centre. Pearl farming took the unpredictability and guesswork out of the pearl industry and thus the novelty, yet today, almost all the pearls sold are cultured.

In Bahrain, natural pearls are garnered from the island's healthy oyster beds in a bid to revive this heritage industry. Occasionally, the sea bed renders up the larger, uniquely coloured pearls that once made the area so famous, but more often than not, Bahraini pearl jewellery features clusters of tiny, individually threaded, ivory-coloured pearls, set in 21-karat gold.

Visit the gold shops of central Manama to see how pearls continue to inspire local jewellers. A perfect pearl can fetch thousands of dollars, but a pair of cluster earrings or a ring can start at a more affordable BD40. Prices for pearl jewellery are more or less fixed, but there's no harm in asking for a discount for oyster shells (BD25 including growing pearl – or free for those willing to dive for their own).

Dare to Dive?

While free diving like the tough old men who used to head out on wooden dhows for weeks on end is an experience you will find difficult to re-create, pearl diving as a touristic pastime is now wholly regulated by the government.

All **Pearl Diving Tours** (☑17 558 800; http://pearldiving.bh; Rd 3469, Ave 65, Samaheej; per person BD32, groups from BD195; ☺hours vary) depart from the Ras Rayyah Port in Muharraq Island and must be booked via the government portal. PADI licensed divers can choose to explore any one of four sites – Sayah, Bu Amamma, Shtayaah and Bulthama in the Gulf – but those who are not licensed can only snorkel at Sayah.

Divers can stay underwater for up to two hours collecting as many as 60 oysters. Each diver must also acquire a BD5 government pass via the government portal before heading out.

Temple (Map p69; ☑17 256 131; off Rd 430, Gold Souq; ☺6-11.30am & 5.15-8pm) really is a one-off experience in Bahrain.

Little India covers an area of 5000 sq m spread over three streets (Bab Al Bahrain Ave, Al Tijjar Ave and Al Hadrami Ave) where historically many houses were built using Indian wood.

Sheikh Hussain Mosque MOSQUE
(Map p60; Bldg 1296, Rd 4134, Block 441, North Sehla, Sheikh Salman Hwy; ☐A1, 19) There are mosques aplenty in Bahrain, but this tiny, perfectly formed Shia mosque has a wonderfully unusual curved design, providing a modern take on the architecture of the famous 9th-century spiralling Malwiya Tower minaret in Samarra, Iraq, a town of huge

spiritual significance for many Shias. The mosque's beautifully carved wooden door is also noteworthy.

Al Khamis Mosque MOSQUE
(Map p60; ☑17 298 777; Tashan Ave, Khamis; ☺24hr, visitor centre 9am-4pm; ☐P; ☐19, A1) This might just be the oldest mosque in Bahrain. It is believed a mosque has stood here since the 8th century, though the current ruins, which include two beautifully restored, climbable minarets, date from the 12th and 13th centuries. The site is particularly evocative when lit up at night. The mosque's name comes from the Thursday market that was held here for centuries. Black-and-white pictures depicting this make up the excellent exhibit in the visitors centre.

Manama

The Gulf

◉9
Bahrain World
Trade Centre

◉5

FADHEL

Government Ave

KANOO

King Faisal Hwy

HAMMAM

Bahrain City
Centre (1km);
Saudi Arabia (30km)

See Central Manama Map (p69)

Fish
Market

Manama
Central
Market

6◉

Central Market Ave

Sheikh Abdullah Ave

BUSIRRA

Lulu Ave

Sheikh Hanad Ave

AN NAIM

MUKHARQAH

Budaiya Hwy

ZARARIE

◉8

Sheikh Isa Al Khebir Ave

Sheikh Mohammed Ave

Cemetery

King Faisal Hwy

Al Mutanabi Ave

Water
Garden

AL QUFOOL

Sheikh Isa Bin Salman Hwy

Salmaniya Ave

Delmun
Roundabout

Salmaniya Ave

AL SULMANIYA

Kuwait Ave

SUQAYA

Oman Ave

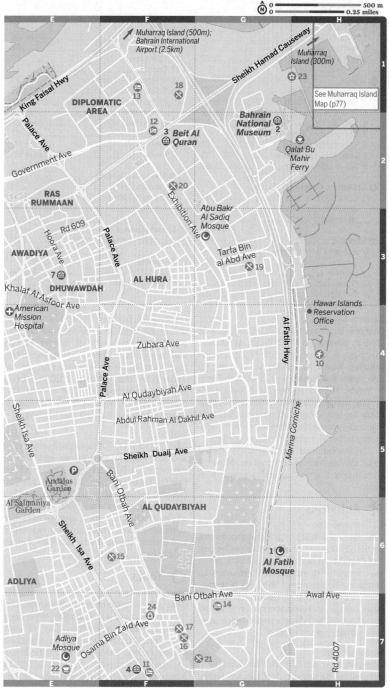

0   500 m
0   0.25 miles

N

Muharraq Island (500m);
Bahrain International
Airport (2.5km)

King Faisal Hwy

DIPLOMATIC
AREA

Sheikh Hamad Causeway

Muharraq
Island (300m)

★ 23

See Muharraq Island
Map (p77)

Palace Ave

13

18

12

3 **Beit Al
Quran**

Bahrain
National
Museum
2

Government Ave

Qalat Bu
Mahir
Ferry

RAS
RUMMAAN

20

Exhibition Ave

Abu Bakr
Al Sadiq
Mosque

Rd 609

Hoora Ave

Palace Ave

Tarfa Bin
al Abd Ave

19

AWADIYA

7

DHUWAWDAH

AL HURA

Khalaf Al Asfoor Ave

American
Mission
Hospital

Hawar Islands
Reservation
Office

Al Fatih Hwy

Zubara Ave

Palace Ave

Al Qudaybiyah Ave

10

Abdul Rahman Al Dakhil Ave

Sheikh Duaij Ave

Sheikh Isa Ave

Marina Corniche

Andalus
Garden

P

Al Salmaniya
Garden

Bani Otbah Ave

AL QUDAYBIYAH

Sheikh Isa Ave

15

1

**Al Fatih
Mosque**

ADLIYA

Bani Otbah Ave

Awal Ave

24

14

Adliya
Mosque

17

Osama Bin Zaid Ave

16

Rd 4007

22

4

11

21

Manama

Yateem Mosque   MOSQUE

(Map p69; Government Ave; ⬛10, 41, 44) Built in 1992 by Sheikh Isa Bin Salman Al Khalifa, this mosque is easily identified by its unique minaret, which (unusually for a mosque) also serves as a clock tower. But the real gem is inside: framed by beautiful Kufic calligraphy, four pillars hold up the twin arches of the mosque's impressive mihrab, which is elaborately carved in different repeating geometric patterns, creating a dizzying effect.

The mosque can be respectfully visited by tourists outside of prayer times. Muslims should note there is no Friday prayer held here.

 Activities

La Fontaine Spa   SPA

(Map p64; ☑17 230 123; https://lafontaineartcentre.net; Rd 639, Dhuwawdah; ⊙9am-10.30pm Tue-Sun) Not only does it nurture the soul with an art gallery and the stomach with a restaurant, La Fontaine also has one of Bahrain's best spas. There are facial and body treatments, reflexology, massages and all manner of body scrubs. Ask about the half-day packages, which combine a treatment with a meal.

Diplomat Spa   SPA

(Map p64; ☑17 525 237; www.radissonblu.com/diplomathotel-bahrain/spa; cnr Sheikh Hamad Causeway & Al Fatih Hwy; ⊙6am-10pm) The Radisson Blu Diplomat Hotel's spa complex evokes Asian zen with its wooden bridges and rock gardens. There is a large swimming pool, gym, steam room, sauna and Jacuzzi. A day pass costs between BD10 and BD15, and spa packages, including a deep Thai massage service, begin at BD35. The spa has separate facilities for men and women.

Wahooo!   WATER PARK

(Map p60; ☑17 173 000; www.theplaymania.com/wahooo; 2nd fl, City Centre Bahrain, Rd 4650, Seef; over/under 1.2m BD13/8.5, under 3yr BD4; ⊙11am-8pm Thu-Tue, to 10pm Wed; ⬛41, A2, A2S, X2) This massive indoor water park guarantees fun for all ages, with a wave pool, water slides, a slow-moving river and a number of heated swimming pools. There are also swimming and surfing lessons. Wednesdays are women only between 5pm and 10pm.

 Tours

Mangroves Tour   TOURS

(Map p60; http://portal.btea.bh/Mangrove; Sitra Park, Sheikh Jabeer A Al Subah Hwy, Nabih Saleh; 30min tour BD5; ⊙8am-4pm) One of Bahrain's most unique sights, the mangrove swamp around Tubli Bay is a major breeding ground for shrimp and small fish, and a haven for migratory birds who come to shelter and feed around the semi-aquatic trees. Drifting through the lush, green, mangroves juxtaposed against Manama's skyline, you'll hear more birdsong here than anywhere else in Bahrain.

In shallower parts, look out for the mangrove's uniquely evolved roots, which stick out of the mud and water like a snorkel.

Tours are weather dependent.

🛏 Sleeping

Manama has a wide range of hotels and apartment-style accommodation, particularly on or around Government Ave. Most high-end international hotels are close to the Diplomatic Area while the few budget options tend to be near Manama Souq (p62), and a range of charming resorts line the city's coastal edges. For real value though, head to Adliya, south of the centre.

Bahrain Carlton Hotel   HOTEL $

(Map p64; ☑17 715 999; www.bahraincarlton.com; Bldg 59, Rd 3601, Block 336, Adliya; r from BD35; [P][🛜]; [🚌43, 45]) You'll put up with the dated, slightly eccentric decor at the Carlton when you see the excellent-value, large, clean and spacious rooms. These, combined with extremely warm and friendly staff, make this an excellent budget choice for those wanting to stay in the heart of Bahrain's artsy Adliya neighbourhood.

Delmon International Hotel   HOTEL $

(Map p69; ☑17 224 000; www.delmonhotel.com; Block 302, Government Ave; s/d BD25/35; [P][🛜][🏊]) The Delmon is a well-located downtown hotel that is great value for money. Rooms tend to feature dark furnishings, but the hotel's nicely decorated Marrakesh restaurant serves excellent Mediterranean cuisine, and there's also a small on-site gym and spa. The best thing about staying here, besides the price, is its proximity to Manama Souq (p62).

Jindol Hotel   HOTEL $

(Map p69; ☑17 227 227; Municipality Ave, Block 315, Manama Souq, cnr Tijjar Ave; s/d BD15/20; [🛜]) This great budget option is on the doorstep of Manama Souq, overlooking its best *chai* shops. The hotel's faux-traditional Bahraini facade makes up for its basic but clean rooms. Stay here and you'll be within walking distance of all the major sights.

★ Fraser Suites Diplomatic Area   APARTMENT $$

(Map p64; ☑16 161 888; https://diplomaticarea-bahrain.frasershospitality.com; Rd 1701, Diplomatic Area; ste from BD62; [P][🛜][🏊]) Outrageously good value, these large serviced apartments have contemporary decor, sitting rooms, kitchens and king-size beds, as well as a good location in Manama's Diplomatic Area. Many also have fine city views. There's another branch in the Seef district.

★ Domain   HOTEL $$

(Map p64; ☑16 000 000; www.thedomainhotels.com; Bldg 365, Rd 1705, Block 317, Diplomatic Area; s/d BD72/78; [P][🛜][🏊]) Slick contemporary furnishings, fabulous views and exemplary service (the floors with suites have butlers) define this excellent hotel on the southern fringe of the Diplomatic Quarter. A stylish spa and a fine selection of restaurants make this an excellent choice, indicated by the scores of repeat guests.

Fraser Suites Seef   APARTMENT $$

(Map p60; ☑17 171 626; https://bahrain.frasershospitality.com; Bldg 2109, Rd 2825, Block 428, Seef; ste from BD50; [P][🛜][🏊]; [🚌41, A2, A2S, X2]) These excellent-value, stylishly decorated suites and apartments come with access to a communal temperature-controlled swimming pool and Jacuzzi that command fabulous views over Manama. Close to the Sheikh Khalifa Bin Salman Hwy and offering tons of child-friendly amenities such as cots and high chairs, this is ideal accommodation for families.

Palace Boutique Hotel   BOUTIQUE HOTEL $$

(Map p60; ☑17 725 000; www.thepalace.com.bh; cnr Mahooz Ave & Sheikh Isa Ave, Adliya; s/d BD55/80; [P][🛜][🏊]) This classy, low-slung place close to the heart of uber-cool Adliya is an excellent choice. Its four-star rooms are large, contemporary in style and supremely comfortable. The on-site restaurant Masso (p71) and stylish cafe the Orangery (p70) are among Manama's best. If you can, bag yourself a poolside terrace room.

C Hotel   BOUTIQUE HOTEL $$

(Map p64; ☑17 312 700; www.coralbaybh.com; Coral Bay Resort, Bldg 491, Rd 2407, Block 322; s/d BD50/55; [P][🛜][🏊]) Shaped like a small moored ferry, this boutique hotel has 14 stylish rooms with great sea views overlooking the resort's private little bay. There's an outdoor bar where live DJs entertain daily, and guests also have access to the onsite spa, outdoor pool, gym, excellent restaurants and sports bar (p74).

Novotel Al Dana Resort
RESORT $$$

(Map p77; ☑17 298 008; https://novotel.accor hotels.com; Rd 2209, Sheikh Hamad Causeway; s/d from BD90/100; [P][🛜][≋]) With distinctive style and character rare in international hotels, the Novotel is built like a *qasr* (castle) around elegant central courtyards and is punctuated at the edges by whimsical Bahraini wind towers. It commands a wonderful view of the bay, and residents have access to their own private beach, a health club and a recently opened international restaurant.

Gulf Hotel
HOTEL $$$

(Map p64; ☑17 713 000; www.gulfhotelbah rain.com; Rd 3801, Block 338, Adliya; s/d from BD80/100; [P][🛜][≋]) Despite being 4km from the city centre, this veteran hotel is the most convenient for the Gulf International Convention Centre and has easy access to bohemian Adliya's cafes, art galleries and popular Western-expat eating haunts. With an extravagant foyer, velvet lounges and marble halls, the interior appears to belong to an Italian palazzo.

Ritz-Carlton Bahrain Hotel & Spa
RESORT $$$

(Map p60; ☑17 588 000; www.ritzcarlton.com; Bldg 112, Rd 40, Block 428, Seef; s/d from BD150/185; [P][🛜][≋]) Arguably Bahrain's most luxurious and opulent hotel, the Ritz-Carlton boasts its own private beach on a secluded island and a host of world-class restaurants. The dark polished interior of black marble and gilt-edged furniture might not be to everyone's taste, but if yours is a Bentley, you'll be in good company.

Regency InterContinental
HOTEL $$$

(Map p69; ☑17 227 777; www.ihg.com; Bldg 130, Rd 1507, King Faisal Hwy; s/d from BD80/90; [P][🛜][≋]) In the heart of downtown Manama, this old favourite continues to get rave reviews. The contemporary black and grey elegance works well, and the pillow count makes up for what the rooms might lack in window size. Bars, restaurants and impeccable service round off a superb package.

✗ Eating

Manama's globally diverse community means the city's cuisine is truly international, offering Michelin-starred dishes alongside delicious budget eateries. The former are in the high-end hotels, whereas those seeking cheap Indian curries, Bahraini *machboos* (spiced chicken and rice) or a delicious shawarma wrap should explore the streets around Manama Souq (p62). The more stylish boutique eateries are in trendy Adliya.

★ Haji's Cafe 1950
MIDDLE EASTERN $

(Al Maseela; Map p69; ☑17 210 647; Government Ave; mains from BD1.5; ⏲5.30am-8.30pm) Balmy Bahraini evenings were created for eating in places like this. Put your feet up (literally), order the house special and tuck into delicately spiced chunks of grilled meat served with a simple salad and bread baked in a clay oven. Why is it so good? This is a recipe unchanged for 70 years.

It's down an alley next to Gulf Pearl Hotel.

Honey's Thai Restaurant
THAI $

(Map p69; ☑39 238 507; Municipality Ave, Manama Souq; mains BD1.5-3.5; ⏲10am-5.30am) Around since the 1980s, Honey's is an award-winning downtown stalwart serving up excellent Thai food at fantastic prices until the early hours. The tom yum soup is exceptional, though there's nothing on the menu that wouldn't win plaudits down a Bangkok foodie alley.

Swagat
VEGETARIAN $

(Map p69; ☑17 263 096; Shop 102, Bldg 1261, Rd 428, Gold Souq; meals BD0.6; ⏲9am-10pm; ☑) Tucked away in a warren of alleyways near the Khrishna Temple (p62) is this delightful slice of downtown Mumbai. Bollywood classics from the 1960s play on a tired stereo as smiling Indian waiters whip up delicious vegetarian *thalis* (spread of dishes) for less than the price of a coffee. Cosy and with no frills, Swagat is popular with local Hindus.

Banana Leaf
THAI $

(Map p64; ☑17 744 172; Shop 41, Bldg 39, Hassan Bin Thabit Ave, Block 326, Adliya; mains from BD2.5; ⏲noon-midnight) The tacky waterfall windows add to the charm of this popular Thai restaurant in the heart of Adliya, where locals come for the fresh mango and green sticky rice, topped with ever-so-slightly-salted coconut milk and a sprinkling of sesame seeds. Like all the dishes here, it's fresh, simple and fragrant.

Golden Plates
INDIAN $

(Tharavadu; Map p64; ☑17 297 575; Rd 2004, Block 320, Hoora; mains from BD2.5; ⏲11.30am-2am; 🛜☑; 🖵41) The ambience at this smart, South Indian eatery is enhanced with mellow music and smiling staff. Dishes include an outstanding beef and green banana cur-

Central Manama

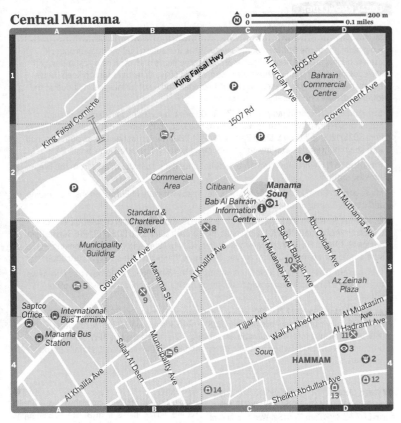

Central Manama

ry, but if you're coming for lunch on Friday, don't miss the *sadiya*, a south Indian *thali* served on a banana leaf, for the princely sum of BD1.5.

Naseef   ICE CREAM $
(Map p69; ☑ 17 223 333; www.naseefrestaurant. com; Bab Al Bahrain Mall, Rd 475, Manama Souq; ice cream from BD1.5; ☺ 8am-11pm; ☏; ☐ 10, 12,

17, 18, 19, 41, 43, 44) Tucked away inside the quiet Bab Al Bahrain Mall at the entrance to Manama Souq (p62) south of the Bab Al Bahrain, Naseef made its name with a vivid-hued mango ice cream, and that's what you should order at the end of a day exploring the narrow alleys of the bustling market. There's also an extensive food menu here.

LOCAL KNOWLEDGE

THE BAHRAIN BRUNCH

A big highlight of the Bahrain foodie's week is the institution that is Friday brunch. It usually begins around noon, runs for around three hours and involves a vast buffet with live cooking stations, and there's often some form of live entertainment to keep things ticking over. Prices vary based on your drinks selection – soft drinks are included at the lower end, wine and beer if you pay top dinar.

Bahrain Bay Kitchen (Map p60; ☑17 115 000; www.fourseasons.com/bahrain/dining/restaurants/bahrain_bay_kitchen; Four Seasons Hotel, Rd 4606, Bahrain Bay; brunch adult/child from BD25/12.5; ⊘7-11am & 12.30-3pm; Ⓟ🛜✒👭) Bahrain's most generous buffet brunch, with seemingly endless variety, great service and even a dedicated kids' area.

Bushido (p71) A local favourite, with a buffet and made-to-order dishes from the live cooking stations.

Masso (p71) Breakfast choices share buffet space with lots of European-inspired mains, and it does it all again on Saturday.

Diplomat Radisson Blu (Map p64; ☑39 945 208; www.radissonblu.com/en/diplomatho tel-bahrain/restaurants; Rd 1701, Diplomatic Area; brunch adult/child BD34/19; ⊘6.30am-10pm, brunch 12.30-4pm Fri; Ⓟ🛜✒) Mexican, Indian, Italian, Asian and barbecue cooking ensure ample variety here. Best of all, you can break things up with a swim in the pool.

Le Domain [34] (p71) In a fabulous setting on the 34th floor, Le Domain has fine views to go with its fabulous French and fusion cooking. It's less family friendly than other options.

Al Waha (Map p64; ☑17 713 000; www.gulfhotelbahrain.com/al-waha; Gulf Hotel, Rd 3801, Block 338, Adliya; brunch per person from BD18; ⊘6-10.30am, noon-3.30pm & 7-10.30pm; Ⓟ🛜✒) The Gulf Hotel may have an astonishing 15 restaurants, but Al Waha dominates proceedings on Friday, when a terrific international buffet takes over. It's family friendly, and there's live music.

★ **Café Lilou**   CAFE **$$**
(Map p64; ☑17 714 440; Rd 3803, Block 338, Adliya; mains BD2.7-8.8; ⊘8am-11pm Sat-Wed, to midnight Thu & Fri; Ⓟ🛜✒) This elegant balconied venue, with its velvet upholstery, wrought-iron banisters and polished-wood floors, is reminiscent of a 19th-century Parisian brasserie, and it's *the* place for a classy breakfast or lunch. The handmade pastries are a stand-out; try the croissants or irresistible French toast soaked in rich vanilla pastry cream topped with mascarpone, almonds and fresh wild berries.

With mains like grilled tamarind hammour skewers served with saffron almond rice and rose petals in dried lime butter and chives, it is easy to see why Café Lilou continues to win local culinary awards. There's another **branch** (Map p60; ☑17 583 939; 1st fl, Al Aali Mall, Rd 2827, Block 428, Seef; mains BD2.7-8.8; ⊘8am-11.30pm Sat-Wed, to midnight Thu & Fri; Ⓟ🛜✒; 🚌41, A2, A2S, X2) in Al Aali Mall, but the lively atmosphere here, especially at weekends, is unmatched.

Orangery   CAFE **$$**
(Map p60; ☑17 369 696; cnr Mahooz Ave & Sheikh Isa Ave, Adliya; mains from BD5.5; ⊘8am-10pm; Ⓟ🛜✒; 🚌43, 45) A delightful terrace overlooking Orangery's neoclassical garden, where the only sound is that of a trickling fountain, helps whisk you off to Europe in this classy, elegantly designed cafe that boasts impressive cakes and a delicious breakfast. It's not cheap, but the clientele here aren't likely to be counting their pennies.

Fish House   SEAFOOD **$$**
(Map p60; ☑17 594 040; Budaiya Hwy, near Ave 27; mains from BD3.5; ⊘11.30am-11pm; Ⓟ; 🚌13, X3) Bahrain's high-end eateries have tried and failed to wrestle the mantle of best seafood spot from this no-frills restaurant. The menu varies with the catch of the day, so it's always fresh, but you can't go wrong with the signature grilled sea bream, which arrives split, spiced and fragrant, with delicious rice, flat bread and a green salad.

My Cafe   MEDITERRANEAN **$$**
(Map p64; ☑77 344 444; https://mycafebh.com; Bldg 1078, Rd 3832, Block 338, Adliya; mains BD4.5-

14.5; ⊙ 8am-11pm Sat-Wed, to 2am Thu & Fri; P 🖥) One of Manama's most sophisticated cafes, My Cafe does dishes like tuna carpaccio and roasted hammour exceptionally well. The experience is enhanced by the lovely and elegant salon and garden terrace setting. It gets very busy during lunch and dinner, so book ahead. After 8pm there is a smart-casual dress code.

La Fontaine
INTERNATIONAL $$

(Map p64; ✉ 17 230 123; https://lafontaineart centre.net; 92 Hoora Ave, Dhuwawdah; mains from BD5.9; ⊙ 11am-10.30pm Tue-Sun; P ✎) This fashionable restaurant, in the outstanding La Fontaine Centre of Contemporary Art, is a magical place to enjoy a meal by a beautiful fountain in one of Manama's best examples of traditional architecture. Highlights from the menu include the grilled halloumi salad and mushroom risotto. There's also an extensive list of mostly European wine.

Isfahani
IRANIAN $$

(Map p64; ✉ 17 290 027; http://isfahanigroup. com; Exhibition Ave, near Rd 1902; mains BD2.8-16; ⊙ noon-midnight; 🚌 41) Excellent Iranian food at an almost-budget price is a winning combination. The Isfahani *juja* kebab (made with spiced boneless baby chicken) served with rice is the signature dish, which can be enjoyed in this pleasant restaurant with simple, tasteful decor that evokes its namesake, the city of Isfahan. Super-friendly staff complete the pleasant dining experience.

Coco's
INTERNATIONAL $$

(Map p64; ✉ 17 716 512; Rd 3803, Block 338, Adliya; mains from BD3; ⊙ 10am-11.30pm; 🖥✎) With indoor and outdoor seating, huge servings and an extensive international menu offering a range of delicious salads, rice dishes, pasta, impressive soup bread bowls and an English brunch, it's not surprising Coco's remains enormously popular. Too popular perhaps? At times staff can appear a little overwhelmed.

Swiss Cafe
BUFFET $$

(Map p60; ✉ 66 310 041; www.swiss-belhotel.com; 10th fl, Swiss Belhotel, King Mohammed VI Ave; buffet BD7-12; ⊙ 12.30-3pm; P 🖥) One of Manama's best deals, the lunchtime buffet here offers a fine salad bar, eight international main courses, and barbecue area and grills, not to mention excellent views from its 10th-floor perch. The Friday version is all about seafood and worth every dinar.

Rayés
LEBANESE $$

(Map p64; ✉ 17 312 700; www.coralbaybh.com; Bldg 491, Rd 2407, Block 322, Coral Bay Resort; mains BD2.2-18.6; ⊙ noon-1am; 🖥) This is one of the most attractive places to sample Lebanese food, right by the water's edge in the Coral Bay complex. The chef prides himself on the variety of salads and cold mezze, but everything's good here. The bread is baked on the premises, and live Arabic music contributes to the convivial Middle Eastern atmosphere.

★ Masso
INTERNATIONAL $$$

(Map p60; ✉ 17 721 061; http://massorestaurant. com; cnr Mahooz Rd & Sheikh Isa Ave; mains BD9-29, brunch BD26-37; ⊙ noon-3pm & 7-11pm Mon-Sat, brunch noon-3pm Fri & Sat; P 🖥; 🚌 43, 45) The kitchen here wins plaudits for its cooking, born in the Mediterranean and making creative use of fresh local ingredients. Standout dishes include Earl Grey–soaked chicken and harissa-marinated lamb chops. It's popular with expats, who thoroughly appreciate the wine specialist on hand to recommend the best red or white for each meal.

Bushido
JAPANESE $$$

(Map p60; ✉ 17 583 555; www.bushido.com.bh; Bldg 52, Rd 38, Block 428, Seef; mains from BD5.9, brunch from BD22; ⊙ noon-2am, brunch noon-3.30pm Fri; P 🖥; 🚌 41) This is where Bahrain first fell in love with Japanese food. As well as the usual suspects, Bushido serves up miso black cod, Wagyu beef cooked on volcanic stone and 'new-style' (lightly cooked) sashimi. Fridays are reserved for an excellent brunch, and there is an ubercool lounge bar with great views that plays down-tempo tunes and serves some of Manama's best cocktails. Dress conservatively; shorts are not allowed.

Rasoi by Vineet
INDIAN $$$

(Map p64; ✉ 17 746 461; www.gulfhotelbahrain. com; Gulf Hotel, Bldg 11, Rd 3801, Adliya; mains BD5.5-16.5; ⊙ noon-3pm & 7-11pm Sat-Thu, 1-4pm & 7-11pm Fri; P 🖥) Michelin-starred chef Vineet Bhatia brings Bahrain's finest Indian food to the table, showcasing what he calls 'evolved Indian' cooking. Try the cashew-crusted asparagus, the 48-hour marinated lamb or his clever adaptation of the Indian tiffin lunch.

Le Domain [34]
BUFFET $$$

(Map p64; ✉ 16 000 200; www.thedomainhotels. com; Domain Hotel, Bldg 365, Rd 1705, Block 317; mains BD8-23; ⊙ 7am-midnight daily, brunch noon-4pm Fri; P 🖥) This is the pick of the restaurants at the Domain hotel, serving fabulous

BAHRAIN MANAMA

HELEN CATHCART/ALAMY STOCK PHOTO ©

1. Arabic coffee
Enjoy coffee and dates at restored Bu Khalaf Coffee Shop in the old Muharraq Quarter (p81).

2. Arabic perfume
The bottles are tempting enough but being daubed in exotic scents is one of Arabia's great experiences.

3. Al Fatih Mosque
Bahrain's grand mosque (p61) was built in honour of the founder of modern Bahrain, Sheikh Ahmed Bin Muhammad Bin Khalifa.

4. Wildlife-watching
Enjoy graceful flamingos at Al Areen Wildlife Park (p84).

ON THE WATER IN BAHRAIN

As you'd expect on an island, the main activities in Bahrain focus on the sea, although very shallow coastal waters mean that swimming, snorkelling and boating are best carried out well offshore.

Dolphin Watching

Both **Bahrain Yacht Club** (Map p60; ☑ 17 700 677; Um Al Saeed Ave, Sitra; ☉ 8am-6pm) and **Coral Bay** (Map p64; ☑ 39 032 975, 39 741 311; Marina Corniche, Rd 2407; BD20-325; ☉ 9am-6pm) will take you onto the stunning blue waters that surround Bahrain in search of playful dolphins, but you must book in advance.

Spotting dolphins is more common than in many other parts of the world, and boats can be chartered for trips lasting 30 minutes, an hour, a half day or a full day. Locals often combine their dolphin-watching with a fishing trip.

Water Sports

Despite being surrounded by stunning crystal-clear blue waters, parts of Bahrain's coast are surrounded by shallow, treacherous coral and rocks that make it unsuitable to engage in water sports close to the coastline.

However, resorts like Coral Bay, Al Bander Hotel & Resort (p86) and Bahrain Beach Bay Resort have all found safe little sections of the coast from where they will happily launch jet skis and inflatables attached to speedboats.

---

seafood inspired by European cuisines. The stunning views over Manama from the 34th floor, especially at night, combined with a knowledgeable wine waiter, ensure this is an exceptional dining experience.

🍷 Drinking & Nightlife

What Manama's nightlife lacks in hard-hitting clubs it makes up for with excellent, lively bars. All top-end hotels have sophisticated bar areas, often with jazz or other live music, and a happy hour or cut-price cocktails.

B28 Bar Lounge
COCKTAIL BAR

(Map p60; 28th fl, Swiss Belhotel, King Mohammed VI Ave; ☉ 4pm-2am Sun-Thu, from 1pm Fri & Sat; ☎) Plush velvet sofas, fabulous views, and brilliant bar food with Aussie steaks and lobster bisque make this intimate venue one of our favourite lounge bars in the capital. Whether it's a vodka martini, the standout mojito or something more extravagant, this is a great spot for sipping a cocktail overlooking Manama.

Candles Cafe
CAFE

(Map p64; ☑ 17 714 844; Rd 2733, Block 336, Adliya; ☉ 10am-2am; ☎; ▣ 45) Candles' comfy, cosy interior is wonderfully complemented by a cool green garden. On balmy Bahraini evenings, ambient Arabic music soothes you as you sit in the shade of a huge palm, puff-puffing away, engulfed in the sweet plumes of shisha smoke, sipping a mocktail or two.

Sherlock Holmes
BAR

(Map p64; Gulf Hotel, Bani Otbah Ave, Adliya; ☉ noon-2am; ☎) The incongruously themed Sherlock Holmes English pub is still going strong, well after other places have folded in Manama's fickle nightlife scene. Regular live music livens things up, and a smart new facelift featuring luxurious leather chesterfield sofas has breathed new life into the venue.

Sports Bay
SPORTS BAR

(Map p64; ☑ 17 312 700; www.coralbaybh.com; Coral Bay Resort, Rd 2407, Block 322, Al Fatih Hwy; ☉ 9am-midnight; ☎) This modern sports bar attracts a lively crowd, especially when there is a football match or live music on. There is a DJ every Thursday, and regional artists regularly perform here. This, combined with the reasonable drink prices, virtually guarantees a good night.

Trader Vic's
BAR

(Map p60; ☑ 17 580 000; www.tradervics.com.bh; Ritz-Carlton Bahrain Hotel & Spa, Bldg 112, Rd 40, Block 428, Seef; ☉ 6pm-2am; ☎) The Polynesian-themed Trader Vic's at the Ritz-Carlton has an appealing outdoor area that's perfect on a warm Bahrain night. They serve good bar food, too.

☆ Entertainment

Bahrain National Theatre
THEATRE

(Map p64; ☑ 17 001 908; www.culture.gov.bh; Sheikh Hamad Causeway; tickets BD15-60) The country's national theatre sits in a stunning location, surrounded by the azure waters of Manama's northeastern bay, and offers an impressive calendar of world-class performing arts, including ballet, classical and traditional music concerts, and opera and musical theatre. Tickets are reasonably priced, and there is a smart-casual dress code (no trainers).

Adjacent to Bahrain National Museum, this stunning architectural showpiece covers nearly 12,000 sq m. It's the third-largest theatre in the region and has a design that owes much to local traditions; the interwoven aluminium strips that allow airflow evoke the roofs of traditional homes here, while the curvaceous interior of the auditorium echoes the seafaring dhows. Even the number of seats is 1001, a nod to that most famous book of stories, *One Thousand and One Nights*.

🛍 Shopping

★ **Kingdom of Perfumes**　　　PERFUME
(Map p69; ✍39 628 006; Sheikh Abdullah Ave; ⊙9am-1pm & 4-9pm) One of the joys of perfume shopping in the Gulf is watching the mesmerising way a perfumer can mix seemingly random oils to produce the very smell you requested. That is the magic you will witness Abdullah perform whether you ask him for a Western waft or a local *oud*. Just sit back and watch the master at work.

Prices for small bottles begin at BD1 to BD4, meaning even a top-of-the-range one won't break the bank.

Abdul Samad Al Qurashi　　　PERFUME
(Map p60; ✍17 177 771; http://new.asqrp.com; The Souq, 2nd fl, Bahrain City Center, Rd 2819, Seef; ⊙10am-10pm Sat-Wed, to midnight Thu & Fri; ◻41, A2, A2S, X2) The most prestigious name in premium Middle Eastern *oud*, musk, agarwood oils and perfumes, this Saudi brand has been around since 1852, dispensing perfumed oils from ornate, sculpted glass holders. Have your credit card ready: ASQ oils are not cheap.

Pearl of Islands Antiques　　　ANTIQUES
(Map p64; ✍38 432 188, 33 057 978; Osama Bin Zaid Ave, Block 326, Adliya; ⊙10am-10pm) Pearl of Islands is the pick of this strip of 'antique' stores selling mostly ornate wood doors and quaint lanterns. That's not because the goods are any different from the others, but because you will have a lot of fun negotiating an agreeable price with cheeky, amiable shop owner Iqbal, who can arrange cargo delivery.

Al Aali Mall　　　MALL
(Map p60; ✍17 581 000; www.alaalimall.com; Rd 2819, Seef; ⊙10am-10pm; 🛈; ◻41, A2, A2S, X2) This small shopping centre next to Seef Mall has gone for quality over quantity. There's a lovely reproduction of an old Gulf souq in the Souq Al Tawaweesh section, as well as designer brands such as Armani, Jimmy Choo and a shopfront for local designer Noof Al Khor. Lovers of Turkish sweets should stop by **Malatya Pazari** (Map p60; ✍17 003 234).

Gold Souq　　　JEWELLERY
(Map p69; Sheikh Abdullah Ave; ⊙9am-1pm & 3.30-9pm Sat-Thu, 9am-1pm Fri) Founded by Indian immigrants who arrived more than 200 years ago, the shops in the Gold Souq are still owned mostly by the families of those early merchants. This is the place to grab yourself a custom-made piece of gold jewellery at a very reasonable price. Look out for the workshops, where goldsmiths can still be seen working.

Spice Souq　　　FOOD
(Map p69; off Sheikh Abdullah Ave; ⊙9am-1pm & 4-7pm) It can be a little hard to find, but this small collection of spice sellers is a wonderfully fragrant place for a stroll as you explore one of the quieter corners of Manama Souq. Walk southeast along Municipality Ave from the Jindol Hotel and take the sixth street on the left.

City Centre Bahrain　　　MALL
(Map p60; ✍17 177 771; www.citycentrebahrain.com; Rd 2819; ⊙10am-10pm Sat-Wed, to midnight Thu & Fri; 🛈; ◻41, A2, A2S, X2) The country's true mega-mall, City Centre Bahrain has something for everyone. If international brands have a presence in Bahrain, you'll most likely find them here, alongside a food court, cinema complex, Carrefour supermarket and a small hub for local designers, including Kubra Al Qaseer and Anmar Couture.

❶ Getting There & Away

AIR
Bahrain International Airport (p93) is on Muharraq Island, approximately 7.5km from central Manama. There are ATMs in the transit lounge and arrivals hall.

❶ Getting Around

Manama's constantly growing traffic borders on ridiculous around rush hour and weekend evenings (Friday and Saturday). If you plan to venture out during these times, add 30 minutes to your journey.

TO & FROM THE AIRPORT

Complimentary hotel shuttles are the cheapest option for getting to and from the airport. Arrange in advance with your accommodation.

Bahrain Bus A2 goes to the centre of Manama (45 minutes), and buses 10 and 11 head to Muharraq (10 minutes) between 6am and 9pm. Tickets cost BD0.3.

A metered taxi to central Manama costs BD5. Ride-hailing services Uber (www.uber.com) and Careem (www.careem.com) charge BD3 to BD5.

BUS

The Bahrain bus system, with its air-conditioned safe and reliable red vehicles, is an excellent option for getting between key spots. Bahrain Bus runs an extensive service all over Manama and beyond. Fares cost BD0.3 when paying in cash and BD0.25 when paying with the rechargeable GO Card, which can be bought from ticket offices and vending machines at the major hubs like **Manama Bus Station** (Map p69; ☑ 66 311 111; https://bahrainbus.bh; Government Ave; ⊗ 6am-9pm; ☑ 12, 41, 44, A1).

TAXI

The heat of Bahrain means most locals drive or jump in taxis to get about. Taxis are easy to hail. There are dedicated stands outside Bab Al Bahrain and many high-end hotels. Taxis are metered; flagfall is BD1 for the first 2km, and thereafter the meter ticks over in increments of 100 fils (or 200 fils per kilometre). You'll pay a BD1 supplement if you take a taxi at a hotel or any other taxi rank. Fares officially increase by 25% after 10pm.

Popular mobile taxi apps Careem (www.careem.com) and Uber (www.uber.com) operate here.

MUHARRAQ ISLAND   جزيرة المحرق

Seen as the spiritual home of all things traditional in Bahrain, Muharraq still feels largely medieval with its narrow alleyways boasting some of the most beautiful historic buildings anywhere in the country. These include former royal residences and the wonderfully restored houses of wealthy pearl merchants. Muharraq is also home to many of the country's galleries and smaller museums. A day spent wandering through Muharraq's atmospheric backstreets is a true highlight of a visit to Bahrain.

Just over the causeways from Bahrain Island, Muharraq is the second-largest island in the archipelago, and its main city was the country's capital until 1932.

Sights

★ Beit Sheikh Isa Bin Ali Al Khalifa   HISTORIC BUILDING

(Map p77; Rd 913, Block 208; BD1.5; ⊗ 8am-2pm Sat-Tue, 9am-6pm Wed & Thu) Offering a fascinating look at pre-oil life in Bahrain, this building was constructed around 1800 and is one of the finest examples of a traditional house anywhere in the Gulf. The chief sitting room downstairs was kept cool in summer by the down draft from the *badqeer* (wind tower), the shutters on which could be closed in winter – stand beneath it to see how effective this system of natural air conditioning really is. There's fine gypsum and woodcarving throughout.

This was the seat of Bahraini power from 1869 to 1932, and its importance is reflected in the four different sections: sheikh, family, guests and servants. These are well captioned in English and a good half-hour could be spent rambling up and down the various staircases admiring the delicate arches, intricate wooden doors, courtyards and palm-trunk ceilings. Note the blackened walls and ceiling of the servants' kitchen.

Sheikh Ebrahim Bin Mohammed Al Khalifa Centre for Culture & Research   HISTORIC BUILDING

(Map p77; ☑ 17 322 549; www.shaikhebrahim center.org; Lane 932, Block 208; ⊗ 8am-2pm & 4-7pm Sat-Thu) **FREE** Inspired by the early-20th-century intellectual of the same name, this elegant centre hosts recitals, lectures and exhibitions throughout the year. It also delivers a summary of Bahrain's history and heritage through an amazing giant electronic book, where a mere wave of the hand turns the pages on Dilmun, pearling and the Tree of Life.

Abdullah Al Zayed House for Bahraini Press Heritage   MUSEUM

(Map p77; ☑ 17 324 117; www.shaikhebrahimcenter. org/en/houses/abdullah-al-zayed-house-for-bah raini-press-heritage-3; Rd 918, Block 208; ⊗ 8am-1pm & 4-7pm Sat-Thu) **FREE** More than 100 years old, this building was the home of the late Bahraini intellectual and 'father' of Gulf newspapers, Abdullah Al Zayed, who founded the region's very first weekly paper. Today the beautifully restored building houses many interesting artefacts related to the country's press heritage, including a copy of the first published Bahraini newspaper.

Muharraq Island

Busaad Art Gallery GALLERY
(Map p77; ☎17 000 020; http://busaad.com; Sheikh Isa Ave, Block 208, cnr Rd 911; ⊙9am-1pm & 4-8pm Sat-Thu) FREE In a wonderfully restored 1930s house, this gallery is the former family home of Ebrahim Mohamed Busaad, who was born here in 1954. On display are Busaad's elegant pieces of calligraphy, as well the more bold and colourful canvases.

There's a small gift shop upstairs and the elaborate wooden balconies are admirable.

Muharraq Souq   MARKET
(Map p77; Rd 1125, Block 208; ⊙ 10am-1pm & 4-7pm Sat-Thu, 4-7pm Fri) Running through the heart of Muharraq city, the souq is an atmospheric old Bahraini bazaar where all the needs of daily life are bought and bartered for. Near its southern end, Souq Al Qaisariya is an important part of the heritage pathway and offers a more historic take on the markets of Muharraq.

Al Korar House   HISTORIC BUILDING
(Map p77; Rd 918, Block 208; ⊙ 9am-1pm & 4-7pm Sat-Thu) **FREE** In this house, Muharraq women work to preserve the craft of *al korar* (gold-thread weaving), which three generations of a local family saved from extinction. The intricate threadwork was once the occupation of all resident women; now only a handful know how to weave the elaborate braid that once adorned Bahraini ceremonial gowns, some of which are on display.

Bin Matar House   MUSEUM
(Memory of the Place; Map p77; ☎ 17 322 549; www.shaikhebrahimcenter.org/en/houses/memory-of-the-place-2; Rd 1129, Block 208; ⊙ 8am-1pm & 4-7pm Sat-Thu) **FREE** This traditional house was built in 1905 on reclaimed land by the Bin Matar pearl trading family, who lived here until 2002. Once surrounded by sea on three sides and now in the heart of Muharraq, it was saved from demolition by the Sheikh Ebrahim Centre for Culture and Research, which reinvented the house as a museum devoted to the history of pearling (on the 1st floor). There's an airy gallery displaying contemporary art grafted onto the back of the building below; exhibitions change two or three times a year. There's an excellent gift shop.

Qalat Arad   FORT
(Arad Fort; Map p77; Ave 29, Block 244, Arad; BD1.5; ⊙ 7am-2pm Sun-Wed, 9am-6pm Thu & Sat, 3-6pm Fri; P) Built in the early 15th century by the Portuguese, Qalat Arad takes its name from the Greek name for Muharraq, Arados. The fort has been nicely restored, but there is little to see inside except the old well. Nonetheless, it's a pleasant location overlooking the bay, especially at sunset when locals flock to the neighbouring park.

🏃 City Walk
Old Muharraq

START BEIT SHEIKH ISA BIN ALI AL KHALIFA
END SOUQ AL QAISARIYA
LENGTH 3KM; TWO TO THREE HOURS

Unesco added Muharraq's pearling tradition to its World Heritage list in 2012, but the country's former capital city (until 1932) is about more than just pearling – it's a wonderful place to better understand Bahrain's cultural heritage. This walking tour leads you through the ancient beating heart of old Muharraq, integrating aspects of the pearling tradition with museums and cultural institutes, relaxing open spaces, historic markets and quaint coffee shops.

1 Beit Sheikh Isa Bin Ali Al Khalifa (p76) is a fine starting point, a splendid example of the power and prosperity that pearling brought to Muharraq. Leaving the house, walk away from the mosque and then turn right onto Rd 916: you'll soon come to the restored **2 Bu Khalaf Coffee Shop** (p81), which serves up thick Arabic coffee, tea and dates. After another 150m or so, turn right, walk a further 50m and then turn left: at this point you will enter an open square. Directly in front of you, overlooking the square's northwestern corner behind a delightfully simple, conical minaret, is the exquisite, semi-restored facade of **3 Beit Seyadi** (p80), a traditional house from the pre-oil period. Back across the square, follow the signs east to **4 Busaad Art Gallery** (p77), on your right as you emerge onto Sheikh Isa Ave.

Retrace your steps to Bu Khalaf Coffee Shop and then take Lane 920 running west for 150m. Where the lane ends (look for the intriguing sculpture high on the wall in front of you), turn left and then take the first right. Just 20m along on your right is the beautifully restored **5 Sheikh Ebrahim Bin Mohammed Al Khalifa Centre for Culture & Research** (p76), its facade adorned with wooden arched windows and carved calligraphy. Directly across the lane from the entrance is **6 Iqra Children's Library**, set up by the centre for the use of local school children. A little further on to the west is the oasis-like **7 Cafe**

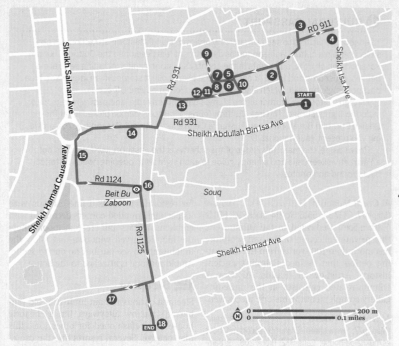

Luqmatina (p81), offering excellent local pastries, coffee and soft drinks in a lovely setting. Just around the corner is **8 Heraf Al Diyar**, a collection of community classrooms and workshops used by local adults. As you wander past, it is worth admiring the restored 1st-floor wooden balconies. Just northeast of this is **9 Al Nukhida House** (p80), where once upon a time visiting divers and ship crews met up ahead of the pearl-diving season.

Return to the Sheikh Ebrahim Bin Mohammed Al Khalifa Centre for Culture & Research and then turn right and wander past the peaceful **10 Water Garden**. This open-air space adds to the beauty of this little stretch. From there follow the signs to the **11 House of Coffee** (p80), a good place to stop if you're feeling peckish or simply want to know the history of coffee: it's a restaurant, cafe and museum. A few doors to the west, **12 Al Korar House** (p78) keeps alive the tradition of gold-thread embroidery. A few doors west again, on the other side of the lane, is **13 Abdullah Al Zayed House for Bahraini Press Heritage** (p76), home of the founder of the first weekly newspaper in the Gulf, now aptly converted into a small museum dedicated to the country's press heritage.

Walk down the gentle slope heading west, keeping the artsy, wavy, low wooden wall on your right, turn left onto Rd 931 where the lane ends, and then right onto busy Sheikh Abdullah Bin Isa Ave. A few metres along on your left is the **14 Vertical Garden**, a green landmark signifying the edge of the city's old quarter. Created by French artist Patrick Blanc, this oasis is home to 200 species of tropical plants from around the world. It comprises a single wall with an arch, planted with salt- and heat-tolerant plants. Continue west and then turn left at the roundabout. The sublime **15 Bin Matar House** (p78), an art gallery and museum of the history of pearling, is clearly visible on your left.

Continue south and then turn left along Rd 1124, past the metal workshops, and then turn right onto Rd 1125, the starting point for Muharraq Souq. Immediately on your right is **16 Beit Bu Zaboon**, which is closed to the public but has a lovely Muharraqi facade. Continue south to Sheikh Hamad Ave, turn right and forsake all other sweet shops on your way to **17 Hussein Mohd Showaiter Sweets** (p81), the king among local sweet merchants. Return east along Sheikh Hamad Ave and follow the signs to the **18 Souq Al Qaisariya**, which is under restoration.

ⓘ CULTURAL PASSPORT

To encourage visitors to see as many of Muharraq Island's historic attractions as possible, Bahrain's culture and antiquities department has developed the Cultural Tourism Passport, which covers 18 sights in the country's historic capital including several old houses, museums and forts. At each site, travellers collect stamps in an impressive blue passport-style booklet, which also contains a pullout map and QR codes.

Foreign visitors who gather all the stamps can enter a raffle, and past winnings have included flights abroad. The free Cultural Tourism Passport can be picked up at the Sheikh Ebrahim Bin Mohammed Al Khalifa Centre for Culture & Research (p76), providing you present your national ID.

Prizes aside, the main advantage of the scheme is the passport itself, which is both an attractive keepsake and a handy guide to each sight, with opening hours, historical background and photos.

Al Oraifi Museum   MUSEUM
(Map p77; ☑ 17 335 5616; Rd 214, Block 202; BD1.5; ⊙10am-5pm) Dedicated to the Dilmun era, this private collection of art and sculpture has more than 100 works from the fascinating period that defined Bahrain's ancient history. Artist-owner Rashid Al Oraifi's Dilmun-related canvases in the museum's gallery complement the historic pieces well.

Al Nukhida House   HISTORIC BUILDING
(Map p77; www.shaikhebrahimcenter.org/en/houses/nukhaida-house; Lane 932, Block 208; ⊙8am-1pm & 4-7pm Sat-Thu) FREE Despite its modest appearance, this captain's (*nukhida*) house was historically a very important place for the pearling industry. Visitors and divers who came to Bahrain were hosted here, and ship crews met up ahead of the pearl diving season. These days it houses a small but interesting exhibit on dive captains.

Qalat Bu Mahir   FORT
(Map p77; ☑ 17 298 777; off Khalifa Al Khebir Hwy; BD1; ⊙9am-4pm) An ancient defence fort built around 1840 to spot invading boats, the Bu Mahir Fort stares out across a bay to the high rises of Manama, making it an ideal spot for photographing the city's skyline. One of the joys is getting here via a small shuttle boat (BD1) from the National Museum (p59), which runs every 15 minutes.

The fort will be the starting point of the walking Pearling Path route, and a new visitors centre has been built in anticipation. Eventually a footbridge will bypass the highway and connect it to old Muharraq.

Beit Seyadi   HISTORIC BUILDING
(Map p77; Central Muharraq) FREE A traditional house from the pre-oil period, Beit Seyadi once belonged to a pearl merchant. The house, located off Sheikh Isa Ave and closed for restoration, boasts a fine exterior, with its peculiar rounded corners decorated with emblems of stars and crescent moons; note the filigree carved windows that allow the inhabitants to see out but no one to see in. An old mosque is attached to the house.

🛏 Sleeping

Sleeping options remain limited in old Muharraq's narrow alleyways, but as historic houses are refashioned for other uses, this may change. Several resorts line the causeways from Manama, but if those don't suit, Manama isn't far away.

Mövenpick Hotel Bahrain   HOTEL $$
(Map p77; ☑ 17 460 000; www.movenpick.com; Rd 2403; s/d BD60/80; P❄☎) It's usually hard to rate a hotel near the airport very highly, but with the chain's usual sensitivity to landscapes, the Mövenpick Hotel Bahrain comes warmly recommended. Built around an infinity pool that overlooks the tidal waters of the Gulf, this hotel says 'holiday' from the front door. Its proximity to the attractions of Muharraq is a plus.

🍴 Eating

House of Coffee   INTERNATIONAL $$
(Map p77; www.shaikhebrahimcenter.org/en/houses/house-of-coffee-2; Rd 918, Block 208; mains from BD3.5; ⊙8am-1pm & 4-7pm Sat-Thu) Housed across three traditional Bahraini buildings, the House of Coffee is a coffee museum, cafe and restaurant. The latter serves up a wide spread of good international staples including biryanis, a passable version of fish and chips, spaghetti and the odd intriguing experiment, such as the surprisingly good baklava cheesecake. They also do an excellent traditional breakfast.

Drinking & Nightlife

Cafe Luqmatina CAFE
(Map p77; ☑17 227 799; www.shaikhebrahim
center.org/en/houses/luqmatina-cafe; Lane 932,
Block 208; ⊙8am-1pm & 4-7pm Sat-Thu) Walk
through the tiny avocado-green wood doors,
past the swing chair and into your very
own light-filled oasis of calm, coffee and
cake. Luqmatina's location near the Sheikh
Ebrahim Centre (p76) and its soothing, understated contemporary design make it the
perfect place for a pit stop on your walking
tour through old Muharraq.

Bu Khalaf Coffee Shop COFFEE
(Map p77; Rd 917, Block 208; ⊙8am-2pm & 4-7pm
Sat-Thu) There are only four things on the
menu at this quaint little coffee shop: tea,
coffee, a chickpea salad and dates, which
is more than enough to refresh you as you
press pause on a wander through old Muharraq. Refuel and admire the collection of
black-and-white photos and intriguing artefacts hanging on the walls.

 Shopping

**Hussein Mohd
Showaiter Sweets** FOOD
(Map p77; ☑17 345 551; Sheikh Hamad Ave, Block
208; ⊙8am-10pm) This is the king among
Muharraqi sweet merchants – just try to
leave without buying something sickly
sweet and sinfully delicious, like the Turk-
ish-inspired baklava or Indian *jelabiya*
(deep-fried sweet). Most of the offerings are
in boxes, but staff may let you try before you
buy if you ask nicely.

❶ Getting There & Away

Muharraq Island is a 10-minute drive from central Manama across either of the two causeways.
Buses A1, 10 and 12 go from Manama's Bab Al
Bahrain (p62) to Sheikh Salman Ave. From there,
all the major sites are within walking distance
of each other. A taxi to the edge of the old town
from central Manama costs BD3 to BD5.

AROUND BAHRAIN ISLAND

Although it's dominated by its capital city,
there's more to Bahrain Island than Manama, as those coming for the Grand Prix
are sure to discover. The island is particularly rich in archaeological sites, and its size
means most of the main sights can be easily
accessed on day trips from the capital by car.

It's hard to get lost because all road signs
point to either Manama or Saudi Arabia!

Bahrain Fort & Museum قلعة البحرين

A 10-minute drive west of Manama, on an
ancient tell (mound created by centuries
of urban rebuilding), the majestic **Bahrain
Fort & Museum** (Qalat Al Bahrain & Site Museum; Map p60; ☑17 298 545; www.culture.gov.bh;
Rd 3863, Block 438, Qalat Al Bahrain Ave, Al Qalah;
foreigner/GCC citizen BD2/1; ⊙8am-8pm Tue-Sun;
P) stares out across the Gulf. Built by the
Portuguese in the 16th century, it is part of
the Unesco World Heritage site believed to
have been the capital of the ancient Dilmun
Empire. As you wander the atmospheric excavations of residential, commercial, public,
military and religious buildings, contemplate this: humans have continuously inhabited this site since 2300 BC.

This is where the most important Dilmun
finds have been made in Bahrain, and it provides an outstanding example not only of
the might of Dilmun, but also its successors
during the Tylos and Islamic periods. The
fort is supported by a stylish, modern visitor
centre and an excellent museum, where you
can pick up a free audioguide. When you're
done wandering the ruins, be sure to enjoy
the glorious sea views with a drink at the
Museum Café (Bldg 3618; ☎).

A'Ali عالي

POP 52,000

A'Ali is a lively residential town distinguished by the large mysterious and extraordinary ancient burial mounds scattered
across it. It's also home to Bahrain's best pottery district, where many of the local Shia
families still run their workshops and fire
their crafts in traditional kilns.

◉ Sights

★**A'Ali Royal
Burial Mounds** ARCHAEOLOGICAL SITE
(Map p60; Ave 42; ⊙daylight hours; ▣14, 15, 16)
FREE There are more than 100,000 Dilmun-era burial mounds scattered across
Bahrain, but none come close to the magnificence of these. That A'Ali was an important place in antiquity is evident from the 17
royal mounds constructed nearly 4000 years
ago, the most impressive of which is royal
mound 8. At 12m high and 50m across, and

housing five separate chambers, it still commands the regal awe it originally inspired.

Visit in the late afternoon when it is cool enough to wander around the neighbouring streets and see how many more of the royal mounds you can find. This isn't that difficult – the gigantic cone-shaped mounds of earth are everywhere!

Pottery District WORKSHOP
(Map p60; Ave 42 & Hwy 71; ⊗8am-1pm & 4-6pm Sat-Thu; 🚌14,15,16) Look out for the giant amphorae and head inwards from the corner of the highway and Ave 42 to explore Bahrain's most famous pottery district, where traditional family-run workshops continue to thrive. Don't distract the potters and no one will stop you from peering in as they go about their daily work and the mud-brick kilns are fired up. The workshop nearest the highway is Mohamed Ja'far's. His son Hasan speaks some English should you require an informal guide.

ℹ Information

There were no safety concerns with travelling around A'Ali at the time of research; however, as a place with a historic reputation for unrest (A'Ali was where some of the Arab Spring riots began), it is worth asking locally before visiting and taking the advice of your taxi driver or guide.

ℹ Getting There & Away

A'Ali is 20km southwest of Manama and is easily reached by car. A number of local buses connect it to surrounding towns.

Saar ساار

Saar Temple & Burial Chambers ARCHAEOLOGICAL SITE
(Dilmun Temple Saar; Map p60; Rd 79, Saar; ⊗daylight hrs; 🅿) **FREE** This extensive site boasts a Dilmun-era temple dating to 1900 BC, surrounded by a host of buildings yet to be formally identified. However, the most exciting excavations are the series of honeycombed burial chambers south of the temple. These have long been plundered with the removal of the coping stones, revealing the fascinating inner sanctums. It's soon to be turned into a major tourist attraction, but for now you can savour the privilege of wandering unchecked among the cradles of the dead.

The site is signposted from Sheikh Isa Bin Salman Hwy, south of Saar. Bus 13 from Manama Bus Station stops at Rd 79; from there it is a short walk to the site.

Al Jasra الجسرة
POP 600

A pleasant and leafy little village on the coast, Al Jasra is visited for the traditional handicraft centre and the former royal home. It is worth sparing some extra time to amble past the villas and small, private plantations to truly appreciate this typical Bahraini community.

◉ Sights

Al Jasra House HISTORIC BUILDING
(Map p60; 📞17 611 454; www.culture.gov.bh; Rd 437, Mazarea Hwy; BD1; ⊗8am-2pm Sat-Tue, 9am-6pm Wed & Thu; 🅿) One of several historic homes in Bahrain restored to their original condition, this one was built in 1907 and is famous as the birthplace of the former emir, Sheikh Isa Bin Salman Al Khalifa. It was constructed using local building materials of coral stone supported by palm-tree trunks, and the gravel in the courtyard is made up of a hundreds-and-thousands mixture of tiny mitre and auger shells. Opening times can be erratic, so it is worth calling ahead.

Al Jasra Handicraft Centre ARTS CENTRE
(Map p60; 📞17 611 900; www.culture.gov.bh; Mazarea Hwy; ⊗8am-3pm Sun-Fri; 🅿) This government-run centre encourages tourists to visit locals trained in age-old traditional skills like model-boat building and basket weaving. The small workshops where the handicrafts are produced represent an admirable attempt to preserve skills that might otherwise be lost. They overlook a pleasant central garden, and there is also a gift shop where a purchase goes a little way to helping Bahrain retain some of its traditional handicraft skills.

ℹ Getting There & Away

Close to the King Fahd Causeway, Al Jasra is easily reached from Manama, 20km northeast. Bus 15 comes through the village as it travels between Budaiya and Isa Town.

Riffa & Around قلعة الرفاع

★ **Riffa Fort** FORT
(Sheikh Salman Bin Ahmad Al Fatih Fort; Map p60; 📞17 322 549; Sheikh Hamood Bin Sebah Ave, Riffa; museum BD2; ⊗8am-8pm; 🅿) **FREE** The completely restored Riffa Fort was built in 1812 by Sheikh Salman Bin Ahmad Al Fatih, the 19th-century ruler of Bahrain. A classic piece of Bahraini fortification, it now boasts

WORTH A TRIP

HAWAR ISLANDS

Approximately 50km southeast of Bahrain Island, close to the Qatari border, the largely uninhabited Hawar Islands are home to some of the rarest wildlife in the Gulf region. This collection of 36 islands, most of which are little more than banks of sand and shingle, was declared a protected area and nature reserve in 1996.

The islands and their surrounding waters are home to a host of endangered animals, birds and marine life, supported by the wetlands, mudflats and sea-grass meadows. The largest island, Jazirat Hawar, is home to introduced Arabian gazelles and oryx.

Jazirat Hawar, the only inhabited island in the archipelago, is almost entirely undeveloped, except for a police garrison and the Hawar Beach Hotel (☑17 641 666; http:// hawarbeachhotel.com; d incl transfers & full-board BD85-250, chalets BD30-45; 🕿🌉), a small resort under the management of the Southern Tourism Company, which also runs the boat to and from Bahrain. Once on the island, visitors must stay on the resort site unless embarking on an organised bus, 4WD or mountain-bike tour. While the lack of independence may feel restrictive, wildlife enthusiasts will thoroughly appreciate these exploratory tours that virtually guarantee sightings of the island's stunning wildlife. The hotel can also organise kayaking to nearby islands, as well as snorkelling in the shallows off the coast.

A boat leaves daily at 8am from Durrat Marina (p93) in the south of Bahrain, returning from Hawar at 4pm. Tickets can be purchased online or at the Hawar Island Reservations Offices (Southern Tourism Company; Map p64; ☑17 641 666; reservation.hbh@sadcbh. com; Rd 2407, Block 320, Al Fatih Corniche; day return BD20; ☉10am-5pm Sat-Wed, 8am-8pm Thu & Fri). Note: day trips are restricted to Fridays and Saturdays and must be booked well in advance.

a small museum with raised walkways leading through a series of interactive spaces that really enhance the visitor experience. A late-afternoon visit is particularly atmospheric, especially if it is finished off on the cafe's outdoor glass terrace overlooking the Hunayniyah Valley, just as the call to prayer engulfs it. If you have the time, pop into the fort's mosque near the northern corner. Riffa Fort is in the east of Riffa and is well signposted.

Al Bahair Mini Canyon & Wetlands
NATURAL FEATURE

(Map p60; btwn Ave 36 & Al Esteglal Hwy; 🚍17, 19, 50) Unlike any other place in Bahrain, these huge, beautiful, natural rock formations of varying shapes are yellowish in colour and sit right in the middle of a bustling residential neighbourhood. During the winter, when shallow wetlands form at their feet, the 'mini canyon', as it is known locally, becomes a bird haven, and locals love to sit atop the rocks in the evenings with a picnic.

Sadly, the dumped rubbish and encroaching development suggest this little urban oasis might not be around for much longer. Care should be taken when exploring as the ground is very soft in parts. For the best views, drive right to the back of the residential area on the western side of the Alba Club.

★ Spicy Village
PAKISTANI $

(Map p60; ☑17 668 248; Bldg 274, Rd 83, Block 909, East Riffa; mains from BD0.9; ☉11am-3.30pm & 5pm-midnight; 🚗) The regular clientele in this clean no-frills establishment speaks volumes: they're all Pakistani, and they're all here for the wholesome, authentic taste of home. Exceptionally good value and conveniently close to the Riffa Fort, this is well worth a detour after a long day of exploring. If you've got the patience, order the slow-cooked mutton biryani – it is out of this world.

Bahrain International Circuit

Bahrain's Formula 1 circuit is among the major attractions of the country and one of the main reasons for getting out of Manama to explore the island (see p85).

⊙ Sights & Activities

Formula 1 Racetrack
STADIUM

(Map p60; ☑17 450 000; www.bahraingp.com; Gate 255, Gulf of Bahrain Ave, Umm Jidar 1062, Sikhar; tours BD6; ☉8am-5.30pm, tours 10am & 2pm Sun, Tue & Thu; 🅿) The Al Sakhir Tower of the Formula 1 Racetrack rises above the desert like a beacon. If you're visiting Bahrain out of season and want to see what a state-of-the-art track looks like, then you can either walk straight into the stand and admire it from afar or join a 40-minute tour of the grounds, media centre, control room and the world-famous track.

Be sure to check the events calendar as the track is also used for drag racing, drifting and superbike races throughout the year.

Bahrain International Karting Circuit
ADVENTURE SPORTS

(Map p60; ☑17 451 745; www.bahraingp.com; Gulf of Bahrain Ave, Sakhir, Al Rifa Wa Al Mintaqah Al Janubiyah; 15min drive BD12; ⊙10am-midnight Tue-Sat, 4pm-midnight Sun & Mon) Get your adrenaline kick on this blistering world-class go-karting track that integrates 14 bends into a winding 1.4 km course. The track and karts are well maintained by the enthusiastic staff, and there are engine options suited to both adults and children. It's a great way for children to experience the thrill of motor racing.

Land Rover Experience
ADVENTURE SPORTS

(Map p60; ☑17 450 000; www.bahraingp.com; off Gulf of Bahrain Ave, Sakhir, Al Rifa Wa Al Mintaqah Al Janubiyah; 1½hr passenger drive BD12.6, 2hr self-drive BD68.3; ⊙9am-5pm Sun-Thu, 10am-4pm Fri & Sat) A great way to learn how to drive off-road, Land Rover Experience lets you go four-wheel driving close to the F1 racetrack with 32 natural and artificial obstacles to negotiate.

Dragster Experience
ADVENTURE SPORTS

(Map p60; ☑17 450 000; www.bahraingp.com; off Gulf of Bahrain Ave, Sakhir, Al Rifa Wa Al Mintaqah Al Janubiyah; per person BD40; ⊙hours vary) Calling all petrol-heads: this one's for you. Strap yourself into a 10,500cc Top Dragster – with a friend if you want – and let the highly qualified driver take you from 0 to 274km/h in just eight seconds. It won't last long, but this is one thrilling ride you will not forget in a hurry. Booking ahead is essential.

Al Areen
العرين

Al Areen was once little more than a desert with a few forlorn native species roaming inside random enclosures, but since being declared a conservation area, the country's only wildlife park and reserve has also developed a decent water park and luxury resort. The area is now popular with day trippers, especially families who come to escape the hustle and bustle of Bahrain's towns.

◉ Sights & Activities

Al Areen Wildlife Park & Reserve
WILDLIFE RESERVE

(Map p60; ☑17 845 480; off Gulf of Bahrain Rd, Al Zallaq; BD1; ⊙8am-4.30pm Sat-Thu, 2-4pm Fri; ℗) Ignore the tacky cardboard cutouts of animals leading up to the entrance – this is a great-value day out for the entire family in one of Bahrain's three conservation areas. The 10-sq-km reserve is home to several species of wildlife indigenous to the region, including herds of Arabian oryx. The park is home to a total of 80 species of birds and 45 species of mammals. Get there early to avoid missing out on the excellent bus tour, which leaves every hour, but fills up very quickly in the afternoons. As you listen to the Arabic and English commentary, passing walkers struggling with the heat, you'll be grateful you chose the bus!

Lost Paradise of Dilmun Water Park
WATER PARK

(Map p60; ☑17 845 100; www.lpodwaterpark.com; Bldg 1663, Rd 6277, Block 1062, Hawrat Ingah; over/ under 1.2m BD17/8; ⊙10am-6pm Mon-Thu, to 8pm Fri & Sat; ⊛) The theme is ancient Dilmun, but the fun is very modern at this excellent water park with stupendously high slides, a rain fortress, fountain, wave pool and sandy beach aimed at keeping swimmers of all ages entertained. There's even a stage where the fun-factor gets ramped up on Friday nights with live DJs (BD1 extra for entry). The park is off Gulf of Bahrain Rd, but is signposted in Arabic only.

⌸ Sleeping

Al Areen's sleeping options are all resorts, and most are not cheap. Those seeking budget options should stay in Manama and visit on a day trip.

★ Al Areen Palace & Spa
RESORT $$$

(Map p60; ☑17 845 000; www.alareenpalace.com; Rd 6277, Hawrat Ingah; r from BD195; ℗ ⟟ ⟨) When the sun sets on the cascading pools of the inner courtyards, a wonderful calm descends on this slice of luxury in Bahrain's southern desert, where the tranquillity is occasionally disrupted by a passing soft-slippered masseuse going from spa to poolside. Three international restaurants and uber-luxurious rooms make this a wonderful treat. When booking ask about the bundle deals that include entry tickets to the local attractions.

BAHRAIN'S F1 STORY

With more than a billion people watching worldwide, the highlight of Bahrain's sporting calendar is undoubtedly the **Grand Prix** (☑17 450 000; www.bahraingp.com; Bahrain International Circuit, off Gulf of Bahrain Rd; ☉Apr). To win the right to host the event, Bahrain fought off competition from rival bidders the United Arab Emirates, Egypt and Lebanon to create the first-ever F1 Grand Prix in the Middle East.

The magnificent Middle Eastern–style stadium, with its 'tented' grandstands and echoes of the country's wind towers, is a fine showcase for modern Bahrain. The stadium holds 70,000 spectators, and the barriers around the track are made up of an astonishing 82,000 tyres. In 2014, the race was held under floodlights, becoming the second track (after Singapore) to have staged a night-time Grand Prix.

There are actually six tracks forming the complex, including a 1.2km-long drag strip and a 2km test oval. The race normally sits at second or third in the Grand Prix calendar, taking place in early April; the usual track is 5.412km (3.363 miles) long and raced over 57 laps.

Authorities insist on respect for local sensibilities, so winners are not sprayed with champagne but with *warrd*, made from locally grown pomegranate and rosewater, and promo models wear less revealing outfits – think Gulf Air crew uniforms rather than your usual pit-lane fare.

Attending the F1 Grand Prix

The place to start when looking for tickets, or for any other information about the Bahrain Grand Prix, is Bahrain International Circuit (p84). Tickets usually go on sale a few weeks before race day – join the mailing list to make sure you don't miss out. Three-day passes that include Friday practice, Saturday qualifying races and the big race itself on Sunday start at around BD30 for the Victory Grandstand and go up to BD75 for a seat in the main stand. Tickets can be purchased online through the main website, though most visitors book their tickets as part of an overall package through a travel agency.

After-Parties

What the official website won't tell you is where the after-parties are. Although venues change each year, there are two mainstays. Manama's five-star hotels will be at the centre of most off-track celebrations, either in their restaurants or, as the night wears on, in their bars. It's also close to guaranteed that one of the best after-parties in Bahrain – every night, but especially Sunday night after the race – will be at Coral Bay Resort (p74). This has often been where the official party was held, with international live acts, DJs and a whole lot of glamour. Tickets for Coral Bay's F1 party cost between BD15 and BD30 per person. Bushido (p71) is another reliable option.

❶ Getting There & Away

Al Areen's attractions are signposted off the Al Zallaq Hwy, 35km from Manama. There is a bus service limited to the weekends that serves the beach area.

Tree of Life   شجرة الحياة

Although the age of the **Tree of Life** (Map p60; off Musakar Hwy; P) **FREE** has now been established, the mystique and allure of this lone, green, desert dweller remains strong. Planted around 1583, the knotty mesquite tree gracefully spreads its ageing limbs over a patch of Bahrain's southern desert, attracting hundreds of visitors daily. They come to take pictures in its shade and enjoy the sunken walkway marked by 19 carved silhouettes of other famous trees around the globe that circumnavigates the Tree of Life, framing it from different perspectives.

It is still not clear what sustains the tree, though the underground water source it is tapped into is probably what once drew the inhabitants of the small village excavations have revealed to be buried close by. Once literally just a tree in the desert, today there is also an informative visitors shelter with toilets and a security guard around the clock.

On special occasions, like the Bahrain International Music Festival (p86), the site's open-air platform hosts cultural events. The tree is best appreciated after dusk, when it is hauntingly lit up to accentuate the mystique

DON'T MISS

BAHRAIN INTERNATIONAL MUSIC FESTIVAL

The long-established Bahrain International Music Festival (www.culture.gov.bh/en/events/FestivalsandAnnualActivities/BahrainInternationalMusicFestival; ☺ Oct) presents a series of regional and international music concerts across the country at various venues including the Bahrain National Theatre (p74) and the Tree of Life (p84). Genres include classic orchestral compositions, traditional Bahraini folk songs, classical Arabic music, and crossover and fusion instrumentals. Many events are free to attend.

that draws people to it. Be careful though, driving away in the dark is tricky in a location where there is no street lighting.

The tree is 40km south of Manama and signposted from the Musakar Hwy, becoming visible as soon as you go off-road. A 4WD is not required but take care not to drive into soft sand.

Oil Museum

The grand white stone building of Dar Al Naft Oil Museum (Map p60; ☑ 17 753 475; off Ave 49; ☺ 9am-5pm Sun-Thu; ℗) FREE, complete with neoclassical pillars, looks odd surrounded by nodding donkeys and sprawling pipelines, but this is where 'black gold' was first struck in Bahrain. The exhibits are informative, albeit a tad dry. The first well, opened in 1932, sits to the left of the museum, and to right is the original, tiny Bapco (Bahrain Petroleum Company) office from 1931.

Ring ahead to check opening times, as the museum is seldom visited. It is a 40-minute drive from Manama along an unmarked road south of Awali off Ave 49.

Sitra & Al Dar Islands

Al Dar Islands   ISLAND
(Map p60; ☑ 17 704 600; www.aldarislands.com; Rd 1507, off Umm Al Saad Ave, Sitra; adult BD5-8, child BD2-5; ☺ 9am-8pm Sun-Thu, to 9pm Fri & Sat) Throughout the day sea taxis whisk visitors to this little desert island, where there are shallow swimming areas, various day-accommodation options (from BD10), a bar,

a covered play area for kids, a gym and two decent eateries. It's a nice break from the mainland and is popular with families, who arrive armed with large picnics, at weekends. Note: you cannot stay overnight.

The port for the island is off Umm Al Saeed Ave at Sitra's Fishing Port.

Al Bander Hotel & Resort   RESORT $$$
(Map p60; ☑ 17 701 201; www.albander.com; Um Al Saad Ave, Sitra; family chalet BD240; ℗ ☎ ☒) Al Bander has all the trappings of an upmarket resort, including a private beach, comfy sun loungers, outdoor swimming pools and a host of leisure facilities. Accommodation is in stylish cabanas or chalets overlooking a private bay. Many users are members with moorings for their own private boats. Guests can book snorkelling, scuba diving, canoeing and fishing in advance.

UNDERSTAND BAHRAIN

Bahrain Today

Until the Arab Spring of 2011, political tensions had been contained – at least overtly – and Bahrain was seen as a model of stability and relative freedom. But since that mask spectacularly fell, Bahrain has been holding its breath. The nation's reputation as a reliable offshore banking centre and commercial hub, as well as its status as a valued member of the UN, Arab League and Gulf Cooperation Council (GCC), are under serious threat. While political spats and simmering tensions are making some investors nervous, there is virtually no risk to travellers.

Political Unrest

Tensions continue to simmer, partly because of the perceived slow pace of political development, but mainly because of ancient sectarian differences that have threatened to boil over (and have done several times) ever since the island of majority Shiite Muslims was taken over by the Sunni Al Khalifa family. Official figures are difficult to come by, but more than half of Bahrain's population today is Shiite.

The government's brutal response to the riots nearly a decade ago continues to be heavily criticised; in 2016, the UN accused Bahrain of 'harassing' its Shiite population. A year later, Bahrain executed three Shiite activists convicted of killing three policemen in a 2014 bomb attack, and in the same year, Bahrain's most prominent Shiite cleric, Isa Qassim, was found guilty of money laundering and illegally raising funds. The main opposition party leader, Al Wefaq's Sheikh Ali Salman, was arrested in 2014; in 2018, his jail sentence was extended to life after he was charged with spying for Qatar, a move that human rights groups believe is politically motivated.

International Relations

In 2017, Bahrain cut its ties with Qatar and asked its diplomats to leave within 48 hours. The reason given was that Bahrain's ministers had come under a cyber attack from its neighbour. However, the move has been widely viewed as toeing the line of their major ally, Saudi Arabia. Travel is no longer possible between Bahrain and Qatar.

History

Dilmun, Ancient Garden of Eden

History in Bahrain is nowhere more intriguing than among the 85,000 burial mounds that now lump, curdle and honeycomb 5% of the island's landmass. Archaeologists have recently confirmed Bahrain as the seat of the lost and illustrious empire of Dilmun (3200–330 BC), whose influence spread as far north as modern Kuwait and as far inland as Al Hasa Oasis in eastern Saudi Arabia.

Dilmun (which means 'noble') was often referred to as the fabled Garden of Eden and described as 'paradise' in the Epic of Gilgamesh, the world's oldest poetic saga. Dilmun's economic success was due in no small part to the trading of Omani copper, which was measured using the internationally recognised 'Dilmun Standard'; the weights can be seen in the Bahrain National Museum (p59).

When the copper trade declined around 1800 BC, Dilmun's strength fell with it, leaving the island vulnerable to the predatory interests of the surrounding big powers of Babylon and Greece.

Pearls & the Founding of Modern Bahrain

Take a stroll through Muharraq, and you'll quickly learn the significance of the pearl trade to Bahrain. Sweet water from springs under the sea mingling with the brackish waters of the shallow oyster beds contributes to the particular colour and lustre of Bahrain's pearls, and it was upon the value of these that Bahrain grew into one of the most important trading posts in the region.

A 'fish eye' (the ancient name for a pearl) dating back to 2300 BC found in the excavations at Saar suggests that pearling was an activity during the days of Dilmun. It was an unglamorous industry in which local divers worked with little more than a nosepeg and a knife in shark-infested waters and were hauled up with their bounty by 'pullers' working long and sun-baked shifts from June to October. At the height of the pearling industry, some 2500 dhows were involved, and loss of life was common.

Pearling was something of a mixed blessing in other ways as well, as it attracted the big naval powers of Europe, who wheeled about the island trying to establish safe passage for their interests further east. In the early 1500s, the Portuguese invaded, building Bahrain Fort, one of their typical seafacing compounds, on the northern shore. Their rule was short-lived, however, and by 1602 they were ousted by the Persians.

Relationship with the British

The relationship began in the 19th century, when piracy was rife in the Gulf and Bahrain had gained a reputation as an entrepôt, where captured goods were traded for supplies for the next raid. The British, anxious to secure their trade routes with India, brought

---

BOOKS ABOUT BAHRAIN

➡ *Looking for Dilmun,* by Geoffrey Bibby, is a celebrated book about Bahrain in the 1950s and '60s, and is arguably the best book ever written about the country.

➡ *A Winter in the Middle of Two Seas: Real Stories from Bahrain,* by Ronald Kenyon, is an enlightening account of the author's four months in the country.

➡ *Footprints in Time: The Story of Indians in Bahrain,* by Reena Abraham, is about the long-established Indian community in Bahrain.

➡ *Bahrain from the Twentieth Century to the Arab Spring,* by Miriam Joyce, takes a fairly dry look at Bahrain's past. Its 2012 publication date means it only touches on the 2011 demonstrations, rather than their fallout.

the island within the folds of the trucial system (the 'truce' or treaty system of protection against piracy, which included states that now form the United Arab Emirates).

In hindsight, this could almost be dubbed invasion by stealth: by 1882 Bahrain could not make any international agreements or host any foreign agent without British consent. On the other hand, as a British protectorate, the autonomy of the ruling Al Khalifa family was secure and threats from the Ottomans thwarted. Bahrain regained full independence in 1971, but it only takes a walk through certain neighbourhoods popular with the sizeable expatriate British community, with its emphasis on full English breakfasts and high teas, to see that the British are not just a part of the island's history.

Oil: Bahrain's Black Gold

Roughly in the middle of the country's main island stands a small museum (p86) sporting marble pillars and a classical architrave, wholly incongruous amid the surrounding landscape of nodding donkeys. But the museum has a right to certain pretensions of grandeur; it marks the spot where, in 1932, the Arab world struck gold – black gold, that is – and with that, the entire financial balance of power in the world was transformed forever.

The discovery of oil could not have come at a better time for Bahrain, as it roughly coincided with the collapse of the world pearl market, upon which the island's economy had traditionally been based. Skyrocketing oil revenues allowed the country to steer a course of rapid modernisation that was a beacon for other countries in the region to follow well into the 1970s and '80s.

When the oil began to run out, the fortunes of the government started to turn, and in the last decade of the 20th century the country was shocked by sporadic waves of unrest. The troubles began in 1994 when riots erupted after the emir refused to accept a large petition calling for greater democracy, culminating in the hotel bombings of 1996. The political tensions have yet to be fully resolved.

Arab Spring Uprising

In the spring of 2011, inspired by the scenes in Tunisia and Egypt, people across the Middle East and North Africa began taking to the streets in an outpouring of anger towards their leaders.

Members of Bahrain's marginalised Shiite community, led by the country's main opposition party, Al Wefaq, took their cue from this, and in scenes that echoed Cairo's Tahrir Sq, demonstrators occupied Pearl Roundabout in central Manama for days, effectively bringing the city to a standstill. The scenes, the worst in the country since the 1990s, led to calls to overthrow Bahrain's ruling family, the Al Khalifas.

A brutal response came on 17 February 2011, as pre-dawn government raids on the demonstrators' encampment left four protesters dead and hundreds injured. A month later, Bahrain called in troops from Saudi Arabia and the United Arab Emirates to clear the protests and destroy the pearl statue that had become the symbol of the demonstrations, before declaring a three-month state of emergency. During this period of high alert, a huge crackdown led

LOCAL CRAFTS

On the face of it, Bahrain is a modern country that looks forward more often than it looks back. This is changing though: with Manama and Muharraq both recent Capitals of Arab Culture, a revival of interest in Bahrain's artistic heritage is gathering momentum. Several cultural centres, such as the Manama Craft Centre (p59), and workshops, such as Al Jasra Handicraft Centre (p82), encourage the continuation of skills. Crafts are generally carried out in cottage industries or cooperatives, with people working from the privacy of their own inner courtyards. If you head out to the following places, especially in the company of a local guide, you may be lucky and see these crafts in progress.

Pottery and ceramics Village of A'Ali

Traditional weaving Villages of Ad Diraz and Bani Jamrah

Basket weaving with palm leaves Village of Karbabad

Pearl jewellery Gold Souq, Manama

Al Kurar metal thread-work (for decorating ceremonial gowns) Al Korar House, Muharraq

to thousands of arrests and the systematic torture of some of those involved, as international governments and human-rights organisations strongly criticised the use of force in dispelling protesters.

Demonstrations continued across the country, emerging from villages and towns with majority Shiite populations, until November 2012, when the government made public gatherings illegal. Since then, sporadic attacks on police stations, arrests of opposition activists and government accusations of Iranian complicity in 'terrorism' on Bahraini soil have continued.

People & Society

Lifestyle

Bahrain is a socially liberal state and, with bars and clubs widespread in the capital city, it might be assumed this liberalism extends to all corners. But many Bahrainis retain conservative views on aspects of social and religious interaction, and this will be apparent to those who venture beyond the capital into the smaller towns and villages.

Bahraini people have enjoyed the spoils of oil for more than half a century, and it's tempting to think that wealth has created a nation of idlers – you won't see many Bahrainis engaged in manual labour, for example. But a modern, enterprising, wealthy nation isn't built on money alone, and the burgeoning financial sector is proof that the locals have chosen to invest their energies and creativity in their traditional trading strengths.

Multiculturalism

Behind Bab Al Bahrain, in the heart of Manama, there is little besides shop signs in Arabic to indicate that this area is indeed part of the Middle East. There are Indian and Pakistani shop owners, Jewish money exchangers, Filipino hotel workers and occasional groups of US service personnel. The long-overdue establishment of Little India, acknowledging the contribution of migrants from the subcontinent, is a testimony to all this.

In a country where an estimated 55% of residents are immigrants, it is surprising that a strong sense of local identity has survived the influx of migrant workers. This imbalance, while harmonious for the most part, has been a source of political agitation too. In 1997, for example, a series of arson attacks were carried out by unemployed lo-

cal Bahrainis who were angry that jobs were being taken by workers from Asia. While the government has since actively pursued a policy of favouring the indigenous workforce, tensions continue as educated Bahrainis find it difficult to compete in sectors with entrenched (and often experienced and skilled) expatriate workforces.

Environment

Most people think of Bahrain (741 sq km) as a single scorched flat island with a couple of low escarpments in the middle of a stony desert, surrounded by a shallow, calm sea. In fact, such is the description of Bahrain Island only, which, at 586 sq km, is the largest in an archipelago of about 33 islands, including the 36 Hawar Islands and a few specks of sand that disappear at high tide. When crossing any of the causeways, including the King Fahd Causeway, which links Bahrain with the Saudi mainland, it is easy to see how the whole archipelago was once attached to the rest of the continent.

Wildlife

Bahrain's noteworthy wildlife includes the Ethiopian hedgehog, Cape hare, various geckos and the endangered Rheem gazelle, which inhabits the dry and hot central depression. The Hawar Islands, with their resident cormorants, serve as a staging post for winter migrants. The Rheem gazelle, the terrapin, the sooty falcon and the seafaring dugong all appear on the endangered-species list, but some of them can be seen, along with a beautiful herd of oryx, at Al Areen Wildlife Park & Reserve (p84).

A unique ecosystem in Bahrain is created by the sea grass *Halodule uninervis*. Important for the dugong and a large number of migrating birds, this tough plant is remarkably resilient against extreme temperatures and high salinity.

Environmental Issues

Bahrain has made a big effort in recent years to clean up its act environmentally, and beautification projects have brought a touch of greenery back to the concrete jungle, although most of the changes are cosmetic rather than meaningful. The main threats to the environment remain unrestrained development, perpetual land reclamation, rampant industrialisation, an inordinate number of cars (about 200 per sq km), pollution of the Gulf from oil leakages and ocean acidification. Little has been done to curb emissions from heavy industry (such as the aluminium smelting plant) to the east of Bahrain Island.

SURVIVAL GUIDE

❶ Directory A–Z

ACCESSIBLE TRAVEL

Bahrain has a long way to go to become more accessible for mobility, visually and hearing-impaired travellers. Efforts are being made in some areas: many high-end restaurants and hotels are more accessible, and the Bahrain bus service is is equipped with a driver-operated ramp for wheelchair users, though pavements are often so poor that no wheelchairs can get to the bus stop. Buses allow trained guide dogs on board.

In most cases, it is best to phone or email ahead and request the specific assistance you require. Most establishments will make an effort to provide this, but in some instances, they simply will not have the resources.

Bahrain International Airport (p93) has services to assist travellers with accessibility concerns. Ask staff for assistance or contact the duty operations manager on ☑ 17 321 444, open 24 hours.

ACCOMMODATION

Bahrain's sights are all day-trip distance from the capital, so most visitors stay in or around Manama.

At the budget end, single/double rooms do not go for less than BD15/25 per night, with some cheaper hotels doubling as brothels for visiting Saudi patrons, especially in central Manama. Midrange accommodation usually includes carpet, minibar, satellite TV and a decent view, and Bahrain has excellent top-end hotels and resorts.

PRACTICALITIES

Magazines *Bahrain This Month* and *Time Out Bahrain* have comprehensive local listings.

Newspapers *The Gulf Daily News* and the less interesting *Bahrain Tribune* are the main English-language dailies.

Weights and measures Bahrain uses the metric system.

Smoking Bahraini law strictly prohibits smoking in all enclosed public areas; anyone breaking the law can be fined.

ETIQUETTE

Bahrain is a liberal Muslim country; however, some parts are more conservative, and it is therefore worth observing a few social norms.

Greetings Men will be happy to shake hands with tourists, as will most women, but male travellers should wait to be invited by the latter, especially in more rural areas.

Dress Men and women should generally dress modestly in public and avoid sheer clothing.

Bargaining Although an expectation in traditional markets, large malls and supermarkets have fixed prices.

FOOD

Food is excellent in Bahrain and has a global flavour. Most restaurants fall within the midrange price bracket, but cheap eats include street shawarma and falafel wraps. Top-end restaurants tend to be attached to luxury hotels in the major cities, where a number of excellent boutique cafes have sprouted. In rural Bahrain, you'll find more eateries than restaurants, and good cafes might be attached to a tourist site.

HEALTH

Before You Go

Some travel insurance may not cover activities like diving (for pearls or otherwise) and drag racing, so check your policy before you arrive, and buy additional cover if needed.

Check your insurance policy's claims procedure for emergency healthcare – in Bahrain, travellers are charged for this and must ensure they have the funds to cover the costs at the time.

In Bahrain

Bahrain has excellent healthcare services. With more doctors and nurses per resident than any other Gulf country, queues tend to be short, too.

There are good hospitals all over Bahrain, such as the **American Mission Hospital** (Map p64; ☑ 17 253 447; www.amh.org.bh; Sheikh Isa Al Kabeer Ave; ▣ A1), and 22 health care centres, which should be a traveller's first point of call for any non-emergency concerns. A visit to see a doctor at one of these will cost no more than BD3.

Tap water in Bahrain is not fit for consumption. Bottled water is readily available but be aware of your plastic impact.

INTERNET ACCESS

Wi-fi is widely available for free. All hotels and most cafes offer free wi-fi access to customers.

LEGAL MATTERS

➡ All visitors to Bahrain must carry photographic ID with them at all times. Failure to do so can result in an expensive fine.

● Bahrain has strict drug laws. Anyone caught using drugs can be imprisoned and/or deported, and anyone caught selling them faces life imprisonment.

● Drunken behaviour is punishable with imprisonment.

● During the day in Ramadan, it is forbidden to eat, drink, smoke, play loud music or dance in public places, and this is punishable by law.

LGBT+ TRAVELLERS

Same-sex relationships between consenting adults over the age of 21 are legal. Bahrain is a liberal country, but many locals do harbour conservative social views and therefore public displays of affection are not advised.

MONEY
ATMs & Credit Cards

Major credit cards are widely accepted throughout Bahrain. Most banks have ATMs that accept Visa, Cirrus and MasterCard, while the Bank of Bahrain and Kuwait has ATMs that take Visa, MasterCard, Cirrus, Maestro and American Express.

Currency

Bahrain's currency is the Bahraini dinar (BD). One dinar is divided into 1000 fils. There are 500-fil and one-, five-, 10- and 20-dinar notes. Coins come in denominations of five, 10, 25, 50, 100 and 500 fils. With huge numbers of Saudi tourists regularly visiting, local businesses in Bahrain also accept Saudi riyals.

Changing Money

Money can be changed at any bank or money-changing office. There is little difference between banks and moneychangers in terms of exchange rates, and it's rare for either to charge a commission. Currencies for other Gulf states are easy to buy and sell.

Tipping

Restaurants A service charge is added to most bills in restaurants and hotels, so tipping is at your discretion. An appropriate tip for good service would be around 10%.

Porters Airport porters expect a small tip of BD1 despite their services being covered by the airport tax.

Taxi Drivers do not expect a tip for short journeys. For longer journeys (more than 5km), 10% is appropriate.

OPENING HOURS

The weekend in Bahrain is Friday and Saturday for most commercial and government organisations.

Banks 7.30am–3pm Sunday to Thursday

Restaurants 11am–3pm and 6pm–1am

SLEEPING PRICE RANGES

The following price ranges refer to a double room with a private bathroom in high season (November to March). Unless otherwise stated, breakfast is included in the price.

$ less than BD40
$$ BD40–80
$$$ more than BD80

Shopping centres 9am–10pm Saturday to Thursday, 10am–10pm Friday

Shops 8am–noon and 3.30pm–7.30pm Saturday to Thursday

PUBLIC HOLIDAYS

In addition to the main Islamic holidays, Bahrain celebrates a number of public holidays.

New Year's Day 1 January

Tasoa'a & Ashura 9 and 10 Muharram (1st month in the Hejira calendar). Ashura marks the death of Hussein, grandson of the Prophet. Processions led by men flagellating themselves take place in many of the country's predominantly Shiite areas.

Labour Day 1 May

Arafa Day Observed on 9 Dhulhijjah (12th month in Hejira calendar). This marks the hajj pilgrimage, which commemorates the Prophet Muhammad's final sermon and completion of the message of Islam.

Islamic New Year 1 Muharram (1st month in Hejira calendar)

Prophet Muhammad's Birthday 12 Rabe'a Alawwal (3rd month in Hejira calendar)

National Day 16 December. Celebrating the country's declaration of independence from the British.

Accession Day 17 December. Celebrating the accession of the late emir Sheikh Isa Bin Salman Al Khalifa to the Bahrain royal throne.

SAFE TRAVEL

Travelling around Bahrain feels safe for foreigners, but take the usual precautions.

EATING PRICE RANGES

The following price ranges refer to a standard main course.

$ less than BD3
$$ BD3–9
$$$ more than BD9

TRAVELLING WITH CHILDREN

Bahrainis welcome visiting children, and a lively expat community means kids are never short of something to do.

Almost all tourist sites in Bahrain offer free or reduced admission for children, but few are pram friendly. Sights that will appeal specifically to little travellers include the **Royal Camel Farm** (Map p60; Janabiya Hwy, Saar; ☺hours vary; [P]; ☐14, 15) **FREE**, where children can get up close and personal with Arabia's most famous animal. In fact, if you tip one of the workers, they may even let the kids ride one. Older kids will love the Bahrain International Karting Circuit (p84), where smaller engines suited to younger drivers are available. Meanwhile those who prefer four legs to two wheels will surely appreciate riding one of the beautiful ponies at **Dilmun Club** (Map p60; ☑17 693 766; https://dilmun-club.com; Rd 7115, Saar; ☺9-10.30am & 3-5pm).

Both the Al Areen Wildlife Park & Reserve (p84) and the spectacular Lost Paradise of Dilmun Water Park (p84) are popular with the entire family, especially the toddler pool in the latter and the bus tour of the park. For younger children, there are some really good indoor entertainment options, such as the Wahooo! (p66) water park and **Magic Planet** (Map p60; ☑17 173 013; www.magicplanetmena.com; 2nd fl, City Centre Bahrain, Rd 2819, Seef; packages BD10-50; ☺10am-10pm Sat-Wed, to midnight Thu & Fri; ☐41, A2, A2S, X2) in central Manama.

Bahrain, like many Gulf countries, is very family orientated, and children are pretty much welcome everywhere; however, this does not necessarily mean facilities specifically aimed at parents are widely available, though this is changing. Most new malls, for example, have baby-changing facilities, as do some well-known restaurant and cafes, but these are often restricted to female toilets and are rarely found outside Manama. Pavements are not very well suited for pushchairs; however, the country's buses do have space for them.

Ongoing tensions with Qatar means there's a curfew in place on the waterways around Bahrain from 6pm to 4am.

TELEPHONE

Bahrain's network runs on the GSM through Batelco and Zain. Visitors can purchase SIM cards for BD1, BD5 and BD10 at Batelco and Zain outlets. Recharge comes in many denominations up to BD20 and is widely available at most supermarkets.

Bahrain's telephone code is 973, and there are no area or city codes. The international access code (to call abroad from Bahrain) is ☑ 00. There are several help lines, including local directory assistance (☑181) and international directory assistance (☑191).

TOURIST INFORMATION

The country's only tourist information office is inside **Bab Al Bahrain** (Map p69; Bab Al Bahrain Ave, Manama Souq; ☺9am-5pm Sun-Thu, 9am-1pm Sat; ☐10, 41, 44, A1). You can also get tourist information via the government websites or by approaching concierges at the bigger hotels.

Bahrain Tourism (www.btea.bh & www.bahrain.com) Official government sites for tourism.

Bahrain Culture (www.culture.gov.bh) Official government site for culture and antiquities.

Bahrain Events and Festivals (www.calendar.bh) Official government site for all forthcoming festivals and events

VISAS

Visas are needed to visit Bahrain; for people of 66 nationalities, these can be obtained on arrival at the airport or at the border with Saudi Arabia. A three-month, multiple-entry visa, valid for stays of two weeks to 30 days, costs BD25 and is payable in cash (either Bahraini dinars or major international currencies).

You can also apply for an e-visa online – follow the links on www.evisa.gov.bh – with the main advantage being that you'll spend less time passing through immigration on arrival.

WOMEN TRAVELLERS

Bahrain is fairly liberal compared to some Gulf countries, which can be both a blessing (less of the staring) and a nuisance (more of the hassle). Muharraq, much of the Manama Souq and Shiite-dominated areas such as Budaiya are much more traditional, and it's best to dress modestly in these areas.

ⓘ Getting There & Away

ENTERING THE COUNTRY

➡ The importation, purchase and consumption of alcohol is permissible.

→ Non-Muslim visitors can import 1L of wine or spirits, or six cans of beer duty free.

→ If planning to enter Saudi Arabia, be aware that alcohol is completely banned there.

AIR

Bahrain International Airport (Map p60; ☎80 007 777; www.bahrainairport.com; Rd 2404) is on Muharraq Island, 12km from the centre of Manama, and handles frequent services to many intercontinental destinations, as well as other countries in the region.

The national carrier is Gulf Air (www.gulfair. com), which flies to destinations worldwide. It has a good safety record and reliable departure times.

LAND

The only 'land' border is with Saudi Arabia, across the King Fahd Causeway.

Tourists are not permitted to drive between Saudi Arabia and Bahrain in a hired car. Residents of Saudi Arabia who have their own cars may use this crossing providing they have car insurance for both countries. For those coming from Saudi Arabia, this can be purchased at the border. A transit visa must be obtained from the Saudi authorities for those travelling by car between the United Arab Emirates and Bahrain. This is not easy to obtain.

Bus

You must have a valid transit visa for Saudi Arabia in advance and an onward ticket and visa for your next destination beyond Saudi Arabia's borders.

The Saudi bus company **Saudi Arabian Public Transport Co** (Map p69; ☎17 226 688; www. saptco.com.sa; Government Ave), runs regular services to cities all over Saudi Arabia for those who have a Saudi visa.

From Manama, Saptco also has daily buses as far as Abu Dhabi, Dubai and Sharjah (UAE) and Kuwait City. All departures are from the **International Bus Terminal** (Map p69; Government Ave) in Manama.

Car & Motorcycle

All drivers (and passengers in taxis) using the causeway to Saudi Arabia must pay a toll of BD2.5 at the **booth** (Map p60; ☎17 796 332; www.kfca. com.sa; King Fahd Causeway; from BD2.5) on the western side of the intersection between Causeway Approach Rd and Janabiya Hwy.

Anyone crossing the border from Bahrain to Saudi Arabia will be given a customs form to complete, and drivers entering Bahrain from Saudi Arabia must purchase temporary Bahraini insurance and also sign a personal guarantee.

🛈 Getting Around

BOAT

There are three boat services open to the general public: the small **Qalat Bu Mahir ferry** (Map p64; Bahrain National Museum; BD1; ⊙9am-4.30pm) that takes passengers from the Bahrain National Museum to the fort and the two services that take passengers to the Al Dar Islands (p86) and the **Hawar Islands** (p83).

BUS

Bahrain now boasts an extensive **public bus system** (Map p60; ☎66 311 111; https://bahrainbus.bh; Depot 1087, Rd 4025, Block 840, Isa Town; ⊙customer services 6am-9pm; 🕿) linking most of the major towns and residential areas. These run daily between 6am and 9pm and arrive every 10 to 15 minutes. Each trip costs BD0.3 when paid for in cash or BD0.25 when paid for using the rechargeable GO Card. Riding a bus in Bahrain is safe.

CAR & MOTORCYCLE

Driving around Bahrain is straightforward and the main sites of tourist interest are well signposted.

Speed limits, the wearing of seat belts and drink-driving laws are rigorously enforced. Speed limits are 60km/h in towns, 80km/h in the outer limits of suburbs and 120km/h on highways. Petrol stations are well signposted, especially along highways.

Hire

Car-hire companies have offices in Manama and at the airport, charging from BD20/70 per day/week for the smallest four-door sedan.

Rates exclude petrol but include unlimited mileage and insurance. To avoid the excess of BD100 to BD200 in case of an accident, it's wise to pay the extra BD2 Collision Damage Waiver (CDW) per day. Companies normally only accept drivers over 21 years old (over 25 for more expensive car models), and foreigners must (theoretically at least) have an International Driving Permit, although a driving licence is often sufficient. There is nowhere to rent a motorcycle.

TAXI

Most visitors get around Bahrain by taxi, although persistence is needed to persuade drivers to use their meters. If you're visiting more than one tourist attraction outside Manama and Muharraq, it's cheaper to hire a car.

Kuwait الكويت

POP 4.1 MILLION

Best Places to Eat

➡ Burj Al Hamam (p113)

➡ Al Boom (p115)

➡ Pick (p112)

➡ Le Nôtre (p113)

➡ Mais Alghanim (p113)

➡ Greenland Vegetarian Restaurant (p112)

Best Places to Stay

➡ Marina Hotel (p111)

➡ Ibis Sharq (p109)

➡ Radisson Blu (p111)

➡ Mövenpick Hotel & Resort Al Bida'a (p111)

➡ Symphony Style by Radisson (p111)

Why Go?

Cradled between Saudi Arabia and Iraq in one of the most ancient and contested corners of the world, Kuwait has a certain cachet. It may be as oil-rich as other Gulf countries, and its architectural landscape as experimental and audacious, but it hasn't embraced glitz and glamour in the same way: perhaps it's the years lost to the Iraqi invasion and its aftermath, or maybe it's a conscious decision not to give in to commercialism.

Geographically, Kuwait lies far enough away from the Gulf travel hubs to the south to mean there are fewer tourists here. The result? A more authentically Arab feel to the country. Kuwait remains an oasis in a land of desert plains, and visitors may be surprised by the intriguing attractions on offer, from excellent museums and galleries to a fine souq, to a corniche with beaches and lively restaurants.

When to Go
Kuwait

Nov–Jan Experience the relief of cool evenings after the burning heat of summer.

Feb Pick up a bargain at Kuwait's Hala shopping festival.

Mar & Apr During spring, the desert is laced in a gossamer of lime green.

Daily Costs

Kuwait is an expensive country to visit. There are few budget accommodation options, and most hotels are aimed at business travellers. Dinner at a local restaurant will cost around KD7 (about US$23), while a meal at a top-end hotel will likely set you back at least KD10 (about US$33).

ITINERARIES

One Day

Potter the length of the corniche (p106), pausing at Layali Al Helmeya (p112) for a shisha and Kuwait Towers (p104) for a quintessential Kuwait photo. Get a feel for the country's Bedouin history with a coffee at Al Sadu House (p107), take lunch in one of the few remaining heritage houses at Beit 7 (p114) and then enjoy the rich Al Sabah collection at Dar Al Athar Al Islamiyya (p100). Sample local desserts in the city's most traditional souq, Souq Mubarakiya (p99), and return to the water for dinner on a dhow at Al Boom (p115).

Two Days

After a day exploring the corniche, head inland and tour the extravagant prayer room of the Grand Mosque (p101). Head further south to Tareq Rajab Museum (p99), where you'll find a collection of ethnographic treasures from across the Islamic world. Afterwards, learn about the curious creatures that live in the Gulf waters at the excellent Scientific Center (p100), and end the day enjoying the scene of promenading locals at nearby Marina Crescent (p105), followed by dinner at Mais Alghanim (p113).

Three Days

Appreciate the archaeological relics salvaged from the 1990 ransacking of the Kuwait National Museum (p106), and learn what a group of young Kuwaitis endured during an Iraqi siege at the Al Qurain Martyrs' Museum (p104). Lift the mood with a visit to the brilliantly bizarre Mirror House (p101) and then unwind at the Hilton Kuwait Resort (p111), on a silky stretch of coastline with sequinned waters, or get away from it all on a boat trip to Failaka Island (p117).

Essential Food & Drink

Hammour or pomfret White fish stuffed with parsley, onions and dill.

Gulf prawns Available late autumn and early winter.

Alcohol Kuwait is a dry state, so the consumption of alcohol is forbidden.

Tap water Safe to drink.

AT A GLANCE

Capital Kuwait City

Country code ☏965

Currency Kuwaiti dinar (KD)

Emergency ☏112

Language Arabic, English

Mobile phones SIM cards widely available

Money ATMs are widespread; credit cards widely accepted

Population 4.1 million

Visas Available on arrival or online for more than 50 nationalities

KUWAIT

Exchange Rates

Australia	A$10	KD2.14
Canada	C$10	KD2.28
Euro zone	€10	KD3.43
Japan	¥1000	KD2.72
New Zealand	NZ$10	KD2.07
UAE	Dhs10	KD0.83
UK	£10	KD4.03
USA	US$10	KD3.04

For current exchange rates, see www.xe.com.

Resources

Bazaar (https://bazaar.town)

Two Forty Eight AM (https://248am.com)

Visit Kuwait (www.visit-kuwait.com)

Lonely Planet (www.lonelyplanet.com/kuwait)

Kuwait Highlights

❶ Souq Mubarakiya (p99) Catching a sense of Kuwait's living history at this bustling, authentic marketplace.

❷ Kuwait Towers (p104) Marvelling at the bulbous towers, an icon of the nation.

❸ Dar Al Athar Al Islamiyya (p100) Admiring ancient artefacts from the region's rich past.

❹ Al Shaheed Park (p104) Strolling a beautifully manicured green urban park, with paths covering 2km.

❺ Tareq Rajab Museum (p99) Marvelling at the fine ethnographic collection that survived the Iraqi invasion.

❻ Grand Mosque (p101) Touring the extravagant prayer room of Kuwait's largest mosque.

❼ Al Qurain Martyrs' Museum (p104) Remembering the Kuwaitis who tried to resist Iraqi arrest at this sobering museum.

❽ Al Boom (p115) Dining in a dhow in the shadow of one of the largest wooden boats on Earth.

❾ Mirror House (p101) Experiencing art-in-action in a house covered with mirrors.

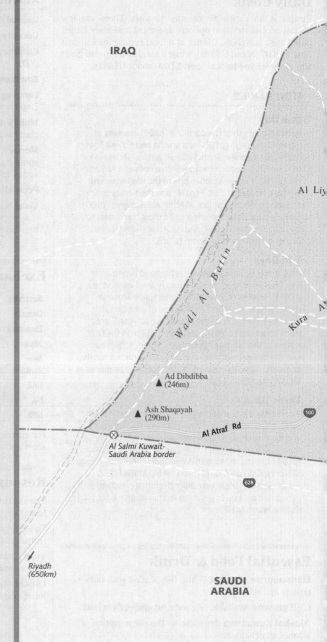

IRAQ

Al Liy

Wadi Al Batin

Kura

A

Ad Dibdibba
▲ (246m)

Ash Shaqayah
▲ (290m)

100

Al Atraf Rd

⊗ Al Salmi Kuwait-
Saudi Arabia border

628

Riyadh
(650km)

SAUDI ARABIA

Ⓝ 0 ————————— 40 km
0 ————————— 20 miles

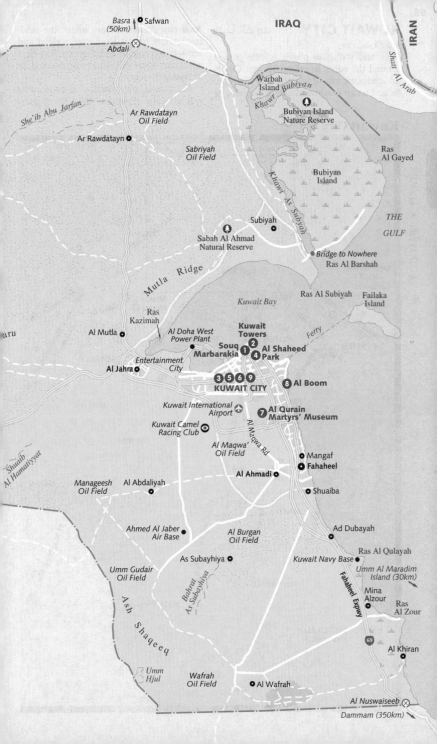

KUWAIT CITY

مدينة الكويت

POP 2.4 MILLION

Slick and stylish in places, a little ragged around the edges in others, Kuwait City is an intriguing mix of wealthy Gulf metropolis and tough neighbourhood of a sprawling Arab city. Attractions are many: the landmark triple towers loom over a clean and accessible corniche, and there's a first-class aquarium, some excellent museums and an atmospheric souq.

Meanwhile, the selection of restaurants will whet the appetite of the fussiest gour-

Kuwait City

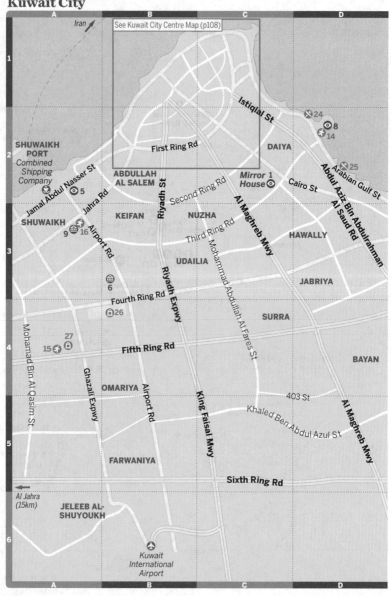

See Kuwait City Centre Map (p108)

mand. Add to its sights and attractions a harrowing layer of modern history, the effects of which rumble invisibly below the surface, and there's enough to keep most visitors intrigued for days.

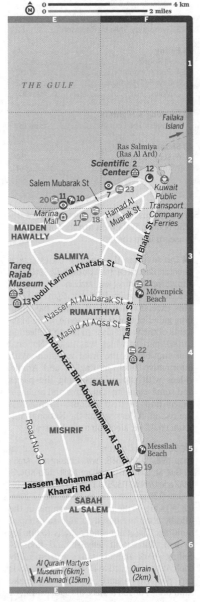

THE GULF

Failaka Island

Ras Salmiya (Ras Al Ard)

Scientific 2
Center 🏛 12

Salem Mubarak St
20 11 10 7 23
Kuwait Public Transport Company Ferries

Marina Mall
17 18
Hamad Al Muarak St
Al Blajat St

MAIDEN HAWALLY

SALMIYA

Tareq Rajab Museum
3 13
Abdul Karimal Khatabi St

21
Mövenpick Beach

Nasser Al Mubarak St
RUMAITHIYA
Masjid Al Aqsa St

Taawen St

22
4

SALWA
Abdul Aziz Bin Abdulrahman Al Saud Rd

MISHRIF
Road No 30
Messilah Beach 5
19

Jassem Mohammad Al Kharafi Rd

SABAH AL SALEM

6

Al Qurain Martyrs' Museum (6km); Al Ahmadi (15km)
Qurain (2km)

0 ——————— 4 km
0 ——————— 2 miles

⊙ Sights

Many of Kuwait's sights are concentrated along the corniche (Arabian Gulf St) and around the National Museum area. While a few of the downtown sights may be within walking distance of each other, the searing heat often prevents exploring by foot. The most convenient way of visiting outlying attractions, or of covering longer stretches of the corniche, is by taxi or ride-hail app Careem (www.careem.com).

★**Souq Mubarakiya**　　　　MARKET
(Map p108; btwn Mubarak Al Kabir, Ahmad Al Jaber & Ali Al Salem Sts; ⊙9am-1pm & 4-9pm Sat-Thu, 4-9pm Fri) Once the centre of trade before the nation found oil, Kuwait City's old souq has retained its sprawling, bustling glory. The historical centre of the market has been added to, with modern buildings and sub-markets of sorts. Wandering around is a wonderful sensory experience, with colourful stalls and air permeated with rich spices. Shoppers haggle over everything from olives and dates to ox tails.

In the area named **Souq Al Hareem**, Bedouin women sit cross-legged on cushions of velvet selling kohl (black eyeliner), pumice stones and gold-spangled dresses in the red, white and green livery of the Kuwaiti flag. Beyond the covered alleyway, the souq opens out into lanes stocked with woollen vests and Korean blankets. The nearby **Souq Ad Dahab Al Markazi** is the city's central gold market, and many shops also glitter with wedding gold and local pearls around the perimeter of Souq Mubarakiya.

★**Tareq Rajab Museum**　　　　MUSEUM
(Map p98; ☑25317358; http://trmkt.com; House 22, Block 12, St 5, Jabriya; adult/child KD2/free; ⊙9am-noon & 4-7pm Sat-Thu, 9am-noon Fri) Housed in the basement of a large villa, this exquisite ethnographic museum should not be missed. There are inlaid musical instruments suspended in glass cabinets, Omani silver and Saudi gold jewellery, headdresses from the humble prayer cap to the Mongol helmet, costumes worn by princesses and goat herders, necklaces for living goddesses in Nepal, Jaipur enamel and Bahraini pearls. Despite all these superbly presented pieces, it's the Arabic manuscripts in the Calligraphy Museum that give the collection its international importance.

The museum was assembled as a private collection of Islamic art by Kuwait's first minister of antiquities and his British wife.

Kuwait City

◎ Top Sights
1	Mirror House	C2
2	Scientific Center	F2
3	Tareq Rajab Museum	E3

◎ Sights
4	Al Hashemi Marine Museum	F4
5	Arab Fund Building	A2
6	Contemporary Art Platform	B3
7	Corniche	F2
8	Green Island	D2
9	Historical, Vintage & Classic Cars Museum	A3
10	Marina Beach	E2
11	Marina Crescent	E2
12	Shaikh Nasser Al Sabah Mosque	F2
13	Tareq Rajab Museum of Islamic Art	E3

◎ Activities, Courses & Tours
	Bike Hire	(see 10)
14	Halloween Beach	D2
	Ikarus Marine	(see 11)
15	Magic Planet	A4
	Marina Skate Park	(see 10)
16	Sirbb Circuit	A3

◎ Sleeping
17	Dalal City Hotel	E3
18	Ibis Kuwait Salmiya Hotel	E3
19	Jumeirah Messilah Beach Hotel & Spa	F5
20	Marina Hotel	E2
21	Mövenpick Hotel & Resort Al Bida'a	F3
22	Radisson Blu	F4
23	Symphony Style by Radisson	F2

◎ Eating
	Al Boom	(see 22)
24	Burj Al Hamam	D2
25	Layali Al Helmeya	D2
	Maki	(see 10)

◎ Drinking & Nightlife
	English Tea Lounge	(see 15)

◎ Shopping
26	Souq Al Juma	B4
27	The Avenues	A4

A pair of ornate doors from Cairo and Carl Haag's 19th-century painting of Lady Jane Digby El Mesreb of Palmyra, who lived in tents in the winter and a Damascus villa in the summer, mark the entrance to an Aladdin's cave of beautiful items.

Many stories arose from the brutal Iraqi invasion and occupation of Kuwait in 1990, many of them too painful or tragic to tell. But there is one good-news story that is remarkable in its simplicity. While the National Museum was being looted by Iraqi soldiers, the custodians of the Tareq Rajab Museum bricked up the doorway at the bottom of the entry steps and littered the steps with rubbish. The Iraqis questioned why the stairs led to nowhere but mercifully didn't pursue the issue and the collection survived intact.

The museum is in Jabriya, near the intersection of the Fifth Ring Motorway and the Abdulaziz Bin Abdulrahman Al Saud Expressway (also known as the Fahaheel Expressway). There is no sign on the building, but it is easily identified by its entrance – a carved wooden doorway flanked by two smaller doors on each side. All four of the door panels are worked in gilt metal.

Allow an hour to visit, although anyone with a passion for textiles will inevitably want to stay longer. Bus 102 stops at the nearby Hadi Hospital. It's a 10-minute walk from here, south along the Fahaheel Expressway and turn right just after the Iranian School. Walk for a further 50m and the museum is on the left.

★ **Dar Al Athar Al Islamiyya** CULTURAL CENTRE
(Amricani Cultural Centre; Map p108; ☑ 22400992; http://darmuseum.org.kw; Arabian Gulf St, Qibla; ☺ 10am-7pm Mon-Thu & Sat, from 2pm Fri) FREE
This exceptional cultural centre has stunning galleries that contain some of the highlights of the world-class Al Sabah Collection (p106), part of which was in the National Museum before the Iraqi invasion. With informative labels in English and Arabic, videos with experts explaining the pieces and some exquisite sculptures and archaeological finds of great antiquity from across the region, it's everything the National Museum could be, albeit on a smaller scale.

★ **Scientific Center** MUSEUM
(Map p98; ☑ 1848888; www.tsck.org.kw; Arabian Gulf St, Salmiya; aquarium adult/child KD4/3, IMAX adult/child KD3.75/3, Discovery Place KD2.25; ☺ 9am-9.30pm Sat-Wed, to 10pm Thu, 2-10pm Fri; P) One of the largest aquariums in the Middle East is housed in this sail-shaped building. The giant spider crabs (3.8m leg to leg), fluorescent jellyfish and floor-to-ceiling shark and ray tanks are especially cool. At the interactive Discovery Place, kids can perform science experiments, make sand dunes or roll a piece of road. An IMAX

DON'T MISS

KUWAIT'S MODERN ARCHITECTURE

Kuwait's extraordinary modern wealth has been expressed in many pieces of architectural civic pride. If you're in town for a while, don't miss at least a drive-by of the following fine buildings.

Kuwait Towers (p104) There are few buildings in the region as iconic as these water towers. Their slender columns and plump reservoirs are symbolic of the way in which a city has blossomed from humble beginnings.

National Assembly Building (Map p108; Arabian Gulf St, Qibla) Designed by Jørn Utzon of Sydney Opera House fame, this landmark building resembles a piece of unfurled silk, evoking both the canopy of a Bedouin tent and a sail-rigged dhow, while expressing modernist concepts of negative space and the sculpture of light and shade.

Arab Fund Building (Map p98; 24959907; www.arabfund.org/aohq; Airport Rd, Shuwaikh; tours 9am-1pm) With its expression of the integrity of space and function, light and communication, this superb building remains true to a traditional Islamic aesthetic all the way through to its modern interior design.

Grand Mosque (p101) Across from Sief Palace on Arabian Gulf St, Kuwait City's main mosque is graced with the tallest minaret in the country and a finely crafted interior.

Fatima Mosque (Map p108; cnr Sanaa & Ibn Abbas Sts) Kuwait's mosques and religious architecture are creative and spectacular, and often financed and built by individuals, including this notable green-and-white domed structure in Abdullah Al Salem.

Shaikh Nasser Al Sabah Mosque (Map p98; Arabian Gulf St, Ras Salmiya) This pyramid-shaped mosque is the stuff of architects' dreams, and it's a fine illuminated example of forward-thinking modern mosque design.

theatre shows 45-minute 3D educational videos about the natural world.

Head outside to the parking lot for one of the Scientific Center's best attractions: a car on a pulley system. Even your smallest kids can have a go at pulling the chains and lifting the car, they won't believe their eyes when it lifts into the air. Parking costs 250 fils.

★**Mirror House**　　　　　　　　HOUSE
(Map p98; 22518522; www.mirrorhouseq8.com; House 17, St 94, Block 9, Qadisiya; adult/child KD3/2; by appointment only Tue-Sun) **FREE**
For a brilliantly bizarre art-in-action experience, visit this residential house covered with mirror mosaics. It's the creation of gloriously eccentric Italian-Kuwaiti artist Lidia Al Qattan, who entertains with her stories and explanations of each room, including a mirror-clad bathroom and cosmos-themed room. Work on the house started in 1966 and was finished in 2006, requiring some 70 tonnes of mirror.

At various points in the tour, guests take a seat while Lidia turns off the lights to reveal glow-in-the-dark displays, hula rings covered in flashing lights, sometimes while creepy galactic music plays. Lidia asks visitors to stare into the mirrors and imagine

they are in a galaxy far far away. It's a trippy experience, certainly one for the open-minded. On the 2nd floor, most rooms are dedicated to the work of Lidia's late husband and politically controversial Kuwaiti artist Khalifa Al Qattan. Part way through the tour, Lidia invites guests to play her self-made game, which involves throwing art-covered tiles at a velcro wall. There's also a gift shop filled with peculiar sculptures made from reused items; some flash and glow.

★**Grand Mosque**　　　　　　　　MOSQUE
(Masjed Al Kabir; Map p108; 22418447; http://thegrandmosque.net; Mubarak Al Kabir St; tours around 5pm, depending on prayer times) The largest of the city's 800 mosques, opened in 1986, completely survived the Iraqi invasion. It cost KD14 million (US$46 million) to build, with extravagant features including a palm tree-lined courtyard, stained glass from France and Italian marble detailing, plus mosaics from Morocco, chandeliers from Germany, teak wood from India and a striking gold-plated central dome. Tours are provided by knowledgeable staff and cover Kuwaiti culture and a peek into the emir's private room. Women must wear an *abaya* (full-length robe-like dress) and a headscarf (both provided).

KIRILL NEIEZHMAKOV/SHUTTERSTOCK ©

MATYAS REHAK/SHUTTERSTOCK ©

. Grand Mosque, Kuwait

he largest of the city's 800 mosques, the Grand
Mosque (p101) has Kuwait's highest minaret
74m) and can accommodate up to 17,000
orshippers.

. Kuwait Towers

esigned by architect Sune Lindström, these
ater towers (p104) are an iconic symbol of
nation that has blossomed from humble
eginnings.

. Eating local

ocal food, including kebabs and hummus, at the
ouq Mubarakiya (p99) in Kuwait City.

. Camel racing

ttend the Kuwait Camel Racing Club (p118) in a
WD, for a thrilling experience where you can drive
longside camels (with electric jockeys) as they
ace at speeds of up to 60km/h.

DON'T MISS

AL QURAIN MARTYRS' MUSEUM

Early one February morning in 1991, an Iraqi militia minibus drew up outside an ordinary house in the Kuwait City suburbs. When no one answered the door, the militia began firing at the doors and windows of the house, trying to rout a cell of the Kuwaiti resistance sheltering inside. They bombarded the house for hour upon hour with machine guns, grenades and eventually a tank, waiting for the young patriots to surrender. Eventually, they got tired of waiting. Nine of those under siege were captured and tortured to death, while four hid in a roof space.

The house, now the excellent **Al Qurain Martyrs' Museum** (✆25430343; House 61, St 3, Block 4, Qurain; ⏱8.30am-12.30pm & 4.30-8.30pm Mon-Thu, 8.30am-4.30pm Fri & Sat) **FREE**, is a sobering memorial to these Kuwaitis who tried to resist Iraqi arrest. The house, still in its post-attack state (fully supported with beams) has the bullet holes and signs of destruction. Markers show where the Kuwaitis fought and hid during the siege, and an exhibition displays the weapons used in the battle, including Kalashnikovs, tanks and shotguns.

Allow at least half an hour to visit. It's around a 20-minute taxi ride southeast of the city centre, or bus 101 stops within a 10-minute walk of the museum. Although signposted with brown signs, it's difficult to find the exact location. Locals should be able to point you in the right direction.

The Grand Mosque has Kuwait's highest minaret (74m) and can accommodate up to 10,000 worshippers in the main hall (open for prayer on Fridays and holidays), and another 7000 in the courtyard. Don't miss the glass cabinet with a replica of the oldest Quran in the world in it.

★**Kuwait Towers**   NOTABLE BUILDING
(Map p108; ✆22081999; Arabian Gulf St, Dasman; adult/child under 4yr KD3/free; ⏱9am-11.30pm; **P**) The Kuwait Towers, with their distinctive blue-green 'sequins', are the instantly recognisable symbols of the nation. Designed by a Swedish architectural firm, they opened in 1979. The largest of the three rises to a height of 187m. Guests can visit a gift shop, viewing platform and an international buffet restaurant. The standard ticket price includes entry to the 360-degree viewing deck at 120m. The entry fee is waived if you eat at the restaurant, offering views at 82m.

Breakfast (adult/child KD8/5) is available between 8am and 11.30am, with lunch and dinner (adult/child KD14/8) served from 12.30pm to 11.30pm. Parking is available for diners only.

Al Shaheed Park   PARK
(Map p108; ✆22461267; www.alshaheedpark. com; Soor St; ⏱5am-midnight; **P**) It's easy to spend a whole day in Kuwait's largest urban park, which has jogging and walking paths covering more than 2km. The green space contains botanical gardens, a lake and palm trees galore, plus restaurants and two museums (the Habitat and Memorial Museums). Just outside the main park area is a cycle track and designated 'resting place' for migrating birds. Fully lit at night, the park is a nice outdoor space to explore of an evening during the warmer months.

Park attendants keep the place immaculate; ask at the visitor centre about upcoming outdoor events being held at the amphitheatre. In the middle of the park, the excellent Three & Barista (p115) cafe makes a great air-conditioned pit stop.

Tareq Rajab
Museum of Islamic Art   MUSEUM
(Map p98; ✆25317358; http://trmkt.com; Dar Jehan, Block 12, St 1, Jabriya; KD2; ⏱9am-noon & 4-7pm Sat-Thu, 9am-noon Fri) A few blocks south of the Tareq Rajab Museum, this sister attraction is also housed in a villa. It has a seriously impressive and beautifully presented range of calligraphy. Typography from different Qurans, collected from all over the Arab world, span two floors and include ancient scripts up to the modern day. An educational video explains the methods of writing.

Curious items in the collection include a special carved cabinet from 1581 used to protect the Quran in Yemen, plus Islamic coins, a 10m-long calligraphy panel, an engraved marble tombstone column from 1044, a number of wall tapestries and various instruments connected with calligraphy –

from pens and quills to knives and etched ink pots.

Fish Market
MARKET

(Map p108; Arabian Gulf St; ⊙10am-10pm Sat-Thu, from 4pm Fri; P) This large market hall has rows of stalls selling all manner of morsels from the sea. Vendors tout their catch of the day, which may include anything from stacks of sardines to 2m-long groupers to buckets of enormous prawns. It's a vibrant place that offers a wonderful insight into local life. There's a fruit and veg section at the front of the building. Find it between the Dhow Harbour, where the catch of the day comes in, and Sharq Marina mall (p116).

Marina Beach
BEACH

(Map p98; Arabian Gulf St; ⊙24hr) Popular beach with great views of the city's skyline. Kiosks serve ice cream and drinks, and there's usually an enormous bouncy playground for kids on the sand, plus bike hire, a skate park and restaurants opposite the beach. Regular swimsuits are fine for women.

Marina Crescent
MARINA

(Map p98; ☑22244666; Arabian Gulf St; ⊙10am-midnight) Attached to Marina Mall, this pleasant palm tree-lined outdoor promenade loops around Kuwait Bay and has a range of restaurants and coffee shops. It's popular in the evening and at weekends.

Contemporary Art Platform
GALLERY

(Map p98; ☑24925636; www.capkuwait.com; Mezzanine level, Life Center, Industrial Shuwaikh, Block 2, St 28; ⊙10am-7pm Sat-Thu) A huge modern space hosting a permanent collection and regular exhibitions featuring Kuwaiti artists, plus occasional international names, talks and panel discussions. Locally regarded as one of the best galleries in Kuwait.

Historical, Vintage & Classic Cars Museum
MUSEUM

(Map p98; ☑24819186; www.kuwaitcarmuseum.com.kw; St 11, Shuwaikh Industrial Area B; ⊙9am-1pm & 4-8pm Sat-Thu) FREE Gearheads won't believe their eyes walking into this exhibition of perfectly polished mint-condition vintage cars covering more than a century of motoring history. See two 1950s Chrysler Imperial models, one used by former US president Eisenhower and the other by Queen Elizabeth. There's also an Aston Martin DB5, which the museum claims was used in the James Bond film *Goldfinger* despite international reports indicating the original vehicle is still missing after being stolen from a Florida airport hangar in 1997.

Other impressive vehicles include a rare 1956 Rolls Royce Silver Cloud used by the emir of Kuwait.

Maritime Museum
MUSEUM

(Map p108; ☑22401459; Arabian Gulf St; ⊙8.30am-12.30pm & 4.30-8.30pm Mon-Thu & Sat, 4.30-8.30pm Fri; P) FREE The entrance to this museum is hard to miss, with its three magnificent dhows (traditional cargo boats) dry docked opposite Kuwait Bay. The place offers insight into the seafaring heritage of Kuwait, which used dhows and boons to bring water from the Shatt Al Arab waterway near Basra to the bone-dry city, making a tidy profit from its thirsty inhabitants. Photographs inside the museum show the transport of water from boon to home before desalination plants brought water to household taps.

Meanwhile, pearling displays recount Kuwait's history of collecting precious objects from the sea and trading with countries around the world. Displays contain a fascinating array of objects used in the industry, such as a heavy lead weight, a turtle-shell nose peg, leather finger ends and a wool suit to guard against jellyfish. These objects speak volumes about the deprivations of a life spent prising pearls from a reluctant seabed. The sieves of tiny mesh used to sift pearls according to size show that the effort was often barely worth the dangers involved.

Al Hashemi Marine Museum
MUSEUM

(Map p98; ☑25673000; Taawen St, Salwa; ⊙9am-5pm Sat-Thu, from 2pm Fri) FREE Maritime fanatics will enjoy this fascinating museum with its impressive collection of large, scale-model dhows, sailing equipment and boards detailing the history of seafaring in the area. *Al Hashemi II*, the huge wooden dhow adjacent to the museum, is the largest handmade wooden boat on earth, measuring a world-record-breaking 80.4m long and 18.7m wide and weighing an estimated 2500 tonnes. The museum has a 2002 *Guinness Book of Records* certificate to prove it.

Commissioned by Husain Marafie, owner of the Radisson Blu hotel, *Al Hashemi II* was completed in 1998 from mahogany and ekki logs from Cameroon, planks from Ivory Coast and pine logs from Oregon. It's worth taking a five-minute walk inside the lavish, parquet-floored interior, which is used for conferences and banqueting.

Al Boom (p115), a smaller dhow in the complex, is a restaurant; and a hugely atmospheric place for dinner. The complex is next to the Palm Gardens hotel inside the grounds of the Radisson Blu hotel.

Dickson House Cultural Centre
HISTORIC BUILDING

(Beit Dickson; Map p108; ☑25725777; Arabian Gulf St; ⊙8am-12.30pm & 4.30-8.30pm Mon-Thu & Sat, 4.30-7.30pm Fri) FREE A modest white building with blue trim, Beit Dickson was the home of former British political agent Colonel Harold Dickson and his wife, Violet, whose love of and contribution to Kuwait are documented in the various archives inside the house. Highlights include a collection of photographs taken during Kuwait's British protectorate era, a replica museum of the Dicksons' living quarters and an archive of Kuwaiti-British relations that dates from the 19th century to the 1960s when Kuwait became independent.

Anglo-Italian explorer Freya Stark spent most of March 1937 in the house and, while she adored Kuwait, she described the house as a 'big ugly box'.

Corniche
WATERFRONT

(Map p98; Arabian Gulf St; P) Comprising more than 10km of winding paths, parks and beaches on Arabian Gulf St (sometimes referred to locally as Gulf Rd), the corniche is marked at its southern end by the Scientific Center and at its northernmost point by Kuwait Towers. Stop off at any of the many beaches, restaurants or coffee shops to watch a desert sunset or, on hot summer evenings, enjoy being part of the throng of people flocking to the sea to catch the breeze.

Kuwait National Museum
MUSEUM

(Map p108; ☑22451195; https://kuwaitnational museum.weebly.com; Arabian Gulf St, Qibla; ⊙8.30am-12.30pm & 4.30-8.30pm Mon-Thu & Sat, 4.30-8.30pm Fri; P) FREE It was the pride of Kuwait and contained one of the most important collections of Islamic art in the world until the 1990 Iraqi invasion. Sadly, the National Museum remains a shadow of its former self and reconstruction works are still nowhere near completion. Only two rooms containing a few archaeological finds are currently open. Among the items are ancient coins, pots, a detailed Bedouin tent and a 17th-century chess game, plus ancient Qurans and a full-sized carved doorway.

The museum was ransacked and largely emptied during the invasion, and it has been under almost complete reconstruction for the past decade. Things here can only get better.

AL SABAH COLLECTION

Many tragic losses were brought about by Iraq's invasion of Kuwait in 1990, but the looting and loss of the Al Sabah Collection must rank alongside the great cultural crimes of the late 20th century.

The collection began in the mid-1970s, when Sheikh Nasser Sabah Al Ahmad Al Sabah, a prominent member of Kuwait's ruling family, bought a 14th-century enamelled glass bottle from a London art gallery. What began as a hobby for the Al Sabahs became a passion for collecting and finally transformed into a world-class collection of Islamic art. By 1983, the Al Sabah Collection became the centrepiece of the Kuwait National Museum. In the space of a few short decades, the collection grew to include more than 20,000 pieces, among them jewellery, textiles, calligraphy, manuscripts, miniatures, coins, ivory, carpets, and wood-, metal- and stonework.

This priceless accumulation of art and archaeological treasures from across the Islamic world was famed throughout the region, and the museum was one of the first places targeted by invading Iraqi troops. The exhibition halls were systematically looted, damaged or set alight. The majority of the museum's collection was eventually returned following intense pressure from the UN, but many pieces had been broken in transit, poorly stored or, some suggest, deliberately spoiled. Others were lost forever.

Until a suitable home can be found for it at the National Museum complex, pieces from the Al Sabah Collection have graced London's British Museum and the Metropolitan Museum of Art in New York. Only a fraction of the collection is back on display inside Kuwait, and it will be some time before the National Museum complex is in a position to house what remains of it under one roof. In the meantime, Dar Al Athar Al Islamiyya (p100) showcases a wonderful, professionally displayed exhibit of some of the pieces.

The quaint **Heritage Museum** (Map p108; ☑22729158; https://kuwaitnationalmuseum.weebly.com/the-kuwait-heritage-museum.html; Arabian Gulf St; ☺8.30am-12.30pm & 4.30-8.30pm Mon-Thu & Sat, 4.30-8.30pm Fri; P) **FREE** is in Building 2, at the rear of the museum complex. It illustrates daily life in pre-oil Kuwait by means of a diorama of full-size figures going about their business – be sure to see the bead maker and what the museum booklet describes as the 'men's over-robe tailor'.

Buses 12 and 16 stop around a 15-minute walk from the museum.

🏃 Activities

Way Out   LIVE CHALLENGE
(Map p108; ☑98788203; https://wayoutkwt.com; Baitak Tower, Ahmad Al Jaber St; 2/3/4/5 players KD15/14/13/12; ☺4-11pm) Solve mysteries and clues within 60 minutes in one of three themed rooms at this escape room game centre. In the 'survivor' room, teams hide inside a cabin during a hurricane and then have to find a way out.

Tech heads will love 8bit, an' '80s-themed room that requires stealing secret computer game plans from a building before the alarm goes off. In the most difficult room, 'outside reality', players find themselves trapped in an alternate universe and have to find their way back to Earth.

Bike Hire   CYCLING
(Map p98; opp Marina Beach, Arabian Gulf St; bike hire per hr/day KD3/15; ☺4-11pm Sun-Thu, 6-10am Fri & Sat; ♿) One of the best ways to explore the corniche is on two wheels. This reliable hut, next to the Marina Skate Park, hires out mountain, BMX and kids' bikes, plus scooters. ID required.

Ikarus Marine   BOATING
(Map p98; ☑22022018, 98762316; Marina Crescent, Arabian Gulf St; solo/group 15-min boat tour KD12/3, day trips to Failaka Island KD20; ☺8am-midnight) This is the place to book short boat trips in Kuwait Bay (day or sunset tours), plus day trips and overnight trips to Failaka Island and the Ikaros Hotel (p117). Day packages include six-hour boat trips to the island featuring a range of activities including a turn on a rowing boat, horse riding, a bus tour and a visit to the military museum.

Day guests get access to the hotel's private beach. Paid-for extras include jet-skiing and banana boating. There's also a small zoo on the island just for kids.

Sirbb Circuit   SPORTS
(Map p98; ☑22274722; Shuwaikh Industrial Area 1, Block 1, St 11; 10min race KD10, 30min race package KD20, courses from KD150; ☺4-11pm) Race around this fun 500m go-kart track, with floodlights for night racing and stands so your friends can watch you in action. There's also a go-karting academy for honing your skills, which teaches the basics of mechanics, driving and controlling the vehicle, and about the fitness required for serious competitions.

Aqua Park   WATER PARK
(Map p108; ☑22431960; Arabian Gulf St; adult/child under 3yr KD4.75/free; ☺10am-10pm Sat-Thu, from 1pm Fri, Apr-Oct) Behind Kuwait Towers, Aqua Park has dozens of fun aquatic attractions including a lazy river, wave pool, flumes and a hair-raising 20m-high water slide. There's also a Flow House wave pool onsite for thrilling board riding, plus a paintball centre (KD7.5 per person, book online at www.paintball-kuwait.com). Tuesdays are for women only and Fridays are for families.

Halloween Beach   WATER SPORTS
(Map p98; Arabian Gulf St; jet ski/flyboard/wakeboarding per hour KD20/50/50; ☺6am-7pm) Find this convenient watersports centre offering wakeboarding, jet ski hire and flyboarding (with a jetpack strapped to your feet) on the beach to the right of Green Island. Bring ID for collateral if hiring a jet ski.

🍽 Courses

Al Sadu House   ARTS & CRAFTS
(Map p108; ☑22432395; www.alsadu.org.kw; Arabian Gulf St; 8-week sadu course KD75, kids sessions free; ☺office & gift shop 8am-1pm & 4-8pm Sat-Thu, kids sessions 11am-1pm Sat; ♿) Craftswomen teach *sadu* (Bedouin-style) and other weaving techniques for both beginners and those with more experience. It's a terrific venue with a relaxing courtyard. There are family and children's workshops on Saturdays, and a gift shop selling handcrafted items, plus the Jumo coffee shop (p115).

🎉 Festivals & Events

Hala Festival   SHOPPING
(www.hala-feb.com; ☺Feb) The city goes crazy with the annual shopping festival. There are lots of draws giving away valuable prizes in the shopping centres, and special promotions lure customers in. Many shops offer discounts of up to 70%. Ask your hotel reception where to go for the best bargains.

Kuwait City Centre

KUWAIT KUWAIT CITY

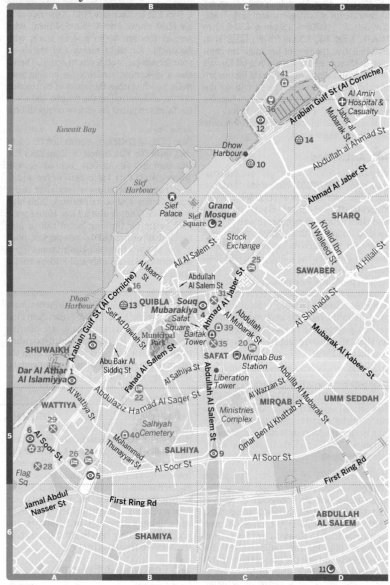

The festival coincides with National Day on 25 February and Liberation Day on 26 February. During this time, there are often fireworks displays, and the city is draped in lights. Arts, sports, a carnival and other activities make this an exciting time to be in town.

🛏 Sleeping

Kuwait City's hotels are of the midrange to high-end variety, with very limited budget options. Most travellers choose to stay near the pleasant Salmiya area, Arabian Gulf St (opposite the corniche and beaches) or the

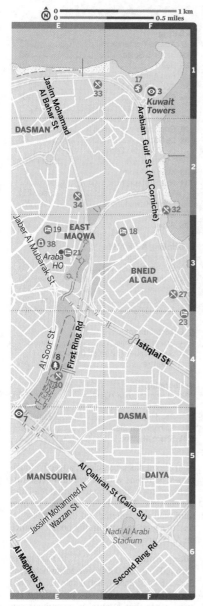

Sharq is clean with modern and light decor typical of the international brand and offers excellent value in a central location, with a good buffet breakfast. There's an Araba HO car hire desk (p128) in the lobby. It's a few minutes walk to the Al Hamra Luxury Center mall (p116).

The friendly desk staff can help you arrange a car with driver (from KD8 per hour).

★ Gulf Rose Hotel   HOTEL $
(Map p108; ☑22444800; www.gulfrosekuwait.com; Abdulla Al Mubarak St; r from KD27; ☎) Gulf Rose Hotel offers views of the city and the Gulf, friendly service and large rooms that would cost more if the hotel was part of an international chain. Room decor – including sheikh pop art, orange couches, brown carpets and exposed brickwork – is a bit random, but for the price, it's pleasant enough.

Ibis Kuwait Salmiya Hotel   BUSINESS HOTEL $
(Map p98; ☑25734247; www.accorhotels.com; Salem Al Mubarak St, Salmiya; r from KD34; [P] ☎) It's not often we recommend this international chain, but its modern rooms are outstanding value for Kuwait. Many on the upper floors have views out over the corniche (you can even see the Kuwait Towers in the distance). It's close to the Scientific Center and Salmiya's shopping district, and a short taxi ride from the centre. The Sharq branch is also a good bet. There's a restaurant, gym and shisha cafe. Reception is on the 3rd floor.

Le Royal   BOUTIQUE HOTEL $
(Map p108; ☑22510999; www.leroyalkuwait.com; 83rd St, Bneid Al Gar; r from KD35; [P] ☎ ☒) This small, tasteful boutique-style hotel, on a slip road off Arabian Gulf St, offers wonderful sea views, a French-rococo foyer and a bright and intimate atmosphere. Rooms have polished floors, floral-design bedsteads, bolster pillows and enormous bathrooms. Guests have access to a gym and a massage service.

There's an atmospheric Middle Eastern seafood restaurant in the basement, with tapestries on the walls and ceilings, plus lots of seafaring memorabilia.

Oasis Hotel   HOTEL $
(Map p108; ☑22465489; www.oasis.com.kw; cnr Ahmad Al Jaber & Mubarak Al Kabir Sts, Sharq; d from KD30; ☎) This central city hotel has simple, clean rooms with dated soft furnishings. It's in a prime downtown location just five minutes' walk from Souq Mubarakiya, and a reliable choice if the top-end hotels are beyond your reach. The upper floors have expansive views – the best are from the

central area of Sharq. Kuwait City is fairly small, so the right location is not as vital as in other capitals.

Ibis Sharq   BUSINESS HOTEL $
(Map p108; ☑22479330; www.accorhotels.com; 155 Jaber Al Mubarak St; r from KD29; [P] ☎) Ibis

KUWAIT KUWAIT CITY

Kuwait City Centre

street-facing rooms, but they're also noisier. There's a basic cafe in the lobby.

Al Hamra Hotel Kuwait   HOTEL $$
(Map p108; ☑ 22021412; www.alhamrahotel.com. kw; Al Shuhada St; r from KD60; P ❐ ❄) Opposite Kuwait's Al Hamra mall, this modern hotel is a decent choice, dressed with glass chandeliers, neutral greys, light browns and marble detailing. Bedrooms come with velvet-style soft furnishings, refrigerators and fruit baskets. It has an international restaurant, a coffee shop, 24-hour room service and a gym, but the stand-out feature is the rooftop pool and cafe.

Dalal City Hotel   HOTEL $$
(Map p98; ☑ 22284777; Salem Al Mubarak St, Salmiya; r from KD35, ste KD55; ❐ ❄) On the 5th floor of a Salmiya office building, this smart hotel has large, clean, attractive business-style rooms with brown and beige furnishings. It's a short hop to Marina Mall and the corniche. The building even has its own mini-mall and cinema, and there's guest access to a gym and swimming pool. Entrance on Al Dimna St.

Adams Hotel   APARTMENT $$
(Map p108; ☑ 22020000; www.adams-hotel.com; Block 3, 64th St, Bneid Al Gar; d from KD50; ❐ ❄) For people who value self-catering and the extra space that a suite or apartment can offer, Adams Hotel is a great choice. Decor is smart-gaudy, and corridors have crystal-style light fittings. There's an indoor pool, a spa, a gym and a Jacuzzi, plus a restaurant serving Turkish and international food. Some rooms have views of Kuwait Towers.

Le Royal Tower Kuwait
HOTEL $$

(Map p108; ☑ 1831831; www.leroyalkuwait.com/tower; Fahad Al Salem St, Wattiya; s/d from KD47/54; � 🛰 ⚉) This stylish, if a little dated, downtown hotel prides itself on being the first 'art and tech' hotel in the Gulf, with a mishmash of styles including a grand piano and a mesmerising shell water feature in the lobby. Rooms are immaculate, with power showers, refrigerators and safes. The illuminated glass panels behind each bed are a fun kitsch addition. The hotel's Cascade Restaurant serves international food. Guests have use of a gym, sauna and outdoor swimming pool.

★ Marina Hotel
HOTEL $$$

(Map p98; ☑ 22230030; www.marinahotel.com; Arabian Gulf St, Salmiya; d from KD88; ⚇ 🛰 ⚉) Situated on the edge of bustling Marina Crescent, within walking distance of Marina Mall, this low-rise hotel floats like a lily on the water's edge and offers many rooms with direct beach access. It's sophisticated, tastefully elegant and modern. There's also a gym, a spa, room service, a pool bar and an international buffet restaurant.

Symphony Style by Radisson
HOTEL $$$

(Map p98; ☑ 25770000; www.radissoncollection.com/en/symphony-style-hotel; Symphony Complex, Arabian Gulf St; d from KD103; 🛰) This bright five-star hotel overlooking Kuwait Bay is filled with colourful soft patterned fabrics and bold accents including gold-coloured bed frames, couches and lampshades. Each room comes with a coffee machine and walk-in rain shower. Three eateries include an international, Italian and chocolate cafe. There's also a gym, pool and excellent Six Senses Spa on site.

JW Marriott Hotel Kuwait City
BUSINESS HOTEL $$$

(Map p108; ☑ 22455550; www.marriott.com; Al Shuhada St; d from KD87; ⚇ 🛰 ⚉) Although the beige room decor could do with an update, the Marriott is a solid luxury choice in Kuwait. Hotel highlights include a spa and fitness centre with a whirlpool and indoor swimming pool. The Courtyard Restaurant offers an enormous buffet (served 7.30pm to 11pm, KD18.5) with lots of serving stations including cuisine from Asia and Europe. It's just 15 minutes from the airport.

Jumeirah Messilah Beach Hotel & Spa
HOTEL $$$

(Map p98; ☑ 22269600; www.jumeirah.com; Al Taawun St; d/ste/villa from KD120/155/180; ⚇ 🛰 ⚉) A good luxury option for families, this 361-room resort has a private beach and tasteful rooms, plus seven restaurants including a seafood option. Its Sinbad's Kids Club is for smaller children with a TV room, games, daily activities and even a babysitter (additional charge). Meanwhile, the Scene Teens Club has Wii, billiards, mini beach football and volleyball.

Radisson Blu
HOTEL $$$

(Map p98; ☑ 25673000; www.radissonblu.com; off Al Taawen St, Rumaithiya; r from KD86; ⚉) Three decades ago, during the Iraqi invasion of Kuwait, there wasn't a window remaining in the Radisson. That's a difficult scene to imagine today at this luxury resort, which has three tranquil pools, a sky lounge serving sushi as diners look out over the sea, plus terrific contemporary rooms with Middle Eastern design touches.

The Al Hashemi Marine Museum (p105) is on site, and the intimate Al Boom restaurant (p115) is located in the back garden – two reasons alone to visit the Radisson Blu.

Mövenpick Hotel & Resort Al Bida'a
HOTEL $$$

(Map p98; ☑ 22253100; www.movenpick.com; Al Taawn St, Salmiya; d with/without pool access from KD121/80; ⚇ 🛰 ⚉) Right on the beach, this large five-star hotel has 280 rooms (some with direct pool access), plus two restaurants, five pools and two shisha terraces. Rooms could do with an update, but they are pleasant and tasteful with beige, brown and dark wood tones. They range in size from doubles to family rooms with kitchenettes and dining areas. Extras include a spa and selection of watersports for guests (paddleboarding, sailing, jet skiing and more), treatments and activities at an additional cost.

Hilton Kuwait Resort
RESORT $$$

(☑ 22256222; www.hilton.com; Coast Rd, Mangaf; studio/d from KD80/85; ⚇ 🛰 ⚉) On a white-sand beach with pristine water, this resort, 35km from the city, makes for a relaxing break. Calm-toned rooms have garden or sea views, and studios come with kitchenettes. A number of restaurants include a Middle Eastern and an international option, plus a cafe next to the gazebo-shaded pool area. Spa fans can enjoy a sauna, crystal steam bath and ice room.

Sheraton Kuwait
HOTEL $$$

(Map p108; ☑ 22422055; www.sheratonkuwait.com; Safat Tower, Fahad Al Salem St; r from KD90;

TRACES OF OLD KUWAIT

Kuwait City's rather scruffy downtown area bears few traces of history amid the vast construction sites, but one street does carry faint echoes of the past. Al Soor St, at the southern end of the city centre, follows the line of the old city wall. Yes, this city that now sprawls seemingly forever was once restricted to the area north of the street (*soor* is the Arabic word for wall). City gates once lined the street, and the four that remain are **Al Maqsab** (Map p108; Block 8, Arabian Gulf St), **Al Jahra** (Map p108; Al Soor St), **Al Shamiya** (Map p108; Abdulla Al Salem St & Soor St) and **Al Shaab** (Map p108; Al Soor St). Trace a line between them on the map and you'll have a clear picture of what Old Kuwait consisted of and just how much it has grown. Despite the gates' ancient appearance, the wall and gates were only constructed around 1920. The wall was demolished in 1957.

Another interesting area lies just south of Dar Al Athar Al Islamiyya (p100), off Arabian Gulf St, with replica 19th-century dwellings that give a good idea of what Kuwait must have looked like before oil was discovered. Their appeal has been diminished somewhat by the new motorway that runs past their front doors and separates the houses from the rest of the downtown area. The restaurant Beit 7 (p114) is part of this island of the past.

P 🛜 🛜) This stalwart central hotel is still one of the best luxury sleeps in Kuwait City, glittering with chandeliers and mirror-polished, gold-detailed marble. Rooms are modern and have all the trimmings (desks, lounge chairs, trouser presses, mini-bars and 24-hour room service), with decor more classic than contemporary. Five hotel restaurants offer Italian, Lebanese, Iranian, international and Indian cuisine.

🍴 Eating

Dining out is perhaps Kuwait City's best-loved activity. There are literally hundreds of restaurants to suit all wallets and palates. Souq Mubarakiya (p99) and Marina Crescent (p105) are lovely places to enjoy a bite with a lively atmosphere. World-class Middle Eastern restaurants are scattered throughout the city, with rare regional specialities thrown into the mix. Hotels serve enormous buffets, and international chains are abundant for the homesick.

★ Greenland Vegetarian Restaurant   INDIAN $

(Map p108; ☑ 22422246; Souq Mubarakiya; mains KD1.75-2.5; ⏱9am-4pm & 6-11pm Mon-Sat, 9am-4pm & 6-10pm Sun; ☑) A real find, this excellent vegetarian Indian restaurant has a light dining area decorated with Gandhi portraits and Indian street art. It does a popular South Indian thali lunch or dinner for just KD1.75 with eight bowls of curry and dips, plus rice, paratha and a pappadam. Wash it down with a fresh orange or lemon and mint juice.

It's left off the main souq thoroughfare as you enter from Abdullah Al Mubarak St.

Pick   HEALTH FOOD $

(Map p108; http://pick.com.kw; Mubarak Al Kabir St; mains KD1-3; ⏱6.30am-11pm Sun-Thu, from 8am Fri & Sat) This slick little spot is best known for its frozen yogurts, smoothies and pancakes, but its concept of healthy fast food extends to ready-made sushi boxes, salads, shawarmas and more substantial dishes that you choose from the fridge. There's another branch in Al Hamra mall (p116).

Beit Ahmed   CAFE $

(Map p108; ☑ 22467373; Souq Mubarakiya; mains KD1.5-2.6; ⏱9am-2pm & 4-10pm Sat-Thu, 4-10pm Fri) We love this place. Inside a stylish homewares shop in the souq, Beit Ahmed is a small but sophisticated cafe with traditional cushions and plush sofas. It serves mint tea and Arabic coffee, plus excellent falafel, cheese platters and lamb kebabs. Signposted only in Arabic, it's just west of Greenland Vegetarian Restaurant.

Layali Al Helmeya   KEBAB $

(Map p98; ☑ 22638710; Arabian Gulf St, Salmiya; mains KD1.75-3.75; ⏱6am-2am) A lovely place to sit and enjoy the view overlooking Kuwait Bay, offering reasonably priced dishes; huge salads, delicious freshly made *muttabal* (aubergine dip) and *shish taouk* (grilled chicken kebab) sandwiches. While the food is good, the place is more popular with shisha smokers than diners.

Naz Restaurant   IRANIAN $

(Map p108; ☑ 22451892; www.nazrestaurant.com/naz; Al Sharq Cooperative Society, Al Soor St; mains KD1.5-5; ⏱8am-midnight) The 'Persian soul food' at this casual eatery is terrific, with the full range of kebabs, salads and stews – of the latter, the tangy fattoush (salad of toasted bread, tomatoes, onions and mint leaves), shawarmas and *khoresht-e bademjan* (a diced-lamb stew with aubergine, onion, garlic and dried lemon) are particularly good. You can access the restaurant by walking through the Al Sharq Cooperative Society grocery store.

Publik Kuwait
INTERNATIONAL $

(Map p108; ☑ 22913222; www.facebook.com/the publik.kw; Mubarak Al Kabeer St; mains KD1.9-4; ⊕9am-11pm) This cool space – with a mosaic tiled floor, exposed pipes and large art murals painted directly onto the concrete walls – is a cafe by day and occasional music venue in the evening, with DJ nights. It serves healthy fusion food including smoothies, desserts, salads and wraps, and eggs benedict for breakfast.

Cocoa Room
BREAKFAST $

(Map p108; ☑ 22083195; www.cocoaroom.co; Flag Sq, Arabian Gulf St; mains from KD4; ⊕8am-11pm; ⓟ) In the grounds of the Sheikh Jaber Al Ahmad Cultural Centre (p116), by the dancing fountain, Cocoa Room serves tasty all-day breakfasts, including short rib benedicts and cornflake croquettes. Lunch options consist of Middle Eastern–inspired tapas, fresh salads and sandwiches. Still have room? Try the monster cakes on the counter, or a red velvet pancake stack.

Ridley's Burger
BURGERS $

(Map p108; ☑ 55036869; M1 level, Salhia Complex, Salhiya St; burgers from KD2.9; ⊕noon-11.30pm; ⓟ) Ridley's is a funky little burger joint inside the Salhia Complex mall, with retro school chairs and bookshelves, plus cutlery stored in classic Tate & Lyle treacle tins. Burgers are named after British gentlemen, like the Mr Holmes beef burger, Mr Bell chicken burger and Mr Campbell cheeseburger with onion rings. The cheesy fries make a good side.

Slice
KEBAB $

(Map p108; ☑ 67009974; www.slicedoner.com; Abdullah Al Jaber St; doner 500 fils-KD2.5; ⊕noon-12.30am) The humble doner has never looked as good as it does at this fast-food kiosk. All of the essential ingredients come into play: flaky pita bread, expertly sliced chicken or beef, the full complement of lettuce, cabbage, tomato and onion. But it's the sauces that make this place stand out – choose from delicately spiced yogurt, tahini, chilli or garlic.

Dukkan Burger
BURGERS $

(Map p108; ☑ 1800011; www.dukkan-burger.com; 83rd St, Bneid Al Gar; mains from KD2.75; ⊕11am-midnight Sun-Thu, to 2pm Fri & Sat) Part burger joint, part modern Kuwaiti *diwaniya* (traditional gathering), Dukkan Burger serves a decent beef burger, plus shawarma burgers with local aioli. Other highlights include cola barbecue beef tips and 'TNT chicken wings' (hot!) with homemade ranch sauce. It's located next to Le Royal hotel (p109).

★ Burj Al Hamam
LEBANESE $$

(Map p98; ☑ 22529095; www.burjalhamam.com.kw; Arabian Gulf St, Dasman; mains from KD3.5; ⊕9am-11.30pm Sat-Wed, to 12.30am Thu & Fri; ⓟ🛜) This unmissable waterfront restaurant is a terrific place to sample Middle Eastern fare. Grilled meat and seafood dominate, but there's also top mezze, like dolma (stuffed grape vine leaves), baked aubergine and aged *shankleesh* (mould-ripened cheese). The focus is the Levant, but you'll find dishes from as far afield as Egypt and Armenia. Adventurous eaters can try lamb testicles and brain.

A relaxing terrace has 270-degree sea views, and a dessert counter touts freshly prepared baklava. Shisha is also available.

★ Le Nôtre
FRENCH $$

(Map p108; ☑ 1805050; www.lenotreparis-kuwait.com; Arabian Gulf St; mains from KD5; ⊕8am-11.30pm; ⓟ) Fantastic views of the Kuwait Towers, a discerning menu, an exclusive chocolatier and a landmark steel-and-glass building make this one of the hippest places in town. Standouts on the iPad menus include granola with crème brûlée or shakshuka in a skillet pan for breakfast, plus veal escalope or shrimp masala and coconut rice for dinner. The desserts are good, too.

The waffles and salted caramel hits the spot, as does the pain au chocolate pudding. Dress smartly. Find it next to Kuwait Towers (p104).

★ Mais Alghanim
MIDDLE EASTERN $$

(Map p108; ☑ 22251155; www.maisalghanim.com; Arabian Gulf St, Sharq; mains KD2.65-6.95; ⊕noon-11pm Mon-Sat; ♿) They've been serving excellent Middle Eastern cooking at this fine place since 1953. Charcoal-grilled meats, seafood and hearty rice dishes are menu highlights, but there's so much good stuff leading up to them (salads, dips, pastries, halloumi and other mezze with all the trimmings). Huge portions are served in a light dining area with classic Middle Eastern decor.

There's a children's play area in a separate room in the restaurant complex with a climbing frame and various games to keep little ones busy while you feast.

Dikakeen
MIDDLE EASTERN **$$**

(Map p108; ☑22996552; www.dikakeen.net; level M2, Salhiya Complex, Mohammed Thunayyan St; mains KD4-7; ☺7am-11pm Sat-Wed, to 11.30pm Thu & Fri) With a genteel air in the upmarket Salhiya mall, Dikakeen serves up classy interpretations of Middle Eastern street food, from tangy *shish taouk* (grilled chicken kebab) and grilled meat platters to more creative East-West hybrids like stuffed meat calzone. There are also breakfasts, shawarma and terrific desserts to draw you in.

Assaha Restaurant
LEBANESE **$$**

(Lebanese Traditional Village; Map p108; ☑22533377; www.assahavillage.com; Al Khalij Al Arabi St, Bneid Al Gar; mains KD3-7; ☺8-11.30am & noon-midnight; ▣🛜) Built to resemble an old Kuwaiti villa, Assaha is an atmospheric place to eat. The stone arches, snugs, *majlis* (reception room) area, tiled floors and antiques provide an experience that's hard to find in the modern Gulf. The food's impressive too, with top mezze, grilled meats and seafood, salads, and even Iraqi specialities. It's just across the corniche near Le Royal hotel (p109). It's hugely popular on weekends, when locals come for the very reasonable Middle Eastern breakfast buffet (KD3.25).

Beit 7
INTERNATIONAL **$$**

(Map p108; ☑22450871; Behbehani Houses No 7, off Soor St; mains from KD5; ☺7.30am-2.30am) Around the corner from the Muse coffee shop, this charming restaurant is tucked away in an interior courtyard. Set in a cor-al-and-gypsum house dating from 1949 (and included on the government's list of heritage sites), with beaded lanterns, palm fans and wicker chairs, it serves French, Italian and Middle Eastern fare, plus good international and local breakfasts, and a rich chocolate fondue.

Baker & Spice
CAFE **$$**

(Map p108; ☑98002331; Flag Sq, Sheikh Jaber Al Ahmad Cultural Centre, Arabian Gulf St; dishes KD3-10; ☺8am-11pm; ▣) Decorated in a light and airy style, like a contemporary French cafe, this pleasant spot from the international artisan chain is a solid lunch choice. The focus is on organic, fresh local produce. Taster salad plates are the healthy choice, but the smell of freshly baked focaccia and pita is difficult to resist. The latter comes stuffed with a choice of five-hour braised lamb, pulled chicken or home-cooked beef sausage. A range of seafood, pasta and meat mains are also available.

Le Relais de l'Entrecôte Salhiya
FRENCH **$$**

(Map p108; ☑22257178; www.relaisentrecote.fr; Mohammad Thunayyan Al Ghanem St; mains from KD9.5; ☺noon-midnight) Outside the entrance of Salhiya Complex (p116), this restaurant is decorated like a classic French bistro, with simple wooden chairs and clean tablecloths. It's renowned for serving only one dish – steak frites with a walnut salad starter. The key to its success? Fine cuts of steak topped with the secret house sauce.

Fayrouzeyat Restaurant
LEBANESE **$$**

(Map p108; ☑22461270; Al Shaheed Park, Soor St; mains from KD4.75; ☺10am-midnight; ▣) Smart Middle Eastern restaurant in a lovely setting with a large terrace and calming

---

KUWAIT'S WATER SHORTAGE

Kuwait has long been known for its fine natural harbour, but, like so many places in the Middle East, it is chronically short of water. Indeed, from 1907 until 1950, traders had to buy fresh water from the Shatt Al Arab waterway near Bubiyan Island, at the head of the Gulf, and ship it by dhow to Kuwait. The trade peaked in 1947, when it was estimated that 303,200 litres of water per day were arriving in Kuwait by boat – thankfully, the country didn't have a golf course.

Early investment of oil revenues into the search for ground water was unsuccessful, but Kuwait's first desalination plant in 1950 signalled the end of the sea trade in water. An exorbitant way to acquire fresh water, desalination nonetheless satisfies the country's huge thirst for water, which (according to some local water-resource experts) has grown to become the highest consumption of water in the world.

Natural resources are precious and, as every Bedouin knows (and any midsummer visitor can guess), in the desert, water is far more valuable than oil. In Kuwait, it's also more expensive.

park views. The menu's mezze offerings are decent, including well-executed stuffed aubergine and cauliflower tahini. Larger plates include stuffed lamb with yogurt and *kibbeh* (meat-filled cracked-wheat croquettes) with rice. It's rarely busy, perhaps because of the park's unpopular nonsmoking rule. It's located above Three & Barista.

Maki JAPANESE **$$**
(Map p98; ☑ 22244560; www.olivermaki.com; Marina Waves, Arabian Gulf St; mains KD5.25-10; ⊙noon-11.30pm) Inside the modern tent-like Marina Waves structure, off the corniche, Maki serves decent sushi, sashimi and Asian mains (noodles, rice, teriyaki chicken and more) from its iPad menu. Guests can choose to eat in the tasteful neutral-toned dining area or, in cooler (for Kuwait) winter evening climes, on the outdoor terrace with views of Kuwait Bay.

★Al Boom SEAFOOD **$$$**
(Map p98; ☑ 25673430; www.radissonblu.com/ en/hotel-kuwait/restaurants; Radisson Blu, Taawen St, Rumaithiya; mains KD18-51; ⊙6-11.30pm) As unique as dining gets in Kuwait, this atmospheric restaurant is set on the huge *Mohammedi II* dhow. Built in Kozhikode, India, in 1979, it's made of fine teak wood, 2.5 tonnes of copper and 8.8 tonnes of iron nails. Dishes include whole Omani lobster, Gulf shrimp skewers and grilled Kuwaiti zubeidi fish. It's a popular experience, so book in advance.

The ship is a replica of one of the largest dhows ever built (*Mohammedi I*, 1915) and took three years to construct. There's steak night on Thursdays, with prime cuts weighed to order, plus a buffet of side salads and sweets for an extra KD7.

🍸 Drinking & Nightlife

This scene was once dominated by traditional Middle Eastern cafes, where mostly men go to chat over numerous small cups of sweet coffee, but these days small, independent cafes and roasters can be found across central Kuwait City. Young Kuwaitis flock to these cool spaces to drink high-quality single-origin coffee brewed by various methods.

Muse CAFE
(Map p108; opp Al Maqsab Gate, off Soor St; ⊙24hr; 🛜) At this chilled, two-tier industrial-styled coffee shop with chipboard tables, concrete walls, exposed pipes on the ceiling and bookshelves, the baristas serve a superb cup of single-origin Ethiopian coffee. It's a

> **ℹ ALCOHOL IN KUWAIT**
>
> Kuwait is a dry state where the consumption of alcohol is strictly forbidden. Penalties if caught in possession of alcohol or appearing under the influence of alcohol are high. There is, however, a fast-developing coffee scene, with many hip cafes around Kuwait City serving single-origin manual brews.

popular hang-out for students, who use it as a study space. Sandwiches and snacks are available at the counter, and there's an outside smoking balcony.

Three & Barista CAFE
(Map p108; ☑ 22061316; Al Shaheed Park, Soor St; ⊙8am-11pm) Opposite Al Shaheed Park's entrance gate is this air-conditioned vintage oasis decorated with an old VW Beetle, bicycle wheels, aeroplane seats, school chairs and bookshelves. Enjoy an Ethiopian-Colombian blend or a 'sparkling' (carbonated) espresso with a slice of homemade marble cake or fresh burrata salad and then peruse the book-exchange corner. Heartier meals are also available.

Bluezone Juice Bar JUICE BAR
(Map p108; ☑ 97377311; Sharq Marina mall; ⊙9am-8pm) Inside the Sultan Center in Sharq Marina mall (p116), Bluezone is run by a Kuwaiti health coach named Khalidah Alessa. Her fresh cold-pressed juices and smoothies hit the spot, as do her homemade cakes and snacks, including gluten- and dairy-free options. It's one of the only places in Kuwait selling fermented products like kombucha and goat-milk kefir, a fermented milk drink.

Euphoria COFFEE
(Map p108; ground fl, Baitak Tower, Ahmad Al Jaber St; ⊙6.30am-10pm Sun-Wed, noon-11pm Thu, noon-10pm Sat) Java connoisseurs will love this hip industrial coffee shop with geometric metal chairs, concrete walls and exposed beams. Speciality coffee can be ordered as a cold brew, manual brew (using the drip coffee method) or a signature brew (the Nutcracker coffee has a smoky caramelised peanut and dulce de leche flavour). Cakes are available, too.

Jumo CAFE
(Map p108; ☑ 99173745; www.jumocoffee.com; Al Sadu House, Arabian Gulf St; ⊙7am-10pm) A tiny artisanal coffee shop inside Al Sadu House

(p107) roasts and serves tasty single-origin Arabica brews. Meanwhile, their more unusual beverage creations include toffee Dutch lattes, cotton candy coffee and charcoal lemonade. Snacks like falafel and lemon chicken wraps are available, too.

Mukha COFFEE
(Map p108; www.mukhacoffee.com; cnr Ahmad Al Jaber & Mubarak Al Kabeer St; ⊘7am-10pm) Minimalist little coffee shop selling single-origin brews from Ethiopia, Brazil, Rwanda and Yemen. Manual brewing techniques range from V60 and cold brew to AeroPress, Chemex and siphon. Croissants and cakes are available at the counter.

English Tea Lounge TEAHOUSE
(Map p98; ☑22597914; The Avenues, Ghazali St, Al Rai, Fifth Ring Rd; ⊘10am-11pm) Run by the Sheraton Kuwait, this plush tea lounge, with chandeliers and dark wooden panelling, could be straight out of a stately manor house. The English-style high tea service includes the classics, from scones with clotted cream to cucumber sandwiches. Dainty tarts and pastries are served on a three-tiered stand with your choice of tea (Assam, Ceylon, Darjeeling, English breakfast and more).

☆ Entertainment

Sheikh Jaber Al Ahmad Cultural Centre CONCERT VENUE
(Kuwait Opera House; Map p108; ☑24835822; www.jacc-kw.com; cnr Arabian Gulf St & Soor St; ⊘reception 8am-11pm) This enormous 214,000-sq-m modern building cost KD235 million (US$773 million) to build and is the largest cultural centre in the Middle East. It contains a music centre, theatres and concert halls that host everything from classical concerts to gigs by the likes of Sting. Its outdoor public park, named Flag Square, has a dancing fountain and is open daily.

🛍 Shopping

Reading Room GIFTS & SOUVENIRS
(Map p108; ☑22461240; https://theyard-kw.com; Al Shaheed Park, Soor St; ⊘10am-10pm Mon-Thu & Sat, from 1pm Fri) A concept store selling carefully curated gifts ranging from Nordic cooking books and inventive kitchenware to tech accessories and locally made birthday cards. It's easy to spend a chunk of time here testing the lotions and potions, and flicking through design journals. There's also a communal

space in which the owners encourage customers to 'lounge, interact and collaborate'.

The Avenues SHOPPING CENTRE
(Map p98; ☑22597777; www.the-avenues.com; Ghazali St, Fifth Ring Rd, Al Rai; ⊘10am-10pm) The largest shopping mall in Kuwait, and the second largest in the Middle East, is quite an experience. Within its different zones, it has long palm tree-lined shopping 'avenues' designed like European streets, with similar shopfront architecture to Venice or London (some with mock 2nd floors, windows, arches, ornate alcoves and flower boxes). More than just a place to shop, it's a destination and hang-out space for Kuwaitis, who promenade these 'streets' of an evening in their national dress.

It's worth stopping at an information desk to pick up a 50-page directory and map, as you'll find 800 stores and counting, plus dozens of eateries and places of entertainment. There are parking spaces for 10,000 cars, but getting into The Avenues can be tricky; expect to queue. Kids love the Magic Planet zone, with fairground-style rides and games. There's also a cinema, five- and four-star hotels, a souq space and the bohemian Soku area – inspired by New York's SoHo neighbourhood.

Al Hamra Luxury Center SHOPPING CENTRE
(Map p108; ☑22270200; www.alhamra.com. kw/luxury-center; Abdulla Al Mubarak St, Sharq; ⊘10am-midnight) In central Kuwait City, this luxury mall has brands like Gucci, Mont Blanc, Hermes and Yves Saint Laurent. It's a mellower shopping experience compared to very busy malls like The Avenues. It has lots of good dining options, plus a branch of **Grand Cinemas** (Map p108; ☑22270333; https://kw.grandcinemasme.com; tickets regular/ VIP KD3/10) on the top floor.

Sharq Marina SHOPPING CENTRE
(Souq Sharq; Map p108; www.souqsharqmall.com; Arabian Gulf St; ⊘10am-11pm) This waterfront shopping mall opposite Kuwait Bay began as a traditional souq and over the years morphed into a full modern shopping mall. It has a small promenade overlooking a marina with yachts and restaurants. Inside are two floors filled with international brands and food outlets including Superdry, Zara and a branch of the Sultan Center supermarket.

Salhiya Complex SHOPPING CENTRE
(Map p108; ☑22996999; www.salhia-complex. com; Mohammed Thunayyan St, Salhiya; ⊘10am-

10pm; 🛜) Located downtown, Salhiya mall specialises in ultra-luxury brands like Cartier, Ermenegildo Zegna, Dolce & Gabbana and Chanel. M1 level has some good independent eateries, and the mall offers free wi-fi.

Souq Al Juma   MARKET
(Friday Market; Map p98; south of Fourth Ring Rd & west of Airport Rd, Shuwaikh; ⊗8am-4pm Fri) The place to buy everything from Afghan coats and antiques to a secondhand sofa, this enormous semi-covered market is a shopping extravaganza – but, more importantly, it offers a look at Kuwaiti life across the board. Shuffle between dusty rails of *abayas* (full-length robe-like dresses) and meet good-natured vendors with insight into the nation's affairs. Note traffic and parking around the market can be frustrating.

Posta Gallery   GIFTS & SOUVENIRS
(Map p108; 🖉 66150140; Mezzanine, Baitak Tower, Ahmad Al Jaber St; ⊗11.30am-9pm) Egyptian- and Middle Eastern–made gifts and goods, from cork laptop cases and leather-bound notebooks with Arabic inscriptions to hand-made canvas bags and household goods. It's a good place to pick up a unique souvenir.

🛈 Getting There & Away

It takes roughly 30 minutes to get from Kuwait International Airport to central Kuwait City. Taxis have a minimum fare of KD5 from the airport (bank on KD7 to central Kuwait City). Careem (www.careem.com), a regional version of Uber, does not pick up from the airport but can drop off (the fare is roughly KD3.5 to KD4).

Kuwait Public Transport Company bus routes 501 and 13 link Kuwait Airport to the city centre and the **Mirqab Bus Station** (Map p108; 🖉 22328866; www.kptc.com.kw; Abdullah Al Mubarak St & Al Hilali St). Buses run every 30 minutes from outside the arrivals hall between 5.30am and 9pm. The journey takes around 30 minutes into central Kuwait City. Fares cost 300 fils and are purchased on board.

City Buses run express services between the airport and destinations like Salmiya and Fahaheel. Buses run every 30 minutes between 4am and midnight and every 60 minutes from midnight to 4am. Fares cost 500 fils to KD1.

🛈 Getting Around

BUS
Two main public bus services operate in Kuwait City: Kuwait Public Transport Company (www.kptc.com.kw) and the less reliable City Bus, which currently only displays routes on its Facebook page (www.facebook.com/citybuskw). Both run air-conditioned buses with fares ranging from 250 fils to 450 fils between the hours of 5am and 10pm. The front seats of these buses are reserved for women. Route maps for KPTC are available online.

Bus 101 goes from the Mirqab Bus Station in the city centre to Al Ahmadi and Fahaheel (the full journey takes around 1½ hours). Bus 103 goes to Al Jahra (one hour).

TAXI
There are several types of taxis operating in Kuwait City. Count on KD2 to KD3 for a trip between Salmiya and the downtown area.

It's possible to hail a taxi from the road or from ranks near malls and hotels, but the wait could be a hot one. For convenience, many with mobile wi-fi prefer to use Kuwait's equivalent to Uber, the car-hailing app Careem (www.careem.com). The app offers fare estimates before your ride, and local rides cost around KD1.5 to KD2 (cash or card accepted). Although it's had some teething issues (cars sometimes arrive a little off location), Careem is easy to use.

AROUND KUWAIT

Failaka Island   جزيرة فيلكا

Failaka Island has some of the most significant archaeological sites in the Gulf. With a history dating from the Bronze Age, evidence of Dilmun and Greek settlements, a classical heritage (the Greeks called it Ikaros) and a strategic location at the mouth of one of the Gulf's best natural harbours, this island could one day be considered one of Kuwait's top tourist attractions.

Alas, recent history has decided otherwise. First, Iraqi forces established a heavily fortified base on Failaka, paying scant regard to the relics over which they strewed their hardware, and then Allied personnel were billeted there, with equally pitiful regard for antiquities.

The island has one resort for visitors and, with future plans to develop it, is beginning to assume its rightful importance at last, although it will be some time before access to the archaeological sites will be possible.

🛏 Sleeping

Ikaros Hotel   RESORT $$
(🖉 22244988; http://heritagevillagefailaka.com; Heritage Village; d incl boat transfers KD80; ⊛) The only hotel on Failaka Island has a range

of facilities, including a petting zoo, a lake, horse riding, camel rides and watersports. Crafts are produced in a living heritage village and are available for sale. The hotel offers an atmospheric stay in its 23 rooms inside a refurbished police station. There's also a small Kuwaiti restaurant serving international food.

In addition to standard hotel rooms, there are 40 traditional heritage houses for groups of up to 15 people. The hotel also offers day rates of KD20. Book via Ikarus (p107), which operates a catamaran transfer service from Marina Crescent (p105) in Kuwait City (next to Starbucks). Day trips last six hours. Booking ahead is essential, and you must arrive 45 minutes before departure.

❶ Getting There & Away

Kuwait Public Transport Company ferries (Map p98; ☑ 22328866, 22328814; www.kptc. com.kw; Hamad Al Mubarak St, off Arabian Gulf St, Salmiya) to Failaka Island depart from Ras Salmiya (also known as Ras Al Ard). The trip takes one hour, costs KD5 on foot or KD30 per car, and leaves twice daily in line with the tides. The ferry terminal in Kuwait City can be reached via buses 15 and 34.

Alternatively, tourist packages can be purchased with Ikarus (p107) and include day trips and overnight options at the Ikaros Hotel (p117). Day trips to Failaka Island cost KD20 per person, including boat transfer and a range of activities. Ikarus trips leave from Marina Crescent (p105).

Al Ahmadi الأحمدي

POP 810,000

The gems in this dusty grid complex of houses and offices built to house the workers of Kuwait's oil industry in the 1940s and 1950s are its oil museums. Named after the emir of the day, Sheikh Ahmad Al Jaber Al Sabah, Al Ahmadi is surrounded by sand and remains, to some extent, the private preserve of the Kuwait Oil Company (KOC). On the border of the municipality is the Camel Racing Club, where those who dare can drive alongside the desert animals as they race at speed.

◉ Sights

KOC Ahmad Al Jaber
Oil & Gas Exhibition MUSEUM
(☑ 23860136; www.kocexhibit.com; Kuwait Oil Company Headquarters; ⊙ 7.30am-5pm Sun-Thu; ℗) FREE Costing around KD18 million (US$59 million) to build, the most recent Kuwait Oil Company exhibition teaches visitors about Kuwait's biggest business. Nine galleries cover themes of oil geology, exploration, extraction and exportation, plus Kuwaiti history and the devastating environmental consequences of burning oil. There are also interactive boards, plus an exciting 15-minute 4D film, with pyrotechnics and surround sound. A viewing gallery offers binoculars looking out onto Kuwait's oil fields. Free tours run every 30 minutes and take 1½ hours.

KOC Oil Display Center MUSEUM
(☑ 23867703; www.kockw.com; Kuwait Oil Company Headquarters, Mid 5th St; ⊙ 8am-2pm Sun-Thu) FREE In this self-congratulatory introduction to the Kuwait Oil Company (KOC) and the country's oil business, bilingual display boards provide an intro to everything from how to dig for oil and trap it to how to transport it. A walk-through tunnel exhibit explains 'The Catastrophe' of 1991 – when Kuwait's oil fields were ignited and became a thick black sky, with sooty rain. Although interesting, the KOC Ahmad Al Jaber Oil & Gas Exhibition nearby has made this smaller exhibit seem redundant.

☆ Entertainment

Kuwait Camel Racing Club SPECTATOR SPORT
(☑ 25394015; off Sulaibiya Rd, Route 604, Al Kabd; ⊙ races 5am Sat May-early Oct, 1-4pm Sat late Oct-Apr) FREE For a thrilling taste of Kuwaiti sporting life, come to this race track in a 4WD on a Saturday and you can drive alongside camels (with electric jockeys) as they race at speeds up to 60km/h. Driving on sand at speed requires skill, and there are other cars to avoid, so make sure you have full insurance.

At the track, ask for the FM radio station used to broadcast the live race, which visitors can listen to as they drive. The track is around 45 minutes south of Kuwait City. It's a 10-minute drive south of Kabad Fire Station, in the desert.

❶ Getting There & Away

Bus 602 runs from Fahaheel to Al Ahmadi, passing the KOC Oil Display Center.

Mina Alzour & Al Khiran
ميناء الزور والخيران

Mina Alzour and Al Khiran have some of the most tempting waters in Kuwait, with watersports fans and clubs making the pilgrimage here to dabble in their favourite activities. The huge, quiet stretches of open sandy beaches in the Mina Alzour area are ideal for a family day out, though some sections are cleaner than others.

Further south is the Sabah Al Ahmad Sea City in Khiran. This Manhattan-sized residential area (set to house 250,000 residents in the next 25 years) is built on reclaimed land, with canals spanning 200km. The whole area is pretty sleepy, save a Saudi Texaco compound, only open to guests of members. In 2020, there are plans to open the fourth-largest oil refinery in the country nearby; construction and day-to-day operations may have an impact on the beaches and surrounding waterways.

🏃 Activities

QBalance WATER SPORTS
(☑ 66130092; www.q8balance.com; Al Khiran; per hr KD35; ⊙9am-5pm Mon-Sat) Learn how to wakeboard with this local adventure-sports outfit, the only one offering lessons off the coast of southern Kuwait. Book in advance as lessons are popular; the exact location will be explained when you book.

ℹ Getting There & Away

Bus route 215 services Mina Alzour from Fahaheel Roundabout on Dabous St, and the journey takes around 45 minutes.

The area can also be reached via car from Kuwait City, via Highway 40 (King Fahad Bin Abdul Aziz Rd) and exiting at Hwy 270 for Mina Alzour or Hwy 278 for Al Khiran. The 96km journey takes roughly 1½ hours.

Al Jahra الجهراء

Al Jahra is the location of a 1920 battle against invading troops from Saudi Arabia. It was also the site of the Gulf War's infamous 'turkey shoot' – the Allied destruction of a stalled Iraqi convoy as it lumbered up Mutla Ridge in an effort to retreat from Kuwait. The highway and surrounding desert are now completely clear of evidence, picked over by scrap-metal dealers and souvenir hunters.

◎ Sights & Shopping

Red Fort FORT
(Al Qasir Al Ahmar; ☑ 24548448; Marzouk Al Metab St, Al Jahra; ⊙8am-noon & 4-8pm; 🅿) **FREE** The grand Red Fort is a fine example of early Kuwaiti architecture. Named for the red clay used to build it between 1914-15, during the

OFF THE BEATEN TRACK
BRIDGE TO NOWHERE
When exploring Mutla Ridge, follow the signs to Subiyah for 30 minutes, and you'll eventually reach the bizarre Bridge to Nowhere, some 50km northeast of Al Jahra. There's a checkpoint in front of it, preventing further exploration, but the bridge spans more than just the narrow passage to Bubiyan Island; it also reinforces Kuwait's claim to the island in the face of erstwhile claims by both Iraq and Iran. So keen was Kuwait to maintain its claim to the uninhabited, flat and barren island and its neighbouring water supply that, when the Iraqis blew up the middle section of the bridge in 1991, the Kuwaitis quickly rebuilt it even though it goes to nowhere.

reign of the seventh ruler of Kuwait, Sheikh Mubarak Al Sabah, it has four watchtowers, surrounded by half-metre thick, 4.5m-high walls. Visitors can enter the surrounding gates to view it from the outside, but cannot go inside.

The fort played a role in a 1920s battle with Saudi Arabia, in which Saudi troops were defeated (with the help of the British). Also known as the Red Palace, the rectangular structure sits near the highway next to Al Jahra Park.

If coming from Kuwait City, follow Al Jahra Rd and take the exit towards Marzouk Al Metab St. The Red Fort is on the right, about 200m south of Jahra Rd.

Mutla Ridge المطلاع

Mutla Ridge is Kuwait's only hilly desert terrain – at more than 300m high, it offers a wonderful view of the full expanse of Kuwait Bay. For a taste of the desert, drive the road to Bubiyan Island that runs along the southeastern flank of the ridge. You may see camels roaming the edge, grazing on the coarse grass that is common to the area. In spring, the slope down to the coastal marshes is pale green with new shoots and wildflowers.

Mutla Ridge is also a popular area for off-road 4WD drivers, who come here to feel the sand under their wheels. Unfortunately, this can disturb the desert silence somewhat. Although the landmines from the Gulf War have officially been cleared, visitors should stick to the paths (both in a 4WD and on foot).

ⓘ Getting There & Away

It takes roughly an hour to get to Mutla Ridge, 50km from Kuwait City via Hwy 80 and Hwy 801 (Saad Al Abdulla Al Sabah Rd). There are no public transport options, but local tour operators may offer custom tours to the area.

UNDERSTAND KUWAIT

Kuwait Today

If Iraq had not invaded in 1990, Kuwait could have been the next Dubai or Qatar, a country made fabulously wealthy by oil and making its name as a travel hub, taking advantage of its position as a bridge between Asia and Europe. Kuwait may not be as glitzy, but it offers a refreshing change from its Gulf neighbours – it's not showy or sparklingly modern and arguably has more Middle Eastern charm as a result.

Democratic Kuwait?

Kuwait has an elected 50-seat National Assembly, which is sometimes described as one of the strongest in the Middle East. The powers of the emir, crown prince and cabinet are tempered by the increasingly vociferous assembly, which must approve the national budget and can question cabinet members.

In 2005, after years of campaigning, women were at last enfranchised and permitted to run for parliament. In 2009, four women were elected to the National Assembly, and despite the reticence of hardline clerics and traditional tribal leaders, the move was viewed by many as a sign of a new era of transparent government. In 2016, however, 15 women ran for the 50 open parliament seats and only one was elected.

Two-Tier Society

The origin of the non-Kuwaiti population has changed considerably in the last two decades. Before the Iraqi invasion, 90% of the expat population was from Arab and/or Muslim countries, but Arab nationalities now make up less than 15% of the expat population.

In recent years, Kuwait has resembled other parts of the Gulf in its mix of mainly Indian and Filipino immigrants. Alas, a two-tier society appears to have developed, wherein some immigrant workers (Filipino maids, in particular) are engaged in virtual slave labour. Filipino workers have garnered much media attention after a married couple were found guilty in 2018 of murdering their Filipina maid. The murder prompted a ban on Filipinos travelling to work in Kuwait, before a new policy on workers rights was agreed between the two countries in 2018.

History

Taking in the view from the top of the Kuwait Towers, it's hard to imagine that 350 years ago this enormous city comprised nothing more than a few Bedouin tents clustered around a stone fort. The discovery of oil helped build a vibrant metropolis that probably would have superseded Dubai in design if it weren't for the Iraqi invasion in 1990, which changed the course of Kuwait's history forever.

Early History

Standing at the bottom of Mutla Ridge on the road to Bubiyan Island and staring across the springtime grasslands at the estuary waters beyond, it's easy enough to imagine why Stone Age humans chose to inhabit the area around Ras Subiyah, on the northern shores of Kuwait Bay. Here the waters are rich in silt from the mighty river systems of southern Iraq, making for abundant marine life. Evidence of the first settlement in the region dates from 4500 BC, and shards of pottery, stone walls, tools, a small drilled pearl and the remains of what is perhaps the world's earliest seafaring boat indicate links with the Ubaid people who populated ancient Mesopotamia. The people of Dilmun also saw the potential of living in the mouth of two of the world's great river systems and built a large town on Failaka Island, the remains of which form some of the best structural evidence of Bronze Age life in the world.

Greeks on Failaka Island

A historian called Arrian, in the time of Alexander the Great, first put the region on the map by referring to an island discovered by one of Alexander's generals en route to India. Alexander himself is said to have called it Ikaros, now known as Failaka. With temples dedicated to Artemis and Apollo, an inscribed stele with instructions to the inhabitants of this high-flying little colonial outpost, stashes of silver Greek coins, busts and decorative friezes, Ikaros became an important trading post on the route from Mesopotamia to India.

Relations with the British

The Kuwaitis and the British were natural allies in many regards. From the 1770s, the British had been contracted to deliver mail between the Gulf and Aleppo in Syria. Kuwait, meanwhile, handled all the shipments of textiles, rice, coffee, sugar, tobacco, spices, teak and mangrove to and from India, and played a pivotal role in the overland trade to the Mediterranean. The British helped to stop the piracy that threatened the seafaring trade, but they were not in a position to repel the Ottoman incursions – that is, until the most important figure in Kuwait's modern history stepped onto the stage.

Sheikh Mubarak Bin Sabah Al Sabah, commonly known as Mubarak the Great (r 1896–1915), was deeply suspicious that Constantinople planned to annex Kuwait. Concerned that the emir was sympathetic towards the Ottomans, he killed him, not minding that he was committing fratricide as well as regicide, and installed himself as ruler. Crucially, in 1899, he signed an agreement with Britain: in exchange for the British navy's protection, he promised not to give territory to, take support from or negotiate with any other foreign power without British consent.

Rags to Riches in the 20th Century

Mubarak the Great laid down the foundations of a modern state. Under his reign, government welfare programs provided for public schools and medical services.

In the 1920s, a new threat in the form of the terrifying *ikhwan* (brotherhood) came from the Najd, the interior of Arabia. This army of Bedouin warriors was commanded by Abdul Aziz Bin Abdul Rahman Al Saud (Ibn Saud), the founder of modern Saudi Arabia. Despite having received hospitality from the Kuwaitis during his own years in the wilderness, so to speak, he made no secret of his belief that Kuwait belonged to the new kingdom of Saudi Arabia. The Red Fort at Al Jahra was the site of a famous battle in which the Kuwaitis put up a spirited defence. They also hurriedly constructed a new city wall, the gates of which can be seen today along Soor St in Kuwait City. In 1923 the fighting ended with a British-brokered treaty under which Abdul Aziz recognised Kuwait's independence, but at the price of two-thirds of the emirate's territory.

The Great Depression that sank the world into poverty coincided with the demise of Kuwait's pearling industry as the market became flooded with Japanese cultured pearls. At the point at which the future looked most dire for Kuwait, however, an oil concession was granted in 1934 to a US-British joint venture known as the Kuwait Oil Company (KOC). The first wells were sunk in 1936, and by 1938 it was obvious that Kuwait was virtually floating on oil. When oil exports took off after World War II, Kuwait's

KUWAIT HISTORY

DIWANIYA: KUWAITI GATHERINGS

An important part of life in Kuwait, *diwaniya* refer to gatherings of men who congregate to socialise, discuss a particular family issue or chew over current affairs. The origins of these gatherings go back centuries, but the rituals remain the same – a host entertains family, friends or business acquaintances in a room specially intended for the purpose at appointed times after sundown. Guests sit on cushions and drink copious cups of tea or coffee, smoke, snack and come and go as they please.

In the early 20th century, on the edge of Souq Mubarakiya, Mubarak the Great (the seventh ruler of Kuwait) held a famous daily *diwaniya*, walking each day from Sief Palace through the old souq to an unprepossessing building amid random coffee houses. Here he would sit incognito, talk to the people and feel the pulse of the street. Sitting near the same place today (a renovated traditional building without signage may mark the spot), with old men nodding over their mint teas, city types trotting to work, merchants hauling their wares to the souq and groups of women strolling in the shade, it's easy to see why he chose this spot.

BOOKS ABOUT KUWAIT

➡ *Modern Architecture Kuwait* (2016) by Ricardo Camacho, Roberto Fabbri and Sara Saragoca Soares. Beautiful photography illustrates the story of how Kuwait became the innovator for design in the Gulf.

➡ *The Bamboo Stalk* (2016) by Saud Alsanousi. Novel set in Kuwait about a Filipina living in Kuwait, offering an unflinching peek into the lives of foreign workers in Gulf countries.

➡ *The Hidden Light of Objects* (2014) by Mai Al Nakib. Personal short stories by a local author on Kuwait's recent struggles.

economy was launched on an unimaginable trajectory of wealth.

As the country became wealthy, health care, education and the standard of living improved dramatically. In 1949, Kuwait had only four doctors; by 1967, it had 400.

Independence

On 19 June 1961, Kuwait became an independent state, and the agreement with Britain was dissolved by mutual consent. In an ominous move, the president of Iraq, Abdulkarim Qasim, immediately claimed Kuwait as Iraqi territory. British forces, later replaced by those of the Arab League (which Kuwait joined in 1963), faced down the challenge, but the precedent was not so easily overcome. Elections for Kuwait's first National Assembly were held in 1962.

Iraqi Invasion

Despite political and economic tensions, by the start of 1990 the country's economic prospects looked bright, particularly with an end to the eight-year Iran–Iraq war, during which time Kuwait had extended considerable support to Iraq. In light of this, the events that followed were all the more shocking to most people in the region.

On 16 July 1990, Iraq sent a letter to the Arab League accusing Kuwait of exceeding its Organization of the Petroleum Exporting Countries (OPEC) quota and of stealing oil from the Iraqi portion of an oilfield straddling the border. The following day, Iraqi president Saddam Hussein hinted at military action. The tanks came crashing over the border at 2am on 2 August, and the Iraqi military was in Kuwait City before dawn. By noon, it had reached the Saudi frontier. The Kuwaiti emir and his cabinet fled to Saudi Arabia.

On 8 August, Iraq annexed the emirate. Western countries, led by the United States, began to enforce a UN embargo on trade with Iraq, and in the months that followed more than half a million foreign troops amassed in Saudi Arabia. On 15 January, after a deadline given to Iraq to leave Kuwait had passed, Allied aircraft began a five-week bombing campaign nicknamed Desert Storm. The Iraqi army quickly crumbled, and on 26 February 1991, Allied forces arrived in Kuwait City to be greeted by jubilant crowds – and by clouds of acrid black smoke from oil wells torched by the retreating Iraqi army. Ignoring demands to retreat unarmed and on foot, a stalled convoy of Iraqi armoured tanks, cars and trucks trying to ascend Mutla Ridge became the target of a ferocious Allied attack, nicknamed 'the turkey shoot'.

An Uncertain Future

During the late 1970s, Kuwait's stock exchange (the first in the Gulf) was among the top 10 in the world, and without knowing it, the nation was the first to use architecture as a symbol of Gulf wealth. Then Iraq invaded, threatening Kuwait's artistic heritage and challenging the very foundations of its wealth. It was only with the death of Saddam Hussein (who was hanged on 30 December 2006) that Kuwaitis were finally able to rest easy.

The rebuilding of the country has been an extraordinary success, but the financial cost has been similarly extraordinary. The result, even three decades later, is a country where museums tell a story of national pain, where artistic treasures are still not on display and where glittering skyscrapers cast long shadows over empty lots and decrepit downtown buildings.

Things have settled down a little in the years since the Arab Spring of 2011 when the prime minister was forced from office, and in 2014 a broad coalition came together to call for full parliamentary democracy. The ruling Al Sabah family largely kept its own counsel, but if the reforms were to be successful, their grip on uncontested power would be all but over.

Behind it all lies a fear that occasional sectarian violence could become more frequent: in 2015, a suicide bomber killed 27 worshippers and injured hundreds more at a Shiite mosque; responsibility for the attack was claimed by Islamic State.

But it is not all doom and gloom. With the country home to 6% of the world's oil reserves, oil and oil-related products naturally dominate the economy and, with more than 100 years' worth of oil remaining, the need to diversify has not been as urgent as it has been in neighbouring countries. The government continues to deposit 10% of its oil revenues into a rainy-day Fund for Future Generations. The question of who will get to decide how to spend it is the issue that will determine Kuwait's future.

People

Lifestyle

In common with the rest of the Gulf, Kuwaiti people value privacy and family intimacy at home, and enjoy the company of guests outside. In many instances, 'outside' is the best description of traditional hospitality: while female guests are invited into the house, men are often entertained in tents at the front of the house. These are no scout-camp canvases, however, but lavish striped canopies made luxurious with cushions and carpets.

Any visitor lucky enough to partake in tea and homemade delicacies in these '*majlis* al fresco' may be inclined to think that life in Kuwait has retained all the charm and simplicity of its Bedouin roots.

Kuwaitis take a different view, however. Some blame the war for a weakening of traditional values: theft, fraudulent practice, problems with drugs, the divorce rate and the incidence of suicidal driving have all increased. Others recognise that the same symptoms are prevalent in any modern society. With a cradle-to-grave welfare system, where 94% of Kuwaiti nationals are 'employed' in government positions, and an economy that has run ahead faster than the culture can adapt to, many Kuwaitis feel their society has become cosseted and indulgent, leaving the younger generation with too much time on their hands to wander off course.

Life in Kuwait has changed out of all recognition in the past decade: women work, couples hold hands in public, formerly taboo subjects find expression, and people wear Western clothes, spend money and raise debts. Indeed, the galloping pace of change is proving a divisive factor in a country of traditionally conservative people. It would be ironic if a society that survived some of the most sophisticated arsenal of the 20th century fell under the weight of its own shopping malls.

Population

Around 30% of Kuwait's population are Kuwaitis (the rest are expats), and many Kuwaitis have Bedouin ancestry. After liberation, the government announced that it would never again allow Kuwaitis to become a minority in their own country, implying a target population of about 1.7 million. However, with an unquenchable desire for servants and drivers, and an equal antipathy for manual labour, it is unlikely Kuwait will achieve this target any time soon.

There are some small inland communities, but for all intents and purposes, Kuwait is a coastal city-state.

Religion

Most Kuwaitis are Sunni Muslims, though there is a substantial Shiite minority. During the 1980s there was considerable tension, mostly inspired by Iran, between the two communities, a worry that has returned with sectarian violence over the border in Iraq.

Before the Iraqi invasion, Kuwait was still governed by a strict code of conduct, steered by a devout following of Islam. The invasion shook belief in all kinds of areas, including religious observance. Materialism is beginning to exert as strong an influence on the young as religion used to affect the customs and manners of their Bedouin or seafaring ancestors. Kuwaiti society certainly can't be described as permissive, but the veil in many areas of social exchange is discernibly slipping.

A tolerance towards other religions is evinced through the provision of services at Coptic, Anglican, Evangelical and Orthodox churches in Kuwait City.

AN ENVIRONMENTAL CATASTROPHE

On 20 January 1991, the third day of the war, Iraqi forces opened the valves at Kuwait's Mina Al Ahmadi Sea Island Terminal, intentionally releasing millions of litres of oil into the Gulf. The resulting oil slick was 64km wide and 160km long. Between six and eight million barrels of oil are thought to have been released, at least twice as much as in any previous oil spill. At least 460km of coastline, most of it in Saudi Arabia and Bahrain, was affected, with devastating consequences for the region's cormorants, migratory birds, dolphins, fish and turtles and large areas of mangroves.

The systematic torching of 699 of the emirate's oil wells contributed to the environmental disaster. By the time the war ended, nearly every well was burning. At a conservative estimate, at least two million barrels of oil per day were lost – equivalent to about 5% of the total daily world consumption. One to two million tonnes of carbon dioxide streamed into the air daily, resulting in a cloud that literally turned day into night across the country.

Like the slick, the fires devastated wildlife throughout the region, but they also had a direct impact on public health. Black, greasy rain caused by the fires was reported as far away as India, and the incidence of asthma increased in the Gulf region.

The slick was fought by experts from nine nations, and oil companies eventually managed to recover, and reuse, around a million barrels of crude oil from the slick. Initial reports that it would take five years to put all the fires out proved pessimistic. A determined international effort, combined with considerable innovation on the part of the firefighters, extinguished the fires in only eight months. The crews did the job so quickly that one well had to be reignited so that the emir of Kuwait could 'put out the final fire' for reporters in November 1991.

Cleaning up the 65 million barrels of oil, spilt in 300 oil lakes covering around 50 sq km of desert, was not so speedily effected. Through a variety of biological processes, which included composting and bioventing, more than 4000 cu metres of contaminated soil were treated, resulting in soil of such high quality that it was good enough for landscaping and could be used as topsoil.

KOC Oil Display Center (p118) and KOC Ahmad Al Jaber Oil & Gas Exhibition (p118) document this disastrous time in history.

Environment

Kuwait is not the most well-endowed patch of earth, in terms of the sublime or the picturesque. The interior consists of a mostly flat, gravelly plain. A grassy fringe greens up prettily across much of the plain late in the spring, providing rich grazing for the few remaining Bedouin who keep livestock. The only other geographic feature of any note in a country that measures 185km from north to south and 208km from east to west is Mutla Ridge, just north of Kuwait City. The coast has a little more character, with dunes, marshes and salt depressions around Kuwait Bay and an oasis in Al Jahra.

Of the nine offshore islands, the largest is Bubiyan Island, while Failaka Island is the most historic: there are plans afoot to develop a container port on the former and a vast tourist complex on the latter.

Wildlife

The anticlockwise flow of Gulf currents favours Kuwait's shoreline by carrying nutrients from the freshwater marshes of Shatt Al Arab and the delta of the Tigris and Euphrates in southern Iraq. The result is a rich and diverse coastline, with an abundance of marine life that even spilt oil has failed to destroy.

Birding highlights along the mudflats include black-winged stilts, teals, lesser crested terns, huge nesting colonies of Socotra cormorants, and flamingos. Inland, birds of prey, including the resident kestrel and the short-toed eagle, roam the escarpments.

Nocturnal desert creatures include caracals, hedgehogs, big-eared fennecs – the smallest canines in the world – and jerboas, which gain all the liquid they need from the plants and insects they eat. It is easier to spot the dhobs, a monitor lizard with a spiny tail, popular as a barbecue snack.

Environmental Issues

While Kuwait shares many of the same environmental concerns as its Gulf neighbours, it has also had to contend with the fallout of war. Unexploded ordnance was diligently removed following the Iraqi invasion, though perversely, campers then began to threaten the environment, discarding rubbish and impacting delicate grazing lands. Much to the dismay of many Kuwaitis, camping restrictions are now in place to help safeguard the desert environment. Camping is now only possible between mid-November and mid-March and in monitored zones. A licence fee (from www.baladia.gov.kw) and hefty deposit is required, which will not be returned if waste is left at the site.

Meanwhile, Kuwait's shoreline has become a major concern. Thanks to relaxed standards regarding waste and oil dumping, pollution threatens swimming and fishing in Kuwait Bay.

Every year on 24 April the country observes Regional Environment Day, with school competitions and raised public awareness regarding marine and land resources.

SURVIVAL GUIDE

ℹ Directory A–Z

ACCESSIBLE TRAVEL

Travellers with mobility issues may struggle in Kuwait. Like many Gulf states, most streets are not designed for pedestrians. Some streets are sandy, some have no pavements and others are impassable because of building works. Buildings have little provisions for people with limited mobility; many have high curbs and narrow doorways.

However, modern hotels and apartment buildings have lifts fitted. Older travellers will find they are treated with respect, with their needs accommodated where possible, but the infrastructure for those needing more accessibility remains poor.

ACCOMMODATION

Kuwait has fewer hotel offerings than other Gulf cities, but demand is low, so there's plenty of choice. Prices are high and usually aimed at a business clientele, with few budget options. Desert camping was once popular in the cooler months, now it's a complicated and costly process. Camping season is between mid-November and mid-March. Register and pay

a large deposit to the municipality (see www.baladia.gov.kw for current details).

ETIQUETTE

As it's a strict Muslim country, there are many dos and don'ts in Kuwait, from wearing a bikini to being open about your sexuality (both big don'ts). Other don'ts won't get you in legal trouble but will serve you well if you abide by them.

Refreshments It is respectful to accept refreshments when offered; try to use your right hand to eat and drink.

Religion Political and religious subjects should be avoided in conversation, as many subjects are controversial and discussion may upset locals.

Shoes It is not required to remove your shoes to enter a reception room.

Soles Revealing the soles of the feet is considered offensive in Kuwait; try not to cross your legs.

FOOD

Although Kuwait doesn't have a reputation as a foodie city, it has some excellent restaurants. The Middle Eastern food is superb, and the malls and hotels have some fine international options, plus decadent buffets. Nearly all of the good dining options are based in Kuwait City.

HEALTH

Health insurance is advisable for travel to Kuwait as medical care is not free for travellers. There are private clinics and hospitals equipped with highly qualified professionals, but it'll cost you.

Common medications such as painkillers, eye drops, and cough medicine are available over the counter. Many anti-depressants, sleeping pills and codeine-based medicines are banned. Oral contraceptive pills, but not the morning-after pill, are available in Kuwait. It's advisable to carry any medications you are dependent on with you, ideally with a letter from your doctor confirming that you need them. Make sure any medication you carry is not banned before you travel to avoid being arrested at customs (contact Kuwait Customs via www.customs.gov.kw for more information).

Kuwaiti tap water is safe to drink.

PRACTICALITIES

....

Smoking Much more prevalent than in neighbouring Gulf countries on buses, in taxis, at the airport, and in restaurants and hotel rooms.

Newspapers *Arab Times*, *Kuwait Times* and *Daily Star* are Kuwait's three English-language newspapers. They include useful 'what's on' listings. International newspapers are available (usually a day or two late) at major hotels.

TV Kuwait TV's Channel 2 is a government broadcast service for English speakers. It broadcasts documentaries, serials and movies programs in English. Many hotels, even the smaller ones, have satellite TV.

Weights and measures Kuwait uses the metric system.

INTERNET ACCESS

Most hotels and many cafes offer free wi-fi, with speeds among the fastest in the world. Be aware that internet usage and browsing is monitored, as in other Gulf countries. At the time of research, Skype was blocked, but WhatsApp could still be used.

LEGAL MATTERS

Kuwait uses a combination of legal systems, deriving from Sharia law, UK law and Egyptian practice, and it also has some legal similarities to the Ottoman system. Kuwait has the death penalty.

Travellers to Kuwait should familiarise themselves with local laws before arriving in the country (see www.visit-kuwait.com/living/laws-regulations.aspx). The most obvious differences between Kuwait and Western countries are bans on importing alcohol, eating and drinking in public during Ramadan, importing pork products, and homosexual behaviour. Public displays of affection between men and women are also illegal. All of these offences could carry jail time.

If you are arrested in Kuwait, the police can detain you for 24 hours to open a file and begin an investigation on the crime they believe you have committed. Authorities may offer a bail release if you can offer a personal guarantee of a Kuwaiti citizen/sponsor.

Those arrested will be provided a telephone call. Travellers should contact their embassy. While your embassy cannot get you out of police custody, they can contact your relatives (if you ask them to) and will provide a list of legal representation. Detainees who do not speak Arabic should be offered a translator and should ask for all statements written in Arabic to be translated before they sign them.

LGBT+ TRAVELLERS

Kuwait is one of the least liberal places in the world. LGBT travellers should avoid making public displays of affection, at risk of imprisonment. While LGBT people do unopenly live in Kuwait, transgender people may find it more difficult.

Article 193 of the Penal Code punishes 'debauchery', which is interpreted as male homosexuality, with up to six years in jail.

Article 198 prohibits 'public immorality', part of which is defined as 'imitating the appearance of a member of the opposite sex'. Transgender people may also face jail time or fines.

MAPS

Arab World Map Library publishes useful maps on Kuwait, available from large online book retailers, plus some car-hire offices, hotels and bookshops in Kuwait City. Google Maps and other app-based map services work here but are often unreliable and don't have up-to-date road information.

MONEY

ATMs & Credit Cards

Visa and Amex are widely accepted in Kuwait, and all major banks accept most credit cards and are linked to the major networks. Most banks accept Visa (Electron and Plus), MasterCard and Cirrus.

Currency

The currency used in Kuwait is the Kuwaiti dinar (KD), which at the time of research was the strongest currency in the world. The dinar is divided into 1000 fils. Coins are worth one, five, 10, 20, 50 or 100 fils. Notes come in denominations of 250 fils, 500 fils, KD1, KD5, KD10 and KD20.

Changing Money

Moneychangers are dotted around the city centre and main souqs, and change all major and regional currencies. The dinar is no longer pegged to the US dollar, but this has made little difference to exchange rates, which remain consistent from one moneychanger to the next.

Tipping

Upmarket restaurants A tip is usually expected, but look out for a 10% service fee that is often already added to the bill.

Cafes and fast food A tip is not expected.

Taxis For longer journeys, 10% is a suitable tip for a taxi driver.

Hotels Tips are not expected, but a small amount is appreciated by baggage handlers.

Petrol station attendants Tips are not expected, but the small change from your bill is appreciated.

OPENING HOURS

These general opening hours prevail throughout Kuwait but will vary by establishment.

Banks 8am to 1pm and 5pm to 7.30pm Sunday to Thursday

Government offices 7am to 2pm (summer), 7.30am to 2.30pm (winter) Sunday to Thursday

Cafes 8am to 10pm

Post offices 8am to 1pm Sunday to Thursday

Restaurants 11am to 3pm and 7pm to 11pm

Shopping centres 10am to 10pm

Shops 8.30am to 12.30pm and 4pm to 7pm or 8pm Saturday to Thursday

PUBLIC HOLIDAYS

In addition to the main Islamic holidays, Kuwait celebrates three public holidays:

New Year's Day 1 January

National Day 25 February

Liberation Day 26 February

SAFE TRAVEL

Exploring Kuwait is safe, but common sense and respecting local traditions and beliefs will help visitors avoid issues.

ID Visitors are required to carry a valid passport and visa with them at all times.

Traffic accidents Kuwait has high road-accident rates, with a third of all deaths driving-related. Only confident drivers should consider self-driving.

Unexploded ordnance The country was reportedly cleared of mines after the Gulf War, but don't pick up any unfamiliar objects in the desert and stick to established tracks to be on the safe side.

Robberies The area of Jleeb Al Shuyoukh has higher levels of crime, so be vigilant.

Stray animals There are a number of stray desert cats and other animals in Kuwait. Don't try to pet them as they may attack you.

Ramadan Eating or drinking during daylight hours in public during Ramadan (this includes chewing gum) is strictly forbidden.

Nudity Don't strip off at the beach, it's an arrestable offence.

Sandstorms If travelling to remote desert areas, be aware that sandstorms can happen at any time. Carry clothing you can use for cover, and ensure your car or a building is nearby for shelter.

TELEPHONE

Kuwait's country code is 965, and there are no area codes. The international access code (to call abroad from Kuwait) is 🖉 00.

SIM cards are widely available.

The main cellular networks are Ooredoo (formerly Wataniya), Viva and Zain. There is an Ooredoo outlet at Kuwait International Airport offering various data packages for visitors. Make sure your phone is unlocked before you travel.

TOURIST INFORMATION

The website www.visit-kuwait.com is a good source of information for visitors, as is the Touristic Enterprises Company (www.kuwaittourism. com).

VISAS

Visas on arrival are available at Kuwait International Airport (p128) for nationals of 52 countries, including Australia, Canada, the EU, New Zealand and the US (valid for 90 days; 30-day maximum stay). Take a number from the Fast Service Desk and buy stamps worth KD3 from the neighbouring machine (free for some nationalities). There's no need to wait again at the immigration desk downstairs, where you'll be waved through. Keep the piece of paper you're given with the visa – you'll need to present it upon departure.

Getting a Visa Online

It is now possible to arrange visas before you travel via the official online portal (https://evisa. moi.gov.kw/evisa/home_e.do). Other online operators also offer this service, however, be aware of fake visa websites. Travellers have recently been caught out, arriving at customs and being refused entry with a bogus visa. It's advisable to either go through the official channels or to queue and get a visa on arrival. Online applications cost more.

Israeli or Iraqi Connections

Anyone holding a passport containing an Israeli or Iraqi stamp may be refused entry to Kuwait.

WOMEN TRAVELLERS

On paper, women in Kuwait are among the most emancipated women in the Middle East (with more than 50% of Kuwaiti women in the workforce). But women only garnered the right to vote properly in 2005, much to the dismay of Kuwait's conservative population.

Women travellers are likely to find the increased attention from men in Kuwait a nuisance. The cultural perception of Western women is exacerbated by the fact that there are fewer women (with a population of around 60% men to 40% women). While most expat and solo

---

EATING PRICE RANGES

The following price ranges refer to a main course.

$ less than KD5

$$ KD5–10

$$$ more than KD10

women travellers won't feel distressed exploring Kuwait, others may find the inevitable unwanted glares disconcerting. Some female travellers have felt harassed, with cases of men following foreign women around shopping malls, tailgating and so on. Even if you dress conservatively and refuse to respond to approaches and avoid eye contact with men, it's still difficult to avoid attracting unwanted attention.

Generally, if the situation becomes uncomfortable, the best way to defuse it is to stop, turn towards the men in question and address them frostily. Better still, if you can speak Arabic, ask the offending parties where they come from and to which family they belong. This is usually so unexpected harassers disappear.

❶ Getting There & Away

ENTERING THE COUNTRY
➡ No alcohol or pork products are allowed.

➡ Up to 500 cigarettes and 500g of tobacco are permitted.

➡ Duty-free items are for sale at the duty-free shop in the arrivals and departures section of the airport.

AIR
Kuwait International Airport (Map p98; 📞 24319829; Gazali Expressway) is around 30 minutes from central Kuwait City. The building is long overdue an upgrade. Construction is underway on a new airport hangar, which is predicted to have capacity for 25 million passengers by 2022.

In the current airport, visas are obtained from a counter on the upper storey level (take a ticket and wait), and then you descend to passport control and baggage claim. On the airside, there is little more than a cluster of fast-food outlets and duty-free shops to keep you entertained.

Major airlines such as British Airways, KLM and Qatar fly into Kuwait. Kuwait also has a no-frills private carrier called Jazeera Airways (www.jazeeraairways.com) with flights to 25 destinations within the Middle East and the Indian subcontinent.

LAND
Kuwait has a border with Iraq in the north, the Abdali/Safwan border along Hwy 80. Also known as the 'Highway of Death', this infamous road was used by Iraqi armoured divisions that invaded Kuwait in 1990. Visitors to Iraq require a visa. Most government foreign offices advise against any, or all but essential, travel to the area. Bus 500 goes to the Abdali/Safwan border from the Hassawi bus stop in Jeeleb Al Shuyoukk (the town next to Kuwait International Airport).

The crossings with Saudi Arabia are in Al Nuwaiseeb (for Dammam and the Al Khafji Customs) and Al Salmi (for Riyadh). Borders are open 24 hours. You must have a valid visa for Saudi Arabia or a transit visa, an onward ticket and a visa for your next destination beyond Saudi Arabia's borders before you can enter. You cannot obtain these at the border.

SEA
Combined Shipping Company (Map p98; 📞 24830889; www.cscq8.com; 1st fl, Office 119, Kuwait Port Authority Bldg, Jamal Abdul Nasser St, Shuwaikh) operates a return service twice a week from Kuwait's Shuwaikh Port to the Iranian port of Bushehr. Prices vary depending on the seasons. You can book online at www.irantravelingcenter.com.

❶ Getting Around

BUS
Kuwait has a cheap and extensive local bus system, but it's designed for the convenience of residents rather than tourists. The routes therefore don't often coincide with places of tourist interest. Nonetheless, if a 10-minute walk either side of the bus stop isn't a problem, pick up a bus timetable from the main bus station in the city centre or on the bus.

Most bus routes are operated by the Kuwait Public Transport Company (www.kptc.com.kw), which has air-conditioned and comfortable vehicles. Intercity trips cost just a few fils per ride. The City Bus (www.facebook.com/citybuskw) alternative follows KPTC routes but isn't quite as reliable. Both services are used primarily by lower-income workers travelling to their jobs.

CAR & MOTORCYCLE
Car and motorcycle hire are affordable and easy with the correct licence, and many of the major car-hire firms have offices in Kuwait.

Hire
Car hire ranges from KD10 (for a Toyota Corolla) to KD30 (for a Toyota Prado) per day. This rate usually includes unlimited kilometres and full insurance. Many people choose to hire luxury sports cars, as daily rates are so affordable. Given the very high incidence of traffic accidents in Kuwait, it is worth paying the extra for fully comprehensive insurance for any car.

Araba HO (Al Mulla Car Rental; Map p108; 📞 24915780; www.almullarental.com; Ibis Sharq, 155 Jaber Al Mubarak St; ⊗ 8am-6pm)

DEPARTURE TAX

There is an airport tax of KD3 for passengers leaving Kuwait. This is usually incorporated into the airfare price.

TRAVEL WITH CHILDREN

In many ways Kuwait is great for children; it has lots of activities and attractions from the Scientific Center (p100) with its educational discovery zone, and **Magic Planet** (Map p98; ☎22597942; www.theplaymania.com; The Avenues Mall, Ghazali St, Al Rai, Fifth Ring Rd; rides from KD1.5, pre-paid packages from KD10; ⏰10am-11pm Sat-Wed, to midnight Thu & Fri; 🚻) at The Avenues with its fairground attractions, to the Aqua Park (p107) for water play, the Sribb Circuit (p107) for go-karting and the **Marina Skate Park** (Map p98; opp Marina Beach, Arabian Gulf St; per hour/day KD1.5/KD3.5; ⏰3-11pm), where kids can burn off their energy on a BMX or scooter. However, while there are plenty of family parking bays close to attractions, and lifts in shopping malls, Kuwait's streets are not pram-friendly. The sweltering heat can also be challenging for parents and kids.

In major shopping malls, mothers will find baby-changing facilities and breastfeeding rooms. Dads may find changing difficult as facilities are often attached to the ladies toilets or to prayer rooms. Breastfeeding in public is possible if you are fully covered, but even then it is still taboo in the Gulf.

and Al Mulla (www.autoalmulla.com) are some of the better local agencies, with desks at the airport and in many of the city's hotels.

Alternatively, some hotels, such as the Ibis Sharq (p109), can arrange cars with drivers for their guests from KD6 per hour.

Insurance

Kuwait's roads are treacherous; the combination of different driving styles, speeding and drivers on their phones results in thousands of fatalities per year. While very careful and experienced drivers should be fine on the roads, it's advisable to pay for fully comprehensive insurance. Dings and scrapes are common, even when you're not driving.

Licenses

If you have an International Driving Permit (IDP), or a licence and residence permit from another Gulf country, you can drive in Kuwait without any further paperwork. With certain licences (including British licences) it may be possible to hire a car for a limited time if you purchase a mandatory temporary licence – your car-hire company will provide details (check when you book). It's usually a one-off payment of around KD10.

TAXI

Taxis fares start from KD1.5 and are a useful, popular and air-conditioned way of getting around. However, they are comparatively expensive when travelling outside the city area, when costs can increase to KD10 per hour. If you want to do some exploring around Kuwait by taxi, it's better to agree on a half- or full-day rate in advance.

Uber is not available in Kuwait, but Dubai-based ride-hailing service Careem (www.careem.com) works here and can be a convenient alternative to a taxi. Download the app, register your details and use the service, which starts from KD1.5 per ride.

Oman عمان

POP 4.65 MILLION

Best Places to Eat

➡ Al Angham (p148)

➡ Bait Al Luban (p147)

➡ Dukanah Cafe (p147)

➡ Ice Cream Mama (p147)

➡ Kargeen Cafe (p147)

➡ Al Mina Restaurant & Bar (p211)

Best Places to Stay

➡ Al Bustan Palace (p146)

➡ Al Baleed Resort (p210)

➡ Misfah Guest House (p186)

➡ Nizwa Heritage Inn (p177)

➡ Alila Jabal Akhdar Oman (p181)

➡ 1000 Nights (p173)

Why Go?

In Muscat's Grand Mosque, there is a beautiful hand-loomed carpet; it was once the world's largest rug until Abu Dhabi's Grand Mosque, in the United Arab Emirates, pinched the record. This is poignant because Oman doesn't boast many 'firsts' or 'biggests' in a region bent on grand-standing. What it does boast, with its rich heritage and embracing society, is a strong sense of identity, a pride in an ancient, frankincense-trading past and confidence in an educated future.

For visitors, this offers a rare chance to engage with the Arab world without the distorting lens of excessive wealth. Oman's low-rise towns retain their traditional charms, and Bedouin values remain at the heart of an Omani welcome. With an abundance of natural beauty, from spectacular mountains and wind-blown deserts to a long coastline, Oman is the obvious choice for those intrigued by the modern face of Arabia, while still wanting to sense its ancient soul.

When to Go
Oman

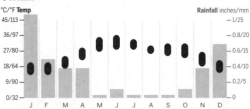

Jan–Feb Muscat Festival brings cultural shows and shopping to the capital.

Jul–Aug Salalah Tourism Festival celebrates the rainy season in Dhofar.

Nov–Mar Balmy days mark the tourist high season.

Daily Costs

Oman is expensive with limited accommodation options outside the capital. Budget hotels average US$70 for single rates but there are cheap options for eating (around US$7) and minimal entry fees to many of the main sites of interest; with a combination of public transport and taxi, a minimum daily cost comes to around US$130. This rises to US$250 staying in midrange hotels with car hire and US$500 for top-end with 4WD hire.

ITINERARIES

Muscat Stopover
Rise with the dawn to see fishermen bring in the weird and wonderful at Mutrah's fish market (p137). Stroll the Corniche (p136) and then duck into Mutrah Souq (p135) to lose your way among the pink, plastic and implausible. Spare an hour for the sights of Muscat proper, the walled heart of the capital, before relaxing at the resorts of Bandar Jissah (p152).

Two Weeks
Begin a mountain tour in the old city of Nizwa (p175). Climb the beanstalk to Jebel Akhdar (p179), famed for giant pomegranates and hailstones. Hike the rim of Oman's Grand Canyon for a spot of carpet-buying on Jebel Shams (p187). Engage with *jinn* (genies) at the remarkable tombs and forts of Al Ain (p389), Bahla and Jabreen (p188). Combine with a visit to the UAE by continuing to the border via Ibri (p191) and Buraimi (p191).

Three Weeks
Begin to follow 1000km of coast by exploring the wadis (dry riverbeds) of Shab (p157) and Tiwi (p158) and the boatyards of Sur (p159). Learn about turtles at Ras Al Jinz (p163) before cutting inland to Sharqiya Sands (p173). Acclimatise to nights under the stars before beginning the epic camping journey south via Duqm (p222) to Salalah (p206) – home of frankincense.

AT A GLANCE

Capital Muscat

Country code ☑968

Currency Omani rial (OMR)

Language Arabic, English widely spoken

Mobile phones SIM cards widely available

Money ATMs widespread; credit cards widely accepted

Population 4.65 million

Visas Available online for many nationalities

Exchange Rates

The rial is pegged to the US dollar and rarely fluctuates. For current exchange rates, see www.xe.com.

Australia	A$10	OR2.7
Bahrain	BD1	OR1
Canada	CA$10	OR2.8
Euro zone	€10	OR4.4
Japan	¥1000	OR3.5
New Zealand	NZ$10	OR2.5
Qatar	QR10	OR1
UAE	Dhs10	OR1
UK	£10	OR4.9
USA	US$10	OR3.8

Essential Food & Drink

Harees Steamed wheat and boiled meat.

Shuwa Slow-roasted marinated lamb, traditionally prepared in an underground oven.

Halwa Confection served at all official functions.

Tap water Safe to drink in all main towns.

Alcohol Available at most tourist hotels.

Qahwa Cardamom coffee – served with dates, it's an essential part of Omani hospitality.

Resources

Destination Oman (www.destinationoman.com) Practical information.

Oman Tourism (www.omantourism.gov.om) Official tourist website.

OMAN

Map labels

IRAN

GULF OF OMAN

Strait of Hormuz

THE GULF

UNITED ARAB EMIRATES

ABU DHABI

Dubai

Ras Al Khaimah

OMAN

Muscat

100 km
50 miles

Tropic of Cancer

Musandam ⑦
Bukha
Khasab
Al Darah/Tibat
Sham
Lima

Dibba
Hatta
Wajaja
Al Jizzi
Buraimi
Al Ain
Hafit

Fujairah
Khatmat Milahah
Shinas
Sohar
Saham
Al Khabura
Hajar ⑨
Mountains
Yankul
Batinah
Coast
Al Hazm
Wadi
Suwayq
As
Barka
Sawadi
Seeb
Daymaniyat
Mussanah Islands

Nakhal ②
Fort
Bidbid
Rustaq
Wadi
Jebel Shams Ghul
Bat
Al Ayn
Ibri
Fahud
Jebel Shams ①
(3075m)
Misfat
Al Hamra
Tanuf
Jabreen
Bahla Fort ③
Nizwa
Birkat
Al Mawz
Jebel
Akhdar
Samail
Wadi
Tayein
Adam
Al Mudaibi
Sinaw

Bandar Jissah
Yitti
Al Seifa
Bandar Khayran
Dibab
Quriyat
Bimmah
Mazara
Qurayat
Ibra
Al Qabil
Al Mintirib

Wadi Shab ⑩
Wadi
Khabbah
Jaylah
Wadi Bani
Khalid

Tiwi
Qalhat
Sur
Al Kamil
Ayijah Ras
Al Hadd
Ras ⑤
Al Jinz
Asselah
Al Ashkarah

Ghaf

Sharqiya Sands ④

Muscat ⑧

Fahud

Oman Highlights

① **Jebel Shams** (p187)
Haggling with carpet sellers on a precipice above Wadi Ghul.

② **Nakhal Fort** (p194)
Surveying the flat panorama

of the Batinah region from the battlements.

③ **Bahla Fort** (p189)
Rambling around the battlements of a Unesco World Heritage Site.

④ **Sharqiya Sands** (p173)
Putting your driving and navigational skills to the test in the dunes.

⑤ **Ras Al Jinz** (p163)
Attending the night-time

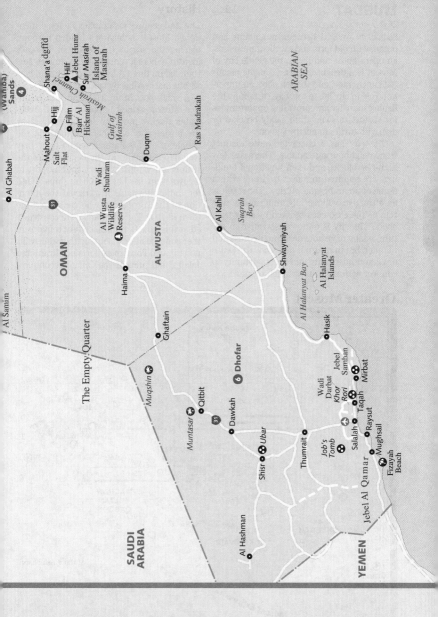

MUSCAT مسقط

📶 24 / POP 1.56 MILLION

Scenically wedged between mountains and ocean, with old forts and excellent museums, an opera house and parks, the gentle city of Muscat is a delight to visit. Its name means 'safe anchorage', and the sea plays an important role in city life to this day, sustaining the fishing industry and providing opportunities for visitors to swim from sandy beaches or dive with turtles in nearby lagoons.

The city has a character quite distinct from neighbouring capitals. There are few high-rise blocks, and even functional buildings are required to reflect tradition with a dome or an arabesque window. The result is an attractive, whimsically uniform city that retains the elegance observed by early travellers. The city is quite conservative in nature, asking of visitors decorum in dress and manner, but in return it offers a warm sense of Omani hospitality and an opportunity to connect with the country's rich heritage.

History

The 2nd-century geographer Ptolemy mentioned Muscat as having a hidden harbour, placing the sea at the centre of Muscat's identity, where it remains today. In fact, surrounded on three sides by mountains, it was all but inaccessible by land for centuries.

A small port in the 14th and 15th centuries, Muscat gained importance as a freshwater staging post, but it was eclipsed by the busier port of Sohar – something the people of today's Batinah region hope may well happen again. By the beginning of the 16th century, Muscat was a trading port in its own right, used by merchant ships bound for India. Inevitably it attracted the attention of the Portuguese, who conquered the town in 1507. The city walls were constructed at this time (a refurbished set remains in the same positions), but neither the walls nor the two Portuguese forts of Mirani and Jalali could prevent the Omani reconquest

OMAN MUSCAT

Greater Muscat

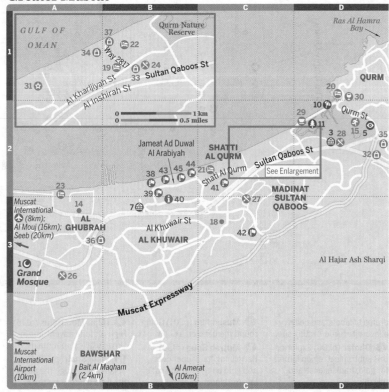

of the town in 1650 – an event that effectively ended the Portuguese era in the Gulf.

Despite becoming the capital of Oman in 1793, and the focus of the country's great sea-faring empire of the 18th and 19th centuries, it became a backwater for much of the 20th century, and the city gates remained resolutely locked against the encroachments of the outside world until 1970. Under the auspices of the current Sultan Qaboos, the city reawakened. To facilitate the growing number of cars needing access to the city, a hole was driven through the city walls. Goods and services flooded in, and Muscat flooded out to occupy the surrounding coastline. Touchingly, the city gates continued to be locked at a specific time every evening, despite the adjacent hole in the wall, until the gates were replaced with an archway. In many respects, that little act of remembrance is a fitting metaphor for a city that has given access to modern conveniences while it continues to keep the integrity of its traditional character.

◉ Sights

Wedged into a relatively narrow strip of land between the mountains and the sea, Muscat comprises a long string of suburbs spanning a distance of 50km or so from the airport to Al Bustan. Visiting the sights can therefore take a bit of planning, and during rush-hour periods (7am to 8.30am, 12.30pm to 3.30pm and 5.30pm to 7pm Sunday to Thursday) you may need to add an extra 45 minutes to get to your destination.

◉ Mutrah مطرح

Mutrah's main sites are clustered along the Corniche, which runs from the fish roundabout to Kalbuh Bay Park, about 4.5km east.

★ Mutrah Souq MARKET
(Map p138; Mutrah Corniche; ⊙8am-1pm & 5-9pm Sat-Thu, 5-9pm Fri) Many people come to the Corniche just to visit the souq, which retains the chaotic interest of a traditional Arab

OMAN MUSCAT

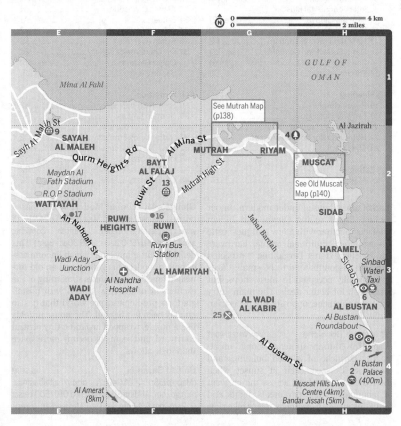

Greater Muscat

OMAN MUSCAT

market albeit housed under modern timber roofing. Shops selling Omani and Indian artefacts together with a few antiques jostle among more traditional textile, hardware and jewellery stores. Bargaining is expected although discounts tend to be small. Cards are generally accepted in most shops, but bring cash for better deals. The main entry is via the Corniche, opposite the pedestrian traffic lights.

★ **Mutrah Corniche**   WATERFRONT
(Map p138) Mutrah stretches along an attractive corniche of latticed buildings and mosques; it's spectacular at sunset when the light casts shadows across the crescent of mountains, while pavements, lights and fountains invite an evening stroll or bike ride.

Ghalya's Museum of Modern Art   MUSEUM
(Place & People Museum; Map p138; ☏24711640; www.ghalyasmuseum.com; Mutrah Corniche; adult/child OR1/500 baisa; ⊙9.30am-6pm) This delightful little museum, which encompasses both a modern art gallery and an old furnished house, encapsulates something of the excitement of the new, tinged with nostalgia for a pre-Renaissance world that has so quickly been left behind. The house unfolds like a puzzle, wrapped around a tiny central courtyard, and seems to occupy more space than logic allows.

Bait Al Baranda   MUSEUM
(Map p138; ☏24714262; http://baitalbaranda. mm.gov.om; Al Mina St; adult/child OR1/500 baisa; ⊙9am-1pm & 4-6pm Sat-Thu) Housed in a ren-

ovated 1930s residence, this museum traces the history – and prehistory – of Muscat through imaginative, interactive displays and exhibits. A 'cut-and-paste' dinosaur, using bones found in Al Khoud area of Muscat and topped up with borrowed bones from international collections, is worth a look. The ethnographic displays help set not just Muscat but the whole of Oman in a regional, commercial and cultural context. The ground floor of the museum is used as an exhibition space.

Mutrah Fort FORT

(Map p138; 500 baisa; ⊙9am-6.30pm Sat-Thu, 9-11am & 2-6.30pm Fri) Built by the Portuguese in the 1580s, this fort dominates the eastern end of Mutrah harbour. Used for military purposes, it has at long last reopened to visitors. There's not much to see inside although the three-tower structure may be of interest to military buffs. Even if you have fort fatigue, it's fun to scale the flank of the building for a good view of Mutrah and the ocean.

Fish Market MARKET

(Map p138; near Samak Roundabout; ⊙6-10am) Despite being the capital's main port, Mutrah feels more like a fishing village. The daily catch is delivered to market, by the Marina Hotel (p144), from sunrise. A lengthy refurbishment has transformed the area from a few crates on the shore to a landmark destination with a purpose-built, wave-shaped building and landscaped addition to the Corniche, completed in 2017. If you want to get an idea of the richness of Omani seas without getting wet, this is the place to do it.

Mutrah Gold Souq MARKET

(Map p138; Mutrah Corniche; ⊙8am-1pm & 5-9pm Sat-Thu, 5-9pm Fri) A visit to Mutrah Souq (p135) wouldn't be the same without a stroll through the narrow alleys that house the glittering gold shops. The bridal gold, worked into bibs, buckles and belts, may not be to everyone's taste, but the sheer accumulation of treasure in the shop windows is exciting on the eye.

⊙ Old Muscat مسقط القديمة

The tiny, open-gated city of Muscat, home to the Sultan's Palace and the *diwan* (royal court), sits cradled in a natural harbour surrounded by a jagged spine of hills. Lying at the end of Mutrah Corniche, it makes a fascinating place to spend half a day with several sights of interest, including the new National Museum.

★National Museum MUSEUM

(Map p140; ☑22081500; Al Saidiya St; tourist/resident OR5/1; ⊙10am-5pm Sat-Thu, 2-6pm Fri) Housed in an imposing new building in the heart of Old Muscat, the National Museum makes a fitting consort for the Sultan's Palace opposite. The emphasis of this contemporary museum is on quality rather than quantity, with space, light and height used to enhance the selective displays showcasing the heritage of Oman. Giant screens and high-tech devices bring the artefacts alive. There's a particularly strong and innovative multimedia section on maritime history.

★Sultan's Palace PALACE

(Al Alam; Map p140; off Al Saidiya St) If you stand by the harbour wall on Mirani St, the building to the right with the delightful mushroom pillars in blue and gold is the Sultan's Palace. On the inland side, an avenue of palm trees leads to a roundabout surrounded by grand royal court buildings and the new National Museum. Although the palace is closed to the public, you can pause in front of the gates, at the end of the colonnaded approach, for a quintessential Muscat selfie.

★Bait Al Zubair MUSEUM

(Map p140; ☑22084700; www.baitalzubair.com; Al Saidiya St; adult/child OR2/1; ⊙9.30am-6pm Sat-Thu) In a beautifully restored house, this much-loved privately owned museum exhibits Omani heritage in thematic displays of traditional handicrafts, furniture, stamps and coins. The museum has evolved into the cultural centre of Muscat, hosting international exhibitions of contemporary art in **Gallery Sarah** within the museum's grounds. A modern cafe and a shop selling quality souvenirs usually entice visitors to stay longer than they expected.

Al Jalali Fort FORT

(Map p140; ☑24641300; www.mhc.gov.om/en; ⊙by permit only) Guarding the entrance to the harbour to the east, Al Jalali Fort was built during the Portuguese occupation in the 1580s on Arab foundations. The fort is accessible only via a steep flight of steps. As such, it made the perfect prison for a number of years, but now it is a **museum of Omani heritage**. Admission is strictly by permit only – apply to the Ministry of National Heritage and Culture, through the contact page on the ministry website.

Mutrah

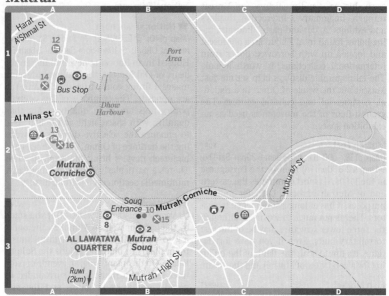

OMAN MUSCAT

Al Mirani Fort   FORT
(Map p140) Sixteenth-century Al Mirani Fort
was built by the Portuguese at the same time
as nearby Al Jalali Fort (p137). Although
closed to the public, its presence looms
large over the harbour and contributes to

A FORT FICTION

Al Mirani Fort has a special place in
history as it contributed to the fall of the
Portuguese. This came about through
a curious affair of the heart: legend has
it that the Portuguese commander fell
for the daughter of a Hindu supplier,
who refused the match on religious
grounds. On being threatened with ruin,
the supplier spent a year apparently
preparing for the wedding, during which
time he worked an elaborate trick on the
commander, convincing him that the
fort's supplies needed a complete overhaul. Bit by bit he removed all the fort's
gunpowder and grain, and when the
fort was left completely defenceless, he
gave the nod to the Omani imam, Sultan
Bin Saif, who succeeded in retaking
the fort in 1649. The Portuguese were
ousted from Muscat soon after, and the
wedding never took place.

---

the iconic view of Muscat captured in 19th-
century lithographs.

⊙ Al Bustan   البستان

The cliffs meet the sea along the rugged
coastline between Old Muscat and Al
Bustan, making for an attractive drive.

Sohar   LANDMARK
(Map p134; Al Bustan Roundabout, Al Bustan) Just
outside Al Bustan Palace Hotel, opposite
the imposing parliament buildings, a small
roundabout is home to *Sohar*, a boat named
after the hometown of the famous Omani
seafarer Ahmed Bin Majid. The boat (a replica of one sailed by Abdullah Bin Gasm in
the mid-8th century to Guangzhou, China)
was built in the dhow yards of Sur from the
bark of more than 75,000 palm trees and
four tonnes of rope. Not a single nail was
used in the construction.

British adventurer Tim Severin is a renowned historian and travel writer who
spent a lifetime retracing legendary voyages
to determine if they were practically feasible. He engaged a crew of Omani sailors
to sail *Sohar* to Guangzhou in 1980. The
journey of 6000 nautical miles took eight
months to complete and helped prove that
the mythical tales of Sinbad may well have
been based on fact.

Marina Bandar Al Rowdha HARBOUR
(Map p134; ☎24737286; www.marinaoman.net; Sidab St, Haramil) Apart from offering a full range of boating amenities, Marina Bandar Al Rowdha is a popular launching point for a range of water sports, including fishing and diving. It is also a pleasant place to enjoy harbour activity and relax at the Blue Marlin Restaurant (p148). The marina offers free use of its pool for those dining at the restaurant, making it a potential day's outing when combined with a boat trip.

Parliament Building LANDMARK
(Map p134; Al Bustan Roundabout, cnr Sidab & Al Bustan Sts, Al Bustan) This elegant building, completed in 2013, is home to the two houses of the Majlis Ash Shura, Oman's parliament. It is not open to the public, but it does make for a fine photo opportunity with its low-rise, Omani-style architecture, backed by Muscat's distinctive russet-coloured ophiolite mountains. The partially elected Majlis Ash Shura assists the state in the formation of policy.

◎ Ruwi روي

Oman's so-called 'Little India' is the commercial and transport hub of the capital, with plenty of budget-priced places to eat, shop (especially along Souq Ruwi St) and socialise.

Sultan's Armed Forces Museum MUSEUM
(Map p134; ☎24312648; www.mod.gov.om/en-us/cossaf/safmuseum; Al Mujamma St, Ruwi; adult/child 500 baisa/free; ☺8am-1.30pm Sun-Thu) Despite the name, this excellent museum is far more than just a display of military hardware. The collection is housed in Bayt Al Falaj, built in 1845 as a royal summer home but used mostly as the headquarters of the Sultan's Armed Forces. The lower rooms outline Oman's history while the upper rooms explore the country's international relations and military prowess. The museum is on the itinerary of visiting dignitaries, and a military escort is mandatory for all visitors.

◎ Qurm & Al Khuwair شاطي القرم و الخوير

Near the Hotel InterContinental Muscat, along Way 2817, there is a highly popular, low-rise shopping complex by the beach. This is where you will find young Omanis cruising the loop in their new 4WDs, families strolling along the beach amid five-a-side footballers, and expats enjoying the Western-style cafe culture and shops. Many ministry and embassy buildings are bunched in this area.

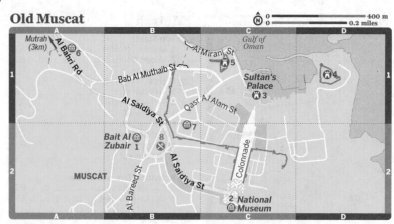

Old Muscat

Qurm Beach   BEACH
(Map p134; Qurm) A road runs along the edge of Qurm Nature Reserve towards the Crowne Plaza Muscat hotel, giving access to a long, sandy beach – a popular place for cruising in the latest on four wheels and for family picnics on the sand. Women bathing on their own may feel uncomfortable here so avoiding skimpy swimwear is advised; all swimmers should take heed of warnings about strong tides. There are cafes along the beachfront with a view out to sea.

Natural History Museum   MUSEUM
(Map p134; ☑ 24641374; Al Thaqafah St, Al Khuwair; adult/child 500/100 baisa; ⊙ 8.30am-1.30pm Sun-Thu, 9am-1pm Sat) The Ministry of National Heritage houses the small but quaint Natural History Museum. The museum is illuminating about the local flora and fauna, and there are some excellent displays on Oman's geography and geology, together with information about environmental protection. Of particular interest is the clump of rudists,

elongated marine fossils that formed giant reefs under the Tethys Sea. These fossils are now to be found only in the remote interior of the Huqf. Entry is off Way 3413.

◉ Al Ghubrah & Bawshar الغبرة وبوشر

With some elegant public buildings, this area is mostly visited for the Grand Mosque – one of Muscat's main attractions.

★ **Grand Mosque**   MOSQUE
(Map p134; www.sultanqaboosgrandmosque.com; Sultan Qaboos St, Al Ghubrah; ⊙ open at prayer times, non-Muslims 8-11am Sat-Thu) Quietly imposing from the outside, this glorious piece of modern Islamic architecture was a gift to the nation from Sultan Qaboos to mark the 30th year of his reign. The main prayer hall is breathtakingly beautiful. The Persian carpet alone measures 70m by 60m wide, making it the second-largest hand-loomed Iranian carpet in the world; it took 600 women four years to weave. Mwasalat buses stop outside the mosque.

The mosque, which can accommodate 20,000 worshippers, including 750 women in a private *musalla* (prayer hall), is an active place of worship, particularly for Friday prayers. Visitors are required to dress modestly, covering arms and legs and avoiding tight clothing. Women and girls (aged seven and above) must cover their hair. An *abaya* (full-length dress) and scarf can be hired from the mosque cafe and gift shop for OR2.5; some form of ID is required as a deposit. Tours are available.

Bait Al Maqham   HISTORIC BUILDING
(end of As Safa St, Bawshar) FREE Open on the whim of the gatekeeper, this fortified residence buried in a plantation in Bawshar is worth visiting for the location. Close to the city's last remaining sand dunes, the fortified residence is a surprise find at the crease of the Hajar Mountains. New houses are slowly encroaching, but for now this little castle presents a fascinating glimpse of Muscat's once-common plantation life. Park opposite Rashan Shopping Centre and follow the signs to avoid getting wedged between narrow plantation walls.

◉ Al Mouj & Mawalih

This up-and-coming sea-board development (Al Mouj means 'the wave') near Muscat International Airport is a relatively new social hub in the capital. Planned as a mixed residential, tourism and commercial development, it remains one of the few locations where expats can purchase property. The result, a decade later, is a thriving community comprising 69 nationalities. There's a marina that hosts Extreme 40 sailing, Seaoman watersports centre, a golf course designed by Greg Norman, fountains, restaurants and leafy pavement coffee shops.

Marsa Plaza   AREA
(The Walk, Al Mouj) The open-air heart of Al Mouj residential and tourism complex, this delightful shaded public space is by the marina and catches the sea breeze. The avant-garde design features a giant pergola with projected images across the walls and pavement, and musical fountains springing from the pavement. Surrounded by restaurants and coffee shops it's the perfect place to begin a waterfront stroll.

Al Sahwa Park   PARK
(cnr Hwy 1 & 15, off Burj Al Sahwa Roundabout, Mawalih; ◷8am-11pm) This perfectly manicured park offers a peaceful retreat from the city. The carefully trimmed trees offer shade, while fragrant shrubs make for a redolent stroll along the extensive walking paths. With water features and abundant flowering annuals in the cooler months, this is the place to head to for a picnic.

🏃 Activities

Hiking

There are some rewarding mountain walks in the Muscat area covered in Anne Dale and Jerry Hadwin's *Adventure Trekking in Oman*. Their Muscat–Sidab route is a one-hour walk that could be added on to our Muscat walking tour (p144).

The Ministry of Tourism (www.omantour ism.gov.om) hiking booklet describes some great routes across Muscat and beyond. Stout shoes, water and a hat are essential at any time of year, even on the shortest route.

Capital Area Hike   HIKING
(Map p138; St 10, Al Riyam Park, Mutrah) The C38 from Al Riyam Park to Mutrah traces the route through Muscat's distinctive ophiolite mountains on a track used by copper miners who were active in the region 5000 years ago. It's an easy 2.5km hike with a rise of only 200m, but it still requires walking shoes.

Water Sports

★**Al Mouj Marina**   WATER SPORTS
(☎24534544; www.almoujmarina.com; Al Mouj; ◷office 9am-6pm, marina access 24hr) Home to Oman Sail, Oman's renowned international sailing team, this marina offers full berthing amenities and outlets that cater for fishing, boat cruises, snorkelling, diving, sailing and wakeboarding among other activities. A water taxi links it to the marina at Bandar Al Rowdha and Jebel Sifah. The marina is surrounded by attractive public space with walking paths, fountains, cafes and restaurants.

★**Seaoman**   BOATING
(Oman Sail; ☎24374201; www.seaoman.com; Al Mouj Marina, Al Mouj; 1hr kayak OR10; ◷9am-5pm) Affiliated with Oman Sail with its emphasis on training and education, this water-sports operator offers courses in sailing, diving, powerboating, waterskiing, kayaking and wakeboarding among others. It operates out of Al Mouj Marina and has outlets at the Millennium Hotel near Barka.

Sea Tours Oman   BOATING
(Map p134; ☎99013424; www.seatoursoman. com; Marina Bandar Al Rowdha, Sidab St, Haramil) Specialising in boat trips, including glass-bottom boats in Muscat, this is now the only company offering the chance to peer into the watering depths without dressing up in rubber.

Crowne Plaza Muscat Health Club   SWIMMING
(Map p134; ☎24660660; www.crowneplaza.com; Qurm St, Qurm; adult/child OR10/6; ◷7am-9pm) The Crowne Plaza Muscat is at the head of a beautiful, sandy bay and has access to a secluded pocket of beach. A day pass includes use of the health club sauna and steam

room, tennis courts and pool. Call one day ahead to check availability.

InterContinental Muscat Health Club
SWIMMING

(Map p134; ☑ 24680000; www.ihg.com; Hotel InterContinental Muscat, off Way 2817, Shatti Al Qurm; adult/child OR10/5; ⊗ 8am-9pm) A day pass gives access to landscaped gardens that offer a shady retreat after lengths of the training pool. Alternatively, there's more relaxed floating in the recreational pool and walks along the beach.

Eurodivers
DIVING

(Gulf Divers; Map p134; ☑ 98194444; www.euro-divers.com; Marina Bandar Al Rowdha, Sidab St, Haramil; half-day 2-dive boat trip incl equipment per person OR42; ⊗ 8am-5pm Wed-Sun) This reputable, worldwide dive company has a lot of international experience to draw upon and offers diving and snorkelling from Marina Bandar Al Rowdha to beautiful Bandar Khayran (p152) in nearby Bandar Jissah. It also runs PADI courses.

Al Nimer Tourism
KAYAKING

(Map p134; ☑ 99550535; Qurm Beach, Shatti St, Shatti Al Qurm; kayak per hr OR5, jet ski 30min/1hr OR20/30) Taking a kayak or jet ski from this dependable, locally run rental agency on Qurm Beach offers a chance to view the mountainous hem of the city from the open sea and makes a fun way to spend an afternoon. Don't forget to take the life-vests on offer as the currents in this area are strong, despite the shallow water.

Horse Riding

Qurm Equestrian School
HORSE RIDING

(Map p134; ☑ 24700844, 99832199; www.qe.hashimani.com; Qurm Park, Qurm; 1hr beach ride OR20; ⊗ 4am-9pm) One of the few horse-riding schools in Muscat, this veteran establishment in Qurm Park offers the joy of cantering an Arabian horse through the surf on the city's long sandy beaches.

☞ Tours

As Muscat's attractions are so spread out, a tour is recommended. Generally, tours can be organised on a bespoke basis by any of the main tour operators. An average price for a full-day city tour including lunch is OR65 per person.

★ UB Cool
TOURS

(☑ 24580117; www.ub-cool.com; Way 6826, NB Bldg, 18 November St, Azaiba) ✈ This locally founded company has taken an innovative approach to tourism in Oman. It offers unique, sustainable tours that help to promote traditional values and ways of life that are less demanding on energy resources and kinder on the environment. It offers fishing trips using traditional boats and fishing methods, and homestays in the ancient village of Wakan.

★ Husaak Adventures
ADVENTURE

(Map p134; ☑ 97123324, 97185288; www.husaak.com; 18 November St, Al Ghubrah) This Omani adventure company has become a leading establishment for outdoor activities. Covering hiking, kayaking, caving and canyoning, they also arrange some interesting geological and archaeological tours ranging from half-days in Muscat to major two-week treks and can tailor-make tours. Weekend trips including food, camping gear and equipment cost around OR200 per person depending on the activity.

★ Big Bus Tours
BUS

(Map p138; ☑ 24523112; www.bigbustours.com/en/muscat/muscat-bus-tours; adult/child/family OR25/17/77; ⊗ 9am-5pm) This popular service aboard air-conditioned, open-top double-decker buses runs through the capital on a hop-on, hop-off basis, taking in 10 of the major sights from Mutrah and Old Muscat to Qurm and offering a free shuttle to the Grand Mosque. A recorded on-board commentary in six languages with free headphones is included in the price.

Toyaan Travel
CULTURAL

(☑ 99881477; toyaantravelguide@gmail.com; per person OR10; ⊗ 5-9pm Sun-Thu & 9am-9pm Fri & Sat) Offering unique walking tours of Muscat and Mutrah, travel guide 'Dr Ahmed' was born in the heart of Mutrah and brings to his tours the tales of his childhood, growing up in an era before education and health-care were widespread. Through witty, personal insights delivered in fluent English, Ahmed shares the love of his neighbourhood in these small-group outings.

Zahara Tours
CULTURAL

(Map p134; ☑ 24400844; www.zaharatours.com; Dawat Al Adab St, Madinat Al Sultan Qaboos) This comprehensive and well-respected tour company has been in business since the 1970s and has won several awards for excellence. Specialising in small-group cultural and adventure tours, it runs a modern fleet of 4WD vehicles and the iconic hotel, The View Resort (p185), in the Hajar Mountains.

MUSCAT FOR CHILDREN

Muscat is a safe and friendly city with a few attractions for children. Most malls have a themed amusement centre, typically open between 10am and 10pm, and costing from around 350 baisa per ride or OR3 for entry.

Children's Museum (Map p134; ☑ 24605368; off Sultan Qaboos St, Qurm; adult/child under 7 yrs OR1/free; ⊙ 8am-1.30pm Sat-Thu; ⓓ) Well-signposted domed building with lots of hands-on science displays. Free for children under seven.

Ice Skating (Fun Zone; Map p134; ☑ 96962422, 24662422; www.funzoneoman.com; Qurm Park, Qurm Rd, Qurm; admission incl skate hire OR4; ⊙ 9am-midnight Sat-Thu, from 2pm Fri) A good way to beat the summer heat. Sessions last 90 minutes. Women-only sessions on Monday from 9am to 6pm.

Marah Land (Map p134; ☑ 22006091, 98000266; Qurm Park, Qurm; admission 300 baisa, per ride 500 baisa; ⊙ 4pm-midnight) Set inside the attractively landscaped Qurm Park, this funfair with Ferris wheel is a local favourite.

Oman Avenues Mall (Map p134; ☑ 22005400; www.omanavenuesmall.om; Sultan Qaboos St, Al Ghubrah; ⊙ 10am-10pm Sun-Wed, to 11pm Thu-Sat; ☎) One of Muscat's most popular malls comes with 150 shops, a large food court open until 1am at weekends and Funtazmo World for kids.

PDO Oil & Gas Exhibition (Map p134; ☑ 24677834; www.pdo.co.om; Sayh Al Malih St, Qurm; ⊙ 8am-3pm Sun-Thu) `FREE` Interactive science displays and a planetarium help kids learn about geology and the cosmos.

Al Riyam Park (Map p138; Mutrah Corniche, Mutrah; ⊙ 4-11pm Sun-Thu, 9am-midnight Fri & Sat) A small funfair entertaining for younger kids under a giant landmark incense burner.

National Travel & Tourism CULTURAL
(NTT; Map p134; ☑ 24660300; www.nttoman.com; Ar Rumaylah St, Wattayah; ⊙ 8.30am-6pm Sat-Thu) Offers an excellent, friendly and comprehensive tour service with several one-week and two-week packages on offer, in addition to popular half-day city tours of Muscat. Next to the Kia showroom in Wattayah, this is one of the best places to ask for tourist information. Staff are experienced and helpful.

Mark Tours CULTURAL
(Map p134; ☑ 24782727; www.marktoursoman. com; Way 2985, off Al Iskan St, Ruwi) One of the most experienced and enduring tour companies in Oman. Can tailor-make study tours and adventure trips.

⭐ Festivals & Events

★ Muscat Festival CULTURAL
(http://en.muscat-festival.com; ⊙ Jan-Feb) Lasting for a month from around the end of January, Muscat Festival is a highlight of the capital's year, featuring nightly fireworks, a 'living' replica of an Omani village with sweet-making and craft displays, exhibitions from regional countries, and events such as laser shows and traditional dancing. A seasonal website (accessible only during the festival) showcases the main features.

Extreme Sailing Series SAILING
(www.extremesailingseries.com; ⊙ Mar) The Oman leg is part of the world series of this high-profile sailing event that takes place from Al Mouj Marina (p141). It invites local interest thanks to the prowess of the excellent local team. Sponsored by Oman Air, this team frequently garners top spots in individual legs and has even won the whole series.

National Day CULTURAL
(⊙ 18 Nov) National Day is marked with fireworks, city buildings are draped with strings of colourful lights, and Sultan Qaboos St is spectacularly lit and adorned with flags. Petunia planting along highway verges, roundabouts and city parks is timed for maximum blooming, transforming the city into a riot of floral colour.

Tour of Oman CYCLING
(www.tourofoman.om; ⊙ Feb) Covering Muscat and Nizwa over six stages, this annual event is gaining in popularity and helping to raise the profile of cycling in Oman. It includes several punishing mountain climbs, including up Jebel Akhdar.

Muscat Marathon SPORTS
(www.muscatmarathon.om; ⊙ Jan) Between Muscat and Seeb, this event attracts only a relatively small number of international

competitors, but takes an inclusive approach with half-marathons and runs for kids.

🛏 Sleeping

Despite belonging to chains, Muscat's main hotels offer a distinctly Arabian experience, with coffee and dates in reception, a beachside location and a penchant for marble, Persian carpets and frankincense. They offer good-value discounts between March and November. Budget hotels in Mutrah are within walking distance of the capital's main cultural attractions. Taxes, wi-fi and breakfast are generally included in the rate.

Beach Hotel   HOTEL $
(Map p134; ☎24696601; www.beachhotelmuscat.com; Way 2818, Shatti Al Qurm; r OR25, 1-/2-bed apt OR35/45; ☎🏊) Few hotels in Muscat offer a genuine Omani experience, but this family-owned hotel, opposite the Opera House (p149), is an exception. With Omani receptionists, premises that resemble a local villa, and a breakfast that includes *fuul medamas* (fava beans) and *khobz* (flat bread), the hotel unfailingly offers a traditional Muscat welcome. Rooms are plain but spacious and arranged around a pool.

Marina Hotel   HOTEL $
(Map p138; ☎24713100; http://marina.muscathotels-om.com; Mutrah Corniche, Mutrah; s/d OR25/30) Balanced like an eagle's nest overlooking the Corniche, this hotel has an enviable bird's-eye view across Mutrah Harbour and Muscat's famous merchant houses. A few clean and simple rooms – admittedly cramped – share the view. Fish so fresh it virtually swims in from the impressive fish market (p137) opposite is a highlight of the hotel's popular Al Boom Restaurant.

Naseem Hotel   HOTEL $
(Map p138; ☎24712418; naseemhotel@gmail.com; Mutrah Corniche, Mutrah; s/d/tr OR18/22/40; ☎) In need of a makeover, this tired old Mutrah stalwart has large rooms, seven with grand views of the harbour. Given its prime location, plumb in the middle of the city's finest row of merchant houses, it's remarkable that this hotel has survived. What it lacks in decor (and clean carpets), it makes up for in friendly, helpful service.

Crowne Plaza Muscat   HOTEL $$
(Map p134; ☎24660660; www.crowneplaza.com; off Qurm Rd, Qurm; r excl breakfast from OR93; 🅿@☎🏊) Draped over the headland at the end of Qurm Beach, this veteran hotel with its west-facing terrace offers the best views

🏃 City Walk
Muscat Coastline

START FISH MARKET, MUTRAH
END AL BAHRI RD, OLD MUSCAT
LENGTH 8KM; FOUR TO FIVE HOURS

Giving a sense of how the sea defines the city, this walking tour follows the coastline through the ancient ports of Mutrah and Muscat. It picks up some of the best of Muscat's sights while following the gulls around the distinctive rocky seafront. Pack a snack and take lots of water. The walk can be segmented if time, energy or summer heat forbid the whole route.

Begin where the morning tide beaches fishermen and their catch at the ❶ **Fish Market** (p137). Stop for something fishy at nearby ❷ **La Brasserie** (p148), with delicious seafood on the menu.

Turn right at Samak roundabout, which means 'fish' in Arabic and is decorated with a pair of generic pisces. Call into nearby ❸ **Bait Al Baranda** (p136) and learn about the history of Muscat's relationship with the sea. Return to the Corniche and head towards the fort. Cast your eye out to sea: His Majesty's Dhow is generally harboured here, cruise ships dock by the harbour master, and large cargo boats unload at the docks beyond. Inland, the merchants' houses of the Lawataya people, who built their fortunes on the seafaring trade, sport balconies that allow the inhabitants a nostalgic glance across the Arabian Ocean.

Turn into ❹ **Mutrah Souq** (p135), where items such as handmade models of silver dhows and ship chandlery are on sale; this souq grew from seaborne cargo and to this day many of the wares (Indian spices and textiles, Egyptian plastic, Iranian crafts and Chinese toys) are shipped in by sea. Return to the Corniche and head east towards 16th-century ❺ **Mutrah Fort** (p137), built by the Portuguese who were unwittingly led to Muscat by the kindness of Ahmed Bin Majid, a famous sailor from Sohar.

At the ❻ **goldfish monument and fountains**, a heron often snacks in view of the royal yacht and the visiting navies of other nations. Continue towards the giant incense burner; Oman's former prosperity was built on Dhofar frankincense, which left the shores of Oman with other precious cargo such as Arabian horses.

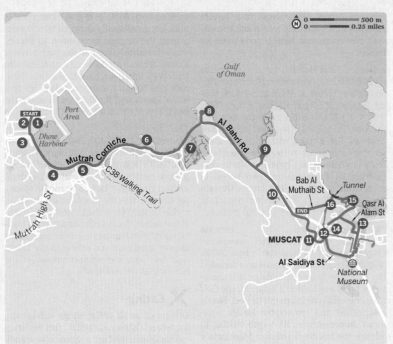

On reaching **7** **Al Riyam Park** (p143) you could, with stout shoes, head back to Mutrah on the Ministry of Tourism's walking route C38, past panoramic views. Alternatively, continue along the Corniche to the **8** **watchtower** (Map p138; Mutrah Corniche, Mutrah) and scan for dolphins – some real and some carved from marble.

After pausing for a rest at **9** **Kalbuh Bay Park** (Map p134; Mutrah Corniche, Mutrah; ⊙9am-10pm), cut inland via Al Bahri Rd and enter the 'city proper' via **10** **Muscat Gate Museum** (Map p140; ☑99328754; Al Bahri Rd, Old Muscat; ⊙8am-2pm Sun-Thu) FREE. Every night until the 1970s the doors to the city were locked at this point, keeping tradition in and those from the interior out.

Turn right towards Sidab on Al Saidiya St and visit **11** **Bait Al Zubair** (p137) for photographs showing the sea's influence on Muscat.

Continue along Al Saidiya St, still heading for Sidab. Pause for fried fish at **12** **City Tower Grill Restaurant & Cafe** (p147) on the corner before turning right along an elegant avenue of date palms.

At the roundabout, march left through the colonnade towards the grand front entrance of the **13** **Sultan's Palace** (p137). Follow the palace walls left, past beautiful gardens and mature trees (a favourite roost of mynah birds) on Qasr Al Alam St.

At the junction, turn left for the **14** **Omani-French Museum** (Map p140; ☑24736613; Qasr Al Alam St, Old Muscat; adult/child 500/200 baisa; ⊙8am-1.30pm Sun-Thu, 9am-1pm Sat) and a display on shipbuilding, or right for Muscat Harbour. The Portuguese built forts, such as **15** **Al Mirani** (p138), towering to the left, and Al Jalali (across the bay), to protect their maritime interests. Look across the harbour for a graffiti logbook etched into the promontory rocks, left by the visiting navies of Great Britain and other countries. This is a good place to admire the back garden of the palace and imagine the spectacle of the military banquets held annually here, complete with ice sculptures on the lawn, a band on each of the surrounding forts, lights from Oman's fully rigged tall ship moored in the harbour for the occasion, and fireworks mirrored in the calm waters of the bay.

Turn left at the harbour wall, and duck under the tunnel before the modern naval base. Turn right under the **16** **old city gate** on to Bab Al Muthaib St. This soon runs into Al Bahri Rd – and from here, it's an easy taxi ride back to Mutrah.

for sundowners. With access to a private strip of sandy beach, big rooms and friendly staff, this competent hotel is good value for money.

Hormuz Grand Hotel
HOTEL $$

(☑ 24350500; www.radissoncollection.com/en/hormuz-grand-hotel; Al Matar St, off Bank Muscat Roundabout, Airport Heights; r from OR95; P@🛜⊠) If you can forgive the fact that the exterior is pink, this good-value hotel, close to the airport with pleasant landscaping and views across the mountains from large, luxurious rooms, is worth considering for those wanting easy access to routes out of Muscat. The hotel's Qureshi Bab Al Hind is a fine-dining restaurant offering excellent northern Indian cuisine.

★ Al Bustan Palace
HOTEL $$$

(Ritz-Carlton Hotel; ☑ 24799666; www.ritzcarlton.com; off Sidab St, Al Bustan; r from OR205; P@🛜⊠) Set in a desert oasis on a secluded bay ringed by rugged mountains, this sumptuous hotel was built as a venue for the Gulf Cooperation Council summit in 1985. Newly refurbished and remarkable for its enormous domed atrium, it's worth visiting to admire the building's interior. More palace than hotel, rooms are a byword for Arabian-style chic and restaurants are top quality.

Kempinski Hotel Muscat
HOTEL $$$

(☑ 24985000; www.kempinski.com/en/muscat/kempinski-hotel-muscat; St 6, Al Mouj; r excl breakfast from OR112; P@🛜⊠) So close to the sea, ospreys settle on the garden lamp posts, and yet with the amenities of Al Mouj complex within walking distance, this modern hotel offers luxurious rooms in a contemporary space. The hotel looks a bit forbidding from the outside, with its honeycombed ballroom and concealed entrance, but unfurls beautifully on to the sea from within.

Hotel InterContinental Muscat
RESORT $$$

(Map p134; ☑ 24680000; www.ihg.com; off Way 2817, Shatti Al Qurm; r from OR130; P@🛜⊠) An excellent hotel in terms of service and amenities, the affectionately known 'InterCon' is so close to the Opera House you can virtually hear the sopranos. While not the prettiest building, this hotel has a fine interior, quality rooms, shady gardens and beach access. Jawaharat Al Shatti Complex – a lively collection of shops, cafes and restaurants – is a stroll away.

Grand Hyatt Muscat
HOTEL $$$

(Map p134; ☑ 24641234; www.muscat.grand.hyatt.com; Way 3033, off Al Saruj St, Shatti Al Qurm; r excl breakfast from OR138; P@🛜⊠) This hotel is pure kitsch. Allegedly designed by a Yemeni prince, the exterior owes much to Disney, while its stained-glass and marble interior is a cross between art deco and a royal Bedouin tent. With luxurious, balconied rooms, Muscat's best Italian restaurant, called Tuscany, water sports and limitless walks along the sandy beach, this is a hotel with attitude.

The Chedi
HOTEL $$$

(Map p134; ☑ 24524400; www.ghmhotels.com; Way 3215, off 18 November St, Al Ghubrah North; r from OR245; P@🛜⊠) With a hint of *kasbah* (desert castle) combined with Asian minimalism (including lack of wardrobe space), the Chedi makes the best of its beachside location. It also boasts the longest pool (103m) in the region. Rooms offer understated luxury, and the restaurants are excellent, but airport flight path and ugly high-rise blocks next door have somewhat compromised the hotel's splendid isolation.

✗ Eating

Dozens of small coffee shops sell kebabs, falafel and dal. Several restaurants featuring typical Omani food are a welcome new addition to capital nightlife, and the city remains a top spot for excellent Indian cuisine, including at the Mumtaz Mahal (Map p134; ☑ 24605907; www.mumtazmahal.net; Way 2601, Qurm; mains from OR10; ⊗noon-3pm & 7pm-midnight Sat-Thu, 1-3pm & 7pm-midnight Fri; P✗).

Al Daleh Restaurant
INTERNATIONAL $

(Classroom Restaurant; Map p134; ☑ 24813141; www.nhioman.com; National Hospitality Institute, St 63, An Nuzha St, Al Wadi Al Kabir; 3-course lunch OR6; ⊗1-3pm Sun-Thu; P✗) Nervous Omani hospitality students practise their culinary and waiting skills at this exceptionally good-value restaurant. Menus comprise mostly top-notch international dishes and include some vegetarian options. Encouraging these youngsters on their chosen career path is a great way to make your visit to Muscat count. Ring to book a table as it gets busy.

Royal House Restaurant
INTERNATIONAL $

(Map p138; ☑ 24714891, 93141672; Mutrah Corniche, Mutrah; mains OR3; ⊗10am-11pm Sat-Thu, from 1pm Fri) This light-spangled restaurant on Mutrah Corniche offers cosy indoor dining on sedans under Turkish lanterns, or at trestle tables alongside Mutrah's busy promenade. Under pressure from cruise-ship diners, the food has become fairly bland and the

LOCATING LOCAL FLAVOURS
....

A recent welcome development to Muscat's food scene is the growing number of restaurants and shops showcasing Omani food. Try the following lesser-known options to sample local flavours:

Breakfast Housed in an old-style Muscat house, Dukanah Cafe (Map p134; ☑ 24502244; Way 3709, behind GMC showroom, Al Ghubrah; breakfast OR3; ⊘ 8am-11pm) specialises in Omani breakfasts.

Coffee Although *qahwa* (Omani coffee) is the national drink it's not found on a menu - the so-called 'coffee shops' all over town are orientated more to snacking than sipping coffee. Try *qahwa* in a hotel lobby instead.

Lunch As if Oman didn't have enough forts, they've just built a new one. Rozna (☑ 95522920; Al Maardih St, Airport Heights; mains from OR4.5; ⊘ noon-10pm) is housed in a crenellated building with a flowing *falaj* – a characterful setting for lunch.

Teatime From a family enterprise based on a single hand-me-down recipe Ice Cream Mama (Map p134; ☑ 91277770; Al Muntazah St, Shatti Al Qurm; scoop 800 baisa; ⊘ 10am-midnight) ✈ has become a successful brand. Flavours include frankincense, and rose water and *laban* (yogurt).

Dinner Camel features among other traditional meats at restaurant Ubhar (Map p134; ☑ 24699826; www.ubharoman.com; Bareeq Al Shatti Mall, Shatti Al Qurm; mains OR5; ⊘ 12.30-3.30pm & 6.30-11pm). In walking distance of the Royal Opera House, it's ideal for a post-show supper.

feral cats can be an issue, but it remains an attractive spot for a late or light bite.

Fastfood 'n' Juice Centre
OMANI $

(Map p138; Mutrah Corniche, Mutrah; sandwiches OR1; ⊘ 24hr) East of the main entrance to Mutrah Souq on the Corniche, this thoroughly typical local-style restaurant with tables on the pavement is an ideal place to people watch over a sandwich, *chai libton* (teabag tea with sweet condensed milk) or *karak* tea (sweetened tea boiled with spices). If the tables here are full, there are a couple of neighbouring eateries that will do just as nicely.

Al Boom & Dolphin Bar
MIDDLE EASTERN $

(Map p138; ☑ 24713100; Marina Hotel, Mutrah Corniche, Mutrah; breakfast OR3, dishes OR6; ⊘ 7.30-10.30am, noon-3pm & 6pm-1am; ☎) This intimate, licensed restaurant, with large windows and a terrace overlooking the fish market, is a good place to get a feel of Muscat's age-old relationship with the sea. A few marine favourites find their way on to the mainly Middle Eastern–style menu. The bar stays open until 3am (2am on Fridays).

City Tower Grill Restaurant & Cafe
CAFE $

(Map p140; Al Saidiya St, Old Muscat; mains OR2, juices 300 baisa; ⊘ 8.30am-7pm; 🅿) Ignore the entirely irrelevant name and have an egg roll-up and fresh orange juice in view of Al Mirani Fort (p138) in this corner street cafe, ideal as a rest stop on a walking tour of Muscat.

★ Bait Al Luban
OMANI $$

(Frankincense House; Map p138; ☑ 24711842; www.baitalluban.com; Hai Al Mina Rd, Mutrah; mains OR6; ⊘ noon-11pm; 🖋) ✈ You know you're somewhere unique when the complimentary water is infused with frankincense. This delightful restaurant is housed in a renovated *khan* (guesthouse), built 140 years ago, that used to charge by the bed not by the room. It serves genuine Omani cuisine (including vegetarian stews and mezze), but you could come just to savour the decor. Opposite Mutrah's fish market (p137).

★ Kargeen Cafe
MIDDLE EASTERN $$

(Map p134; ☑ 24692269, reservations 99253351; www.kargeen.com; Madinat Qaboos complex, Madinat Al Sultan Qaboos; mains from OR4; ⊘ 8am-1am Sat-Thu, noon-1am Fri; 🖋) With a choice of open-air and *majlis*-style dining (on sedans in small rooms), this Muscat favourite has spilt into a courtyard of illuminated trees to create a thoroughly Arabian experience. Make sure you try Kargeen's take on the traditional Omani *shuwa* – a succulent banana-leaf-wrapped lamb dish. Also worth a try are the hibiscus drinks and avocado milkshakes.

Zahr El Laymoun
LEBANESE $$

(☑ 24543311; cnr St 4 & Way 449, Al Mouj; mains OR5; ⊘ 10am-11pm) Bench seats with colourful cushions spill on to the pavement at this excellent Lebanese restaurant, inviting diners to make a night of it. That's easily done as there are lots of different hot and cold mezze on offer that can be rolled out slowly over the course of an evening. It's situated in a prime spot next to trendy Marsa Plaza (p141).

La Brasserie
FRENCH $$
(Map p138; ☑24713707; Mutrah Corniche, Mutrah; mains OR8; ☺9.30am-10pm) Serving delicious French food in a small wooden den of a restaurant opposite the fish market (p137) in Mutrah, La Brasserie is the perfect venue for coffee and a pastry on a walking tour of Muscat. Alternatively, try the excellent homemade bread and soups for lunch.

Blue Marlin Restaurant
INTERNATIONAL $$
(Map p134; ☑24740038; Marina Bandar Al Rawdar, Sidab St, Haramil; meals OR6; ☺8am-11pm; ⓟ) With cheerful cloth-covered tables under brollies alongside the harbour, the Blue Marlin offers consistently delicious light bites at lunchtime – perfect after a boat trip from the marina. Breakfast aficionados take note: this place serves real bacon. Diners are offered free access to the marina's pool. There's a cool, blue-lit interior for unbearably hot summer days.

★ Al Angham
OMANI $$$
(Map p134; ☑22077777; www.alanghamoman. com; Opera Galleria, Sultan Qaboos St, Shatti Al Qurm; mains OR16; ☺noon-4pm & 7-11pm; ⓟ♪) This exquisite restaurant next to the Royal Opera House offers just the kind of refined fare demanded of a special occasion, such as a night at the opera. From the Omani silver napkin rings to the carved wooden ceiling, this stylish restaurant showcases national cuisine at its best.

★ The Beach
SEAFOOD $$$
(Map p134; ☑24524400; www.ghmhotels.com; The Chedi, off 18 November St, Al Ghubrah North; meals from OR45; ☺7-10.30pm Sep-May; ⓟ♪) This top-class restaurant, with superb Arabian ambience created by fire pits and subtle lighting, serves exciting, complex fare in a luxurious beachside location. The French pastry chef at The Chedi's indoor restaurant makes wicked confections, including delectable handmade chocolates if your sweet tooth tempts you. The multicourse tasting menu is excellent.

🍷 Drinking & Nightlife

Most tourist hotels have a bar where alcohol is unrestricted but expensive. The best of these are the John Barry Bar (Map p134; ☑24641234; Grand Hyatt Muscat, Way 3033, off Al Saruj St, Shatti Al Qurm; ☺4pm-2am), named after the raised ship and its booty of silver treasure that made the fortunes of the hotel's owner; Al Ghazal Bar (Map p134; ☑24680000; Hotel InterContinental Muscat, off Way 2817, Shatti Al Qurm; ☺6pm-3am), popular with Western expats; Duke's Bar (Map p134; Crowne Plaza Muscat, off Qurm Rd, Qurm), perfect for sundowners with a sunset view; and Rock Bottom Café (Rockies; Map p134; ☑24651326; www.rameehotels.com; Ramee Guestline Hotel, Way 1622, Qurm; ☺noon-3pm & 6pm-3am) with a nightly DJ.

★ Trader Vic's
COCKTAIL BAR
(Map p134; ☑24680080; www.tradervicsmuscat. com; Hotel InterContinental Muscat, off Way 2817, Shatti Al Qurm; ☺6pm-2am) When it comes to cocktails (try the Samoan Fogcutter or Honi Honi), nowhere competes with this fun and lively Polynesian-style venue. Resident expert stirrers and shakers have been making 'em how you like 'em for more than a decade. With live Latin music (except Friday) and Mongolian barbecued choice cuts, you'll probably be seduced into staying for dinner.

★ On the Rocks
LOUNGE
(☑24346765, 97983333; www.ontherocksmuscat. com; Golden Tulip Hotel Seeb Hotel, Exhibition St, Airport Heights; ☺6pm-midnight Sat-Wed, to 3am Thu, to 2am Fri) This novel lounge restaurant, with its giant psychedelic TV screen, serves a spirited cocktail and a fine-dining menu for modest prices, but it's the music that draws the crowds. Every Tuesday is steam-and-beer night, with dim sum and pulse and soul music; every Wednesday there's live music, and DJs pitch in from 8.30pm to 2am on other nights. Smart-casual dress is strictly enforced.

Café Bateel
CAFE
(☑24558839; www.bateel.com; Way 447C, Al Mouj Marina, Al Mouj; ☺8am-midnight) This stylish cafe overlooking the marina has brought a touch of class to the new esplanade that is slowly expanding around the fashionable Al Mouj complex. Having made its name from the retail of fine quality dates, Bateel is a regional favourite, offering local flavour with international flair. This branch, with its wrap-around marina-view windows, also serves light bites.

Grand Hyatt Muscat
CAFE
(Map p134; ☑24641234; Grand Hyatt Muscat, Way 3033, off Al Saruj St, Shatti Al Qurm; ☺3-8pm) If you sit sipping tea long enough in the extrav-

agent foyer of this sumptuous hotel, chances are you'll worry that the tea was laced: the statue of the *Arab on Horseback* that graces the central podium moves just slowly enough to make you suspect you've joined the flight of fancy that inspired the architects. The afternoon tea is an elegant affair.

Al Makan Cafe
COFFEE

(Map p134; ☑24662924; Al Shatti St, Shatti Al Qurm; ☉10am-2am) This branch of a popular chain of local-style coffee shops has a magnificent view of the sea and a small garden for shisha smokers, banished from the cafe's rather cavernous interior. Drop by for mixed-juice sundowners with the locals.

☆ Entertainment

Other than the Royal Opera House, Muscat is rather thin on entertainment options. A local free magazine called *Y* (available from cafes) is the best source of information on the latest events in Muscat.

★Royal Opera House Muscat
OPERA

(Map p134; ☑24403300; www.rohmuscat.org.om; Sultan Qaboos St, Shatti Al Qurm) Some of the most famous names in opera and ballet have performed within this beautiful building since its inauguration in 2011, and the quality of the productions here (the season extends from September to May) regularly wins international acclaim. There's an efficient online reservation system with ticket collection on arrival. Note: there's a strict dress code for attending a performance.

City Cinema Shatti
CINEMA

(Map p134; ☑24567668; www.citycinemaoman.net; Hayy As Saruj, Shatti Al Qurm) One of several modern cinemas in town, this complex shows the latest Hollywood releases; follow with a scoop from Ice Cream Mama (p147) and a stroll on the beach.

🛍 Shopping

Muscat has a few classy shops such as those in Opera Galleria (Map p134; www.rohmuscat.org.om/en/operagalleria; Sultan Qaboos St, Shatti Al Qurm; ☉10am-10pm Sat-Thu, from 4pm Fri) adjacent to the Royal Opera House Muscat, and some big sprawling malls including Oman Avenues Mall (p143). Mutrah Souq is the obvious destination for crafts but these are also available from the Sabco Centre (Map p134; Qurm Shopping Complex, off Sultan Qaboos St, Qurm; ☉10am-10pm Sat-Thu, from 4.30pm Fri) and the recommended, not-for-profit Omani Heritage Gallery (Map p134; ☑24696974;

Way 2817, Jawaharat Al Shatti Complex, Shatti Al Qurm; ☉10am-8pm).

★Asmaa Collectionz
ARTS & CRAFTS

(Map p134; ☑22020111; www.asmaacollectionz.com; 1st fl, Opera Galleria, Sultan Qaboos St, Shatti Al Qurm; ☉10am-10pm Sat-Thu, from 4pm Fri) Spicing up a piece of bland furniture with a display of traditional silver jewellery, the owner of the Asmaa brand realised that the table would be more useful if the jewellery was photographed and laminated onto the surface. The concept was an instant success with friends, and now the collection of finely crafted pieces is a Muscat success story.

Jawahir Oman
JEWELLERY

(Map p134; ☑24563239; Al Wilaj St, Qurm; ☉9am-1pm & 4.30-9pm Sat-Thu) Selling prized Omani silver, this shop's exclusive contemporary jewellery and gift items are handcrafted in a workshop in Muscat.

Amouage
PERFUME

(Map p134; www.amouage.com; Sabco Centre, Qurm Shopping Complex, Qurm; ☉9.30am-1pm & 4.30-9.30pm Sat-Thu, 4.30-10pm Fri) Amouage sells the most expensive (and exquisite) perfume in the world, produced from frankincense, musk and other exotic ingredients in premises. You'll find the ultimate Arabian gift here or better still, at the Visitors Centre & Factory (☑24534800; www.amouage.com; Hwy 15, Mawalih; ☉8.30am-4.30pm Sun-Thu) on Hwy 15 (the main road to Nizwa), 3km west of Burj Al Sahwa Roundabout, where they offer guided tours of the factory.

Bateel
FOOD

(Map p134; ☑24601572; www.bateel.com; Oasis by the Sea complex, Shatti Al Qurm; ☉10am-10pm) For a regional gift with a difference, the chocolate dates from Bateel are world class, presented in high-quality packaging.

ℹ Information

INTERNET ACCESS
All of the main cafes, coffee shops and hotel foyers offer free wi-fi. Even the new public transport service, Mwasalat, offers this service on city buses.

MEDICAL SERVICES
International-standard healthcare is available at the main city hospitals. Initial emergency treatment may be free, but all other healthcare is charged. English is spoken in all hospitals and clinics in Muscat.

Pharmacies rotate to provide 24-hour coverage in all regions; check the English dailies to learn which ones are on duty on a given day. Pharmacies can advise which local doctors or dentists are on duty.

Emergency cases are generally brought to **Al Nahdha Hospital** (Map p134; ☑ 24837800, 22503333; Al Nahdha St, Wattiyah; ⊙ 24hr).

TELEPHONE
Omantel and Ooredoo are the main operators. SIM cards (from OR2 with OR2 credit) are available from the arrival hall at the airport and in malls, supermarkets and corner shops.

TOURIST INFORMATION
Brochures and maps are available from the tourism counter at Muscat International Airport and in the foyers of many hotels. The **Ministry of Tourism** (Map p134; ☑ 22088000, toll free 80077799; www.omantourism.gov.om; Ministries Area, Thaqafah St, Al Khuwair; ⊙ 7.30am-1.30pm Sun-Thu) has a very informative website.

Getting There & Away

AIR
Situated 37km west of Mutrah is **Muscat International Airport** (☑ 24351234; www.muscatairport.co.om; Airport Rd, off Hwy 1, Al Azaiba). Operating from a beautiful, brand-new terminal shaped like a manta ray, the airport offers international and domestic flights. Oman Air (www.omanair.com), the national carrier, flies between Muscat and Khasab, Duqm and Salalah, and there is a service between Muscat and Salalah on Salam Air (www.salamair.com), a local low-cost airline.

BUS
Mwasalat, the national bus company, provides comfortable intercity services throughout Oman. It has three main bus stations in Muscat, all of which are interconnected: **Ruwi Bus Station** (Map p134; ☑ 24708522, 24701294;

http://mwasalat.om/en-us; Al Jaame St, Ruwi) is the main city hub for local buses, **Azaiba Bus Station** (Hwy 1, Sultan Qaboos St, Al Azaiba) is the hub for national and international routes, and **Burj Al Sahwa Bus Station** (Hwy 15, off Burj Al Sahwa Roundabout, Mawalih) is the hub for the western suburbs and Seeb. Timetables in English (with fares) are available on the website (http://mwasalat.om/en-us/Bus-routes).

CAR
Car hire can be arranged with many agencies in Muscat, including **Alwan Tour Rent-a-Car** (☑ 99833325; www.alwantour.com) and Mark Tours (p143), as well as at the usual desks in hotels and at the airport in Muscat.

Getting Around

TO/FROM THE AIRPORT
Many hotels offer complimentary shuttle services. Mwasalat taxis (red and white) run from the airport, and flagfall is OR3 (400 baisa per kilometre), with a minimum charge of OR5. Taxis await passengers outside the arrivals hall – avoid the orange-and-white taxis, which are not licensed to operate from the airport. Taxi apps are not available from the airport.

Mwasalat public buses (www.mwasalat.om) stop here for city routes (every 30 minutes, 500 baisa) and various national routes.

BUS
Muscat is served by a local bus service with modern, air-conditioned buses that depart every 15 or 30 minutes, depending on the route. Routes connect all three bus stations and cover the whole of Muscat and the suburbs, including Seeb.

Bus stops are marked with red-and-white Mwasalat logos. Buses stop outside most main tourist attractions including the Royal Opera House (Route 1), Mutrah Corniche and Mutrah Souq

MAIN INTERCITY BUS ROUTES FROM MUSCAT

Mwasalat buses connect the capital with many regional cities. The main routes leave from Azaiba Bus Station.

TO	FREQUENCY (DAILY)	ROUTE	TIME (HR)	SINGLE (OR)	RETURN (OR)
Buraimi	5	41, 53	4¾	3.5	7
Duqm	1	52	6½	5	9.5
Ibri	4	53, 54	4½	3.9	7.5
Nizwa	8	54, 62, 100, 101	3	5	9
Rustaq	2	63	1½	1.3	2.6
Salalah	3	100	12	7.5	12
Sohar	3	41	2½	3.5	7
Sur	4	36, 55	5	4	8
Dubai	3	201	5½	5.5	9

(Route 4), Sultan's Palace and National Museum (Route 4), Grand Mosque and Muscat International Airport (Route 1) and Al Mouj (Route 10). Fares cost between 200 and 500 baisa, payable to the bus driver in cash.

The Mwasalat website (http://mwasalat.om/en-us) has a helpful destination-planning feature showing the schedule, tariff and duration of journeys. A bus app is due to be released in 2019 showing all routes and bus stops.

TAXI

Mwasalat taxis are red and white and are metered. The daytime flagfall is OR1 (OR1.3 at night) and 200 baisa per kilometre. A Mwasalat taxi app can be downloaded from Google Play or the App Store but other apps, like Uber and Kareem, are not available in Oman.

Other Muscat taxis are orange and white and do not have meters. Even if you bargain you will inevitably pay two or three times the going rate for locals but this can still be less than a metered taxi – fix the rate before you get in. These are currently more abundant on Muscat's streets than metered taxis.

Landmarks (eg the HSBC in Qurm, or Burj Al Sahwa Roundabout) are more useful for navigational purposes than street addresses when travelling by public transport or taxi.

WATER TAXI

Call ahead to book a place on the **water-taxi service** (Map p134; ☑ 24749111; www.sifawy hotel.com; Marina Bandar Al Rowdha, Sidab St, Haramil; per person OR8; ☉ to Al Seifa 7.30am, 9.30am Thu & Sun, 10am Fri & Sat, to Al Mouj Fri & Sat, 7.30am) between Marina Bandar Al Rowdha and Al Seifa (Jebel Sifah). There is an additional service between Al Mouj and Al Seifa.

AROUND MUSCAT

Oman's northern coast showcases a couple of the nation's beauty spots, including a set of lagoons referred to locally as Bandar Jissah (home to attractive resorts) and Bandar Khayran (a popular anchorage for boat trips from Muscat). The coast itself assumes something of a split personality in this region: south of Muscat (around Al Seifa and Qurayat) the sea is often rough, with high waves pounding against rocky coves that hint at the high drama of the Indian Ocean, while west of Muscat, near the typical Omani town of Seeb, the waters share the more limpid characteristics of the Gulf as they flood gently across limitless stretches of shell-studded sands. All the region's attractions are accessible as day trips from Muscat.

Seeb السيب

☑ 24 / POP 237,800

If you're looking to experience a typical Omani town close to Muscat that barely sees a tourist, you can't do better than a trip to Seeb. A 20-minute drive northwest of Muscat's international airport, this thriving coastal town has much to offer: there's a watchtower, a lively shopping district (Wadi Bahayis & Souq Sts; ☉9am-1pm & 4-9pm) with colourful textiles, bridal gold and traditional Omani hat shops. There are also two corniches, either side of the harbour – the northwestern corniche is dotted with coffee shops, such as the Ciastro Café (☑24613764; Dama St; ☉8am-1am).

Despite the town's proximity to the capital, small-scale fishing continues to be a major industry here and nets being dragged to shore between two tiny boats is a time-honoured sight all along Seeb's coastline. Watch fishermen mending their nets by the light of a lantern, and it's easy to forget that Muscat is just a bus ride away.

◉ Sights

★ Old Souq   MARKET

(Dama St; ☉9am-1pm & 4-9pm) Between the main road and the sea, this traditional souq is housed under some makeshift awnings in a sandy-coloured complex of buildings just off the corniche, and is a fun place to explore. Selling camel ropes and walking sticks, piles of spices, fruits and vegetables, it's very much a locals' market, but there are a couple of shops selling bright-coloured headdresses that make good souvenirs. The wet fish market has its own building further west along the corniche.

★ Seeb Corniche   WATERFRONT

(Dama St) This 2km corniche, to the west of Seeb, has a landscaped area for walking, enjoying sea views, sniffing drying sardines and watching the fishermen mending nets while footballers compete for a pitch on the sand. Various ad hoc coffee shops come alive in the evenings. Swimming is possible anywhere along the beach – in discreet swimwear.

⎙ Sleeping

Al Bahjah Hotel   HOTEL $

(☑24424400; www.rameehotels.com/our-hotels/oman; off Wadi Bahayis St; s/d OR23/35; ☏) Right in the heart of town, this simple hotel has basic but spotless rooms (a tad on the dark side) within easy walking distance of the old souq

OMAN AROUND MUSCAT

and the beach. A cosy Indian restaurant here, with an alcohol licence, is a popular meeting place for Western expats.

Ramee Dream Resort
HOTEL $

(☑ 24453399; www.rameehotels.com; Dama St; s/d OR30/35; ☎ ✿) Guests can watch herons parachute into the adjacent tidal pools at this local hotel. The term 'resort' is a bit far-fetched, although there's a pool and an enjoyable sense of space around the low-key buildings. Better still, the corniche is only a five-minute walk away. Rooms are comfortable, with big bathtubs, but are windowless (though they face onto a glass corridor).

✖ Eating & Drinking

★ Al Bahjah Restaurant
SOUTH INDIAN $

(☑ 24424400; off Wadi Bahayis St; mains from OR2; ☺ 6pm-midnight; ☑) Seeb has a large expat community from India, and this is reflected in the presence of this very good Indian restaurant. It showcases dishes mostly from Kerala, in southern India, but there are also international options including chicken tikka masala all the way from Bradford, UK. The restaurant is dimly lit and atmospheric, and unusually serves alcohol.

Seeb Waves Restaurant
MIDDLE EASTERN $

(☑ 24425556; Dama St; mains OR2; ☺ 9am-2am) Near the harbour in the heart of Seeb, this is a cheap and cheerful venue for roast chicken, chopped salad and hummus.

Mirzab Restaurant
BREAKFAST $$

(Dama St; Omani breakfast under OR10; ☺ 8am-1pm & 3-11pm Sat-Thu) Occupying an attractive location at the end of the corniche and helping to keep local traditions alive, this new Omani-run restaurant specialises in breakfast. With homemade Omani bread of differing types, pies with meat and chickpeas, and an assortment of Omani sandwiches served on wooden platters, it provides a welcome opportunity to try local dishes.

ⓘ TAILORING TIP

Seeb is an excellent place to find a tailor. Bring a favourite shirt or skirt, and buy some material in a textile shop here. The cloth merchant will advise you which tailor to visit to make a replica (in half a day for under OR20). If you have a special event on, a dinner jacket can be made for a bargain OR75.

🛍 Shopping

Wadi Alahlam Trading
GIFTS & SOUVENIRS

(Wadi Bahayis St; ☺ 10am-1pm & 5-10pm Sat-Thu, 2-10pm Fri) In the town centre, this tiny shop has a small selection of silver souvenirs and camel sticks. It also has some pieces of old Bedouin jewellery that are becoming hard to find.

ⓘ Getting There & Away

Mwasalat city bus 10 runs from Muscat's Burj Al Sahwa to the bus stop near Seeb Souq every 30 minutes from 6am to 8pm Monday to Thursday, and to 9pm on Friday and Saturday. A taxi from Muscat International Airport takes 20 minutes along Sultan Qaboos Hwy (28km, OR14).

Bandar Jissah
بندر الجصة

☑ 24 / POP 3000

Bandar Jissah is the name given to the promontory that juts out sharply into the sea beyond Muscat's Al Bustan. This mountainous rump of russet-coloured rock is corrugated at the edges, creating picturesque bays and lagoons. Out to sea, layers of weathered sandstone, eroded by rough waters, have been fashioned into odd shapes such as cliffs with scooped-out channels near their bases and a sea arch that local fishermen delight in charging through at high speed. Small fishing villages have occupied the bays here for centuries, but they now share the striking landscape with the prestigious Shangri-La and Muscat Hills resorts and water sports complexes. A road, cut spectacularly through the mountains, links Bandar Jissah with Yiti and Bandar Khayran. The whole area offers a relaxed holiday experience, a weekend retreat from Muscat or a day's outing from the city.

◉ Sights

★ Bandar Khayran
MARINE RESERVE

(via 94 St) Beyond Mutrah, the headland close to Muscat shatters into a series of *khors* and *bandars* (natural harbours), the most extensive of which is Bandar Khayran. It's possible to reach the *bandar* from the Yiti–Jebel Seifa road, but the mangrove-fringed lagoon is more usually visited by boat from Bandar Jissah or Bandar Al Rowdha. It's a popular spot for snorkelling, and at sunset the sandstone and its reflection in the water seemingly vibrate with colour. Three-hour guided kayaking trips (OR25) through the bioluminescent plankton are offered here at sunset through Husaak Adventures (p142) or you can hire your own kayak for OR15.

Yiti
BAY

Yiti boasts a beautiful, sandy beach surrounded by craggy mountain scenery that makes an attractive spot for a swim or picnic. The beach is at the end of a large, muddy inlet that is regularly picked over by wading waterbirds. If the tide is low, you can wade to a sandbar and look left for a great view of Bandar Jissah's famous sea arch.

Sea Arch
NATURAL FEATURE

Created by rough seas working against the sandstone, this sea arch at the end of the Bandar Jissah headland is a famous landmark of this coast. Fishermen in speedboats from Qantab village make it a point to thrill their passengers by heading at great speed for its narrow aperture (OR10); at high tide, it's just large enough to allow a boat to pass between jagged coral and low roof, but it's not unknown for skippers to misjudge the depth!

Wadi Mayh
NATURAL FEATURE

For a taste of a typical Omani wadi within an afternoon's drive of Muscat, look no further than Wadi Mayh. With towering limestone cliffs forming a canyon, sand-coloured villages, back-garden date plantations, straying goats and feral donkeys – not to mention a compulsory watchtower or two – Wadi Mayh is also a geological wonder. Look out for a pair of stout *aflaj* (irrigation channels) that follow the course of the wadi, carrying water from one village plantation to the next.

Bandar Jissah Viewpoint
VIEWPOINT

(Map p134) This viewpoint (yet to be properly developed) on the road between Al Bustan and Bandar Jissah offers a fine panoramic vista of the chocolate-coloured mountains that distinguish the area. Comprised of ophiolite, these low peaks present a jagged edge to the sea and contrast with the grey limestone of the Hajar Mountains further inland. Directly opposite, a paved track leads to a cycling trail offering even better views.

Activities

Muscat Hills Dive Centre
WATER SPORTS

(24853000; dive@muscathillsresort.com; half-/full-day snorkelling trips incl sofa trips OR30/60; 8am-5pm) In addition to snorkelling and diving trips to Bandar Khayran, PADI courses are available from this competent dive centre. A range of water sports are also on

offer including boat charters; banana-boat, doughnut, sunset and sofa trips (30 minutes, OR10 to OR30); kayaking and stand-up paddleboarding (from OR20); water-/jet-skiing and knee/wakeboarding (from OR30).

Sleeping & Eating

★ Shangri-La Barr Al Jissah Resort & Spa
RESORT $$$

(24776666; www.shangri-la.com; off Al Jissah St; Al Waha/Al Bandar/Al Husn r excl breakfast from OR105/130/165; P@⊛≋) This resort complex comprises three kasbah-style hotels set around a beautiful shared beach and landscaped gardens. Al Waha Hotel is easygoing, family accommodation, accessed via a tunnel through the cliff; Al Bandar Hotel is the more business-oriented of the three hotels; while the sophisticated six-star Al Husn Hotel is perched on the headland with a private beach and complimentary afternoon tea.

Meandering between the hotels, a lazy river offers a fun way of getting from one watering hole to another. The richly carpeted foyers, marble corridors and designer bedrooms and bathrooms in all three hotels make choosing one over the other a matter of whim. The resort includes some of the country's top restaurants: the **Bait Al Bahr** (seafood), **Samba** (international buffet) and **Shahrazad** (Moroccan), and there's a range of low-key water sports on offer.

Al Husn Hotel offers some interesting luxury tours, including a private yachting trip to Bandar Khayran (9am to 3pm Mondays) and an off-road drive through Wadi Arbeieen (p157; 9am to 2pm Thursday).

Muscat Hills Resort
RESORT $$$

(24853000; www.muscathills.com; off Al Jissah St; cabins OR146; P≋) This attractively landscaped resort, tucked into a shallow sandy lagoon, offers rustic huts with private open-air showers and sea-view porches. You can enjoy the extensive beach, chiselled-out under-cliffs, pool and trendy beach-bar facilities as a non-guest for a day rate of OR10 for adults and OR5 for children (including towels and sunbeds) and stay on for a sundowner.

★ Beach Restaurant
SEAFOOD $$

(24853000; www.muscathills.com; Muscat Hills Resort, off Al Jissah St; mains from OR8; 7-11am, noon-5pm & 7-10pm Sun-Thu, 7am-11pm Fri & Sat) This elegant outdoor restaurant, designed in shades of white with wood decking and sepia photographs, is a perfect venue for lunch. Oysters and lobster compete with

AHMED AL-SHUKAILI/GETTY IMAGES ©

1. Grand Mosque, Muscat
A gift from Sultan Qaboos to mark the 30th year of his reign, the quietly imposing Grand Mosque (p140) has a breathtakingly beautiful main hall.

2. Ayn Athum Waterfall
In a magical spot, regardless of the season, the Ayn Athum Waterfall (p214) only occurs after heavy rains.

3. Beehive tombs
Little is known about the 'beehive tombs' of Bat (p190) but archeologists believe they were built to protect the remains of up to 200 people.

4. Omani culture
Omani girls in traditional dress celebrate at a cultural festival in Muscat.

other local seafood for pride of place on the menu. On the last Friday of each month the restaurant hosts 'Beats by the Beach', with a DJ (2pm to midnight).

❶ Getting There & Away

There's a complimentary shuttle bus from the Shangri-La to shopping areas in Muscat and a shuttle service (45 minutes) to and from Muscat International Airport. It's a 15-minute drive by car to Bandar Jissah from Mutrah, and taxis are willing to make the journey for around OR10. There's no public transport serving this area.

Jebel Seifa   جبل السيفة

In an isolated part of the Hajar Mountains, looming Jebel Seifa towers over a rocky plain that frays into the sea in a series of tiny bays. Each of these are dusted with yellow sand and scattered with rocky pavements. In fact, all the beaches here are a rock hound's dream, with pebbles of yellow ochre, burnt sienna and olive green begging to be picked up. For those interested in bugs, the giant skipper butterfly frequents the surrounding wadis in spring and the whole area bristles with tiny wildflowers after rain.

Visitors, however, don't come for the rocks, the bugs, or the little village bearing the same name (Al Seifa): they come for the resort and residential complex at the water's edge. Arranged around a marina, the elaborately designed **Sifawy Boutique Hotel** (☏ 24749111; www.sifawyhotel.com; r OR94, incl half-board OR140; 🅿🛜🏊) offers a retreat from Muscat with a growing number of activities to entice a longer stay. A day pass is available for nonguests (weekdays/weekends OR5/10).

Occupying a breezy spot on the edge of the complex, independent of the neighbouring hotel, is the stylish **Bank Beach Club** (☏ 97368425; www.jebelsifah.com/dining/the-bank; ⏰9am-11pm) **FREE**. There's a palm-shaded infinity pool here that pulses with colour at night – much like the cuttlefish that lurk in the adjacent sea. Admission is free, but use of the pool costs OR6.5, and the minimum spend per person is OR10. The club has a recommended restaurant which offers, in addition to poolside dining, a romantic dinner on the beach (OR50 for three courses, including a bottle of wine and water).

❶ Getting There & Away

The village of Al Seifa is clearly signposted off the Bandar Jissah–Yiti road (St 94); it's only about 25km from Yiti, but it takes a good 40 minutes to drive because of the winding road and some steep descents. You will need 10 minutes more and preferably a 4WD to find your own beach beyond Al Seifa along unpaved tracks. There is no public transport, but a taxi to or from Bandar Jissah costs OR8, OR11 from Mutrah (45km), and OR31 from Muscat International Airport (73km). **Sinbad Water Taxi** (☏94414438; to Marina Bandar Al Rowdha OR4, to Al Mouj Marina OR8; ⏰departures from Seifa at 8.30am & 4pm Thu & Sun, 3pm Fri & Sat) runs a service to and from Sifawy Boutique Hotel – phone for a current schedule.

Qurayat   قريات

📍 24 / POP 21,500

Famous for exporting horses that were reared on the surrounding desert plains, the attractive coastal town of Qurayat was once an important port, although it's difficult to imagine from the sleepy corniche today. Sacked by the Portuguese in the 16th century (and more recently devastated by tropical cyclone Gonu in 2007), the town has never regained its status. Despite sinking into relative oblivion, Qurayat still has one claim to fame: its basket-making. The porous baskets, made from the local mangrove that grows in abundance in the town's large *khor*, are used for keeping bait fresh aboard the small fishing boats that pack the harbour.

Presided over by a 19th-century **watchtower**, the boats make an attractive sight moored along the corniche. There are other points of interest dotted around the area, including a **fort** (Al Hesn St; 500 baisa; ⏰8.30am-2.30pm) in the centre of town, a landscaped **park** (⏰9am-11pm Sun-Thu, to midnight Fri & Sat) with water features and a beautiful stretch of empty sandy beach – follow the signs for misnamed **Al Khobaar Lake Resort**.

❶ Getting There & Away

Mwasalat buses run from Muscat's Azaiba Bus Station (OR3) daily at 1.50pm, returning at 8.30am. The journey (110km, two hours 40 minutes) is via Wadi Aday and continues on to Tiwi (160km, three hours 50 minutes) and Sur on the coastal Hwy 17. Taxis from Muscat cost OR22.

The journey from the Wadi Aday roundabout in Muscat is through the colourfully striated Eastern Hajar foothills on a fine multilane highway.

Mazara   مزارع

📍 24 / POP 1000

Positioned halfway along Wadi Dayqah, once protected by a now ruined **fort** (⏰24hr) and surrounded by copper-toned mountains, the village of Mazara is highly picturesque. Much of the village lies half-buried under densely packed date palms, but it emerges blinking into the bright sunlight at either end of the plantation.

Most people come to the area to visit Oman's largest **dam** (☉8am-10pm) FREE. A road winds up to the reservoir, the edges of which have been pleasantly landscaped into a park with a decent **coffeeshop** (snacks from 500 baisa; ☉8am-8pm). The panoramic view of the mountains reflected in the plate-glass-like water is a rare sight in the desert, and this is the largest stretch of fresh water in the country.

In and around Mazara, a few ad hoc adventures beckon, including walking downstream (away from the dam) through the narrowing shoulders of Wadi Dayqah as it slithers towards the sea. Or there are off-road routes that lead past desert mushrooms and other **wind-eroded features** to the mountain villages above **Wadi Arbeieen**.

A combination of spring and rain water collects in deep pools along the length of this wadi. It's accessible (from Hwy 17) by 4WD along the wadi bottom from Dibab, though after prolonged rains may only be navigable for a few kilometres. Any outing in this area, however, is rewarding for the beautiful mountain landscape, turquoise pools and birdlife that congregates in the waterside reeds and bushes. Hiking trips here can be organised through Husaak Adventures (p142).

ⓘ Getting There & Away

Brown signs indicate 'Wadi Dayqah Dam' 19km off Hwy 17 near Qurayat. To reach the crumbling fort in Mazara, follow the road through the village from the dam and cross the wadi. There is no public transport to this inland area, but taxis in Muscat are often willing to make the 110km journey for around OR50, with waiting time.

EASTERN COAST

This easternmost region of the Arabian Peninsula holds some of Oman's main attractions, including beautiful beaches, spectacular wadis, turtle-nesting sites and the strawberry-blonde Sharqiya sand dunes. Sharqiya has a distinct culture built on an entrepreneurial, seafaring past. Indeed Sur, the main town in the region (and home to Oman's modern gas industry), was once a major collection point for the export of Arabian horses.

HOUSE OF THE DEMON

The blue-green, brackish water at the bottom of the peculiar 40m-by-20m limestone hole at pleasant **Sinkhole Park** (Hawiyat Najm Park; off Coastal Hwy 17, Bimmah; ☉8am-8pm) invites a swim and a snorkel. The intrepid can inch round the ledges that surround the pool and dive into the deep unknown. The sinkhole, the depth of which is still uncertain, is known locally as Bayt Al Afreet (House of the Demon). If the demon eludes you, look out for the equally elusive blind cavefish instead..

The route along the coast road to Sur ideally forms the first day of a two- or three-day circular tour, returning to Muscat via Sharqiya Sands and Ibra. Alternatively, it makes the first leg of an epic camping trip along the coast to Masirah: the coastal road cuts across the Sharqiya Sands in a remarkable feat of modern engineering and ambles on through fishing communities, the growing port of Duqm and vast tracts of wild Dhofari (southern Oman) desert all the way to Salalah.

Tiwi طيوي

🚗 25 / POP 1950

The little village of Tiwi is an unassuming fishing community that looks much like any other in Oman: a large flotilla of fibreglass boats are protected by a new harbour wall and there's a sleepy main street designed largely as a conduit for goats and donkeys. There's only one hotel, outside of town, and no public transport to Muscat or Sur. Don't be fooled, however, by its appearance: being flanked by two of Oman's beauty spots, Wadi Shab and Wadi Tiwi, it has found itself very much on the tourist map, and is transformed into a busy thoroughfare at weekends.

◉ Sights

Wadi Shab　　　　　　　　NATURAL FEATURE

Aptly named in Arabic as the 'Gorge Between Cliffs', Wadi Shab is one of the most lovely destinations in Oman, despite Hwy 17 slung across the entrance. The wadi rewards even the most reluctant walker with turquoise pools, a busy *falaj* (irrigation channel), waterfalls and terraced plantations; kingfishers add glorious splashes of colour and year-round trusses of pink oleander

OMAN TIWI

bloom by the water's edge. A five-minute boat ride (OR1 return) is required to cross the mouth of the wadi to the trail head.

Wadi Tiwi   NATURAL FEATURE

With its string of emerald pools and thick plantations, Wadi Tiwi almost rivals its neighbour, Wadi Shab, in beauty, especially in spring when the allotments either side of the wadi turn a vivid green. It's known as the 'Wadi of Nine Villages', and there's a sealed road along the wadi bottom and up through the villages. Although it's accessible by car, villagers prefer visitors to approach the upper villages on foot as it's easy to get large vehicles stuck between plantation walls.

Bibi Miriam's Tomb   TOMB

(off Hwy 17, Qalhat) The ruined tomb of Bibi Miriam is about all that remains of the 2nd-century settlement of Qalhat, one of the most ancient sites in Oman. There's not much left to see, but if you pay the site a visit, you'll be in excellent company: both Marco Polo in the 13th century and Ibn Battuta in the 14th century stopped here on their travels. A site restoration began in 2014 and is ongoing. Until it's complete, you can spot the tomb from the highway.

If you make it over to the outlying grounds that extend to the sea, you'll have the satisfaction of knowing that your journey to Qalhat was a tad more adventurous than that of your travelling forebears. In Marco Polo's day, Qalhat was a busy port frequented by merchant ships from India and a hub for the trade in horses from the interior. Today only the tomb, water cistern and remnants of city walls are visible, and in place of barques and dhows, all that the sea brings to the shore are sharks, sardines and rays. If you camp nearby, you'll find the water is often spangled at night with green phosphorus.

 Activities

Two-Wadi Hike   HIKING

(Rte E35) For the intrepid hiker, a strenuous but scenic two-day, 28km hike begins at Sooee, the last of the nine settlements in Wadi Tiwi. The route over the mountain to Wadi Bani Khalid has become a popular camping excursion with walking groups, but a guide is essential. Brown signs indicate the trail head from the village of Tiwi.

DON'T MISS

WADI SHAB وادي شاب

The celebrated four-hour, moderately challenging hike through Wadi Shab is more of a wade than a walk at times, depending on the amount of rain received high up in the Eastern Hajar Mountains. It begins with a boat ride across the deep water at the wadi's entrance, organised by enterprising locals, and continues through plantations, criss-crossing the wadi several times before reaching a small pumping station. Be prepared to wade up to your knees in places and beware of slipping on algae-covered rocks. After heavy rains, it may be impassable; at any time, bring dry clothes and a bag for your camera.

The path has been concreted for part of the way and passes close to several villages that are hidden in the plantations. For much of the way, the path follows an impressive *falaj* (traditional irrigation system) complete with underground sections and laced with ferns. The wadi eventually broadens into an area of large boulders and wild fig trees, with many pools of deep water. While swimming in the lower pools is forbidden as these are a source of drinking water, there is an opportunity for discreet swimming (but no skinny dipping!) here. A large pool, a two-hour walk from the car park, offers a bit of underwater adventure: look for a ladder into the water from which you can duck through a small channel into a partially submerged cave.

It's possible to walk beyond the pools to other small villages clustered along the wadi floor, but the paths are not so well trodden and they follow goat tracks over the wadi cliffs. Walking shoes and plenty of drinking water are essential. The wadi becomes drier the higher you climb into the mountains.

Guided hikes though the wadi (OR25 per person) can be arranged from Wadi Shab Resort, with discounts offered for groups. Sadly, this beauty spot has been marred in places by thoughtless visitors leaving their rubbish after picnics. There are no facilities within the wadi, and hikers are urged to use the toilets at the wadi entrance (7am to 7pm) and take all litter home. Lighting a barbecue and camping are not permitted in the wadi.

🛏 Sleeping & Eating

Tiwi Beach   CAMPGROUND **$**
(White Beach; off Hwy 17; free camping) Given the moniker 'White Beach' because of its fine, powdery sand, this is the most popular beach for wild camping along this part of the coast. There are no facilities, but the wide stretch of beach is accessed by a good track, and there are plenty of suitable places to pitch a tent. Basic supplies can be found in Tiwi.

★ Wadi Shab Resort   HOTEL **$$**
(☎24489853; www.samaresorts.com; standard/deluxe/ste OR68/86/135; 🅿🛜🏊) The small but modern and stylish rooms of this low-key hotel are arranged in two tiers down a hillside, with views of the sea from each veranda. Deluxe rooms represent the best value and are arranged around the pool. A gate gives access to the beach at the bottom of the incline.

Anwaar Tiwi Restaurant   MIDDLE EASTERN **$**
(Main St; dishes from 400 baisa; ⊙6am-1am) On the village's main street at a sharp bend in the road, this small local-style restaurant offers Middle Eastern staples, including mezze and some Indian biryani and dal dishes. Its terrace sits above the road, making it a good place to drink a fresh mango or lemon-and-mint juice and watch the goats jostle by.

ℹ Getting There & Away

Mwasalat buses (OR3) run from Muscat's Azaiba Bus Station to Tiwi along the coastal highway at 1.50pm, returning from Tiwi to Muscat at 7.40am (170km, 3½ hours). Passengers for Tiwi alight at the Sur-bound bus stop on the western side of Hwy 17, not in town. Muscat-bound buses from Sur arrive at the bus stop on the eastern side of the highway. Taxis from Muscat via the coastal highway cost OR34.

Tiwi and the two flanking wadis make an easy day trip from Sur; the Muscat–Sur Hwy (Hwy 17) passes the very doorstep of the town, unfortunately marring the entrance to both wadis somewhat because of the giant pylons where the road rests. You might be able to persuade a taxi driver from Sur to take you to Tiwi (OR45, 60km, 40 minutes) and wait for an hour or so while you explore either Wadi Shab or Wadi Tiwi. Alternatively, hotels in Sur can arrange a tour from OR25 per person.

Sur   صور

☎25 / POP 71,150
Once famous for dhow-building, Sur's boatyards are still functioning and open to visitors. Given this, plus a fine corniche, two

forts, souqs and excellent beaches nearby, Sur is generally included on tours of Oman. It serves as a convenient base for beauty spots around Tiwi and the turtle reserve at Ras Al Jinz.

Ask what people associate with Sur today, however, and there's a high chance the giant gas plant on the edge of town will be mentioned. The large industrial fringe that creeps along the undercliff of the Eastern Hajar Mountains has been something of a blight to a small section of coast, but it has also brought wealth to the town, bringing in long-stay expats who spend money in the town's growing number of shops. For visitors, the town's growth has led to a choice of hotels from which to explore Sur's many attractions.

◉ Sights

Fatah Al Khair   SHIP
(Corniche; ⊙daylight hrs) **FREE** Built in Sur 70 years ago and brought back from its retirement in Yemen, this historic wooden fishing vessel has been meticulously restored and now sits permanently on dry land as part of an open-air museum dedicated to Sur's shipbuilding lineage. It's not possible to climb aboard *Fatah Al Khair*, but it's interesting getting up close to the flanks of the dhow: traditionally, these vessels were made by hand without nails and using handwoven ropes to shore up joins.

Corniche & Dhow Yards   WATERFRONT
The corniche affords a picturesque view across to the village of Ayjah. Dhows used to be led to safety by Ayjah's three watchtowers, which mark the route into the lagoon. It is still possible to see the boats being made by hand alongside this passage. To reach the dhow yards, follow the corniche in a crescent past the suspension bridge to the great lagoon. The road circles back eventually to the New Souq, passing by restored dhow Fatah Al Khair.

Sur

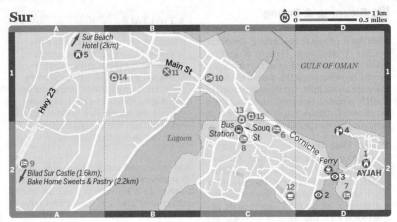

Sur

◉ Sights

🛏 Sleeping

⊗ Eating

◉ Drinking & Nightlife

🛍 Shopping

Sunaysilah Castle   CASTLE
(Hwy 23; 500 baisa; ⊙7.30am-6pm Sun-Thu)
Crowning a rocky eminence in the centre of
town, this 300-year-old castle is built on a
classic square plan with four round watchtowers. It was the most important part of
the defensive system of Sur, a town that
was greatly fortified to protect its illustrious
overseas trade. A few traditional artefacts,
such as pottery, Quran stands and carpets,
help bring some of the rooms to life. You
can't miss the castle, as its presence looms
over the town centre.

Bilad Sur Castle   CASTLE
(off Hwy 23) Built to defend the town against
marauding tribes from the interior, 200-year-
old Bilad Sur Castle boasts unusually shaped
towers. It has been closed for an extended
period for restoration, but you can wander
around the outside. To reach the castle, turn
left off Hwy 23 (Main St) at an elaborately

kitsch residence, 1.3km from the clocktower
roundabout at the Muscat end of town.

🛏 Sleeping

★**Sur Hotel**   HOTEL **$**
(☏25540090; www.surhotel.net; off Souq St; s/d/
tr/q OR13/15/16/18; 🖥) In the middle of the
souq, this well-managed, good-value budget
hotel has neat and comfortable rooms. Some
rooms are a bit noisy and others dark, but
visitors rate this hotel highly not for its
rooms, but for the friendly Omani welcome
and the help with onward journeys. The hotel is also convenient for the bus stop, cinema and corniche.

Turtle-watching trips can be arranged
through the hotel (OR25 per car) as can trips
to Wadi Shab (OR25), Wadi Tiwi (OR60)
or Wadi Bani Khalid (price negotiable). A
booking and transport service to Wadi Bani
Khalid and the Sharqiya Sands is available

(OR45, or OR75 for both), and camels can be arranged for OR10 an hour per camel.

Al Afiah Corniche Hotel Apartment HOTEL $
(☑25561666, 94444515; Corniche; s/d OR20/25) Don't get excited by the sparkling pillars holding up the porch: the glamour doesn't extend to the plain and cavernous interior. That said, rooms are decent enough, most with private bathroom and some with a kitchen. They all sport tiled floors and wooden furniture.

⭐**Zaki Hotel Apartments** APARTMENT $$
(☑25545924; www.zakihotelapartments.com; Hwy 23; s/d OR38/55; ℗ @ ☎) Excellent value for money, this new hotel in the middle of town has been boldly designed, with primary-coloured seating, abstract artwork and giant vases decorating the foyer. The rooms are huge and boast three TVs (presumably to save family squabbles over viewing choice), and there's a kitchen for self-catering. There's also an adjoining coffee shop and a popular restaurant.

⭐**Sur Beach Holiday** HOTEL $$
(☑25530300; www.holidayhotels.com; Beach Rd; s/d OR53/65; ℗ ☎ ▣) This somewhat dated old favourite benefits from its location on the beach and its excellent staff. All rooms have balconies overlooking the sea, from which to watch for phosphorescent waves at night. Some self-catering chalets come with kitchens. Reasonable international fare is served in the restaurant, and there are two bars, one of which sees its fair share of male nightlife.

'Veg' (OR4.5) and 'non-veg' (OR6.5) picnic boxes save the bother of self-catering. Every Friday there's a poolside barbecue (OR7). An ATM is in the foyer.

Sur Plaza Hotel HOTEL $$
(☑25543777; www.omanhotels.com; off Hwy 23; s/d/ste OR35/45/90; ℗ ☎ ▣) This hotel, with comfortable rooms and giant oyster-shaped sinks in bathrooms, is popular with tour groups despite being inland. The hotel's Oysters Restaurant (p162) is licensed to serve alcohol, which can be taken poolside to make an evening of it. Turtle-watching trips can be arranged (OR20 per person); these depart at 7.30pm. Ask reception for a list of other tours.

✖️ **Eating**

⭐**Mersal Café & Lounge** BREAKFAST $
(☑25536665; Hwy 23, City Centre Sur; breakfast from OR2; ⊙10am-midnight) This stylish new cafe occupying a bright, multi-windowed corner of City Centre Sur is a great place to sample Middle Eastern–style breakfasts. With soft cheeses, *fuul medamas* (a bean dish), fresh falafel and *karak* (sweetened black tea boiled with milk and spices), it sets you up well for a long day's travel.

Bake Home Sweets & Pastry BAKERY $
(Hwy 23, Global Village, opp Clock Tower; tray of local home bakes OR2; ⊙8am-11pm) It takes about five minutes to walk the length of the counter in this bakery: not because it's particularly large, but just because of the complex array of assorted local sweetmeats on display. If you're undecided about what to try, opt for a tray of homebakes, made of date purée, semolina and condensed milk – they're perfect for a picnic.

Sur Sea Restaurant SEAFOOD $
(☑92126096; mains OR1.5; ⊙7.30am-2am) On the ground floor of the Sur Hotel (the entrance faces the other side of the block), this is a popular and lively local restaurant. It serves tasty bean dishes and biryanis for under OR2, plus delicious fresh juices. Its main staples, however, are delicious fish dishes, including a fiery fish curry. There's a shaded pavement terrace for cooler months.

Zahrat Bilad Al Sham Restaurant KEBAB $
(Hwy 23; mains OR4; ⊙9am-2.30am) Right beside the main road, this popular semi-open-air venue offers sizzling Turkish kebabs

SUR'S BOAT-BUILDING HERITAGE

Watching the boat builders in Sur's dhow yards hand-planing planks of wood, it's easy to recognise a skill inherited from master craftsmen. Sur has long been famed for its boat-building industry, and even in the 19th century – when the Portuguese invasion and the division of Oman into two separate sultanates had delivered a heavy blow to the port town's trading capability – Sur still boasted an ocean-going fleet of 100 or more vessels. Demand for ocean-going boats declined once the British India Steam Navigation Company became pre-eminent in the Gulf and the town's fortunes declined accordingly. Sur is currently enjoying a resurgence, however, thanks to the ever-growing liquid-gas plant and a fertiliser factory, which have generated many jobs.

marinated in the chef's best spices, reputedly of Ottoman origin, and triple-decker fruit juices (from 800 baisa). It attracts a crowd later in the evening.

Zaki Restaurant
OMANI **$**

(off Hwy 23; mains around OR3; ⊘noon-1am; P🚭🛜)
Located next to the Oman Oil petrol station, this popular local chain serves Omani, Indian and Chinese cuisine, including a signature fried-chicken dish (OR3). Seating is in a bright, pleasantly designed restaurant with lots of windows and upholstered seats. It's buzzing with families later in the evening.

Oysters Restaurant
INTERNATIONAL **$$**

(✒99351467; www.omanhotels.com; off Hwy 23, Sur Plaza Hotel; mains from OR5; ⊘6-11.30am, noon-3pm & 6-11pm; P🛜) One of the few venues in Sur where you can dine with a glass of wine, Oysters is a sociable gathering point. The Friday lunch buffet (OR6) includes fresh fish dishes (and free use of the pool) and is a popular event for expats. Tables spill outside the restaurant around the pool area, which doubles as an ad hoc bar.

🍷 Drinking & Nightlife

Zaki Café
COFFEE

(✒79011186; ⊘24hr) This modern coffeeshop, in front of the trendsetting Zaki Hotel Apartments, is attractively decked out with homely tables and chairs and specialises in iced cappuccinos, among a choice of a dozen coffee blends. Someone at the cafe must like football, as giant European club emblems are emblazoned across the wall at the entrance. Delicious home-made biscuits cater for those with a sweet tooth.

Bab Al Hara
CAFE

(Corniche; ⊘1pm-2am) This simple open-air coffeeshop offers the typical local brand of nightlife: plastic seats, a tree or awning of some description, *chai libton* (a disposable cup of teabag black tea), a *mushkak* (kebab) or shawarma, freshly made mint-and-lemon juice, a TV grumbling in the background, a gurgle of scented shisha, and of course the company of friends.

🛍 Shopping

Ladies' Souq
MARKET

(Main St; ⊘10am-noon & 5-10pm) With its traditional perfume shops, gold souq and Arab clothing stores, the Ladies' Souq is a fascinating part of town to wander around. There are many textile shops here, some selling braided ankle parts, for traditional women's trousers, which make a good souvenir.

Al Haramain Perfumes
PERFUME

(Souq St; ⊘10am-1pm & 4.30-9pm) The elaborate bottles alone are temptation enough to enter this shop, and being daubed in exotic musk and ambergris is one of Arabia's great experiences. It's adjacent to the Ladies' Souq.

City Centre Sur
SHOPPING CENTRE

(Hwy 23; ⊘10am-10pm Sat-Wed, to midnight Thu & Fri) This attractive new mall has brought a touch of modernity to shopping in Sur. There's a Carrefour (open 9am to midnight daily) selling a more international range of foods for resupplying the cool box, and a number of attractive cafes and restaurants.

ℹ Getting There & Away

Buses leave from the bus station near the Sur Hotel off Souq St.

Mwasalat buses run from Muscat's Azaiba Bus Station (OR4) twice daily at 7.50am and 2.50pm, returning at either 6am or 2.30pm. The journey (312km, four hours and 50 minutes) is via Ibra.

Mwasalat buses also travel to Sur via Tiwi on the coastal highway (OR3, four hours and 10 minutes). These leave Muscat at 1.50pm, returning from Sur at 7am (200km).

Taxis from Muscat via the coastal highway cost OR40. Taxis from Sur cost OR20 to OR30 to Muscat International Airport. A taxi ride to Ayjah costs OR3.

From Sur, day trips can be organised from any of the hotels to Wadi Tiwi, Wadi Shab and the turtle reserve at Ras Al Jinz. Sur also makes a good halfway stopover on a round trip from Muscat via the desert camps of the Sharqiya Sands.

Speedboats leave from the ferry terminal near the suspension bridge (OR10 for a 20-minute journey around the lagoon).

ℹ Getting Around

Taxis cost 300 baisa per ride in a shared taxi anywhere around Sur.

Ayjah
العيجة

📱 25 / POP 5000

Lying on the other side of the lagoon from Sur and boasting its own **fort** (500 baisa; ⊘8.30am-2.30pm Sun-Thu) and watchtowers, the pretty, whitewashed village of Ayjah is well worth a detour from Sur, if only to enjoy the view across the lagoon. At sunset and sunrise, if you wander over to the **lighthouse**, there is a fine view of Sur and of the wooden dhows setting out to or returning from sea.

The village has the good-value **Al Ayjah Plaza Hotel** (☑25544433; www.alayjahplazahotel.com; s/d/tr/q OR25/35/50/60; ▣ @ 🔊), and a highly recommended Turkish eatery called **Sahari Restaurant** (☑25541423, 96281508; mains from OR4; ⊘8.30am-1am). With its hand-painted murals and breezy terraces overlooking the lagoon, it's a delightful place to watch dhows beaching at low tide.

❶ Getting There & Away

To reach Ayjah from Sur, you can either cross (by car or on foot) the 240m-long **Khor Al Batah Bridge** – Oman's first and only suspension bridge – or drive 10km around the lagoon. Ayjah is a gateway (with a literal gateway signifying as much) to the Coastal Highway (Hwy 17), which continues from Sur to Al Ashkharah via Ras Al Hadd and Ras Al Jinz (home to the Turtle Reserve). There's no public transport passing this way. Taxis from Sur cost OR3 – if you can find one!

Ras Al Jinz Turtle Reserve

محمية راس الجنز

Ras Al Jinz (Ras Al Junayz), the easternmost point of the Arabian Peninsula, is an important turtle-nesting site for the endangered green turtle. More than 20,000 females return annually to the beach where they hatched in order to lay eggs. Oman has an important role to play in the conservation of this endangered species and takes the responsibility seriously, with strict penalties for harming turtles or their eggs. The whole area is under government protection.

Turtles don't approach the beach during the day, so for the best chance of seeing a turtle join a **night eco-tour** (☑96550606; www.rasaljinz-turtlereserve.com; Visitors Centre; adult/child over 5 yrs OR7/1, Oman residents OR5/1, children under 5 yrs free) 🐢, from 9pm each evening, through the Turtle Reserve, bookable in advance online or by phone. The beach is a 900m, 15-minute walk from the reserve visitors centre across soft sand (cars can't proceed beyond the parking lot). Flash photography is forbidden. Groups are limited to 25 people per guide, with no more than eight guides in each session, but despite the reserve's best efforts, some groups can be off-putting. Gawping at such an intimate act as the laying of eggs, when flippers are lifted out of the way for better viewing and the frightened turtles are chased down the beach by mobile-phone-wielding individuals, may not be an experience to everyone's taste.

There's an interesting **museum** (adult/child OR2/1; ⊘9am-9pm) here charting, through video and display, the history of local interaction with turtles since ancient times. The **beach** (Ras Al Jinz Reserve; OR1), with its impressive cliffs, is accessible during the day (between 8am and 1.30pm). It's often possible to spot turtles between the waves, waiting for nightfall before approaching the beach.

Food and accommodation is available at the **Reserve guesthouse** (☑96550606; www.rasaljinz-turtlereserve.com; r incl breakfast OR95,

---

BEST TIME TO SPOT TURTLES

Turtle-watching aficionados time their visit to Ras Al Jinz to witness maximum traffic on the beach. This is what they recommend:

Go in July This is the peak laying season for the green turtle, when more than 100 females come ashore each night.

Go between September and November Although at least one turtle arrives on the beach every night of the year, this is the best time to witness both laying and hatching at Ras Al Jinz.

Go at new moon Full-moon nights make it easier to walk and to witness the spectacle, although turtles prefer dark nights so as not to attract the unwanted attention of predators, which often dig up the eggs as soon as they are laid.

Go at dawn There is a tour at 5am, perfect for seeing the last of the latecomers. At this time of day, there are fewer visitors, and you can set your own limits of discretion around the few remaining laying turtles.

Go regardless If the turtles have already departed, then don't be too disappointed: at dawn the sandstone cliffs are burnished rose-red by the rising sun, and the turtle tracks of the previous night's heavy traffic inscribe the sand like ancient calligraphy – a rare sight that few people get to enjoy.

TURTLE-WATCHING ETIQUETTE

Watching turtle labour and delivery on Oman's sandy beaches can be an awe-inspiring sight. Serene and patient, the female turtles that quietly lumber up the beach are sure to win the hearts of anyone lucky enough to see the spectacle of egg-laying. Witnessing these gentle giants slip back into the darkness of the returning tide is one those unforgettable wildlife experiences – at least, that is, if the turtles are permitted to make their exit *after* rather than *before* the job is done, and without the disheartening spectacle of bullish tourists trying to take a photograph at any cost.

Turtles are no land-lovers, and they are very easily dissuaded from making the journey up the beach. In fact, any disturbance during the turtle's approach to the shore will most probably result in a U-turn, and it may be days before the turtle plucks up the courage to try again. Once the digging of pits is over and the laying has begun, however, the process cannot be interrupted.

The following actions should be avoided:

➡ touching or approaching a moving turtle

➡ standing in front of a nesting turtle

➡ riding or sitting on a turtle (it happens)

➡ lighting a fire or using a torch near a turtle beach

➡ taking photographs with a flash or a mobile phone (cameras are not permitted on the beach at Ras Al Jinz)

➡ leaving garbage – turtles often mistake plastic bags for jellyfish, a favourite food

2-/4-person luxury tent OR120/140; P @ 🗢). The room rate includes the cost of an evening and dawn guided tour of the turtle beach (9pm and 5am respectively). The reserve also offers 10 luxury, air-conditioned **tents** with en suite bathrooms.

❶ Getting There & Away

Ras Al Jinz can be visited as an evening or dawn trip from Sur, organised through Sur Hotel (p160) and Sur Plaza Hotel (p161). The journey time is 40 minutes each way. There is no public transport.

If you have your own vehicle, follow the signs to Ayjah and Ras Al Hadd. Ras Al Jinz can also be reached from the Arabian Sea Motel, in Asselah near Al Ashkharah (about a 45-minute drive to the south).

Ras Al Hadd
رأس الحد

🚗 25 / POP 3000

Surrounded by the mighty Indian Ocean to the east and a giant inlet, Khor Garami, to the west, the headland upon which Ras Al Hadd sits feels like an outpost of Oman – and in many ways it is. This, together with neighbouring Ras Al Jinz, is the most eastern point, not just of Oman, but of the whole Arabian Peninsula. If you're expecting a slight leaning towards the subcontinent of India, however, you'll look in vain, as the flat rocky plain that rambles into the sea here, dotted by the odd acacia, trimmed by roving camels, is quintessential Arabian desert. A derelict runway left over from WWII is about the only reminder of the world beyond. The town encompasses its own lagoon, Khor Haja, where dhows shelter during storms. The lagoon landscape and an old fort make it worth a stopover en route to or from Ras Al Jinz.

◉ Sights

Ras Al Hadd Fort FORT
(500 baisa; ⊙ 7.30am-6pm Sun-Thu) Built between 1560 and 1570, this is one of many hundreds of similar picturesque forts dotted around Oman. Although the fort is empty inside, it's easy to picture the isolation of its inhabitants, marooned on this flat coastal plain before the small settlement grew up around it. It's located near a large lagoon, which is a haven for wildlife. At night, foxes pursue hedgehogs and disgruntled herons flap by, chased off their perches by rivals.

🛏 Sleeping & Eating

Ra's Al Hadd Holiday HOTEL $
(🚗 25569111; www.holidayhotelsoman.com; r OR44; P 🗢 🐾) Offering good-value accommodation wedged between a calm lagoon full of waders and a sea bobbing with turtles queuing up to come ashore after dark, this simple hotel is signposted from the castle in Ras Al Hadd. Rooms are comfortable, if

a bit dated, and wi-fi is only available in the lobby. The hotel is set back some distance from the sea. Two-hour fishing-boat trips can be arranged for OR25 per boat for up to five people, and there are jet skis (OR25) that can seat two people.

Ras Al Hadd Guesthouse HOTEL $
(☑ 25530440; www.gghotels.com; s/d OR21/25; P ⓧ) Housed in a multi-storey building, this budget hotel is marooned in the *bondu* (waste ground), alongside the old WWII runway. The communal area is decked out with bucolic murals of temperate climes that contrast wildly with the desert outside. Rooms (some smell of fish so ask to see a few first) are comfortable enough for the bargain price. There's no lift.

★ **Turtle Beach Resort** CAMPGROUND $$
(☑ 25544900; www.tbroman.com; s/d incl half-board OR50/65; P ⓢ) Sitting like a full stop at the end of the Ras Al Hadd peninsula, this resort commands the high ground at the point where Khor Hajar pours into the open sea and gives access to miles of sandy beach. Rooms are in low-rise, air-conditioned concrete huts, made rustic with *barasti* (palm-frond) cladding and each with a small covered porch. The camp, which unusually has a bar, is signposted left immediately after entering Ras Al Hadd. A one-hour dolphin-watching trip in a fibreglass boat costs OR20 per boat (up to five people).

★ **Dolphin Bar &**
Restaurant INTERNATIONAL $$
(☑ 25544900; Turtle Beach Resort; meals from OR8; ⊙ noon-3pm & 6pm-midnight Sat-Thu, 2pm-midnight Fri; ⓢ) This sea-salted restaurant, with its open-air terrace overlooking the sea, has a licence to serve alcohol, something of a rarity in Oman's hinterland. A range of Middle Eastern, Indian and international dishes are prepared by competent chefs and served with a smile by the helpful Indian waiters.

🛍 **Shopping**

Al Fouz Hypermarket SPORTS & OUTDOORS
(Main St; ⊙ 8am-10pm) Camping equipment and food supplies are available from this supermarket. Don't expect too much from the name 'hypermarket', however: it's a small shop with a little of all sorts.

ℹ **Getting There & Away**

To reach Ras Al Hadd from Sur, follow the signs for Ras Al Jinz after the village of Ayjah but veer left after Khor Garami. It is clearly signposted. There is no public transport to this area.

Al Ashkharah الأشخرة

☑ 25 / POP 10,000

Wedged between two beautiful white-sand beaches, Al Ashkharah is a lively fishing village and an important supply point for the Bedouin communities of the Sharqiya Sands. The village itself is weather-beaten and scruffy, but it's a good place to buy provisions for the onward journey. The sea south of Al Ashkharah is much rougher and more characterful than the beaches north of town, so if you choose to break your journey here you can look forward to large waves and flocks of gulls itching to join your picnic.

Wild camping is possible along the coast or you can put up at the recommended **Arabian Sea Motel** (☑ 97794244; www.arabiansea motel.com; off Ras Al Hadd-Al Ashkharah Rd, Asselah; s/d with sea view from OR30/40, per person camping OR6; P ⓢ ⓧ). This low-rise surfers' lodge, northwest of town, looks like a government school from a distance, but don't be put off: it's in a superb location at the top of the high-tide line and fresh seafood is on the menu daily (from OR4.5). Thanks to the high waves in summer, the hotel (15km north of Al Ashkharah) is often full between May to October. You can hire a surfboard (OR15 per day) and book a ticket for the night tour at Ras Al Jinz Turtle Reserve, a 45-minute drive in your own transport.

Al Ashkharah has two other places to stay: the budget **Al Ashkarah Hotel** (☑ 25566222; Hwy 35; s/d/ste OR12/15/18; P) in town, and the attractive **Al Ashkara Beach Resort** (☑ 25535666, 94082424; www.ashkhara. com; Hwy 17; r/ste from OR30/50; P ⓢ ⓧ), located 15km to the south. This small, isolated resort has been tastefully designed around the ocean views and offers indoor games, quad bikes (OR10 per hour) and horse riding (OR6 per hour). It also has its own delightful **coffeeshop** (7.30am to 11pm) with a full espresso bar – a perfect pit-stop along Coastal Hwy 17, which is a striking but desolate desert drive.

ℹ **Getting There & Away**

Al Ashkharah is located at an important junction. This is where Coastal Hwy 17 meets inland Hwy 35 from Al Kamil. Most people heading south to Masirah or Salalah from Sur are likely to pass through this town. There is no public transport.

OMAN SHANA'A

DUNES ROAD

Dubbed the Dunes Rd, Hwy 17 is almost a destination in its own right. This feat of engineering cuts a corridor through the auburn Sharqiya Sands linking Al Ashkharah with Shana'a, Hijj and Mahout. Crossing some of the most inhospitable terrain in the country, the road passes small fishing villages, outcrops of aeolite (fossilised sand) blown into extraordinary formations, and the tracks of the Bedouin, which ignore the road and continue across it as if it were a minor interruption to age-old caravan routes. The whole route is laced with beautiful beaches, perfect for wild camping.

Hijj and Mahout are the nearest towns of any size at the southern end of the route and these act as staging posts for intrepid excursions into desolate **Barr Al Hickman** (off Hwy 17), an area of coastal mud flats celebrated for bird-watching. Nearby **Filim** (off Hwy 17) showcases *barasti* (palm-leaf) houses. Only recently abandoned, these dwellings give an idea of typical traditional housing in this seldom-visited area before the days of air-conditioning.

The journey from Sur, via Ras Al Hadd, to Al Ashkharah is 120km and takes about two hours to drive. From Al Kamil (70km) it takes about one hour to drive.

Shana'a شناعة

📞 25 / POP 500

Little more than a tiny collection of houses in the middle of a vast area of flat *sabkha* (salt pan), the tiny hamlet of Shana'a is studded with shallow, salty pools tinged bright red with blooms of algae; these are used for harvesting salt, a back-breaking, eye-damaging occupation carried out under a fierce sun and with no shade.

Shana'a is perhaps better known, however, as the location of the ferry terminal for the island of Masirah, which can be seen from here on a clear day, 20km off the coast.

There's nowhere to stay in Shana'a and wild camping here is just that – wild! Alternatively, **Saqla Resort** (📞 97874331; www.saql-resort.topomanhotels.com; Hwy 17, Dunes Rd; r excl breakfast from OR27; 🅿), off the Dunes Rd an hour's drive north, offers a desert retreat with windsurfing, horse riding and hiking and accommodation in attractive individual stone cabins. An hour's drive south, there's **Al Jazeera Tourist Guesthouse** (📞 25427555, 99820882; Hwy 32, Mahout; r small/large OR15/20; 🅿🛜); part urban boutique, part rural outpost, it's located at the Hijj junction, and offers a handy stopover en route to or from Duqm.

🛈 Getting There & Away

Mwasalat buses run from Muscat's Azaiba Bus Station (OR4) daily at either 9.40am or 10.40am, returning at either 4.15pm or 5.15pm. The journey (450km, six hours) is via Sinaw, Mahout and Hijj.

There's no public transport along the Dunes Rd. From Al Ashkharah it's a two-hour drive (175km) to the ferry in Shana'a.

Ferries for the island of Masirah leave from **Shana'a Port** (Masirah Ferry Terminal; 📞 National Ferries Company 98111162) several times a day more or less when full.

South of Mahout, Hwy 32 leads to Duqm, with beautiful beaches lying a short distance from the main road at Filim, Khaluf, Sarab and Ras Sidrah. However it is best, even in a 4WD, to drive along Hwy 32 and make side trips to the shore rather than risk getting stuck in soft sand and perilous *sabkha* on the erratic coastal tracks.

Masirah Island جزيرة مصيرة

With its rocky interior of palm oases and gorgeous rim of sandy beaches, Masirah is the typical desert island. Used variously as a staging post for trade in the Indian Ocean and as home to fishermen attracted by the rich catches of kingfish, lobster and prawn, Masirah is home to flamingos and herons that patrol the coast by day and armies of ghost crabs that march ashore at night. With a rare gastropod, the Eloise, and large turtle-nesting sites, the island is justifiably fabled as a naturalist's paradise.

Expats stationed in the main town of Hilf affectionately termed Masirah 'Fantasy Island' – not because of the wildlife, but because anything they wanted during the long months of internment was the subject of fantasy only. Now better supplied, Masirah is still remote, with minimal facilities. As such it continues to offer a rare chance to see nature in the raw.

Just getting to Masirah can be an adventure, especially during holidays when the jetties teem with vehicles impatient to board the boat ramps. Expect practised queue jumping, wedging of cars to within an inch of their paintwork, and the endless wait for the last car to appear from across the desert to complete the load before sailing.

◉ Sights

Ras Abu Ar Rasas   BEACH

With no sights to speak of, you may be wondering why anyone comes to Masirah, but stand on the headland at Ras Abu Ar Rasas and the reason becomes apparent. The ocean pounds the rocky shore on the angry eastern side of the island, while the shallow waters of the western coast are a beautiful limpid turquoise. It's magnificent in its wild beauty.

Hilf   VILLAGE

The small town of Hilf, a 3km string of jetties, shops and fish factories in the northwest of Masirah, is home to half of the island's tiny population. Car ferries from the mainland dock at any of the three main jetties that line up along the corniche, which runs parallel with the main street in town. There are no sights here as such, but visitors drive through it, to or from the ferries.

Jebel Humr   MOUNTAIN

Jebel Humr (274m) is the highest point of Masirah's hilly backbone and a climb up this flat-topped mountain is recommended for the wonderful view of the island it affords, especially at sunset. The plateau is strewn with fossils. Wear good shoes as the scree can be quite dangerous towards the top. It takes about 30 minutes to hike up the left rump of the mountain and scramble over the rim. To get here, head out of Hilf in the direction of Sur Masirah, turn left at the sign for A'Samar and scout around the wadi until the mountain comes into view.

Safa'iq Grave Site   CEMETERY

Little is known about the history of Masirah island, except that it was once inhabited by Bahriya tribespeople, shipwrecked from Salalah. They were wiped out by an epidemic around 300 years ago, and their tombstones can still be seen at this grave site in Safa'iq. Two rocks are usually the only indication of a grave for men, with three rocks for women, so the elaborate inscriptions are surprising. The site is easy to miss: look uphill from the island road, 6km north of Sur Masirah.

🏂 Activities

Masirah Beach Camp   KITESURFING

(☑96323524; www.kiteboarding-oman.com; Sur Masirah; kite hire OR39.5, cabins OR19) This kiteboarding camp, with its Caribbean-coloured huts, occupies a salt pan that hasn't flooded for at least a decade, with spits of sand running far into the shallow turquoise sea. Run by Kite Board Oman, the camp offers a peaceful retreat and various courses.

🛏 Sleeping

Danat Al Khaleej Hotel   HOTEL $

(☑25504533; www.danat-hotel.com; Main Rd, Hilf; s/d/tr OR25/30/35; P 🛜) This delightful hotel, near Al Maha petrol station on the road leading southeast out of town, has large, fancy rooms with exotic reproduction furniture. The custard-yellow walls and red carpet are an unusual design choice, but the rooms have sea views, and the management is both competent and helpful.

Serabis Hotel   HOTEL $

(☑25504699; dira2008@omantel.net.om; Corniche, Hilf; r excl breakfast OR25; 🛜) The gloomy lobby of this Egyptian-run hotel is a bit dispiriting, as are the basic, cavernous rooms. It is clean, however, and the location at the end of the corniche (next to Al Maha petrol station) is convenient for night-time strolls in town.

OMAN MASIRAH ISLAND

SHIPWRECKED!

Masirah must be the only place in Oman without a fort – unless the air base counts. The local population tolerates the few remaining overseas militia with good grace, but outsiders have not always been welcome. In 1904 a British ship called the *Baron Inverdale* was wrecked off the rugged eastern coast. The crew struggled ashore, expecting the usual Arab hospitality, but found a very different reception. A monument to their massacre in the shape of a concessionary Christian cross is all that remains of the luckless crew. There were rumours of cannibalism and as a result the sultan decreed the destruction of all local houses – there are surprisingly few permanent settlements, even for the tiny population. A royal pardon was only granted to the islanders in 2009. You'll be glad to know that nowadays the only meat on the kebabs is likely to be camel or goat.

Masirah Hotel HOTEL **$**
(25504401; www.almajalioman.com; Main Rd; s/d/tr excl breakfast OR18/20/25;) With multiple beds, commodious bathrooms and a lot of Arab chintz, you can forgive the goats sitting on the doorstep. This is the biggest and most established of Hilf's three budget hotels, and it has a reasonable in-house restaurant.

Masira Island Resort RESORT **$$**
(25504274; www.masiraislandresort.com; Cross-Island Rd; r OR65;) This attractive, landscaped resort is a 10-minute walk across soft sand to the water's edge; turtles nest on the beach. Large, comfortable rooms are available in the main block, while the chalets offer more privacy. The restaurant is the only place on Masirah for international cuisine, and there's a bar. You'll need your own transport to reach the hotel.

Eating

Turkish Restaurant TURKISH **$**
(Main St, Hilf; mains OR2; 10am-midnight) For kebabs and whole roasted chickens, this restaurant, on the main street near Masirah Hotel and a prominent crossroad, is an old favourite.

Abu Shabeeb SUPERMARKET **$**
(Main St, Hilf; 8am-1pm & 4-10pm) Abu Shabeeb is the most comprehensive supermarket in town (useful for camping provisions), but if you require any 'must haves' it's best to bring them with you.

Information

Banks with ATMs (surrounded by the post office, pharmacy and modern hospital) are all within walking distance of the crossroads on the main street through Hilf.

Getting There & Away

The ferry to Masirah leaves from Shana'a. By car it takes about five or six hours from Muscat to the ferry departure point, or three hours from Sur.

Mwasalat buses run from Muscat's Azaiba Bus Station (one-way/return OR4/7.5), once daily at 10.40am (Wednesday to Saturday) and at 9.40pm (Sunday to Tuesday), returning at 5.15pm and 4.15pm. The bus journey is 450km from Muscat and takes six hours, stopping at Mudaibi, Sinaw and Mahout.

On the old ferries, the journey costs OR10 (1½ hours) each way per car; foot passengers travel free. The last ferry leaves when full at around 6pm to/from Hilf. If you don't relish the ad hoc approach, you can book a ticket on a faster,

scheduled roll-on-roll-off service with **National Ferries Company** (www.nfc.om; one way per person OR3.6, per saloon car/4WD OR8/10) and travel in air-conditioned comfort.

There are three jetty terminals on the island side, all in the town of Hilf. There's no rhyme or reason about which jetty is used for what – just spot where the fishers' trucks are heading and follow suit.

Getting Around

Masirah is 63km long, 18km wide and lies about 15km off the mainland coast. The only way to explore the island is by car or on foot – the taxis only service Hilf. There is no car-hire service on Masirah, so the most feasible option for getting around is to bring your own vehicle. A sealed road circumnavigates the island, but you'll need a 4WD to get close enough to the sea to enjoy it or to camp by it. The northwestern tip of the island is a military zone and is off limits.

Jalan Bani Bu Ali
جعلان بني بو علي

25 / POP 35,000
This town, which blends seamlessly into neighbouring Jalan Bani Bu Hassan, comprises a conglomeration of watchtowers, old fortified houses, a **castle** (Bani Bu Hassan; 500 baisa; 7.30am-6pm Sat-Thu) and ancient plantation walls, all of which lie crumbling in various states of beloved dereliction. There has been little attempt to court the modern world and none at all to woo the visitor, making a visit to these sites all the more interesting. Look out for elaborately painted metal doors and traditional carved wooden gates sported by the town's residences – both are a feature of the region.

The most important sight here is the aged and revered **Jami Al Hamoda Mosque**. The low-lying prayer hall is unique due to its profusion of 52 domes. Non-Muslims aren't permitted to enter, but it's possible to gain a vantage point across the mosque roof from the neighbouring buildings. A *falaj* used for ablutions runs through the courtyard and goats assemble in the shady lanes nearby. Getting to the mosque (follow the brown signs) is half the fun as the road rides the fault line between settlement and sand.

Brown signs dot the edge of town, wistfully stating 'You are on the fringe of the sands' and warning you not to go further without 4WD. Tracks lead into a uniquely wooded area of the Sharqiya Sands but should not be attempted without a guide as these routes are seldom explored by visitors and it's easy to get lost or mired in sand.

If the quiet authenticity of Bani Bu Ali or its gateway location to the sands appeals, then consider a stopover. With fancy tiling, arched corridors and carved doors, the Tourist Motel (☑ 25553307; d/tr excl breakfast OR15/20; P) in Jalan bani Bu Ali has pretensions above its ability to deliver, but it does at least offer a clean bed for the night. Better still, head into the gently undulating sands for a night at the recommended Al Reem Desert Camp (☑ 96666703; www.alreem-desert camp.com; r incl half-board/Bedouin tent with shared bathroom OR52/48; P). This lovely little camp, signposted off Hwy 35 and usually accessible by saloon car, is on the fringe of a unique hem of desert, marked by an abundance of native *ghaf* (a desert tree with pendulant branches). The location offers a blissfully quiet, authentic experience, in a neighbourhood frequented by the Bedouin.

❶ Getting There & Away

Mwasalat buses run from Muscat's Azaiba Bus Station (OR3) daily at 1.50pm, returning at 5.30am. The 290km journey is via the coastal highway (Hwy 17) and the town of Sur and takes 4½ hours.

Jalan Bani Bu Ali is 17km from Al Kamil and 36km to Al Ashkharah and makes a good diversion to or from Ras Al Jinz in a tour of the Sharqiya region. This is only possible, however, with your own transport, as these towns are not yet linked by public transport. Local taxis are available, however, for around OR10 to OR20 per journey.

Selma Plateau   هضبة سلمى

Along the coastal highway around Tiwi, several roads zigzag up the mountainside and into the clouds that often top the Eastern Hajar range. These roads mostly connect with small villages, such as Umq, from where there is no onward route except by foot. One or two roads, however, lead on to the remote Selma Plateau, a semi-arid, undulating mountain top, dotted with tiny hamlets and hollowed out with caverns (including the famous Majlis Al Jinn). The plateau is the location of an ancient burial site, Jaylah, where a cluster of beehive tombs (resembling those at Al Ain and Bat) mark a dramatic spot on a cliff edge.

If you're feeling brave, and have a good sense of direction and spare petrol, you can ascend to the mountain top at Tiwi, follow the growing network of roads and tracks across the plateau to Jaylah, and descend towards Ibra on the other side of the mountains. There's nowhere to stay or eat up here but wild camping is possible.

◉ Sights

★ Jaylah Tombs   TOMB
(⊘24hr) The 90 or so meticulously crafted stone towers scattered across the Selma Plateau are tombs dating back to the Umm An Nar culture of 2000 to 2700 BC. Standing about 3m tall and conical in shape, they command a dramatic position on the edge of the plateau and provoke plenty of unanswered questions. Local belief has it they were built by the spirit Kebir Keb – as good a way as any of describing the collective consciousness of the ancients.

Jaylah is a rewarding destination as much for the journey as the tombs, striking as they are: the route curves through crumbling cliffs and past remote mountain villages in a region that is still very seldom visited. Myriad car tracks thread from village to village on the top of the plateau, and numerous small communities survive on very little on the more or less barren plain. Until relatively recently the only access to many of these villages was by foot, with an occasional helicopter bringing supplies and/or health officials.

Parts of the same mountain range are home to rare species of goat, including the *tahr* and the Arabian ibex, and lucky visitors may just spot a gazelle or two grazing the plateau.

🏃 Activities

Mountain Drive   SCENIC DRIVE
This circuitous route leads from Wadi Kabbah, near Ibra, up to the Selma Plateau and is something of a 4WD adventure given the roughness of the route, the navigational difficulty and the steepness of some of the inclines. For a weekend of challenging off-roading, the route can be combined with the cliff drive (p170) down towards Tiwi.

The route begins at a right turn for Souqah, just before the town of Ash Shariq (also known as Simayiah), located at the entrance of Wadi Kabbah. The start of the track moves each time it rains: look for a track across the wadi adjacent to a water station signposted for Saih Ar Rak. Make sure you have water, a map, a compass and a full tank of petrol.

OMAN SELMA PLATEAU

Around 3km after you leave the sealed road, take the right fork for Jaylah (sometimes spelt 'Gaylah' or 'Al Gailah'). The track traces a precarious route through walls of unhinged black shale, waiting for a good storm to collapse. The last 6km of the ascent to the plateau, past shepherd enclosures, is poorly graded and progress is slow. At 21.4km, turn steep left by the water filling 'station' and follow the road to the top of the plateau.

Cliff Drive
SCENIC DRIVE

Near Tiwi, there is a graded track carved out of the rock face that leads to the cliff-hugging village of Qaran at the top of the Eastern Hajar Mountains. The route is strictly 4WD and is not for the faint-hearted, as the last part of the ascent is a near-vertical climb with sharp hairpin bends and no margin for error.

The ascent to the arid Selma Plateau, though, offers fantastic panoramic views of the coastal plain and gives access to the ancient tombs of Jaylah.

Look out for a brown sign to 'Qaran' or 'Kbaikab Graveyard and Al Jayla Village' off the Muscat–Sur Hwy, 5km northwest of Wadi Shab, and follow the brown signs. Water, a map, a compass and a full tank of petrol are essential.

Majlis Al Jinn
CAVING

Recognised as the second-largest cave chamber in the world, this vast cavern, discovered in 1983, offers Oman's longest rappel. Cheryl's Drop descends 158.2m into the cave. Sliding down the rope (with a shaft of sunlight that spears the blackness) is relatively easy but being winched back up is a bit more of an adventure!

ⓘ Getting There & Away

No public transport reaches this isolated region, and the tracks here can only be negotiated by 4WD. The plateau can be reached either from the coast near Tiwi on a daring cliff drive or via a long and meandering mountain drive from the entrance of Wadi Khabbah, near Ibra.

If you'd rather put your faith in a local driver who knows the road, Mark Tours (p143) offer a visit to the plateau as a day trip from Muscat, and Husaak Adventures (p142) offers overnight trips to Majlis Al Jinn.

Al Kamil
الكامل

☑ 25 / POP 17,800

With some interesting old architecture, including a unique castle museum and watchtowers, this small but pivotal town at the junction between Hwy 23 and Hwy 35 is a gateway to local beauty spot, **Wadi Bani Khalid** (off Hwy 23), and well worth a stop-off on the journey between the coast and the Sharqiya Sands.

Sights in Al Kamil include the not-to-be-missed **Old Castle Museum** (☑ 25557773, 93200166; Al Kamil Wa Al Wafi; adult/child OR2/200 baisa; ⊙ 9am-7pm), housing the personal collection of Sheikh Khalfan Al Hashmi. The sheikh's great grandfather owned the 250-year-old castle and donated it to the government; it was restored to its former glory under the current Sultan Qaboos, who gave it back to the Al Hashmi family. The present owner lives in the castle, and has embellished the rooms with meticulously arranged collections of copper, ceramics, mirrors, electronics, wood and palm crafts, gleaned from homes around the country.

Owned by the Al Hajri family, the delightful **Oriental Nights Rest House** (☑ 92896363; onrhoman@gmail.com; Hwy 23, btwn Bidaya & Al Kamil; r OR25-70; P ⓢ ⓧ) on Hwy 23, opposite the junction for Wadi Bani Khalid, offers the only accommodation in the area. Indian and Middle Eastern fare plus a few international dishes are served in the hotel's restaurant (open 6am to 10pm) and some excellent **desert tours** are offered from here. These include a sunrise tour (OR30 for up to four people), a three-hour sunset drive by 4WD (OR40 for up to four people) and, for the more adventurous, a five-hour, 8km wadi adventure that involves

GORGEOUS GHAF

The windblown town of Al Kamil is something of a rarity in Oman for being one of the few in the country surrounded by trees other than date palms. The low-lying acacia and *ghaf* (*Prosopis cineraria*; a native tree of the highly arid Arabian desert) both thrive here and the dense woodland is a special feature of the area. The *ghaf*, which can grow to heights over 5m, are particularly prized by the Bedouin, who use the wood for shade, shelter (as props for their tents) and firewood. Their camels nibble the nutritious new shoots and livestock lick the moisture from the small leaves in the early morning, saving the need to drink.

WADI BANI KHALID وادي بني خالد

Justly famed for its natural beauty, this wadi just north of the town of Al Kamil makes a rewarding (and well-signposted) diversion off the Muscat–Sur road (Hwy 23). The approach road, which climbs high into the Eastern Hajar Mountains, zigzags through some spectacularly colourful **rock formations**, green with copper oxide and rust-red with iron ore, and passes by a roadside *ayn* (natural spring) accessed via steps.

Most people visiting Wadi Bani Khalid head for the springs that collect in a series of **deep pools** in the narrow end of the wadi. The pools have been developed into a tourist destination with a (too) small car park, a concrete pathway and a series of picnic huts. Swimming is possible here but only if clothed appropriately in shorts and T-shirt over the top of a swimsuit. While the scenery is beautiful, the picnic site is heavily visited.

If you want to beat the crowds at Wadi Bani Khalid, then **Moqal Cave** in the upper reaches of the wadi is a curiosity to head towards. There's not much to the cave itself, but the hike along the wadi bottom is something of an adventure. Look for the lower path above the picnic area and then be ready to scramble over and squeeze under boulders and to ford the water several times. Goat herders may or may not show you the way, as locals are not keen on tourists venturing beyond the pools. Then again, they may just be worried you'll be lured into the land of gardens and cool streams revealed to all who strike the rocks of Moqal Cave and utter the magic words 'Salim Bin Saliym Salam'. The cave, however, is more likely to reveal evidence of bats and previous visitors. The cave's narrow entrance is accessed by a stairway – best entered with a guide.

You can continue walking above the wadi on the 28km **Hiking Route E35**. This eventually leads to Tiwi by the coast and takes 14 to 18 hours. This popular hike generally takes two days and is offered by tour agents in Muscat who also organise donkeys to transport camping equipment. It's hard to find the way without a guide.

OMAN AL MINTIRIB

leaping into pools with no possibility of returning the same way (OR60 per person). There's also a seven-day, 180km camel trek from Bidaya to Gehed on the Sharqiya coast.

❶ Getting There & Away

Mwasalat buses run from Muscat's Azaiba Bus Station (OR4) twice daily at 7.50am and 2.50pm, running in the opposite direction at 6.50am and 3.20pm. The journey from Muscat (275km, four hours) is via Ibra (170km, 1¾ hours) and continues on to Sur (55km, 50 minutes).

There is no reliable public transport from Al Kamil in any other direction.

Al Mintirib المنترب

☑ 25 / POP 11,200

This small village, on the edge of the dunes and often semi-buried in sand, has some sights of interest including a picturesque old quarter, a **fort** (currently closed for restoration) and the delightful **Bidaya Museum** (OR1; ⊘ 8.30am-1.30pm & 4-6pm). This quirky little museum preserves the history of the Hijri Tribe, written in Arabic on goat skins. A collection of spears and swords dating back 300 years, together with household items such as Chinese ginger jars and dishes (an essential part of Omani households in the last century) are well displayed in this cavernous house.

There's nowhere to stay in the village of Al Mintirib itself but it's a gateway to the Sharqiya Sands. Camp representatives often meet their guests in town and help them navigate (by 4WD only) to their site – often impossible to find independently.

There are lots of local-style coffee shops in Al Mintirib but for tasty Lebanese food, head to **Al Saula'ee Restaurant & Grills** (☑ 91163777; Hwy 23; mains from OR2; ⊘ 6am-midnight). Distinguished by a white-picket fence enclosing a small tree-shaded yard, it has a terrace and air-conditioned indoor seating, and also offers takeaways.

❶ Getting There & Away

Mwasalat buses run from Muscat's Azaiba Bus Station (OR4) twice daily at 7.50am and 2.50pm, running in the opposite direction at 7.30am and 4pm. The journey is 200km from Muscat and take 3¼ hours. The bus continues on to Sur (120km, 1½ hours), stopping at Al Kamil on route.

Al Mintirib is the access point for two parallel dune corridors and the desert camps that are located there. The 18km off-road track to Al Raha Tourism Camp (p173) is a difficult drive over severe washboard, interspersed with soft sand.

LOCAL KNOWLEDGE

AD HOC SHOPPING

On the edge of the sands near Al Mint-irib, Bedouin women, still wearing their traditional peaked-mask costume, sell handicrafts from a small goat-hair tent by the side of the road. Items at this **stall** (☉hours vary) begin at around OR1 for hand-woven woollen key-fobs, while flat-loomed carpets can cost around OR20 depending on size. As inveterate traders, these women are unlikely to offer much discount, however hard you bargain!

Similarly keeping no fixed opening hours, the **Arkan Modern Shop** (☑95111156; ☉10am-5pm) is run by Bedouin owners. This tiny shop sells two-person tents and other basic camping supplies, including blankets, torches and firewood. It's opposite a smart, clean public-toilet block and opens pretty much at the whim of the owner.

It requires care, but not special sand driving experience, to reach the camp. The onward section, however, to 1000 Nights Camp (p173), a further 20km deeper into the sands, is a much more challenging soft-sand drive over the dunes and should be approached with caution.

Al Wasil الواصل

☑25 / POP 2500

A gateway into the sands, this tiny village boasts a large **fort** with a mighty round tower with a unique, detached (and arched) external stairway and extensive rambling walls. There is little to draw a visitor here, however, other than the access it affords to some major desert camps. It also comes briefly alive when the annual **Desert Marathon** (www.marathonoman.com; ☉Nov) passes through town.

For those not keen on overnighting in the sands, there's the **Al Wasal Hotel** (☑25581243; Hwy 23, Al Qabil; r OR30; P�}). This old faithful, located on Hwy 23, 10km northwest of Al Wasil, has simple rooms with elaborate furniture crowding the courtyard and open-kitchen dining. Desert trips can be arranged from here.

❶ Getting There & Away

Sur-bound Mwasalat buses stop at nearby Al Mintirib, from where pre-booked camp transport can meet guests.

Al Wasil is the access point for four parallel dune corridors and the desert camps that are located there. In the most northerly of these corridors lie **Sama Desert Camp** and **Al Salam Camp**. This valley is reached via a sealed road just north of Al Wasil.

The next dune corridor south is the location of the **Bidayah Desert Camp**. This is signposted from the middle of Al Wasil (a left turn by the fort), and can be reached via a sealed road followed by 2km of bumpy graded track, just about possible in a saloon car, if driving with care.

Also reached from the centre of town, the next corridor south houses **Sama Al Wasil Camp**. Reaching here involves a challenging dune drive requiring a 4WD and some desert driving experience.

The most southerly dune corridor, accessed from the southwestern outskirts of Al Wasil, leads to two neighbouring camps, **Desert Nights** and **Arabian Oryx Camp** (1km apart). Access to these two camps requires a 4WD trip across 11km of miserably bad washboard road that takes patience to drive safely.

If a Bedouin suggests an alternative route to a camp, expect to pay for the privilege of following in his (or her) tracks – generally across some pretty extreme dune terrain.

Ibra ابراء

☑25 / POP 25,260

Ibra, the hub of the Sharqiya region, enjoyed great prosperity during Oman's colonial period as aristocratic locals set sail for Zanzibar and sent money home for plantations and luxury residences. These are still in evidence in the atmospheric old quarter of town, which makes for a fascinating place to wander. The tradition of farming is continued today, with rich plots producing vegetables, bananas, mangoes and, of course, dates. A watchtower punctuates the top of each surrounding hill, indicating the prior significance of the town – an importance it is beginning to enjoy again with a university, a large regional hospital and a lively souq area. All in all, Ibra is a pleasant stop-off for those heading to the Sharqiya Sands or simply wanting to get a sense of provincial life in Oman.

❍ Sights

Ibra Old Quarter RUINS

The old part of Ibra is a honeycomb of crumbling mud-built houses of two or three storeys. There's a paved walkway of several kilometres through some of the best parts of the old village, accessed by a double archway; note the well on the right of the

SHARQIYA SANDS رمال الشرقية

Home to the Bedouin, these beautiful sands offer visitors a glimpse of a traditional way of life that is fast disappearing as modern conveniences limit the need for a nomadic existence. It is possible to visit the sands as a day trip, but the majesty of the night sky and the pleasure of dawn in the dunes makes a stay at one of the desert camps a better bet. Access is by 4WD and knowledge of sand driving is required to reach many camps.

Desert Experiences

Various desert experiences are available through tour companies and through the desert camps, either as day excursions or as overnight safaris. Activities include camel rides (OR10 for 30 minutes), dune-driving (from OR25 for a sunset trip with a near-vertical descent), quad-biking (from OR5 for 30 minutes for a 90cc vehicle), wild camping (OR40 per person), full-day camel safaris (OR88), sandboarding and trips to Bedouin settlements.

A full-day, guided desert drive through the sands from Desert Nights Camp to the coast costs OR160 (up to four people). Huge convoys also ply the sands, with up to 100 cars ripping through the desert with little or no thought of the damage this causes to the fragile desert environment, and as such cannot be recommended. The sands are a unique habitat for wildlife and may be better approached more as a case study in desert survival than as an adventure playground. Opting for something four-legged rather than four-wheeled may help a visitor come closer to the desert's soul while protecting the environment.

Recommended Camps

Accessed from Al Wasil

Sama Desert Camp (www.samaresorts.com; P) On the edge of a silver sand dune, with local Bedouin villages nearby.

Al Salam Camp (J 96995117, 92675707; www.alsalam.om; r incl half-board OR50; P) New and rather raw camp with rows of concrete cabins. A peaceful retreat, however, along a particularly attractive corridor of silverish sand.

Bidiyah Desert Camp (J 99382914; www.bidiyah-desert.com; per person incl half-board OR25; P) Good-value camp, 12km into the sands, popular with Omani families.

Sama Al Wasil Camp (www.desertpalmoman.com.; d chalet incl half-board OR50; P) Comprising a ring of attractive stone chalets surrounding a covered *majlis* (reception area). The stone entrance gives this remoter camp a sense of the *kasbah*.

Desert Nights Camp (J 92818388; www.desertnightscamp.com; s/d incl half-board OR145/164; ⊙ Aug-May; P @ ⬡) Luxury camp with canvas-roofed cabins and boutique furnishings. There's a bar and fine-dining restaurant serving hot plates and wine (OR20).

Arabian Oryx Camp (J 94421500; www.oryx-camp.com; s/d tent incl half-board OR40/60, cabin OR60/80; P) Pretty camp with welcoming, traveller-friendly service. Lets the dunes creep in at the edges with well-thought-out excursions and facilities.

Nomadic Desert Camp (J 99336273; www.nomadicdesertcamp.com; per person incl half-board & shared bathroom OR35; ⊙ Oct-Apr; P) Run by a Bedouin family, accommodation is in *barasti* huts with shared bathrooms. No generator – no noise!

Accessed from Al Mintirib

Al Raha Tourism Camp (J 99551155, 99343851; www.alrahaoman.com; tent incl half-board per person OR15, with air-con OR20; P) In a corridor of orange sand. Concrete huts decorated with palm fronds are basic and tired, but it's a friendly camp.

1000 Nights (J 22060243, 99448158; www.1000nightscamp.com; incl half-board d OR85, with shared bathroom OR75; P ⬡ ⬡) This highly recommended camp lies deep in the heart of the dunes. Offers Bedouin-style tents, Arabian-style seating areas...and a swimming pool.

entrance and the old **Al Qablateen Mosque** 500m along the narrow lane. Several houses have been restored by local residents. Wander on foot as it's a struggle to get around the corners in a car. You can reach the old quarter by walking across the wadi next to Ibra Souq and following your nose. Alternatively, follow the brown signs past the souq area and turn right for the local villages of Al Munisifeh and Al Kanatar. This route meanders round the lanes and ends in a parking lot. The double archway marks the village entrance, and it's easy to navigate around the village *falaj* (irrigation channel). There are clean public toilets here (200 baisa).

Wadi Khabbah   NATURAL FEATURE
This wide and luscious wadi meanders along the western base of the Eastern Hajar Mountains and provides a fascinating alternative route between Muscat and Sur. A 4WD is needed to navigate the off-road sections, which invariably involve fording water. The picture of rural wadi life that unfolds as you travel through the spectacular mountain scenery is a highlight. There are numerous plantations and small villages in this broad wadi, and sensitivity is needed when driving through them.

Ibra Souq   MARKET
(⊙6am-2pm) Ibra has a lively souq that is at its most active on a Wednesday morning. Arranged around a double courtyard, the greengrocery takes pride of place in the centre, with local melons and aubergines making colourful seasonal displays. To reach the souq by car, turn right off the Muscat–Sur Hwy at a sign for Al Safalat Ibra, just past the Sultan Qaboos Mosque, and the souq is about 500m on the right.

A working silver souq, where *khanjars* (traditional curved daggers) and veil pins are crafted, occupies several of the shops around the outer courtyard, muscling in between carpentry shops where elaborately carved doors are still made. Look out for a shop called 'Sale and Maintenance of Traditional Firearms & Rifle Making': there's always an energetic huddle of old men engaged in comparing ancient weaponry around the tables outside. You will probably also notice piles of flattened and dried fish – a local delicacy, still prized despite the modern road system that brings fresh fish to Ibra via the neighbouring wet fish market.

If trying to reach the souq by bus, say you're heading for the souq and ask to be set down near Al Yamadi turning.

Women's Souq   MARKET
(⊙6am-1pm Wed) Once a week this souq, opposite the main market, attracts women-only buyers and sellers from all over the region, selling a variety of handicrafts such as baskets, woven cushions and camel bags. Men are not welcome, and photographs are prohibited here in the only souq in the country dedicated to female shoppers.

Activities

Devil's Gap   HIKING
Near the point where Wadi Kabbah runs into Wadi Tayein are the villages of Tam and Tool. Tool is the gateway to high-sided Wadi Dayqah, which makes for an interesting hike. Old cave dwellings are still used by shepherds here and there's all kinds of wildlife (toads, dragonflies, jewel beetles) congregating around the deep pools.

The pools also invite a swim, but don't for a minute think you're alone – the steep ravine is a favourite with silent-walking shepherds. The hike runs along the wadi bottom towards Dayqah Dam and is often impassable. Tool lies 10km east of the town of Mehlah, at the end of the sealed road through Wadi Tayein.

Sleeping

Ibra Motel   HOTEL $
(☑25571666; ibramtl@omantel.net.om; Naseeb Rd; s/d excl breakfast OR18/20) It's cheap and central but best of all, the owner epitomises Omani hospitality. The custard-yellow walls of this modest hotel need a repaint, but there's a fancy foyer of extravagant gilded furniture, and rooms are clean, with smartly tiled bathrooms. Each room has a kettle and free tea and coffee, and breakfast is available (from 500 baisa) in the adjoining coffeeshop.

Al Sharqiya Sands Hotel   HOTEL $
(☑25587000; www.sharqiyasands.com; Old Hwy 23 & Hwy 28; s/d OR27/30; P🖥❄) Arranged around a simple, unlandscaped pool, this hotel, set within its own grounds, is in need of refurbishment, but the rooms are clean, and it makes a convenient stopover en route to Sharqiya Sands. There are two loud 'local' bars, and a family-oriented licensed restaurant with an international menu. The hotel is more friendly than the dark lobby suggests.

Ibra Hotel   HOTEL $
(☑25571873; s/d excl breakfast OR25/35; P@🖥❄) The artist engaged to work on the exterior of this hotel must have been

homesick as the overflows are decorated with cashew nuts and tropical birds, while the downpipes are painted to look like palm trees. It adds character to an otherwise unexceptional hotel with plain rooms. It's set back from the road (connecting Ibra's main roundabout with the bypass).

Eating

Rawazen Restaurant　　　　　TURKISH $
(📞98077980; Old Hwy 23; mains from OR3; ⏰8am-2am; 🅿) This popular upstairs restaurant on the main road in Ibra (opposite the Ibra Motel) offers cosy dining for reasonable prices. Particularly good value is the daily lunchtime buffet from 10.30am to 2pm, which offers 11 different dishes from four different cuisines (Turkish, Middle Eastern, Indian and Chinese) and free soft drinks. Mind the unmarked plate-glass window at the bottom of the stairs!

**Al Shariq Restaurant &
Coffeeshop**　　　　MIDDLE EASTERN $
(📞92372684; Old Hwy 23; mains around OR2; ⏰6am-midnight) This typical local-style restaurant, with its attractive red-painted exterior, has tiny, screened cubicles for private family dining. There's a huge selection of local fare, including *shuwa* (slow-roasted meat) and *mandi* (meat stew). There are also dozens of sandwiches (OR1.5), Indian dishes and fresh juices to choose from. The menu is illustrated.

ℹ Getting There & Away

Mwasalat buses run from Muscat's Azaiba Bus Station (OR4) twice daily at 7.50am and 2.50pm, returning at 8.25am and 4.55pm. The journey is 150km from Muscat and takes two hours and 20 minutes. The bus continues on to Sur (160km, two hours and 10 minutes), stopping at Al Mintirib and Al Kamil en route.

Taxis are available from Muscat (OR31), and local taxis run from the middle of town (outside Rawazen Restaurant). Note that new Hwy 23 bypasses Ibra, but old Hwy 23 continues to be the main road through town.

HAJAR MOUNTAINS　　جبال الحجر

This dramatic, mountainous region is one of Oman's biggest tourist destinations, and for good reason. Historic Nizwa boasts a grand souq and elegant Grand Mosque and acts as the gateway to spectacular mountain destinations including Jebel Shams

(Oman's highest mountain), Wadi Ghul (the Grand Canyon of Arabia) and Jebel Akhdar (the fruit bowl of Oman). Nearby Bahla and Jabreen are famous for their rambling forts – two of the country's best.

Many of the sights around Nizwa can be visited on a long daytrip from Muscat, and all tour companies in the capital organise coach tours. The region deserves more than just a fleeting visit, however, especially if adding 4WD excursions into the mountains. One scenically rewarding two-day 4WD excursion from Muscat involves an overnight stop in Nizwa and an exciting off-road mountain drive (p183) via Hatt and Wadi Bani Awf to Rustaq and the Batinah Plain.

Nizwa　　نزوى

📋 25 / POP 72,100

The historic town of Nizwa, with its giant fort and high-walled souq, lies on a plain surrounded by a thick palm oasis and some of Oman's highest mountains. Only half a century ago, British explorer Wilfred Thesiger was forced to steer clear of Nizwa: his Bedouin companions were convinced that he wouldn't survive the ferocious conservatism of the town and refused to let him enter. He would be amazed to find that Nizwa is now the second-biggest tourist destination in Oman. The seat of factional imams until the 1950s, Nizwa, or the 'Pearl of Islam' as it's sometimes called, is still a conservative town, however, and appreciates a bit of decorum from its visitors.

Marked by a grand double-arched gateway, Nizwa forms a natural access point for the historic sites of Bahla and Jabreen, and for excursions up the mountain roads to Jebel Akhdar and Jebel Shams.

For those with a special interest in Nizwa, www.nizwa.net offers some locally produced information.

◉ Sights

★ **Nizwa Fort**　　　　　　　FORT
(Main St; 500 baisa; ⏰8am-6pm Sat-Thu, 8-11.30am & 1.30-6pm Fri; 🅿) Built over 12 years in the 17th century by Sultan Bin Saif Al Yaruba, the first imam of the Yaruba dynasty, Nizwa Fort is famed for its distinctive 40m-tall round tower. By climbing to the top of the tower, it's possible to gauge the scale of the surrounding date plantations and to admire the view of the Hajar Mountains that loom over the town. All Nizwa tours include

IRRIGATION IN A DRY LAND

As you travel around northern Oman, be sure to look out for Oman's ancient irrigation system – an engineering highlight of such sophistication and complexity that it has earned Unesco World Heritage status.

Comprised of channels, known locally as *aflaj* (plural) or *falaj* (singular), cut into mountainsides, running across miniature aqueducts and double-deckering through tunnels, this irrigation system is responsible for most of the oases in Oman. The precious water is diverted firstly into drinking wells and then into mosque washing areas and at length to the plantations, where it is siphoned proportionately among the village farms. Traditionally, a *falaj* clock, like a sundial, was used to meter the time given to each farm; nowadays, some *aflaj* are controlled by automatic pumps.

There are more than 4000 of these channels in Oman, some of which were built more than 1500 years ago. The longest channel is said to run for 120km under Sharqiya Sands. Although they can be seen throughout the mountains, some of the most easily accessible examples include **Falaj Daris** (off Hwy 21; ⊙24hr) and Falaj Tanuf (p182) near Nizwa, and those running through Misfat Al Abriyyin (p185), Wadi Bani Awf (p197) and Wadi Shab (p157).

the fort in their itinerary, helping to make sense of this giant building.

★**Nizwa Souq**　　　　　　　　　MARKET
(Main St; ⊙7am-12.45pm & 4-9pm Sat-Thu, 4-9pm Fri; P) The site of one of the oldest souqs in the country, this extensive marketplace is dedicated mostly to fruit and vegetables, meat and fish, all of which are housed in separate blocks behind the great, crenellated piece of city wall that overlooks the wadi. Part of the souq (nearest the fort) is dedicated to handicrafts and caters specifically to the passing tourist trade.

You'll have to try hard to find a bargain for antiques and silver, but local craftsmanship is good. Nizwa is particularly famous for crafting the silver *khanjar* (traditional curved dagger). Today Indian or Pakistani silversmiths often work under an Omani master-craftsman, especially for pieces designed for tourists, but the workmanship is often exquisite. Prices range from OR50 for a tourist piece to well over OR500 for an authentic piece.

Livestock Market　　　　　　　MARKET
(Nizwa Souq, Main St; ⊙6-8am Fri) If you're not put off by the smell of heaving bulls and goats, the livestock souq is well worth a look. The livestock market occupies a small plot of land beyond the main market walls, left of the entrance, and the brisk trading in goats, sheep and cattle is a centuries-old tradition.

Al Qala'a Mosque　　　　　　　MOSQUE
(Main St) Nizwa was once a major centre for Islamic scholarship, and two aged mosques, among the oldest in the world, have survived since the early 7th century. Nestled up against the souq and the fort, the mosque (closed to non-Muslims) forms part of a fine ensemble of buildings in the middle of the town.

Nizwa Gateway　　　　　　　　GATE
(Hwy 21) This grand double-arched gateway straddles Hwy 21, along the original Muscat–Nizwa road. The watchtowers that form the uprights of the gateway seem aged, but in fact the gateway was built in 2015.

🎉 Festivals & Events

Haute Route　　　　　　　　　CYCLING
(www.hauteroute.org; ⊙Mar) This three-day international cycling event cuts through the Hajar Mountains. The starting point is Nizwa and the route covers a total distance of 370km, with more than 6500m of climbing – including an ascent of Jebel Akhdar (p179).

👉 Tours

Tijwal Tours　　　　　　　　　TOURS
(☑95605764; sultan19941190@gmail.com; 3½hr city tour OR30) Offers half-day walking tours or longer six-hour excursions to Al Hamra (OR58). Four-wheel drive tours to Birkat Al Mawz and Jebel Akhdar cost OR60.

Bike & Hike Oman　　　　　　CYCLING
(☑24400873; www.bikeandhikeoman.com) Offers a number of spectacular cycling and hiking tours in the Hajar Mountains.

🛏 Sleeping

Tanuf Residency　　　　　　　HOTEL $
(☑25411601; www.tanufresidency.com; Hwy 21; s/d/ste OR25/32/37; P🕸) With a sparkling

white marble lobby and bright corridors, this hotel (refurbished in 2018) has had a complete overhaul. The result is a modern, well-run establishment with very comfortable rooms (with free tea and coffee) for budget prices. The top-floor restaurant is good enough for breakfast, and the excellent **Turkish restaurant** (mains from OR2; P ✳) next door is perfect for supper.

Nizwa Residence Hotel Apartments
HOTEL $

(☑ 79164116; Hwy 21; s/d/apt OR21/25/45) This brand-new hotel, in a modern block on the way into town, advertises an eight-minute walking time to the souq and indeed, a view of Nizwa's grand trio of fort, souq and mosque graces the view from many of the rooms. The double rooms are business-like, but the 19 apartments furnished with kitchen and lounge offer the best value.

★ Nizwa Heritage Inn
HERITAGE HOTEL $$

(☑ 25448999; nizwainn@gmail.com; Al Akhbar St, behind Nizwa Souq; r with shared/private bathroom OR30/from OR35; tr OR50; P 🛜) Comprising four, newly converted old townhouses, this characterful hotel (booked by email) is located immediately behind the souq and is helping to save Nizwa's old quarter from being abandoned. Rooms are dark, many without windows, but they offer – with their internal pillars, timbered ceilings, alcoves and Omani artefacts – a privileged glimpse into traditional life in this historic town.

★ Falaj Daris Hotel
HOTEL $$

(☑ 25410500; www.falajdarishotel.com; Hwy 21; s/d OR59/64; P @ 🛜 ☀) This ever-friendly hotel, 4km east of the town centre, is wrapped around two swimming pools and a **bar**. With a vista of serrated mountains looming beyond, it's one of the best hotels in Nizwa. The rooms are better in the newer block, but the older courtyard often hosts an evening buffet – a sociable, tasty affair with long tables for tour groups.

Al Diyar Hotel
HOTEL $$

(☑ 25412402; www.aldiyarhotel.com; Hwy 21; s/d/ste OR35/45/90; P @ 🛜 ☀) There is some charm in the gypsum-and-marble foyer with its hand-painted lozenges on wall and ceiling, but it doesn't extend to many of the plain, large, no-nonsense rooms. In a popular town with few beds, however, this is no criticism. Rooms in the new wing sport modern comforts. The hotel lies 3.5km east of the town centre.

✕ Eating

★ Al Mandi Al Dhahabi
MIDDLE EASTERN $

(☑ 25414121; opp Nizwa Souq; mains OR2.5; ⊙ 10am-midnight Sat-Thu, 6am-noon & 1pm-midnight Fri; 🛜) A popular venue with expats and visitors, this friendly restaurant serves standard Middle Eastern fare despite its billing as a specialist in Omani and Zanzibari food. That said, the *mandi* dishes are authentic and all meals are delicious. Tables on the roadside terrace make the best of the souq view.

Boom Burger & Sweets
BURGERS $

(☑ 97560333; Hwy 21; burgers from OR1.5; ⊙ 11am-midnight Sat-Thu, from 1pm Fri; P) Roughly opposite the Falaj Daris Hotel, this modern, attractive restaurant with calligraphic walls caters to a growing national appetite for burgers. This burger bar has a local twist, however, with a camel patty on the menu. There are pancakes for 'afters'.

Al Zuhly Restaurant
OMANI $

(opposite Nizwa Souq; meals OR2.5; ⊙ 8am-midnight) This simple venue with seating on the pavement has one of the best night-time views in Oman. Situated opposite the souq, the cafe overlooks the fort and mosque, both of which are lit up spectacularly at night. It sells shawarma and kebabs, and is always busy with locals, who generally pull up in the car and sound the car horn for a takeaway.

Bin Ateeq Restaurant
OMANI $

(☑ 25410466; off Main St; meals OR2.2; ⊙ 11am-midnight) Part of a small chain of Omani-style restaurants, this is one of the few places where you have the opportunity to sample genuine local dishes. Dining is also Omani style, seated on the ground on carpets that have seen better days. Set menus offer a wide range of tasting opportunities for two people.

🛍 Shopping

Omani Craftsman's House
ARTS & CRAFTS

(next to Nizwa Fort; ⊙ 8am-1pm & 4-8pm Sat-Thu, 8am-noon & 4-8pm Fri) One of a number of shops in the craft section of the souq, this shop occupies a refurbished old building next to the fort. It has a fine range of traditional crafts including leather and basketwork bowls from southern Oman as well as locally crafted silver and earthenware pots from Bahla.

Al Diwaniya Omani Sweets
FOOD

(Main St, opp Nizwa Souq; ⊙ 7.30am-11pm) With a traditional diet that relied heavily on dates,

OMAN NIZWA

OMAN

Hajar Mountains

20 km
10 miles

N

Mutrah

MUSCAT

See Greater Muscat Map (p134)

17

Shat

Ulyah

Naqsi

Al Ulya

Samad

Gharyan

Samad

Murayrat

Sarur

Muscat International Airport

Seeb

23

Nida

Samail

15

Masqad

33

Barka

Wasit

Muslima Nakhal

Said

Imti

Izki

Al Mawz

Birkat

Al Akhdar

Saiq

Al Aqor

Nizwa

Mussanah

Al Abiyad

13

Wadi Mistal

Sunaybah

Sunnar

Al Ayn

Sawadi

1

Al Awabi

Wadi Bani Kharus

Sharfat al Alamayn

Tanuf

21

Muladdah

Al Hazm

Falaj Al Sharah

Rustaq

Wadi Bani Awf

Hatt

Bilad Sayt

Al Hamra

Al Hoota Cave

Bahla

11

Wadi Hoqain

Wadi Sahten

Misfat

Al Ayn

Jabreen

Nattalah

Al Tayib

(2777m)

Jebel Shams (3075m)

Wadi Ghul

Al Ayshah

Halhal

10

Rumaylah

Sint

Maqniyat

Jebel Misht

Al Ayn

Jebel Kawr (2730m)

21

Ghab

9

Miskin

Bat

Maqabil

Kubarah

Khadal

Omanis have a particularly sweet tooth. A favourite confection is *halwa*, a thick, gelatinous sweet laced with cardamom and nuts. This shop has a sampling station of seven or eight varieties. The most expensive is a deep red colour, stained with slivers of saffron. Earthenware *halwa* bowls are sold here, too.

ℹ Getting There & Around

Mwasalat buses stop outside Nizwa Souq. These run from Muscat's Azaiba Bus Station (OR4.5, three hours) twice daily at 9.15am and 3.15pm, returning at 11.40am and 8.40pm via Fanja. The Muscat bus continues on to Bahla (40km, 30 minutes), Ibri and Buraimi. Taxis from Muscat to Nizwa (160km, three hours) cost OR32.

Salalah-bound Mwasalat buses (originating in Muscat, OR7) stop almost opposite Nizwa Grand Mall at 9.10am (arriving in Salalah at 7.55pm), noon (arriving at 11.15pm) and 9pm (7.40am). They travel via Haima (370km, four hours 20 minutes). While it's possible to board at Nizwa, it's worth bearing in mind that the best seats for the 10-hour journey will have been taken in Muscat, so it's best to reserve a seat.

Microbuses (300 baisa) link the hotels that lie along Hwy 15, the old Muscat–Nizwa road, with the town centre.

Birkat Al Mawz   بركة الموز

🕿 25 / POP 7600

Sheltered in the hinge between plain and mountain, this pretty village has retained much of its aged charm (despite recent modernisation). Birkat Al Mawz roughly translates as 'Banana Pool', an appropriate name as a drive through the village plantation will reveal. Most people only venture here to begin the 4WD drive (or strenuous day hike) up Wadi Muaydin to the Saiq Plateau on Jebel Akhdar. This is a pity because there are several interesting things to see, including a 17th-century fort, Bait Al Radidah, an active *falaj* (irrigation channel), some interesting old village that is in the process of being saved from ruin, and a thick plantation of date palms that invite a quiet stroll.

The village also offers practical assistance to visitors heading up the mountain such as 4WD hire, supermarkets and camping gear, available from Al Azbal Supplies (🕿 93908582; Main Rd; ⊘ 7am-1pm & 4-10pm Sat-Thu, 7-11am & 2-10pm Fri).

The Golden Tulip Nizwa (🕿 25431616; https://nizwa.goldentulip.com; Hwy 21; s/d OR71/82; 🅿 @ 🛜 🏊) offers recommended, good-value accommodation nearby. This attractive Arabian Nights-style hotel once hosted members of the royal family and it has a sociable pool, four bars and a souvenir shop. Between October and March the Al Fannar Restaurant here offers a poolside barbecue (OR14). Within Birkat Al Mawz, Time of Tea (Main Rd; sandwich 500 baisa; ⊘ 10am-10pm) is a good spot for a cuppa before heading up the mountain.

ℹ Getting There & Away

Birkat Al Mawz lies on the old Muscat–Nizwa Rd, 111km from the Burj Al Sahwa Roundabout in Muscat and around 25km from Nizwa. There's no public transport to the village, nor up Jebel Akhdar. Car hire (4WD is required) is possible from here for the paved but unremittingly steep ascent; Al Jabal Al Akhdar Rent-a-Car (🕿 92220990; Hwy 21; 24hr car incl petrol with/without guide OR50/40, 24hr 4WD incl petrol with guide OR100; ⊘ 7am-8pm) has several vehicles to choose from.

Jebel Akhdar   الجبل الاخضر

Without a guide or some inside information, Jebel Akhdar (Green Mountain) may seem something of a misnomer to the first-time visitor. Firstly, Jebel Akhdar refers not to a mountain as such, but to an area that encompasses the great Saiq Plateau, at 2000m above sea level. Secondly, the *jebel* (mountain) keeps its fecundity well hidden in a labyrinth of wadis and terraces. There, the cooler mountain air and greater rainfall encourage scented Damask roses (which flower in March and are the source of the region's celebrated rose water), prize pomegranates, apricots and other fruit to grow in abundance. Temperatures during December to March can drop to -5°C, and hailstones are not uncommon.

With a day or two to explore this 'top of the beanstalk', the determined visitor will soon stumble across the network of mountain villages and their well-tended gardens and orchards that make this region so justly prized.

◎ Sights

Diana's Viewpoint   VIEWPOINT
The rim of the cliff here, with its celebrated panoramic view of the farmed terraces below, has a royal connection. Diana, Princess of Wales, enjoyed this spot on a royal visit to Oman with the future British king in 1986. The tourist office receives numerous enquiries about the location, a point not lost on two neighbouring hotels that both encircle

a potential viewpoint. They may be capitalising on Diana's memory, but this doesn't detract from the spectacular vista.

Seeq
VILLAGE

Not to be confused with the main town of Saiq, this small village has a rose-water distillery, making it an interesting place to visit during production time in spring. It's also a trailhead for the Village Trail.

Ash Shuraiqa
VILLAGE

Growing an abundance of pink Damask roses that bloom in spring (late March, early April), this village is linked to neighbouring villages by the irrigation channels that keep the terraces watered. The village has a particularly stunning vantage point over Wadi Muaydin many meters below, making it a popular spot for a photograph. It's best to park outside the village and walk down as there's very little turning or parking space.

Wadi Bani Habib
VILLAGE

Wadi Bani Habib refers less to the wadi of walnuts and pomegranates that are still grown here, and more to the ruined village that lies wrapped around the bottom of the valley. An easy walking path leads down 200 steps to the wadi bottom, across the irrigation channel that keeps the orchards fertile, and up to a cluster of slowly decaying mud buildings on the other side. The whole area is picturesque but best avoided at weekends when it gets crowded and parking is difficult.

Al Aqor
VILLAGE

This tiny hamlet clinging to the edge of the cliff, below Diana's Viewpoint (p179), is typical of the villages on the Saiq plateau. Growing an assortment of vegetables and fruit in terraced allotments, it is kept fertile by water conducted along ancient irrigation channels known as *aflaj*. It's not possible to drive into the village, but there's a wonderful walking path that edges around the Jebel Akhdar crescent to the village of Ash Shuraiqa.

🏃 Activities

Village Trail
HIKING

This delightful 4km hike (numbered W18b) inches around the fertile crescent of Jebel Akhdar between the mountain villages of Al Aqor and Seeq and can be continued on to Wadi Bani Habib . Following paths that have linked these tiny settlements for centuries, this route among rose blooms (in spring)

offers an insight into the tenuous nature of high-altitude farming.

Wadi Al Muaydin Hike
HIKING

Access to Jebel Akhdar is by mandatory 4WD. The only alternative is a 17km walking trail through the terraced villages of Wadi Al Muaydin to the Saiq Plateau. You'll need a guide, and beware: it's an unrelenting uphill slog. Thankfully, it is also a magical way to sense the eerie-like retreat of the villages that dangle around the mountain crescent.

Discovery Trail
HIKING

This pleasant 5.3km downhill route leads from Hayl Al Hadab to hotel Alila Jabal Akhdar Oman along a marked trail (look for red, white and yellow tabs on the rocks). To understand why this is dubbed the 'Discovery Trail', you have to train your eye towards the minutiae of the walk, from the high-altitude desert plants with their tiny pin-prick flowers, to the footprints of hedgehogs. The hotel can arrange guides to identify the unique flora sprinkled across this rocky terrain.

Mirage in the Mountains Trail
HIKING

With a 200m rise involved, this 6.5km trail over rocky terrain requires a bit of fitness. It is worthwhile, however, for the close-up it affords of a wadi bottom and the vegetation that thrives in this semi-arid landscape. The trailhead is at Alila Jabal Akhdar Oman, where guides are available.

🛏 Sleeping

Khab Hail Mahlab
CAMPGROUND

FREE Encompassing a large tract of flat open space, ringed with magnificent mature juniper trees, this area makes a perfect wild campground. It neighbours the Sultan's experimental farm, where prize pomegranates are grown (harvested between August to October). The site is busy at weekends with local families who picnic around the edge of the space. There are no shops or facilities here.

The juniper trees are more than 100 years old and grow to 18m in height. The berries are harvested between March and June.

Green Mountain
APARTMENT $

(☎ 25429888; www.jahotelapartments.com; 1/2-bed apt excl breakfast OR45/65) Offering apartment-style accommodation, this new Omani-run hotel in the middle of Saiq offers either one-bedroom or two-bedroom flats. The flats are comfortable and come with kitchen and lounge, and represent good value for money for families looking to spend some time getting to know Jebel Akhdar. There's no food provided, but restaurants are within walking distance.

Sama Al Akhdar Hotel
HOTEL $$

(☎ 22507681; www.shanfarihotels.com; r incl half-board OR80-200; P🅿️🛜❄️) This large hotel, built in the local grey stone and with paths that are constructed from the distinctive fossilised pavement that is a unique feature of the area, has one of the best views on Jebel Akhdar. Overlooking the terraced villages below, and claiming Diana's Viewpoint (p179), it offers large balconied rooms in a main block and more attractive chalets.

Stone House Saiq
HOTEL $$

(☎ 94400904; Saiq; r excl breakfast OR45; 🛜) This new villa offers simple, sparsely furnished but clean rooms with tiled floors in the middle of Jebel Akhdar's main town. No food is provided, but it's within walking distance of coffee shops and restaurants.

Jebel Al Akhdar Hotel
HOTEL $$

(☎ 25429009; www.shanfarihotels.com; s/d/tr OR40/55/65; P) Near the junction to the upper plateau and without a view, this hotel feels empty even when full. With an open fire in the lobby in winter and a wind howling around the wacky stained-glass domes, the hotel (the first to be built on Jebel Akhdar) at least has character. Rooms are utilitarian but comfortable, and there's a licensed restaurant.

Buffet lunch and dinner cost OR8 and are open to nonresidents, and picnic boxes (OR5) can be ordered. Mountain bikes are available for hire (OR10 for six hours).

★ Alila Jabal Akhdar Oman
BOUTIQUE HOTEL $$$

(☎ 25344200; www.alilahotels.com; r incl half-board for 2 from OR280; P🅿️@🛜❄️) This is one gorgeous hotel. Overlooking a dramatic rift in the mountain floor, the 86 luxury rooms of this refined hotel command views of the 2000m desert canyon below. Built of locally hewn basalt, with hints of the juniper wood for which the upper plateau of Jebel Akhdar is renowned, the resort lives up to its Sanskrit name, 'Surprise'.

A *falaj* runs past the licensed Juniper Restaurant, which offers buffet and barbecue dining (OR15) from noon to 3pm (4pm on Fridays) and a fine dining à la carte menu (dishes around OR10) at other times (clos-

es 11pm). An open fire roaring in the lobby takes the nip out of the high-altitude air, and a spa (OR45 for a one-hour therapeutic Balinese massage) helps ease the aches from wilderness hiking with local guides. A range of three-hour hikes can be organised through the Leisure Concierge (from OR15 per person) to the abandoned village of Sarab and beyond. There is a library sporting large slabs of polished fossilised coral from the *jebel* and a shop selling a few tasteful Omani crafts.

Anantara Al Jabal Al Akhdar Resort
HOTEL $$$

(☎ 25218000; www.anantara.com/en/jabal-akhdar; r incl half-board from OR225, 1-bedroom villa from OR332; P🅿️@🛜❄️) This exclusive address is positioned on the edge of the Jebel Akhdar crescent with eagle-eyed views of the mountain's famous terraces below. Accommodation is in luxurious rooms or villas with their own heated private pool. Romantic dining at the canyon's edge can be arranged at Diana's Viewpoint (p179) – also claimed by the neighbouring hotel! Rose tours are organised in season.

🍴 Eating & Drinking

Robo'u Alsaab Restaurant
MIDDLE EASTERN $

(mains from OR1.5; ⏰ 9am-11pm) Serving simple but well-prepared fare such as shawarma and whole roasted chickens (OR2.8), this local-style restaurant has tables under colourful awnings along the main road through Saiq and is popular with independent travellers.

Jebel Nights
MIDDLE EASTERN $$

(☎ 90505866; www.layalialjabal.com; platter for 2 OR6.5; ⏰ 10am-10pm) Despite being on the edge of the cliff near Diana's Viewpoint, (p179) this restaurant doesn't in fact have a view even from the rooftop terrace. What it does have is very tasty Middle Eastern and Iranian food. Don't be put off by the kitsch European decor, nor the lingering smell of cooking – the steaming stews and bread easily compensate.

Da'an Al Pesaiteen Coffee Shop
CAFE

(⏰ 24hr) This tiny coffee shop – one of a series of government-built outlets all over Jebel Akhdar, located in pretty picnic spots – offers tea, coffee, soft drinks and basic snacks such as egg rolls (in bread) and dal. It makes a good drinks stop, particularly as there are attractive picnic shelters to enjoy the view with some shade.

DON'T MISS

AL HOOTA CAVE
كهف الهوتة

At the bottom of the ascent to Sharfat Al Alamayn, between Tanuf and Al Hamra, lies one of Oman's main tourist attractions, **Al Hoota Cave** (كهف ال; ☑ 24391284; www.alhootacave. om; adult/child 6-12 yrs OR12/3.5; ☉ 9.30am-5pm; ℗). Embellished with stalactites and stalagmites, and the habitat of tiny, blind cave fish, it's something of a gem. A narrow-gauge railway runs into the cave, delivering visitors to a trailhead from where you walk the 850m (via staircases totalling 230 steps and an ascent of 65m) in a 45-minute loop back towards the entrance. Humidity is high (85%), but the cave is well - and sensitively – lit.

Pause for 10 minutes in the excellent **geological museum** at the visitors centre before leaving; it showcases features that have made Oman internationally renowned among geologists. There's a climbing wall, souvenir shop and restaurant here making a trip worthwhile even when the cave is closed with flooding.

ⓘ Information

Knowledgeable staff demonstrate typical Omani hospitality (serving local coffee and dates) in the reception of the purpose-built **Tourism Information Centre** (☑ 80077799; www.omantourism.gov.om; ☉ 9am-4pm Sat-Thu, 8-11am Fri). They offer advice on accommodation, sights and hikes, and free maps and brochures are available. It's located at the beginning of the ascent to Jebel Akhdar, beside the police checkpoint.

ⓘ Getting There & Away

Access to Jebel Akhdar is by 4WD only, via the town of Birkat Al Mawz (p179). Follow the brown signs for Wadi Al Muaydin, off Rte 15, and head for the fort. After 6km you will reach a checkpoint where you will have to satisfy the police that your car has 4WD. Saiq is about 30km beyond the checkpoint and the main road, after a series of steep switchbacks up the mountainside, leads straight there.

The upper plateau is reached via a road (currently being widened) to the right just after Jebel Al Akhdar Hotel.

There have been many fatal accidents caused by people trying to make the long descent in a 2WD, using their brakes rather than changing gears, and for this reason, 4WD is mandatory despite the good paved roads that thread across the mountain top.

As yet there is no public transport to the area, but several tour companies, including National Travel & Tourism (p143), offer day trips from OR65 per person (for a minimum of two). It is cheaper and more rewarding to hire a 4WD in Birkat Al Mawz and stay at one of the hotels.

Tanuf
تنوف

☑ 25 / POP 300

Home to one of Oman's most-famous mineral-water plants, Tanuf is nestled at the crease between plain and mountain around 35km northwest of Nizwa. The village is sprinkled across the plain with a concentration of date palms and cornfields close to the mountains and offers an interesting glimpse of plantation life.

Tanuf makes for an interesting visit for two further reasons. The crumbling old village of mud-brick houses, abandoned after attack in the local wars between sultan and imam in the 1950s, makes a rich auburn foreground at sunset to the grey slab of *jebel* (mountain) behind. If you walk behind this atmospheric collection of old houses, there is one of the best examples of an active falaj in the region. The watercourse doubles in and out of the rock high above the wadi en route to the small water bottling plant nearby.

ⓘ Getting There & Away

There's no public transport to Tanuf, but the village is an easy 30-minute drive from Nizwa and included in some tour itineraries. For those with 4WD, the route continues on past a dam, high into the mountains beyond.

If you're happy to follow your nose, a small rural road leads through Tanuf's plantations to Al Hoota Cave, at the bottom of the road to Sharfat Al Alamayn, giving an interesting glimpse of plantation life.

Sharfat Al Alamayn
شرفات العلمين

Straddling a saddle between Oman's two highest mountains, Jebel Shams and Jebel Akhdar, Sharfat Al Alamayn overlooks some of the most spectacular mountain scenery in the region. Reached from the south via by a well-paved, zigzag road from Al Hamra (near Al Hoota Cave), Sharfat Al Alamayn can also be reached from the north along a tortuous off-road mountain route via Wadi Bani Awf and the tiny village of Hatt. At the point where the off-road route connects with the paved road, there is a high-altitude **viewpoint** (Shorfet Al Alamin Pass) with a 360-degree view across the limestone terrain. It's a joy to stand here and watch Egyptian vultures wheeling around on the thermals, and to see the sun carve deep shadows across the crumpled vista in the late afternoon.

Two friendly budget hotels, **Al Hoota Resthouse** (☑ 92822473; hootaoman@hotmail.com; r excl breakfast OR35; ℗) near the top of the paved ascent to Sharfat Al Alamayn, and **Shorfet Al Alamin Hotel** (☑ 99449071; www.shorfetalalamin.com; r OR40; ℗ 🛜) on

the ridge (although curiously designed to miss the view), offer the only accommodation near here. Beside Snake Gorge, on the off-road descent, there's delightful **Bait Bimah** (☑ 95915555, 97929963; www.baitbimah oman.com; Bimah Village; dm/s/d incl half-board OR25/30/50; ℗) which can organise transfers from Muscat (OR100).

❶ Getting There & Away

A saloon car can make the ascent from Al Hamra to Sharfat Al Alamayn (30km, 40 minutes) as the road is paved and not too steep. To descend to Wadi Bani Awf on the other side of the mountain, however, a 4WD (and confidence in off-road driving) is essential. There is no public transport in this region, but some tour companies, such as Mark Tours (p143) offer this as a day-trip from

---

MOUNTAIN ROAD VIA HATT اهات ووادي بني عوف

You don't need to see the mangled heaps of metal at the bottom of the vertical cliffs to realise that this is one off-road driving route that needs extreme concentration. If impossible inclines, narrow gaps and heart-stopping drop-offs appeal, this five-hour, truly spectacular road over the western Hajar Mountains is for you. It can be driven (strictly 4WD) as a long round-trip from Muscat or as a more leisurely outing from Nizwa to Rustaq. The route passes through remote, rugged country, and you should take the necessary precautions (spare tyre, jack, water, warm clothing, walking shoes and basic provisions). Check weather conditions before you leave and do not attempt the journey during or after rains.

Follow the signs for Al Hoota Cave from the Nizwa–Bahla road. You'll see a brown sign, just before reaching the cave, indicating Bilad Sayt (Balad Seet). The road, zigzagging up the mountain in front of you, is sealed for the entire ascent. Zero your odometer at the base of the road and at 24km, you will come to the Sharfat Al Alamayn viewpoint, on the saddle of the ridge: this is the highest point in the road and the view is exceptional.

Descend off road into the village of **Hatt**. This traditional mountain oasis is best explored on foot or, to avoid being intrusive, admired at a distance. After Hatt, the road continues for another 6km, skirting past **Bilad Sayt**, which makes a good detour. With its picture-postcard perfection of terraced fields and sun-baked houses, it's one of the prettiest villages in the area. The villagers prefer visitors to park outside and walk in, or simply view the village from a distance.

At around 44km, the road passes the entrance to aptly named **Snake Gorge**, a popular destination for adventure hikers and climbers. From here the main track meanders around the mountain to the exit of Snake Gorge at 50km, signalled by a neat row of trees. If you're here in April, look out for a beautiful yellow-flowering tree, a subspecies of *Tecomella undulata*, commonly known as 'Rajasthan teak'.

Continue along the main track into Wadi Bani Awf (p197), ignoring the left fork at 57km that leads into Wadi Sahten (p197). Wadi Bani Awf runs through a magnificent canyon, with limestone cliffs towering above the wadi bottom. Plantations of dates, lemons and mangoes cling to the wadi's edge, providing a livelihood for small settlements that lurk in the perpetual shadow of the *jebel* (mountain). At 60km you will join a sealed road that leads eventually to Hwy 13 at 70km. Turn left for Rustaq, or right for Nakhal and Muscat.

Adventure tour companies can arrange guides and transport in the area, and there is accommodation and wild camping opportunities near Snake Gorge. Husaak Adventures (p142) offer an overnight trip via Nizwa and Sharfat Al Alamayn for OR200 including camping gear, equipment, food and transport.

MOUNTAIN ADVENTURES

Most people would be content with peering gingerly over the rim of Wadi Ghul (p187) – Oman's Grand Canyon – but there are those for whom this isn't close enough. If you are the kind who likes to edge to the ledge, then try some of the following adventure activities in the Hajar Mountains.

Balcony Walk (p187) The return hike along route W6 from the rim village of Al Khateem (3km beyond Jebel Shams Resort) to the so-called 'hanging village' of Sap Bani Khamis, which clings to the side of Wadi Ghul, is a favourite with thrill seekers. Abandoned more than 30 years ago, it is reached along the popular but vertiginous balcony walk: one false step in this five-hour 'moderate hike' will send you sailing (without the 'ab') 500m into the void.

Haute Route (p176) For those with lungs built to withstand punishing altitude, try the high-altitude cycling tour that pedals between 1600m to 2300m above sea level with two canyons thrown in.

Snake Gorge (p183) If you're comfortable with an extreme angle of dangle, then you might like the climbing opportunities in the upper reaches of this narrow gorge. Enthusiasts have thrown up via ferrata lines allowing those with a head for heights to pirouette on a tightrope 60m above certain death.

Majlis Al Jinn (p170) The 158m drop into this cavern is like a descent into Hades. Fabled as the second-largest cavern in the world – bigger than St Peter's Basilica in Rome, bigger than Cheops' pyramid in Giza – this is one mighty hole. Don't count on a *jinn* (genie) for company; the only spirit you're likely to feel is your own, petering out with the rope as you reach for rock bottom. Named after the first person to descend into the shaft of sunlight at the bottom of the cavern, **Cheryl's Drop** is the deepest free-fall rappel in Oman.

With dozens of challenging hikes, 200 bolted climbing routes and an almost uncharted cave system, Oman is one adrenaline rush still pretty much waiting to happen. If you want to be in with the pioneers, contact the mountain camps on Jebel Shams (guided hikes cost from around OR50 from the camps for a maximum of four people). Alternatively, contact Husaak Adventures (p187) or Bike & Hike Oman (p176), offering exciting pedal-power tours.

Muscat. Husaak Adventures (p187) offers a two-day round trip from Muscat via Nizwa with camping at the top of the pass (OR225 per person).

Al Hamra

الحمراء

📰 25 / POP 9300

This venerable village at the foot of the Hajar Mountains is one of the oldest in Oman, and it is interesting for its well-preserved row of two- and three-storey mud-brick houses built in the Yemeni style. There are many abandoned houses in the upper parts of the village, which make for an atmospheric stroll, especially at sunset when the honey-coloured buildings appear to melt into one.

Visitors are welcome, and there's a museum devoted to domestic pursuits that helps open up the inner life of this 400-year-old community. As with most rural villages in Oman, it's best to explore on foot.

Al Hamra has a new as well as an old quarter; these are located either side of a large plantation of dates. The route through the old quarter is best explored on foot by following the *falaj* at the bottom of the village.

🅞 Sights

★ Bait Al Safah
MUSEUM

(OR3, discounted entry with guide OR2; ⊙ 9am-5.30pm) This quirky museum is more open house than historical display. Three ladies accompany guests around their traditional house in the aged and crumbling village of Al Hamra. They demonstrate the culinary arts of juniper-oil production, Omani bread-making and coffee-bean grinding, and there's an opportunity for a photo shoot in traditional regional costume. Sitting cross-legged in the *majlis* (reception room), surrounded by photos of local sheikhs, sampling coffee and dates, and exchanging sign language with the ladies is an experience not to be missed.

The museum is in the old part of Al Hamra. Park by the roundabout at the western end of town and walk along the street past the historic old Yemeni-style buildings. The ladies will spot you before you see them in the interior gloom of the downstairs entrance.

At the time of writing, bread-making courses were being planned and local women were about to take up their traditional crafts in the cool basement of this newly extended, 400-year-old building.

Al Hamra Viewpoint VIEWPOINT
Bathed in the golden light of sunset, with the limestone 'dip slope' of Jebel Shams as backdrop and a thick plantation of date palms in the foreground, the old village of Al Hamra is magnificently framed for a photograph from this viewpoint above town. Little surprise, then, that this has become a regular stop on most tours of the area. With a couple of awnings for shade, it also makes a good place for a picnic.

🛏 Sleeping

⭐ Beit Al Jebel
Hospitality Inn HERITAGE HOTEL $
(📞 92962660; baiit.aljabal@gmail.com; Old Hamra; r incl half-board with shared/private bathroom OR40/50) This atmospheric lodging, located in old Al Hamra, offers a chance to experience the usually hidden interior of Al Hamra's famous tall buildings. Saved from crumbling to dust, the hotel is the project of four local lads and comprises traditional rooms with mattresses on the floor and beds in the cosy basement. The rooftop view of the surrounding plantations is splendid.

⭐ The View Resort RESORT $$$
(📞 at the lodge 97233189, booking office 24400873; www.theviewoman.com; r incl half-board with full/half view OR140/120; 🅿 🛜 🏊) This resort lives up to its name with panoramic views over Al Hamra basin, a dizzying 1400m below. Don't be put off by the cabins cantilevered over the drop: the spacious interiors offer an unparalleled vista from both luxury bed and bathtub. The 7.5km signposted ascent from Al Hamra is steep – 4WD is essential or hotel transfer costs OR25 return.

With a temperature-controlled infinity pool that appears to hover in the sky and an upmarket restaurant with a 'pasta station', where the chef prepares Italian dishes in view of delighted diners, this resort is an attractive place to relax, which is just as well as there's almost nothing else to do. That said, there is a 1km walk from The View that leads to some interesting villages. Alternatively bikes are for hire (OR10 per hour) or book an onward itinerary through Zahara Tours (p142), which owns the resort.

🍷 Drinking & Nightlife

Juice Village JUICE BAR
(📞 99617910; ⊙ 8am-10pm) Selling delicious banana, mango and pomegranate juice to take away, this tiny juice shop is one of several along the main road in new Al Hamra.

❶ Getting There & Away

The only way of reaching Al Hamra is by car or with a tour from Nizwa or Muscat. Parking is possible at either side of the long strip of aged houses. The new part of town (and the gateway for the village of Misfat Al Abriyyin) is about 1km from the old quarter.

Misfat Al Abriyyin مسفاة العبريين

📋 25 / POP 2000

A sealed road leads from Al Hamra up to this mountain-hugging village (sometimes shortened and spelt Misfah), making it one of the few mountain villages accessible without 4WD. The mountain flank, draped in date plantations and with a terraced sequence of stone houses in the foreground, is very picturesque and often seen in promotional literature on Oman.

It's possible to visit one of the guesthouses for lunch or, for an introduction to life among the date palms on the flank of Oman's highest mountain, a hike alongside the *falaj* (irrigation channel) is highly recommended. This is one of the few old villages that actively welcomes tourists, but in return visitors are urged to stick to the well-marked trails, respect marked no-go areas and to refrain from smoking, drinking alcohol and picking fruit – the village's main livelihood. It is also necessary to dress modestly (covering knees and shoulders) to avoid causing offence.

◉ Sights & Activities

Misfat Viewpoint VIEWPOINT
For the best view of Misfat, turn right by the campground before entering the village.

The ancient stone buildings, half buried in a thick date plantation and framed by grey limestone slopes behind, makes for a quintessential Hajar Mountain composition.

★ **Plantation Circuit Trail** HIKING
This path loops through the date palms, ascending and descending the plantation steps in a circuit around the southern part of the village. The experience is one of brilliant sunlight splintering through the trees, lime-green allotments and the sound of water tumbling along the *aflaj*.

☞ Tours

Canyon Adventure Tours CULTURAL
(⌨ 99412660;   2.5hr village/agricultural tour OR25/30 per group (up to 10 people)) ✒ Escorted by locals born in the area, the tours offered by this company offer genuine insights into Omani culture and the traditions of the Hajar Mountain settlements. The company also arranges a full-day trek along walking trail W9 to Sharfat Al Alamayn, an unrelenting uphill slog made easier by stretching it over two days and taking a donkey (OR120 per person, minimum of two).

★★ Festivals & Events

Titan of the Hill CYCLING
(www.redbull.com/toth; ☉ Nov) This downhill mountain-bike event (in a time-trial format) commences above Misfat and threads a path through the middle of the village and down steep plantation steps. It's still a new race (inaugurated in November 2017) but is already attracting attention for the extreme nature of the course.

🛏 Sleeping & Eating

★ **Misfah Guest House** GUESTHOUSE $$
(Misfah Old House; ⌨ 99338491; bandb.misfah@gmail.com; s/d incl half-board & shared bathroom OR35/55, d incl half-board & private bathroom OR70; ☎) ✒ This tiny guesthouse – the first to bring tourism income to the village – is set within a beautiful plantation. It's housed in two old buildings, family heirlooms of the Al Abri family. Rooms are small but quaint, and all have air conditioning. Bring only what you need overnight as it's a 10-minute walk from the car park. Reservations are essential.

Al Misfah Hospitality Inn GUESTHOUSE $$
(⌨ 91104466; www.canyonadventurestours.com; d/tr incl half-board & shared bathroom OR50/70)

Joining the growing number of accommodation options in this tiny village, and securing a future for a way of life that is slowly ebbing away as the younger generation move to the city, this characterful guesthouse on the edge of the plantation occupies a typical old building with wooden ceilings and a cave room. Rooms are cosy and have air conditioning.

Al Husn Guesthouse GUESTHOUSE $$
(⌨ 92173611; r incl half-board & private/shared bathroom OR85/65, 4-/6-bed dm OR20 per person) The tallest of several guesthouses capitalising on the success of the original, this multistorey restoration project requires a bit of fitness just to reach the rooms. These are attractively fitted into the caves and rock rooms around which the 300-year-old dwelling was built – the reception was once a donkey's stable. There's a fantastic view from the rooftop restaurant.

Ideal Ambitious BUFFET $
(buffet OR3; ☉ 9am-10pm Fri-Sun) This unlikely campground at the entrance to the village doubles as a restaurant at weekends. Buffets include Omani rice and Indian dishes. Sleep off supper by pitching a tent (own/hired OR2/5) in the minimal but thankfully level grounds. Blankets are available, and there's hot water in the shared shower block. The site also has clean toilets (200 baisa for nonguests).

🛍 Shopping

Bait Al Nahal FOOD
(⌨ 99442104; ☉ 8am-6pm) ✒ Active beehives form the centrepiece of this open-sided shop. As the worker bees collect their precious cargo, their keepers demonstrate the magic properties of honey and give tastings. The honey is available to buy in even very small quantities, along with fresh honeycomb. There's also wild herbs, date syrup, neem juice and some crafts for sale in this health-promoting haven.

ℹ Getting There & Away

There's no public transport, but the village is clearly signposted from Al Hamra and the 7km uphill drive is navigable in a saloon car. Understandably, locals insist on visitors parking on the edge of the village and you'll see why as you begin to climb down through the narrow alleyways of the village and along the edge of the encompassed plantations.

Jebel Shams   جبل شمس

Oman's highest mountain, Jebel Shams (Mountain of the Sun; 3009m), is best known not for its peak but for the view into the spectacularly deep Wadi Ghul lying alongside it. The straight-sided Wadi Ghul is known locally as the Grand Canyon of Arabia, as it fissures abruptly between the flat canyon rims, exposing vertical cliffs of 1000m and more.

Until recently, there was nothing between the nervous driver and a plunge into the abyss, but now an iron railing at least indicates the most precipitous points along the track, and rough car parks pick out some of the best viewpoints into the canyon. Near the summit, the terrain flattens out into a large plateau making an ideal place to camp and picnic...or buy a carpet (p188)! There are also a couple of well-established hikes here, the most famous of which is the Balcony Walk just below the canyon rim.

◉ Sights

★ Wadi Ghul Viewpoint   CANYON
The term 'Grand Canyon of Arabia' is wholly deserved for this quintessential feature of Oman's spectacular mountain scenery. A short path leads to the edge of the limestone cliffs with a vertiginous 1000m drop into Wadi Ghul below. There are no safety barriers, but the cliff edge is stepped at the top allowing visitors to sit in safety while contemplating the view. There are other viewpoints along the Jebel Shams road, but this is the most expansive.

There's a colourful carpet stall opposite selling key fobs and small rugs.

Ghul Village   RUINS
Affording one of the most lovely vistas in the Hajar Mountains, the abandoned village of Ghul dusts the shoulder of a cliff at the foot of Wadi Ghul, the Grand Canyon of Arabia. The lime-green fields in the foreground contrast with the camouflaging grey of the ruined houses, making for a wonderful photograph in the morning light. The village is just before the Jebel Shams road begins its ascent and a carpet stall (p188) marks the spot.

It's possible to drive into Wadi Ghul (a popular local picnic spot) for around 7km to enjoy the pools of water that collect here. The road terminates in the village of A'Na-khar with views of the towering canyon cliffs above. A walking path (numbered 6A) threads deeper into the mountains.

🏃 Activities

★ Husaak Adventures   ADVENTURE SPORTS
(☑97123324; www.husaak.com; Sama Heights Resort; four-hour walk per person from OR20, 2-day hiking tours from OR150) This Omani company has a mission to rebrand the country as a world-class adventure destination. To this end, it offers treks with various degrees of difficulty on Jebel Shams and elsewhere in the Hajar Mountains. Hikers are accompanied by experienced local guides and routes range from easy four-hour walks to challenging 12-hour, 15km hikes with 1400m ascents.

A popular two-day tour (OR150) involves a strenuous 20km, 1500m-ascent hike to the top of Jebel Shams. The tour includes transport from Muscat, camping equipment and food.

Balcony Walk   HIKING
The most popular of several well-established routes on Jebel Shams, this 5km hike (in each direction) requires some nerve because of the 1000m drops but is not technically difficult. The route (numbered W6) ends at an abandoned village with a permanent pool of water in the rocky overhang above. A small rug stall marks the entrance.

Jebel Shams Circuit   SCENIC DRIVE
For a rewarding off-road drive with spectacular views, the rugged loop around the top of Jebel Shams can be completed in about two hours. This gives enough time to walk over to various precipices to admire the view. The route is very steep and narrow but requires no particularly technical 4WD skills – just a head for heights!

Clockwise, follow the signs for Sunrise Resort, passing tiny terraced hamlets clinging to the steep cliff face, until you come to a T-junction where a left turn leads to the Sunrise Resort. Turn right here for the villages of Krub and Al Marrat: the track passes the entrance to the radar site at the top of Jebel Shams and descends past the junction for Jabal Shams Resort (and the canyon viewpoint) to complete the loop.

At dusk, keep an ear open for hoots in the scrubby bushes – a recently discovered endemic species of owl inhabits the area.

🛏 Sleeping

★ Sama Heights Resort   TENTED CAMP $$
(☏24489853; s/d tents incl half-board OR35/45, s/d chalets OR70/85; P 🏊) This delightful camp, attractively landscaped in sympathy with the wilderness setting, is thriving under new ownership. A range of accommodation is on offer, from goat-hair tents and small bungalows to a grand chalet that sleeps 10. There's hot water, a restaurant and the chance to barbecue in the camp cave, while Jebel Shams' key sights are within walking distance.

Situated at the start of the walking route to the summit of Jebel Shams (route W4, seven to 12 hours), Sama Heights Resort is perfectly placed for outdoor activities, and a branch of Husaak Adventures (p187) facilitates a number of off-the-beaten-track walking options. If hiking up 1000m to the summit of Jebel Shams (2990m) seems too much of an effort, the edge of Wadi Ghul is an easy stroll away. Transport from Al Hamra costs OR40 for a return trip.

Sunrise Camp   TENTED CAMP $$
(☏94100900; www.sunriseresort-om.com; tents/chalets OR30/40; P) In a tranquil location near a dramatic mountain precipice, this remote camp makes for a peaceful retreat. Beds are offered in Arab-style tents or simple concrete chalets, all with private bathrooms. Guests huddle inside the dining room during bitter winter nights or round their own campfires. Pitch your own tent for OR8 (including breakfast) – dinner costs OR8.

Jebel Shams Resort   TENTED CAMP $$
(☏99382639; www.jebelshamsresort.com; s/d tents incl half-board OR35/50, s/d cabins OR55/70; P 🛜 🏊) Offering cosy stone cabins with bathrooms, verandas and heaters, plus some Arab tents popular with Omanis at weekends, this camp is so close to the canyon rim that you'll have to be strapped down if you're a sleepwalker. Mountain-bike hire (OR5 per hour) is available. Pitch your own tent for OR10 (OR18 with food).

🍴 Eating & Drinking

Coffee Shop   CAFE $
(snacks from 800 baisa; ☉7am-10pm) By the signpost for Dar Lawi, across from some picnic shelters (and derelict toilets best avoided), this simple one-storey establishment with a *barasti* (palm-frond) fence and small terraced sitting area is a favourite with water-tanker drivers. Join them for tea, fresh paratha and dal of the day (OR1) – and the chance to use a clean toilet.

Alstromeria Cafe   CAFE
(☏25422880; ☉6.30am-10.30pm) This smart, modern cafe on the approach road to Jebel Shams is something of a surprise find, given the traditional nature of the neighbourhood. As a result, it attracts a young crowd (mostly male) and has quickly become the local meeting place of choice. A range of coffees, teas and cakes are served in the cosy interior or under umbrellas outside.

🛍 Shopping

Rug Stall   ARTS & CRAFTS
(☉sunrise-sunset) Entrepreneurial carpet sellers have set up open-air shop at the bottom of Jebel Shams, capitalising on the fact that most people stop at Wadi Ghul to take a photograph of the abandoned village opposite. They sell rugs handwoven from coarse goat hair in natural colours, produced for generations on Jebel Shams.

ℹ Getting There & Away

There is no public transport ascending Jebel Shams, but tours with Husaak Adventures (p187), or just about any tour agency in Muscat or hotel in Nizwa, can be arranged. Alternatively, it's possible to hire a 4WD from Muscat or from Birkat Al Mawz.

If driving, the junction for Jebel Shams is clearly signposted off Hwy 21, the Nizwa–Bahla Rd, 30km or so from Nizwa. A paved road follows the bottom of the wadi, climbing through a series of sharp hairpin bends before eventually giving way to a well-graded track that climbs to the military radar site on the summit (closed to visitors). There's a right turn just before the summit that leads, after 10-minutes' drive along a paved road, to the plateau and canyon rim. The whole route is a 30km uphill climb from the start of the paved road and takes about 45 minutes.

Some people wish to attempt Jebel Shams without a 4WD, but car-hire agencies won't thank you for the uninsurable abuse of their car. It's also dangerous, with big holes opening up in the track after rains.

Bahla & Jabreen   بهلاء وجبرين

Located on the edge of a flat plain, just at the point where the foothills of the Hajar Mountains run into the dust of the desert, the small town of Bahla is dominated by a disproportionately large fort. But ask anyone in Oman what Bahla means to them, and only historians will single it out for the fort; expats may name the potteries, but any Omani not resident in the town will be sure to respond with '*jinn*'. These devilishly difficult spirits are blamed for all manner of evil-eye activities, but you're unlikely to encounter them unless you understand Arabic, as they form part and parcel of the country's oral folklore.

Nearby Jabreen is linked to Bahla by a triumphal gateway – an enormous double-arched construction over the road with grand views of Bahla, the mountains and the desert beyond. Jabreen is plagued by no such reputation, but does boast its own impressive fort.

◉ Sights

★ **Jabreen Castle** CASTLE
(Jabreen; adult/child 6-12 yrs 500/200 baisa, audio tour OR1; ☺ 9am-4pm Sat-Thu, 8-11am Fri) Rising without competition from the surrounding plain, Jabreen Castle is an impressive sight. Even if you have had a surfeit of fortifications, it's worth making the effort to clamber over one more set of battlements – Jabreen is one of the best-preserved and whimsical castles of them all. Head for the flagpole for a bird's-eye view of the latticed-window courtyard at the heart of the keep; the rooms here have distinctive painted ceilings.

Built in 1675 by Imam Bil-Arab Bin Sultan, Jabreen Castle was an important centre of learning for astrology, medicine and Islamic law and, unusually for Oman's forts and castles, there's quite a lot to discover inside the vast battlements. There is an interesting date store, for example, to the right of the main entrance on the left-hand side. The juice of the fruit would have run along the channels into storage vats, ready for cooking or to assist women in labour.

The most interesting feature of this castle is the elaborately painted ceilings. Several rooms, that seem to spring illogically from different courtyards in the heart of the keep, sport ceiling timbers with the original floral motifs. Finding these hidden rooms is part of the fun – and the original defensive mechanism – of Jabreen. Try to locate the burial chambers, remarkable for their carved vaults, and the room earmarked for the sultan's favourite horse.

Jabreen's location, trapped between the mountain and a particularly arid part of the desert, roasts under a ferocious sun for much of the year, hence the *falaj* (irrigation channel) running through the outer courtyard, which was not used for water supply but as an early air-con system.

★ **Bahla Fort** FORT
(Nizwa–Bahla Rd; 500 baisa; ☺ 8.30am-4pm Sat-Thu, 8-11am Fri) After many years of restoration, Bahla Fort, one of the largest in Oman, makes a grand sight looming over the sprawling modern settlement of Bahla. Built by the Bani Nebhan tribe who were dominant in the area from the 12th to the 15th centuries, it was granted Unesco World Heritage status in 1987. There are a few interpretative panels, but the chief attraction of this enormous fort is its scale and the panoramic view from the battlements.

The surrounding mud-brick houses are a fine example of a medieval Islamic community organised around the *afalaj*. It is best to explore the twisting lanes here on foot.

Battlements WALLS
(Nizwa–Bahla Rd) Said to have been designed by a woman 600 years ago, Bahla's remarkable battlements are noticeable at every turn of the main road through town. The walls extend for several kilometres from the fort along the adjacent wadi, making Bahla one of the most comprehensively walled towns in the world.

Bahla Potteries WORKSHOP
(☺ 8am-1pm & 4.30-6pm Sat-Thu) All over Oman, terracotta pots with simple ribbed motifs decorate the entrances to smart villas and hotels. The potteries where these beloved vessels are made are humble in comparison, buried in Bahla's backstreets. To reach them, follow the main road through the town centre towards the plantations. After 500m, you'll come to a number of potteries. Beware, the streets are very narrow, and it's easy to get a 4WD stuck. Better to walk if you're not planning on a big purchase.

The traditional unglazed water pots, designed to hang on a rope rather than sit on a table, cost a couple of rials; a large 'Ali Baba' pot fetches around OR40.

Bahla Old Souq MARKET
(☺ 6-10am) Opposite Bahla Fort, on the other side of Nizwa–Bahla Rd, rows of low-rise, arched buildings hide the entrance to a tiny traditional souq. A giant tree shades the central courtyard and a series of small workshops sell homemade ropes and *fadhl* (large metal platters used for feeding the

whole family). It's not always open, but it's an interesting place to wander if waiting for the bus back to Nizwa.

🛏 Sleeping & Eating

Jibreen Hotel
HOTEL **$**

(📞 25363361, 25363340; www.jibrenhotel.com; Hwy 21, Bahla–Ibri Rd; s/d/tr OR26/32/38; 🅿 🛜) With sky-blue roundels in the ceiling, rag-rolled walls, Egyptian gilt-edged furniture and luxurious drapes in the wi-fi-equipped bedrooms, this hotel is often full. With little alternative accommodation nearby, it's worth calling ahead. The attached River Nile Restaurant is the best place for supper in the area. It's conveniently situated on the main Bahla–Ibri road by the Jabreen junction.

Bahla Hotel Apartments
BUSINESS HOTEL **$**

(📞 25421017; www.bahlahotel.com; Hwy 21, Nizwa–Bahla Rd; s/d OR20/25; 🅿 🛜) Modern and clean, this business hotel offers spacious rooms with tiled floors arranged off large bright corridors. Some rooms sport a sliver of balcony, and all are comfortable if not exactly glamorous. The hotel has a restaurant, but its best asset is the detailed model of Bahla Fort in the foyer.

River Nile Restaurant
MIDDLE EASTERN **$$**

(📞 25363371; Hwy 21, Bahla–Ibri Rd, Jibreen Hotel; mains OR3; ⏱ 6.30-9.30am & 7.30-10pm; 🅿) With a rather elegant dining room, tables draped with cloths and upholstered chairs, this restaurant is a cut above the norm in a region of utilitarian dining. The menu focuses on grilled meat and filling rice dishes, and a range of mezze bring some distinctive Middle Eastern flavours to the largely Egyptian fare.

❶ Getting There & Around

➡ **Mwasalat buses** (Hwy 21/Nizwa–Bahla Rd) run from Muscat's Azaiba Bus Station (OR4.5), twice daily at 9.15am and 3.15pm, returning at 11.20am and 8.15pm. The journey is 190km from Muscat and takes 3½ hours via Nizwa (40km, 30 minutes). The bus continues on to Buraimi (257km, four hours), stopping at Ibri (100km, one hour) en route.

➡ Taxis are available from Muscat (OR38, three hours), and local taxis run from Nizwa to Bahla (OR15, 30 minutes).

➡ Jabreen is clearly signposted 7km off the Bahla–Ibri road. A return taxi from Bahla with an hour's waiting time costs around OR15.

Al Ayn
العين

📞 25 / POP 1000

The tiny village of Al Ayn, on the plain at the foot of the Hajar Mountains, would pass as typical but not particularly noteworthy were it not for the fact that it is located in an extraordinarily striking location. The Hajar Mountains can boast more than their fair share of dramatic landscapes, but at Al Ayn the scenery is given an ancient, human dimension thanks to a set of beehive-shaped tombs that crest a nearby ridge.

The whole area, with rocks tinged with deeply saturated bands of colour, feels highly charged, especially at sunset when the tooth-edged mountain behind the tombs, **Jebel Misht**, appears to catch alight. This striking lump of rock is one of Oman's so-called 'exotics' – a limestone mass that is out of sequence with the surrounding geology.

The whole area is spectacular. Just east of Al Ayn, there's a small roundabout, beyond which lies **Wadi Damm**, a local beauty spot

---

> **WORTH A TRIP**
>
> ### BEEHIVE TOMBS
>
> Unlike the discreet modern cemeteries of Oman, where a simple, unmarked stone indicates the head and feet of the buried corpse, the ancient tombs around the villages of Al Ayn and Bat rise defiantly from the tops of the surrounding hills, as if in a bid for immortality.
>
> Little is known about these 'beehive tombs' (so called on account of their shape) except that they were constructed between 2000 and 3000 BC, during the Hafit and Umm An Nar cultures. Archaeologists believe, however, that the free-standing structures of piled stones were designed to protect the remains of up to 200 people.
>
> It can be hard to spot the tombs, best seen silhouetted along a low red-stone ridge at sunset, but a two-bay parking slot opposite a mosque in Ayn helps focus your eye in the right place. While Al Ayn has the best-preserved beehive tombs, the largest concentration of these Unesco-listed structures is to be found around Bat in neighbouring Wadi Hajir (accessed by 4WD only) where there is barely a hilltop without one.

offering a hike by a small dam fed by waterfalls; a right turn here leads up a winding paved road to a broad fertile plateau on top of **Jebel Al Kawr**. At 2700m, this limestone massif offers spectacular views of neighbouring mountains, Jebel Misht and Shams, but attracts nothing like the same number of visitors. Several date-palm villages dot the plateau, including Sint and Sant, watered by springs and supported by tiny farms.

❶ Getting There & Away

Al Ayn lies around 30km north of Hwy 21 from the junction of Al Amlar. With a 4WD and an off-road guide, there are some exciting mountain drives in this area, but the steep tracks are often washed out after heavy rains. There is no public transport.

Ibri
عبري

📵 25 / POP 101,650

Ibri is the capital of the northern Al Dhahirah region. A sprawling town with a major highway (Hwy 21) linking it to the border town of Buraimi in the northwest and Nizwa in the southeast, it has a few sights to keep a visitor busy – including two impressive forts. The enormous 600-year-old **Sulaif Castle** (off Hwy 21; ⊙9am-3pm) on the edge of Ibri has been sensitively restored to give a flavour of the original without rebuilding all its parts, while imposing **Ibri Castle** (500 baisa; ⊙8.30am-2.30pm Sun-Thu) lies in the heart of an interesting old quarter **souq** (⊙7am-1pm & 5-9pm Sat-Thu, 4-8pm Fri) and has been fully restored. The town mostly features on itineraries as a friendly stopover en route to or from the United Arab Emirates.

There are a couple of places to stay in Ibri, helping to break a journey to or from UAE. The every-friendly **Ibri Oasis Hotel** (📵25696172; iohotel@omantel.net.om; Hwy 21; s/d excl breakfast OR28.3/38.9; 🅿🛜) is on the Buraimi side of town and serves tasty English breakfasts an **Al Majd Hotel** (📵25688272; www.almajdhoteloman.com; Hwy 21; d/tr excl breakfast OR20/25, q with kitchen OR30; 🅿🛜). With powder-blue roundels and a wealth of rather quaint decoration, this hospitable if labyrinthine hotel sports an elaborate ceiling on the 5th floor and cosy rooms with kettles and free tea. To experience local culture, head to **Arab World Restaurant** (📵99043578; Hwy 21; mains from OR1; ⊙8am-1am): men and women sit apart (or in family groups) at this highly popular restaurant serving Omani dishes, such as chicken mandhi (OR1.7), and Indian favourites.

❶ Getting There & Away

Mwasalat buses run from Muscat's Azaiba Bus Station (p150) via Nizwa (OR4.5, 280km, 4½ hours) twice daily at 9.15am and 3.15pm, returning at 10.15am and 7.20pm. The bus journey between Nizwa and Ibri is 160km and takes 1½ hours. The Muscat bus continues on from Ibri to Buraimi (200km, 2½ hours).

If you have plenty of time to explore Oman, a loop can be made from Muscat via Nizwa, Al Ayn and Ibri, through the mountains along Hwy 8 to Sohar and back along the coast to Muscat – a trip of at least three days.

Buraimi
البريمي

📵 25 / POP 73,700

Buraimi has the atmosphere of a frontier town, with its busy strip of cheap and uninspiring hotels, cargo trucks plying the main road through town, and large congregations of semi-lost travellers, idling away the time until they can recross into the United Arab Emirates on a new visa. In fact, the 'visa run' (where expatriates from the across the border enter Oman for a couple of days just to renew their visa), has become a good source of income for Buraimi and every other building in the centre of town appears to be either a budget hotel or a restaurant. It's fair to say that there's not much reason to make a special visit to Buraimi unless you're using the UAE border for Al Ain and Abu Dhabi, but there are a couple of forts, the moated **Al Khandaq Fort** (Buraimi Fort; ⊙9am-4pm Sat-Thu) **FREE** and **Hela Castle** (500 baisa; ⊙8.30am-2.30pm Sun-Thu), that are of passing interest and an **old souq** (⊙7am-1pm & 4-6pm) that sells a few handicrafts.

If you find yourself stranded in Buraimi, then **Al Buraimi Hotel** (📵25642010; Hwy 7, Sohar–Buraimi Rd; r OR35; 🅿📶🛜🏊), with split-level villas arranged around a small garden, offers a clean and friendly night's stay. There are dozens of coffee shops near the fort, the marginally best of which is **Aroos Damascus Restaurant** (📵25655207; mains from OR2; ⊙8am-midnight).

❶ Getting There & Away

Mwasalat buses run from Muscat's Azaiba Bus Station (p150) (OR3.5, four hours 40 minutes) three times daily at 6.50am, 1.20pm and 4.20pm, returning at 7am, 1pm and 5pm via Sohar (100km, 1¾ hours). Buses also connect Buraimi with Ibri; these leave Ibri at 1.45pm and 7.45pm and depart Buraimi at 7.50am and 5pm (200km, 2½ hours).

BATINAH PLAIN سهل الباطنة

The flat and comparatively fertile strip of land between the Hajar Mountains and the Gulf of Oman is the country's breadbasket and most populous area. It's been settled for centuries and even hosted Oman's capital city – at both Rustaq and Nakhal – before Muscat assumed the responsibility. All towns in the region have impressive forts, either guarding the coast or protecting the inland routes to the interior. It may not look like it from the plain (as the mountains appear as a continuous rock face with little in the way of foothills), but these routes find unlikely access into the heart of the mountains via a series of wadis (dry river beds) that periodically flood. For the visitor, these wadis, and the tiny hamlets they protect, offer exhilarating off-road exploration, while the coastal towns of Barka and Sohar exhibit an interesting culture, sharing much in common with Baluchistan across the water.

Sohar صحار

📞 26 / POP 108.300

The rumoured home of two famous sailors, the historical Ahmed Bin Majid and the semi-fictional Sinbad, Sohar is proud of its illustrious past. A thousand years ago, it was the largest town in the country: it was even referred to as Omana, though its ancient name was Majan (meaning 'seafaring'). In the 3rd century BC, the town's prosperity was built on copper that was mined locally then shipped to Mesopotamia and Dilmun (modern-day Bahrain). Little more than legend and a triumphal arch over Hwy 1 marked Sohar's place in history, however, until the new port transformed the town into a city, bringing jobs and creating wealth.

For the visitor, Sohar has a few sights of interest, while shopping opportunities and some good hotels make it a relaxed destination on a tour of northern Oman. It's also the perfect stopover on the long drive between the United Arab Emirates and Muscat.

⊙ Sights

Sohar Fort   FORT

(Al Hijra St; 500 baisa; ⊙ 9am-4pm Sat-Thu, 8am-11pm Fri) Built in the 13th century, Sohar's distinctive square-towered fort allegedly boasts a 10km tunnel intended as an escape route during a siege. Easier to find is the small **museum** in the fort's tower, which outlines local history, and the tomb of Sayyid Thuwaini Bin Sultan Al Busaid, ruler of Oman from 1856 to 1866. The fort has recently been well restored, with several rooms furnished to give an idea of military life in 19th-century Oman.

Corniche   WATERFRONT

Sohar is often congratulated for being well-kept, and the Corniche is an example of this civic pride. Providing an attractive pavement along which to stroll, this coast road is the social heart of town – joggers use it for exercise, visitors come for lunch at the cafes or lean against the sea wall to watch fishermen land their catch, while Sohar's youth parade from fort to fish market in jeeps, waving flags for National Day or celebrating football victories.

Sallan Silver Jubilee Park   PARK

(Sultan Qaboos St; ⊙ sunrise-sunset) **FREE** This park neighbours Sohar's glorious beach with its glossy, smooth strands of sand that runs without interruption into the distance. Look under the hedges of this park, which extends along the extensive Wadi Sallan, a *khor* that is often dry, for the mighty minotaur, the largest beetle in Arabia.

Fish Market   MARKET

(⊙ 7am-noon) The fish market, built in the shape of a dhow, punctuates the northern end of the Corniche. It's fun to visit early in the morning when haggling over the night catch is at its liveliest. Omani traders in *kumar* (embroidered hats), Indian fishermen in *wizar* (cotton sarongs) and women in traditional dress make for a colourful scene. Fish of all shapes and sizes are heaped on the slabs and include tuna, bream and a pipe-nosed fish without an English name.

🛏 Sleeping

Al Wadi Hotel   HOTEL $

(📞 26840058; www.omanhotels.com; Al Barakah St; s/d OR28/35; 🖎 🏊) With a lively atmosphere (partly because of the popular 'taxi bar' – frequented exclusively by male taxi drivers), Al Wadi has nicely refurbished poolside rooms and a welcoming foyer with homely sofas. A buffet (OR8) is offered when occupancy is high. The hotel (10km from the town centre) can arrange rooms at its popular Desert Nights Camp (p173) in Sharqiya Sands.

★ **Sohar Beach Hotel** HOTEL **$$**
(☎ 26841111; www.soharbeach.com; Sultan Qaboos St; r from OR45, chalets OR100; P @ 🛜 🏊) Shaped like a fort with watchtowers and a central courtyard, this hotel brings some welcome local character to Sohar's rather bland accommodation. Rooms in the main building are a bit old-fashioned, but the chalets are good value and there are pretty gardens leading to the beach. All in all, it makes a peaceful retreat a few minutes' drive from the town's attractions.

Radisson Blu Hotel, Sohar HOTEL **$$**
(☎ 26640000; www.radissonblu.com/hotel-sohar; r from OR55; P @ 🛜 🏊) While the grand staircase, marble lobby and five-star amenities (landscaped pools, rooftop bar and fine dining) are familiar prerequisites of most luxury hotels in the region, this excellent-value hotel steals a march on its rivals with the beach location. Most of the luxurious rooms have sea views, and at night the fishing boats on the horizon sparkle with Sinbad magic.

Crowne Plaza Sohar BUSINESS HOTEL **$$**
(☎ 26850901; www.ihg.com/crowneplaza/hotels/gb/en/reservation; Al Falaj Rd, off Hwy 7; r from OR55; @ 🏊) Tiers of bougainvillea lead to the domed porch and grand foyer of this predominantly business-oriented hotel. Rooms are functional rather than elegant and staff are used to catering to those in town for the nearby industrial plants. The location, on the highway to Buraimi about 15km from the town centre and near Sohar Airport, is helpful to visitors in transit.

✗ **Eating**

Thala Cafe CAFE **$**
(Corniche; mains from OR2; ⊙ 3pm-3am Fri & Sat, 8am-2pm Sun-Thu) This tiny cafe serves up tasty shawarma (pockets of bread filled with shaved meat and salad) into the small hours of the night. During the day, it offers breakfast with a good view of the sea. It also caters for the current local craze for burgers.

Wardat Al Fatah Trading TURKISH **$**
(☎ 97231990; Sultan Qaboos St; mains OR2.5; ⊙ 11am-midnight) For a partial sea view and newly caught *hamour* (a type of grouper) from the fish market opposite, this simple eatery serves delicious Turkish food at outdoor plastic tables. It began with just a couple of chairs on a concrete forecourt, but its growing reputation has helped it extend across the neighbouring *bondu* (waste ground).

DON'T MISS

CASTLE MUSEUM NEAR NAKHAL

The fortified residence **Al Ghasham Museum House** (adult/student & child OR3/500 baisa; ⊙ 9am-5pm Sat-Thu, 9am-noon & 3-5pm Fri) has hosted royalty on two occasions in its 300-year history. Now the sensitively restored, mud-brick house has been converted into an interesting museum. An active *falaj* runs through the courtyard and many of the rooms have been decorated with furniture from Zanzibar. A guided tour is included in the admission fee – helpful in identifying the best features, including a hidden passage exiting the castle, a library and a room of donated antiquities.

★ **Cornish Restaurant** SEAFOOD **$$**
(☎ 71932618, 93535077; Corniche, opp Corniche Park; mains from OR2.5; ⊙ 11am-4pm & 6pm-midnight, live rooftop BBQ station from 7pm; 🍴) In the heart of the busy fish market, this attractive, bright-windowed restaurant serves up the best of the catch, fresh from the incoming fishing boats. Preparations range from Indian and Chinese to fish and chips with plenty of nonfish and vegetarian options. Forget any thoughts of Cornish pasties – the name is a misspelling of Corniche.

Karim Beirut LEBANESE **$$**
(☎ 94625825, 90145145; Corniche; mezze OR1.3; ⊙ 10am-12.30am) Located along the seafront with a bright, no-nonsense interior and a few tables on astroturf on the pavement outside, this small Lebanese restaurant is all about the food. Popular with family outings at the weekend, the restaurant serves generous portions of delicious hot and cold mezze (starters) – meals in their own right.

🍷 **Drinking & Nightlife**

Wow Cafe CAFE
(Sultan Qaboos St; ⊙ 1pm-midnight Sat-Thu, from 2pm Fri) Ladies will feel at home in the darkened interior of this tiny cafe by the fish market – it caters for a largely female clientele. Dimly lit and with a spangled roof, it offers a trend-setting space to relax and enjoy good coffee and homebakes. There's an outdoor deck shaded with coloured

brollies for those (of either gender) who prefer blue skies.

v6O Cafe   CAFE

(☑96963102; Corniche; ◷6.30am-midnight Sat-Thu, from 9am Fri) This stylish new cafe with its sofas and urban chic interior is perfectly located on the Corniche to provide refreshment during a stroll of the seafront. It plans a broader menu of snacks, but at the time of writing was offering only a range of coffees and tasty crêpes.

Shopping

Sohar Souq   ARTS & CRAFTS

(◷9am-1pm & 4.30-10pm) Neighbouring the fort, Sohar's revamped heritage souq boasts a covered walkway with a fine wooden ceiling and an arcade with shops that sport wooden doors. Some shops are dedicated to men's tailoring but are yet to be rented. Shops number 7 (☑98128668) and 25 (☑95431143) have some beautiful textiles from Kashmir and lots of potential souvenirs; telephone if they're closed.

Traditional Handicraft Souq   MARKET

(Al Shizaw St & Sohar Rd; ◷8am-1.30pm & 4.30-8pm) Only half the workshops in this modern arcade are open, but there's a few mat-weaving establishments (shop nine) and an apothecary (shop 10), where you can pick up some *bukhorr hassad* (a mixture of natural ingredients to ward off the evil eye). Try sage for sore throats, frankincense for constipation and myrrh for joint pains.

❶ Getting There & Away

➡ Most of Sohar's sites of interest lie along or near the Corniche, 3km from Hwy 1, the Muscat–Sohar Hwy.

➡ Mwasalat buses run from Muscat's Azaiba Bus Station (one-way OR1.3, return OR1.6, 2½ hours) three times daily at 6.50am, 1.20pm and 4.20pm, returning at 8.45am, 2.45pm and 6.45pm. The Muscat bus continues on to Buraimi (100km).

➡ Taxis are available from Muscat (250km, 2¼ hours, OR45), and local taxis run along Hwy 1 from the City Centre mall.

➡ Sohar has a small international airport (p235), which sees a few flights daily. Air Arabia (www.airarabia.com) links Sohar with Sharjah in the United Arab Emirates four times per week, and Qatar Airways (www.qatarairways.com) connects Sohar with Doha daily.

❶ Getting Around

Mwasalat (www.mwasalat.om), the national bus company, is introducing an in-city service. The two routes will link the port with the city centre and will hopefully thread between some of the sights of touristic interest.

Nakhal   نخل

☑26 / POP 18,100

Nakhal is an attractive traditional town caught in the crease between the flat Batinah Plain and the Hajar Mountains. The mountains rise almost vertically behind the settlement, making a striking backdrop to one of Oman's most dramatic and best-loved forts.

Built on the foundations of a pre-Islamic structure, the towers and entrance of **Nakhal Fort** (500 baisa; ◷9am-4pm Sat-Thu) were constructed during the reign of Imam Said Bin Sultan in 1834. There are excellent views of the Batinah Plain from the ramparts, and the *majlis* (reception room) on the top 'storey' of the fort makes a cool place to enjoy the tranquillity. The windows are perfectly aligned to catch the breeze, even in summer. There are many features to look for: gaps where boiling cauldrons of honey would have been hinged over doorways, spiked doors to repel battering, round towers to deflect cannonballs and *falaj* in case of a siege.

Worth a day trip from Muscat in its own right, the fort was well-placed to protect the large date plantations that flourish here thanks to the presence of abundant spring water. A road leads through the thick plantations to **Ain Al Thawarah** (Ath Thowra Hot Spring; ◷24hr) **FREE**, a hot spring that makes for a popular picnic point at weekends. Enough light passes through the feathery canopy of palms to allow for allotments of corn, alfalfa, edible greens, bananas and citrus trees to thrive in the small plots below. Even wild ferns and an occasional lily put in an appearance. The drive makes for an interesting close up of plantation life, where water is still diverted by rocks according to ancient principles.

There's nowhere to stay in Nakhal but snacks are available from **Keytha Café** (☑99887762; sandwiches from 600 baisa; ◷8am-midnight) by the hot springs or **Oasis Shathoon Coffee Shop** (◷8am-1.30am Sat-Thu, 4pm-1am Fri) by the fort. Local-style takeaway lunch is also on offer inside **Souq Nakhal**

(☑ 99336001; ◉ 8am-1pm & 4-8pm), which also sells a small selection of crafts.

There's no reliable public transport to Nakhal, which lies off Hwy 13. Taxis from Muscat (97km, one hour) cost OR21.

Wakan وكان

☑ 26 / POP 1000

This tiny mountain hamlet is a celebrated beauty spot, boasting some of the most awe-inspiring views over the Batinah Plain of any village in the Hajar Mountains. Wrapped around by verdant terraces of vegetables, and fringed by grape, pomegranate and citrus trees, the village has changed little over the years and only now is adapting to life under the tourist gaze. The growth in visitor numbers is largely because of the delightful, paved Walking Route 25 that leads right through the pedestrian centre of the village to a viewpoint on the edge of the Jebel Akhdar massif.

Village folk are forgiving of most misdemeanours, but they do not appreciate inappropriate clothing (cover shoulders, cleavage and knees). Visitors are further expected to refrain from taking photos of people without permission, to remove all litter and to avoid picking fruit – however temptingly a pomegranate dangles over the path!

The village has charming lodgings. With only three rooms available, the tiny **Wakan Guesthouse** (☑ 24489853; r OR60) is likely to be booked up for most of the year so call ahead. The rooms are small but attractively decked out, and best of all there's a snug, communal sitting room with leather chairs

and an open fire. The mountain views from the **restaurant** terrace are superb.

🛈 Getting There & Away

The only way to reach Wakan is by 4WD via Wadi Mistal, which is signposted off Hwy 13, the main road from Nakhal to Rustaq. The drive from the highway takes about 40 minutes. There's no public transport. Locals leave their saloon cars at the bottom of the steep climb and ascend in shared 4WDs.

There's only one small car park at the top of the off-road track, beneath the village watchtower, so it's best to avoid a visit during the weekend or on national holidays if possible.

Al Awabi العوابي

☑ 26 / POP 2000

The small village of Al Awabi straddles Hwy 13, the road that links the important towns of Barka and Rustaq. With some attractive modern houses painted in pastel hues, in defiance of the national 'white only' regulation, this is a typical Batinah Plain village. It boasts a tiny **castle** but not very much else by way of sights, but it has an important function as the gateway to Wadi Bani Kharus.

This important wadi extends over 20km into the depths of the Hajar Mountains and is famed for its **petroglyphs** and its geological features such as a 'classic unconformity', where the sequence of geological layers has been interrupted – proof, some suggest, of tectonic plate theory. Regardless of your interest in rocks, a drive from Al Awabi to Al Aliya offers plenty of dramatic mountain vistas and showcases a tough rural life lived

OMAN WAKAN

WORTH A TRIP

THE WAKAN WALK

Walking Route 25 (W25) is one of the most celebrated short walking routes in Oman. The good news is that it is also one of the easiest. A well-paved, signposted path leads from the watchtower through Wakan village, across allotments of vegetables and up through orchards of peach, pomegranate and orange. A running *falaj* (irrigation channel) follows the route, filling up cisterns beside the path, ready to be diverted to the terraces below. The path ends at a picnic shelter with superb views.

Offering panoramic views of the Hajar Mountains along its entire length, the route is a virtual poem to village life and gives an indication of just how stoic the mountain people of this area need to be to survive life on the edge. Despite the challenge of driving to Wakan, the walking route – mostly via steps with several sitting areas – is easy for anyone with a reasonable level of fitness, although the altitude can cause a headache for those unused to mountain paths. It takes about 45 minutes to walk to the picnic shelter and back – longer with stops for photographs.

beneath the shadow of the mighty mountain of Jebel Shams.

There is no public transport of use to the visitor, but Wadi Bani Kharus is one of the few wadis that can be easily accessed in a saloon car.

Rustaq الرستاق

26 / POP 79,400

Rustaq enjoyed a spell as Oman's capital in the 17th century, and it remains an important regional centre. An imposing fort (one of the most impressive in Oman) dominates this friendly town, and some famous hot springs – Ain Al Kasfah (p197) – feed into neighbouring public baths. The town has a distinct older portion around the fort, and a newer part, linked by a giant decorative gateway.

Rustaq is an important access point to some mighty wadis, including Wadi Hoqain and Wadi Sahten. Threading along the base of the Hajar Mountains behind Rustaq, Wadi Sahten eventually connects with Wadi Bani Awf via an impressive rock arch. With Jebel Shams towering above the wadi, and impossibly lofty villages perched on high-altitude ledges, a 4WD drive through this region is an off-road highlight. Parts of all three wadis, however, are paved and accessible by saloon car.

◉ Sights

★ Rustaq Fort
FORT

(500 baisa; ⊙9am-4pm Sat-Thu, 8-11am Fri) Two cannons mark the interior courtyard of this enormous fort – the entrance alone signals its former importance. Built on top of pre-Islamic foundations, the massive outer walls date from the 18th century while the inner keep is of much earlier vintage. The fort has been carefully restored and is an impressive sight looming above the town, with the mountains as backdrop. The interior is a fort-lover's dream, with hidden passages, vertical stairways and massive ramparts.

★ Qasra Museum
MUSEUM

(Al Bayt Al Gharbi; ⊙9am-1pm & 4.30-8pm) **FREE** Tucked into the unlit and crumbling old quarter of Rustaq, behind the fort, this unique museum is the personal project of the owner, Zakia Al Lamki. Left the aged house by her father and reluctant to let her inheritance slide into dust, Zakia has opened up this remarkable 300-year-old time capsule to the public. The house is a popular venue for video shoots, and every

---

OMAN'S GEOLOGICAL HERITAGE

If geology seems like a frankly 'anorak' pursuit, then a trip through the wadis of the western Hajar Mountains might change your mind. Seams of iridescent copper minerals; perfect quartz crystals glinting in the sun; stone pencils and writing slates loose in the tumbling cliff; walls of fetid limestone that smell outrageously flatulent when struck; pavements of marine fossils, beautiful for their abstract design and the pattern of history they reveal – these are just a few of the many stone treasures of Batinah's wild wadis.

Although many of these features can be spotted in Wadi Bani Awf, it is neighbouring **Wadi Bani Kharus** that excites geologists. They go in search of the 'classic unconformity' that is revealed halfway up the canyon walls, a few kilometres into the wadi. At this point, the upper half of the cliff is a mere 250 million years old while the lower half is more than 600 million years old. What created this hiatus, and what it reveals about tectonic forces, is the subject of speculation in numerous international papers. For the layperson, what makes Wadi Bani Kharus remarkable is that it appears to have been opened up as if for scientific study: the opening of the wadi comprises the youngest rocks, but as you progress deeper into the 'dissection', some of the oldest rocks in Oman are revealed, naked and without the obscuring pelt of topsoil and shrubs. While you're inspecting the rocks, look out for petroglyphs – the ancient images of men on horseback are a common feature of all the local wadis.

All the main wadis in the area – **Wadi Mistal**, Wadi Bani Kharus, Wadi Bani Awf and Wadi Sahten – have their share of geological masterpieces and can be easily accessed with a car (4WD required for pottering off the road), a map and an off-road guidebook. Take along Samir S Hanna's *Field Guide to the Geology of Oman*, too, to help identify some key features.

item has a story to tell of a bygone era, including the 1970s lack-and-white television.

Brown signs lead the way through a labyrinth of narrow lanes from the car park to the house.

Wadi Bani Awf   NATURAL FEATURE
(off Hwy 13) This spectacular wadi is a major artery through the mountains and often flows year-round with spring water. It looks particularly gorgeous when mountain rain causes the *falaj*, which parallels the entire lower reach of the wadi, to cascade over its walls. With its towering cliffs and plantation settlements huddled along the wadi banks, mature native trees and striking rock features, the wadi offers a fascinating glimpse of rural life in Oman's hidden interior, beyond the populous plain.

A brand new paved road leads into the wadi from Hwy 13, but a 4WD is required to explore beyond the end of the road. Just beyond the paved section of road, the track veers right for Wadi Sahten, via a rock arch, and left for the upper reaches of Wadi Bani Awf at a signposted junction marked by a stand of ancient *Ziziphus* (native 'Christ thorn trees', popular with goats).

The track through the upper reaches of this wadi (p183) is a thrilling off-road drive along narrow ledges. There's often no room to pass another vehicle and backing round a hairpin bend, with a 500m drop if you get it wrong, is not for the faint-hearted! The route passes by Snake Gorge and climbs up, via Bilad Sayt and the village of Hatt, to Sharfat Al Alamayn (p183) – a celebrated viewpoint more usually reached by paved road from Al Hamra.

Rock Arch   NATURAL FEATURE
(Wadi Sahten) Referred to locally as a rock arch, this striking natural feature is in fact a fissure in the cliff. There is just enough space at the bottom of the crack in the mountain for the track through Wadi Sahten to slither, linking this wadi with neighbouring Wadi Bani Awf. Scattered at the base of the fissure are stone shards of limestone known as stone pencils – they 'write' well on a piece of loose slate from the friable cliff walls nearby.

Thorn Tree Copse   NATURAL FEATURE
(Wadi Bani Awf) Where the paved road through Wadi Bani Awf ends, a magnificent stand of trees comes into view. These are *Ziziphus spina christi*, or 'Christ thorn trees' – a tree associated with the biblical crown of thorns. These gnarled and knotted old specimens

are a welcome sight in the middle of an arid section of the wadi and are thought to be hundreds of years old. Near the junction for Hatt, they are perfectly located for a shaded picnic.

Wadi Sahten   NATURAL FEATURE
The exciting route through Wadi Sahten begins near Rustaq and winds through a narrow corridor that is often flowing with water. A paved road opens out into a huge basin at the foot of the Hajar Mountains. From here, the radar station at the top of Jebel Shams, Oman's highest mountain, is clearly visible. The Sahten basin is a beautiful spot from which to enjoy the 360-degree mountain vista.

Rough tracks lead from the basin up the cliffs to a number of tiny settlements that appear to defy gravity. To visit these traditional settlements or to continue on to Wadi Bani Awf via an off-road track and a rock arch, a 4WD vehicle (and a map) is essential. The 70km circular drive from Rustaq takes at least two hours.

Al Hazm Fort   FORT
(Hwy 11) With Nakhal and Rustaq, Al Hazm is one of the three great Batinah Plain forts and like them, it protects a large plantation. Currently closed for a lengthy restoration project, it's still of interest for its giant ramparts and position in the middle of the arid Batinah Plain.

Rustaq Gateway   LANDMARK
(Hwy 13) Befitting a town of its size, Rustaq has a fine gateway similar to those in Nizwa, Bahla and Sumail. Wedged between a cut in the mountains, this landmark links old Rustaq with its fort and new Rustaq, which is marked by an elegant Grand Mosque.

Ain Al Kasfah   HOT SPRINGS
(⊗9am-9pm) **FREE** These hot springs attract visitors who believe the water issuing from under the ground at Al Kasfah has therapeutic properties. As a result, the unglamorous hammam (public baths) alongside the spring are thronged at weekends with towel-wielding locals. The site may be of some touristic interest for those who haven't had the chance to dip fingers in naturally hot water before.

Wadi Hoqain   NATURAL FEATURE
(off Hwy 10) This fertile wadi, accessible only by 4WD, offers one of the easiest off-road experiences of the region and an intimate view

OMAN RUSTAQ

of life under the date palms. A reasonable graded road meanders through wadi-side plantations and villages, bustling with activity in the late afternoon. Add to the rural mix copper-coloured cliffs and a ruined **castle** (which on closer inspection turns out to be a walled settlement), and it's a wonder that this wadi has remained a secret for so long.

🛏 Sleeping & Eating

Shimook Guesthouse HOTEL **$**
(📞26877071, 92809101; alshomokh234@gmail. com; Hwy 10; r OR35) The only place to stay in Rustaq is Shimook Guesthouse, opposite Rustaq's new public park. This unexceptional two-storey hotel is accessed via a steep drive; it's home to a few long-stay teachers, so it's worth ringing ahead to check availability. Rooms are large and bland but clean, and the hotel at least offers a base from which to explore the local wadis.

Rawabi Coffee Shop MIDDLE EASTERN **$**
(shawarma 300 baisa; ⊘9am-1am) Tucked under three giant neem trees behind Rustaq Fort, this large coffee shop cooks up a giant doner kebab each night and offers a range of fruit juices which are a meal in themselves. Seating with an excellent view of the fort is at tables under the trees or in an air-conditioned restaurant.

🔒 Shopping

Souq MARKET
(⊘6am-noon & 3-6pm) This enormous souq is flooded with vegetable and grain sellers for half the day and virtually abandoned for the rest. One or two shops stay the course, among them a couple of handicraft shops selling handmade ropes and belts (used for

---

climbing and tending to date palms), rice mats, baskets and earthenware pots, all of which make interesting souvenirs.

Cobbler SHOES
(⊘9am-1pm & 4-6pm Sat-Thu) For a pair of handcrafted leather sandals, look no further than the cobbler opposite the souq. Sitting cross-legged and still producing shoes with a knife, needle and thread, the shoemaker creates traditional men's sandals in premises that are unmissable. Decorated with quirky carpentry, the shop is accessed via a somewhat bizarre miniature bridge covered in artificial grass.

ℹ Getting There & Away

Mwasalat buses run from Muscat's Azaiba Bus Station (one-way OR1.3, return OR1.6) twice daily at 4am and 3pm, returning at 5.45am and 4.35pm.

Taxis are available from Muscat (137km, OR28, 45 minutes), and local taxis run from the middle of town.

Rustaq is at the junction of three important thoroughfares: Hwy 10 from Ibri, Hwy 11 from Mussanah (on the coast) and Hwy 13 from Barka via Nakhal. The Muscat Expwy has cut the journey time between the capital and Rustaq in half and it now takes just 45 minutes to drive between the two.

Mussanah المصنعة

🚹 26 / POP 3000

Mussanah is the home of Oman's navy, docked at Wudum naval base. Quite fittingly, then, the town has also earned itself a name as the destination of choice for nautical adventures. Indeed, the **Millennium Resort** (📞26871555; www.millenniumhotels.com; r from OR84, r with sea view OR95; 🅿@🛜🌊), which punctuates the flat shoreline of Mussanah at the edge of the shrubby Batinah Plain, was initially established to accommodate athletes during the second Asian Beach Games of 2010, and that event left behind a legacy of sailing, kayaking and swimming that has since been supplemented with a range of other water sports. **Oman Sail** (www.omansail.com), the country's world-class, government-supported sailing enterprise, has a base in the resort's private harbour. There's a small zip line here and a water course of floating buoys of all shapes and sizes, called **Aqua Fun** (1hr OR5; ⊘11am-1pm & 2-6pm) which, judging by the squeals of

---

delight from water-confident kids, lives up to its name.

The resort makes a good base for diving and snorkelling off the **Damaniyat Islands**. These government-protected rocky islands, around an hour's boat ride off the Batinah coast, are rich in marine life, including magnificent whale sharks (often seen between August and October). Day trips can be arranged through the resort's **Seaoman** (☑24274201; www.seaoman.com; two dives from boat OR45, plus equipment OR16, snorkelling incl equipment OR30) or through dive centres in Muscat. A permit is required to visit, but this is usually included in the cost of the excursion.

It has to be said that other than visiting the resort, or eating in its excellent buffet restaurant, **Al Bahar** (lunch buffet OR10, dinner buffet Sat & Sun OR12, Mon-Fri OR14; ⊙12.30-3.30pm & 6.30-10.30pm), there isn't too much to see or do in the surrounding area. That said, a couple of forts, including the enormous **Husn Al Tharmad** (Tharmad Fort; 500 baisa; ⊙8.30am-2.30pm Sat-Thu), dot the salt-blighted date plantations and are of passing interest.

ⓘ Getting There & Away

Mwasalat buses ply Hwy 1 from Barka to the inland portion of Mussanah, and the fort of Husn Al Tharmad is walkable from the Wudum Junction. The Millennium Resort, however, lies too far off Hwy 1 to be practically reached except with your own transport or by taxi from Muscat (OR60, 1½ hours); transport by taxi can be organised through the resort.

Barka بركاء

☑26 / POP 81,650

Barka is a thriving coastal town that has become something of a crossroads between the regional centres of Sohar and Rustaq. The old part of town, near the sea, is looking a bit sad as the traditional mud-built houses are being torn down to make way for a new corniche.

That said, there's still a traditional market of interest to visitors, and the fort restoration is nearing completion. As further compensation, the new suburb of Bahla has sprung up along the Muscat–Sohar Hwy with big shops and new restaurants transforming life in this once sleepy town. Many people head to Barka during the annual Muscat Festival (p143) around January or February, as nearby Naseem Park hosts many of the festival's attractions.

◉ Sights

Barka Market MARKET
(Beach Rd; ⊙6-10am Fri, to noon Sat) This traditional market is a fascinating place to stand on the sidelines and watch. Giant tuna are lugged across the fish slabs of the open-air premises, while bundles of vegetation are carried aloft on the heads of farmers as livestock are ushered in and out of the thronging crowds.

Bayt Nua'man HISTORIC BUILDING
(500 baisa; ⊙8am-3pm Sun-Thu; ℙ) This multistorey, imposing merchant house from the 18th century sports a fine archway and a pair of unique, quirky turrets and is protected by high mud walls. It has been restored and now doubles as a local **museum**, with a small collection of typical household items – that's if you find it open, as the posted opening hours are seldom observed. The turnoff for the house is signposted off Hwy 1, the Muscat–Sohar road, 7km west of the Barka flyover.

Naseem Park PARK
(Hwy 1; ⊙9am-11pm Sat-Wed, to midnight Thu & Fri) **FREE** Off the main Muscat–Sohar Hwy, this large formal park has mowed lawns trimmed with flower beds and is shaded by mature trees. It makes a pleasant retreat for a picnic.

It hosts part of the annual Muscat Festival (p143) with shopping stands, funfairs and live entertainment in January/February each year.

Barka Fort FORT
(Beach Rd) With its unusual octagonal tower and a location fending off incursions from the sea, Barka Fort cuts a dash along Barka's busy coastline, flanked by several adjacent watchtowers. It has been closed for restoration for some time but is still impressive from the outside. The fort is by the coast, around 5km from the town centre, next to the market.

🛌 Sleeping

Barka Hotel Apartments BUSINESS HOTEL **$**
(☑26984888; barka_hotelapartments@hotmail.com; off Hwy 13, opp Al Salam Mosque; 1-/2-bed r OR25/35; ℙ🛜) This new hotel in a modern block in the centre of new Barka is convenient for an early getaway for explorations

of the Batinah Plain. Rooms are bland but huge with tiled floors and simple furnishings. There's no breakfast on offer, but a small kitchen makes DIY meals possible.

Al Nahda Resort & Spa RESORT **$$**
(☑ 26883710; www.alnahdaresort.com; off Hwy 13; r from OR65; P @ 🛜 🏊) A night spent in a luxurious low-rise chalet amid the 30 acres of verdant gardens at this well-established resort, off the Barka–Nakhal road, may trick you into forgetting the surrounding desert plain. The chalets have their own patios from which to watch the abundant birdlife. There's a spa and a good restaurant. A taxi from Muscat International Airport costs OR15.

★ **Dunes by Al Nahda** BOUTIQUE HOTEL **$$$**
(☑ 97235700; http://dunesbyalnahda.com; off Muscat Expwy, Wadi Al Abiyad; luxury tents OR170; P 🛜 🏊) Many residents of Muscat are unaware that there are sand dunes just 45 minutes west of the capital, and this luxury camp has made the best of their hidden location. With an open-sided reception and restaurant surrounded by lily ponds, a sand-therapy unit and attractive rooms designed to resemble tents, this dune-top establishment makes for a peaceful retreat.

With a day's notice, breakfast or a barbecue dinner (an extra OR15 per person) can organised at the top of a private dune. Activities include quad biking (from around OR20 per person per hour for a 100cc vehicle), camel rides (OR10 for 15 minutes), a one-hour visit to a camel farm (OR75 per vehicle), and a lesson in making *shuwa* – a local favourite involving marinated lamb, wrapped in banana leaves and slow 'roasted' underground in a sand pit (OR17). There are also opportunities to explore Wadi Abyad (OR40 per vehicle), famous for its pools of opaque white water.

Access to Dunes involves 1km of gravel track from the expressway and is best attempted with a 4WD. Transfers from Muscat International Airport cost OR53.

✕ Eating

Al Batinah Restaurant & Coffee Shop CAFE **$**
(off Beach Rd, Barka Fort Grounds; mains from OR1.5; ⊙ 6am-11pm) Serving delicious grilled meat, steaming piles of biryani, whole fried chicken and fish scooped from the sea by the fishermen mending their nets nearby, this restaurant also prepares its own fresh paratha. It's conveniently located across the *bondu* (open land) from the fort and the market, both of which can be enjoyed as a backdrop from the terrace.

Fleur INTERNATIONAL **$$**
(☑ 97235700; Dunes by Al Nahda, off Muscat Expwy; light lunch OR10; ⊙ noon-3pm & 7-11pm) The best part about this restaurant is that it is open-sided – and on top of a sand dune. Licensed to serve alcohol, the restaurant offers a short menu of international favourites. Follow up lunch with a camel ride or a hike in the sands and it makes for a fun day trip from Muscat.

🛍 Shopping

Barka Factory for Omani Halwa FOOD
(⊙ 7am-10pm) Barka is renowned for its *halwa*, Oman's traditional sweet, which is made in industrial quantities at an attractive-looking factory (with spangled pillars) in Barka. Many outlets along Hwy 1 near the Barka flyover sell this sticky confection. Flavoured with cardamom, dates and saffron, it's dispatched all over the country – there's even a **Barka Sweets** (Sultan Qaboos St; ⊙ 7am-1pm & 5-9pm Sat-Thu, 4-10pm Fri) shop in Salalah, 1000km away.

ⓘ Getting There & Around

Public Mwasalat buses run from Muscat's Azaiba Bus Station (800 baisa, one hour) twice daily at 4.20am and 3.15pm, returning at 5.40am and 4.45pm.

Metered taxis are available from Muscat (80km, OR17). Local taxis can be found around the T-junction in town and at the Barka roundabout on the highway.

It's not possible to reach any of the sights by public transport. The best bet is to take a taxi from the Barka flyover on Hwy 1.

Al Sawadi السوادي

☑ 26 / POP 5400

A popular day trip an hour or so drive west of Muscat, Al Sawadi is a beautiful spot: two gorgeous, gently sloping golden beaches slowly elide into each other at a sand bar that, at low tide, extends to some islands scattered offshore. There's good snorkelling off the islands, and local fishermen line up by the sand bar to take visitors to the best sites. At low tide, you can walk to a **watchtower** on the largest of the islands, none of which are inhabited. But beware: the tide returns very quickly leaving a very strong chance of being marooned.

Shell collectors will love Al Sawadi, as drifts of tiny pink top shells, interlaced with spiny murex and sundials, are a common sight here. Pick up a shell guide by the late Donald Bosch (available in Muscat bookshops) if you want help identifying the treasures on the beach.

ℹ Getting There & Away

Lying midway between Barka and Mussanah, Al Sawadi is signposted off Hwy 1, reached via a 12km road. The road often becomes log-jammed in the early evening at weekends (especially from October to March). There is no public transport to Sawadi. Taxis will make the trip from from Muscat (100km, OR21, 45 minutes).

MUSANDAM   مسندم

Separated from the rest of Oman by the east coast of the United Arab Emirates, and guarding the southern side of the strategically important Strait of Hormuz, the Musandam Peninsula is dubbed the 'Norway of Arabia' for its beautiful *khors*, small villages and dramatic, mountain-hugging roads. Accessible but still isolated in character, this beautiful peninsula with its cultural eccentricities is well worth a visit if you're on an extended tour of Oman, or if you're after a taste of wilderness from Dubai.

In a couple of days you can either do justice to the mountains around Jebel Harim by 4WD, or you can focus on the water and explore the *khors* (most easily by boat). With an ordinary saloon car, the drive along Musandam's western coast gives a taste of both, with its dramatic limestone scenery and reticulated coastline.

Khasab   خصب

🕿 26 / POP 12,100

The provincial capital of Musandam is small but far from sleepy. Its souq resounds to a babble of different languages, including Kumzari (a compound language of Arabic, Farsi, English, Hindi and Portuguese), and its harbour briefly bursts with activity each time a cruise ship arrives. Fishing boats and dhows amble in and out of the creeks, picking up lobster pots or casting nets in the surrounding bays. Since the lifting of the trade embargo with Iran, the mad dash in

fibreglass boats across the 55km strait has pretty much brought the semi-illicit trade in goats and cigarettes to an end, but piracy may yet stage a comeback if international sanctions are reapplied. The town has a great location wedged between steep cliffs and the sea, a feature you can't fail to appreciate when arriving by air or entering the harbour by boat.

◎ Sights

★ **Khasab Fort**   FORT
(500 baisa; ⊙ 8am-3pm Sat-Thu, to 10.30am Fri) With its command of the bay sadly diminished since Lulu Hypermarket was built on reclaimed land opposite, Khasab Fort nonetheless cuts quite a dash with its four stone turrets and fine crenellations. Built by the Portuguese in the 17th century around a much older circular tower, this well-preserved fort now houses one of the best little ethnographic museums in Oman. The central tower displays the peninsula's flora and fauna and a video highlighting the famous sea chants of local fishermen.

Bassa Beach   BEACH
Located a 2km walk from the ferry terminal, this sandy beach has shade and toilets and is the nearest place to Khasab for a swim. Wild camping is permissible here, and

OMAN KHASAB

Musandam Peninsula

beautiful shells often wash up at campers' tent flaps when the weather is rough. Some enterprising kebab sellers set up shop here on the weekends.

Khmazera Castle   CASTLE
(⊘8am-2pm Sat-Wed; **FREE**) Buried in the heart of town (brown signs show the way), this small fortified house sports two cannons at the doorway, a renovated well in the courtyard and giant oyster shells in one of the rooms. It's underwhelming compared to Khasab Fort but worth a pause during a walk or drive around town.

🏃 Activities

Khasab Sand Tours   WATER SPORTS
(☑91956010; www.khasabsandtours.com; Hwy 2; ⊘9am-9pm) This competent and friendly agency near the port offers kayaking, banana boating and wakeboarding (OR15 for one hour). Some activities require chartering a boat to Khor Al Sham, which costs around OR40 for a two-hour trip. Snorkelling trips cost from OR14 for a half-day trip depending on the size of the group. Many activities require a minimum of two people.

Rubba   BOATING
(☑26730424; www.msaoman.com; 2 nights/3 days standard d cabin full board per person OR410) Musandam Sea Adventure Tourism offers an exciting three-day cruise aboard *Rubba*, their luxury yacht. The interior resembles a traditional dhow, but facilities include en suite toilets, showers and air-conditioning. Snorkelling, kayaking, traditional fishing and an end-of-trip mountain safari are included. *Rubba* sails with a minimum of four people or as scheduled on the first and third Sunday of every month between October and April.

Musandam Discovery Diving   DIVING
(☑99682932; www.musandamdiscoverydiving.com; 2-/3-dive trips incl equipment OR48/58; ⊘8.30am-noon & 3.30-7.30pm) Described as friendly, efficient and safe by divers, this outfit offers trips to Khor Al Sham (good for novice divers and accessible by dhow) and the northern coast (where leopard sharks and torpedo rays inhabit the deep sea; better for experienced divers and accessible by speedboat). Visibility is good between October and January; jellyfish or cold currents are challenging at other times of year.

👉 Tours

There are two main activities accessible from Khasab: dhow cruising around the *khors* and 4WD mountain safaris to the top of Jebel Samhan. All the tour companies in Khasab offer both if you're looking for a 'one-stop' service. Book online, through your hotel or at the agencies in Khasab.

Khasab Travel & Tours   TOURS
(☑99103144, 26730464; www.khasabtours.com; Atana Khasab Hotel, Hwy 2; ⊘8am-8pm) Situated at the Atana Khasab Hotel, this agency is highly efficient and has many years of experience. City tours, dhow tours and mountain safaris are on offer and staff can organise transfers to the UAE border.

Khasab Sea Tours   BOATING
(☑26731123; www.kstoman.com; ⊘8.30am-6pm) This long-established agency offers half-day dhow rides to Khor Al Sham (9.30am to 1.30pm, OR15 per person) that come highly recommended by travellers. Full-day trips (10am to 4pm) press on to Seebi Island; these cost OR20 and include lunch. Snorkelling equipment is provided on board. Half-/full-board beach camping (OR40/50 per person) with all equipment provided is a popular way of engaging with the wilderness.

Musandam Sea Adventure Tourism   BOATING
(☑26730424; www.msaoman.com; off Hwy 2; ⊘8am-8pm) Dhow trips can be booked through this recommended agency. The owner is a proud local who employs knowledgeable Omani captains who speak a variety of languages. An overnight camping trip on a beach in one of the *khors* costs OR55 per person (minimum two people) and includes all equipment, dinner and breakfast.

🛏️ Sleeping

Khasab Hotel   HOTEL $
(☑26730267; www.khasabhotel.net; s/d OR30/36; P🛜❄) Located 1km inland, near the airport, this traveller-friendly hotel, with its wacky mini-fort entrance, offers bright rooms with views of the mountains. There's a small restaurant on-site. Payment is preferred in cash, but card is possible. Cheap tours are on offer and there's a free shuttle to and from the ferry or airport.

⭐ **Atana Khasab Hotel**   HOTEL $$
(☑26730777; www.atanahotels.com; Hwy 2; d with mountain/sea view OR82/94; P@🛜❄)

Perched on a headland just outside Khasab on the Khasab–Tibat road, this old favourite is surrounded on three sides by water and makes the most of the crystal-clear water and mountain scenery. At sunset the cliffs on the opposite side of the bay dissolve like liquid gold. Some rooms have split levels, windows for walls and balconies aligned to the sunset.

Diwan Alamir Hotel HOTEL $$
(☑ 26833995; www.diwanalamir.com; Hwy 2; r/ste OR60/75; P ☀) There are good views here from the small rooms, but what really distinguishes this hotel is the chocolate-caramel swirls of the marble basins. The average restaurant serves average international fare. The hotel is close to Khasab Fort and walking distance from the ferry.

Atana Musandam Resort HOTEL $$$
(☑ 26730836; www.atanahotels.com; off Hwy 2; r from OR120; P ☀ ☲) Using local materials, this appealingly rustic hotel attempts to blend into the environment with its sandstone-clad rooms, wooden beams and *bar-asti* ceilings. Arranged along the edge of two creeks that slice through the reclaimed land upon which it sits, this resort echoes twice a day with the sound of powerboats as they set out or return from fishing.

✗ Eating & Drinking

Al Shamalia Grill & Restaurant GRILL $
(☑ 26730477; mixed grill OR3; ☺ 9am-2am) Near the big mosque in the new souq area, this brightly lit local favourite, with seating inside and on a small terrace outside, does a roaring trade in takeaway platters. It has a huge menu of tasty kebabs and a wide range of fruit juices.

Lulu Hypermarket SUPERMARKET $
(☺ 9am-11.45pm) This supermarket sells fresh biryani, tandoori chicken, salads and pastries – all the ingredients needed for a picnic. It's also handy for camping supplies, including tents and cool boxes.

★ Aroos Musandam Restaurant SEAFOOD $$
(☑ 26831331; www.aroosmusandam.com; mains from OR3; ☺ 8am-2am) This cosy restaurant in the centre of town is a cut above the rest in terms of decor and service. There's an emphasis on the catch of the day (lobster, prawns, crab, fish of several varieties), but there are also Omani and Indian dishes too, including melt-in-the-mouth mutton. Deli-

cious juices are on offer and there's complimentary soup for larger orders.

Darts Bar BAR
(☑ 26730777; www.atanahotels.com; Hwy 2, Atana Khasab Hotel; ☺ 6pm-midnight) This cosy spot in the basement of the Atana Khasab Hotel was the only place to buy a beer in town at the time of research. Bar-goers either sit inside watching sport on the TV or wander out to the poolside terrace overlooking the sea.

🛍 Shopping

Hormuz Flower ARTS & CRAFTS
(☑ 92834168; Lulu Hypermarket; ☺ 9.30am-11pm) This shop inside Lulu Hypermarket is one of only a couple in Musandam to sell souvenirs and crafts of any kind. Camel sticks, traditional axes and Omani incense are sold here, with a good selection on offer.

ℹ Getting There & Away

For a weekend break from Muscat, Oman Air Holidays (www.omanair.com) offers flights both ways for OR300 for two people, including one night at the Atana Musandam Resort in Khasab.

AIR

Oman Air (www.omanair.com) has daily flights in either direction between Khasab and Muscat costing from OR35 one way (1¼ hours). These leave Muscat at 7.40am and Khasab at 9.45am. There are two flights daily on Thursday and Saturday. Flights depart and arrive from Khasab's military air base (p235).

BOAT

National Ferries Company (☑ toll free 800 72000; www.nfc.om; Hwy 2) operates a service every Thursday and Sunday from Muscat. This service leaves by bus from Muscat's Burj Al Sahwa Bus Station (p150) at 10am (report in at 9am) for a 3pm sailing from Shinas, arriving at 8pm.

From Khasab, the ferry leaves at 1pm every Tuesday and Saturday, arriving in Muscat (via Shinas and bus ride) at 9.20pm.

A one-way ticket costs OR13/24/36 in economy/business/1st class, and there's no price discount on return tickets. It is possible to take a car (including rental cars) on the ferry for an extra OR48.

CAR

Driving between Muscat and Tibat (530km, eight hours) involves insurance for two countries, and passing through checkpoints no fewer than eight times. On an Omani-visit visa, this is not the best use of your time. It is a feasible drive, however, from Dubai. The only border post allowing access to the Musandam Peninsula is at Al Darah/Tibat, on the western coast of the Musandam Peninsula.

TAXI

There is no public transport operating in Musandam. You can book a taxi, though, through your hotel to Bukha (OR25) or Tibat and to Khor Al Najd (OR25) or Jebel Harim (OR60). A taxi to Dubai costs OR90 for up to three people.

ⓘ Getting Around

Car rental (2WD/4WD OR13/40) is available from the ever-obliging Omani owner of **Khasab Rent-a-Car** (☑ 99726565, 99447400; Khasab Rd; ⊙ 8am-1pm & 5-10pm). A 4WD with a driver costs OR60 per day. Cars can be delivered to your hotel and dropped off at the ferry terminal.

Rahaal Khasab (☑ 99441700, 91323440; rahalkhasab@gmail.com; Khasab Rd; ⊙ 8am-1pm & 4-10pm) offers saloon-car and 4WD options, as does **Al Rehab** (☑ 91119573; alrehabrc@gmail.com; Khasab Rd; ⊙ 8am-midnight).

The only other way of getting around town or beyond is to ask your hotel to arrange transport for you.

The Khors
اخوار مسندم

Musandam is justly renowned for its rugged inland beauty, but it is just as famed for the extraordinary landscape out at sea. The whole northern coastline is deeply incised with inlets that are so convoluted it's easy to get disoriented when navigating them by boat. Known as *khors,* these fjord-like deep-water bays are home to dolphins that often accompany dhows and tour boats as they potter around the coast.

The most popular boat trip is from Khasab to Khor Al Sham, but it's also possible to visit Kumzar, the peninsula's isolated northern settlement. A few other tiny fishing villages are scattered across the tip of Oman, but mostly this is a sparsely populated region. Only one *khor* is accessible by road – Khor Al Najd – and it features on inland tours of the peninsula, but to experience the *khors* at their best, a boat trip is a must.

◉ Sights

★ Khor Al Sham
BAY

This beautiful inlet is interesting for its stone fishing villages, accessible only by boat, and for Telegraph Island, which dots the middle of the bay. Huge flocks of seabirds, particularly cormorants, gulls and terns, can be seen along the cliffs surrounding the entrance to this inlet. It's best visited on a dhow cruise from Khasab.

★ Khor Al Najd Viewpoint
VIEWPOINT

Located 24.5km southeast of Khasab, Khor Al Najd is the only *khor* accessible by vehicle (preferably 4WD). You can camp on the rim of this wild bay, although it's often too shallow and muddy for a good swim. The viewpoint at the top of the graded road, however, is stunning, especially when clouds pattern the surrounding cliffs. This is the view that is most often chosen in tourist literature to promote Musandam.

Telegraph Island
ISLAND

(Khor Al Sham) This tiny spit of land is only accessible at high tide, and it's easy to imagine how those posted on the island, when it housed a British telegraphic relay station in the 19th century, went mad from isolation. There's nothing to do on the abandoned island, but snorkelling and swimming in the pristine surrounding waters is a highlight.

LOCAL KNOWLEDGE

GOING ROUND THE BEND

Ever wondered about the term 'going round the bend'? If you take a trip to Khor Al Sham you'll learn first-hand what the saying means. In the middle of the *khor* (inlet), the tiny island here was home to a British telegraphic relay station in the 19th century. The utter isolation of so-called Telegraph Island, tucked around the bend of this remote inlet, with no diversions other than sleeping and swimming, drove many of the workers stationed here to madness. The saying 'going round the bend' persists to this day – and so perhaps does the associated implication of being 'driven round the bend'. From time to time, the military sets up camp on the rocks to see how long it takes to run out of things to do. Personnel stationed here run straw polls estimating the number of days endurable at a stretch. One volunteered the improvement of their fishing skills, and another stated that counting cormorants became a favourite pastime!

HOUSE OF LOCKS

An interesting feature of Jebel Harim is the type of local stone-built house known as *bait al qifl* or 'house of locks'. So called on account of their elaborate locking mechanisms, the homes (traditionally left empty during summer months) are built low to the ground, and the floor is excavated to about 1m below the door, with beds and an eating area raised on platforms. There's a good example in the middle of Rawdah Bowl, near the road and a grave site.

Furniture and vital earthenware water jars are often placed inside a house of locks just before the roof is added, ensuring that no one makes off with the contents during summer migration. Some of the rocks used in these buildings are 1m thick and take six to eight men to lift. The roof is made of tree trunks and insulated against the heat and cold by mud.

Kumzar
VILLAGE

Set on an isolated *khor* at the northern edge of the peninsula, the surprisingly modern town of Kumzar is accessible only by boat. The villagers speak their own language, known as Kumzari – a combination of Farsi, Hindi, English, Portuguese and Arabic. There are no sights of special interest in the town, but it is nonetheless fascinating to wander around the old stone houses and the new souq area to see how this outpost has developed its own unique character.

Al Khalidiyah
NATURAL FEATURE

From the base of the track to Khor Al Najd, a road leads to the village of Sal Alaa and Al Khalidiyah, an inland bowl full of magnificent mature trees that makes for a rare shaded (and often grassy) picnic or camping spot. This is classic 'bowl' landscape – a flat cul-de-sac plain encased in an amphitheatre of mountains. Musandam is marked by several of these features.

ⓘ Getting There & Away

The best way to explore the *khors* is by boat from Khasab, with a company such as Khasab Sea Tours (p202).

Water taxis travel between Khasab and Kumzar, charging an outrageous OR200 for the harrowing trip in a speedboat with no seats and a maximum clearance between deck and gunwale of 15cm. At least life jackets are now provided.

To reach the only *khor* accessible by road, head inland past the airport for 15km and follow the sign for 'Khor An Najd 6km'. Turn left and head for the obvious graded road that winds up the mountain, through colourfully striated rock. After a couple of kilometres you come to the pass, from where a steep 3km descent brings you to the water's edge.

Jebel Harim
جبل حارم

The mountain scenery surrounding Musandam Peninsula's highest peak, Jebel Harim (Mountain of Women), is very striking, with strong striations in the rock face and spectacular vistas across the arid landscape. In spring the scenery softens as a tinge of green touches the mountainside and delicate blooms such as wild geraniums and miniature iris contrast with the rugged backdrop.

The mountain can be accessed from Khasab via a graded road (4WD only) and makes for a spectacular off-road day trip. The route switchbacks through limestone formations until it reaches the Sayh plateau, a startling patchwork of green fields and grazing donkeys surrounded by stone settlements.

The road climbs a further 8km to a pass below the telecommunications tower (off limits to the public) that marks the top of the mountain. It's worth unravelling the helter-skelter of road for a few kilometres on the other side of the pass: the views of improbable homesteads, clinging to the crescent-shaped canyons, with terraces in various states of livid green or grey abandonment, are spectacular.

Beneath Jebel Harim, a gap in the mountains leads to an almost circular plateau known as the Rawdah Bowl. A beautiful depression filled with mature acacia and *ghaf* trees, the bowl has a long history of settlement, as can be seen from the pre-Islamic tombstones lying close to the road. The entire area, with its diagonal slants of striated sedimentary rock, takes on a surreal quality at sunset.

ℹ️ Getting There & Away

Jebel Harim can only be accessed in a 4WD. Many Musandam tour companies, such as Khasab Travel & Tours (p202), organise trips here, and it's possible to hire a 4WD through one of the Khasab hotels, but there is no public transport. At the bottom of the eastern descent from Jebel Harim, a right turn leads towards Dibba via the Omani checkpoint, but note that neither this nor the UAE border area in Wadi Bih can currently be accessed by non-Omanis. Access to Ziggy Bay is from Dibba.

Western Coast

Musandam's western coast, together with the cliff-hugging 42km, 90-minute drive along its rim from Khasab to Tibat, is a highlight of a trip to the Musandam Peninsula. The sealed road is a feat of engineering and affords spectacular views across the Strait of Hormuz.

There are a few sites of interest along the way, including **Burka Fort** (Hwy 2, Khasab Coastal Rd, Burka), where prisoners used to be pegged to the lower courtyard and drowned by the incoming tide. Nearer to Khasab, there are some **petroglyphs** (off Hwy 2, Khasab Coastal Rd, Wadi Qida) in the village of Tawi. To reach them, follow the road through Wadi Qida for 2.3km. The images of horses and camels are etched into two rocks on the left of the road, just before a large white house with outdoor ovens. There are lots of examples of traditional houses here, and there's also a virtual goat hotel in the wadi pavements at the end!

You could spend a day pottering along the coastal road, enjoying a swim at one of the many glorious sandy beaches, and watching very large sharks basking in the shallows. The beachside settlements are often inundated by the listing flanks of sand dunes blown back from the shore. The road ends in Tibat at the Al Darah border with the United Arab Emirates.

ℹ️ Getting There & Away

The magnificent road (currently being inched away from the cliff in a widening project) connecting Khasab with the UAE **border crossing** (⌚ 24hr) is a destination in its own right. The good news is that, unlike other places in the rest of the Musandam Peninsula, it's also accessible by saloon car. No public transport runs along the road, but taxis to the border (OR25, 26km) are available from Khasab through tour agencies.

DHOFAR ظفار

The southernmost governorate of Oman is a world away from the industrious north and separated geographically by an interminable gravel desert. Edged by the sand dunes of the Empty Quarter to the north and an escarpment encircling the main city of Salalah in the south, this region is a fascinating place to visit, particularly during or just after the *khareef* (rainy season) when mists and light rains transform the hillsides from desert brown to luscious green.

If travelling between July and September, try going overland to Salalah and returning by plane. This is the best way to sense the full spectacle of the *khareef* across the top of the escarpment; after eight hours of gravel plains, Dhofar seems like a minor miracle. With lots of historical interest – from the city of Ubar in Shisr to Al Baleed Archaeological Park in Salalah – Dhofar is a must on most itineraries of Oman.

Salalah is sandwiched in the middle of a plain between the mountains and the Indian Ocean. This plain, embraced by a horseshoe crescent of hills, extends east towards Jebel Samhan, and west towards the Yemeni border. In a day trip it's feasible to visit the many sights of interest east or west, but not to tackle both.

Salalah صلالة

📞 23 / POP 163,150

Salalah, the capital of the Dhofar region, is a colourful, subtropical city that owes much of its character to Oman's former territories in East Africa. Indeed, flying into Salalah from Muscat, especially during the *khareef* (rainy season), it's hard to imagine that Oman's first and second cities share the same continent.

From mid-June to mid-August, monsoon clouds from India engulf Salalah in fine drizzle. As a result, the stubble of the encircling plain and the desert escarpment beyond (referred to locally as the *jebel*) is transformed into a verdant oasis where huge herds of camels graze alongside cattle and goats in the engulfing mists. Gulf visitors flock to Salalah at this time to enjoy the long-running tourism festival (p209) and to picnic under the rain clouds. All year round, however, Salalah's coconut-fringed beaches, banana plantations and sociable Dhofari culture offer an attractive flavour of Zanzibar in the heart of the Arabian desert.

MUSCAT TO SALALAH OVERLAND

It doesn't matter which of the two routes you choose between Oman's two major cities (Muscat in the north and Salalah in the south) – both involve a journey across remote desert that can seem interminable at times. Most people go by bus, or opt out of the overland experience altogether by taking a 45-minute flight over the monotonous central plains. With time, patience and your own vehicle, however, driving between the two cities can be rewarding – if only to understand the true nature of the desert before human beings tamed the edges. Ideally it's worth driving the inland route in one direction and returning via the coast: a trip of at least a week involving wild camping.

Inland Route: 1000km, 10 hours

It comes as some surprise to see a sign off the Burj Al Sahwa roundabout in Muscat that says 'Salalah 998km'. Salalah may be Oman's second city, but there are few destinations that are sign-posted from such a distance. The sign implies that there is precious little in between – that once on the lonely Hwy 31 from Nizwa, there is nothing between you and Salalah. And that's pretty much the case. The eight-hour journey between Nizwa and Thumrait across Al Wusta region is punctuated by one lone hump near Adam, the excitement of a scruffy little town at Haima and very little else. Dubbed by some as the most forgettable journey in the world, it's hard not to agree as you gaze across the big sky, midpoint along Hwy 31, without a rock, a bush, or any kind of interruption of the level plain. With your own 4WD, however, there are a few points of interest along the 'road across nowhere' and some basic but friendly hotels in Haima. There's no need to book ahead.

Oasis of Muqshin Relatively easy access to the magnificent *ghaf* woodlands and seams of Sodom's apple that decorate the edge of the Empty Quarter.

Oasis of Muntasar (near Qitbit) Famous for the daily fly-by of sand grouse.

Shisr (p220) A chance to exercise your imagination at the supposed site of the fabled gold-pillared city of Ubar, a shortish detour along Hwy 43.

Top Tip If you drive this route between July and mid-September, there is a point along Hwy 31, just after Thumrait, where you will notice something quite remarkable: the *jebel* (mountain) suddenly, unexpectedly and with ruler-like precision, turns green. After hours of hard desert driving, it is an unforgettable, almost zen-like experience. In the words of the Bedouin proverb, 'There's nothing sweeter than water after drought'.

Coastal Route: 1500km, 16 hours

There is an altogether more scenic way of getting to Dhofar, along the shores of the beautiful Arabian Sea, but it is not for those in a hurry. It takes at least three days to do the coastal trip from Muscat to Salalah justice, and the beauty of the coast will make you wish you'd allowed more time. There are hotels at Al Ashkharah, Mahout and Duqm, but you'll need camping equipment for the last leg. The route includes the new, spectacular, coast-hugging road from Shwaymiya to Hasik, wrapped around brooding Jebel Samhan. To explore the best of the coastal route, you'll need a 4WD to reach the shore or explore the wadis. For full descriptions of how to make the best of this area, refer to an off-road guide. Some of the highlights include the following:

Wadi Shuhram Blue-green algae (the earth's original animate form) can be seen in the cliffs here.

Duqm (p222) The wind-eroded rock garden here is a national treasure.

Ras Madrakah The shell coves of this candy-striped headland invite cosy camping.

Al Kahil Pink lagoons here make seasonal homes for flamingos.

Shwaymiya This basket-weaving village cowers under the looming presence of Jebel Samhan, lair of the leopard.

Hasik (p217) A limestone stalactite formation is visible from the road.

⊙ Sights

★ Al Baleed

Archaeological Park   ARCHAEOLOGICAL SITE
(Museum of the Frankincense Land; www.omantourism.gov.om; As Sultan Qaboos St; per car OR2; ⊙9am-9pm Sun-Thu, from 3pm Fri & Sat) Well-labelled and atmospherically lit at night, the ancient ruins of Al Baleed belong to the 12th-century trading port of Zafar. Frankincense was shipped from here to India in exchange for spices. Little is known about the port's demise, but the excellent on-site **Museum of the Frankincense Land** charts the area's settlement since 2000 BC and illustrates the nation's maritime strength, including its recent renaissance. The site includes several kilometres of landscaped paths and the adjoining reed beds make for good birdwatching.

Sultan Qaboos Mosque   MOSQUE
(23 July St; ⊙8am-11pm Sat-Thu) **FREE** This newly completed, single-dome mosque

with two minarets is a gift from His Majesty to the people of his mother's hometown, Salalah. It's open to visitors on weekday mornings and makes an impressive sight when the sun glances off the mosque's large dome.

Plantations   GARDENS
(As Sultan Qaboos St) Salalah is famous for its plantations of coconuts, papayas and bittersweet, small bananas. Stroll through the plantation roads near the corniche (2km from the town centre), and it's hard to remember Salalah is Oman's second city. For refreshment, stop off at one of the many colourful fruit stands that stay open until late in the evening along As Sultan Qaboos St and enjoy the juice of a king coconut.

Sultan's Palace   LANDMARK
(As Sultan Qaboos St) This enormous palace complex, with villas and landscaped gardens along the beach front, is home to the family of Oman's ruler, Sultan Qaboos Bin

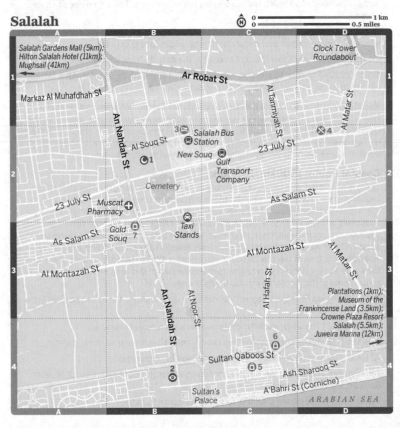

Salalah

Said. While not open to the public, it is noteworthy for the visitor because its crenellated walls dominate the southern end of town, making for an unmissable landmark for the adjoining souq.

🏃 Activities

Anantara Spa   SPA
(www.anantara.com; Al Baleed Resort, Al Manurah Rd; 60min massage OR59) Elemis products are used in this luxurious spa with its Moroccan-style hammam. There are separate pools for men and women, and a range of pleasurable and therapeutic massages on offer.

No Boundaries Oman   FISHING
(📱 95951810; www.noboundariesoman.com; Shwaymiya Village; B&B OR35; 3-day full-board fishing trip per person OR700) This respected tour company specialises in game fishing (including world class GT or Giant Trevally) with conservation in mind and a strict policy of tag and release. Run by an expat couple, Ed and Angela Nicholas, the company operates from Shwaymiya – a village that sits alongside a beautiful bay of the same name, three-hours' drive from Salalah.

ABT Divers   DIVING
(📱 23238000, 99894031; www.abtdivers.com; Crowne Plaza Resort, Al Khandaq St; 1 dive with/without equipment OR41/25, two dives OR58/40) This respected outfit offers boat dives around China Wreck near Mirbat, and near Donkey Head and Mughsail. Turtles, manta rays and moray eels are common sightings and visibility is good (7m to 15m). Snorkelling with equipment costs from OR20 (9am to 2.30pm), and there are dolphin-watching and fishing trips.

Salalah

◉ Sights

🛏 Sleeping

🍴 Eating

🛍 Shopping

☞ Tours

Given the current lack of useful public transport and the difficulty of driving in the *khareef*, Dhofar is one region that repays the expense of taking a tour. These can be organised through hotels or travel agencies along An Nahdah St in Salalah.

Most tours explore the plain east of Salalah (Khor Rori, Taqah and Mirbat) or the plain west of Salalah (Job's Tomb and the Mughsail blowholes) and cost from around OR80 for a day-trip. For the romantic, there is a 4WD visit to the lost city of Ubar (p220) in Shisr, 175km from Salalah (OR120), but be warned: you'll need a lively imagination or Ranulph Fiennes' book *Atlantis of the Sands* to make any sort of sense of the site.

For a more rewarding experience, spend the night in the **Empty Quarter** camping near Al Hashman (p220); from OR75 including half board. Prices quoted are for a vehicle with an English-speaking driver and a maximum of four people. Recommended tour agencies for more-adventurous Empty Quarter expeditions include Oman Day Tours (p221).

★ Arabian Sand Tours   ADVENTURE
(📱 99495175, 23235833; www.arabiansandtoursservices.com; Arabian Sea Villas, Salalah Beach) For help with more adventurous Empty Quarter expeditions, contact desert specialist Mussallem Hassan, who runs this experienced agency. Born in the sands, he organises full-board five-day trips (OR150 per day, one to three people). For a modern-day Thesiger experience, driving the whole Saudi–Oman border to the UAE takes seven days (OR400 per day for a group; OR2000 per trip for two people).

Al Fawaz Tours   TOURS
(📱 23294324, 97235285; www.alfawaztours.com) Operating from Salalah, this company offers tours all over the Dhofar region and beyond. They are recommended particularly for their six-day camping tour from Salalah to Muscat (OR435 per person, minimum of two). Providing equipment and meals, the tour offers all the excitement of a desert journey without the attendant worries of DIY camping along this often remote route.

🎊 Festivals & Events

Salalah Tourism Festival   CULTURAL
(Khareef Festival; 📱 23383333; Ittin Rd; ⊙ 21 Jun-21 Sep) During the *khareef*, Ittin Rd is the main location of the Salalah Tourism

OMAN SALALAH

LAND OF FRANKINCENSE

Oman's early heritage was built on the sap of the ungainly *Boswelia sacra*, a tree that usually grows little bigger than a bush and is native to the Dhofar region. The precious resin is known the world over as frankincense (*luban* in Arabic) and it continues to be highly prized to this day for its exquisite fragrance.

Sites associated with the ancient trade in frankincense include **Wadi Dawkah** (off Hwy 31). This small reserve, 40km north of Salalah, protects a 5km grove of ancient frankincense trees – in fact more than 1200 trees are dotted around the arid wadi that lies just beyond the cooling mists of the *khareef* (summer rains). The trees have fewer leaves as a result, but equally the sap has a better fragrance and therefore the trees are all the more prized. Sign boards at the site explain how the tapping of sap is carried out. Trees are bled for sap when they reach 10 years in age, and each tree yields 3kg to 4kg of *luban* each season. The beads of incense range from yellow to the highly prized milky-blue nuggets; some are even the colour of jade.

Other sites associated with frankincense include the remains of the caravan oasis of Shisr (p220), site of Ubar; the ports of Sumhuram (p214), in today's Khor Rori; and Al Baleed (p208), from where cargo vessels loaded with beads of resin would have sailed for China. Unesco have honoured these sites with heritage status, as together they bear witness to the sophistication of early Arabian Peninsula inhabitants since neolithic times.

Festival. Arab families from across the region come to picnic in paradise. Their favourite haunt is under the street lights of Ittin Rd, where a large festival complex includes funfairs, clothes stalls, cultural villages, a theatre, restaurants and lots of small stands selling kebabs and shawarma.

🛏 Sleeping

★ **Salalah Beach Villas** HOTEL $
(📞 23235999; beachspa@omantel.net.om; Beach Rd; s/d OR30/35; 🅿🏊☀🐾) This welcoming family-style hotel, run by an amiable Tunisian manager who speaks English, Italian and French, has lovely views: the sea is so close you can taste it through the window. Walk off breakfast along the magnificent white sand and splash in the surf on calmer days. This is one of the few hotels in Oman where pets are welcome.

This guesthouse is linked to the 65-room Beach Resort next door, which has the benefit of an all-day restaurant and beach sunbeds. Tours (from OR70 per car) and car hire (2WD/4WD from OR14/37, including 200km free mileage) are available, including a guided overnight camping trip to Al Hashman for OR140 per car.

Salalah Hotel BUSINESS HOTEL $
(📞 23295332; salalahhotel123@gmail.com; Al Souq St; r OR15; 🅿🛜) This hotel is a bit tired, but it has large, comfortable rooms and friendly staff. Close to the new souq area and almost opposite the bus station, it is a good choice for the early-morning bus back to Muscat. There's a free (and not altogether welcome) light show from the front windows, courtesy of the fancy fairy lights on the building opposite.

Beach Resort HOTEL $$
(📞 23236170; www.beachresortsalalah.com; Beach Rd; r with/without sea view OR50/40; 🅿🛜☀) Located in a not-particularly-attractive block, this hotel nonetheless offers simple but large rooms with unparalleled sea views from the balcony. All rooms are nonsmoking. With the sea virtually rolling up to the lobby, the hotel has a few shaded sunbeds on the beach and guests can use the pool at the neighbouring Salalah Beach Villas. A buffet dinner costs OR6.

Salalah Gardens Residences HOTEL $$
(📞 23381000; www.safirhotels.com; Salalah Gardens Mall, Ar Robat St; s/d/ste OR117/129/176; 🅿🛜) At the heart of the city's busiest shopping enterprise, this hotel offers easy access to all the amenities of Salalah Gardens Mall. It is also a short distance from Ittin Rd, home of the Salalah Tourism Festival. With longer-stay options available, it represents good value for money out of season.

★ **Al Baleed Resort** HOTEL $$$
(📞 23228222; www.anantara.com/en/al-baleed-salalah; Al Mansurah St; standard r OR216, garden/lagoon/beach villas OR375/433/539; 🅿@🛜☀) Wedged between beach and bird-filled lagoon, this beautiful spa resort is a

study in refined elegance and landscaped luxury. A series of arches leads to a low-rise reception building wrapped around an infinity pool that appears contiguous with the Indian Ocean. Given the general cost of a stay, the one-bedroom villas with their own private pools represent the best value.

Crowne Plaza
Resort Salalah   RESORT $$$
(☑ 23238000; www.ihg.com/crowneplaza; Al Khandaq St; r mountain/sea view from OR110/120; P@ⓢⓦⓧ) The main rendezvous for Western expats, this sociable and highly competent hotel, with roundels of local scenes and coloured glass, is an old favourite among the large hotels in Salalah. It has a small golf course, a beach and a terraced restaurant overlooking a magnificent sandy beach, with waves illuminated each evening beneath the palms.

 ## Eating

Pottery Restaurant & Café   SEAFOOD $
(☑ 98585407; Ar Robat St, opp Salalah Gardens Mall; meals from OR2.8; ⊙ 11am-2am) This smart little restaurant, with two floors of seating, has created a friendly, homely atmosphere with its cheerful and quaint interior. There is no good reason for 'pottery' being included in the name – the owner just liked the sound of it! Shrimp tagines and other seafood dishes are recommended here.

Al Baleed Restaurant   MIDDLE EASTERN $$
(☑ 23227887, 91152518; As Sultan Qaboos St; mains from OR4; ⊙ 9am-9pm) This local favourite (not related to the hotel of the same name) is a popular venue for an excellent brunch buffet (OR7) served between 9am and 1pm. The cavernous dining hall has some stylish Arabian features such as a lantern made up of dozens of *kumar* (embroidered caps). There's a huge deck overlooking Al Baleed *khor*.

Al Jood Restaurant   LEBANESE $$
(☑ 23295656; 23 July St; mains from OR3; ⊙ 9am-2am) With dishes of fresh *kunafeh* (an addictive syrup-and-cheese dessert) on display and fresh bread flipped from the ovens on to the plate, this restaurant warrants a trip into town. There's a fresh fish counter and seating for families in the basement – or order a takeaway. Good value mixed mezze per person costs OR9 for two or OR12 for four people.

Annabi Shisha Lounge   LEBANESE $$
(☑ 23381000; www.safirhotels.com; Salalah Gardens Mall, Ar Robat St; mains from OR3; ⊙ 12.30-11pm) Tuck behind an arabesque screen for private dining or sit outside on the landscaped terrace and watch the shoppers go by at this attractive restaurant. You don't have to be a smoker to enjoy a whiff of peach shisha from neighbouring tables as you savour hot mezze, lavish mixed grills (OR10) and mocktails.

★ Al Mina
Restaurant & Bar   MEDITERRANEAN $$$
(☑ 23228252; almina.aabs@anantara.com; Al Baleed Resort, Al Mansurah Rd; mains around OR12; ⊙ 10am-midnight; Pⓢ☑) One of the best restaurants in Salalah, this open-sided terrace-style restaurant has an exotic ambience, with waves thundering on the shore and moonlight captured in the adjoining infinity pool. Seafood and vegetarian dishes from Spain, Italy and Greece are given an Arabian flourish. Live bands play cool blues and Latin music from 7pm every day except Sunday. Book by email.

Yamal Seafood Restaurant   SEAFOOD $$$
(☑ 23381000; www.safirhotels.com; Salalah Gardens Hotel, Ar Robat St; lunch/dinner buffet OR12/13; ⊙ 12.30-4pm, 7-11pm) Located inside a busy mall, teeming with visitors during the *khareef*, this modern and no-nonsense restaurant serves good, locally caught seafood. The daily buffets are particularly good value.

OMAN SALALAH

WORTH A TRIP

DHOFAR'S SPRINGS

The whole area surrounding Salalah is dotted with *ayun* (springs) and any of these make a good half-day trip from the city. Some of the most picturesque springs include Ayn Razat (p213), set in gardens, Ayn Tabraq (p214) and Ayn Athum (p215), in the heart of a subtropical thicket, all of which are signposted off the Salalah–Mirbat road. There is also Ayn Garziz (p219), which can be visited off the Ittin Rd on the way to Job's Tomb. With eccentric limestone cliffs, gnarled with wild fig-tree roots and hanging with maidenhair ferns, these are good spots to appreciate the transformation brought about by a drop of water.

Drinking & Nightlife

Dolphin Beach Bar
COCKTAIL BAR

(☑23238000; Crowne Plaza Resort Salalah, Al Khandaq St; ⊙noon-3pm & 6pm-midnight) One of the few places to serve alcohol in Salalah, this open-air bar is shaded by palms. Enjoy sundowners here before the nightly buffet and watch the waders dash in and out of the flood-lit waves, finding their supper as you eat yours. Refurbishments to bar and restaurant were underway at the time of research.

Italian Barista Café
COFFEE

(Salalah Gardens Mall Rd; ⊙11am-midnight Sat-Wed, to 1am Thu & Fri) This fun little cafe is decked out more like an Arizonan rather than Arabian desert diner, with small cubicles for a cosy chat indoors and some outside seating from which to spot the odd elusive mongoose scuttling across the car park. Despite the decor, the menu is broadly Italian.

🛍 Shopping

Don't visit Dhofar without treading in the paths of ancient traders. A small bag of locally harvested frankincense costs from 500 baisa, and a decorative locally made pottery incense burner costs OR6 to OR10. There are different grades of incense: Somali frankincense is cheaper but not so aromatic, while the milky, greenish resin from Dhofar is highly prized. A whole kit with burner and charcoal costs OR2, or buy a local perfume made from frankincense (per bottle OR5 to OR50).

Baskets made of rush and camel's leather, from the fishing village of Shwaymiya, make another good souvenir (OR8 to OR30), together with colourful woven rice mats. Among Dhofar's most distinctive souvenirs are small, bead-covered *kohl* (black eyeliner) bottles (OR4 to OR10).

Gold Souq
JEWELLERY

(An Nahdah St; ⊙10.30am-1.30pm & 4.30-11pm Sat-Thu, 4-11pm Fri) There's a charm to this 1970s-style parade of shops, with their windows glittering with rows of 22-carat gold bangles, wedding necklaces and headdresses. Some shops sell traditional Salalah silver, but today's silversmiths, once famous in Dhofar, now mostly make bespoke jewellery. Some Bedouin silver is on offer, as well as rings set with semi-precious stones – for Omani men, who wear silver, not gold.

Salalah Gardens Mall
MALL

(Salalah Gardens Mall Rd; ⊙10am-10pm Sat-Thu, 2pm-midnight Fri) This attractive mall encompasses a hotel (handy for visiting the Salalah Tourism Festival), recommended restaurants, a branch of Carrefour supermarket (open 9am to midnight) and a small souq selling *luban* (frankincense) and local handicrafts. There's also a large modern cinema showing English-language films and Fun Station (admission OR2, plus 200 baisa per ride; ⊙10am-10pm Sun-Wed, to midnight Thu & Sat, 2pm-midnight Fri) amusement park for kids.

Al Husn Souq
MARKET

(Sultan Qaboos St; ⊙10am-1pm & 4.30-9.30pm) Head for this souq to rub shoulders with the jovial Dhofari people who have been assembling in this spot, albeit under different awnings, for centuries. The souq, spread over a number of alleyways next to the sultan's palace (p208), flaps with colourful cotton headdresses, smokes with aromatic frankincense and sparkles with imitation jewellery. Traditional ceramic incense burners and spices are on sale here.

ℹ DHOFAR DANGERS

Despite numerous bulletins from the Royal Oman Police, every year people are killed on the Ittin or Thumrait roads, driving too fast in the summer mist. It's imperative to take extra caution driving anywhere on the escarpment leading into Salalah between mid-June to mid-August. Camels loom out of the fog on to the road and are a major hazard.

Another regional danger is the strong tidal undertow. This is especially perilous during the *khareef* but takes lives at any time of the year. Even if you're a strong swimmer, heed the red flag warnings on the beaches of Salalah and swim in the hotel pool instead.

Don't be tempted to have a dip in any of the freshwater pools scattered across the Eastern Salalah Plain – bilharzia (snail fever) occurs here, carried by small snails that infest the water. If infected, the disease can cause permanent intestinal damage.

If you run into problems, Muscat Pharmacy (An Nahdah St; ⊙24hr Thu-Sun) is just near the Gold Souq and Salalah has good, modern medical facilities at Sultan Qaboos Hospital (Sultan Qaboos St).

❶ Getting There & Away

AIR

The **Salalah International Airport**
(📞 24518072; www.salalahairport.co.om) is
housed in a splendid new building.

Oman Air (www.omanair.com) flies to Muscat
(one way/return from OR32/64, 1½ hours)
around six times daily at variable times. Salam
Air (www.salamair.com) offers similar flights.

Qatar Airways, Fly Dubai and Air Arabia all
offer international connections with Gulf cities.

The 20-minute journey into town by taxi costs
around OR10.

BUS

Mwasalat (www.mwasalat.om) buses to Muscat
(one way/return OR7.5/12) cover the 1021km
in 12 hours, travelling via Nizwa (860km, OR6).
They leave from the **bus station** (📞 23297103;
www.mwasalat.om; Al Souq St) in the new souq
at 7am, 10am and 7pm. You can store luggage in
the adjoining ticket office free of charge. Mwasalat runs air-conditioned, nonsmoking buses
with toilet and TV on all services.

Gulf Transport Company (p236) services
on modern buses to Muscat leave Salalah for
Muscat at 7am, 10am, 1.30pm and on the hour
between 5pm and 9pm (one way/return OR7/13,
12 hours). A service to Dubai leaves at 3pm (one
way/return OR10/18/16 hours). Tickets should
be bought in cash a day in advance of travel.

Microbus fares from Salalah include Mirbat
(OR2), but there's a long walk from the dropoff
point into Mirbat.

❶ Getting Around

The main car-hire companies can be found on
arrival at the airport, and Budget is represented
at the Crowne Plaza Resort. Many local companies offer cars for hire, especially along 23 July
St. For competitive rates and help with where
to explore, Salalah Beach Villas (p210) hires
2WD/4WD from around OR14/37, with 200km
free and reductions for week-long hire.

A microbus ride within the city costs around
500 baisa. Salalah's taxi stands are behind HSBC
on As Salam St. Some sample taxi fares from the
city centre include Crowne Plaza (OR5), Hilton
(OR6), Juweira Marina (OR7), Taqah (OR15), Mirbat (OR25) and Salalah Marriott Resort (OR30).
No taxi apps work in Salalah at present.

Eastern Salalah Plain سهل صلالة الشرقي

The Salalah Plain extends in one large flat
crescent for more than 70km east of the
city towards the town of Mirbat. The plain

receives only light drizzle between July and
September, so while it may take on a green
tinge in the *khareef* (rainy season), it doesn't
enjoy the same fertility as the escarpment
that encases it. This doesn't stop the Jebbali grazing their camels here, watered by
the many *ayun* (springs) that usher from
the hillside. These springs make interesting
places to visit as they are havens for wildlife
and offer a pleasing contrast to the starkness
of the plain itself.

Wadi Darbat is another important source
of water and a celebrated picnic spot: in a
good year, water flows over the cliff and out
to the sea at Khor Rori. Once an ancient
port, this lonesome archaeological site is of
historical interest and well worth a visit.

◎ Sights

★ **Wadi Darbat** LAKE
A popular picnic site during the *khareef*
and a great place to enjoy the *jebel* in any
season, Wadi Darbat is a grassy plateau in
the hills marked by Oman's largest natural
permanent lake. This is the source of the
estuary that flows into Khor Rori, and during a good *khareef*, water cascades through
a series of limestone pools before tumbling
over the plateau's edge in a long drop to the
plain below.

In the dry months, October to May, the
Jebbali tribespeople set up their camps in
this area. The surrounding caves were used
by the sultan's forces, together with the British SAS, to infiltrate areas of communist
insurgency in the mid-1970s. Now the most
surreptitious activity you are likely to see is
the scuttling away of a small, fur-clad rock
hyrax (an unlikely relative of the elephant)
that lives among the rocks. Chameleons
share the same territory and are equally
clandestine, changing colour when abashed.

Boat trips (OR4 per hour) are available,
but don't be tempted to swim in any of the
pools in Wadi Darbat – the snails bearing
bilharzia occur here. Lots of tiny biting insects often make the site challenging during the rains. A tiny coffee shop selling tea,
water and sandwiches opens between noon
and 11pm at the very end of the road.

★ **Ayn Razat** SPRING
(north of Al Ma'murah Roundabout) The most
striking of all the springs scattered across
the Salalah Plain, Ayn Razat flows copiously from the hillside at all times of year
and rolls across the limestone pavement in

something close to a permanent river. The water collects in a set of lily ponds, the pink and blue blooms of which attract bright-orange dragonflies, which in turn are watched by kingfishers with beaks of a similar hue. There's a beautiful garden here, popular with picnicking locals.

★ **Sumhuram**
Archaeological Park   ARCHAEOLOGICAL SITE
(Khor Rori; per car OR2; ☺9am-9pm) Looking across one of Dhofar's prettiest bays at peacefully grazing camels and flocks of flamingos, it's hard to imagine that 2000 years ago Khor Rori was a trading post on the frankincense route and one of the most important ports on earth. Today little remains of the city except the painstakingly excavated ruins of Sumhuram Archaeological Park. This fascinating park is part-museum and part-archaeological site, and you can wander around the ruins and watch the archaeologists at work.

Visit the gallery within the site to see some of the 1st century BC to 3rd century AD finds from the site, including some evocative Kursi inscriptions. There are toilets and a small coffee shop inside the grounds, and there's a track down to the beautiful beach.

Ayn Tabraq   SPRING
One of the prettiest springs sprinkled across the eastern Salalah Plain, this one ushers from a bare rock and is channelled through a zigzagging concourse before trickling through the valley. Hoopoes and dippers are among the many birds that frequent the site. The Jebbali people descend from the mountain during the *khareef* and camp nearby, driving their livestock back up the *jebel* (escarpment) after the rains have ceased.

Wadi Darbat Waterfall   WATERFALL
Every few years, steady rains across the *jebel* result in a torrent of water racing across Wadi Darbat and falling over the edge, 300m to the Salalah Plain below. Once every decade the waterfall consists not just of one stream but of a whole wall of water – a spectacular phenomenon reported in the national press. For months after the water has stopped flowing, the cliff edge remains bright green with moss and vegetation.

The road to the bottom of the waterfall is not signposted but is obvious as it meanders towards the cliff from the main coastal road. From the car park, there's a rugged path

that leads over rocks towards the best view points. To access the top of the waterfall, follow the brown signs from the coastal road up the hill and turn into Wadi Darbat.

Ayn Athum Waterfall   WATERFALL
Just before reaching a spring of the same name, a small car park appears on the right-hand side of the road and a paved path disappears mysteriously into the wooded undergrowth. At the end of the path, there's a surprise find: a limestone waterfall (15m) slides down the cliff, forming stalactites and filtering through maidenhair ferns, segmented cacti and various creepers. The waterfall only occurs after heavy rains, but it's a magical spot even when stilled by the season.

Khor Rori Beach   BEACH
A celebrated local beauty spot, this *khor* is often partitioned from the sea by a sandbar that shrinks and grows according to the season. In the summer, water chasing through Wadi Darbat sometimes breaches the bar, dissolving the lagoon back into the sea. After a heavy storm surge, it can take months for the beach to rebuild. As tempting as it looks, swimming here is very dangerous as the waves are powerful and there is a strong undertow.

Taqah Castle   CASTLE
(Al Hosn St; 500 baisa; ☺9am-4pm Sat-Thu, 8-11am Fri) This small but well-preserved castle was built in the 19th century. With a furnished interior, good signage and an accompanying booklet explaining the history of this sardine-producing town, this is one of the better fort museums in Oman. The fort is located in the pretty fishing village of Taqah, which boasts a white-sand beach, a landscaped *khor*, a fine corniche, another fort on the hill (closed to visitors) and, for some inexplicable reason, a multistorey branch of Bank Dhofar.

Ayn Humran   SPRING
Tiny compared with its more bountiful neighbours, this spring collects in a small well in the middle of a rural road at the northern rim of the plain. Of more interest is the beautiful avenue of tall coconut palms and a giant breadfruit tree that leads towards it, a peaceful place to watch wagtails and bulbuls splashing in the outflow. There are public toilets here but, as with the other springs, no other facilities.

Ayn Athum
SPRING

One of several issuing from the hills above the plain to the east of Salalah, this spring trickles into a reservoir at the end of the road. The spring itself is less of a feature than the drive to reach it, as the road passes across the plain through a hidden valley of dense vegetation. It's alive with birds and insects in summer.

Activities

Juweira Marina
BOATING

(Taqah Rd) Encompassing an ever-increasing set of shops, cafes, restaurants and ice-cream parlours, this marina is becoming the social hub of the Eastern Salalah Plain. It also (as you'd expect) offers a range of water sports and boating activities as well as berthing for yachts, giving a broader dimension to a beach holiday here.

Around the Ocean
BOATING

(☑99334207; www.aroundtheocean.om; Juweira Marina, Salalah Beach; 1hr dhow cruise adult/child OR20/10; ◷9am-5pm Sat-Thu) Offers the only dhow cruises currently operating in Salalah. In addition to their one-hour sunset cruise, a 10-hour snorkelling trip to Mirbat runs from 8am to 6pm is on offer for OR48. Two-hour dolphin-watching trips (OR20 per person) leave at 8am, 10am and 3pm. Four-hour fishing trips (OR160) are also available.

Hawana Water Park
WATER PARK

(☑23276870; www.hawanasalalah.com; Taqah Rd; adult/nonswimmer/child OR7/OR4/from OR4, under 3yr free; ◷10am-6.30pm Sun-Wed, to 7.30pm Fri & Sat, 10am-4.30pm & 5-10pm Wed) A number of giant slides and a wave pool offer a range of thrills for swimmers in this family-oriented water park, currently the only such park in Oman. Piped pop music, burgers from the snack bar and free shuttles from Taqah Rd hotels make this a good place to placate travel-weary kids. It's busiest on a Friday, and Wednesday nights are women only.

Sleeping

Salalah Rotana Resort
RESORT $$

(☑23275700; www.rotana.com/rotanahotelandre sorts/oman/salalah/salalahrotanaresort; Juweira Marina, Taqah Rd; r from OR65; P@☎⌗☒) Often full, this enormous, chic, marble-clad hotel plays on its *Arabian Nights* theme with lanterns, pointed arches and *majlis* (reception room) seating on Arabian-style couches. Rooms are large and tastefully designed,

and there are attractive pools, good on-site restaurants and a popular beach bar.

★Souly Lodge
LODGE $$$

(☑94972220; www.soulyecolodge.com; Taqah Rd; bungalow incl half-board with side/sea view OR152/175, extra bed OR20; P☎) ⌖ Run by an Egyptian family, this beachside lodge is tastefully decked in natural materials and comprises upmarket cabins with minibar and outside bathrooms. It's not exactly an ecolodge, but it is a welcome break from neighbouring concrete behemoths and offers a glamping experience for those wanting to be close to nature but not to the crabs and scorpions who inhabit it.

Juweira Boutique Hotel
RESORT $$$

(☑23239600; www.juweirahotel.com; Juweira Marina, Taqah Rd; r from OR100; P@☎⌗☒) In the middle of Salalah Beach, some 13km from town, this attractive hotel is surrounded by luxury apartments, shops and restaurants clustered around Juweira Marina. The hotel, shaped rather like a fort, has stylish rooms and top-end facilities but the term 'boutique' is something of a misnomer.

Eating & Drinking

Beach Bar & Restaurant
SEAFOOD $$$

(Salalah Rotana Resort, Taqah Rd; mains OR8; ◷6.30pm-1am) This popular beachside restaurant offers tasty grilled seafood. It makes the perfect palm-tree setting for a four-course romantic dinner (OR58.5). The menu focuses mainly on seafood, and the candlelit evening begins at 6.30pm and ends at 10.30pm.

★Island
BAR

(Juweira Marina, Taqah Rd; ◷6pm-3.30am) The island may be artificial, only one bar wide and accessible by a humpback bridge so small that you could almost span it in one stride, but the sense of this being a little piece of revelry cut adrift from the marina makes it highly attractive. Open-sided and on stilts, it draws a lively crowd from Salalah.

ⓘ Getting There & Away

There's very limited public transport linking Salalah with Taqah and Mirbat. The best option is to take a taxi, hire a car, or go on a tour of the sights east of Salalah through a company such as **Al Qasim Travel** (☑23238799, 24hr 94900666; www.alqasimtravel.com; Crowne Plaza Resort Salalah, Al Khandaq St; Dhofar tours per person from OR25; ◷8am-5pm). If driving, brown signs help navigate the entire region, and free maps of the Dhofar region are available from most hotels and travel agents.

Jebel Samhan   جبل سمحان

Remote Jebel Samhan (2100m), the mountain that towers over the eastern portion of the Salalah Plain, is more plateau than peak. The desolate flat top of the *jebel* is home to the elusive Arabian leopard. Critically endangered, this magnificent animal is protected in a vast sanctuary covering much of Jebel Samhan, which is closed to the general public. Visitors can drive, however, to the stunning 1300m-high viewpoint on the edge of the reserve. The upper plateau suddenly ends here in a vertiginous drop more than 1000m to the coastal plain below. Barely a ledge interrupts the vertical cliff, and it seems impossible that there should be any route down from here that didn't involve a rope and crampons. But in fact that is not the case: locals, armed with nothing more than a snake stick and a kettle, have been climbing from plain to *jebel* for centuries along their own hidden paths.

The rump of Jebel Samhan is riddled with caves and sinkholes, the most notable

---

LOCAL KNOWLEDGE

JEBEL SAMHAN'S FLORA

The approach road to Jebel Samhan climbs up through a variety of different flora, including rocky fields of leafless desert roses. Sometimes known as elephant plants, they have huge bulbous trunks and beautiful pink flowers. If you're wondering about the occasional spiky tree dotted over the plateau, they're called dragon trees and are confined to high, semi-arid elevations.

Botanists may also be surprised to find a small stand of baobab trees gracing the thickets just above the Salalah Plain. These magnificent giants, their trunks sometimes ringed with snails, stand head and shoulders over the more typical Dhofari vegetation and are the only such trees on the Arabian Peninsula. This grove can be spotted among a thicket of trees and bushes off the Tawi Atayr–Mirbat road (currently under repair), and there's a viewpoint marking the spot.

---

of which is Taiq Cave. Identified in 1997, this 90 million cu metre–sinkhole is one of the largest of its kind in the world. Elliptical in shape, it has a depth of 250m and is part of a vast limestone complex deep in the hills above the Salalah Plain. Look out too for Tawi Atayr. This deep sinkhole (1 million cu metres), known as the Well of Birds, gapes without warning in a corrugated landscape of rock, covered in thicket. A small path leads from the car park to a viewing platform, but the sinkhole is really only accessible with a guide, available from a tour company in Salalah.

ℹ️ Getting There & Away

Although you need a permit and a good reason to visit the leopard sanctuary at Jebel Samhan, the sealed road up to the reserve entrance makes a rewarding day trip from Salalah, passing through tiny hamlets and bucolic scenery. There is no public transport linking anywhere of use for the visitor, but the places of interest are easy enough to find with your own transport – just follow the brown signs from Hwy 49, the main road that crosses the eastern part of Salalah Plain from Salalah to Mirbat.

Mirbat   مرباط

📞 23 / POP 7300

The town of Mirbat is something of a backwater these days, but it has considerable historical significance. This was the scene of fierce fighting during the 1970s, when communists fought a war of independence from the rest of the country. Today, there is little evidence of those hostilities, and the only unrest a visitor is likely to experience is the summer sea crashing against the beautiful white-sand beach. Some old merchant houses with their wooden, latticed windows are of passing interest, and there's the onion-domed Bin Ali's tomb, 1km off the main road, marking the entrance to the town.

◉ Sights

Bin Ali's Tomb   ISLAMIC TOMB
(Bin Ali St) Housing the remains of Mohammed Bin Ali, a descendant of the Prophet Muhammad, this tiny tomb, with its two distinctive onion domes, marks the old entrance to town. The white-washed building makes a striking contrast against the russet-coloured rock of the headland, making it impossible to miss when driving along the

old road to Mirbat. As with most such tombs in Oman, the interior is plain with a simple green cloth covering the holy burial site. A cemetery surrounds the site.

Mirbat Castle   CASTLE
(Al Hisn St) The town's main fort is now derelict despite being the site of the well-documented Battle of Mirbat. Nine soldiers kept 300 insurgents from taking Mirbat during this battle in 1972, during the Dhofari insurrection. The British armed forces were called in by the Sultan to assist and two British Victoria Crosses were earned by the Special Air Service (SAS) but not awarded, to help keep the war out of the public eye.

Merchant Houses   NOTABLE BUILDING
(Mirbat St) Of passing interest in the town of Mirbat is the old quarter, where some merchant houses still stand proud along the beach front. Some are still lived in, but many are derelict as modern residents opt for concrete lodgings over the traditional mud and wattle. Some of the old buildings have kept their fine doors and latticed window frames, illustrating the former wealth of this Dhofari outpost.

Mirbat Fort   FORT
(Mirbat St) Recently restored, this old crenellated castle is set square to the sea as if designed to repel invaders. It's closed to the public but makes a photogenic foreground in a seascape composition.

🏃 Activities

Extra Divers   DIVING
(https://extradivers-worldwide.com/en/dive-center/country/oman/dive-center-karaiba-royal-mirbat-resort_360.html; Karaiba Mirbat Resort, Fath St; 2-tank boat trip OR40, 3hr snorkelling & dolphin-watching trip OR21, dive course OR89; ⊘ 8am-noon & 1-6pm) This experienced dive centre facilitates access to a range of snorkelling and diving sites from the Karaiba Mirbat Resort. There are 25 dive sites, including the Chinese wreck, which are home to corals, octopus and tuna. The area's distinctive kelp forest harbours big fish from October to December, including humpback whales.

Note that it is not possible to dive or snorkel in the summer months (June to September) because of dangerous currents. Free transport is offered from Juweira Marina (p215) to Mirbat.

🛏 Sleeping

Kairaba Mirbat Resort   RESORT $$$
(☎ 23275500; reservationsmanager.mirbat@kairaba-hotels.com; off Al Fath St; r incl half-board from OR67; @ ⊠) Bringing comfort to the coastal experience for those who'd rather not camp, this resort and dive centre, a 10-minute drive east of Mirbat, is located on a pretty, sandy cove. The spacious rooms have tiled floors and balconies overlooking the sea. At the time of writing, the hotel was looking tired, something the brand-new German management will hopefully address.

ℹ Getting There & Away

Ad hoc microbuses to Mirbat from Salalah cost OR2 (1½ hours); taxis cost OR30 to cover the 75km (one hour) but both are infrequent. To avoid being marooned in this far-flung outpost, it's better to drive.

Hasik   حاسك
POP 3000

Positioned at the most eastern end of the Dhofar coast before the cliffs of Jebel Samhan interrupt, Hasik is worth the two-hour drive from Salalah for the journey more than the destination. The road is sealed and not particularly exceptional between October and June, but in the remaining months, luminous clouds billow down from the *jebel* (mountain) and high winds whip across the water, sending the surf backwards as the waves roll forwards. Glossy cormorants cluster like oil slicks in the coves and waders shelter from the seasonal fury amid drifts of pink-top shells.

There's not much to see in Hasik itself, but if you continue along the road towards Hadraban, look out for an interesting limestone **formation** (Coastal Hwy) overhanging the cliffs. This remarkable feature affords the opportunity of seeing a living stalactite in the making without having to clamber through a cave to do so. Water running off Jebel Samhan, the mountain plateau above, drips constantly throughout the year, even in the hottest months, causing the limestone to melt like candle wax down the cliff face. After heavy rains, a waterfall rushes over the tongues of limestone, much to the delight of the resident swifts. A small car park and toilet block marks the spot.

The spectacular road that leads on from here, across Jebel Samhan and linking Hasik to Shwaymiya, is a tourist attraction in its own right.

ⓘ Getting There & Away

Hasik lies 200km from Salalah and 400km from Duqm along one of the remotest stretches of the coastal highway. There is no public transport of any kind and next to no passing traffic to speak of, either. The 40km of coast between Hadbeen and Hasik hugs the coastline and is very pretty indeed, while the Hasik to Shwaymiya stretch of road represents a fantastic feat of engineering as it is virtually cut into the cliff.

Western Salalah Plain سهل السلالة الغربي

To the west of Salalah, the plain extends 60km along the coast to Port Salalah, a busy international cargo terminal that also hosts Gulf-bound cruise ships, and ends abruptly in the cliffs of Mughsail. Beyond that lies the impressive zigzags of the Sarfait Rd en route to the Yemeni border. The road is open to visitors only until just past the turning (at the top of the cliff) for Fizayah Beach, but this is far enough to gain an idea of the distinctively different kind of landscape that characterises this part of the plain.

Indeed, both plain and surrounding hillsides here are a fascinating product of human interaction with centuries of livestock grazing (mostly camels, cows and goats) helping to shape the contours, while nature has taken care of the rest. Ancient trees and striking limestone formations (including blowholes) are just some of the unique natural wonders of this area.

◉ Sights

★ Mughsail   NATURAL FEATURE
Oman's most spectacular bay ends in a set of sheer cliffs that reaches towards the Yemeni border. Immediately below the start of these cliffs the rock pavement is potholed with blowholes that are active year-round, but

particularly volatile during the high seas of the *khareef*. A path has been paved around these petulant vents allowing for a close encounter with the jets of sea spray; the woofs of water against rock is a memorable part of Mughsail's soundscape.

Sarfait Road   VIEWPOINT
The Sarfait road, which links Salalah with the Yemeni border via Mughsail, is one of Oman's many impressive engineering projects. Zigzagging nearly 1000m from the Salalah Plain, it reaches the top of the cliff via 14 steep bends. A few kilometres beyond the road's summit there are stunning views back towards Mughsail and inland across some of the wildest wadis in Arabia. Just beyond the turning to Fizayah Beach, there's a police checkpoint preventing tourist access to the Yemeni border.

The vegetation in this area is entirely different from that on the Salalah Plain, with yuccas and succulents clinging to the limestone ledges and frankincense trees in the lower reaches of the wadis.

Fizayah Beach   BEACH
(off the Sarfait Rd) Separated from the rest of the Salalah Plain by the vertical cliffs of Mughsail, and accessed via the Sarfait Rd, Fizayah Beach is one of the most dramatic spectacles in Dhofar. Lunging cliffs and limestone pinnacles, decorated at the base with perfect sandy coves, make for perfect wild campsites – a fact not lost on the local Jebbali (the indigenous residents of Dhofar's mountains) who graze their numerous camels here and set up camp under the trees.

A small cargo ship, marooned during Cyclone Mekunu and pushed closer to the shore by Cyclone Luban, looks set to become a permanent wreck in the first cove of Fizayah Beach. This may spoil the view a little, but it shows the power of the sea when provoked.

KHAREEF – DESERT RAINS

While the rest of Oman suffers the summer slump in visitors, the result of insanely high temperatures, one small corner of the country enjoys an isolated high season. Dhofar, in the far south of the country catches the edge of an annual monsoon carried on winds from India. There is not much volume to the clouds as they reach the shore of Oman, but enough to disperse as a light rain or drizzle that generally persists for 60 days or so over the months of July and August.

The rain brings mists and cooler temperatures, which between them transform the generally hard-baked landscape into a green oasis of flowering shrubs and grasses. This annual phenomenon is known locally as the *khareef* and is celebrated in Salalah's popular summer festival.

The beach is signposted off the Sarfait Rd, 13.5km from the Al Maha petrol station in Mughsail. Access to the beach involves a 6km steep descent on a rough track, so it's safer to travel here in a 4WD.

Ayn Garziz
SPRING

(off Ittin Rd) One of the most visited of the springs issuing from the foothills surrounding Salalah, Ayn Garziz often has a generous flow of water collecting at the bottom of the knotted cliffs. With stunted fig trees and limestone formations, it's an interesting site, however, even when dry. The spring can visited off the Ittin Rd on the way to Job's Tomb.

Job's Tomb
ISLAMIC TOMB

(⊙ sunrise-sunset) **FREE** In religious terms, this tomb is probably the most important site in Dhofar. The tomb of Prophet Job, mentioned in the Old Testament and venerated by Muslims, Jews and Christians, is situated on an isolated hilltop overlooking Salalah. Regardless of your religious convictions, the site is a must-see for the beautiful drive, especially during the *khareef*, and for the view over the Salalah Plain on a clear day. The tomb is around 30km northwest of Salalah.

Ayoon Pools
NATURAL POOL

Below the village of Ayoon there are some natural pools surrounded by tall stands of reeds and other vegetation. The pools are accessed along a 3km off-road track and make for a pleasant picnic spot. The site lies right on the edge of the monsoon catchment, and the contrast between the green slopes towards Salalah and the desert floor that stretches inland is remarkable. There are no facilities here.

🏃 Activities

Donkey's Head Beach
DIVE SITE

This distinctive headland juts out to sea just beyond Salalah Port. The lonesome beach under this promontory can be reached by a very bumpy off-road track, but most people head there by boat as, just off shore, is a popular deep-sea dive site of the same name.

🛏 Sleeping & Eating

Hilton Salalah Hotel
RESORT $$$

(☑ 23211234; www.hilton.com; Sultan Qaboos St; r with/without sea view OR135/123; P@⊛⛵) This hotel lies within view of Raysut Port, but despite cargo boats queuing up on the horizon, it represents a retreat from the city and camels occasionally charge along the hotel's beach. Rooms and amenities are tired and dwarfed by the yet-to-open neighbouring resort, but it's a sociable spot (and a hit with Nordic holidaymakers) offering family-centred activities.

Etienne Cave Park Restaurant
CAFE $

(Ittin Rd; snacks 800 baisa; ⊙ 2pm-2am; P) One of a couple of basic coffee shops on top of the incline above the Ittin Rd, this simple establishment offers a few seats under shady trees that bob with the inhabitants of weaver-bird nests. The panoramic vista of the Western Salalah Plain is green in the summer (if visible through the ubiquitous mists) and grizzled for the rest of the year.

Mughsail Coffee Shop
CAFE $

(off Hwy 47; snacks from OR1; ⊙ 7am-7pm) This simple coffee shop serves black tea, tea boiled with milk, soft drinks and a few basic snacks. With a shaded terrace, it's a good spot from which to watch locals delighting in dashing in and out of the spray from the blowholes while trying to take a selfie.

🍷 Drinking & Nightlife

Whispers Bar
BAR

(☑ 23211234; Hilton Salalah Hotel, Sultan Qaboos St; ⊙ 8pm-3am Sat-Thu, to 2am Fri) A highly popular venue for a drink, the indoor bar at the Hilton Salalah Hotel hosts DJs on Thursdays and Fridays between 11.30pm and 2am. There's an outdoor beach bar, too, if this small venue becomes too crowded.

Mayfair Cafe
COFFEE

(☑ 23211234; Hilton Salalah Hotel, Sultan Qaboos St; ⊙ 9am-11pm) This stylish cafe with indoor seating offers some respite from the midday heat and serves excellent coffee, cakes and a range of tasty mocktails.

ℹ Getting There & Away

There is no public transport linking Salalah with any of the sights to the west of the city, but good paved roads thread throughout the area. The coastal road to Mughsail was broken during the 2018 cyclone, but the diversion inland works just as well. Although you'll see Dhofaris taking their saloon cars west from Mughsail, it's best to have a 4WD if you want to tackle the Sarfait Rd and the rough track down to Fizayah Beach. Tours, through a company like Al Qasim Travel (p215), cover this area from Salalah. Cruise ships dock at **Port Salalah** on their way up the coast towards Muscat.

OFF THE BEATEN TRACK

DHOFAR'S LOST CITY

An archaeological site of potentially great importance, **Ubar** (Wubar; ⊘24hr) **FREE** was lost to history for more than 1000 years. The rediscovery of the remains of this once important trading post on the frankincense route was one of the great archaeological sensations of the 1990s. Today it may be hard for the ordinary mortal to appreciate what all the fuss is about, as there is little to see. An insightful video (in the small information centre, opened in 2017) helps but imagination and curiosity are the most useful tools in exploring this atmospheric site.

The Quran states that God destroyed Ubar because the ancient people of the Ad civilisation were decadent and had turned away from religion, but archaeologists are more inclined to believe that it fell into a collapsed limestone cavern or sinkhole. The site of this calamity is easy to see today, the remains shored up rather unsympathetically in concrete.

You can wander around the unearthed settlement walls and get a feeling for the old walled community. The fabled golden pillars of antiquity, however, are probably just that: a fable elaborated from Bedouin tales and predictably, there are many who dispute the rediscovery of Ubar. Excavations at the site have shown nothing of sufficient age to verify the claims and some chess pieces suggest a much later period of habitation.

So is it worth the effort of bouncing along a graded track into the middle of nowhere to see not very much? For the historian, the romantic, or the plain curious, the site, in the middle of a great stony plain, offers the chance to peer through a hole in the desert at a legend laid bare.

The route from Thumrait is now paved and signposted from the main road.

Shisr الشصر

📳 23 / POP 800

The tiny desert hamlet of Shisr has little of note other than some experimental farms that peter out into wilderness...and the fact that it may be built on the ancient caravan post that some have identified as legendary Ubar. In 1992 the British explorer Ranulph Fiennes, together with a group of US researchers led by Nicholas Clapp, announced the discovery, with the aid of satellite imagery, of the remains of Ubar, one of the great lost cities of Arabia.

According to legend, Ubar, otherwise known as the Atlantis of the Sands, was the crossroads of the ancient frankincense trail. Scholars are fairly certain that the place existed, that it controlled the frankincense trade and was highly prosperous as a result, but therein lies the end of the certainties. Suffice to say, if you travel out here, bring with you an imagination and a dose of healthy scepticism.

ⓘ Getting There & Away

There's no public transport to Shisr. A sealed road leads here, but it's a long journey from Salalah (168km, two hours)...and even further from anywhere else.

Al Hashman الحشمان

POP 500

The tiny settlement of Al Hashman feels like frontier country – given its proximity to the Yemeni and Saudi Arabian borders, in many ways that's exactly what it is. Although nearby as the crow flies, the borders are kept at a distance by the dunes of the legendary Empty Quarter, which start to rise in increasing height the further north you travel from Al Hashman. Bedouin have settled permanently in the area, raising rare black camels and surviving on very little other than the milk and meat these animals provide. For the visitor, the main interest lies beyond the settlement in the corridors of sand blown into classic desert shapes by the ever-present prevailing winds.

The sands of the Empty Quarter begin to curl around the road on the approach to Al Hashman, then very quickly collect into small mounds and ergs (wind-blown dunes) around the settlement. From here, a track leads north along a soft sand corridor with dunes rising dramatically either side and offering superb desert vistas from their summits. This is the fringe of the largest sea of sand in the world, and the landscape is exquisite in its silence and enormity. There is very little rock or vegetation here, but an occasional white geode (cauliflower-shaped rock formation, sometimes harbouring crystals) breaks the uniformity of the sands.

At the time of writing, it was best to avoid travelling further west than Al Hashman as the border with Yemen is considered unsafe.

❶ Getting There & Away

There is no hint of public transport in this remote fringe of the Empty Quarter. The off-road track means, furthermore, that there's very little traffic of any other kind. The only way to access Al Hashman is by 4WD along an hour's worth of very badly corrugated track from Shisr. To reach the surrounding sand dunes (which begin within sight of the village), it's important to let air out of the tyres – there's a petrol station in town for reinflation before heading back to the road – and to be confident in driving safely (p487) in soft sand.

Several tour agencies, such as **Oman Day Tours** (☑ 97710486; www.omandaytours. com; Empty Quarter & Lost City Tour OR300 per person) and Arabian Sand Tours (p209), in Salalah, run out this way, offering the safest way to explore this beautiful region.

AL WUSTA الوسطى

There's a point along legendary Hwy 31 – the often-deserted ghost road linking the northern town of Nizwa with Salalah, 870km to the south – where you could be forgiven for thinking the road had left planet Earth and resettled on the moon. Not a tree nor a bush, not a rock nor a sand dune, rises above the flat, gravelled disc of land. This is Al Wusta: Oman's arid central region.

Despite appearances from this central artery, however, the region does have features of interest. There's the port of Duqm, focus of an ambitious urbanisation and tourism project; a string of beautiful beaches that stretch along the entire length of Al Wusta, and there is the Quqf, a magnificent escarpment that's the home of the Arabian oryx. Factor in a share of the Empty Quarter offering opportunities for wild camping, and this remote, desert region rewards an adventurous spirit.

Haima هيماء

☑ 23 / POP 11,100

Haima is the chief town of the region and an important transit point between the in-

terior and the coast; it also marks the halfway point of the journey between Muscat and Salalah. In fact, the town has largely grown up around the highway, servicing the passing trucks and buses, and there is little to commend the straggling settlement other than the convenience of the amenities it offers. These include basic accommodation, some good Asian restaurants and a useful supply point for trips into the Empty Quarter.

The dunes of that mighty sand desert, best visited on a tour or at least in a convoy of two or more 4WD vehicles, lie tantalisingly close, just 70km or so to the west. Haima also makes a good base for visiting the (relatively) nearby Huqf escarpment, home to the wildlife reserve with its dwindling population of oryx and gazelle.

◉ Sights

Al Wusta Wildlife Reserve   NATURE RESERVE
(formerly Jaluni Arabian Oryx Reserve; ☑ 99356002, permit info 24296626; half-/full-day guided tour in own vehicle OR25/40; ⊗ 7am-1pm & 3-5pm, or by arrangement) **FREE** In the middle of a spectacular desert escarpment, this reserve is home to a small herd of reintroduced oryx. It offers a rare chance to see this magnificent desert antelope up close as there is a large herd of over 600 animals in the reserve's breeding centre. The reserve, access to which is by 4WD with prior permit only, is 50km off the Haima–Duqm road (Hwy 37) on a poorly graded track marked 'Habab', 110km from Haima. After 23km along the track, veer right.

Visitors, who must make their own way to the reserve, are welcome – but permission has to be gained in advance from the Office for Conservation of the Environment. A guided tour, usually by a retired ranger and member of the Harasis tribe, is the only way to visit the reserve although you can visit the portacabin information centre and captive oryx herd for free. The guides often don't speak English and act as navigators only.

A full day's tour includes the remarkable windblown formations of the **Huqf Escarpment**, deep in the reserve, and there is an increasing chance, thanks to intense conservation efforts, of spotting gazelles, hares, ibex or even one of the oyrx that live outside the enclosure.

Wild camping with your own equipment outside the reserve is the only accommodation at present, and you need to bring all your own supplies of food and water. Keep clothes under canvas as there is always a heavy dew by the morning – this is how the animals survive in the absence of surface water.

🛏 Sleeping & Eating

Arabian Oryx Hotel   HOTEL $
(☑92860775, 23436379; arabianoryxhotel@gmail.com; Hwy 31; s/d excl breakfast OR15/25; 🅿🛜) On the opposite side of the highway from the town of Haima, this basic hotel, arranged around a courtyard, offers a clean bed for the night. The English-speaking manager at reception can arrange a barbecue for a group of travellers if you call ahead.

Arabian Sand Hotel   HOTEL $
(☑23436314; arabiansandswrs@gmail.com; off Hwy 31; r excl breakfast OR20; 🅿🛜) Rooms are basic in this concrete block on the highway, and indeed there's not much to recommend with its institutional-style rows of dark corridors. Still, the beds are clean, and it has working air-con if some hours of kip are needed for the inevitably long onward journey.

Al Falah Restaurant   ASIAN $
(Junction Hwy 31 & Hwy 37, near Shell Petrol Station complex; meals OR2.5; ⊙6am-1am) This bright, jolly restaurant, with its cheery staff, faux leather seats and whitewashed walls, attracts travellers all times of the day and night. Acting rather like the watering holes of ancient caravan routes that passed near here, it's abuzz with news of the road. Meals (biryani, sandwiches, kebabs) are basic but filling.

❶ Getting There & Away

Public 'Mwasalat' buses run from Muscat's Azaiba Bus Station to Haima every day. There are two routes.

On the longer route (735km, 10 hours, OR6) buses leaves Muscat daily at 11.10am and travel via Duqm. In the other direction, buses leave Haima for Muscat via Duqm (180km, 2 hours from Haima) at 10.30am.

On the shorter route (550km, 6½ hours, OR6) buses leave Muscat daily at 7.10am, 10.10am and 6.25pm and travel via Nizwa. In the other direction, buses leave Haima for Muscat via Nizwa (370km, 4 hours 20 minutes from Haima) at 12.20pm, 4.15pm and 1.20am. Many private Salalah-bound bus companies also use this route.

Despite its location at a major junction between Hwy 31 and Hwy 37, Haima acts only as a pit stop for buses. Your own transport is required, therefore, for any kind of exploration around Haima.

Duqm   الدقم

☑23 / POP 11,200

Duqm's port may not yet have reached anything like its hyped potential, but it has transformed the once-tiny fishing community into a sprawling, busy town, set to become a city of 40,000 people. Construction is taking place across the barren shores of this wild coastline with three hotels and sets of improbable luxury housing cropping up in various scattered developments. For now, it's best visited as a stopover if travelling to or from Salalah via the coastal highway.

Thankfully, construction teams are being mindful to preserve Duqm's main attraction, the beautiful natural **rock garden** (Hwy 32) of wind-eroded forms. Partly fenced off as the future location of a cultural centre, the site is accessible through gaps in its eastern perimeter. There are some fine beaches both in Duqm and along the shore either side of town, but there are no facilities and 4WD is required to access most of the nearby coast.

Duqm makes a good place to break the long coastal journey. The recommended **Crowne Plaza Duqm** (☑25214444; www.ihg.com/crowneplaza; Resort St, off Tourist Rd; r from OR60; 🅿@🛜⛱) offers first-class amenities in a beautifully landscaped location. With a fine buffet and a bar with live entertainment, this hotel altogether offers surprising luxury in the middle of the desert fastness. Set back from the shore with no ready access to the sea, the **Park Inn & Residence** (☑22085700; www.parkinn.com; Resort St, off Tourist Rd; r excl breakfast from OR53; 🅿@🛜⛱) has chalet-style rooms and a pleasant pool bar (7pm to 9pm), attractive gardens and a spa. At the more budget-conscious end of the spectrum, **City Hotel Duqm** (☑25214900; www.cityhotelduqm.com; Tourist Rd; s/d/tr OR45/75/85) is a low-key, modern business hotel nearer to Hwy 32 that can rustle up takeaway biryanis if you call ahead.

❶ Getting There & Away

Oman Air (www.omanair.com) has daily flights into **Duqm Airport** (☑24341000; www.duqmairport.co.om; off Hwy 37), a desert airport with few amenities. Car hire is available from the tiny terminal building, and a courtesy shuttle bus operates to and from the hotels.

Mwasalat buses run from Muscat's Azaiba Bus Station (630km, OR6) daily at 11.10am, returning at 12.45pm in the afternoon. The journey from Muscat takes 7¼ hours, including a short stopover in Sinaw. The bus continues on to Haima (180km, 2 hours).

Happy Line Oman (www.happylineoman.com) has modern, air-conditioned buses covering the same journey from Muscat (OR10, 8¼ hours), departing at 7am and arriving at 3.15pm. The return service leaves at 6am, reaching Muscat at 1.15pm.

UNDERSTAND OMAN

Oman Today

'Renaissance' is a term any visitor to Oman will hear, as it refers to the current period under Sultan Qaboos Bin Said Al Said, a leader venerated by most of the population for easing the country into modernity. Before he came to the throne in a bloodless coup in 1970, Oman had no secondary schools, only two hospitals and a meagre 10km of sealed roads. In addition, the country was in a state of civil war. Today Oman is a forward-thinking, peaceful success story.

There have been challenges – not least some protests during the Arab Spring of 2011, and ongoing economic concerns driven by the falling price of oil and the challenges of diversification – but there have been many successes, too. In the 2010s Oman has stepped from out of the shadow of more media-savvy neighbours to promote its own brand of modern Arab culture. Pursuing a modernising agenda without surrendering links to a proud heritage, and with an increasingly highly educated, globally connected workforce that is hungry to embrace change, Oman is strategically well-positioned to meet the social, economic and environmental goals of its Vision 2040.

Good Governance

Throughout the political and economic challenges of the past decade, Sultan Qaboos has remained a popular, if not always visible, leader and his reign is celebrated with due pomp and ceremony during National Day in November each year. Despite his age and recently failing health, the Sultan still manages to steer the country forward and his citizens are by and large willing him to reach his half century at the helm (in November 2020).

Much of the Sultan's popularity stems from his human touch and willingness to engage with his subjects. For decades of his reign, the Sultan insisted on an annual 'meet the people' tour, where he and his ministers would camp each year in different regions of the country to listen to local requests. Representing a good metaphor for his success, these tours, during which any visiting dignitaries were also obliged to go camping, were often marked by pennant-carrying camel riders bringing their petitions across the desert with gifts of goats for His Majesty. Requesting lighting in their village on day two of the sultan's visit, petitioners were often gratified to see the pylons delivered by day four of the same trip. It was this accessibility on the part of the sultan, together with his reputation for delivering promises, and for promoting tolerance and dialogue in a region not wholly typified by either quality, that has made him the national treasure that he is today.

Sultan Qaboos is not married and has no children. As he nears his half century of benign and enlightened reign, thoughts are inevitably turning to what the country will do without him. He is still consulted as an oracle of wisdom, but whereas five years ago his eventual demise was a source of anxiety, recent delegation to selected ministers has suggested the legacy of sound governance that he has put in place will endure.

Investing in Human Capital

In building a modern state, Sultan Qaboos' chief strategy has been to create a highly trained local workforce through intensive investment in education. Schooling is free, even partially at tertiary level, and provision is made for children of even the remotest villages. There has been no distinction in this approach between the genders. Indeed, girls account for almost half of the students in public and private schools while around half of the students at Sultan Qaboos University, the country's leading educational establishment, are women. Women are outperforming male students in engineering and medicine, traditionally seen as male disciplines: the first female flight engineer in the region is from Oman, and women are performing to a high level in the military.

With limited oil revenues, Oman cannot sustain costly expatriate labour, so a policy of 'Omanisation' in every aspect of the workforce is rigorously pursued. In contrast to the rest of the region, it is refreshing to find locals – often of both sexes – working in all sections of society, from petrol-pump attendants to senior consultants.

Youth unemployment is now one of the biggest challenges facing the government, as highly educated graduates often fail to find work in an economy dominated by cheap imported labour. Employability training and work-placement schemes ensure that graduates leave university with life skills that prepare them for the workplace, but the fact remains that without incentives to develop small- and medium-sized industries, it is unlikely that the unemployment issue will be resolved any time soon.

Economic Diversification

Two central planks of the economy are self-sufficiency in food production, realised through intensive agriculture along the Batinah coast, and diversification of the economy. These schemes include the export of natural gas from a plant near Sur, giant ports in Salalah and Duqm, and methanol and aluminium plants in Sohar. The decision to disperse new economic initiatives across the regions has helped keep local communities buoyant and helped slow the exodus of villagers migrating to the capital. Tourism is the one major plank of the economy that enjoys a mixed fortune, vulnerable as it is to the negative effect on tourism confidence of Middle Eastern security concerns.

Much investment continues to be made in Oman's infrastructure – no mean feat given the challenges presented by the country's size, remoteness and terrain. It is now possible to drive on sealed roads to most towns and villages across the country. A similar surge in IT infrastructure is ensuring that Oman is connected effectively to the world's information highways, with e-government and telecom developments revolutionising the way business is conducted at home and abroad.

It is probably fair to say that Oman's approach to investment in new projects is cautious and this has slowed the recent pace of development, to the frustration of many who see the country's potential. That said, a new government-led emphasis on entrepreneurialism is helping to create a sector of small- and medium-sized enterprises, run by Omanis for Omanis, which will inevitably lead the way to a more sustainable, home-grown future.

History

When Oman began to modernise in the 1970s after a long period of deliberate isolation by the former sultan, investment from oil revenues were spent on infrastructure, education, healthcare...and fort restoration. This simple fact represented an ongoing commitment to heritage and the way in which history is valued in the present and shapes the course of the future. History in Oman is not something confined to museums: it is alive in the country's arts and culture.

Gold, Frankincense and...Copper

The term 'renaissance' as applied to Sultan Qaboos' reign is an appropriate one, as it suggests equally rich periods through Oman's long history.

As far back as 5000 BC, southern Oman (now called Dhofar) was the centre of the lucrative frankincense trade. This highly prized commodity, produced from aromatic tree sap, was traded for spices with India and carried by caravans across Arabia. While the trees also grew in Yemen, they grew best in the monsoon-swept hills of Dhofar, where they continue to be harvested to this day. So precious was frankincense that the part-mythical Queen of Sheba gave it to King Solomon and three wise men of biblical report brought it to a babe in Bethlehem.

The Bible also mentions the golden-pillared city of Ubar (p220), built by the people of the ancient civilisation of Ad. This fabled city, which has excited the curiosity of explorers for centuries, grew out of the frankincense trade to become one of the most powerful in the region. The remains of the city were rediscovered in the 1990s by English explorer Ranulph Fiennes. The presumed descendants of Ad still occupy the surrounding desert, speaking the distinct and ancient language of Shehri (or Jebbali), whimsically known as the 'language of the birds'.

Oman, or 'Majan' as it was then called, enjoyed further prosperity in pre-Islamic times through the trading of copper. Oman is referred to in some sources as 'the Mountain of Copper', and the Bahrain National Museum provides evidence of vigorous trading in copper between Oman and its Gulf neighbours.

Hostilities: the Portuguese

After the introduction of Islam in the 7th century AD, Oman came under the leadership of the Bani Nabhan dynasty for half a millennium (1154–1624). This period was typified by frequent civil wars between the sultan's forces and tribal factions, which left the country vulnerable to outside hostilities. These eventually came in the form of the Portuguese.

Alarmed by Oman's naval strength and anxious to secure Indian Ocean trade routes, the Portuguese launched a succession of attacks against Omani ports; by 1507 they managed to occupy the major coastal cities of Qalhat (near Sur, and mentioned in the journals of 14th-century explorers Ibn Battuta and Marco Polo), Muscat and Sohar. Ironically, it was a talented sailor from Sohar, Ahmed Bin Majid, who unwittingly helped Vasco da Gama navigate the Cape of Good Hope in 1498, leading to the Portuguese invasion a few years later.

Over the next 150 years, Oman struggled to oust the occupying forces. Eventually, under the guidance of the enlightened Yaruba dynasty (1624–1743), Oman was able to build up a big-enough fleet to succeed. The Portuguese were interested in Oman only as a sentry post for their maritime adventures and had barely ventured into the country's interior and were therefore easily routed. The Portuguese left little behind, although their legacy of military architecture dominates Muscat and fort construction across Oman.

Unified & Wealthy

Between the 17th and 19th centuries Oman became a settled, unified state of considerable wealth and cultural accomplishment. It had a sizeable empire that controlled strategic parts of the African coast, including Mombasa and Zanzibar, and parts of what are now India and Pakistan. Today it is easy to see the influence that Oman had on the coastal areas of those countries, and even more tangibly, the extent to which its own culture and population was enriched by the contact. The Batinah coast, for example, is home to the Baluchi people, and mosque design along the highway between Barka and Sohar bears more resemblance to the florid architecture across the neck of the Gulf than it does to the more austere Ibadi tradition of Oman's interior.

When 19th-century Sultan Said died, the empire was divided between two of his sons. One became the Sultan of Zanzibar and ruled the African colonies, while the other became the Sultan of Muscat and ruled Oman. The division of the empire cut Muscat off from its most lucrative domains, and by the end of the 19th century, the country had stagnated economically, not helped by British pressure to end its slave and arms trades.

A Rebellious 20th Century

The 20th century in Oman was marked by a rift between the coastal areas, ruled by the sultan, and the interior, which came to be controlled by imams (religious teachers). It fell to Sultan Said Bin Taimur, who came to the throne in 1932, to regain control of the restive areas around Nizwa and Jebel Akhdar – a mission he accomplished with the help of long-term ally, the British. Said celebrated the reunification of Oman in the first motor tour of the country in 1955 (as captured in a travel account by author Jan Morris). The celebration proved somewhat premature with two further rebellions in 1957 and 1959; both of these, however, were successfully quelled.

If successful in uniting the country in all other respects, Said reversed Oman's fortunes with policies that opposed change and isolated Oman from the modern world. Under his rule, a country that a century earlier had rivalled the empire builders of Europe became a political and economic backwater. While neighbouring countries were establishing welfare states, Oman slumped into poverty, with high rates of infant mortality and illiteracy. Even the communist insurgency in Dhofar during the 1960s failed to rouse Said from his reclusive palace existence in Salalah, and by the end of the decade his subjects, the most powerful of which had been imprisoned or exiled, lost patience and rebellion broke out.

The unrest led to a palace coup in 1970 when Said's only son, Qaboos, covertly assisted by the British, seized the throne. With a face-saving shot in the foot, Said was spirited off to London's Grosvenor Hotel, where

OMAN HISTORY

he lived out his days. Some suggest that Said was not bad, just fiercely protective of his country's conservative traditions which he feared would be eroded by rapid modernisation. Perhaps the country's contemporary balance between old and new, so skilfully maintained by his son in what amounts to the peaceful and productive cultural revolution of the past 50 years, owes something to Said's cautious approach to Western influence.

Rapid Development

Since 1970 Oman has flourished under the leadership of Sultan Qaboos, but it was a somewhat cautious start. Enormous challenges faced the young sultan, including the need to build the economy, create infrastructure, and introduce education and healthcare systems while still mustering troops to quash the Dhofar Rebellion (1962–1976). By the end of his first decade on the throne, the rebellion was successfully concluded and the country was beginning to bridge the gap with its more affluent neighbours in terms of development. It's to the enormous credit of Sultan Qaboos that Oman today is peaceful and boasts efficient, locally run hospitals, respected colleges and universities, electricity in even the remotest villages, and an excellent and ever-improving infrastructure of roads and ports.

In January 1992 an elected Majlis Ash Shura (Consultative Council) was convened as a first step towards broader participation in government. Women were represented on the council (Omani women were the first in the Gulf states to participate in this way) and invited to hold high office in government, including at ministerial level, beginning a trend for female inclusion in decision-making that continues into the present day. Indeed, at the time of writing, the current ministers of education and higher education are both women. In addition to political inclusiveness, the country enjoys a peaceful civil society, evidenced through enviably low crime rates, and a well-trained and highly educated workforce.

While the country is peaceful and successful, not to mention well respected abroad, this is not to suggest that modern Oman has been without problems. The demonstrations in Oman during the so-called Arab Spring of 2011 began largely in sympathy with Arab neighbours but quickly turned into local protests against corruption and lack of opportunity, particularly in the northern town of Sohar. In contrast to unrest elsewhere in the region, however, the demands of protesters in Oman focused less on calls for greater democracy (the sultan is the ultimate authority, with jurisdiction over even minor policy decisions) than on the lack of opportunities for job seekers and the slow progress of Omanisation (the process of replacing expatriates with Omani nationals in the workplace in all sectors of the economy).

The government response to the 2011 unrest was to offer a generous scholarship system for Omani citizens to study at tertiary level free of charge, with the result that a very large proportion of the population have now graduated with under- and postgraduate degrees. There is some speculation that free education may not be sustainable for much longer, as the low price of oil continues. For the present, however, with the higher education sector now being held to account by comparison against internationally benchmarked standards, Oman is enjoying something of an intellectual renaissance.

People & Society

The National Psyche

Since Sultan Qaboos came to power in 1970, Oman has trodden a careful path, limiting outside influence while enjoying some of the benefits that it brings. The result has been a successful adoption of the best parts of the Gulf philosophy, marked by a tolerance of outside 'customs and manners'. This has been achieved, thanks to the slower pace of change, without the sacrifice of national identity that often characterises rapid modernisation.

Oman takes pride in its long history, consciously maintaining customs, dress, architecture and rules of hospitality, as well as meticulously restoring historical monuments. With relatively modest oil revenues, Omani people have had to work hard to make their country what it is today, and perhaps that is why the arrogance that may be seen in neighbouring countries is conspicuously absent here.

OMAN DRESS

While many modernising countries have rushed headlong into international-style cloth-ing, marked by business suits or jeans and a t-shirt, the people of Oman have made a conscious effort to maintain their sartorial heritage. While this is beginning to change in certain circumstances (in Muscat women often wear trousers under their full-length *abaya* dresses), on the whole visitors can't fail to note the uniformity – not to mention the elegance – of the costume worn by young and old alike.

Traditional Omani dress is revealing of ethnic and regional origins. Heads, arms and legs are always covered, but costumes for women range from a long velvet train tradi-tional in Dhofar, to a transparent *abaya*, worn over colourful tunics, with a peaked face mask worn by the Bedouin. During festivals, sisters and even friends often wear clothes cut from the same fabric. Elaborate trouser cuffs with silver embellishment, embroi-dered tunic yokes and long veils bedecked with gold jewellery form dazzling ensembles on special occasions.

Men wear a *dishdasha* (shirt-dress, officially white but in an increasingly wide array of neutral colours off duty) and a white *kumar* (cotton, brimless hat), traditionally em-broidered by a loved one. At work, men sport a pastel-coloured *masar* (turban) made of Kashmiri pashmina (goat's wool), wrapped according to the traditions of their home region. During ceremonies, a silver *khanjar* (traditional curved dagger) is tucked into the belt and on an especially formal occasion, a *bisht* (transparent silk outer garment with gold trim) is worn while carrying a short, simple camel stick.

Lifestyle

It would be hard to imagine any country that has changed so dramatically in such a short space of time. Within the living mem-ory of most middle-aged people outside Muscat, travelling to the next village meant hopping on a donkey or bicycle, education meant reciting the Quran under a tree, and medication comprised of a few herbs (albeit very effective ones) from the mountainsides. Modern farmers contemplate GM crop rota-tions, yet also look at the cloudless sky and realise that their grandmothers and chil-dren haven't been praying loudly enough. Modern medics administer the latest drugs while nipping back to grandmother for a herbal remedy for their own headaches. Lit-tle wonder that some families have buckled under the pressure of such an extraordinary pace of change; alcoholism, divorce, drug abuse and manic driving are all social ills that have increased proportionately.

On the whole, however, Oman is a success story; it has embraced the new world with just enough scepticism to allow people to return to their villages on the weekend, park their Toyotas at the end of the tarmac and walk the rest of the way to see grandfather.

Multiculturalism

Oman's population is predominantly Arab, although the country's imperial history has resulted in intermarriage with other groups, particularly from East Africa. As such, some Omanis speak Swahili better than Arabic. An Indian merchant community has existed in Muscat for at least 200 years, and people of Persian or Baluchi ancestry dominate the Batinah coast, with many still speaking the Baluchi language or Farsi.

The people living in the escarpments of Dhofar form another, distinct ethnic group. Known locally as the 'Jebbali' or 'mountain people', and tracing their heritage to the an-cient people of Ad, many still live a mostly nomadic life rearing camels. They have their own distinct customs and speak their own, unwritten language, 'Jibbali' (also known as Shehri), which is believed to be spoken still by over 50,000 people. At the other end of the country, those living in the Musandam Peninsula form another distinct group; they too speak a unique language, called 'Kumzari'. A mixture of Portuguese, Arabic and Farsi, this colourful language is sadly on the decline as younger generations are opt-ing to use more mainstream Arabic.

Omani people have a strong sense of tribe, many of which can be traced back to Bedouin roots. Their tribal names (for ex-ample, Al Nabhani, Al Wahaybi, Al Balushi) indicate very clearly to which area they be-long. Some families, such as Al Abris from Wadi Sahtan, can be pinpointed to specific wadis in the Hajar Mountains, while the

Bedouin Al Wahaybis still consider themselves to be guardians of the Sharqiya Sands.

Attracted by work and modern amenities, many people are moving to the capital, Muscat, which is spreading westward, along the coast towards Seeb. In an effort to stem this flow, graded roads, electricity and water have been supplied to even the smallest *willayat* (village). It is not unusual in even these far-flung outposts of the country to see expatriates, mostly from India, working in shops, schools and clinics.

Religion

About 75% of Omanis follow the Ibadi sect of Islam, an austere form of the religion that eschews decadence of any kind, even in mosque architecture. That said, modern Omanis tend to be pragmatic in their interpretation of religion, are tolerant of other forms of Islamic worship and allow expats to express their own religions discreetly in and around Muscat.

Magic plays a tangible role in the spiritual life of many Omanis. The 'evil eye' is not mere superstition; it is regarded as a hazard of everyday life. Amulets containing verses from the Quran, or hung around the necks of infants, are considered an effective way of warding off such adversities, and it's not uncommon to see a tiny hole in an infant's ear (not in the lobe but near where the ear joins the head) or *khol* (mascara) around a baby's eye, helping to keep trouble at bay.

Arts

In a village between Dibab and Tiwi on the old Qurayat–Sur coast road, the porches of several houses sport splendid pink or lime-green bathroom tiles, complete with fern motifs. Next door to one of these houses, the remains of an intricately hand-carved door lay disintegrating for years until weather, or an entrepreneur from Muscat, or both, put paid to it.

It's not a case of 'out with the old and in with the new', but a demonstration of Oman's commercial relationship with art: a job lot of Indian tiles for a camel-bag of incense (or the modern-day equivalent) is the kind of international exchange that has characterised the pragmatic nature of Omani arts and crafts for centuries. It's not unusual, for example, to find the family silver (particularly grandmother's jewellery) making the journey to Muscat because wife number two prefers gold. Before they became items of tourist value, exquisite pieces of silver were readily melted down and returned in kind from the gold souq. In fact, for centuries most silver jewellery was fashioned from Oman's old currency (smelted *thalla*, or Maria Theresa dollars), prized for its 80%-plus silver content.

In other words, Oman's arts and crafts are all about the living rather than the dead, the practical rather than the purely decorative. Whether this heritage can withstand rapid modernisation is another matter, but craft shops in Muscat and heavy investment through a dedicated government ministry are helping to give this important cultural expression a chance of being relevant in the future.

Traditional Crafts

There are many crafts in Oman, all of which have been meticulously documented through the Omani Craft Heritage Documentation Project, under the auspices of His Highness Sayyid Shihab Bin Tariq Al Said and endorsed by Unesco.

Each region of Oman is associated with a different craft – Bahla is famous for pottery, Nizwa for silver jewellery, Jebel Shams for rug-weaving, Sur for boat-building, Shwaymiya for basket-making. For a definitive survey of Omani crafts, the twin-volume *The Craft Heritage of Oman*, by Neil Richardson and Marcia Dorr, makes a weighty souvenir. Avelyn Forster's book *Disappearing Treasures of Oman* focuses on the silver Bedouin jewellery of Oman.

For more information on Oman's rich craft industry, see the website of the Public Authority for Craft Industries (www.paci. gov.om).

Music & Dance

There are dozens of traditional song and dance forms in Oman, more than 130 of which have been documented by the Oman Centre for Traditional Music, founded in 1984 to preserve the country's musical heritage. Oman was the first Arab country to become part of the International Council for Traditional Music, under Unesco.

Oman's music is diverse because of the country's seafaring and imperial heritage. The *naham* is a particularly famous call to crew members to pull together during a long sea voyage.

Sultan Qaboos is a lover of Western classical music. The Royal Oman Symphony Orchestra set up in his honour has been a surprising success, given the difficulties involved in learning a completely different musical idiom. The opening of the magnificent Royal Opera House Muscat (p149) in 2011, to mark the occasion of the 40th anniversary of the sultan's reign, has enabled the hosting of world-class opera, ballet and classical-music orchestras from around the world.

Each branch of the armed forces has a band of international calibre, including the highly popular bagpipe contingent – no official ceremony in Oman would be the same without the pipes and drums. The massed bands perform annual tattoos, giving lavish horse- and camel-back displays. Some of the military bands have regularly participated in international events, such as the Royal Edinburgh Military Tattoo in the UK, to much acclaim.

Architecture

Oman may no longer boast pillars of gold, like the fabled city of Ubar, but it does have another architectural trump card: its forts. There is barely a village without one, and crenellations turn up as a motif in many public buildings, from bus stops and telephone kiosks, to ministries and courts of law.

The country has mercifully largely escaped the skyscraping obsession of its neighbours, settling for more restrained public buildings in keeping with a more modest budget. However, what the buildings lack in multiple floors, they make up for in imaginative design. Muscat, in particular, abounds with serene and elegant examples, such as the ministry buildings and embassy buildings in Al Khuwair. The Grand Mosque in Al Ghubrah, completed in 2001, is the ultimate expression of restraint, with the simplicity of its exterior masking an exuberantly rich interior.

Barasti (palm-leaf) and other palm-constructed housing is no longer common, but a few examples can still be seen along the coast from Duqm to Shwaymiya. In the Sharqiya Sands, the Bedouin use goat-hair tents, and a few people in the mountains continue to live in caves with an improvised front door.

Finding a balance between old and new is a challenge. Young Omani engineers are disappointed in the low-rise constructions of their capital, and yet at the same time it has been difficult convincing some communities to move the goats out of the municipal housing built for their benefit. For the time being, at least, architectural ambition is held in check by the falling price of oil, and visitors will appreciate the resulting and unique homogeneity of the built environment, invariably enhanced by delightful landscaping and public parks.

Environment

Oman is blessed with a remarkable environment of spectacular desert landscapes and a wealth of flora and fauna. However, it doesn't render up its treasures easily and a 4WD is required to visit many of the places of natural beauty and interest. Accommodation near these places is often restricted to ad-hoc camping, but many regard this as a joy in its own right. Indeed, waking up to the sound of a turtle retreating down the beach, or falling asleep to the croak of toads, is an unforgettable experience.

The Land

Geographically, Oman is large and diverse, with a coastline more than 2000km in length, rugged mountains in the north, a share of the Empty Quarter and a unique monsoon catchment in the far south. The country extends from the fjords of the Musandam Peninsula, separated from the rest of Oman by the United Arab Emirates (UAE), to the seasonally green Dhofar region and includes a tiny enclave in the middle of the UAE.

Most of the country's population is concentrated on the Batinah coast, a semifertile plain that runs from the border with the UAE to Muscat, and is separated from the rest of Arabia by the Hajar Mountains. These mountains are internationally famed for their geological heritage, and even the layperson will enjoy the candy-striped rocks. The highest peak is Jebel Shams (Mountain of the Sun), officially measured at 3075m, alongside which runs Wadi Ghul, dubbed the Grand Canyon of Arabia. On the slopes of nearby Jebel Akhdar (Green Mountain), temperate fruits are grown.

OMAN'S ORYX HERD – A TALE OF TWIN ANTLERS

Watching the magnificent oryx paw the dust in the summer heat, or slip gracefully through the dawn mists in winter, makes the long journey to the desolate Jiddat Al Harasis plain worthwhile. Watching a mature bull, with rapier-like antlers and white, summer coat, level up to a rival in profile, you could be forgiven for thinking you'd seen a unicorn. In fact some trace the unicorn myth to the ancient Egyptian practice of binding the antlers of young oryx so they fuse into one. Fact or fiction, there's no doubting this magnificent animal caught the public imagination and great efforts were made to protect the species.

In 1962 the Fauna and Flora Preservation Society captured the last remaining oryx in Oman close to the border with Yemen, and sent them to a zoo in the USA. By 1982, protected by new laws banning the hunting of wild animals, a herd of 40 Arabian oryx was returned to Jiddat Al Harasis. Despite intermittent bouts of poaching the program met with initial success, in part because of the commitment of the Harasis tribe designated to look after them, and earned the reserve Unesco World Heritage status.

That should have been the happy end of the tale but alas, poaching proved harder to control than anticipated and the discovery of oil in the reserve resulted in a drastic 90% reduction in the oryx's protected habitat. As a result, and to the country's embarrassment, in 2007 the reserve became the first Unesco site ever to be delisted. This was bad news not only for the oryx, the population of which shrank from a herd of 450 in 1996 to only around 60 (with only four mating pairs) two decades later, but also for the endangered houbara bustard, honey badger and caracal that also called the diminished Huqf wilderness their home.

Thanks to the concerted efforts of the Office for Conservation of the Environment over the past decade, the fortunes of the Huqf is once again beginning to be reversed. Oryx numbers have now increased to over 600 and, for the first time in many years, a calf has been born outside the breeding enclosures. Other animals currently spotted in the reserve include gazelle, caracal, badger, fox and wolf. These naturally prove elusive, but visitors are still welcome to visit the Al Wusta Wildlife Reserve (p221) and share in the knowledge of the Huqf's knowledgeable retired rangers.

Much of the country between the Hajar Mountains and Dhofar is flat and rocky desert, but there are also areas of sand dunes. Most notable are the Sharqiya Sands, informally known as Wahiba Sands, and the less-accessible sands of the Rub Al Khali (Empty Quarter). Oman is not as rich in oil as its neighbours, but it does have some extensive fields in the gravel plains around Marmul in Al Wusta region and Fahood in Al Dakhiliyah region.

Thriving and diverse marine life exists off Oman's long coastline and there are many islands, the chief of which is the desert island of Masirah.

Wildlife

Oman's isolated mountains and wadis are a haven for a variety of animals. These include more than 50 types of mammals, such as wolves, foxes, hedgehogs, jerboas (long-legged desert rodents) and hares. The largest land mammal that a visitor is likely to see is the gazelle, which occupies the Huqf in Al Wusta region.

There are 13 different species of whale and dolphin in Omani waters, including the world's biggest living creature, the blue whale – a skeleton of which can be seen in Muscat's Natural History Museum (p140). Oman also has an important biodiversity of molluscs: it's quite possible to identify more than 30 different species along a 1km stretch of beach, even in the capital.

The *Oman Bird List* is updated regularly and published by the Oman Bird Records Committee (available in Muscat bookshops); there are nearly 500 recorded species. Spoonbills and flamingos frequent salt lagoons, even in Muscat, but the country is internationally renowned for its migrating raptors. For more information, *Common Birds in Oman,* by Hanne and Jens Eriksen, is an excellent resource produced by two expats renowned for their superb bird photography. Keen ornithologists may like to refer to their website (www.birdsoman.com).

There is a wide diversity of insects in Oman – from the mighty minotaur beetle to the fig-tree blue, orange pansy and other butterflies – attracted to Oman's fertile wadis or desert acacias. Dhofar, with its unique microclimate, is particularly rich in entomological interest, much of which is yet to be fully documented.

ENDANGERED SPECIES

Oman is of global importance to the survival of the endangered green turtle and has one of the largest nesting sites in the world at Ras Al Jinz (p163). There are five endangered species of turtle which inhabit the coasts of Oman, all protected by royal decree.

Oman's varied terrain is home to a large number of endangered species, including houbara bustard, ibex, tahr (an Omani species of a goatlike animal) and the magnificent Arabian leopard, which is native to Dhofar and the subject of intense conservation efforts. There are also declining numbers of sand cat, caracal, honey badger and mongoose.

Al Wusta Wildlife Reserve (p221) in Jiddat Al Harasis houses a highly protected herd of wild oryx (p230), reintroduced in the 1980s. The future of this magnificent antelope is looking brighter now that poaching has been brought under control.

FLORA

Oman built an empire on the frankincense trees that grow in Dhofar around Wadi Dawkah (p210). The trees are still bled for the aromatic sap, but dates, covering 49% of cultivated land, have overtaken them in economic importance. Oman has a very rich plant life thanks to its fertile wadis, many irrigated year-round by spring water. It is common to see tall stands of pink oleander flowering in the wadis throughout the year.

A government-sponsored herbal clinic in Muscat uses many locally occurring plants and shrubs to treat a wide range of illnesses, most commonly diabetes and hypertension.

A national collection of plants is being assembled as part of the world-class Oman Botanic Garden (www.bgci.org), the first of its kind in Arabia. When complete, every habitat in Oman will be represented in two giant biomes on the outskirts of Muscat.

National Parks

While there are several reserves, such as the Qurm Nature Reserve (Map p134; alongside Al Shatti St, Shatti Al Qurm) in Muscat, set up to protect the endangered mangrove, there are no formal national parks. The Damaniyat Islands are designated as a national nature reserve, and access to this marine environment is controlled.

Environmental Issues

Oman used to enjoy an enviable record with regard to its protection of the environment – a subject in which the sultan has a passionate interest. His efforts were even acknowledged by the International Union for Conservation of Nature (IUCN), which awarded him the John C Phillips Memorial Medal in 1996 and cited Oman as a country with one of the best records in environmental conservation and pollution control. The sultanate's first environmental legislation was enacted in 1974, and in 1984 Oman was the first Arab country to set up a ministry exclusively concerned with the environment. The prestigious Sultan Qaboos Prize for Environmental Preservation, first awarded in 1991, has been given every two years to a conservation body or individual chosen by Unesco for environmental performance. On 8 January each year the sultanate celebrates Environment Day, when children learn about habitat erosion, rubbish dumping and depletion of freshwater reserves.

Despite this exemplary record, increased tourism has led to a recent increase in littering, especially of plastic, and oil waste is being washed up on Oman's hitherto pristine beaches, dumped illegally from container ships. Despite heavy penalties if caught, offenders often get away with it, as it's almost impossible for Oman's military services to police such a long and exposed coastline.

Landfill and waste-management issues are being tackled through various research initiatives, together with schemes to make water conservation more sustainable and solar energy more reliable in a dust-blown climate. A circular economy of recycling and energy generation through waste, however, is still a long way off.

To find out more about the steps Oman is taking to preserve the environment and the unique flora and fauna within it, contact the Environmental Society of Oman (www.eso.org.om). There is also a highly successful Outward Bound initiative, endorsed by the government, bringing environmental awareness to the nation's youth.

OMAN ENVIRONMENT

Food & Drink

Local restaurants selling genuine Omani food, with its emphasis on fish and dates, represent a new trend in the cities prompting the question 'What exactly *is* Omani food?'. This little-known cuisine was pretty much hidden from view until recently, as Omanis traditionally tend to cook and eat at home or otherwise choose to go out to a restaurant (international in cities, Indian in interior towns) to eat something different to the local cuisine. The chain of restaurants called Bin Ateeq were once the only way of sampling Omani dishes, but now a modern interest in culinary history, together with more women seeking careers outside the home, has helped give wider exposure to the rich national cuisine.

While sharing much with Arab cuisine in general, including the staples of rice and unleavened bread, Omani cooking is nutritious and varied with a heavy emphasis on cardamom, saffron and turmeric, reflecting the country's ethnic diversity. With access to a long coastline, Omanis are particularly fond of fish – sardines can be seen drying in noisome piles from Sohar to Salalah. Until recently, shellfish, including the local lobster (actually a large, clawless crayfish), were not considered fit for eating. Tastes have now changed and lobster is a popular dish even in small regional restaurants. One common delicacy from southern Oman is *rabees,* which is made from boiled immature shark, stripped and washed of the gritty skin, then fried with the liver.

One of the most typical Omani dishes is *harees,* made of steamed wheat and boiled meat to form a glutinous concoction. It is often garnished with *owaal* (dried shark) and laced with lime, chilli and onions, and is a popular dish to break the fast during Ramadan. Few Omani dishes are especially spicy, although some form of chilli paste usually crops up as a garnish.

The dish of parties and festivals is *shuwa:* goat, mutton, calf or camel meat is marinated with date juice and spices, wrapped in banana leaves and buried in an earthen or underground oven. The result, at least 12 hours later, is a mouth-wateringly tenderised piece of meat, aromatically flavoured with wood smoke and spices. It is served with *rukhal* (wafer-thin Omani bread) and rice on a *fadhl* (giant, communal eating tray), and eaten, of course, with the right hand only.

As Oman grows its own prize pomegranates, together with bananas, apricots and citrus fruit, mainly on the terraced gardens of Jebel Akhdar, fruit is not surprisingly an important part of an Omani meal. What is surprising to many visitors, however, is that it is traditionally served before the meat course.

Guests traditionally eat first, followed by men, who are expected to reserve the best pieces for women, who eat with the rest of the family after the guests are gone. This does not represent as long a wait as it might seem, as traditionally guests, having dispensed with all the news before the meal commences, 'eat and go'.

SURVIVAL GUIDE

❶ Directory A–Z

ACCESSIBLE TRAVEL

Outside Muscat, Oman does not cater particularly well for the needs of disabled travellers, with ramps and disabled parking being the exception rather than the rule. New malls in each city are more accommodating.

ACCOMMODATION

Accommodation in Oman, which outside Muscat is limited and expensive, should be booked in advance from November to March (or June to August in Salalah). Note that some towns have no hotels at all, although wild camping is often possible close by.

Heritage Homes are helping to preserve Oman's architectural heirlooms and these family-run enterprises offer a retreat from the region's rampaging modernity. A relatively new phenomenon in Oman, they can now be found in several towns in the Hajar Mountains. Traditional rooms tend to be dark and windowless (to keep out the heat) but generally have air-conditioning and are invariably decked with local artefacts.

SLEEPING PRICE RANGES

The following price ranges refer to a double room with a private bathroom in high season (November to March). Unless otherwise stated, breakfast is included in the price.

$ less than OR45

$$ OR45–100

$$$ more than OR100

PRACTICALITIES

Newspapers Oman has two main local English-language newspapers: *The Times of Oman* (www.timesofoman.com), *Oman Daily Observer* (www.omanobserver.om).

Photography Discretion is required when photographing people, especially women in rural and remote areas.

Radio The local English-language radio station broadcasts on 90.4FM (94.3FM from Salalah); High FM (95.9FM) is Oman's most popular English-language commercial radio station and the BBC World Service (103.2FM) is also available in Muscat.

Smoking A no-smoking policy is enforced in interior public places. This includes inside restaurants and on public transport.

Telephone Phonecards are available from grocery stores and petrol stations.

Weights & Measures Oman uses the metric system.

The home cooking included in the price is a highlight.

EMERGENCY NUMBERS

Ambulance, Fire & Police	📞9999
Country Code	📞968
International Access Code	📞00

LEGAL MATTERS

Driving offences (including crossing a red light, using a mobile phone while driving, and drink driving) result in heavy fines and even prison sentences. Drug use is strictly prohibited and has severe consequences.

All fines must be paid before departure, and passengers are not permitted to pass through immigration until they have paid their dues. Note that these are payable by credit card only – cash is not accepted.

Arresting police tend to be polite and helpful; in return they expect similar courtesy. Bribes are not expected or accepted.

LGBT+ TRAVELLERS

Homosexuality is illegal in Oman. Visitors, however, are unlikely to meet with prejudice as room sharing is considered acceptable as a form of economising. Condoms are widely available. Global Gayz (www.globalgayz.com/middle-east) has more information relevant to LGBT+ travellers in the region.

MAPS

Up-to-date maps are hard come by in Oman. The Ministry of Tourism desk at the airport offers a reasonably accurate free road map, also available from many hotels, but it doesn't cover many off-road routes. Online services such as Google Maps are becoming ever-more extensive in coverage and, in remote areas such as the Hajar Mountains, are helpful in picking up unmapped routes in satellite view.

MONEY

➺ ATMs are widespread.

➺ Money changers (open between 4pm to 7pm in Muscat) are slightly more competitive than banks.

➺ The most popular credit card in Oman is Visa, but MasterCard is also widely accepted. American Express is not accepted in many shops, and you may incur a fee of 5% for using it in some restaurants and hotels.

➺ The official currency is the Omani rial (OR, but also widely abbreviated as RO or OMR). One rial is divided into 1000 baisa (also spelt baiza and shortened to bz). There are coins of 5, 10, 25 and 50 baisa, and notes of 100 and 200 baisa. There are notes of a half, one, five, 10, 20 and 50 rials.

Tipping

Tipping in Oman is not as widespread as it is elsewhere in the region and is uncommon in smaller establishments.

Hotels OR1 for baggage handling and room service; gratuity for cleaning staff is uncommon and discretionary.

Restaurants In large hotel restaurants, 10% is expected if a service fee hasn't been included in the bill.

Taxis Tipping taxi drivers is discretionary.

EATING PRICE RANGES

The following price ranges refer to a standard meal. Service charge and tax are included in the price.

$ less than OR5

$$ OR5–10

$$$ more than OR10

OPENING HOURS

Oman's weekend is on Friday and Saturday.

Banks 8am to noon Sunday to Thursday

Government Departments & Ministries
7.30am to 2.30pm Sunday to Thursday; closing at 1.30pm during Ramadan

Malls 10am to 10pm

Post Offices 8am to 4pm Sunday to Thursday

Restaurants 11.30am to 2pm and 5pm to midnight Saturday to Thursday; 5pm to midnight Friday

Shops 8am to 1pm and 4pm to 7pm Saturday to Thursday; 5pm to 7pm Friday

Sights 9am to 4pm Saturday to Thursday; many sights open on an ad hoc basis – timings change frequently.

POST

Sending a postcard to any destination outside the Gulf Cooperation Council (http://www.gcc-sg.org) costs 150 baisa. Postage for letters is 250 baisa for the first 10g and 400 baisa for 11g to 20g. For parcels of up to 1kg it is around OR5.

Oman Post (www.omanpost.om) includes Matjar (www.matjar.om), a virtual mailbox company, offering courier services at competitive prices so that you can send all your online shopping in one consignment.

PUBLIC HOLIDAYS

Public holidays in Oman are generally characterised by an exodus from the main cities as people drive home to their regional villages to spend time with their extended families. For the visitor, this means that roads are busier before and after the holiday, and public offices are closed. Shops and restaurants, however, remain open. Oman's sights (the best-known wadis and the Sharqiya Sands in particular) are also busier at this time – largely with expatriate visitors.

In addition to Islamic holidays shared across the region, Oman celebrates **Renaissance Day** (23 July), when a day's holiday is given to mark the beginning of the reign of Sultan Qaboos, generally credited for the modern rebirth of the country, and **National Day** (18 November) which is marked by at least two days of holiday, camel racing, military parades and flags decorating the highway.

SAFE TRAVEL

Oman is a very safe country with low crime rates and people who go out of their way to help strangers. Take the usual precautions regarding walking late at night in unlit, urban areas. Dangers are related mostly to road use and natural events. In particular, watch out for high volumes of traffic accidents because of tailgating and speed; flash floods that can appear at great speed coursing along wadis (don't camp in the bottom of a wadi); the isolation of many off-road destinations; and extreme summertime temperatures (particularly from May to October), which can quickly lead to heat exhaustion and heat stroke.

TOILETS

➡ Generally public toilets are something of a rarity, with highway service stations offering the best chance of clean amenities (the ladies' loo is generally kept locked – ask the petrol-pump attendant for the key).

➡ Smart new public toilets are beginning to put in an appearance – some in unlikely places, such as on the top of a sand dune in the Sharqiya Sands.

➡ Most accommodation types – even in tented camps – offer en suite bathrooms and almost all have Western-style toilets. Squat toilets (which local doctors advocate as being more conducive to natural bodily functions) are the norm in restaurants outside the big cities.

➡ Toilet paper is reserved for drying purposes only and is therefore not always available – using it for any other purpose than drying is considered a barbaric Western practice. Water (generally via a hose) is provided instead.

VISAS

Visas (OR5/20 for 10/30 days) are required for most nationalities and must be applied for in advance. Applications can be obtained through Omani embassies abroad or, more easily, online through the Royal Oman Police website (www.rop.gov.om). The visa should be printed, ready for presentation at the immigration desk on arrival at the airport or land border.

WOMEN TRAVELLERS

Women travelling alone are made welcome but it is still uncommon to see solo travellers outside the main cities. You may feel uncomfortable in the interior of Oman, particularly on public transport, eating in restaurants and when visiting public beaches. Omani men mostly ignore women out of respect, and it's hard to meet Omani women.

Harassment is not a big problem. It helps, however, in addition to being culturally sensitive, to be discreetly dressed in loose-fitting clothing, and to wear shorts and a T-shirt for swimming.

ⓘ Getting There & Away

AIR

There are three international airports in Oman, but the only one connecting major international destinations is Muscat International Airport (p150). Qatar Airways (www.qatarairways.com) offers direct flights between Doha and both Sohar and Salalah. Fly Dubai (www.flydubai.com) offers direct flights between Dubai and Salalah.

The national carrier is Oman Air (www.omanair. com) and other airlines that fly to Oman include: British Airways (www.ba.com), Emirates (www. emirates.com), Gulf Air (www.gulfair.com) and Saudia Airlines (www.saudia.com)

LAND

Oman borders the United Arab Emirates, Saudi Arabia and Yemen. Current practicalities mean, however, that you can only enter UAE. The situation changes frequently, and it's worth checking with the Royal Oman Police (www.rop.gov.om) before planning your trip to see which crossings are open to non-GCC visitors. Note that visas for Oman must be obtained online in advance. Currently, a Dubai tourist visa permits entry to Oman within the validity of the visa.

Border Crossings

There are six border crossings (open 24 hours) currently open to foreigners, only four of which are commonly used by tourists. These posts are between the UAE and Oman:

Wajaja The post that Dubai-bound buses use. It takes about an hour for a full bus to clear through immigration. The route between Wajaja and Dubai takes you in and out of Omani territory (the border is not a straight line) with checkpoints at each crossing, but this usually involves a quick wave of your passport.

Khatmat Milahah More useful for those with their own transport wanting to explore the eastern coast of the UAE.

Buraimi The post mostly used for Abu Dhabi.

Tibat Currently the only post open for foreigners between UAE and Musandam.

The rules regarding entry and exit formalities change frequently so check with the Royal Oman Police (www.rop.gov.om) before travelling.

Bus

Mwasalat (http://mwasalat.om/en-us) offers an Oman–Dubai express service at 6.20am, 3.20pm and 11.20pm (OR5.5, 5½ hours) departing from Azaiba Bus Station (p150) in Muscat.

Sea

There are currently no passenger services to/ from Oman but a new car ferry service is rumoured to be launched soon between Kuwait, Doha and Sohar as a result of the Qatar embargo. Khasab, Sohar, Muscat and Salalah are ports of call for cruise liners.

Car & Motorcycle

It's possible to drive through any of the open borders in your own vehicle if you obtain insurance to cover both countries. You need extra insurance if you wish to take a hired car over the border to/from UAE, and you must return the car to the country in which you hired it (unless you're willing to pay a huge premium).

ℹ Getting Around

AIR

Besides Muscat International Airport, there are airports in Salalah (p213), Duqm (p223), **Sohar** (☏ 26840807; www.soharairport.co.om; off Hwy 1) and **Khasab** (Airport Rd).

Oman Air services the domestic airports, as well as a selection of Middle East and subcontinental destinations. Tickets can be booked through any travel agent or online.

Salam Air (www.salamair.com) is the only Oman-based low-cost carrier; it operates between Salalah and Muscat, as well as a handful of other regional destinations.

BICYCLE

Cycling in Oman is not feasible for much of the year, on account of the extreme heat. As such, it tends to be a dangerous form of transport as motorists are unaccustomed to sharing the road with cyclists. Local expats tend to cycle on the wrong side of the road, including on roundabouts, with the slightly odd logic of being able to see a potential accident! This practice should not be emulated.

The Tour of Oman (p143) is helping to raise awareness of cycling, and interest in mountain biking is growing in popularity with events such

---

ℹ BORDER CROSSING TIPS

➤ Bring a photocopy of your passport and a pen – you may find that this helps speed up the process, which can be lengthy at weekends and during holidays.

➤ You can take a hire car across the border if you have insurance (available from booths at Wajaja and Khatmat Milahah crossings) but it is much quicker to clear immigration if you have arranged insurance in advance.

➤ Don't forget to empty your cool box of beer when crossing borders.

➤ There's no exit tax for Oman; exit tax from the UAE costs Dh35, payable only by credit card.

as the Titan of the Hill (p186) downhill race from Misfat Al Abriyyin.

BOAT

There are two ferry services, operated by National Ferries Company (www.nfc.om), connecting Shinas in northern Oman with Khasab. This is accessed via a bus service from Muscat. Another service connects Hilf, the main town of the island of Masirah, with Shana'a on the mainland. Water taxis connect Muscat's marinas (Al Mouj and Bandar Al Rowdha) with the marina at Jebel Seifa.

BUS

City and intercity buses are operated by Mwasalat (www.mwasalat.om), which has daily services to/from the main provincial cities for less than OR10. Buses are usually on time, comfortable, air-conditioned and safe. Tickets can be bought with cash from the bus driver, but it is better to make a reservation for longer journeys. City bus services are currently only operating in Muscat but are being introduced into Salalah and Sohar.

A few other bus services operated by private companies, such as **Gulf Transport Company** (☑ 23293303; Jct 8, 23 July St; ⊘ 5am-11pm), provide competition on main routes to Dubai, Salalah and Duqm; they tend to leave at similar times to Mwasalat.

CAR & MOTORCYCLE

Road signs are written in Arabic and English (with inconsistent spelling) throughout Oman. Brown signposts signal most sites of tourist interest. Petrol, all of which is unleaded, is widely available and comparatively cheap. Most petrol stations have modern, well-stocked shops and clean(ish) toilets. Tow-ropes (OR5) are available from any large supermarket.

Carrying water is essential (a box of a dozen 1.5L bottles costs OR1.7 from petrol stations). 'Freezer packs' (around 600 baisa each) will keep cool boxes cold for a day, even in summer, and hotels will refreeze the packs at night.

Most foreign driving licences are accepted in Oman.

Car Hire

International car-hire chains in Oman include Avis, Budget, Europcar and Thrifty, but dozens of local agencies offer a slightly reduced rate. Daily rates for 2WD cars start at about OR15 and 4WD vehicles at OR40. Alwan Tour Rent-a-Car (p150) has a large selection of saloon and 4WDs and Mark Tours (p143) is another reliable local rental agency. Check the small print on all car-hire documents to see if you are covered for taking the vehicle off-road. Extra insurance is required if taking the hire car across the border to UAE.

Road Hazards

Potential problems on the road include aggressive tailgating and fast, aggressive driving; camels and goats wandering onto the road; exceptionally slippery conditions after rain; failing brakes on mountain roads (low gear is a must); soft sand and a salty crust called *sabkha* that looks and feels hard until you drive on it, and flash flooding that occurs frequently in wadis.

Road Rules

The following traffic laws are strictly enforced, especially in Muscat:

➡ Seatbelt use and child-safety seats (under four years of age) are mandatory.

➡ Mobile-phone use is forbidden while driving.

➡ The drink-driving limit is zero.

➡ The maximum speed limit is 120km per hour.

➡ Speeding and parking fines must be paid by credit card before exiting airports.

➡ An OR5 fine is levied for a dirty car.

HITCHING

Hitching is never entirely safe, and we don't recommend it. Travellers who hitch should understand that they are taking a small but potentially serious risk. This is particularly the case in Oman: many routes are isolated with little traffic and potentially lethal temperatures if you get stranded. If you're driving, you will often be asked to give a ride to locals, but this is not recommended either.

Qatar قطر

POP 2.7 MILLION

Best Places to Eat

➡ Argan (p254)

➡ Morimoto (p255)

➡ Al Aker (p251)

➡ IDAM (p255)

➡ Turkey Central (p252)

➡ Drawing Room (p254)

Best Places to Stay

➡ Arumaila Boutique Hotel (p249)

➡ W Hotel Doha (p251)

➡ Banana Island Resort (p241)

➡ Najd Boutique Hotel (p249)

➡ Sharq Village & Spa (p251)

➡ Mondrian Doha (p250)

Why Go?

In steeped-in-tradition Qatar, you can learn about the ancient pursuit of falconry, watch camels race across the desert and admire traditional dhows (wooden cargo boats) bobbing on the water. But the country is developing rapidly, with the capital Doha a world-class city in the making, thanks to its spectacular modern skyline, peerless Museum of Islamic Art, a fine and expansive traditional souq, and burgeoning arts and culinary scenes. On any given day you could sample a portfolio of sophisticated restaurants and then watch the sun set over sand dunes that seem to spring from a fairy tale.

As Qatar prepares to host the 2022 World Cup, there's a flurry of activity and controversy in the air – as the nation uses imported labourers for construction of roads, rail routes and stadiums for the future fans. The recent Saudi-led blockade of Qatar makes most onward Gulf travel from this once-popular stopover destination much more difficult.

When to Go
Qatar

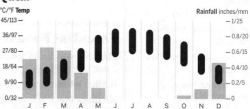

°C/°F **Temp**

45/113 —
36/97 —
27/80 —
18/64 —
9/90 —
0/32 —

J F M A M J J A S O N D

Rainfall inches/mm

— 1/25
— 0.8/20
— 0.6/15
— 0.4/10
— 0.2/5
— 0

Oct–Mar Cool off from scorching summer heat as temperatures decrease.

Mar & Apr Cheer as dromedaries speed along during the Emir's GCC Camel Race.

May–Sep Stick to indoors; outdoor temperatures can be unbearable and dangerous for extended periods.

AT A GLANCE

Capital Doha

Country code 974

Currency Qatari riyal (QR)

Emergency 999

Language Arabic, English

Mobile phones SIM cards widely available

Money ATMs are widespread; credit cards widely accepted

Population 2.7 million

Visas Waivers available on arrival for more than 80 nationalities

Exchange Rates

Australia	A$1	QR2.58
Euro zone	€1	QR4.18
Japan	¥100	QR3.23
Kuwait	KD1	QR12
UK	UK£1	QR4.73
US	US$1	QR3.64

For current exchange rates, see www.xe.com.

Resources

Lonely Planet (www.lonely planet.com/qatar)

Visit Qatar (www.visit qatar.qa)

I Love Qatar (www.ilove qatar.net)

Al Jazeera (www.aljazeera.com)

Daily Costs

Qatar is an expensive destination, particularly in terms of accommodation. It's tough to find budget digs, and there are no hostels whatsoever, but Doha does have a few atmospheric and less-spendy options (under QR500, about US$140) around Souq Waqif. Doha has no shortage of high-end and Michelin-starred restaurants, but inexpensive Middle Eastern eats are in abundance as well.

ITINERARIES

One Day

Absorb the best of modern central Doha on a morning promenade along the Corniche (p243), watching the stellar skyline dance in the heat. Spend the afternoon in cooler contemplation at the Museum of Islamic Art (p241), Doha's priceless treasure house. Seek out gems of a different kind among the silks and spices of Souq Waqif (p239), and admire the plumage on display in the Falcon Souq (p239). Complete the evening with a meal at one of the souq's bustling restaurants.

Three Days

On day two, recharge by the beach at Katara (p245), where there are also fine restaurants and art galleries to fill your time before a sunset dhow trip.

On day three, hire a car and tour the peninsula, stopping off at Al Khor (p263) for lunch at Al Sultan Beach Resort. Afterward, head north to explore the ancient rock carvings at Al Jassasiya (p262) and far-flung Al Zubarah Fort (p263), returning to Doha at night.

Four Days

On day four, get your thrills at Sealine Beach Resort (p262), zooming along the water on a jet ski or racing around the soft desert dunes via dirt buggy. Alternatively, catch the relaxing luxury catamaran boat to Banana Island Resort (p241), where opaque waters and nearly a kilometre of pristine sand await.

Essential Food & Drink

Machboos Rice and spices with chicken, lamb or fish in a rich sauce.

Grilled lobster Local crayfish are a popular choice.

Khabees Dates in a variety of sizes, colours and stages of ripeness.

Tap water Safe to drink.

Alcohol Available in five-star hotels only.

Coffee Traditionally served pale and spiked with cardamom, or dark, strong and with plenty of sugar.

DOHA

الدوحة

POP 1.35 MILLION

It's rare to see a great city in the making these days, but here's your chance. Whether it's the stunning and constantly changing skyline or the massive investments Qatari authorities are making in landmark cultural icons, Doha is a city oozing confidence and style, and it's as much ease with its modern shopping malls as it is with its heritage and traditional souqs.

Wander the fabulously atmospheric Souq Waqif, wonder at the sheer beauty of the world-class Museum of Islamic Art and its exhibits or head out to Katara to explore Doha's art culture. Wherever you look, Doha is threatening to eclipse Dubai as the Gulf's most dynamic city. Throw in a new metro system in the making and the 2022 FIFA World Cup on the horizon, and even despite the Gulf-Qatar diplomatic crisis, chances are Doha is going to come out on top.

◉ Sights

★ Souq Waqif   MARKET

(Map p246; btwn Al Souq & Grand Hamad Sts; ⊗7.30am-10pm Sat-Thu, 4-9pm Fri; P) This vibrant complex is without doubt one of the most atmospheric places to explore in Qatar. Built on an ancient market site, the area remains the social heart of Doha. Centuries ago, Bedouin would bring their sheep, goats and wool here to trade for essentials, and the entire market area has been cleverly redeveloped to look the part of a 19th-century souq, with mud-rendered shops and exposed timber beams, plus some authentic and beautifully restored original Qatari buildings.

With booming prosperity, the advent of vast air-conditioned shopping malls and Qatar's rush to embrace the new, Souq Waqif fell into serious decline by the 1990s, and much of the market was destroyed in a fire in 2003. An outcry from Qataris prompted the authorities to undertake a massive rehabilitation program, one that continues to this day. Such has been the success of this venture that the souq keeps growing to accommodate new 'old alleyways'.

Despite the ongoing gentrification of the area, the chief business of the souq continues unabated, and it remains one of the most traditional marketplaces in the region. This is the place to look for national Qatari dress, including the beautifully embroidered *bukhnoq* (girl's head covering), spices, perfumes and *oud* (incense made from agarwood).

Until land was reclaimed along Doha's waterfront in the 1970s, the waters lapped at the entrance to Souq Waqif, where traders were just as likely to arrive by boat as by camel. The first semi-permanent shops here were built around 250 years ago. Before that, vendors stood and sold their wares from makeshift stalls, as the market often flooded, and it is from this tradition that the souq's name derives: *waqif* means 'standing' in Arabic.

The Falcon Souq is a highlight, but falconry is not the only traditional Qatari leisure pursuit you can see around the market. Nearby **stables** (btwn Jasim Bin Mohammed St & Al Jasra St) house Arabian horses and just off the Corniche end of Al Jasra St, a **pen** (cnr Al Jasra St & Abdulla Bin Jassim St) is filled with feeding camels most of the day.

Animal lovers beware: located behind the colourful spice section of Souq Waqif is a collection of caged birds, and sometimes cats, rabbits, tortoises and dogs, kept outside in all weather: hot, hot and even hotter.

QATAR DOHA

DON'T MISS

FALCON SOUQ

For a glimpse of Qatari heritage, don't miss the Falcon Souq (Map p246; Al Jasra St; ⊗9am-1pm & 4-8pm Sat-Thu, 4-8pm Fri; P). You only have to see the scale of the market, afforded its own traditional arcaded building off Souq Waqif, to understand the place of falconry in Qatari society. Evenings are the best time to come, especially on Thursdays, when you can watch customers examining the birds – most of them hooded in black leather and perched on posts or railings – and discussing the finer points of falconry with the shopkeepers.

You may see shopkeepers crafting leather falcon helmets or enjoying tea on the cushioned benches at each store. Next door to the Falcon Souq is the Souq Waqif Falcon Hospital – if you stop by when things are quiet and ask nicely, the staff are usually pleased to show visitors around.

Qatar Highlights

1 Souq Waqif (p239) Stepping into the past in the cardamom-scented alleyways.

2 Museum of Islamic Art (p241) Viewing the world's largest collection of Islamic art.

3 Falcon Souq (p239) Ruffling feathers by bidding for a peregrine.

4 Corniche (p243) Gazing at a skyline-in-the-making on this waterside walk.

5 Katara Cultural Village (p245) Enjoying an exhibition, live show or relaxing meal.

6 Sheikh Faisal Bin Qassim Al Thani Museum (p260) Perusing a life's collection of artefacts in a fort-like building.

7 Banana Island Resort (p241) Dipping your feet in opaque waters and walking along a golden sandy beach.

8 Qatar National Library (p241) Entering a spaceship-like building with two million books and a maze of ancient literature.

9 MIA Park (p241) Walking through beautiful green spaces along Doha's waterfront.

10 Khor Al Adaid (p262) Using a dune for a pillow and the stars for a blanket.

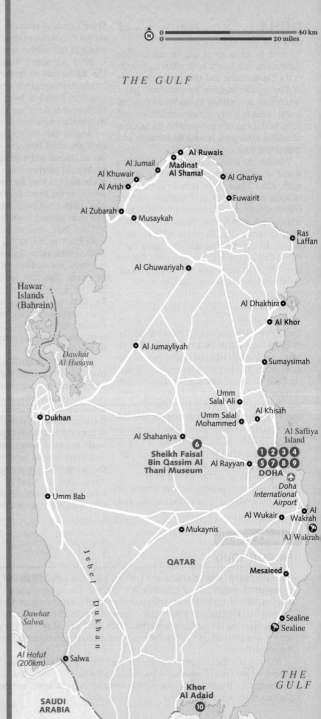

Some of the shops are like museums, displaying artefacts (such as swords and shipping memorabilia), plus jewellery from around the Arab world. Many shops and stalls in the souq close around 1pm and reopen at 4pm, but the area, and its many cafes and restaurants, remains open all day.

★ **Museum of Islamic Art** MUSEUM
(Map p246; ☑442 24444; www.mia.org.qa; off Al Corniche; ⊙9am-5.30pm Sat-Thu, 1.30-7pm Fri; ℗) FREE With the largest collection of Islamic art in the world, drawn from three continents, this fabulous museum is so rich in treasure that it rewards short, intense visits. Rising from its own purpose-built island, and set in an extensive landscape of lawns and ornamental trees off the Corniche, the museum is shaped like a postmodern fortress with minimal windows (to reduce energy use). The views across the water are splendid.

The museum was designed by IM Pei, the architect of the Louvre pyramid in Paris, and you know that something special awaits from the minute you lay eyes on the grand, palm-tree-lined entrance. Inside, the building is a masterpiece of light and space, drawing your eyes up to the dome, a clever modern take on an element so prevalent in Islamic architecture.

The collection is spread over three floors: the 1st and 2nd floors house the permanent collection, which includes exquisite textiles, ceramics, enamel work and glass, all showcased conceptually. A single motif, for example, is illustrated in neighbouring display cases in the weave of a carpet or a ceramic floor tile, or adapted in a piece of gold jewellery, allowing visitors to gain a sense of the homogeneity of Islamic art.

Pace yourself by visiting the cafe downstairs or finish at the top-floor IDAM restaurant (p255). On the ground floor there's a large museum shop. There are free 40-minute guided tours (English and Arabic) of the permanent collection on Thursday at 2pm.

Both men and women should avoid strappy tops or vests and shorts because you may be refused admission.

MIA Park PARK
(Map p246; www.mia.org.qa/en/mia-park; off Al Corniche; ℗) One of the best and most beautiful green spaces along the Doha waterfront, Museum of Islamic Art Park is home to Richard Serra's vertical steel sculpture, known as 7, this celebrated artist's first public piece of art in the Middle East. It's also home to cafes with some of the finest city views in Doha, including the MIA Park Cafe (p252), as well as pop-up food trucks. Runners enjoy the 1km crescent pathway around the park, and there's also a kids play area.

Renting a picnic basket inside the park costs QR50; you can fill it up with goodies from the local cafe. Check the website for upcoming events, from weekend markets and outdoor cinemas to kayaking tours and fitness sessions.

★ **Banana Island Resort** ISLAND
(☑404 05050; www.doha.anantara.com; Banana Island; day pass QR200) With its opaque waters and 800m golden-sand beach, the crescent-shaped Banana Island is one of the best excursions in Qatar, even if you're not staying at the luxury hotel (p251). Covered in tropical plants and greenery, it's reached via catamaran. Six restaurants on the island, from traditional Middle Eastern and American to Italian, keep guests fuelled up for the many activities on offer, including Segway rides (QR250), beach diving (from QR700), bowling (QR50) and flowrider wave riding (QR150 for 30 minutes).

Day passes include a QR100 food voucher.

Qatar National Library LIBRARY
(Map p242; ☑445 40246; www.qnl.qa; Al Luqta St, Education City; ⊙8am-8pm Sat-Thu, from 4pm Fri; ℗) One of the best libraries in the world, this incredible, spaceship-like structure contains a literary wonderland of two million books, including ancient maps and Qurans and literature dating back to the 15th century. You enter the building though a futuristic hatch; inside, the bookshelves appear to almost float on the wall of the library. In the centre of the expansive room is a labyrinth-like pit where all the ancient heritage books are kept on a maze of carefully positioned shelves.

The library also contains egg chairs, work stations, exhibition spaces (with rotating shows by modern artists), a children's library and a cafeteria-style restaurant. An innovation station has a recording studio filled with instruments; it's free to use, but bookable by residents only. Likewise, anyone can read the books while visiting the library, but only Qatari residents may borrow them from the building.

Mathaf GALLERY
(Arab Museum of Modern Art; Map p242; ☑440 28855; www.mathaf.org.qa; Rawadat Al Qada St, Education City, off Al Luqta St; ⊙9am-7pm Sat-Thu, from 1.30pm Fri; ℗) FREE This exceptional

QATAR DOHA

Greater Doha

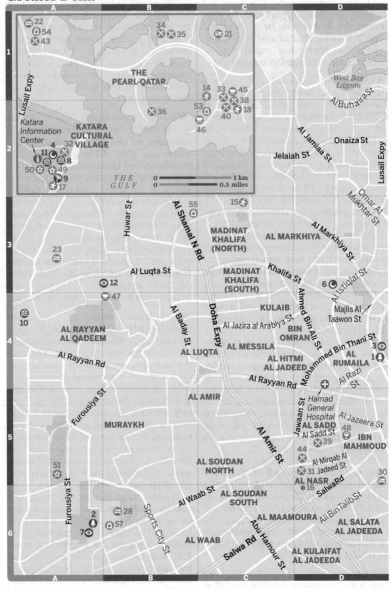

QATAR DOHA

modern exhibition space provides a home for international art with an Arab connection. Housed in an old school near Education City, the sleek building was redesigned by French architect Jean-François Bodin. The venue hosts a variety of exhibitions ranging from interactive multimedia works to a permanent collection of modern and contemporary art from the Arab world on its 2nd floor. Visitors should expect to leave their bags in a free locker upon arrival. The museum can be hard to find, so watch the YouTube video with detailed driving directions on the museum's website before setting off.

galleries that have been organised into three 'chapters': Beginnings, Life in Qatar and Building the Nation. Exhibits focus on Qatari history and heritage, celebrating the nation's past, present and future on the world stage. A thrilling, immersive and educational experience that should not be missed.

Corniche   WATERFRONT
(Map p242; Doha Bay; **P**) Doha makes full use of its attractive waterfront promenade, which stretches 7km along Doha Bay and was carefully constructed from landfill to make a pleasing crescent. The best views are from the water's edge close to the Museum of Islamic Art (p241), with dhows in the foreground and the skyscrapers of West Bay across the water. The best time to come is late afternoon on Friday, when families of all nationalities throng here.

The 5km walk from the Museum of Islamic Art to the Sheraton on West Bay is a wonderful late-afternoon stroll in a city not known for its pedestrian-friendly streets. Allow a good hour and a half.

At the southern end of the Corniche is the National Museum of Qatar. The collection of whitewashed traditional-style buildings on the far right belongs to the exquisite five-star Sharq Village & Spa. A must-stop down this end is the traditional **Halul Coffeehouse** (☑773 11587, 554 90464; ⊗6am-2.30am Mon-Sat, to midnight Sun), a local-style cafe that has escaped the modernisation of the area.

Further north is the 'sea' zone of the Corniche, with Doha's busy **port** marked by the monumental anchors on the shore and the cream-coloured flour mills at the end of the jetty. North of the Museum of Islamic Art, the entrance to the **dhow harbour** is marked by the famous **pearl monument**, a popular spot for photos. Enjoy the spectacular view of West Bay from the end of a jetty full of lobster pots and lazy dhows, moored between night-time fishing trips.

Al Bidda Park   PARK
(Map p242; off Al Corniche) One of the best green spaces in the city, with lots of walkways and cycle lanes, plus manicured lawns, a children's play area and views of the **Diwan** (Map p246; ☑443 88888; www.diwan.gov. qa), Doha's version of parliament. Desert wildflowers are abundant, and there's basketball, tennis courts and an outdoor gym. Best of all, barbecues are allowed. Al Bidda is planned to be a 'fan zone' for the upcoming 2022 FIFA World Cup.

National Museum of Qatar   MUSEUM
(Map p246; ☑(+974) 445 25555; www.nmoq.org. qa; Museum Park St) The much-anticipated opening of the National Museum of Qatar took place in March 2019. French architect Jean Nouvel's sprawling desert-rose-inspired structure is spectacular and houses 1.5km of

QATAR DOHA

Greater Doha

Hotel Park PARK
(Map p242; ☎ 445 67665; www.hotelparkdoha.
com; 1 Al Corniche; Ⓟ) This pleasant, manicured city-centre park with more than five
football pitches' worth of greenery is both
family friendly and modern, with design features such as bubbling water fountains and
geometric flower beds. The playgrounds are
pristine, plus there's a fitness zone, prayer
rooms and accessible toilets. It's tucked behind the iconic Sheraton Hotel at the centre
of Doha's bustling business district.

The park hosts festivals and community
events throughout the year, from a Bollywood
Festival to a Pizza and Pasta Festival. Check
the park's website for upcoming events.

Aspire Park PARK
(Map p242; ☎ 441 38188; www.aspirezone.qa; Al
Waab St, Aspire Zone; ☉ 8am-midnight) Doha's
largest park, covering 88 hectares, Aspire
has something to keep every member of the
family entertained: extensive lawns, walking
and running tracks, children's playgrounds,
exercise equipment and eateries. The park
is also home to the distinctive Torch Doha
hotel (p250), and to Doha's only lake, where
ducks, geese and other birds flock to cool off
from the desert heat. The park hosts various
events and festivals throughout the year,
particularly fun runs and other health- and
fitness-related activities.

Gallery Al Riwaq GALLERY
(Map p246; ☑445 25555; www.qm.org.qa/en/
project/qm-gallery-al-riwaq; Al Corniche; ⊙9am-
7pm Sat-Thu, from 1.30pm Fri; **P**) This modern
gallery space hosts some terrific temporary exhibitions – previous artists to show
their work here include Damien Hirst and
Takashi Murakami. Check the website to see
what's on before you visit the gallery, located
at the edge of MIA Park (p241).

Gold Souq MARKET
(Map p246; Ali Bin Abdullah St; ⊙9am-1pm &
4-10pm Sat-Thu, 4-10pm Fri; **P**) This modern
mall a stone's throw away from Souq Waqif (p239) has one of the largest clusters of
gold-jewellery vendors around. The glorious
designs and spectacular craftsmanship are
fun to look at even if you've no intention to
buy. The souq comes alive in the evenings,
especially before holidays, when men traditionally buy 22-karat gold bangles, or a 'set'
comprising earrings, necklace and a brace-
let, for the women in their family.

Qatari bridal jewellery can cost thousands of dollars, but sometimes pieces can
be traded back after the wedding for something more readily usable. Find the souq
between Al Nakheel Hotel and Souq Waqif.

◉ The Pearl

This pristine, pedestrian-friendly artificial island is a wonderful hang-out spot, and it's *the*
place to be seen during the cooler evenings
and winter months. The outdoor area, shaped
like a pearl and surrounded by ocean, covers
a distance of around 4 sq km, and its pavements are full of European-style street-facing
shops and restaurants. There's a lovely promenade opposite a large yacht-filled harbour,
where locals and tourists stroll.

Tempted to get out on the water? **Blue
Pearl Watersports** (Blue Pearl Experience; Map
p242; ☑666 02830; https://bluepearlexperience.
com; Porto Arabia, Gate 22), a respected outfit
situated in the harbour, will hook you up
with a boat or a board. Meanwhile, the marina's walkway is the perfect place to stroll
of an evening. Alternatively, hop on one of
the golf buggies (free) or if you'd rather go
by water, a boat taxi service runs from six
points of the crescent-shaped marina between 9am and 11pm (return ticket QR25).

TaliaMare Beach Club BEACH
(Map p242; ☑448 88370; https://taliamare.com;
Qanat Quartier, Lido Venezia Beach; umbrellas/
sunbeds QR25/65, towels QR15; ⊙8am-11.30pm;

OFF THE BEATEN TRACK

EAST-WEST / WEST-EAST BY RICHARD SERRA

Worth the trip if you're interested in
unique art set in unusual landscapes,
sculptor Richard Serra's **East-West /
West-East installation** (www.qm.org.
qa/en/project/east-west-west-east-richard-
serra; Brouq Nature Reserve) comprises
four steel plates, each more than 14m
tall, spread out over a kilometre of the
desolate western Qatari desert. You may
even spot an ostrich or gazelle in the
surrounding Brouq Nature Reserve. The
1.5-hour drive west of Doha includes a
bit of off-roading.

P) One of Doha's best hangout spots, Talia-
Mare is set on a pretty beach, among pastel-coloured houses, and has a chilled-out
vibe and music reminiscent of Ibiza's Cafe
Mambo. Guests pay for an umbrella or a
sunbed and get use of showers, lockers and
other facilities, including beach toys for kids.
Smoke shisha as the sun sets or have a bite
to eat in the trendy cafe.

The kitchen serves up excellent shakshuka, pancakes and omelettes for breakfast,
plus seafood mains and salads (breakfast/
dinner plates from QR36/79). Wash your
meal down with a cooling mocktail.

◉ Katara

Katara, a custom-built cultural village on
West Bay north of downtown Doha, has
some stunning replica architecture on show
from across the Islamic world and is fast becoming one of the most important creative
hubs of the Gulf region. It has a buzzing gallery scene, dozens of places to eat, an opera
house and even a striking open-air amphitheatre facing the sea that's a fantastic venue
for concerts and other live entertainment.
For more details, stop by the **Katara Information Center** (Map p242; ☑182; www.katara.
net; ⊙9am-4pm Sun-Thu). The website also has
helpful event listings and booking options.

Katara Beach BEACH
(Map p242; www.katara.net; ⊙9.30am-sunset;
P 👪) **FREE** If you fancy a swim but don't
want to go too far from the city, the 1.5km
beach at Katara Cultural Village is a pleasant sandy stretch with inflatable play structures for kids (purchase a day pass for QR50
from the kiosk), plus watersports (p247)

Central Doha

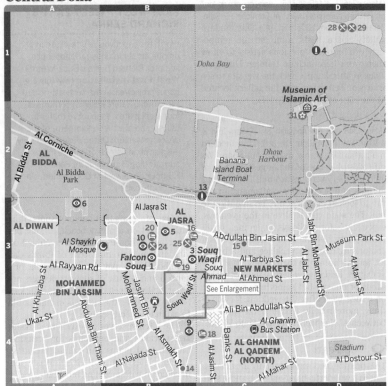

from parasailing to wakeboarding on offer. Women can't swim here unless they are completely covered. Men aren't allowed to wear speedos.

Golden Mosque　　　　　　　MOSQUE
(Map p242; ☑ 440 80000; www.katara.net) Covered in thousands of golden tiles, this striking Ottoman-style mosque shimmers in the sun. While non-Muslims can't go inside, it's one of the most spectacular mosque designs in the city, and the exterior is worth a closer look if exploring the Katara area.

Qatar Fine Arts Association　　　GALLERY
(Map p242; ☑ 440 81469; Bldg 13; ☉ 9am-12.30pm & 5-9pm Sun-Thu) **FREE** This organisation draws some of the better-known artists from across the region. Visitors are free to wander around the current gallery shows and displays, which range in vibrancy and theme. It's pot luck what you may stumble upon. Call ahead for details of upcoming exhibitions.

Katara Art Center　　　　　　GALLERY
(KAC; Map p242; ☑ 440 30101; www.dohakac.com; Bldg 5; ☉ 10am-9pm Sun-Thu, from 4pm Fri & Sat; **P**) **FREE** Local contemporary art and design are the focus of this cultural hub inside Katara Cultural Village. The venue hosts regular talks and classes, including workshops on caricature clay sculpture, recycled art and basic brush calligraphy, plus regular exhibitions. Find it on the northeastern side of the Katara Amphitheatre.

🏃 Activities

★**Majlis Al Dama**　　　　　　BOARDGAMES
(Map p246; Spice Souq, Souq Waqif; ☉ 7am-1pm & 4-10pm Sat-Thu, 4-10pm Fri) **FREE** They don't get many tourists here, but that's the point. This old-school government-funded place is where folks pop in for a free, thick Arabic coffee or tea and a game of aldama (a blend of draughts and backgammon). Be a fly on the wall when there are people at the boards – or if you know what you're doing, it's free to play.

The drop zone is roughly 45 minutes north of Doha off Al Shamal Rd; exact directions are provided after booking.

Bounce Doha ADVENTURE SPORTS
(Map p242; ☑ 440 86500; https://bounce.qa; 2nd fl, Al Markhiya St, Tawar Mall, Al Duhail South; per person QR90; ⊙ 10am-10pm Sat-Wed, to midnight Thu & Fri) The largest trampoline park in the Middle East, with more than 4000 sq metres of wall-to-wall trampolines. The space includes a crazy obstacle course to put your ninja warrior skills to the test, a trampoline basketball court and caged football pitch, huge inflatable landing pads for practicing wild trampolining moves, a zip line, a free-running area and much more besides.

Sessions run on an hourly basis and it's worth booking your tickets online to avoid queues.

🍽 Courses

**FANAR Qatar Islamic
Cultural Center** LANGUAGE
(Map p246; ☑ 442 50173, 444 47444; www.binzaid.gov.qa; Abdullah Bin Jassim St; 2-month courses from QR300; ⊙ 5am-8pm Sun-Thu) Courses in Arabic language and Qatari and Islamic culture are offered at the striking spiral FANAR building, where you can also take a free tour that includes an Arabic coffee, a 10-minute educational video and a visit to the mosque. The free exhibition about Islam is also worth a look; it includes a replica of the world's oldest Quran. Tours must be booked in advance by phone or email.

🍴 Tours

Doha Bus BUS
(Map p242; ☑ 444 22444; https://dohabus.com; Al Amir St; adult/child from QR180/90; ⊙ office 9am-6pm Sun-Wed, to 2pm Thu, bus tours 9am-7pm Jul-May) A city has made it as a tourist destination when it gets its own hop-on, hop-off open-top sightseeing bus. Doha's goes from the Marriott Hotel, south of the city centre, to The Pearl, a recent development in the north. The full journey takes 2½ hours, not taking into account time for sightseeing. There are audio guides on board, plus drinks.

Major stops include the Museum of Islamic Art (p241), Souq Waqif (p239), City Center Doha mall (p260), Katara Cultural Village (p245) and The Pearl. Buses pass every 40 minutes. Choose between tickets good for 24 hours or 48 hours. Tickets can be booked online.

Katara Beach Watersports WATER SPORTS
(Map p242; Katara Beach, Katara; actvities from QR100-1500; ⊙ Nov-Mar) At this modest beach hut offering a range of aquatic activities, you can opt to explore Doha's calm waters by hiring a boat or gondola, or to zip along the surface via waterski. Futuristic jet-levitation 'flying' (using an Iron Man–style pack to float on top of the surface of the water) is also on offer here, but it's pricey!

Skydive Qatar SKYDIVING
(☑ 403 29173; www.skydiveqatar.com; tandem jumps from QR1999; ⊙ booking hours 7am-4pm, jumps Oct-Feb) See Qatar from an entirely different perspective: nearly 4000m in the air while hurtling towards the ground at around 200 km/h. It's not for the faint of heart, and it's not cheap, but you'll remember this adrenaline-filled experience for a lifetime. Jump videos and photos are included in the tandem price. Courses are offered for those wanting to jump solo.

Central Doha

The Doha Bus company has also expanded into other tours, including a north Qatar tour, a tour of Sheikh Faisal Museum (p260), a jaunt around the Camel Track & Equestrian Club , and a 'culinary Qatar' tour, among others. Another Doha Bus branch (p262) in Mesaieed offers monster truck and 4WD tours in the desert.

Arabian Adventures TOURS
(Map p246; ☑443 61461; http://arabianadven turesqatar.com; Al Asmakh St; tours QR160-600; ☉office 9am-5pm Sun-Thu) This recommended operator offers a range of tours, including dhow cruises, Doha city tours, and half- or full-day desert safaris, plus a north Qatar tour that includes a visit to Al Zubarah Fort (p263) and the Al Thakira mangroves.

🎇 Festivals & Events

Emir's Sword Race CULTURAL
(www.qrec.gov.qa; Doha Racing & Equestrian Club; ☉Feb) FREE Qatar's answer to the Royal Ascot or Kentucky Derby is the Emir's Sword Race, where purebred Arabian horses race for glory. One of the biggest annual international events of the year, it's held in Doha, usually at the Racing & Equestrian Club (Map p242; ☑448 03016; Al Furousiya St; ☉office

7am-2pm Sun-Tue, to 9pm Wed & Thu) FREE; tickets are not required.

Emir's GCC Camel Race SPORTS
(☉Mar or Apr) FREE Riders compete for the prestigious 'Golden Sword' in one of the most important events on Qatar's sporting calendar, held at Al Shahaniya's camel race track (☉training sunrise Mar-Nov, races from 1pm on Fri & Sat Oct-Feb) FREE, 60km west of Doha. Some 6000 camels from Qatar and around the Middle East participate in exciting races held over 4km, 6km and 8km distances, with camels speeding along at up to 60 km/h.

Qatar Winter Dragon Boat Festival SPORTS
(☑550 52204; http://qatardragonboat.com; Grand Hyatt Doha; ☉Dec) Watch teams battle it out through Qatar's waterways in narrow boats that originate in south China and were traditionally made out of teak. These unusual vessels are propelled by up to 20 people (in the largest boats) with oar power alone.

🛏 Sleeping

While budget sleeping options are scarce (there are no hostels at all), good deals can be found at some of the city's boutique lodgings. Midrange accommodation is conveniently located around Souq Waqif. Meanwhile, Doha's luxury accommodations are arguably the best in the Gulf, from stunningly converted heritage hotels in the souq to five-star palaces in the skyscrapers. The city even has its own island resort.

★ Najd Boutique Hotel   BOUTIQUE HOTEL $

(Map p246; ☑️ 443 36666; www.tivolihotels.com; Souq Waqif; r from QR383; 🕾) Najd gives an excellent first impression with its beautiful lobby's stained-glass windows, coloured stone floor, feature wall covered with vases and relaxing areas for lounging. Rooms have tasteful arabesque patterns, velvet and silky cushions, wooden furnishings – some of which are stunning – and plenty of space.

★ Zubarah Hotel   HOTEL $

(Map p242; ☑️ 444 70000; www.zubarahhotels. com; Al Rawabi St; d/ste from QR299/349; 🕾) Zubarah is proof that excellent value still exists in Doha, despite the profusion of pricey five-star hotels. The rooms here are excellent, with some showing contemporary designer touches, while service is also good. There's a 1st-floor spa (massages from QR400), a gym, an Middle Eastern–Argentinian restaurant and plenty of repeat visitors.

Al Najada Hotel   BOUTIQUE HOTEL $

(Map p246; ☑️ 443 36444; www.tivolihotels.com; Souq Waqif St, Souq Waqif; r from QR429; 🕾) This superb hotel done up in contemporary Arab style has nice touches including atmospheric thatched roofs in the rooms, marble details in the bathrooms and a courtyard layout in the public areas. The rambling Qatari-style 1930s building also has stylish walls of water. A five-minute walk south of Souq Waqif (p239), it offers a haven of quiet near the bustling marketplace.

Al Najada is located opposite the Gold Souq (p245), with dozens of restaurants a few steps away.

Arumaila Boutique Hotel   BOUTIQUE HOTEL $

(Map p246; ☑️ 443 36666; www.tivolihotels.com; Souq Waqif; r from QR385; 🕾) One of the loveliest and friendliest hotels in Doha, the Arumaila inhabits a gorgeous old souq building whose stunning rooms have wooden floors, soothing grey concrete walls and beautiful lamps and partitioning with elaborate filigree design. There's a mini gym and guests have access to spa facilities nearby at other boutique hotels run by the same owners in Souq Waqif.

Premier Inn Doha
Education City Hotel   HOTEL $

(Map p242; ☑️ 400 78333; https://premierinn.com; Wadi Ad Salamiya St, Education City; r from QR210; 🅿️🕾🏊) You can't beat the value of this global chain in Doha's Education City. Its simple, comfy rooms have purple accents, and there's an international restaurant and a gym. That said, it's in an awkward location, with a lot of construction taking place in the area. Getting from here into the central city takes longer than it should.

Musheireb Boutique Hotel   BOUTIQUE HOTEL $

(Map p246; ☑️ 443 36666; www.tivolihotels.com; Al Jasra St, Souq Waqif; r from QR410; 🕾🏊) This 14-room boutique hotel just outside the hubbub of the main souq is decorated with extravagant Qatari design features, studded velvet sofas, plush carpets, gilded mirrors and lush purples and sky blues, which ensure it's neither dark nor overwhelmingly heavy. There's an on-site spa and gym, too.

Owned by the Tivoli Hotel group, it's located next to the horse and camel pens.

Al Jomrok Boutique Hotel   BOUTIQUE HOTEL $

(Map p246; ☑️ 443 36666; www.tivolihotels.com; Souq Waqif; r from QR362; 🅿️🕾) The simple but sophisticated rooms here are large, with dark wooden panelling behind the beds and attractive wooden floors and furnishings. But the hotel's best feature is its rooftop

QATAR DOHA

BOUTIQUE HOTELS IN SOUQ WAQIF

As Souq Waqif expands further with each passing year, one of the more welcome developments has been the conversion of old or remodelled market buildings into boutique hotels that combine intimacy, luxury and traditional Qatari decor. There are nine in all, all with distinct individual heritage style. Some are larger, some smaller, some come with excellent restaurants or a spa, and some have standout features including thatched roofs, a rooftop cafe or delicate design details. They're run by the same owners and share a website (www.tivolihotels.com). The conversions of such places into hotels has added considerable depth to Doha's accommodation scene, making it one of the most impressive anywhere in the Gulf region.

restaurant (p259) – the only one with views above the souq. Al Jomrok is located by one of the entrances to the Souq Waqif opposite the Corniche.

★ Mondrian Doha
HOTEL **$$**

(Map p242; ☑404 55555; www.morganshotel group.com; West Bay Lagoon; r from QR563) The Mondrian, clad in thick metal mesh, is meant to evoke the image of an eagle's nest, and the radical design continues on the inside. With a black glossy staircase that leads to nowhere, gold eggs dotted around and a white-tree indoor forest, it has to be seen to be believed. Rooms include sand-dune-inspired carpets and designer vanity desks.

All of the brilliantly wacky design creations are courtesy of Dutch powerhouse Marcel Wanders. Spectacular views over Doha from the rooms and kaleidoscopic rooftop pool and **Skybar** complete the experience; they gaze onto the snaking artificial waterways and spaghetti-like highways in the distance. Dining options at the hotel are world-class: choose from steakhouse Cut by Wolfgang Puck (p258), **Magnolia Bakery** or Morimoto (p255)'s Japanese restaurant – all have striking design features that will amaze.

★ InterContinental Doha
HOTEL **$$**

(Map p242; ☑448 44444; www.ihg.com; off West Bay St, West Bay; d/ste from QR650/1500; **P**🅿🛜🏊) This genteel, good-value, high-end hotel may have been dwarfed by the neighbouring St Regis, but it continues to thrive. Rooms are decorated in neutral tones, many with panoramic views of the Gulf. Ten dining options include a tea room, pool bar and the popular Belgian Cafe, serving steaming pots of *moules marinières* (mussels in white-wine sauce) and cold Belgian beers.

Marsa Malaz Kempinski
HOTEL **$$**

(Map p242; ☑403 55555; www.kempinski.com; Costa Malaz Bay, The Pearl; d/ste from QR800/1575, day pass QR250) Occupying its own artificial island connected to The Pearl, the Marsa Malaz has decadent palatial dimensions, including an 18m-tall bronze horse sculpture on the grounds. Rooms are regal with contemporary touches. Outside guests visit for its popular international brunch, inviting pool area, beach water sports and bike hire. **Illusion**, the outdoor roof lounge and nightclub, is popular in winter. Cake stands are stacked for afternoon tea in the lobby, while tapas fans may enjoy the **El Faro** Spanish restaurant.

St Regis Hotel
HOTEL **$$**

(Map p242; ☑444 60000; www.stregisdoha.com; West Bay; r from QR810; 🏊) An enormous metal oryx welcomes visitors to the St Regis, a hotel with fantastic eating establishments (including an indoor and outdoor weekend brunch in winter), a wonderful beach and Doha's only Olympic-sized pool. Rooms are well appointed, with butler service, while **The Rooftop** (winter only) is a great place to grab a cocktail. Gordon Ramsay has a restaurant here.

Ritz-Carlton Hotel
HOTEL **$$**

(Map p242; ☑448 48000; www.ritzcarlton.com; West Bay Lagoon; d from QR746; **P**🛜🏊) On its own island surrounded by the Gulf, the Doha Ritz is as grand as you'd expect from the American hotel giant. Enormous windows, polished floors and bulbous chandeliers decorate the lobby, while rooms have French-oak hardwood floors and Tuscan-marble bathrooms. The **Club Lounge** is regarded as one of the best in the city, for both food and service. Cigar fans can smoke up a storm at **Habanos** bar. There's a rather good kids club here.

Al Mirqab Boutique Hotel
BOUTIQUE HOTEL **$$**

(Map p246; ☑443 36666; www.tivolihotels.com; Souq Waqif; r from QR800; 🛜🏊) Elegant, spacious rooms with marble floors and minimalist arabesque decor offset occasional flourishes such as filigree stonework at this fine hotel. There are no views here, but there is a sense of refinement and privacy, in keeping with the large Doha houses of old. There's a secluded pool, and the souq location is ideal.

Torch Doha
HOTEL **$$**

(Aspire Tower; Map p242; ☑444 65600; www. thetorchdoha.com.qa; Aspire Plaza Rd, Aspire Zone; r from QR600; **P**🛜🏊) The Torch, at 300m high, is the tallest structure in Doha, and its sleek grey rooms are well known for their panoramic views over the city and the desert. Other highlights include the **Torch Tea Garden** and Three Sixty (p255), a rotating restaurant on the 47th floor. Hotel guests can swim in a sky-high swimming pool overlooking the city. At night, the entire structure lights up in bright neon colours and is a recognisable sight on the horizon when looking out towards the desert from West Bay. The 40,000-seat Khalifa International Stadium, which will host matches through to the quarter finals of the 2022 FIFA World Cup, sits next door in the Torch's impressive shadow.

★ **Banana Island Resort**   RESORT $$$
(📞 404 05050; www.doha.anantara.com; Banana Island; r/ste QR1221/1515, villas QR4166-10,098; 🛜🕸) Choose from a number of uber-luxury rooms at this excellent private island retreat, including sea-view rooms, junior suites or private villas on stilts over the turquoise ocean (the villas have their own pool, boat jetty and private butler). Guests have use of plenty of facilities, including a cinema, mini-golf course and volleyball court.

Extras include massages at the island's spa, and classes including yoga and meditation sessions, plus meals at the resort's Middle Eastern, Italian and American restaurants. Children will be well entertained with beach games and football, plus a kids club. With a phone call's notice, drivers with golf buggies will pick guests up and take them wherever they need to be on the island. Service is excellent, with the little details considered throughout, starting with dates and refreshments on the boat transfer to the resort.

Boats leave for Banana Island from the Dhow Harbour in front of Souq Waqif and take 25 minutes (tip: book the sunset journey for hazy sky views).

★ **Four Seasons Hotel**   HOTEL $$$
(Map p242; 📞 449 48888; www.fourseasons.com/doha; Al Corniche; r from QR1250; 🅿🛜🕸) Occupying a prime position at the edge of the Corniche overlooking the Gulf, the Four Seasons has a regal feel. Rooms are classic (and slightly chintzy) in design, with gold-coloured trimmings and marble-topped bathroom units. Extensive pools, a pristine beach, excellent spa, tennis courts, world-class dining – including the world's largest Nobu (p255) – and a fantastic kids club are big pulls.

★ **W Hotel Doha**   HOTEL $$$
(Map p242; 📞 445 35000; www.whoteldoha.com; Bldg 262, St 831, West Bay; r from QR999; 🛜🕸) Coloured lanterns adorn the lobby of this hotel, with its attractive floral water features and spiral staircase to the mezzanine level. Furniture throughout is bold and sleek: platinum black tables, dark purple carpets and soft furnishings. Rooms are equally as appealing. Jean-Georges heads up the hotel's international restaurant; other foodie hangouts include the chic pink-doused southeast Asian eatery **Spice Market**.

For drinks, join the stylish clientele at **Crystal Lounge** (www.crystaldoha.com; ⏱ 8pm-2am), where there's mingling and dancing to DJs until the wee hours.

★ **Sharq Village & Spa**   RESORT $$$
(Map p242; 📞 442 56666; www.ritzcarlton.com/sharqvillage; Ras Abu Abboud St; r from QR920; 🅿🛜🕸) With its heritage architecture, exquisite desert landscaping and beach location, this is one superb hotel. The intimate, super-luxurious rooms with four-poster beds and diaphanous silken drapes are arranged around sand-coloured courtyards and cactus gardens. Lanterns, shadows dancing across the marble and Ali Baba pots bubbling with water all play their part in creating an *Arabian Nights* atmosphere.

The agarwood-perfumed **spa**, with mysterious alleys leading to the treatment rooms, rounds off the decadent experience. The spa menu is extensive, with massage, hammam steam bath and exfoliation, beauty therapies and physical therapies on offer (treatments start from QR300). One thing's for sure, you won't want to leave the relaxation areas.

Sheraton Grand Doha Resort   HOTEL $$$
(Map p242; 📞 448 54444; https://sheraton.marriott.com; Al Funduq St, Al Corniche; r from QR807; 🛜🕸) The pyramid-shaped Sheraton Doha is more than a place to stay; it's an institution. The oldest of Doha's five-star hotels, it still has one of the best locations, with wonderful views from its light-filled, clean, simple rooms with balconies (and some with split levels). Unwind at the private beach or with Italian cuisine (including wood-oven pizzas) at **La Veranda**.

In the evening, venture to the basement for some live music at the **Irish Harp pub** (www.irishharpdoha.com; ⏱ 5pm-2am). One of the most unusual features of this hotel is the display cabinets full of antiques along one of the corridors leading to the pool area. Stop and marvel at beautifully ornate ancient jugs, boxes and other artefacts.

✖ Eating

Many of Doha's more celebrated restaurants inhabit the city's five-star hotels, with offerings from famous international chefs increasingly turning up here. Inexpensive Middle Eastern options are in abundance too. Three excellent areas to wander in search of a meal are Souq Waqif (p239), The Pearl (p245) and Katara Cultural Village (p245). At the weekend, don't miss brunch at one of the five-star hotels.

★ **Al Aker**   DESSERTS $
(Map p246; Souq Waqif Rd, Souq Waqif; sweets per 500g around QR60; ⏱ 10am-midnight Sat-Thu,

LOCAL KNOWLEDGE

DOHA BRUNCH

Brunch is an institution in Doha: not simply a late-morning breakfast, but rather a sit-down marathon meal with limitless food that continues for four or five hours. It mainly happens in five-star hotels, where the booze is available and free flowing. Typically, brunch takes place on a Friday or Saturday and the majority of the diners are groups of expats, who dress up for the social occasion of the week and then gorge and drink themselves silly, like they're at a banquet with Henry VIII.

Each hotel's buffet is first-rate, usually with food stations offering the best cuisine from around the world: think lobster and shellfish, fine cheese varieties and chefs preparing fresh Wagyu steak in the background. Entertainment comes in the form of bands and DJs – the InterContinental Doha (p250) and Sheraton Grand Doha Resort (p251) brunches are particularly known for their entertainment – while children's performers or activities may be laid on for families, consider Mondrian Doha, (p250) Sheraton Grand Doha or the Ritz-Carlton Hotel (p250) if you have kids in tow.

Brunch is a lavish and decadent affair that requires a degree of decorum, but with alcohol hard to come by in everyday life in Qatar, and reasonably high price tags for what is essentially a large buffet lunch, many guests see it as a rare chance to let loose and consume to excess.

Brunch deals change seasonally, and many of the hotels hold their largest and most luxurious brunches between October and March, when the weather is cooler – the Grand Friday Brunch at St Regis Hotel (p250) is particularly spectacular; it covers a whopping 2500 sq metres of space on and around manicured lawns. Brunch must be booked in advance; check with the hotel for current themes, prices and timings.

---

from noon Fri) Now here's somewhere special. Those with a sweet tooth should make a beeline for these splendid Middle Eastern and Turkish filo pastries such as baklava, which are freshly made in-house to perfection. Salivatingly good sweets are laid out on the counter – the melt-in-the-mouth *kunafeh* (a soft or crispy pastry filled with white cheese and soaked in syrup) is our favourite.

The staff can also box up a selection of sweets for you to take away and enjoy. Ask nicely, and you may get to try a sample before you buy. A couple of large pieces should set you back around QR15.

★ **Turkey Central**   TURKISH $
(Map p242; ✆ 444 32927; Al Mirqab Al Jadeed St; mains QR10-50; ⊙11am-1am) No-frills but utterly delicious Turkish food, including fantastic breads (cooked on-site) and mezze in truly epic portions that may leave little room for the kebabs, which would be a terrible shame. It's always packed, with a refreshingly mixed clientele – Middle Eastern families, folks from the West and southeast Asia all dining together.

★ **Bandar Aden**   MIDDLE EASTERN $
(Map p246; ✆ 443 75503; www.bandaraden.com; Souq Waqif; mezze QR10-50; ⊙8am-11pm Sat-Thu, from 12.30pm Fri) The fabulous food has made this basic, very casual restaurant an institution in Souq Waqif. Traditional Yemeni cooking draws a local crowd, who share mounds of rice and all manner of meats. The stews, too, are exceptionally good. Plus, there are salads, fresh breads, fish and very reasonably priced breakfasts (like egg shakshuka).

MIA Park Cafe   CAFE $
(Map p246; www.mia.org.qa/en/mia-park/kiosks; MIA Park, off Al Corniche; light mains from QR12; ⊙6pm-midnight) Glorious views of the city's modern skyline from a pretty, calm spot in the park. Tables and chairs are positioned on a patio opposite the bay, with coloured egg lights and chill-out music playing in the background. It's the perfect spot at dusk when the sky turns hazy as the sun sets. The menu includes salads, mezze and sandwiches. Picnic baskets and blankets are available for hire from the cafe for QR50; you can fill a basket with food and drinks for two for QR110.

Al Jazeera Media Cafe   CAFE $
(Map p242; ✆ 403 42220; www.aljazeeracafe.com; Bldg 4, Katara; mains from QR45; ⊙8am-11pm Sat-Thu, 8-11am & 1-11pm Fri, studio 4-10pm; 🛜) This cafe operated by news broadcaster Al Jazeera serves decent salads and mains, from chicken tikka and fish and chips to pan-roasted salmon and tenderloin steak. The main reason to visit, however, is to use the interactive

studio, where visitors can pretend to be a news anchor and record a broadcast. Cafe tables double as work stations (with power outlets). Bring a flash drive so you can save your news broadcast and take it home with you. The cafe is located northeast of the Katara Amphitheatre.

Afghan Brothers Restaurant　　AFGHANI $
(Map p242; ☑448 88556; Al Mirqab Al Jadeed St; mains from QR28; ☺7am-1am) It's not a fancy place, but the rice and meat dishes here are truly delicious – and it's a chance to dine in a typically Middle Eastern atmosphere, surrounded by patterned carpets and woven upholsteries. It's popular with locals, who tuck into full goat platters with vegetables, or lamb with flavoursome *majboos* rice (cooked with spices and herbs). Portions are hearty. Don't miss the sides, including enormous plates of olive salad and fresh bread.

Halo Donuts　　DESSERTS $
(Map p242; near Calle Vivaldi & Quartier Chanal Dr, The Pearl; doughnuts from QR18; ☺8am-11pm) Devour scrumptious designer doughnuts at this trendy industrial-chic hang-out spot on The Pearl. The inventive, and beautifully presented, flavours include glazed maple-butter pecan and chocolate brownie, plus stuffed creations like birthday cake, crème brûlée, dulce de leche and lotus cheesecake. Halo also bakes cronuts (a cross between a croissant and a doughnut) and cookies, and serves a good cuppa joe.

Mokarabia Coffee　　CAFE $
(Map p242; ☑449 84264; http://mokarabia.com. qa; Bldg B14, Marbella St, Medina Centrale, The Pearl; mains from QR32; ☺8am-1am Sat-Thu, to midnight Fri) A cool hangout decorated with books, picture frames and random vintage items such as a small penny-farthing bike and an '80s TV set. Choose from salads, breakfasts, sandwiches and pastas on the iPad menu, but it's the desserts that are really special. The chocolate-slathered creations include a chocolate shawarma and a black forest chocolate ball that oozes chocolate goo.

**Sukar Pasha
Ottoman Lounge**　　MIDDLE EASTERN $
(Map p242; ☑440 82000; Katara; mezze QR25-90; ☺8am-1am) Grand armchairs, comfy couches and an indoor fountain filled with petals give this place a royal feel. It serves good Middle Eastern breakfasts, plus more unusual dishes to ignite your palate like *bostan salatası* (tomato, cucumber, mint, pars-

ley, lemon juice, pomegranate), *otlu nohut* (chickpeas with herbs and spices) and *has paşa lamb* (kofta with tomato sauce, breadcrumbs, cheese and yoghurt).

Sugar and Spice　　CAFE $
(Map p242; ☑441 14456; http://sugarandspice qatar.com; Lagoona Mall, Pearl Blvd; mains QR35-45; ☺9.30am-10pm Sun-Thu, 1.30-11pm Fri, 9.30am-10.30pm Sat; ℗) Owner Saleh Alayan launched Sugar and Spice after looking for good carrot cake and failing to find any in Qatar. His deliberately chintzy place resembles a country kitchen. The sweet treats on offer are good, but the breakfasts are even better, including eggs benedict, waffles, beetroot shakshuka and Lebanese scrambled eggs. Burgers and sandwiches are also on the menu.

June Cafe　　CAFE $
(Map p246; MIA Park, off Al Corniche; snacks QR10-20; ☺5pm-1.30am) A range of snacks like chapatis, samosas, potato squares and curious lolly waffles (potato shapes on sticks) are served with a view of Doha's skyline as impressive as that from the next-door MIA Park Cafe. June Cafe's mini chocolate-filled pancakes are rather special – bite into them for an oozing sweet treat.

Bosphorus　　TURKISH $
(Map p246; ☑332 66194; Souq Waqif; mains QR32-79; ☺9am-1am) Specialising in slow-cooked tajines served in copper pots, plus grills and salads, this casual place has indoor and outdoor seating for souq-watching. More unusual dishes include *arnavut ciğer* (slow-cooked fresh liver cubes with spices) or *ali nazik* (juicy chunks of veal on a layer of baba ganoush with fresh pide bread).

MIA Cafe　　CAFE $
(Map p246; www.mia.org.qa/en/visiting/cafe; ground fl, Museum of Islamic Art; mains QR15-55, afternoon tea QR60; ☺10.30am-5.30pm Sun, Mon & Wed, noon-8pm Thu & Sat, 2-8pm Fri) Cafeteria-style, above-ordinary salads and snacks nicely complement the light Middle Eastern and French mains that fill the short menu at the cafe at the Museum of Islamic Art (p241). The fresh baba ganoush with tahini is especially good. The tiny treats served with the afternoon tea (2pm to 6pm) are popular. Tables in the light-filled atrium gaze out across the water.

Cafe-Tasse　　ITALIAN $
(Map p246; ☑444 47017; Souq Waqif; mains QR35-60; ☺8am-12.45am Sat-Wed, to 2am Thu & Fri; ☑) Set in a colonial-style house, this venue is

different from other eateries in Souq Waqif, with its winding staircase, large chandelier and different living rooms (dining areas) decorated with patterned wallpaper, ornate alcoves and comfy armchairs. Dishes include tagliatelle, lamb chops and lasagne. A quick bite generally turns into something longer as patrons lounge and chat in the relaxing spaces.

★ **Drawing Room** CAFE $$
(Map p242; ☑401 73367; Medina Centrale, The Pearl; mains QR32-74; ☺noon-10pm) Part shop, part cafe, this cute and atmospheric spot would fit in London's hip Shoreditch area. It's adorned with crafted trinkets and vintage goods, from an old gramophone to a retro typewriter. The cafe serves hot drinks in chintzy teacups, plus fresh, well-prepared meals – ranging from kale quinoa to chicken schnitzel potato salad – on enamel serving plates and parcel-paper tablecloths.

In the shop area, upcycled wooden stepladders display bundles of classic used books wrapped with strings, and birthday cards with mix tapes attached to them. Everything in the store is carefully curated and thought about. It's all overpriced, but pretty darn wonderful.

★ **Evergreen Organics** VEGAN $$
(Map p242; ☑447 20437; www.evergreenorganics. qa; Palazzo 1, Mercato Qanat Quartier, The Pearl; mains QR35-75; ☺7am-10pm; ☞☑) Doha's first vegan and veggie cafe, Evergreen Organics is the brainchild of two young Qataris who are passionate about changing the health of the nation. From the Instagrammable hardwood interiors to the innovative plant-based menu of consciously sourced, artisanal vegan whole foods like date and pear granola, buckwheat pancakes, kale salads and healthy smoothies, this spot is a winner.

★ **Argan** MOROCCAN $$
(Map p246; ☑443 36686; Al Jasra Boutique Hotel, Souq Waqif, Al Jasra St; mezze QR25-85; ☺1-11.30pm) One hell of a dining experience, Argan serves tasty Moroccan cooking in a classy, convivial *majlis* (reception room), with mauve couches and patterned cushions. The seafood tajine is spectacular, the lamb couscous outstanding and the *taktouka* salad (peppers marinated with tomato, garlic, onions, coriander and cumin) flavourful. Save room for a sweet *mhensha* (filo pastry with almond paste) to finish.

Jones The Grocer INTERNATIONAL $$
(Map p242; ☑440 77175; www.jonesthegrocer.com; Gate Mall, Al Bidda St; mains QR35-83; ☺8.30am-10.30pm Sat-Thu, closed 11.30am-1.30pm Fri) This Aussie-born gourmet cafe has a simple industrial-style space with metal chairs and serves high-quality ingredients. Excellent breakfast and lunch dishes include the king prawn egg florentine, which is super tasty, as is the hoisin duck wrap. For dinner, splash out on a Wagyu beef burger with smoked-beef bacon and cheddar cheese. Single-origin manual-brew coffee is also available.

Damasca One SYRIAN $$
(Map p246; ☑447 59088; www.damascarestaurant.com; Souq Waqif; mains QR86-137; ☺9am-1am Mon-Thu & Sat, 1-11pm Fri) One of the most atmospheric places to eat in Souq Waqif, with blue chairs, flowery upholstery and historic scenes of Damascus on screens, Damasca One serves traditional Syrian dishes. Choose from Middle Eastern breakfasts or the subtle flavours of paprika-inflected hummus, salads such as *fattoush* (toasted bread, tomatoes, onions and mint leaves) and perfectly grilled meats.

Al Bandar SEAFOOD $$
(Map p246; ☑443 11313; Souq Waqif Rd, Souq Waqif; mains from QR56; ☺9am-midnight) With perhaps the best seafood in the souq – or anywhere in downtown Doha, for that matter – this little place is a wonderful choice. Its casserole is tasty and packed with morsels from the sea, but best of all is the fresh fish, grilled and unadorned. The red snapper, kingfish steak, and rock lobster hit the spot.

Jwala Restaurant INDIAN $$
(Map p242; ☑443 78437; http://jwalarestaurant.com; Bldg B12, Andalucia Way, Medina, The Pearl; mains QR45-86; ☺9am-1am Sat-Wed, to 2am Thu & Fri) One of the most attractive Indian restaurants in town, shabby-chic Jwala has Indian illustrations on the walls, upcycled oil barrels as tables and auto-rickshaws at the rear of the building. Order shrimp biryani, butter chicken and chicken tikka or unusual dishes like Jwala bunny curry chow: brioche stuffed with curry meatballs, rice, cheese and béchamel sauce.

Isla Mexican Kitchen MEXICAN $$
(Map p242; ☑440 952854; http://hdc-global.com/restaurants/isla.aspx; Parcel 1, Unit 22 & 23, The Pearl; mains QR30-100; ☺noon-11.30pm) Internationally renowned chef Richard Sandoval, called the father of modern Mexican cook-

ing, has brought his authentic techniques to Qatar with the opening of this restaurant. The menu includes modern flavours with a twist, such as a *chimichanga de deshebrada* (pan-fried burrito with Monterrey-style beef and charro beans). On cooler Thursday and Friday evenings, there's live rumba between 6pm and 9pm.

Little Yee Hwa
ASIAN $$

(Map p242; ☑ 444 26868; www.facebook.com/yee HwaDoha; Al Jazzera St, Bin Mahmoud; dishes QR17-88; ⊙ 11.30am-10.30pm Sat-Thu, from 12.30pm Fri) Established in 1998 under its former name, Moon Palace, Yee Hwa was the first Korean and Japanese restaurant to open its doors in Qatar. It's a favourite amongst expats and locals because it's affordable, authentic and unique in the country. Little Yee Hwa is a spin-off of the original restaurant and serves mighty fine noodles, sushi and bento boxes.

Khan Farouk Tarab Cafe
EGYPTIAN $$

(Map p242; ☑ 440 80840; http://khanfarouk tarabcafe.com; Bldg 7, Katara; mains QR15-98; ⊙ 9am-midnight) You'd half expect to find prize-winning Egyptian writer Naguib Mahfouz working on a novel at a corner table in this low-key, unfancy, Old Cairo–style restaurant. Instead, there's often live traditional Egyptian *tarab* music in the evenings and a menu brimming with *kushari* (noodles, rice, black lentils, fried onions and tomato sauce), falafel and signature Egyptian dishes like grilled pigeon.

★ IDAM
FRENCH $$$

(Map p246; ☑ 442 24488; www.mia.org.qa/en/visiting/idam; 5th fl, Museum of Islamic Art; mains QR155-375, mezze from QR45, set lunch menu QR200; ⊙ 12.30-3pm & 7-10pm Sat-Thu) Famed French chef Alain Ducasse's restaurant crowning the Museum of Islamic Art (p241) is one of Doha's best. Try the whole blue lobster, or the tender camel with duck foie gras, black truffle and soufléed potatoes. Enjoy dining in an impressive, light space with a floor-to-ceiling window and Philippe Starck designer furniture. The mezze dishes are also incredible. Don't know what to order? Let the chef decide for you with the 'experience menu' (QR690).

★ Nobu
JAPANESE $$$

(Map p242; ☑ 449 48600; https://noburestau rants.com; Four Seasons Hotel, Diplomatic St; small plates & sushi QR90-295; ⊙ 6.30-11.30pm) One of the city's most talked-about dining destinations, this is the world's largest – and arguably most architecturally outstanding – branch of chef Nobu Matsuhisa's globally acclaimed Japanese restaurant. Shaped like a shell, it has stunning views of the city from its iconic rooftop bar. The food is outstanding; yes, it's pricey, but this is once-in-a-lifetime stuff. Entry is strictly by reservation only. Arrive at the Four Seasons Hotel (p251), where the staff will arrange a golf-cart transfer to the restaurant. The dress code is smart casual.

★ Morimoto
JAPANESE $$$

(Map p242; ☑ 404 55999; www.morganshotel group.com; Mondrian Doha, West Bay Lagoon; small plates & sushi QR60-350, tasting menus QR590; ⊙ 6.30-11.30pm Mon-Sat) 'Iron Chef' Masaharu Morimoto's first restaurant in the Middle East is inspired by ancient Japan, with interiors adorned with rose-gold pillars, artwork by Japanese painter Hiroshi Senju and an impressive low-hanging chandelier as a centrepiece. Sit at the 16-seat sushi bar and watch the master chefs at work, while tucking into exquisite sushi, seafood, steak, noodles and soups.

Prime
STEAK $$$

(Map p242; ☑ 447 74542; www.ihg.com; 1st fl, Intercontinental Doha The City, Dafna; mains QR80-820; ⊙ 6-11pm) A steakhouse that delivers more than just steak, Prime imports choice cuts of Wagyu, which are some of the best in the city. Its menu also contains innovative dishes such as crab-and-sweet-pea panna cotta or triple-cooked lamb ribs. Sides include heirloom tomato salad and chowder soup, and there's an extensive wine list.

Three Sixty
MEDITERRANEAN $$$

(Map p242; ☑ 444 65600; www.thetorchdoha.com. qa; Torch Doha, Aspire Zone, Aspire Plaza Rd; mains QR75-215; ⊙ noon-3pm & 7-11pm) This posh and novel restaurant on the 47th floor of the iconic Torch building (p250) slowly rotates a full 360 degrees during a meal, offering a different perspective with every bite. Pricey but satisfying dishes include a seafood extravaganza – with Omani lobster, hammour, scallops and prawns – and slow-cooked venison with caramelised vegetables. Bookings are advisable.

Diners sit in a narrow, brown-and-beige circular corridor, but forget the decor – the floor-to-ceiling windows offer staggering views of Qatar.

Cut by Wolfgang Puck
STEAK $$$

(Map p242; ☑ 404 55999; www.morganshotel group.com; Mondrian Doha, West Bay Lagoon; lunch

QATAR DOHA

1. Khor Al Adaid
The beautiful Khor Al Adaid (p262) is accessible by 4WD only and is best visited with someone who knows the area well.

2. Doha Corniche
Doha's attractive waterfront promenade (p243), popular with families, stretches 7km along Doha Bay.

3. Al Jassasiya
The Al Jassasiya rockcarvings (p262) – around 900 in total – have been seen by very few visitors.

4. Souq Waqif
Built on an ancient market site, and still the social heart of Doha, Souq Waqif (p239) is one of the most atmospheric places to explore in Qatar.

mains QR55-120, dinner mains QR115-425; ⊘6.30-10.30am, noon-3.30pm & 7pm-midnight) This restaurant by eponymous steak connoisseur Wolfgang Puck is set within the quirky Mondrian hotel (p250). The avant-garde interior is in keeping with its surroundings - enormous gold-lined, platinum-white lampshades hang over selected tables. The food is largely good; the ingredients are key to the restaurant's success, with fine hunks of meat on the menu. That said, it's on the pricey side.

Save a few bucks with the happy-hour deals (offered 4pm to 7pm) that include daily selected drinks for QR30 and bites from QR35, or the two-course business lunch including a starter, main and dessert for QR95.

Opal by Gordon Ramsay BISTRO **$$$**
(Map p242; ☑444 60116; www.opalbygordon ramsaydoha.com; St Regis Doha, West Bay; mains QR75-345, 2-course Fri brunch from QR200; ⊘noon-4pm & 6-11pm) Gordon Ramsay's bistro specialises in burgers and Australian steaks; try the lamb burger with harissa mayonnaise, homemade tomato ketchup, fresh green mint, *zaatar* (a blend of spices that includes hyssop, sumac and sesame) and pomegranate. Salads and pizzas and a raw bar (with sushi and cold cuts) also available.

L'Wzaar SEAFOOD **$$$**
(Seafood Market; Map p242; ☑440 80710; www. lwzaar.com; Bldg 27, Katara; side dishes from QR48, fish by weight; ⊘noon-4pm & 7-11.30pm Sat-Thu, 1-4pm & 7-11.30pm Fri) Choose your own fish from the catch of the day at L'Wzaar, which claims to serve Doha's best, freshest seafood. Just back from the beach in Katara Cultural Village, it offers a rare opportunity to mingle with Qatari families. The traditional fish soup followed by grilled mixed seafood is a solid choice, and there's excellent sushi and good fish and chips, too.

🍷 Drinking & Nightlife

Five-star hotels are the only places allowed to sell alcohol to tourists. A third-wave coffee scene is also emerging in Doha - a boon for fans of single-origin brews.

★**Backyard** BEER GARDEN
(Map p242; www.facebook.com/TheBackyardDo ha; Sheraton Hotel, Al Funduq St; entry incl 1 drink women/men QR65/100; ⊘6pm-midnight Oct-Feb) Set in a lush garden under trees, and lit with fairy lights, this place has a different feel from the other bars in Doha. It hosts acoustic sets, which guests listen to on garden

benches or floor blankets, and has a chilled-out vibe. When international DJs play, it turns into more of a festival atmosphere.

The dress code is come as you are. Entry is free for women before 7.30pm.

★**Belgian Cafe** BAR
(Map p242; ☑448 44919; InterContinental Doha, Al Isteqlal Rd, West Bay; ⊘12.30pm-2am) One of the few casual pubs in Doha, Belgian Cafe gets packed to the rafters on Thursday and Friday nights. The crowds are here for the imported Belgian ale and other European beers, great bar food (classic mussels or waffles) and laid-back atmosphere. There's a large smoking area out back. The decent happy hour runs between 12.30pm and 6.30pm daily, with beers from QR30.

Flat White COFFEE
(Map p242; ☑402 91965; www.flatwhite.qa; Unit 346, 27 La Croisette, Porto Arabia, The Pearl; ⊘7am-11pm Sun-Wed, to 11.30pm Thu, 7am-11.30am & 12.30-11.30pm Fri) A homegrown artisanal coffee house kickstarting Doha's third-wave coffee scene, Flat White is the brainchild of two Qataris who, after travelling the world to source the best coffee and learning the techniques required, opened their first coffee shop at The Pearl. Try the excellent manual brews and cold brews. This place is always busy. There's another branch (Map p242; Student Centre, Education City; ⊘7.30am-3.30pm).

Rise BAR
(Map p242; ☑404 55777; www.morganshotel group.com; Mondrian Doha, West Bay; ⊘6pm-1am Tue-Thu, from 5pm Fri & Sat) The spectacular bar on the 27th floor of the Mondrian Doha (p250) has stunning views out onto the artificial waterways and buzzing highways in the distance. Like the rest of the hotel, its design is bold and whimsical with kaleidoscopic black-and-white printed walls, soft red chairs, chandeliers hanging throughout and a pool view. The cocktail menu includes flavoursome champagne-based drinks.

Eden COFFEE
(Map p242; ☑335 97541; www.theedencoffee.com; Medina Centrale, The Pearl; ⊘9am-midnight; 🛜) This little coffee shop serves single-origin coffee from Panama, Ethiopia, Colombia, Guatemala and Brazil, among other coffee-growing nations. Enjoy your cup amid exposed brickwork, indoor plants and wooden floors. Bites include a range of pastries, cakes and some excellent homemade chocolates.

Wahm Lounge Doha
LOUNGE

(Map p242; www.wahmdoha.com; W Doha Hotel, Diplomatic St; ⊙noon-2am Sun-Fri, to midnight Sat) A trendy set hangs out at this poolside lounge bar, sipping cocktails while listening to Latin roots music and chill-out beats. The cocktails, such as Source of Nature – a mix of honeydew melon, jasmine flowers, thyme, lemon and gin – are rather good.

Al Shurfa Arabic Lounge
LOUNGE

(Map p246; top fl, Al Jomrok Boutique Hotel, Souq Waqif; ⊙12.30pm-midnight) Souq Waqif's only rooftop lounge serves shisha, mocktails (our fave is the Al Shurfa with fresh ginger, lemongrass, lemon juice, mint leaves and raspberry puree) and mezze, plus mixed-grill mains. The balcony tables are ideal for people-watching in the souq.

Sky View
BAR

(Map p242; ☑442 88888; www.lacigalehotel.com; La Cigale Hotel, 60 Suhaim Bin Hamad St, Bin Mahmoud; ⊙7pm-2am) The well-to-do young and professional crowd at the rooftop bar of La Cigale Hotel doesn't flinch at the tab for what are some of Doha's pricier drinks – served with an incredible perspective on the city's skyline. Great sushi-bar food, house music and clientele dressed to impress adds to the atmosphere.

Al Mandarin
CAFE

(Map p246; Souq Waqif Rd, Souq Waqif; ⊙8am-1.30am Sat-Thu, 8-11am & 1pm-1.30am Fri) Covered in brightly coloured mosaics, this place serves some of the best juices in the souq, with a range of fruity non-alcoholic cocktails on its long menu.

☆ Entertainment

Katara Amphitheatre
THEATRE

(Map p242; ☑440 80000; www.katara.net; Katara) This grand arabesque/Greek outdoor theatre at the heart of the Katara Cultural Village is a sight to behold. It has around 30 rows of deep steps and seats and views down onto a large circular stage with a sea-view backdrop. Performances here are among the most atmospheric in the city, especially when it's a full house with some 5000 people. Visitors are welcome to walk around the amphitheatre at any time of day. Check the Katara website for upcoming shows and events.

Doha Film Institute
CINEMA

(Map p246; ☑442 00505; www.dohafilminstitute.com; MIA Auditorium; tickets QR35) Holding screenings of local, independent and cul-turally relevant movies, many of which are by filmmakers from the Arab world, this independent, not-for-profit company was also behind the very successful Doha Tribeca Film Festival. Screenings take place in the MIA Auditorium, plus other areas of the city.

Qatar Opera House
THEATRE

(Map p242; www.katara.net; Bldg 16, Katara; tickets QR75-200) The grand interior with red chairs, ornate balconies and a striking ceiling design has space for 550 guests, who come to enjoy philharmonic orchestras and solo classical musicians. International artists, from Andalusian guitarists to the Orchestra of the Filipino Youth, play here, too.

🛍 Shopping

Villaggio Mall
SHOPPING CENTRE

(Map p242; ☑442 27400; www.villaggioqatar.com; cnr Al Waab St & Al Numan St; ⊙9am-10pm Sun-Wed, to 11pm Thu & Sat, 9-11am & 2.30-11pm Fri; ⚐) In this Venetian-themed mall, you can shop under a 'sky' of fluffy white clouds, eat pizza at Paul, and take a ride on a gondola (QR10 per person) along the indoor grand canal and peruse items in shops with European-style facades. Entertainment includes an IMAX cinema and indoor theme park Gondolania, with fairground-style rides, games and amusements for kids.

Good Life Market
FOOD

(Map p242; The Pearl; ⊙6.30am-10pm Sun-Thu, 9.30-11.30am & 1.30-10.30pm Fri, 10am-10pm Sat) The first health-food store in Qatar sells organic, gluten-free, nutritional and vegan products, plus health drinks (like kombucha and fresh juices) and grab-and-go salads and dishes such as grilled salmon and rice. There's a very small seating area if you wish to eat in.

Al Galaf
ANTIQUES

(Map p246; Souq Waqif; ⊙8am-12.30pm & 3.30-9.30pm Sat-Thu, 6-10pm Fri) This half-museum, half-shop boasts a remarkable collection of antiques, some for sale, others for viewing purposes only. It has old medals, pocket watches, historic fishing and boat memorabilia, vintage cameras, telephones and TVs, plus rare items such as a photo of the UK's Prince Charles in Souq Waqif in 2007.

Arumailah Gifts & Masterpieces
GIFTS & SOUVENIRS

(Map p246; Shop 418 & 419, Souq Waqif; ⊙7.30am-12.30pm & 3.30-10pm Sat-Thu, from 6pm Fri) A wonderful place to rummage around in

SHEIKH FAISAL BIN QASSIM AL THANI MUSEUM

The **Sheikh Faisal Bin Qassim Al Thani Museum** (☎ 448 61444; www.fbqmuseum. org; Al Samriya St, off Dukhan Rd; adult/child QR20/free; ⊙ 9am-4.30pm Mon-Thu, 2-7pm Fri, 10am-6pm Sat, 9am-4pm Sun) offers the very rare opportunity to step onto a rich sheikh's property and take a peek at his personal belongings. Sheikh Faisal has spent a lifetime collecting beautiful things. His vast, remarkable collection of artefacts includes carpets, furniture, swords, ancient tapestries and Bedouin outfits, plus a whole Syrian house (transported and placed inside the museum). The whole lot is displayed in an enormous fort-like building, which was hand-cut from limestone purely to house all these weird and wonderful items.

The seemingly endless displays include dozens of classic American cars, dhows, motorbikes, full-sized stuffed camels and other desert creatures, plus controversial pieces such as an elephant's foot. Visitors will need a good few hours to take everything in, starting with the 10-minute educational video in which Sheikh Faisal talks about Qatari culture and heritage. There's a small cafe at the end of the museum.

Tour operators in Doha run excursions here, or it's roughly 45 minutes by car from central Doha. You will have to show ID when entering the grounds, and entry is permitted up to an hour before closing time.

QATAR DOHA

Souq Waqif, this Ali Baba-style grotto sells swords, daggers, belts and bags, plus painted bowls, carved boxes and lanterns.

Spices & Sweets Souq　FOOD
(Map p246; Souq Waqif; ⊙9am-1pm & 4-7pm Sat-Thu, 4-9pm Fri) This particularly fragrant corner of Souq Waqif (p239) has little boundary between its two specialities. Vendors display large containers of herbs and spices outside their stores – walking though these stone alleys is an olfactory sensation, as immense flavours fill your nostrils.

Souq Waqif Art Center　ART
(Map p246; ☎441 76204; www.facebook.com/souq waqifartcenter; btwn Souq Waqif Rd & Ali Bin Abdullah St, Souq Waqif; ⊙8am-2pm & 4-10pm Sat-Thu, 4-10pm Fri) Housed in an attractive two-storey lantern-lit building that fronts onto Souq Waqif (p239), this centre is filled with galleries and artists' studios. Artists work on paintings, sculpture and other creations onsite, and there are often artists in residence.

City Center Doha　SHOPPING CENTRE
(Map p242; ☎449 33355; www.citycenterdoha. com; Conference Center Rd; ⊙10am-10pm Sun-Wed, to midnight Thu & Sat, 10am-11am & 1pm-midnight Fri; ⊛) A trip to City Center Doha is more event than errand for its congregations of juice-sipping Qataris and huddles of homesick expatriates. In addition to its 350 shops, tented architecture, marble flooring and glass-fronted lifts, there's an ice-skating rink, bowling alleys and climbing walls. Kids will especially enjoy the basement den filled with pool tables, arcade games and PlayStation consoles.

ⓘ Getting There & Away

AIR
Doha's swish, five-star-rated Hamad International Airport (p271) opened in 2014 and has quickly grown into one of the region's busiest airports. It was ranked fifth-best airport in the world at the SKYTRAX World Airport Awards 2018.

The airport cost US$17 billion to build, and the investment shows throughout, from its sleek modern curves to its Apple Mac desktops for passengers to use. Throughout the terminals are pieces of world-class modern art to admire. A bronze statue of a 20-tonne teddy bear with its head inside a lamp is one of the most notable; it was created by Swiss artist Urs Fischer and bought by the Qatari royals for a staggering US$6.8 million.

ⓘ Getting Around

There are ambitious plans for an extensive underground metro system that will connect all points of Doha, from the airport to The Pearl, revolutionising travel within the city. It's scheduled to be completed in 2019.

TO & FROM THE AIRPORT
Many top-end hotels and resorts provide free transport to and from Hamad International Airport, located 13km southeast of the city centre.

Karwa buses between the airport and the Al Ghanim Bus Station and other locations in the city leave every 20 minutes between 4am and midnight. Journeys to the city take around 30 minutes. Travellers must buy a Karwa Smartcard at the airport (a QR10 card is valid for two inner-city trips within 24 hours).

Taxis (turquoise in colour) are clean, safe and metered, and the journey between the airport and central Doha starts at QR25 and costs QR1.20 per kilometre between 5am and 9pm, rising to QR1.80 per kilometre between 9pm and 5am. The journey takes roughly 15 to 20 minutes into Doha, traffic depending. Avoid taking unofficial taxis from the touts at the airport who illegally claim business for their private car.

An Uber (www.uber.com) from Hamad International Airport to central Doha costs around QR40.

BUS

The government-run national bus company, Karwa Public Bus (www.mowasalat.com), provides comfortable city services around Doha in environmentally friendly vehicles. Timetables are displayed at each of the sheltered bus stops.

Buses operate every 15 to 30 minutes along many city routes; most start from **Al Ghanim Bus Station** (Map p246; ☑ 445 88888; www.mowasalat.com; btwn Al Ashat St & Ibn Malik) and have stops every 750m. To travel by bus, you must purchase a Karwa Smartcard. Without a card, there's a QR10 fee for a single journey. Cards are available at the bus station and at some supermarkets (you need ID to purchase).

The free West Bay Shuttle loops through the West Bay area and can be handy for getting from one end of the bay to the other. Route maps are posted at bus stops and are available on www.mowasalat.com and http://qatar.transit-guide.com.

CAR & MOTORCYCLE

Many major car-hire brands are located in Doha and in the arrivals area of the airport.

Driving in Doha is easy enough if you watch out for impatient drivers overtaking on both the left and right, honking the horn, flashing their lights and exhibiting a general disregard for roundabouts and free-roaming pedestrians. Parking is not too much of a problem, except in the souq areas. Most hotels and malls have car parks or parking services. Ongoing construction and a lack of street signs can make navigation difficult. Most people navigate by landmark, not by road sign.

TAXI

Despite the efficient bus system, most people get around Doha by taxi or Uber. If you don't use an app, taxi journeys in theory cost QR4 plus QR1.60/1.80 per kilometre during daylight/nighttime hours, although very few taxis use their meters these days. In practice, agree a price before getting in. The minimum fare is QR10, and waiting time costs QR8 for each 15 minutes.

Bright-turquoise taxis can be hailed by the side of the road or found at the airport and outside malls and hotels. Short Uber trips start at QR15.

AROUND QATAR

Al Wakrah & Al Wukair الوكرة و الوكير

The old pearling villages of Al Wakrah and Al Wukair are rapidly sprawling out to meet the Doha suburbs and make a pleasant afternoon outing from the capital. There are several interesting old mosques and traditional houses in and around the gracious modern villas. The old souq along the shoreline is the area's main attraction, with dozens of atmospheric alleys and a nice seafront promenade with restaurants and shops.

The beaches south of Al Wakrah offer glorious stretches of sand, interspersed with the odd *khor* (creek). The shallow water makes paddling a better option than swimming. At least the determined wader is in good company: small flocks of flamingos roost along the coast between Al Wakrah and Mesaieed during winter. Fishing is a popular pastime in the area, as the limestone shallows act as fish traps when the tide goes out.

◉ Sights

Souq Al Wakrah MARKET

(Al Ghawwas St, Al Wakrah Seafront, Al Wakrah; ⊙24hr, shops & restaurants 4pm-midnight) Al Wakrah's enormous and enchanting souq is a maze of alleyways and courtyards, full of aged clay structures, traditional architecture, a mosque and stables, and shops selling everything from honey, spices and dates to perfumes and souvenirs. It's easy to spend an evening wandering the alleys, soaking up the atmosphere and imagining what life would have been like hundreds of years ago in these lands. The seafront promenade beside the souq is dotted with authentic (but mediocre) restaurants.

⛏ Sleeping

Souq Al Wakra Hotel BOUTIQUE HOTEL $

(☑ 442 87888; www.tivolihotels.com; Souq Al Wakrah, Al Wakrah; d from QR308; [P][☎]) With superbly finished rooms and the same heritage style as the Tivoli-brand hotels in Doha's Souq Waqif, this hotel is by far the top place to stay in the Al Wakrah area. Rooms are simple and light, with dark wood features and crisp linen. There's a good all-day dining restaurant, palm trees and water features on the grounds.

AL JASSASIYA ROCK CARVINGS

This profusion of **petroglyphs** (off Al Shamal Rd; ☉ sunrise-sunset) – some 900 rock carvings depicting fish, cups in rows, rosettes, ships and foot marks – in northern Qatar has been seen by very few visitors. Until very recently, their whereabouts was all but a secret and only those in the know with a 4WD could find them. Up close some may feel underwhelmed by the poorly preserved shapes, but imagining communities here hundreds (perhaps thousands) of years ago is still an evocative experience.

Some archaeologists have suggested the petroglyphs could date back to the 3rd century BC, while other experts believe they were created between the 10th and 18th centuries AD. The petroglyph site is located 60km north of Doha near the Buzwair Industrial Gases Factories. A 4WD is essential. Plan a trip with a local guide or tour operator as they will have the necessary permissions to enter the fenced-off site.

❶ Getting There & Away

The 109 and 129 buses depart from Doha's Al Ghanim Bus Station (p261) every 30 minutes.

Mesaieed   مسيعيد

POP 37,550

Industrial Mesaieed is not particularly attractive in itself, but its surrounding landscape offers some appealing adventures. The deep water at a nearby beach makes for some of the best swimming in Qatar, while the area's dunes are what desert-buggy and 4WD adventures are made of. Divers can take a trip with a Doha-based scuba-diving company to see four sunken GMC cars, which have turned into underwater reefs. There's also one popular resort here, favoured by expats wanting a getaway from the big city.

☞ Tours

Doha Bus   ADVENTURE
(☑ 740 91694, 444 22444; https://dohabus.com; Sealine Rd; monster bus adult/child QR180/90, min 4 people; ☉ office 9am-5pm, trips Thu-Sat at various times) A thrilling way to experience Qatar's desert is to book a trip across the sand dunes with Doha Bus via 'monster bus' (the bus equivalent of a monster truck; a one-hour trip) or 4WD (1¾ hours). Various routes go over floodplains and a motocross track to desert viewpoints and came-grazing areas, and to Qatar's inland sea.

🛏 Sleeping

Sealine Beach Resort   RESORT $$
(☑ 447 65299; www.sealinebeachqatar.com; Sealine Beach Rd; day admission Thu-Sat adult/child QR100/50, Sun-Wed QR75/25; ⓟ🛜🏊) This lovely low-rise, beachside resort just south of Mesaieed is a favourite among expats wanting to escape the city for the weekend. Far enough away to be unaffected by Mesaieed's heavy industry, it's ringed by glorious amber sand dunes, plus lawns and palm trees on the grounds. There's a gym, spa and smart, modern and clean rooms with wooden floors.

❶ Getting There & Away

The 109 bus leaves from Al Ghanim Bus Station (p261) in Doha every 30 minutes and takes around an hour to reach Mesaieed Industrial City. From here to the beach is another 20 minutes by taxi.

Khor Al Adaid   خور العديد

This beautiful 'inland sea' is one of the major natural attractions in Qatar, and it takes on an almost mystical quality under a full moon, when the *sabkha* (salt flats) sparkle in the gaps between the sand. Often described as a sea or a lake, the *khor* is in fact neither: rather it is a creek surrounded by silvery crescents of sand (known as *barchan*). A night under the stars on a camping expedition here is a special experience.

Not everyone goes to this area to enjoy the tranquillity: sand skiing, quad biking and 4WD racing compete with the time-honoured picnic and a song, much to the consternation of some and the pleasure of others. The area is big enough, thankfully, to satisfy all, although environmental concerns are being expressed as more travel agencies make the area the central attraction of their tours.

This region is only accessible by 4WD, and independent travellers should go with someone who knows the area, such as a company like Doha Bus, and can drive a 4WD. Being stuck in the sand is no fun after the first hour and in summer is very dangerous.

If you're determined to do it yourself, make sure you have at least a box of water bottles on board for each passenger, a map and compass, very clear directions of the best route currently navigable, a tow rope and a shovel. If you get stuck, don't dig: let out the air in the tyres and return to the nearest petrol station immediately to re-inflate.

Al Khor الخور

POP 202,000

Once famous as a centre for the pearling industry, Al Khor is a pleasant town with an attractive corniche, a small dhow yard and a lively fish market. Several old watchtowers are scattered around town, and many have been restored to their original form. The nearby mangroves are a good place for birdwatching.

Sights

Baladna Farm FARM
(📞403 58833, 501 40268; http://baladna.co; North Rd, exit 44, Umm Al Hawaya; park adult/child QR55/35, visitor hall free; ⊗8am-8pm Sun-Thu, to 9.30pm Fri & Sat Sep-May; P🔧) Qatar's biggest and best-known dairy and meat producer is the only place in the country where you can experience life on a real working farm. Watch the cows being milked in the state-of-the-art milking parlour from the visitor hall and then try some farm-sourced meats at the excellent on-site restaurant. Kids will love the amusement park, where there's a petting zoo, horse riding, a high-wire obstacle course and a playground.

Baladna Farm started as a goat and sheep farm, but since the blockade, Qatar – which used to get its milk from Saudi Arabia – has had to become self-sufficient, importing cows to the desert (via boat and even plane), so residents could continue to enjoy dairy products. The **farm restaurant** sells succulent meat and rice dishes cooked in clay pots, a range of grills, plus 'Baladna Trays' with lots of little pots of goodies you can try (mains from QR81).

Sleeping

Al Sultan Beach Resort RESORT $$$
(📞447 22666; www.alsultanbeachresort.com; Safa Al Tawg St; r from QR1100; P🏊) This four-star resort just off the corniche is a fine getaway, if eclectically decorated, with cast-iron horses in the drive and abstract art and Middle Eastern scenes adorning the rooms. The clean, inviting rooms centre around an indoor courtyard with desert plants and modern sculptures; they have neutral soft furnishings, windows onto an infinity pool and stunning sea views.

There's tennis, basketball and volleyball courts on-site, along with the **Blue Brasserie Restaurant**, with its trippy sky ceiling and fish tank, which serves an international buffet and shisha in the afternoons. Kayak hire is available for QR150 per hour.

If you just want to visit for the day, entry costs QR125 for adults and QR75 for children.

❶ Getting There & Away

Buses 102 and 102X leave from Al Ghanim Bus Station (p261) in Doha every 30 minutes.

Al Zubarah الزبارة

Al Zubarah Fort FORT
(www.qm.org.qa/en/project/al-zubarah; Al Areesh Rd; ⊗6am-6pm; P) FREE Qatar's first and only Unesco World Heritage site appears in the desert as if out of nowhere. The impressive structure, built in 1938, has four striking towers and stands alone in a sea of sand. Inside are cabinets of artefacts containing pearl merchants' boxes and simple yet utterly genius divers' nose pegs – used for pearling decades ago. A large commercial and pearling port was located here in the 18th and 19th centuries.

Info boards at the fort, which was used by the military until the 1980s, contain information on how remote villages like Al Zubarah used to find water in this stark and barren landscape. Archaeological excavations of the old pearling village are ongoing, but not open to visitors.

Bir Zekreet بئر زكريت

There's not much in the way of altitude in Qatar, which only serves to exaggerate the little limestone escarpment of Bir Zekreet, on the northwestern coast of the peninsula, near Dukhan. Here, the wind has whittled away softer sedimentary rock, exposing pillars and a large mushroom of limestone, like a geography lesson in desert formations come to life. The surrounding beaches are full of empty oyster shells, with rich mother-of-pearl interiors, and other assorted bivalves. The shallow waters are quiet and peaceful and see relatively few visitors, making the area a pleasant destination for a day trip.

The remains of the 9th-century Murwab Fort, about 15km further up the northwestern coast from Dukhan, may be worth a visit with a guide. Five groups of buildings, including two mosques and an earlier fort, have been partially excavated, but a lack of information makes the site of limited interest.

❶ Getting There & Away

To reach Bir Zekreet from Doha, head west past Al Shahaniya and take the signposted turn-off on the right about 10km before Dukhan. The journey takes roughly 1½ hours. A 4WD is advisable for exploring the escarpment.

To reach the desert mushroom, turn right 1.5km past the school at a gap in the gas pipes and bear left before the trees, or ask locals for directions.

UNDERSTAND QATAR

Qatar Today

Qatar's desert peninsula has been utterly transformed over the past 20 years. Bedouin charm remains in the culture, but the ruling family has modernised the landscape with glitzy skyscrapers and malls. Despite controversy around Qatar's 2022 FIFA World Cup, the country is investing an estimated US$220 billion to host the tournament, including country-wide construction. A

diplomatic crisis that broke out in 2017 has resulted in a trade and travel blockade with other Gulf nations that may impact visitors' onward travel plans.

Gulf–Qatar Diplomatic Crisis

Diplomatic, trade and travel ties with Qatar were severed by Saudi Arabia, the United Arab Emirates, Bahrain and Egypt in 2017 after Saudi officials claimed that such a blockade would protect their national security from Qatar, a nation they alleged has terrorist links.

Qatar has consistently rejected this allegation and claimed that Saudi Arabia was instead trying to ruin Qatar's trade relationship with the US. Leaked emails from the UAE to the US later appeared to support the claim that the blockading nations had intentions to discredit Qatar.

Visitors to Qatar will see most residents in full support of their leader, Emir Tamim Bin Hamad Al Thani, and standing by his decision to reject the long list of demands from the blockading countries. Enormous Qatari flags and portraits of the emir have been hung from skyscrapers to show their united front, and his face appears on car stickers all over the country.

The land, sea and air blockade forces Qatari planes and ships to make major detours. Qataris can no longer live in or travel to the countries involved in the blockade. Visitors cannot directly travel to countries involved in the blockade, but can transfer in Oman, Kuwait or other nations further afield.

AL JAZEERA

Al Jazeera, which means 'the island', was launched in 1996 as an Arabic-language news satellite-TV channel, funded with a grant from the emir of Qatar. It has been subsidised by the leader of Qatar on a year-by-year basis since, despite airing criticism of his own government. The station was originally staffed by many former members of the BBC World Service, whose Saudi-based Arabic-language TV station collapsed under Saudi censorship.

Al Jazeera is widely watched across the Middle East, where it gives audiences rare exposure to debate, independent opinion and alternative perspectives on regional issues. It has always been viewed with suspicion or contempt by ruling parties across the Arab world. On one occasion, in 1999, the Algerian government reportedly pulled the plug on its capital city's electricity supply to prevent the population from hearing a live debate that alleged Algerian military collusion in a series of massacres. Critics also accused Al Jazeera of spurring on the unrest in Tunisia and Egypt that led to the Arab Spring.

More recently, the network has become a bargaining chip in the Gulf–Qatar diplomatic crisis, with the blockade countries demanding its closure as a condition for lifting the embargo on trade. Saudi Arabia and Jordan have both closed their Al Jazeera bureaus.

Qatar & the 2022 World Cup

Qatar's winning bid for the 2022 FIFA World Cup will make it the first country in the Middle East (and the first majority-Muslim nation) to ever host the tournament.

The event, though, has already been shrouded in controversy. Under pressure from tournament sponsors, FIFA investigated bribery allegations, eventually publicly clearing Qatar of any wrongdoing, though corruption claims continue.

Meanwhile, human-rights groups have accused Qatar of modern-day slavery, saying that the migrant workers building the tournament's stadiums have had their passports seized by their employers and are working in extreme heat, with no water or food provided – conditions that have reportedly led to many worksite deaths. Qatar has rejected many of these claims, but also arrested and held for two days four BBC journalists who attempted to report on migrant workers' conditions in 2015. A law was changed in late 2018 to allow most migrant workers to leave the country without permission from their employers.

Human-rights advocates have also voiced concerns about the dangers faced by members of the LGBT community who might want to travel to Qatar, where homosexuality is illegal, for the event.

Usually occurring in the summer months, the World Cup in Qatar will be held from late November until mid-December to beat the region's scorching summer heat. The decision to hold the event later in the year was also partly made to avoid clashing with the holy month of Ramadan, during which it is forbidden to eat or drink in public in Qatar during daylight-hour fasting. The World Cup final will take place on 18 December 2022, which is also Qatar National Day.

Much to the dismay of hardline religious groups in Qatar, the chief executive of the country's World Cup bid, Hassan Abdulla Al Thawadi, said the nation would reverse its ban on alcohol consumption during the tournament. Whether this means drinking will be restricted to designated zones remains to be seen.

History

Little physical evidence remains of Qatar's early history, but the heritage of its semi-nomadic Bedouin population lives on in beloved traditions such as falconry and camel racing. The rise to power of the Al Thani family, which established a capital at Al Bida (now a district of Doha) in the mid-19th century, laid the foundations for the modern country. Still under Al Thani rule, Qatar has been undergoing rapid change over the past two decades, with no sign of stopping.

Early Inhabitants

The written history of Qatar begins in grand fashion with a mention by the 5th-century Greek historian Herodotus, who identifies the seafaring Canaanites as the original inhabitants of Qatar. Thereafter, however, Qatar appears to be the subject more of conjecture than of history. Although there is evidence – in the form of flint spearheads, pottery shards, burial mounds near Umm Salal Mohammed and the Jassasiya Rock Carvings – of the early habitation of Qatar (from 4000 BC), the peninsula has surprisingly little to show for its ancient lineage.

The Rise of Islam

Documents indicate that Qatar played an important role in the early spread of Islam through the assembling of a naval fleet used to transport the warriors of the Holy Jihad. The Portuguese, who left forts in every country in the Gulf like modern businessmen leave calling cards, bequeathed only hearsay to Qatar's coastline. The Turks helped drive out the Portuguese in the 16th century, and Qatar remained under the nominal rule of the Ottoman Empire (and the practical governance of local sheikhs) for more than four centuries. Yet the comings and goings of even that great empire made little impression on Qatar's sands of time, metaphorically or physically.

Al Thani Family Dynasty & the British

The transience of historical record changes in the mid-18th century with the arrival of the charismatic Al Thani family, which remains in power to this day.

A branch of the ancient Tamim tribe of central Arabia, Al Thani were originally nomadic Bedouin, but the region's sparse vegetation led them to settle in the peninsula's coastal areas around Zubarah, where they fished and dived for pearls. The first Al Thani emir, Sheikh Mohammed Bin Thani, established his capital at Al Bida in the mid-19th century, thereby laying the foundations of modern Doha.

Sheikh Mohammed strengthened his position against other local tribes by signing a treaty with the British in 1867. In 1872, the second Al Thani emir, Jasim, allowed the Turks to build a garrison in Doha (Doha Fort), but they were expelled under the third Al Thani emir, Sheikh Abdullah, after Turkey entered WWI on the opposite side to Britain. Thereafter, the British guaranteed Qatar's protection in exchange for a promise that the ruler would not deal with other foreign powers without British permission, an agreement that endured until independence was proclaimed in 1971.

Rags to Oil Riches

Qatar's history from WWI to the end of the 20th century reads rather like a fairy tale. Life in Qatar, even before the collapse of the pearl market in the 1930s, was marked by widespread poverty, malnutrition and disease. The arrival of oil prospectors and the establishment in 1935 of Petroleum Development Qatar, a forerunner to today's state-run Qatar General Petroleum Corporation (QGPC), signalled the beginning of a brave new world, even though WWII delayed production of oil for another 10 years.

Although not huge in comparative terms, the oil revenue instantly turned the tiny, impoverished population into citizens of one of the richest per-capita countries in the world. Qatar's first school opened in 1952 and a full-scale hospital followed in 1959, marking the beginning of long-term investment in the country's modernisation.

Arab Spring

In 2011, Qatar was notable among its regional neighbours for the lack of Arab Spring protests, despite having no elected representatives in government and key government posts being occupied by members of the emir's family. The most likely explanation for Qatar's lack of protests is the ruling family's generosity in spreading the country's wealth and its allowing a degree of (albeit limited) free speech.

People

Just 25% of Qatar's population is under age 25, a far smaller proportion than in other countries in the region. More than 99% of the population lives in urban areas, there are three Qatari males for every female, and foreign workers make up around 88% of the population. Indians comprise the largest such group, followed by Nepalis and Bangladeshis. Under a new law, 100 foreign expatriates will be granted permanent residency each year, a first for any Gulf nation.

Lifestyle

While observant of a conservative form of Islam, many Qataris will extend hospitality to those of a different mind. While it is still unusual to see Qataris drinking alcohol, there is a certain tolerance of visitors who do. Local men and women are very discreetly dressed, and women who are not fully covered will likely experience unwanted stares. Indirect campaigns about dress code are prevalent on social media and signage around Doha and promote conservative attire. That said, modestly dressed women can walk around freely in Qatar, and no activities are off limits to women.

A significant difference is Qatar's press, which compared to its neighbours has enjoyed a certain amount of freedom of expression since 1995, resulting in one of the most controversial and celebrated media phenomena in the Middle East: Al Jazeera (p264).

In public, the country reflects the espousal of Western materialism while paradoxically retaining something of the Bedouin simplicity of life: the day can stop for tea with a stranger, and family life still lies at the heart of Qatari society.

Multiculturalism

An arriving visitor will be stamped into the country by a Qatari, but thereafter they could be forgiven for thinking they had stepped into another country – or at least pockets of many. There are car-hire attendants from Pakistan, shopkeepers from India, nightclub entertainers from the Philippines and Brits turning pink in the afternoon sun during a day off from the oil and gas industries. Qatari men are recognisable in the multiethnic crowd by their impeccable white *thobe* (floor-length shirt-dress), *gutra* (white headcloth) and long, black-tasselled *agal* (head rope), and Qatari women by their narrow-eyed *yashmak* (veil).

The relative broadmindedness of an otherwise conservative nation stems not only

ALCOHOL VS COFFEE

Around the country, locals in national dress can be seen drinking Arabic coffee at various atmospheric coffeehouses and restaurants, while playing aldama (a board game with similarities to both draughts and backgammon) and smoking shisha. It's a fascinating (if almost entirely male) scene and visitors wanting to experience local culture should take part during any trip to Qatar.

In direct contrast, and a controversial subculture among Qatar's hardline Muslim population, are the expats who head to five-star hotels with themed bars, pubs, swanky lounges and lively DJ nights, where revellers drink and party into the wee hours. When the clubs kick them out, problems can occur. Qatar has a zero-tolerance policy towards people being visibly drunk in public, and those who break the rules could face jail time.

For now, Qatar's coffee drinkers and boozers remain in two separate worlds that exist in parallel. However, tensions may rise during the 2022 World Cup, a tournament known for its big drinking culture. Qatar officials have said they will take a more lenient approach to those drinking alcohol during the tournament, although what this means remains to be seen.

While a cup of coffee or a shisha costs a few riyals, alcohol is imported and isn't cheap: a 100% alcohol tax went into effect in January 2019, doubling the price of a drink overnight. However, deals can be found most nights of the week at the hotels' many bars, including ladies' nights, happy hours and themed nights.

from interaction with the thousands of immigrant workers who have helped build the country but also from the fact that so many Qataris have travelled or studied abroad. Alas, that broadmindedness doesn't always translate into fair treatment of the immigrant population, many of whom continue to be considered second-class citizens. This issue came to the fore in 2013 when the International Trade Union Confederation published a report claiming that 1200 workers from India and Nepal alone had died while working on construction projects associated with the 2022 FIFA World Cup.

Qatar denied the accusations, but the fact remains that migrant workers very often live and work in appalling conditions that have everything and nothing to do with the glossy facade that Qatar likes to present to the world. Under international pressure, a Qatar law changed in late 2018 to allow most migrant workers to leave the country without permission from their employers, but 5% of contractors still may have their passports retained. Further regulations were due to be announced regarding workers who remain under their employers' complete control, and unable to travel freely.

Arts

Although Qatar's rapid modernisation has encouraged a certain Westernisation of culture, some distinctive elements of traditional cultural expression remain, particularly in terms of music and dance. This is especially evident during the Eid Al Adha and Eid Al Fitr religious holidays or on social occasions such as weddings. Only a specialist is likely to pick up the nuances that distinguish Qatar's music or dance from that of other Gulf states, given their shared Bedouin inheritance, but numerous events throughout the country make Qatar one of the easier places to encounter these art forms. Check listings in the *Gulf Times,* the *Peninsula* or the *Qatar Tribune* to see what's happening where.

Interest in orchestral music is enjoying a revival with the Qatar Philharmonic Orchestra (www.qatarphilharmonicorchestra. org), sponsored by the charitable Qatar Foundation and playing at the Qatar Opera House (p259) and other venues around town.

Environment

One would expect the land area of a country to be finite. Not so in Qatar, where extensive reclamation programs keep adding to the total with each passing year. The area of the Qatar peninsula is generally given as 11,571 sq km – about 160km long and 55km to 90km wide – with 700km of shallow coastline. It includes one or two islands, but not the neighbouring Hawar Islands, which were a bone of contention until the International Court of Justice awarded the oil-rich

QATAR ARTS

islands to Bahrain in 2001. While Qatar is mostly flat, the oil-drilling area of Jebel Dukhan reaches a height of 75m.

The sand dunes to the south of the country, especially around the inland sea at Khor Al Adaid, are particularly appealing. Much of the interior, however, is marked by gravel-covered plains. This kind of desert may appear completely featureless, but it's worth a closer look: rainwater collects in *du-hlans* (crevices), giving rise intermittently to exquisite little flowering plants. Roses even bloom in the desert, though not of the floral kind: below the *sabkha* (salt flats that lie below sea level), gypsum forms into rosettes, some measuring 20cm to 25cm across. These roses are the inspiration for the look of the new National Museum of Qatar (p243).

Environmental Issues

Qatar has virtually no naturally occurring fresh water and relies upon desalination plants for its burgeoning water needs. And what little water there is may be getting harder to find. Qatar is now 2m higher than it was 400 years ago thanks to 'geological uplift', a phenomenon by which movements in the Earth's crust push the bedrock up. As a result, the underground water table sinks, or at least becomes more difficult to access.

There are also human-caused issues such as the 24-hour air-conditioning found in virtually every building (at least in the summer months), which releases greenhouse gases into the environment and consumes lots of electricity.

SURVIVAL GUIDE

 **Directory A–Z**

ACCESSIBLE TRAVEL

Little provision has been made in Qatar for travellers with disabilities, although the new resorts have tried to make accommodation wheelchair-accessible. The Corniche area of Doha and the new malls are easily accessed, but many of the other sights and souqs are not. No provisions are made for the visually or hearing impaired.Download Lonely Planet's free Accessible Travel guides from http://lptravel.to/AccessibleTravel.

ACCOMMODATION

Qatar's main sights are all within day-trip distance of the capital. Unless you plan on camping out overnight in the desert (something you'll need to arrange through a travel agency), your best bet is to stay in Doha or West Bay, where the choice of accommodation is exceptional. Boutique hotels are carved from traditional buildings in the souq, the five-stars are temples to luxury, and there's even an offshore resort.

ETIQUETTE

Conversation Steer clear of politics and religion, two contentious and sensitive topics in the Middle East.

Hospitality Graciously accept refreshments when offered by Qatari hosts.

Taboos Don't show the soles of your feet (or shoes) in public, or use your left hand when passing food – these things are considered rude.

Clothing Women should cover their shoulders, upper arms and knees in public. Men should cover their shoulders, torso and upper legs.

Greetings Men and women don't usually shake hands. If a hand is offered and a Qatari doesn't feel comfortable, they may instead put their hand over their heart.

Ramadan Never eat or drink in public during this religious holiday; this is bad etiquette and is also illegal.

PRACTICALITIES

Smoking Popular in Qatar, but new laws prohibit smoking tobacco in covered public places, with hefty fines for offenders. Shisha is an exception to this rule in establishments with the proper permits. The ban includes smoking in cars where there are children under 18 years old.

Magazines The quarterly *Marhaba* (www.marhaba.qa) is an excellent source of information regarding events in Qatar and includes some interesting feature articles on local life and culture. It costs QR20. *Time Out Doha* has comprehensive listings for dining and entertainment; it costs QR9, with some content online at www.timeoutdoha.com.

TV Channel 2 on Qatar TV (QTV) broadcasts programs in English, and international satellite channels are available at the majority of hotels. The widely respected Al Jazeera satellite channel is broadcast in English and Arabic from Doha.

Weights & measures Qatar uses the metric system.

FOOD

Doha is a world-class dining destination, with some of the most esteemed chefs on the planet heading up restaurants in the city. Along with excellent high-end dining options, there's affordable and delicious Middle Eastern food, with flavours from throughout the region on offer. Meanwhile, the malls are filled with international food outlets for all budgets, from fast-food burger joints to high-street pizza restaurants, hailing from Europe, the US and beyond.

HEALTH
Before You Go

Full travel insurance is advised for travel to Qatar, as medical bills can add up to be extremely expensive. International medical insurance is available for those staying for long periods of time.

In Qatar

Healthcare standards in Qatar are good. Foreigners must be insured for healthcare via travel insurance, independent medical insurance or by their employer in Qatar. There are more than a dozen medical centres and hospitals in and around Doha.

Hamad General Hospital (Map p242; ☑443 95777; www.hamad.qa; Al Rayyan Rd) has an emergency room. Medical and dental treatment is available for tourists on a walk-in basis.

Tap water is safe to drink in Qatar.

INTERNET ACCESS

There's wi-fi (usually free) at most coffee shops, hotels, some restaurants and malls in Doha. Outside of the capital, opportunities for internet access can be few and far between.

LEGAL MATTERS

Check the law before you go to Qatar: taking alcohol into the country, engaging in extramarital relationships or public displays of sexuality, nudity, consuming pork products, homosexual behaviour and blasphemy are all illegal. Qatar has the death penalty for certain crimes (including apostasy), although execution is rare.

Breaking the law can have severe consequences. In the case of an arrest, if the detainee requests it, Qatar must notify the embassy for the detainee. Your embassy should help you contact a lawyer, contact friends and family on your behalf and will check on your welfare. Consular staff cannot get you out of prison, give you money or give you legal advice.

LGBT+ TRAVELLERS

LGBT+ travellers should avoid public displays of affection and being open about their sexuality in Qatar, where homosexual acts are illegal. Men who engage in homosexual behaviour may face up to three years in prison. People committing adultery, fornication and any speech considered offensive (including LGBT+ activism) could also be arrested and punished under Qatari law. Cross-dressing is also considered a sin and may be an arrestable offence.

In 2017, *The Danish Girl* – a movie in which Eddie Redmayne plays a transgender artist – was banned after public outcry. The Ministry of Culture thanked the public for their 'unwavering vigilance' in bringing the matter to their attention. Interestingly, though, openly gay people have been invited to perform in the country, including pop singer George Michael in 2008.

MONEY
ATMs & Credit Cards

All major credit and debit cards are accepted in large shops. Visa (Plus and Electron), MasterCard and Cirrus are accepted at ATMs of HSBC, the Qatar National Bank and the Commercial Bank of Qatar, which also accepts American Express and Diners Club cards.

Currency

The currency of Qatar is the Qatari riyal (QR). One riyal is divided into 100 dirhams. Coins are worth one, five, 10, 25 or 50 dirhams, and notes come in denominations of one, five, 10, 50, 100 and 500 riyals.

Tipping

Tips are not expected in bars, hotels or taxis. A service charge of 10-15% is usually added to top-end restaurant bills. If no tip is included, 10% is appreciated, but be discreet, as some establishments have begun to reduce wages in anticipation of tips.

OPENING HOURS

Qataris love their siesta, and Doha resembles a ghost town in the early afternoon.

Banks 7.30am to 1pm Sunday to Thursday

Restaurants 11.30am to 1.30pm and 5.30pm to midnight Saturday to Thursday, 5pm to midnight Friday

Shopping centres 10am to 10pm Saturday to Thursday, 4pm to midnight Friday

Shops 8.30am to 12.30pm and 4pm to 9pm Saturday to Thursday, 4.30pm to 9pm Friday

PUBLIC HOLIDAYS

In addition to the main Islamic holidays of Eid Al Adha and Eid Al Fitr, which are set based on the lunar calendar and thus rotate throughout the Gregorian calendar, Qatar observes the following public holidays.

National Sports Day 12 February

Accession Day 27 June

National Day 18 December

SAFE TRAVEL

Qatar is safe, and petty crime is minimal. However, it's worth checking government travel advice before your trip, in light of the Gulf-Qatar diplomatic crisis (p264).

➡ Drivers in Qatar are aggressive. If you're driving, you may be tailgated and beeped at. Cars may flash their lights at you to get out of the way.

➡ Speeding and dangerous manoeuvres are common. Pedestrians beware: drivers are unlikely to stop.

➡ Off-roaders beware of pockets of soft sand, which your 4WD may get stuck in.

➡ Women travellers may find men staring at them, though dressing modestly can alleviate this to a degree.

TELEPHONE

➡ All communications services are provided by Ooredoo (www.ooredoo.qa) and Vodafone (www.vodafone.qa).

➡ Internet calling services, such as Skype and WhatsApp, are blocked.

➡ SIM cards are available at the airport.

➡ Qatar has a fast 4G data speed.

VISAS

➡ Entry to Qatar is visa-free for citizens of 83 countries, including Australia, many EU nations, New Zealand, the UK and the US. Visa waivers are issued on arrival and are single entry.

➡ Visitors from some of these countries will be granted a 30-day visa, while others will be issued a 90-day visa. Check the Visit Qatar page for your country: www.visitqatar.qa/plan/visas-requirements.html.

➡ Visitors from countries for which visa requirements have not been lifted can apply for a tourist visa online (https://portal.moi.gov.qa/qatarvisas) for QR100.

➡ People from Saudi Arabia, Bahrain and the United Arab Emirates are currently banned from travelling to Qatar by their governments.

TRAVEL WITH CHILDREN

Qatar is a safe, easygoing, family-oriented country, and children are welcome and catered for in most places, especially malls, where there are changing facilities and activities.

There's an animal-themed **Jungle Zone** (Map p242; ☑ 449 99699; www.hyattplaza.com; Al Waab St, Hyatt Plaza; rides/activities from QR15; ⊙ 9am-10pm Sun-Wed, to midnight Thu, 1pm-midnight Fri, 9am-11pm Sat; 🅿 🚼) in Hyatt Plaza, a trampolining wonderland (p247) inside Tawar Mall, an ice rink and den of activities in the basement of City Center Doha (p260) and the Gondolania amusement area filled with fairground-like games in Villaggio Mall (p259).

Outside of the malls, kids can burn off steam at Katara Beach (p245), with its inflatable play structures, or the Megapolis Entertainment Center (p51) on The Pearl, with bowling and arcade games, and the water rides at **Aqua Park** (☑ 449 05872; www.aquaparkqatar.com; Salwa Rd, exit 29; height 90-120cm/above 120cm QR120/180; ⊙ 10am-8pm Mon, Wed & Thu, 1-10pm Tue, 10am-10pm Fri & Sun; 🚼).

Large resorts also have plenty of activities for young children, and sometimes kids clubs with daily schedules. At brunch (p252), some Doha hotels offer kids entertainers, face painting and other activities so parents can catch up with friends.

Doha is not a pedestrian-friendly place, and visitors with prams may struggle on the streets' uneven surfaces and big curbs. Nearly all public attractions have ample parking facilities, however, and the parks and Corniche are buggy-friendly.

WOMEN TRAVELLERS

Qatar is a safe place for women to travel and women can move about freely. Harassment of women is not looked upon kindly by officials. However, leering and unwanted attention is a daily occurrence for some women, especially those with fair features. It's a sad reality that the more conservatively women dress (the minimum being covering shoulders and knees) the fewer unwanted stares and less attention they will receive from men in Qatar. Although it's not necessary, women travelling solo may prefer to wear a headscarf in more rural parts of Qatar, simply to better blend in.

❶ Getting There & Away

ENTERING THE COUNTRY

No alcohol, narcotics, pornographic materials or pork-related products may be brought in through customs. Goods originating in Israel may also pose problems.

AIR

Hamad International Airport (☎ 446 56666; https://dohahamadairport.com; off F Ring Rd) is a world-class airport and Doha's international gateway. National carrier Qatar Airways (www.qatarairways.com) has transformed itself into one of the world's best airlines.

LAND

Saudi Arabia closed its land border to Qatar in 2017 due to a major diplomatic rift (p264) that's still ongoing.

SEA

Cruise ships usually dock at Hamad Port on Doha Corniche. As Saudi Arabia, the UAE and Bahrain have closed their territorial waters to Qatar, sea transport remains difficult. Travel on routes between neighbouring countries involved in the diplomatic crisis has ceased.

❶ Getting Around

BUS

The public bus system operates from Doha's central Al Ghanim Bus Station (p261), with air-conditioned services to Al Khor, Al Wakrah and Mesaieed among other destinations. Karwa Smartcards start from QR10 (including two inner-city journeys) or QR20 for unlimited bus trips around Qatar in a 24-hour period; the card can also be topped up. Routes and maps can be found at http://qatar.transit-guide.com.

CAR

Visitors can rent a car if they have a driving licence from home – but only within seven

---

❶ QATAR BLOCKADE

Because of an ongoing diplomatic rift, it is currently not possible to travel between Qatar and Saudi Arabia, the United Arab Emirates or Bahrain.

---

days of arriving in Qatar. After seven days, a temporary driving licence – issued by the Traffic Licence Office – must be obtained. It lasts for the duration of your visa, and rental agencies can arrange this for you.

Major car-rental brands are located in Doha and charge about QR100 per day for the smallest car. The cost of a 4WD is higher (around QR300 per day); an ordinary car is perfectly suitable for reaching most of Qatar's attractions, with the exception of Khor Al Adaid and some of the sand-dune seas.

Fully comprehensive insurance is highly recommended.

If you're driving around Doha, you'll discover that roundabouts are very common, treated like camel racetracks and often redundant in practice. Finding the right way out of Doha can also be difficult, as construction is happening all over town, and new roads are popping up that don't exist on GPS yet. You may find it best to look at an overview of where you are going and head in the general direction, until GPS catches up. Once out of Doha, there are far fewer roads and navigating is much easier.

TAXI

The easiest way to catch a taxi is to ask your hotel to arrange one, although technically you can wave one down from the side of the road. To visit most sights outside Doha, it's better to hire a car or arrange transport with a tour company as it usually works out considerably cheaper.

The turquoise taxis belonging to Mowasalat-Karwa offer good service. Uber (www.uber.com) is available in Doha, and short trips start at QR15.

TRAIN

The Qataris have big plans for transport around the island. Once Doha's urban metro system is complete (a planned 300km of rail and 100 stations, to open in 2019), there are plans for a rail system that connects most of Qatar's population centres. A long-distance network was also planned, connecting neighbouring countries with Qatar, but this is on hold in light of the Gulf-Qatar diplomatic crisis (p264).

Saudi Arabia
المملكة العربية السعودية

POP 32.9 MILLION

Best Places to Eat

➡ Najd Village (p279)

➡ Globe Lounge (p279)

➡ Spears (p286)

➡ Makkah Restaurant (p285)

➡ Parkers (p308)

➡ Al Marsah Seafood Restaurant (p298)

Best Places to Stay

➡ Al Koot Heritage Hotel (p307)

➡ Park Inn by Radisson (p307)

➡ Ritz-Carlton Riyadh (p279)

➡ Waldorf Astoria Qasr Al Sharq (p283)

Why Go?

If there is a final frontier of tourism left, it's Saudi Arabia. The birthplace and spiritual home of Islam, Saudi Arabia is rich in attractions and stirring symbolism. For Muslims, the cities of Mecca and Medina, rich in Prophetic significance, have no equal, while the carved temples of Madain Saleh, known as the second Petra, and the sophisticated rock art at Jubbah are the Kingdom's greatest pre-Islamic treasures.

Other wonders abound, from echoes of TE Lawrence (Lawrence of Arabia) along the Hejaz Railway to the sculpted red dunes of romantic deserts. Fascinating Riyadh is a showpiece for modern Saudi Arabia, while Jeddah's World Heritage coral architecture whisks you back to the history of this bustling pilgrim port. The pristine, azure waters of the Red Sea ache to be explored and in the south, the jewel in the Kingdom's crown, Asir, reveals breathtaking mountain scenery where mysterious and spectacular villages wait to be discovered.

When to Go
Saudi Arabia

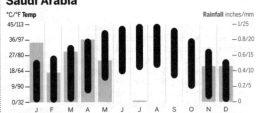

Nov–Mar Cooler temperatures make daytime weather bearable and nights surprisingly chilly.

Apr–Oct Daily temperatures above 40°C, high coastal humidity and April sandstorms.

Year round Excellent visibility on Red Sea dives; in summer morning dives are best.

Daily Costs

Saudi Arabia is not a budget destination although it is possible to eat cheaply, find budget accommodation and use the limited public transport system for around SR450 per day. Sights are cheap, however, and with an upgrade to midrange accommodation good value is to be had for SR450 to SR850 per day. Throw in some luxury accommodation, scuba diving and car hire and the budget is more likely to be over SR1000 per day.

ITINERARIES

One Week

Begin in the capital Riyadh (p276), where you'll appreciate the contradiction that is Saudi Arabia as you explore the modern architecture, indulge in world-class cuisines, and make sense of the country's history at Diraiyah. Fly to mystical Al Ula (p299), where pre-Islamic Arabia awaits in a surreal landscape. Flying south, make for Jeddah (p281), the historic pilgrim port and home of the country's biggest souq, where you can wander beneath the city's stunning Red Sea coral architecture or enjoy the region's best diving.

Two Weeks

After exploring the Unesco World Heritage Sites of Riyadh (p276) and Madain Saleh (p300), fly to the country's south to visit the beautiful Farasan Islands (p312) for a Red Sea diving odyssey. In between dips, look for pearl merchants' houses. Head to the mountain town of Abha (p310), to explore Asir National Park (p311) and its legendary villages. Climb the Kingdom's tallest peak, Mt Soudah (p311), before meandering north, taking in the region's spectacular scenery en route to Jeddah (p281). Resume a coastal excursion by heading north towards Yanbu (p295), stopping at desolate beaches and enjoying excellent seafood.

Essential Food & Drink

Mezze Truly one of the joys of Arab cooking and similar in conception to Spanish tapas, with infinite possibilities.

Fuul Mashed broad beans served with olive oil and often eaten for breakfast.

Shawarma Ubiquitous kebab- or souvlaki-style pita sandwich stuffed with meat.

Baby camel Among the tenderest of Saudi meats, it's a particular speciality of Jeddah and the Hejaz.

Red Sea seafood Fresh and varied and at its best when slow-cooked over coals or baked in the oven

Khouzi A Bedouin dish of lamb stuffed with rice, nuts, onions, sultanas, spices, eggs and a whole chicken.

AT A GLANCE

Capital Riyadh

Country code 966

Currency Saudi riyal (SAR)

Language Arabic

Money ATMs widespread; credit cards widely accepted.

Visas Business and pilgrimage visas, and some visitor visas

Exchange Rates

Australia	A$1	SR2.69
Canada	C$1	SR2.83
Euro zone	€1	SR4.29
Japan	¥100	SR3.43
New Zealand	NZ$1	SR2.56
UK	UK£1	SR4.90
US	US$1	SR3.75

For current exchange rates, see www.xe.com.

Resources

Lonely Planet (www.lonely planet.com/saudi-arabia) Destination information, hotel bookings, traveller forum and more.

Arab News (www.arab news.com) Up-to-the-minute news from a Saudi perspective.

Saudi Tourism (www.saudi tourism.com.sa) Some useful information and pointers.

Saudi Arabian Information Resources (www.saudinf. com) History, culture, economics and helpful links.

Saudi Arabia Highlights

1 Jeddah (p281) Wandering beneath coral architecture and hunting bargains in the country's biggest souq.

2 Jubbah (p305) Admiring the country's greatest open-air gallery of ancient rock art.

3 Mecca (p288) Staring in awe at the hypnotic *tawaf* inside the world's biggest mosque.

4 Asir National Park (p311) Standing atop the Kingdom's tallest peak and exploring its mysterious villages.

5 Yanbu (p295) Diving the dazzling Seven Sisters.

6 Hejaz Railway (p298) Listening for the ghost of TE Lawrence and exploring Arabia's romantic railway remnants.

7 Farasan Islands (p312) Admiring the islands' beautifully carved houses.

8 Dammam (p307) Enjoying world-class opera and theatre here at the country's premiere performing-arts venue, Ithra.

9 Madain Saleh (p300) Marvelling at the evocative rock-hewn tombs and sublime desert setting of the 'other Petra'.

10 Diraiyah (p280) Reliving the capital's capture beneath the ruins where modern Saudi Arabia was born.

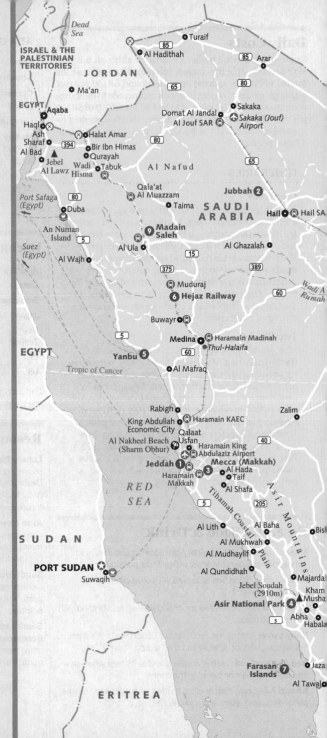

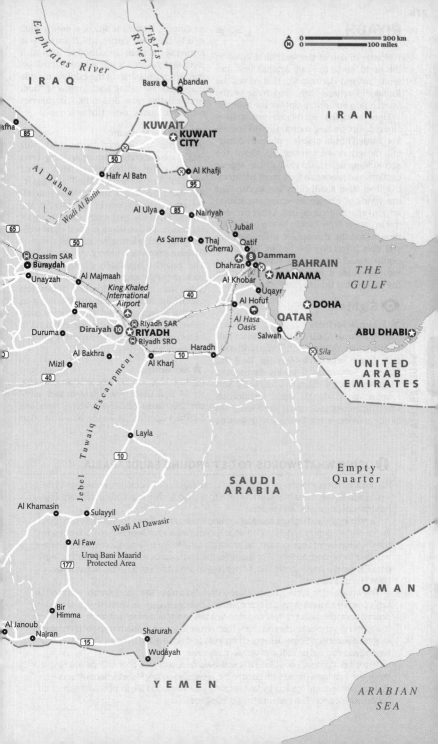

RIYADH

الرياض

⟲ 011 / POP 5.3 MILLION

Welcome to one of the wealthiest cities in the world, home to Saudi Arabia's best museum, a World Heritage Site that relates the Kingdom's genesis story, and some of the finest hotels and restaurants in the country.

Once a walled, mud-brick way station along desert trading routes, Riyadh (meaning 'garden') from afar is a picture of soaring modern towers rising up above the surrounding desert. Up close, it can appear cautious and sober and feels more conservative than other Saudi cities like Jeddah. But the winds of change sweeping the nation are also affecting the capital. A long overdue metro system is on its way, as is a public bus service, and the atmosphere is far more liberal than it has ever felt before. Riyadh recently hosted the country's very first music festival, where a female singer performed live for the first time in Saudi history.

◉ Sights

★ Masmak Fortress
HISTORIC SITE

(Qasr Al Masmak; ⟲ 011 411 0091; Al Imam Turki Ibn Abdullah Ibn Muhammad St; ⫼ victory.detained. cable; ⊙ men 8am-noon & 4-9pm Sun, Tue & Thu, 9am-noon Sat, women & families 8am-noon & 4-9pm Mon & Wed, 4-7.30pm Fri & Sat) **FREE** Surrounded by sand, this squat fortification was built around 1865 and is like a scene out of the movies: a big fortress representing

an empire. It was the site of a daring 1902 raid by Ibn Saud, during which a spear was hurled at the main entrance door with such force that the head is still lodged in the doorway. Highlights among the exhibits include maps and fascinating photographs of Saudi Arabia dating from 1912 to 1937, in galleries converted from *diwans* (living rooms).

★ National Museum
MUSEUM

(King Abdul Aziz Historical Center; ⟲ 011 402 9500; www.nationalmuseum.org.sa; King Faisal St, Al Murabba; ⫼ voucher.skews.twists; adult/child SR10/free; ⊙ noon-8pm Mon-Thu, 4-8pm Fri, 8am-8pm Sat, noon-2pm Sun; ℗) This state-of-the-art museum is one of the finest in the Middle East. Encased within modernist architecture, its two floors contain eight well-designed and informative galleries covering Arabian prehistory, history, culture and art. The galleries beautifully display evocative rock carvings, engaging models and even a full-scale reconstruction of a Nabataean tomb from Madain Saleh (p300). Films in English shown on 180-degree screens complement the exhibits, as do virtual visits to historical sites and other excellent interactive displays.

★ Sky Bridge
VIEWPOINT

(⟲ 011 211 2222, ext 109; www.kingdomcentre.com. sa; 94 St, Al Olaya; ⫼ velocity.handy.slap; adult/child 2-9yr/under 2yr SR63/21/free; ⊙ noon-11pm Sat-Thu, 4-11pm Fri) Not for the faint-hearted or

---

❶ USING WHAT3WORDS TO GET AROUND SAUDI ARABIA

It's not always easy to find your way around in a region with sometimes downright confusing addresses, roads that seem to wish to remain anonymous and no standard English transliteration of Arabic words.

To help locals and visitors navigate around the country, Saudi Tourism has partnered with a digital address system called what3words (www.what3words.com). Developed in the UK, what3words has divided the entire planet into 3m by 3m squares that each have a unique three-word address. For example, the what3words address for Riyadh's Kingdom Centre is ///talker.basin.last. Wherever you are in the world right now has its own what3words address.

The what3words system is particularly useful in a place like Saudi Arabia, which often lacks precise address details and consistent spellings in English. Whether you're tracking down a nomadic desert retreat or ordering a taxi to a specific mall entrance, what3words is also much simpler to use and share than remembering a random string of latitude and longitude numbers. Some delivery companies and ride-hailing services in Saudi Arabia have already signed up to the what3words system.

To try it out yourself, download the what3words app to your phone. Once you have the three-word address (listed with each of the reviews in Lonely Planet's Saudi Arabia information), enter it into the app by text or using your voice, and the location will appear on your mobile device. The system also works offline.

sufferers of vertigo, here high-speed lifts fly you at 180km/h to the 99th-floor Sky Bridge, inside the Kingdom Centre. The views from the highest place in Riyadh are truly breathtaking. Avoid weekends and evenings after 6pm, when it can get very crowded. Tickets can be bought at the booth on the 2nd floor near the Carolina Herrera shop or at the machines nearby. Both only accept cash.

Antiquities Museum   MUSEUM
(☏ 011 467 4942; College of Tourism & Antiquities, King Saud University, Ash Shaikh Hasan Ibn Abdullah Al Ash Shaikh; ⊕ mindset.indicate.marshes; ⊙ 8am-2pm Sun-Thu; ℗) **FREE** This museum is home to objects found during the Faw and Rabdha excavations (sites in the south and north of Saudi Arabia) by King Saud University in the 1970s. These include beautiful little Roman and Hellenic statues of Hercules and Apollo. There are also ancient inscriptions yet to be deciphered, porcelain, pottery, jewellery, coins, frescoes: items that suggest a highly cultured society once lived at the excavated sites.

Souq Al Jamal   MARKET
(off Hwy 80, Al Janadriyyah; ⊕ working.barefoot.free; ⊙ sunrise-sunset; ℗) One of the largest in the Arabian Peninsula, Riyadh's camel market is a fascinating place to wander. Late afternoon is when the traders really find their voices. If you want to put in a bid, you'll need SR5000 to SR10,000. The market is north of the Dammam road 30km from the city centre (take the Thumamah exit), but check with locals first as the development in this area means the location can be moved.

Globe Experience   NOTABLE BUILDING
(Al Faisaliah Tower; ☏ 011 273 3000; King Fahd Branch Rd, Al Mathar Ash Shamali; ⊕ showcase.poet.lace; viewing platform adult/child SR60/free; ⊙ 11am-11pm) The Globe Experience is a spectacular viewing platform inside an enormous glass ball that's 24m in diameter, made of 655 glass panels and suspended just below the top of Al Faisaliah Tower. The panoramic views of Riyadh from inside the Globe are most magical at sunset and early evening. Designed by British architect Norman Foster and built in 2000 by the Saudi Bin Laden construction company, the Al Faisaliah was the first of Riyadh's major skyscrapers.

Kingdom Centre   NOTABLE BUILDING
(☏ 011 211 2222; www.kingdomcentre.com.sa; 94 St, Al Olaya; ⊕ talker.basin.last) Riyadh's land-

---

RIYADH ACTIVITIES

For indoor fun, there's lively dance tracks, a big-screen TV, a billiards table and a swank interior at **Strike Bowling Alley** (☏ 011 802 8333; www.ritzcarlton.com; Ritz-Carlton Riyadh, Makkah Al Mukarramah Rd; ⊕ frizz.pines.unity; per person SR120; ⊙ 4pm-midnight Sun-Wed, families only noon-midnight Thu & Fri, women only 4pm-midnight Sat). For outdoor activity, try a stroll in **Addiriyah Park** (Al Imam Abdulaziz Ibn Saud Rd, Al Bujairi Quarter; ⊕ certainty.tunes.emailed), in view of historic Al Diraiyah, or take the kids on a mini-train tour of **Riyadh Zoo** (☏ 011 477 9523; Mosab Ibn Umair St, Az Zahra; ⊕ forms.tanked.falls; adult/child SR10.50/5.25; ⊙ 8.30am-5pm Tue-Sat, 8.30am-1pm Mon; 🛝), where highlights include the native but nearly extinct bird, the houbara bustard.

---

mark tower, rising 302m high, is a stunning piece of modern architecture – it's particularly conspicuous at night, when the upper sweep is lit with constantly changing coloured lights. Its most distinctive feature is the steel-and-glass 300-tonne bridge connecting the two towers. High-speed lifts fly you (at 180km/h) to the 99th-floor Sky Bridge, from where the views are breathtaking.

☞ Tours

The award-winning **Haya Tours** (☏ 011 229 1181; www.hayatour.com; 1st fl, Alia Plaza, Thumamah Rd, An Najris; ⊕ blanket.awards.sparkle; per person SR126-1260; ⊙ 9am-4pm Sun-Thu) can arrange trips to almost every corner of Saudi Arabia with English-speaking guides. For trips round town, there are open-top **City Sightseeing** (www.citysightseeing-riyadh.com; Olaya St, Al Olaya; ⊕ glory.sheet.winners; 1-day ticket adult/child/family SR112/68/294; ⊙ red & blue 4pm-midnight Mon-Thu, from 2pm Fri & Sat, green 2pm-midnight Fri & Sat) buses.

⚝ Festivals & Events

Janadriyah National Festival   CULTURAL
(www.janadria.org.sa; off Hwy 550; ⊕ advising.joker.eclectic; ⊙ Feb/Mar) Saudi Arabia's largest cultural festival runs over two weeks at Al Janadriyah heritage village, 42km northeast of Riyadh. Commencing with the King's Cup (an epic camel race with up to 2000

Riyadh

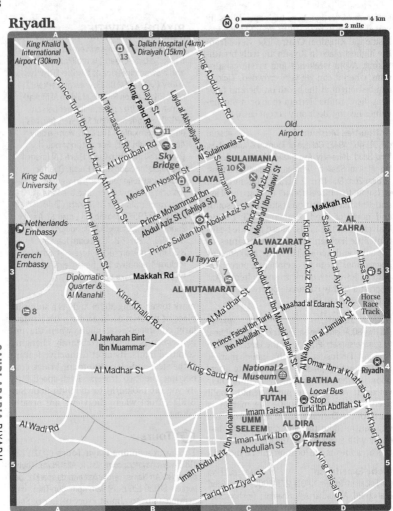

participants racing across a 19km track), the program includes traditional songs, dances and poetry competitions, as well as falconry demonstrations and exhibitions of traditional crafts from around the Kingdom.

🛏 Sleeping

Coral Olaya Hotel   HOTEL **$**
(☑ 011 465 5656; www.coralolayahotelriyadh.site; Abdulmalik Ibn Marwan St, Al Olaya; 🖥 regard. bonkers.saloons; r/ste SR278/552; 🅿🛜) With large, smart rooms, a hearty breakfast included in the price and a central location, the Coral Olaya Hotel is a great budget option.

★ **Al Khozama Hotel**   HOTEL **$$**
(☑ 011 465 4650; www.alkhozamahotels.com; Olaya St, Al Olaya; 🖥 twist.mash.guardian; r from SR400; 🆒) Though the rooms here aren't large, they are comfortable, well furnished and squarely aimed at the modern business traveller. With a lively lobby, a good bakery and two reputable restaurants, it's a popular choice.

Doubletree by Hilton – Al Muroj Business Gate   HOTEL **$$**
(☑ 9200 09681; www.doubletree3.hilton.com; Northern Ring Branch Rd, Al Muruj; 🖥 teach.havens. spinning; r from SR579, ste SR734; 🅿🛜) Located

Riyadh

in northern Riyadh, Doubletree Al Muroj provides easy access to the city centre and most tourist sites. As expected from this international brand, it doesn't skimp on luxe furnishings or in-house eating options, and the customer service is exceptional. All the rooms come with great views, but it's the spacious suites that make this an excellent choice.

★ Ritz-Carlton Riyadh   HOTEL $$$
(☑ 011 802 8020; www.ritzcarlton.com; Makkah Al Mukarramah Rd, Al Hada; ⊞ paddings.defends.plotted; r from SR1500; ℗ ⊛ ⊛) This hotel sums up Riyadh 'luxury'. A Hollywood-like driveway greets you at the entrance to grounds that boast 210,000 sq metres of pristine, landscaped gardens. The rooms, as you might expect, are huge and sumptuous, with many including butler service. Staff are attentive and considerate, and there is an excellent buffet in the restaurant.

It was here in 2017 that Crown Prince Mohammed Bin Salman locked up around 200 people, including 17 princes, as part of an anti-corruption sweep, earning the hotel the title of the 'world's most luxurious prison'.

Al Faisaliah Hotel   HOTEL $$$
(☑ 011 273 2000; www.alfaisaliahhotels.com; Al Faisaliah Tower, Rd 38, Al Olaya; ⊞ showcase.poet.lace; r from SR1815; ℗ ⊛ ⊛) All the details of a fabulous modern hotel are present at Al Faisaliah, including fresh orchids and chocolates delivered daily to your room, and your own butler available 24 hours a day. Il Terrazzo restaurant enjoys a fine reputation and the hotel is hugely popular with Riyadh's upper crust for celebrating weddings and birthdays.

✗ Eating & Drinking

Zaatar W Zeit   MIDDLE EASTERN $
(☑ 9200 03542; www.zaatarwzeit.net; Prince Muhammad Bin Abdulaziz Rd, Al Wurud; ⊞ surveyed.siesta.crunch; wraps SR25-43; ⊙ 6am-1.30am) This little eating outlet built its reputation on its delicious, freshly baked *manakeesh* (flatbread), which can come stuffed with a host of ingredients, including chicken, steak, falafel and the restaurant's namesake, *zaatar* (thyme and sesame seed). Try it mixed with *labneh* (yoghurt) for a delicious local snack.

★ Najd Village   MIDDLE EASTERN $$
(☑ 9200 33511; www.najdvillage.com; Abi Bakr As Siddiq Rd, Al Mursalat; ⊞ inquest.pine.wording; mains SR21; ⊙ noon-12.30am) This place serves Saudi food in a Saudi setting, where some rooms even have a traditional fireplace. It's the perfect place to sample popular regional dishes such as *kabsa* (meat with rice) or *hashi* (baby camel). The set menu (SR125; minimum five people) includes 14 mains, coffee, dates and *bakhoor* (incense). Fridays and Saturday are the only days when families are welcome.

★ Globe Lounge   INTERNATIONAL $$$
(☑ 011 273 2222; www.alfaisaliahhotels.com; Al Faisaliah Tower, Rd 38, Al Olaya; ⊞ showcase.poet.lace; mains from SR210; ⊙ noon-2.30pm & 8pm-12.30am; ☎) One of five restaurants in Al Faisaliah Tower, the Globe Lounge has spectacular views that make it the most romantic spot in town. Cosy and dimly lit, this is one of the best places to dine in Riyadh. Offerings from the international menu include delicious Wagyu steaks and Canadian lobster.

WORTH A TRIP

DIRAIYAH

The ancestral home of the Al Saud family in Wadi Hanifa, the Turaif district in Diraiyah, west of Riyadh, was declared a Unesco World Heritage Site in 2010 and is one of the most evocative places in the Kingdom. The site has been closed to the public for restoration, with plans to reopen in early 2020.

Special permission to enter and explore the site with a private guide (arranged through travel agencies) may be possible. The southwestern Turaif quarter is the historic heart of the site, while the Ghusaiba quarter was the Saudi capital until 1683. On the eastern bank of Wadi Hanifa a visitor centre and museum were under construction at the time of research. There's no public transport to Diraiyah, which is 25km northwest of Al Bathaa. A one-way taxi from central Riyadh costs SR50 (or from SR200 return, including waiting time).

Maharaja East by Vineet　　　INDIAN $$$
(☑ 011 464 1111; www.maharajaeast.com; King Mohammed V, Al Olaya; ⓜ dialect.chef.surviving; mains SR130-275; ⊗ noon-3.30pm & 6.30-11pm Mon-Sat; ☎) One to book for a special occasion, this upscale restaurant offers a refreshing spin on standard Indian cuisine. Creating dishes such as classic Punjabi butter chicken to the innovative spinach tikki with fig chutney, Vineet Bhatia, a three-starred Michelin chef, knows how to please every palate (and you might even get to meet him).

Spazio 77　　　INTERNATIONAL $$$
(☑ 011 211 1888; www.spazio77.com; Kingdom Tower, 94 St, Al Olaya; ⓜ spray.assets.physical; mains from SR120; ⊗ 9am-1pm & 4pm-1am Sat-Thu, from 1pm Fri) In the nook of the 'necklace' of the Kingdom Tower, Spazio 77 is a combination brasserie, coffee house and luxury restaurant serving fine-dining dishes that use ingredients such as veal and truffles. It's where the great and the good come when they are in town. Enter via the mall's ground floor.

Al Masaa Cafe　　　CAFE
(☑ 050 684 0235; Al Urubah Rd, Al Wurud; ⓜ snippet.pumps.miss; ⊗ 6am-2am Sat-Thu, 6-10.30am & 2pm-2am Fri; ☎) This vibrant cafe in the heart of Riyadh is all about the views of the Kingdom Tower opposite. Arrive before the sun sets, sit with a coffee and delicious cheesecake, and watch as the tower and its 'necklace' feature slowly light up in an array of pinks and blues. The cafe also serves food.

☆ Entertainment

King Abdulaziz Racetrack　　　HORSE RACING
(☑ 011 477 3802, 050 300 8044; www.frusiya.com; Al Janadriyah Rd, Equestrian Club Riyadh; ⓜ bribes.bridges.column; SR10; ⊗ 2-6.30pm or until last race, Fri & Sat Sep-Mar) A popular weekend destination, the King Abdulaziz Racetrack exemplifies the Kingdom's rich equestrian heritage. The 5000-seat grandstand flanks the finish line, and results from each of the 10 daily races are displayed via the electronic leaderboard. Trackside viewing areas offer the best vantage point of the finish line, as well as up-close encounters with the racing talent.

🛍 Shopping

In a country where public diversions are few, shopping has become a national sport, and there is no shortage of high-end shopping centres and malls in Riyadh, including **Al Nakheel Mall** (☑ 9200 00262; www.arabiancentres.com; Uthman Ibn Affan Rd, Al Mughrizat; ⓜ game.calculating.waffle; ⊗ 9.30am-midnight Sat-Thu, from 4pm Fri; ☎) and **Kingdom Tower** (☑ 011 211 2222; www.kingdomcentre.com.sa; 94 St, Al Olaya; ⓜ talker.basin.last; ⊗ 9am-midnight Sat-Thu, from 4pm Fri; ☎) with 40 exclusive women's boutiques. For gold, head to **Uwais Souq** (☑ 011 470 0001; Olaya St, Al Olaya; ⓜ stubble.bought.magpie; ⊗ 10am-10pm Sat-Thu, 5-10pm Fri) and to **Souq Al Thumairi** (Al Thumairi St, Ad Dirah; ⓜ ticking.whom.afford; ⊗ 9am-noon & 4-9pm Sat-Thu, 4-9pm Fri) for coffee pots and silvery jewellery. **Jarir Bookstore** (☑ 9200 00089; www.jarir.com; Olaya St, Al Olaya; ⓜ blankets.brush.scraper; ⊗ 9am-11pm Sat-Thu, 4-11pm Fri) has the best collection of English-language books on culture and history.

ⓘ Information

Al Tayyar (☑ 9200 12333; www.altayyargroup.com; Al Takhassusi Rd, Al Olaya; ⓜ overtime.half.stubble; ⊗ 9am-1.30pm & 4.30-8pm Sat-Thu) The largest travel company in Saudi Arabia and one of the most reputable, Al Tayyar can organise car hire, air tickets, accommodation and tours.

Medical services These are excellent in Riyadh, with hospitals and pharmacies widespread and easy to get to.

Saudi Commission for Tourism & National Heritage (19 988; from overseas 011 261 4750;

www.sauditourism.sa) A contact centre dedicated to assisting tourists.

ℹ️ Getting There & Away

Riyadh's **King Khalid International Airport** (☑ 9200 02016; www.kkia.gov.sa; King Salman Rd, An Narjis; ⓦ vicinity.journeying.empires) is 25km north of the city centre, and the recent growth in budget airlines means there are now regular flights to every corner of Saudi Arabia.

Riyadh has two train stations. The oldest, **Riyadh Railway Station** (SRO Rail; ☑ 9200 08886; www.sro.org.sa; Hasan Al Shawri St, As Sinaiyah; ⓦ endings.scary.wipes), is for trains to Dammam via Hofuf and Abqaiq, while the new **SAR Railway Station** (☑ 9200 00329, WhatsApp 05 331 04455; www.sar.com.sa; Ath Thumamah Rd, Al Munsiyah; ⓦ contact. workshop.totally) serves the country's western interior, passing through Majmah, Qassim, Hail and Jauf.

Riyadh's main **Saptco bus station** (☑ 9200 00877; www.saptco.com.sa; off Southern Ring Branch Rd, Al Aziziyah; ⓦ camped.home.void) has buses regularly leaving for Dammam, Buraydah, Jeddah, Mecca and Medina.

TO/FROM AIRPORT

Buses (SR15, every two hours) run from 8am to 10pm between the Saptco bus station (p281) and the airport, via the main **local bus stop** (☑ 9200 00877; www.saptco.com.sa; Al Bathaa St, Al Amal; ⓦ feels.magnets.native).

A taxi from the airport to the city centre costs SR50 to SR80, depending on the traffic, and Uber (www.uber.com) and Careem (www.careem.com) also operate here.

ℹ️ Getting Around

Riyadh's white taxis charge around SR10 for a journey of 1km to 2km; always make sure the meter is turned on.

Increasingly popular and often far more convenient are Uber (www.uber.com) and Careem (www.careem.com). The latter is marginally cheaper.

HEJAZ   الحجاز

Meaning 'barrier', the Hejaz region's name is taken from the huge escarpment that separates it from the great plateaus of the interior. Outward looking, cosmopolitan and home to the most important pilgrim sites for nearly two billion people, the Hejaz is one of the most visited regions anywhere in the world. But even if you're not Muslim, you'll be wowed by Jeddah's World Heritage architecture, blown away by awesome Red Sea dive sites and unable to resist the amazingly diverse cuisine brought about by cultural cross-pollination.

Jeddah   جدة

☑ 012 / POP 3.5 MILLION

The historic crossroads of pilgrims and traders, and the traditional gateway to Mecca, Jeddah is the most fascinating of Saudi Arabia's major cities, with a cosmopolitan and liberal air not present anywhere else in the Kingdom. Visitors will love the city's World Heritage Red Sea architecture, its bustling souq, the laid-back coastline that's home to fantastic dive sites, and its diverse, world-class cuisine.

The commercial capital of Saudi Arabia, modern Jeddah is more than a thousand times the size of the ancient city where it is believed the mother of humanity, 'Eve', was laid to rest. These days Jeddah is fast-paced and a bit rough around the edges, with high-rises and a waterfront culture that are symbols of the Kingdom's modernisation. This blend of old and new is what makes the 'bride of the Red Sea' such an appealing destination, and often the first Saudi city foreigners like to visit.

👁️ Sights

The **Corniche** (Corniche Rd, Al Naeem; ⓦ belonged.wished.drop; Ⓟ) in northern Jeddah has a great new walkway that begins near the Hilton. The coastal area is also home to a series of famous contemporary sculptures that line the wide pedestrian pathways for approximately 30km north of the port. Among the highlights are four bronzes by British artist Henry Moore and works by Spaniard Joan Miró.

⭐ **Al Tayibat City Museum for International Civilisation**   MUSEUM
(Map p282; ☑ 012 683 0049; Mansur Al Katib, Al Faisaliyyah; ⓦ imported.tribune.headed; SR50; ☺ 8am-noon & 5-9pm Sat-Thu) This privately owned four-floor collection has displays ranging from pre-Islamic artefacts, exquisite Islamic manuscripts, old coins and weaponry to stunning furniture, pottery and traditional Saudi dress. Replicas of home interiors from every region are also featured. Exhibits are accompanied by excellent information panels, as well as dioramas of the Kingdom's provinces. If you get here

Jeddah

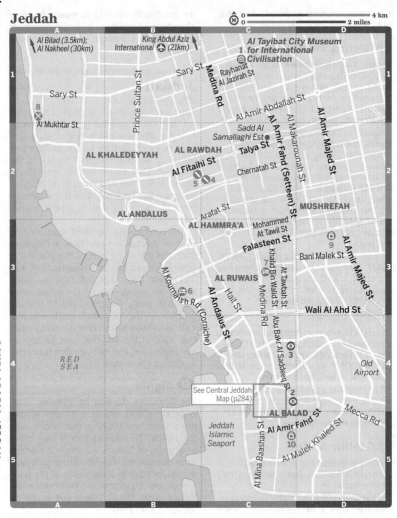

Jeddah

◎ Top Sights
1 Al Tayibat City Museum for
International Civilisation C1

◎ Sights
2 Bab Makkah C4
3 Little India C4

✦ Activities, Courses & Tours
4 Blue Reef Divers C2
5 Red Sea Divers B2

🛏 Sleeping
6 InterContinental Hotel B3
7 Radisson Blu....................................C3

✕ Eating
8 Al Nakheel Restaurant A1
Makkah Restaurant ....(see 3)
Spears ....(see 6)

🛍 Shopping
9 Jarir Bookstore D3
10 Souq C5

JEDDAH'S OLD TOWN

Jeddah's main attractions are all within the old town or 'Al Balad', with its amazing series of narrow medieval alleys, where beautiful houses made of Red Sea coral have stunning *mashrabiyya* (wooden lattice balconies). A recreated **city gate** (Map p284; Abu Inabah, Al Balad; ⓜ sympathy.cute.eats) marks the northern entrance to Al Balad, and is surrounded by some of the most beautiful historic houses, including the **Sharbatly House** (Map p284; Al Matt'haf Lane, Al Balad; ⓜ times.pothole.muffin), while **Bab Makkah** (Map p282; Old Makkah Rd, Al Balad; ⓜ shut.defeat.grounded), historically the most important gate for Jeddah, Arabia's official pilgrim port, stands at the eastern entrance at the beginning of the road to Islam's holiest city. In the last 14 centuries, billions of pilgrims have passed beneath it.

Within the old town, the most accessible house is occupied by the privately owned **Matbouli House Museum** (Map p284; ☑ 5056 23933; Souq Al Alawi, Al Balad; ⓜ follow.diverts.digs; SR10; ⊘ 5pm-midnight) (with its old gramophones and telephones and uneven floors, stairwells and beautiful wood ceilings), while the finest example is **Naseef House** (Map p284; ☑ 012 647 2280; Souq Al Alawi, Al Balad; ⓜ chef.weddings.pass; SR25; ⊘ hours vary), where the country's founding father King Abdul Aziz lived. Look out for the ramps installed by the king to allow his camel-mounted messengers to ride to the upper terrace, and the huge tree left of the door. As recently as 1920 this was the only tree in the whole of Jeddah.

The old town has some of the country's most beautiful historic mosques – or at least remnants of them – including the snow-white, Ottoman-era **Hanafi Mosque Minaret** (Map p284; off Al Basha, Al Balad; ⓜ truly.branded.slipped; ⊘ prayer times) and the tastefully restored **Al Shafee Mosque** (Map p284; Suq Al Jami, Al Balad; ⓜ passing.stews.winner; ⊘ daylight hrs; Ⓟ), both named after famous Sunni theologians. Non-Muslim visitors can enter the latter freely outside of prayer times, but must dress modestly and remove shoes. The mosque is close to the bustling ancient **Souq Al Alawi** (Map p284; Al Balad; ⓜ comb.harvest.napkins; ⊘ 8am-1pm & 5-9pm Sat-Wed), the Kingdom's most extensive bazaar, where you can buy anything from footwear to exotic spices.

early enough, you may get lucky and receive a private tour.

Al Rahma Mosque
MOSQUE

(Corniche Rd, Al Naeem; ⓜ shiver.random.slug; ⊘ daylight hours; Ⓟ) This mosque in the north of Jeddah sits on stilts and seemingly floats on the Red Sea. Visitors come to wander in the open courtyard and enjoy the cooling sea breeze, especially at sunset. The mosque is equally impressive inside, where modern twists on classical Andalusian patterns decorate the main hall and a pretty dome sits in the centre on a ring of stained glass. When the sun shines through it's as if the dome is floating as well.

Little India
AREA

(Map p282; cnr Ras Tanurah & King Fahd Rds, Al Baghdadiyah Al Sharqiyah; ⓜ funnels.weep.stew) There is a distinct air of the subcontinent in this square mile just off the King Fahd Rd. Clothes shops sell saris, grocers stock fresh curry leaves and hawkers refer to everyone as *vhai* (Hindi for 'brother'). You'll get the best curries and the sweetest *karak chai*

(sweetened tea boiled with spices) here as you soak up a taste of Jeddah's South Asian culture.

🛏 Sleeping

Radisson Blu
HOTEL $$

(Map p282; ☑ 012 652 1234; www.radissonblu.com; Medina Rd, Al Sharafeyah; ⓜ vampire.student.runner; d SR500; Ⓟ 🛜 ☀) Smart, spacious rooms in a central location, with all the politeness and professionalism expected of this international chain. The hotel has even tried to blend into the locality with an impressive effort at recreating Hejazi *mashrabiyya* (covered balconies) all over its large building. There's also a great Japanese restaurant here.

★ Waldorf Astoria
Qasr Al Sharq
HOTEL $$$

(☑ 9200 09565; www.waldorfastoria.com; Al Kurnaysh Rd, Ash Shati; ⓜ whips.download.rivers; s/ste SR2255/4850; Ⓟ 🛜 ☀) Decorated by the same designer who worked on Dubai's famous sail-shaped Burj Al Arab, this five-star hotel

Central Jeddah

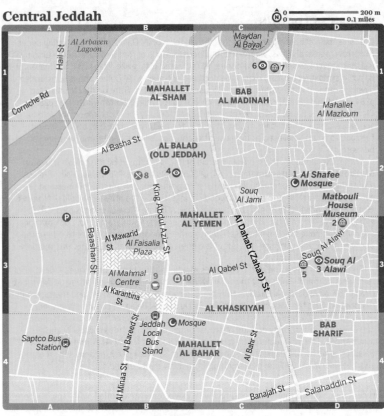

Central Jeddah

prides itself on luxury. The dazzling decor includes no less than 60kg of gold leaf, silk curtains and a 12m Swarovski crystal chandelier. All the rooms have a 42-inch plasma TV (with obligatory gold panelling) and 24-hour butler service.

InterContinental Hotel HOTEL $$$
(Map p282; ☎ 012 229 5555; www.ihg.com; Al Kurnaysh Rd, Al Ruwais; ⅲ mincing.promote.party;

r/ste SR1225/1676; P⊅≋) The chic Inter-Continental boasts three main drawcards: a waterside location with a private beach, good facilities (including decent restaurants) and great attention to detail – right down to complimentary underwater cameras and playing cards for kids. It is also home to the excellent Brazilian restaurant Spears (p286).

🍴 Eating & Drinking

To catch the buzz surrounding Jeddah's burgeoning food scene, head to the Al Rawdah district in North Jeddah – it has virtually become restaurant row. Consult www.jeddah food.com for up-to-date reviews of Jeddah's eateries.

⭐ **Wong Solo**   INDONESIAN $
(Map p284; ☎ 5660 19911, 5360 19441; www.wong solo.com; Al Mawared Alleyway, Al Balad; 🔳 hidden. echo.starch; buffet SR20, mains SR17-30; ☉10am-2pm & 4-10pm) 'The man from Solo' (a city in Java Island, Indonesia) is an excellent budget Indonesian restaurant close to the start of Al Balad. It's been wholly claimed by visiting Indonesian pilgrims who arrive in hordes and will tell anyone who listens that it's the closest taste of home in all of Saudi Arabia.

⭐ **Makkah Restaurant**   PAKISTANI $
(Map p282; ☎ 012 604 0016; Ras Al Ayn, Al Bagh-dadiyah Al Sharqiyah; 🔳 busters.aimless.majority; mains SR12-24; ☉1-3.30pm & 6pm-midnight) The secret's out with this no-frills Pakistani restaurant, once frequented only by Little India's South Asian community. Now you'll be rubbing shoulders with Saudis and Western expats digging into delicious spicy dishes from the subcontinent, such as the signature mutton *makhni karai* (lamb curry), served with freshly baked, warm flatbread, and the excellent *chana dhal* (split lentils).

⭐ **Al Nakheel Restaurant**   MIDDLE EASTERN $$
(Map p282; ☎ 012 606 3161; off Al Kurnaysh Rd, Ash Shati; 🔳 pastime.suffice.overhaul; mains SR30-80; ☉8am-1am Sat-Thu, to 1.30am Fri; 🛜) Styled like a traditional tent, with open sides to let the sea breezes in, the huge courtyard with large traditional couches is popular, especially on weekends, when groups of friends dine from the excellent traditional menu (though even the spaghetti bolognese is good) before reclining to puff away on fruity shisha. This really is the place to spend a balmy Jeddah evening.

RED SEA DIVING

Top Dive Sites in Saudi Arabia

Featuring clear year-round visibility, superb reefs and an abundance of sharks, rays and smaller tropical fish:

Sharm Obhur Coral Popular for night dives. Near Jeddah.

Abu Madafi Includes the *Staphonos* wreck. Expansive site, 40km north of Jeddah.

Abu Faramish Famous for the wreck of *Ann Ann*. Two hours north of Jeddah.

Seven Sisters Sightings of hammerhead sharks. Off the coast of Yanbu.

Jabal Al Lith Whale sharks from March to June, 200km south of Jeddah.

Farasan Banks Depths from 10m to 500m, abundant fish. Near Jazan.

Trusted Operators

Blue Reef Divers (Map p282; ☎ 012 618 1777; Al Buraydi, Al Andalus; 🔳 foil.notebook.broke; half-day diving per person SR250; ☉9am-11pm Sat-Thu, 7am-11pm Fri & Sat) Offers classes for beginners.

Red Sea Divers (Map p282; ☎ 012 660 6368; redseadivers@arabnet.com.sa; Abdul Majid Shubukshi, Al Andalus; 🔳 back.bowls.admires; half-day diving per person SR350; ☉8am-10.30pm Sat-Thu) One of the oldest dive shops in Jeddah.

Dolphin Free Divers (☎ 054 642 0600, 054 772 2400; King Abdullah Rd; 🔳 voucher.observer.dragging; half-day/1-week course from SR200/1800; ☉10am-noon & 5-11pm Sat-Thu, 5-11pm Fri) Family-run outfit in Yanbu with freediving expertise.

Dive Time (☎ 014 425 3000, 014 421 3132; www.thedivetime.com; Ubbadah Ibn As Samit St; 🔳 watches.clothed.tribune; 1 day diving SR300, 1-week course SR1500; ☉8.30am-12.30pm & 4-11pm Sat-Thu, 4-11pm Fri) Operates from Tabuk.

Jazan Diver (☎ 056 833 5114, 050 066 0852; www.jazandiver.net; King Fahd Rd, Jazan Harbour; 🔳 leopard.parks.pounding; half-day/7-day course SR500/1800; ☉9am-11pm Sat-Thu, 5.30-10pm Fri) Local knowledge of the Farasan Islands.

★ **Spears** BRAZILIAN $$$
(Map p282; ☑ 012 229 5555; www.ihg.com; 1st fl, InterContinental Hotel, Al Kurnaysh Rd, Al Ruwais; ⊞ mincing.promote.party; buffet adult/child SR225/110; ⊗ 1-4pm & 7pm-1am; ☎) Jeddah's introduction to the Brazilian *churrascaria* is an excellent dining choice. Keep your wooden indicator in the upright green position and the delicately spiced choice cuts of grilled meat will just keep coming to your table at this all-you-can-eat buffet-style restaurant on the 1st floor of the elegant InterContinental Hotel (p284).

Qadah Cafe CAFE
(Map p284; 6th fl, Al Mahmal Centre, King Abdul Aziz St, Al Balad; ⊞ struck.edits.gala; ⊗ 9am-11pm Sat-Thu, from 4pm Fri; ☎) This cafe is all about the great views over the dome and minaret of the Al Mahmal Centre mall's mosque and out across the south of Old Jeddah. It's a good spot to take a breath and grab a coffee and a slice of their excellent biscotti cake ahead of tackling Al Balad.

🛍 Shopping

★ **Jarir Bookstore** BOOKS
(Map p282; ☑ 9200 00089; www.jarir.com; Falasteen St, Bani Malik; ⊞ fixed.sailed.minder; ⊗ 9am-11pm Sat-Thu, from 4.30pm Fri) Jeddah's best bookstore, with the city's widest selection of English-language books including guidebooks, maps and excellent titles on local and national history and heritage.

Souq MARKET
(Map p282; off King Fahd Rd; ⊞ poems.lamps.changed; ⊗ 10am-11pm) Jeddah's souq, immediately south of King Fahd Rd, is well worth seeking out. It's subdivided into sections, some populated by different immigrant groups, such as Yemenis selling coffee and *jambiyas* (ceremonial daggers). Don't miss it if you're here around hajj season, when visitors from across the globe arrive to bargain in a thousand tongues and create a fascinatingly unique spectacle.

Khayyam Al Rabie Est FOOD
(Map p284; ☑ 012 647 6596; Qabel Trail, Al Balad; ⊞ nobody.lake.reacting; ⊗ 9am-2pm & 4.30-11pm Sat-Thu, 4.30-11pm Fri) For dates, nuts and nibbles at discount prices, head straight for the famous Khayyam Al Rabie Est. With its fairy lights and floor-to-ceiling rows of goodies (including more than 50 varieties of date in all shapes, colours and textures), it's like an Aladdin's cave for the sweet-toothed.

ℹ Tours

Sadd Al Samallaghi Est (Map p282; ☑ 012 668 5054; www.samallaghi.com; Flat 8, Hassan Al Dabei St, Al Faisaliyyah; ⊞ gravel.sector.curbed; ⊗ 9am-noon & 4-8pm Sat-Thu) A one-stop shop that arranges flights around the peninsula, day trips around Jeddah, car hire, diving, desert safaris and boat trips. It's one of Saudi Arabia's best operators.

ℹ Getting There & Away

AIR

Jeddah's **King Abdul Aziz International Airport** (☑ 9200 11233; www.jed-airport.com; Airport Rd; ⊞ sympathy.prefix.embarks) is 17km north of the city centre. As the main airport for the holy city of Mecca, the airport receives daily flights from all over the world.

A taxi from the town centre to the airport terminal costs SR75 to SR100.

BUS

For Al Ula, some services travel via central Medina, which is off limits to non-Muslims. If you are non-Muslim, inform the ticket vendor and you'll be advised as to which buses avoid this route.

Buses for the following destinations depart daily from the **Saptco Bus Station** (Map p284; ☑ 9200 00877; www.saptco.sa.com; Baashan St, Al Balad; ⊞ gripes.slams.pictured).

BUSES FROM JEDDAH

DESTINATION	DURATION (HR)	FREQUENCY	COST (SR)
Abha	9	every 2hr	137
Dammam	14-15	3 daily	231
Jazan	9	every 2hr	137
Riyadh	12	every 2hr	173
Taif	3	hourly	47
Yanbu	5	every 2-3hrs	74

BUSES WITHIN JEDDAH

NO	DESTINATION	FREQUENCY
7	Saudi Airlines (Al Khalidiyyah)	every 15min
8	Vegetable Circle (Al Safa)	every 20min
9	Periodic Inspection (Al Marwah via Al Makarunah Rd)	every 15min
9B	Periodic Inspection (Al Marwah via King Fahd Rd)	every 15min
10	National Guard Hospital (KAA Med City)	every 10min
11	Alkhaleejiah Company (Industrial Area)	every 10min

❶ Getting Around

BUS

Jeddah has a new public bus system, with all services departing from the **local bus stand** (Map p284; ☑ 9200 00877; www.saptco.sa.com; King Abdul Aziz St, Al Balad; ⊚ catch.loose.channel; SR2; ⊙ 5.30am-11.30pm) in the old town. Buses run from 5.30am to 11.30pm and one-way fares cost SR2. Buses are 'hail and ride' in between their main destinations (listed below). There are some bus stops, but hailing a bus at any point along the route normally gets the driver to stop if it is safe to do so.

TAXI

A short hop in town by taxi costs around SR20. Uber (www.uber.com) and Careem (www.careem.com) also operate here.

Taif الطائف

☑ 012 / POP 987,900

The gentle, temperate climate of Taif, situated 1700m above sea level, is its biggest attraction. It can seem like a breath of fresh air in summer, and compared to humid Mecca, it truly is. The area is popular for the mountain roadside's wild baboons, which many locals stop to feed. The baboons are relatively tame and have become accustomed to humans. Taif is renowned for its agriculture, producing pomegranates, grapes and roses. The city is family friendly, with numerous garden parks scattered throughout. In the evenings the open spaces in Taif Souq and the surrounding parks are packed with people enjoying the cool climate. In summer Taif becomes Saudi Arabia's unofficial capital when the king relocates here.

◉ Sights

★ **Taif Souq**   MARKET
(King Faisal Rd; ⊚ strain.nurture.rails; ⊙ 9am-2pm & 4.30-11pm Sat-Thu) The Taif souq is one of the largest in Saudi Arabia and well worth a wander. Set in the tastefully renovated historic centre, where wonderful little squares with dancing fountains are filled every evening by the chatter of locals, the souq is a great spot to buy local products such as honey and rose water, as well as handicrafts. When the shopping's done, grab a mint tea and pitch up at one of the squares. People-watching here is a real delight.

Al Shafa   MOUNTAIN
(Ash Shafaa Rd; ⊚ insulated.gaskets.doglike; ℗)
Al Shafa, 25km southwest of Taif, is the highest mountain in the region and is accessed by paved roads. The 10,000-sq-metre Daka Mountain Park sits on the peak and offers stunning views over the local mountain range. The area's popularity means visitors can now ride camels, 4WD sand buggies and dine on a host of street food. There are also terraces for barbecues and picnics, and for those that want to stay a little longer, several basic resorts.

Al Gadhi Rose Factory   FACTORY
(☑ 012 733 4133; Adam St; ⊚ faded.considerable.prickles; ⊙ 9.30am-2.30pm Sun-Thu) [FREE] The largest rose factory in Taif, the 120-year-old Al Gadhi Rose Factory is well worth a visit, particularly at harvest time (May to July), when it's open 24 hours and visitors can witness how the flower petals transform into rose water, scent and other domestic products, all of which are available for purchase here.

Shubra Palace   MUSEUM
(☑ 050 371 5949, 012 732 1033; Shubra St; ⊚ destiny.tolls.talked; ⊙ 9am-1pm Sun-Thu; ℗) [FREE] The city's museum occupies a beautiful house built in 1905 on the orders of Sharif Ali Pasha. The palace is the most stunning vestige of old Taif, with latticework windows and balconies, and interior marble from Carrara. King Abdul Aziz used to stay here, and the palace was later the residence of King Faisal.

WORTH A TRIP

WAHBA CRATER

The result of an underground volcanic explosion, this spectacular crater (250km north of Taif) is in the middle of the desert. It measures 1.3km across and 200m deep. In the middle, white sodium phosphate crystals create a milky lake whenever rain collects, and palm plantations can be seen growing along the eastern edges. A new road leads up to a visitors centre with picnic spots; and there is a tricky, hidden hiking trail leading to the bottom: note that the path is in a bad state. The crater is approached off Hwy 80, along Hwy 8454.

Festivals & Events

Camel races

(www.arabnews.com) Truly an experience unique to this region, camel races are held from 3pm to 5.30pm every other weekend (Friday and Saturday) during July and August. Follow local media for dates and venues.

Souk Okaz Festival

(www.soukokaz.sa) A 10-day culture fest of poetry readings, dancing, sport, theatre and markets with 6th- to 8th-century origins.

Sleeping

Tulip Hotel   HOTEL $

(☏012 733 5533; www.tulip-inn-taif.goldentulip. com; King Saud St; ☷shelter.equality.stable; r SR270; P☎) In a city with very limited accommodation options, this hotel is a step up from the lower end of the budget scale. Rooms are generally cleaner, and decor is marginally better. There are some rooms with decent views over the city, and a modest breakfast is included in the price.

InterContinental Hotel   HOTEL $$

(☏012 750 5050; www.intercontinental.com; Airport Rd; ☷dating.theme.fussed; r/ste from SR869/1080; P☎) Around 10km from Taif's airport, the refurbished InterContinental is Taif's only international-standard hotel. The entrance of this '70s-chic place is arranged like a classical North African *riad* (open central courtyard), with balconies looking down on a central fountain. Rooms are beautifully decorated with renaissance-style European furniture, giving them an old-world elegance, and the restaurant is of a high standard.

Eating & Drinking

As Shafa   MIDDLE EASTERN $

(☏012 734 5569; off Shubra St; ☷pigment.shorter.swaps; mains from SR8; ☉noon-1am) As Shafa serves delicious Saudi and Turkmen dishes, including *manti* (similar to ravioli), at unbeatable prices. It's much admired locally, but there's no family seating. It's located behind the Saudia office.

Mirage Indian Restaurant   INDIAN $$

(☏012 748 4444; Ash Shafaa Rd; ☷insect.pelting. twists; mains SR20-57; ☉1pm-1am) Although light on atmosphere, with small touches of Indian decor, the Mirage is still very popular with locals and offers an excellent biryani (rice dish cooked with saffron and accompanied by marinated chicken or lamb). A traditional treat for the timid diner is the tandoori chicken cooked in yoghurt and spices.

Crepe Cafe   CAFE

(☏055 458 4556; cnr Al Hassan Ibn Ali St & Ash Shafaa Rd; ☷reaction.twists.purely; SR20; ☉4pm-midnight; ☎) A nice little alternative to the food, including sweet options. in Taif, the crêpes here are made fresh and to perfection. Get them stuffed with your favourite fruit and covered in melted chocolate and top it off with some excellent coffee. It's popular with local young men on the weekends when it can get quite busy and noisy.

Getting There & Away

Taif Airport (☏9200 11233; www.gaca.gov.sa; Airport Rd; ☷premises.ages.soaped) is 25km northeast of the town and has daily domestic flights. The **Saptco bus station** (☏9200 00877; www.saptco.com.sa; Airport Rd; ☷bring.foam.solids) has buses that connect it to all the Kingdom's major towns and cities.

There are no public transport options in Taif, and local taxis charge SR20 for short journeys around town. Uber (www.uber.com) and Careem (www.careem.com) are also available here.

Mecca   مكة

☏012 / POP 1.3 MILLION

Mecca is only accessible by Muslims, who often describe the moment they first lay eyes on the city's sacred Kaaba as an overwhelmingly emotional experience. For those living outside the Kingdom, a visit to Mecca – generally spelt 'Makkah' by Muslims and in Saudi Arabia – is a lifelong dream. Coming here to perform the hajj pilgrimage is a

Mecca

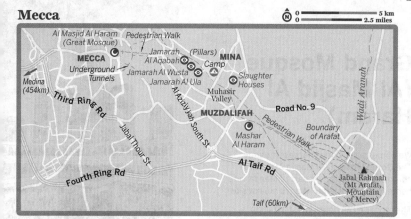

religious obligation for all Muslims who are financially and physically able to do so.

The birthplace of the Prophet Muhammad, Mecca is awash with monuments of religious symbolism. Born of the desert, this is a modern city with the heart of an ancient Arabian village. Despite the immense construction projects around the city's sacred Kaaba – the most controversial being the clock tower – sun-bleached homes still nestle in the rocky hillsides and everywhere you look men dressed in two simple cotton sheets wander its streets.

Sights

★ Al Masjid Al Haram
MOSQUE
(Grand Mosque; Al Masjid Al Haram Rd, Al Haram; ⧆ dull.given.somebody; ◷ 24hr; P) The focal point for every Muslim and the biggest mosque in the world, Al Masjid Al Haram is able to host a million worshippers and covers an area of 356,800 sq metres. At its epicentre is the Holy Kaaba, covered in black and gold cloth, around which Muslims can be found circumnavigating night and day (known as *tawaf*). It's the holiest structure in all of Islam, and is at the heart of the Islamic pilgrimages (hajj and umrah).

The Kaaba predates the Prophet Muhammad's lifetime; Muslims believe it was built by the Prophet Ibrahim and his son Ishmael. The foundations of the mosque around the Kaaba date to at least the 7th century, when the second caliph, Omar Bin Al Khattab, built a structure to accommodate the growing number of pilgrims each year.

Set into the Kaaba's eastern corner is the Black Stone, a relic Muslims believe fell from

the heavens and was placed into the corner by the Prophet Ibrahim. The stone came away from the Kaaba during the Prophet's lifetime, and it is said he then personally placed it back into the corner, where it sits today. At the Kaaba's northwestern edge, a curved area known as the *Hatem* or *Hijr Ishmael* represents the area believed to have been part of the Kaaba's original boundary when it was built by the Prophet Ibrahim. The mosque is in the midst of the Third Saudi Expansion, which will increase the mosque's area to 400,000 sq metres and allow 2.5 million people to pray inside it.

★ Exhibition of the Two Holy Mosques
MUSEUM
(☑ 012 560 2188; www.gph.gov.sa; Old Makkah Jeddah Rd, Oum Al Jood; ⧆ wants.grow.parkway; ◷ 9am-8pm; P) FREE This little museum is brimming with relics from the two holy mosques, Al Masjid Al Haram in Mecca and the Prophet's Mosque (p293) in Medina. These include pillars, marble insignia and historical photos. Some items date as far back as the 13th-century Abbasid period. There are two standout items: the ornate teak wooden stairwell on wheels, which the Ottomans used to access the Kaaba in the 1820s, and a historic pair of the Kaaba's spectacular giant gilded metal doors.

Makkah Museum
MUSEUM
(☑ 012 547 1815; Al Madinah Al Munawarah Rd, Az Zahir; ⧆ cautious.january.agreed; ◷ 8am-8pm Sun-Thu, 4-8pm Fri & Sat) FREE Formerly Al Zahir Palace, the 3435-sq-metre Makkah Museum has a collection ranging from images of Saudi Arabia's important archaeological

Grand Mosque (Al Masjid Al Haram)

Welcome to the world's largest mosque. The Grand Mosque (Al Masjid Al Haram) complex is the beating heart of Mecca, and home to the ❶ **Kaaba**, Islam's holiest site.

The mosque can hold almost a million worshippers at once, and plans for colossal expansion are underway to accommodate the huge numbers of pilgrims who visit the site each year.

During these pilgrimages, the flow of humanity never stops as worshippers try to get close enough to the Kaaba to touch or kiss it. If crowds – or sometimes security – prevent them from touching the black, veiled cube, they point at it instead.

This is part of the ritual of ❷ **tawaf**, one of the most significant parts of hajj and umrah. To perform the ritual, worshippers circle the Kaaba seven times counterclockwise, keeping it on their left.

Once they have completed the seventh round, they offer a prayer of two units, called rak'ahs, at the ❸ **Station of Ibrahim**, a small structure sitting about 1.5m from the door of the Kaaba.

Next is a refreshing drink of the ❹ **Zamzam Well's** sacred water, taken from one of the fountains on the periphery. Finally, pilgrims move on to perform ❺ **Sa'ee**, which entails walking seven times back and forth between the hills of Safa and Marwah.

TOP TIP

Zamzam's water is thought to have healing properties, and many pilgrims take at least a litre home with them.

AZAHAR PHOTOGRAPHY/GETTY IMAGES ©

Kaaba
The Kaaba was not always an Islamic place of worship but stood in the pre-Islamic era as a pagan shrine. Some scholars also claim that the Kaaba was once dedicated to the Nabataean deity Hubal.

Station of Ibrahim
Enclosed in glass and metal, this stone is where Ibrahim, often with his son, Ishmael, is believed to have stood while building the Kaaba. The stone contains his sunken footprint.

SAMET GULEY/SHUTTERSTOCK ©

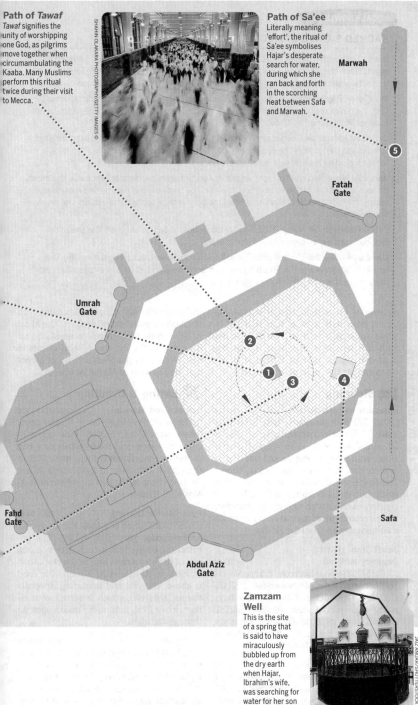

Path of *Tawaf*

Tawaf signifies the unity of worshipping one God, as pilgrims move together when circumambulating the Kaaba. Many Muslims perform this ritual twice during their visit to Mecca.

SHAHIN OLAKARA PHOTOGRAPHY/GETTY IMAGES ©

Path of Sa'ee

Literally meaning 'effort', the ritual of Sa'ee symbolises Hajar's desperate search for water, during which she ran back and forth in the scorching heat between Safa and Marwah.

Marwah

5

Fatah Gate

Umrah Gate

2

1

3

4

Fahd Gate

Abdul Aziz Gate

Safa

Zamzam Well

This is the site of a spring that is said to have miraculously bubbled up from the dry earth when Hajar, Ibrahim's wife, was searching for water for her son Ishmael.

JAIZ ANUAR/SHUTTERSTOCK ©

LOCAL KNOWLEDGE

SACRED SIGHTS IN MECCA

In a city rich with religious sites, it can be difficult for the first-time visitor to absorb the significance of each place. Complement your time at Al Masjid Al Haram (p289) with trips to key sites in and around Mecca to better appreciate the city's religious narrative.

Masjid Al Bay'ah (off Al Jawhara St, near Mina Train Station 3; ⊞ blinking.predict.sediment) Visit the remains of the spot where Mecca's tribal leaders pledged their allegiance to the Prophet Muhammad in AD 621.

Jannat Al Muallaa Cemetery (Al Masjid Al Haram Rd, Al Hujun; ⊞ jumbled.bliss.catching; ⊙ hours vary; P) It won't be easy to get into, but this is where many of the Prophet's family, including his first wife, Khadija, are buried.

Jabal Al Nour (Mountain of Light; An Nur, Al Adel; ⊞ talents.bills.firm; P) Probably the most famous mountain in Islamic tradition. It was in the small cave of Hira on this mountain, during the month of Ramadan, that Muslims believe the Prophet received his first revelation from God.

Jabal Rahmah (Mt Arafat; Rd 62, Suq Al Arab; ⊞ apricot.decoder.drip; P) The site of the Prophet's last sermon shortly before his death.

Cave of Thor (Ghar Thor; off Jabal Thawr Rd, Al Hijrah; ⊞ backpack.trying.darling; P) The small mountain where the Prophet and his friend Abu Bakr hid for three days when they were being chased by the Quraysh tribe.

---

discoveries to exhibits on pre-Islamic history. A presentation traces the origins of Islamic calligraphy with references to Arabic fonts and samples of inscriptions discovered in archaeological digs. A hall on Islamic art complements the calligraphy displays.

Sleeping

Palestine Hotel Makkah HOTEL $
(☎ 012 530 8888; Ibrahim Al Khalil St, At Tandabawi; ⊞ sushi.nickname.curated; d/tr/ste SR230/362/471; P ◈) The huge Palestine Hotel, with many rooms decked out in reds and creams, is a reasonably priced choice. The lower-priced rooms can be somewhat small, but the suites are spacious. It has a concierge service with tour-guide assistance and an around-the-clock business centre. It's a 20-minute walk from the Kaaba.

Jabal Omar Hyatt Regency Makkah HOTEL $$
(☎ 012 577 1234; www.hyatt.com; Ibrahim Al Khalil St, Jabal Omar; ⊞ coaster.heave.most; r SR415-1780; ◈) This high-end hotel offers large rooms with partial views of Al Masjid Al Haram from its floor-to-ceiling windows. The bathrooms are the height of luxury, with walk-in marble rain showers.

Hotel Fairmont Makkah HOTEL $$$
(☎ 012 571 7777; www.fairmont.com/makkah; Abraj Al Beit, Ajyad St; ⊞ pitchers.copycat.gent; r SR595-20,600; ◈) The Fairmont may have an air of

controversy around it for its association with the modern architectural design of the Abraj Al Beit complex, but there's no question that it's every bit the five-star hotel it claims to be. Rooms offer panoramic views of Mecca and the Kaaba in Al Masjid Al Haram.

Eating & Drinking

Street-Food Stands STREET FOOD $
(off Ibrahim Al Khalil Rd, Al Haram; ⊞ detail.steers.cubes; wraps SR2-5; ⊙ 24hr) Pick up delicious shawarma and falafel wraps or a bag of freshly fried samosas for a mere SR2 at these great little 24-hour food stands selling the best cheap street eats anywhere near Al Masjid Al Haram.

Paradise Restaurant PAKISTANI $
(☎ 055 043 3252; off King Abdul Aziz Rd; ⊞ chip.sporting.huddle; mains SR15; ⊙ 24hr) This no-frills little eating spot is tucked away along one of the backstreets east of the clock tower, close to Al Masjid Al Haram. The food is cheap, cheerful and delicious, especially the meat *karahi,* which is served with either rice or fresh flatbread. Plus it's open all through the night.

Al Deyafa MALAYSIAN $$
(☎ 012 571 4444; Abraj Al Beit, Ajyad St; ⊞ outwit.sooner.flat; buffet adult/child SR168/84; ⊙ 6-10.30am, 1-3.30pm & 7-11pm) On the 12th floor of the Al Marwa Rayhaan hotel, commanding spectacular views over Al Masjid Al Haram,

Al Deyafa offers a great Malaysian buffet that is popular with Southeast Asian pilgrims.

Abak Kahva CAFE
(☑056 702 5001; cnr Al Akhlaq & Abdullah Arif Sts; 🌐cove.bunny.youngest; ⊘7-11.30am & 4.30-11.30pm Sun-Thu, from 4.30pm Fri & Sat; ☎) The trendy baristas of the Western hemisphere have arrived in Mecca, and Abak, with its quirky branding and hipster interior, is leading the way. Popular with middle-class Saudi youths, who can be seen sitting inside on most weeknights staring at their laptops and cradling a hot cup, this is a welcome, local alternative to the big American brands.

🛍 Shopping

Abraj Al Beit Towers MALL
(Fairmont Makkah Clock Royal Tower; Abraj Al Beit, Ajyad St; 🌐punks.chatting.motion; ⊘10am-noon & 5-11pm) These towers feature a prayer hall that can accommodate up to 10,000 people and – perhaps incongruously – a five-storey mega shopping mall. The 601m-tall, post-modern towers have been criticised for their modern architectural design overlooking historic and holy Al Masjid Al Haram, but they're one of Mecca's most visited nonreligious landmarks.

ℹ Information

Money exchange is available from **Hatem Sulaiman Money Exchange** (☑012 570 1888; flr B1, 104-5 Al Safwa Towers, Ajyad St; 🌐jumbled. deeper.figure; ⊘9am-11pm), and medicines from **Nahdi Pharmacy** (☑012 541 0520; www. nahdi.sa; off Ibrahim Al Khalili Rd, Al Haram; 🌐club.lawn.lentil; ⊘24hr), close to Al Masjid Al Haram.

ℹ Getting There & Around

The nearest international airport is in Jeddah, which has a train station connecting it directly to Mecca's Makkah Haramain station. Other options are to get a Saptco bus or a taxi (taxi fares from the airport to Mecca start at SR150).

Saptco Al Haram bus station (☑9200 26888; www.saptco.com.ksa; Jabal Al Kaabah Rd, Al Haram; 🌐prowess.riots.altitude) has services to and from all major towns and cities in the Kingdom.

Mecca's new **Makkah Haramain train station** (☑9200 04433; www.hhr.sa; Ash Shafaah St, Ar Rusayfah; 🌐bleak.balloons.herb) is 10km west of Al Masjid Al Haram and connects directly to Jeddah's international airport and the city of Medina. Trains run from Thursday to Sunday.

There are also shuttle buses (SR3) from Mecca's train station to the city centre.

There is no public transport in Mecca, although most hotels away from the centre offer free shuttles to Al Masjid Al Haram. Taxi rides in Mecca start at about SR20. Other options are to use Uber (www.uber.com) and Careem (www. careem.com).

Medina المدينة

☑014 / POP 1.3 MILLION

Medina (often spelled Madinah) is known as the 'city of the Prophet'. It is where Islam's founder, Muhammad, was given refuge after being exiled from Mecca. Here he lived, built his mosque, fought pivotal battles, and it's where he was finally laid to rest. Monuments to this seminal period of his life are what pilgrims from all over the world come to visit, but the city's central area is off limits to non-Muslims. The significance of the Prophet's time here is acknowledged by the fact that the Islamic calendar starts from 622, the year he arrived in Medina.

The modern city, like Mecca, is centred around a grand mosque, the Prophet's Mosque, which has a series of large numbered gates often used to navigate the pedestrianised area in and around it. It's surrounded by high-end hotels and eating outlets, with the rest of Medina sprawling out from here.

👁 Sights

⭐**Prophet's Mosque** MOSQUE
(Al Masjid An Nabawi; Al Haram; 🌐sunroof.ab acus.comment; ⊘24hr; 🅿) One of only two mosques in the world that can accommodate a million people, the Prophet's Mosque holds deep significance for Muslims all over the world. It is said to have been built by the Prophet himself in AD 622 and not only encompasses his final resting place (alongside the first two caliphs) beneath the iconic green dome built by the Ottomans, it also covers where his house once stood, adjacent to the mosque when it was just a modest square mud-and-wood building.

Masjid Miqat MOSQUE
(Omar Bin Al Khattab Rd,, Dhul Hulaifah; 🌐attracts.pickles.identity; ⊘24hr; 🅿) The biggest *miqat* (pilgrim station) complex in the whole of Saudi Arabia, this fort-like mosque rises up like a North African *kasbah* on the southwestern edge of Medina,

SIGHTS IN MEDINA

In addition to the Prophet's Mosque and the Masjid Miqat, Medina has a number of other sights. These are complemented by exhibitions on Islam at the beautifully restored **Ottoman Hejaz Railway Station** (☑011 880 8855; Sikkat Al Hadid, As Suqya; ⓦadmiral.hills.gripes; ⊙8am-4pm & 5-10pm Sat-Thu) and at **Dar Al Madinah Museum** (☑014 865 3049; Safwan Ibn Malik Al Tamimi, Al Mabuth; ⓦdirt.painters.dude; SR25; ⊙9am-8pm Sat-Thu; Ⓟ). A hop-on-hop-off **city sightseeing bus** (☑9200 14044; www.csmadinah.com; near Gate 21, King Fahd Rd, Badaah; ⓦmoth.shirts.archive; ticket adult/child SR80/40; ⊙24hr) links most of these sites.

Uhud Martyrs Cemetery (King Fahd Rd, Uhud; ⓦenjoyable.competent.feels; Ⓟ) Around 85 martyred soldiers from the Battle of Uhud (a battle the Muslims lost because a group of archers left their post prematurely to claim war spoils) were buried here.

Masjid Al Qiblatain (Khalid Ibn Al Walid Rd, Al Qiblatayn; ⓦroutines.trucks.ranches; ⊙24hr; Ⓟ) The Arabic word *qibla* means 'direction' of prayer, and this mosque is said to have two as, in AD 624, the Prophet received a revelation to change the direction of prayer from Jerusalem to Mecca.

Quba Mosque (Qiba Rd, Al Khatim; ⓦbasic.scarred.proofs; ⊙3am-midnight; Ⓟ) In AD 622 the Prophet reportedly laid the foundation stone here for the world's first mosque.

marking the point at which would-be pilgrims have to assume the state of *ihram* (purity) ahead of making their journey south to Al Masjid Al Haram and the Kaaba in Mecca. This stunning world-class mosque has almost 2000 showers, toilets and ablution stations integrated into the perimeter wall, which is styled like an ancient city wall.

🛏 Sleeping

Ewan Dar Alhejra Hotel   HOTEL $

(☑014 869 0757; King Fahd Rd, Al Madinah; ⓦsector.good.thorax; r SR160; Ⓟ🛜) It's the little touches in this smart, budget option, away from the centre behind Awaji Mosque, such as the slippers, mini dental kit and hairdryer, and the kindly nature of the staff, that make all the difference. The hotel isn't close to the Prophet's Mosque, and that's reflected in the prices. If you don't mind the location, it's a great option.

Madinah Hilton   HOTEL $$

(☑014 820 1000; www3.hilton.com; King Fahd Bin Abdul Aziz Rd, Al Haram; ⓦbikers.clearing.movies; d/ste SR675/800; Ⓟ🛜) The Hilton appears to be craning its neck to get a look at the Prophet's Mosque, such is its design. This means some rooms have the view everyone craves, making this an excellent mid-range option within a minute's walk of the mosque. Being a Hilton hotel, its rooms are well designed and comfortable, and the service is impeccable.

★ Dar Al Taqwa   HOTEL $$$

(☑014 829 1111; www.taqwamadinah.com; near Gate 20, Al Haram; ⓦundulation.apply.glides; d/ste SR1075/2150; Ⓟ🛜) The pick of the hotels near the Prophet's Mosque, Dar Al Taqwa is highly sought after during peak periods, when prices can double, so book well in advance. The luxuriously spacious rooms have large, comfortable beds and fantastic views over the grand mosque, and offer an oasis-like calm high above one of the busiest spots on earth.

🍴 Eating

★ Meraj Hyderabadi Restaurant   SOUTH INDIAN $

(☑012 866 1116; Sayyid Ash Shuhada St, Ar Rayah; ⓦpaying.regime.date; mains SR25-32; ⊙1-4pm & 8pm-1am) The astonishing takeaway traffic tells its own story at this cosy South Indian restaurant, just north of the centre. It's popular with locals, and you'll see every section of Saudi society tucking into the restaurant special – a sizzling grill that's heard before it's seen. Little wonder, given the prices here are as good as the food. There's also a family section.

★ Abu Zaid   MIDDLE EASTERN $

(☑9200 03670; www.abuzaidrest.com; Prince Abdulmajeed Ibn Abdulaziz Rd, Al Iskan; ⓦwires.transfers.merchant; mains SR4-19; ⊙5-11am & 6pm-2am) The ultimate spot for an authentic taste of what has become classic Saudi fare.

Fuul (thick broad-bean soup), *masoob* (a Yemeni sweet of bread, banana and honey) and *muthabbak* (omelette pancake) are the staples here. Each is cooked fresh to order and tastes so good you'll begin to understand why the restaurant is always full.

Route 66　　　　　　　　　　　　　AMERICAN **$$**
(Zunayrah Ar Rumiyah St, Bir Uthman; [w]annoys. speeds.feathers; mains SR40-80; ⊙6am-noon & 1pm-1.30am) This pseudo-American restaurant serves up nice alternatives to the South Asian and Middle Eastern options everywhere else. The portions aren't big, but you do get to sit in half a Cadillac to eat them. Try the hearty breakfasts if you're here before noon. It's north of Masjid Al Qiblatain.

🛍 Shopping

For high-quality rugs, prayer mats, prayer beads, local dates, honey and spices head to the highly recommended **Madina Made** ([✓]9200 07664; www.madinamade.com; Al Haram, Abu Ayyub Al Ansari; [w]acid.tests.fattest; ⊙5.30am-midnight). No Muslim visits Medina without purchasing some of the city's famous dates, best bargained for at the **Central Dates Market** (King Faisal Rd, An Naqa; [w]founders.engage.cobras; ⊙5.30am-midnight). For perfume, the 167-year-old shop **Abdul Samad Al Qurashi** ([✓]9200 07173; www.store. asqgrp.com; King Fahd Rd, Badaah; [w]central.sleep. grew; ⊙9am-11pm Sat-Thu, 4-11pm Fri) sells luxurious Arabian oud and musk.

ℹ Information

ATMs are quite common around the Prophet's Mosque. Many pilgrims arrive with foreign currency, and the **Zuhairi Exchange** ([✓]014 820 8000; King Fahd Rd, Badaah; [w]aged.slower. mice; ⊙6am-11.30pm) is one of the closest places to exchange this. It also offers some of the best rates.

Al Safia Health Center (opp Gate 5, Al Ayyub Al Ansari, Al Haram; [w]unfair.lunged.whoever; ⊙5.30am-midnight) For medical nonemergencies.

Bab Jebreel Health Center (Al Haram; [w]warriors.dubbing.bigger; ⊙5.30am-midnight) For medical emergencies.

Haj & Umra Services ([✓]014 832 0275; www. haj.gov.sa; Al Haram; [w]somebody.glory.record; ⊙5.30am-midnight) The main tourist information point, located in the southeastern corner of the Prophet's Mosque.

Nahdi Pharmacy ([✓]800 119 1198; King Fahd Rd, Badaah; [w]finally.modules.rooting; ⊙24hr)

ℹ Getting There & Away

Medina's **Prince Mohammad Bin Abdulaziz International Airport** ([✓]014 813 8555, 014 813 9999; www.madinahairport.com; Abdullah Ibn Wadiah Rd; [w]memo.coffee.regatta) is outside the Muslim-only boundary, northeast of the city. It also has a **train station** ([✓]9200 04433; www. hhr.sa; King Abdul Aziz Rd, Al Hadra; [w]rests. softly.explains; 🛜) linking it to the other holy city of Mecca and the port city of Jeddah. Medina's **Saptco bus station** ([✓]9200 00877; www. saptco.com.sa; Abi Dhar Al Ghafari, Bani Abdul Ashhal; [w]intend.cycled.types) has regular services to Yanbu, Tabuk, Hail, Riyadh, Jeddah and Mecca.

ℹ Getting Around

Medina has two bus services useful to visiting pilgrims. Public buses 6, 7 and 37 go to Quba Mosque and bus 22 goes to the Uhud Martyrs Cemetery from the **bus stop** (www. mda.gov.sa; King Fahd Rd, Badaah; [w]scuba. gossip.mailbox; one-way ticket SR3; ⊙3-11pm Sat-Thu, 10am-10pm Fri) near the northern entrance of the Prophet's Mosque. The other option is to board the City Sightseeing Bus (SR80), which covers more of Medina's key pilgrim sites.

A short trip in a taxi costs SR20. Uber (www. uber.com) and Careem (www.careem.com) are also available in Medina.

Yanbu　　　　　　　　　　ينبع

[✓]014 / POP 299,000

Yanbu is fast becoming an appealing tourist destination, due to amazing dive sites and pristine white sandy shores, many with resorts and private beaches. However, at first glance, the backdrop of refineries and petrochemical plants hardly paints the area in an attractive light. Fortunately, this is the 'new' Yanbu, which sits 15km south of 'old' Yanbu. Old Yanbu has a lengthy history dating back 2500 years to when it was a staging post for the marine spice and incense routes. In more recent history it is remembered as the place where TE Lawrence (Lawrence of Arabia) stayed.

Yanbu's modest old town is small but quaint, with an unhurried atmosphere not apparent in larger cities, and the **historic houses** (off King Faisal Rd; [w]tenses.export.hang) – one of which belonged to Lawrence – display elegant *mashrabiyyas*. Just north of the town is vast, open desert that gives way

1

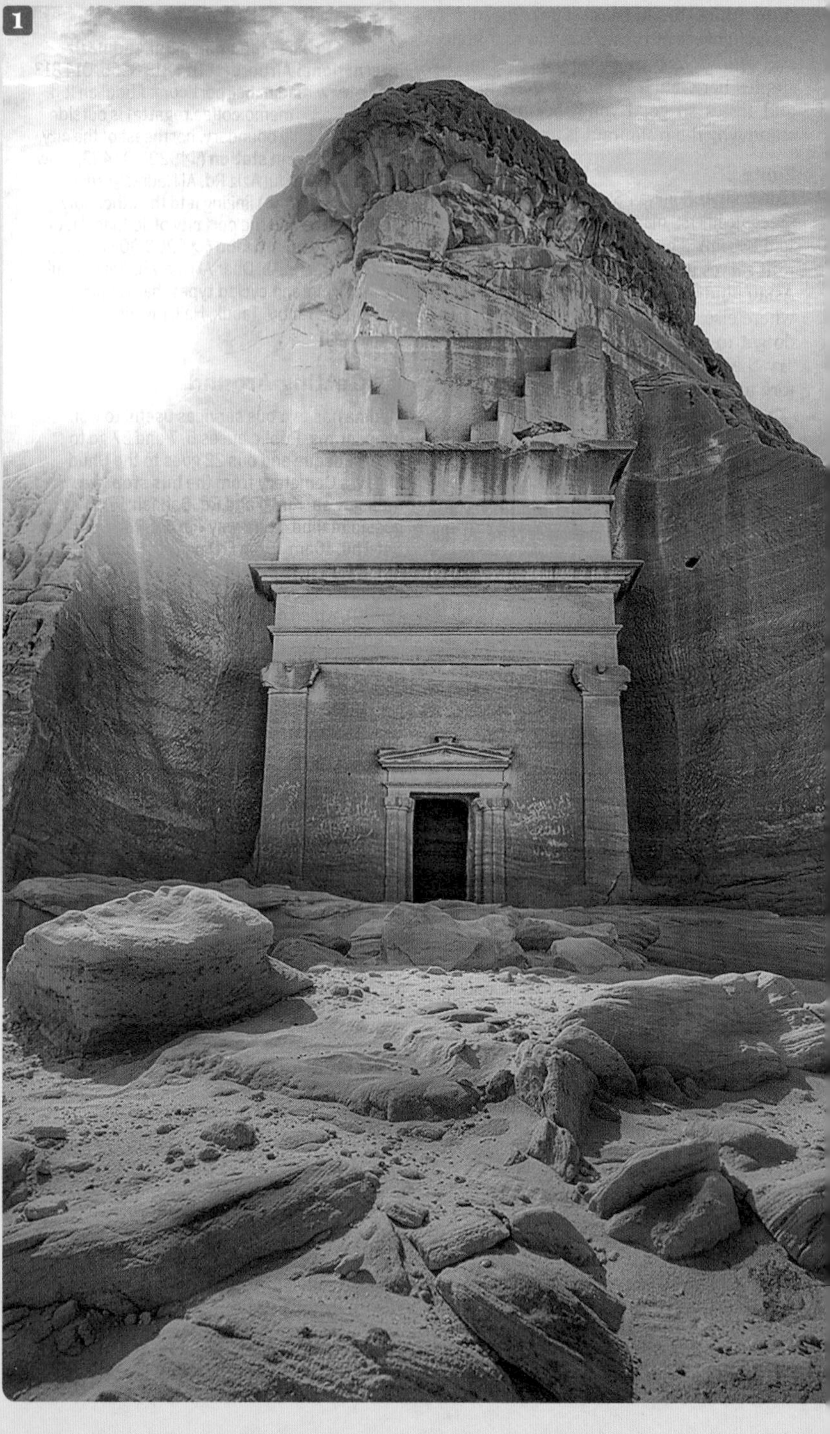

FARID SUHAIMI/SHUTTERSTOCK ©

CRYSTAL EYE STUDIO/SHUTTERSTOCK ©

1. Madain Saleh
Often called the 'second Petra', Madain Saleh (p300) has 131 enigmatic tombs.

2. Dates
Dried dates, often consumed with nuts and coffee, are a good source of energy and keep well in the heat.

3. Sky Bridge at Kingdom Centre
Riyadh's landmark tower (p277), rising 302m high, has a steel-and-glass bridge offering stunning views.

4. Red sea diving
The laid-back coastline of Jeddah (p281) is home to some fantastic dive sites.

ABDULLAH AL-EISA/GETTY IMAGES ©

WORTH A TRIP

THE HEJAZ RAILWAY

The doomed Ottoman Hejaz Railway, with its echoes of British Army officer TE Lawrence (Lawrence of Arabia) and the Arab Revolt, cuts across northwestern Saudi Arabia in the form of abandoned and evocative stations, garrison forts and the odd bridge.

The railway was meant to make life easier for pilgrims trying to reach the two holy cities of Medina and Mecca. It dramatically cut journey times and made it difficult for waiting bandits to carry out raids. The line, begun in 1900, finally arrived in Medina in 1908, covering 1600km from Damascus in Syria, though the planned final leg to Mecca would never be realised.

Despite many Arab tribes supporting the railway for its economic potential, during WWI, the Hashemite ruler of the Hejaz at the time, Sherif Hussein, made an alliance with the British to drive the Ottomans out of the region, and their new flagship project became an obvious target. Harnessing the hostility of local Bedouin, TE Lawrence helped orchestrate the Arab Revolt's successful attacks on the railway, and by 1918 – less than two decades after the project had started – the line lay in ruins.

The stations (now restored) in both **Medina** and Tabuk (p303) were the biggest in Saudi Arabia and are the most accessible sites, with locomotives on display. Around Al Ula (check locally for directions), there's **Al Buwayr station and fort** (⧈unfasten. megabytes.closes), with an almost-complete train and several wagons. Near Huraymil, a huge **rusting locomotive** (⧈urgings.earned.derails; ⊙daylight hours) lies on its side, as if blown up by the Arab revolters yesterday, surrounded by the ruins of a substation and fort. Nearby lies a beautiful 150m long **Ottoman railway bridge** (⧈divergence.encrypt. openings) that spans a dry riverbed. Surrounded by barren desert and connecting an invisible track from one bank to the other, the bridge is a poignant picture of what has been and gone.

to blue waters, and this area is where most visitors spend their time.

🛏 Sleeping

⭐ Ibis Yanbu
HOTEL **$**

(📞014 354 0666; www.ibishotel.com; 2874 King Abdul Aziz Rd; ⧈turkeys.nights.swinging; r SR350; 🅿🛜🛗) An excellent budget choice close to the centre of Yanbu and run by friendly, warm staff who know their city well. Rooms are clean and comfortable, with some commanding impressive views across town. There is also an excellent restaurant and a vibrant shisha cafe set around the outdoor pool.

Arac Yanbu Resort
RESORT **$$$**

(📞014 328 0888; www.arac.com.sa; Corniche Rd; ⧈repairs.mergers.recounts; r/villa/chalet from SR990/1890/2200; 🅿🛜🛗) A family-only resort 17km from Yanbu and 10km from the airport, Arac boasts a good location and great facilities. These include a private beach where women can swim in modest attire, a host of water sports, a cafe and a restaurant. Two-storey chalets are on the waterfront and are comfortable, if a little bit tired.

🍴 Eating

⭐ Al Marsah
Seafood Restaurant
SEAFOOD **$**

(📞014 357 3555; off King Abdullah Rd; ⧈bangle. explorer.shams; mains from SR25; ⊙11am-1am) Eating here, in one of the old town properties overlooking the seaport, is as much about the location as the food, which is excellent. Beautifully renovated, Al Marsah backs on to ruins and recently restored historic buildings. The nautical decor adds to the charm when dining on the roof in one of the private booths on a warm evening.

Iskenderun Restaurant
TURKISH **$**

(📞014 322 8465; King Abdul Aziz Rd; ⧈crunch. candles.respect; mains SR14-25; ⊙10am-midnight) Canary coloured, cheap and cheerful, this is Yanbu's favourite eating establishment. Try the speciality, the *shawarma iskandar*, served with a secret sauce. Mixed grills, Turkish pizza, barbecued hamour fish and fresh fruit juices are also served.

ℹ Getting There & Away

Prince Abdul Mohsin Bin Abdulaziz Airport (📞9200 11233; www.gaca.gov.sa; King Fahd Rd; ⧈tramples.giant.outspend) is 10km north-

SAUDI ARABIA YANBU

east of the town centre and is connected to most major cities in Saudi Arabia. Yanbu also has a **Saptco bus station** (⬚ 9200 00877; www.saptco.com.sa; Khalid Bin Alwalid; ⬚ stew.joggers.egging) with good onward connections.

NORTHERN SAUDI ARABIA

المملكة العربية السعودية الشمالية

Northern Saudi Arabia is the region with the richest pre-Islamic sites in the entire country. While Madain Saleh will rightly continue to take all the headlines, with its Petra-like carved tombs in spectacular desert settings, the lesser-known town of Al Ula is also an impressive ode to ancient civilisations. It sits hemmed in by a forest of palms and stunning red cliffs. And then there are the awesomely isolated stretches of the Red Sea, where the desert seemingly walks into the sea, camels and all.

Al Ula العلا

⬚ 014 / POP 32,413

Nestled in a large, spectacular valley, where palm groves run down the centre of a *wadi* (dry riverbed) and forbidding redsandstone cliffs rise up on either side, Al Ula has a delightfully mysterious air about it. It is also the gateway to Saudi Arabia's very own 'Petra', Madain Saleh, with most visitors to the World Heritage Site staying here in town.

Al Ula's old-town ruins are among the best examples of traditional northern Arab architecture, and with a history that stretches back to the 6th century BC, the town is surrounded by a host of fascinating pre-Islamic sites.

Founded as 'Dedan' by the Lihyanites, the town became the capital of their kingdom. Al Ula's strategic location meant it also sat along several trade routes for spices and incense coming from the Levant, Egypt and North Africa.

◉ Sights

★ **Al Ula Viewpoint** VIEWPOINT
(King Abdulaziz Park; off Junction for Routes 375 & 70; ⬚ rodents.amending.frill; P) The views as you wind your way up to this gem of a spot offer glimpses of what's to come. At the top, the road plateaus through a windswept, lunar landscape of black basalt rock, before arriving at a sad-looking park with a precarious fence at its edge. Suddenly the breathtaking view comes into sight and the entire Al Ula valley, surrounded by majestic red-rock mountains disappearing into the horizon, sprawls out before you like a surreal painting.

★ **Al Ula Heritage Village** RUINS
(off Route 375; ⬚ dentures.slump.lockets; ⊙ daylight hours; P) There are plans to make this a formal tourist venue in the near future, but for now you can enjoy freely wandering among the beautiful mud ruins where people (the ancestors of the current residents of Al Ula) lived for centuries. As well as visiting Al Ula Fort, it is worth trying to locate the *tantura* (sundial) and old mosque. The ruins are dissected by the highway: those on the upper west side have been renovated considerably, while the lower east side is wonderfully raw.

Al Ula Fort CASTLE
(off Route 375, Old Al Ula; ⬚ ever.workaholic.incomers; ⊙ daylight hours; P) To protect the ancient village, inhabitants in the 6th century used red-sandstone blocks to build this castle on a promontory that gives a 360-degree view of the surrounding valley. The 45m climb to the castle is of moderate difficulty but worth the effort once you see the red-tinged cliffs of the sweeping valley below.

Jebel Khuraibah MOUNTAIN
(⬚ staffers.basing.straws; P) The fortress and three peaks of Jebel Khuraibah once formed part of the capital of the ancient Kingdom of Lihyan. Rock-cut tombs squat at the foot of the peaks, the most impressive being the 'Lion Tomb', named for the two lions carved on either side of the entrance. At Khuraibah is a huge, headless sandstone figure, while climbing to the top of the central peak reveals stone stairs and walls linking all three crags together into a ruined fortress city.

There is a small visitors centre near the entry point that's open daily from 8am to 5pm.

Al Ula Antiquities & Heritage Museum MUSEUM
(⬚ 014 884 1536; King Fahd Rd; ⬚ outdo.cushion.voted; ⊙ 8am-8pm Sun-Thu; P) FREE This small museum is attractively designed, with some intriguing and informative displays on the history, culture, flora and fauna of the area, as well as on Madain Saleh and Nabataean culture.

⌖ Tours

Two recommended local tour guides are **Shahad Bdyr** (☑ 050 353 2869; shahad-bdyr@ hotmail.com), a proud resident of Al Ula who can trace her family roots back to the old town, and **Fayiz Al Juhani** (☑ 055 764 7773; fayizjoh@gmail.com), a warm, friendly man with years of experience in guiding tourists.

🛏 Sleeping & Eating

Al Harbi Apartments   APARTMENT $
(☑ 014 884 3100; alharbihotel@hotmail.com; King Fahd St; 🔲 microphones.demographic.resisted; apt from SR180; P 🔊) In an area where any tourist-ready accommodation is scarce, these apartments/hotel rooms in the heart of Al Ula's new town are good value for money. The rooms are clean, cheap and spacious, but most of the toilets are squat-style, so ask ahead when booking. The receptionist speaks enough English to be helpful and knows the area well.

★**Shaden Resort**   RESORT $$$
(☑ 050 604 3344, 050 066 3388; www.shaden-re sort.com; off Route 70; 🔲 dreading.cautioned.contingency; r/tents/chalets SR2137/1600/10,000; P 🔊♨) Although it's more desert glamping than camping, this new resort close to Al Ula and Madain Saleh is all about the location. It's hidden away inside the same tall, dramatic red rocks from which nature has hewn the nearby Elephant Rock – staying here feels like you're getting up close and personal with this dramatic landscape.

★**Al Ula Heritage Restaurant**   ARABIC $
(☑ 055 837 0888; Al Hameediya, off Route 375; 🔲 motives.receives.reframe; mains SR12-24; ☺ 9am-midnight Sat-Thu, from 1pm Fri) This busy little restaurant is set in a mock-traditional house, as so many serving local Saudi food tend to be. The key draw though is the cook making delicious fresh *kunafeh* (a vermicelli and cheese sweet dish). In the evenings he rarely stops putting the metal dishes onto the open burners as the orders keep coming.

ⓘ Getting There & Away

Al Ula's **Prince Abdulmajeed Bin Abdulaziz Airport** (☑ 9200 11233; www.gaca.gov.sa; off Route 375; 🔲 horizon.manifold.finer) is 30km southeast of the town centre. **Saptco** (☑ 9200 00877; www.saptco.com.sa; cnr King Faisal Rd & Khalid Bin Walid St; 🔲 rounds.hilarious.alleys) runs regular, daily buses between Al Ula and major Saudi towns and cities including Tabuk, Medina, Yanbu, Jeddah and Riyadh.

Madain Saleh   مدائن صالح

Often dubbed the 'second Petra', **Madain Saleh** (Al Hijr; ☑ from overseas 011 261 4750, tourism contact centre 19988; www.sauditourism. sa; off Route 375; 🔲 mooing.wizards.divots; P), for many, is on a par with – if not more impressive than – its famous cousin across the border in Jordan. Both were major trading cities along the ancient Nabataean trade routes, as confirmed by recent excavations that have revealed the foundations of houses and a market area for traders and caravans. However, it's the 131 enigmatic tombs, which combine elements of Graeco-Roman architecture with Nabataean and Babylonian imagery, that grab all the attention.

At the time of research the site was closed for refurbishment and due to reopen in early 2020, when the Hejaz Railway station within the site will become the new visitor centre for the signposted main entrance off Route 375. Given Saudi Arabia's track record of abruptly closing and opening major tourist sights, however, it is best to call the contact centre ahead of any attempted visit.

At the main entrance of the site is the **Madain Saleh station** of the Hejaz Railway (p298), soon to become the visitors centre. Built in 1907, it consists of 16 buildings and includes a large workshop (with a restored WWI-era engine), shells of train carriages and a rebuilt Turkish fort that served as a resting place for pilgrims travelling to Mecca.

Qasr Al Saneh reveals many of the essential elements of Nabataean funerary architecture: a relatively unadorned facade, two five-step motifs at the top, a simple interior burial chamber with shelves for corpses, and inscriptions above the doorway. Built around AD 50, Qasr Al Saneh was in use for just 50 years before the Nabataean kings were overwhelmed by the Romans.

Al Khuraymat, about 750m north of Qasr Al Saneh, has some of the best-preserved tombs in Madain Saleh – around 20 tombs are carved into the rock face. Look out for elegant gynosphinxes (spirit guardians with women's heads), lions' bodies and wings adorning the corners of pediments. There is some archaeological evidence of plasterwork on the facades and a suggestion that people feasted outside familial tombs – a Nabataean 'Day of the Dead'. The Nabataeans were masters of hydrology and manipulated rain run-off and underground aquifers to thrive in the desert landscape. The great

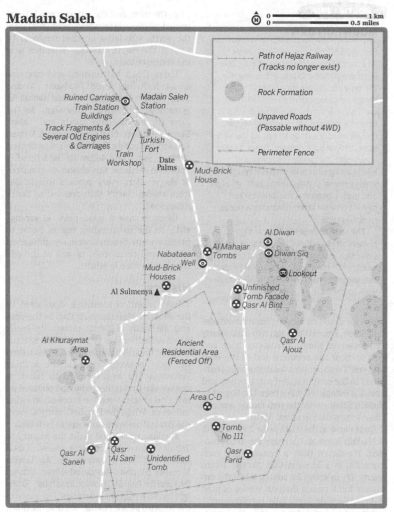

Nabataean Well was one of more than 60 wells currently known of in the city. The wall supports – added in the 20th century – were built from railway sleepers pilfered from the Hejaz Railway. The **Al Mahajar tombs** are especially photogenic and some of the oldest at Madain Saleh.

Al Diwan, carved into a hillside to shield it from the wind, is one of the few extant examples of nonfunerary architecture in Madain Saleh. The name (*diwan* means 'living room') owes more to modern Arab culture than to the Nabataeans, who probably used the area for sacred feasts. Opposite the hollowed-out room, which contains three benches and a large entrance suggesting that the feasts extended outdoors, are niches cut into the rock where Nabataean deities were carved. Exposure to the elements has badly weathered these carvings.

Running south from Al Diwan is the **Siq**, a narrow passageway measuring about 40m wide between two rock faces lined with more small altars. At the far end is a striking **natural amphitheatre**. Climb along the southeastern slope up to a number of altars. From here, look west and soak in the breathtaking views.

Qasr Al Bint (Palace of the Daughter) consists of a wonderful row of facades that

WORTH A TRIP

MOUNTAIN DRIVE

Rising 2580m above sea level, **Jebel Al Lawz** (Almond Mountain; off Hwy 394; 🌐 relieve.admire.unblock; **P**), is one of the only accessible mountains in the Kingdom to experience snowfall in winter. This is what many visitors driving up the windy road through the Midian mountain range hope to see. At the very least, they are guaranteed spectacular views over the range. Camping and hiking along unmarked trails through valleys home to pre-Islamic petroglyphs and inscriptions are also popular but should only be attempted with an experienced guide.

The road to Jebel Al Lawz is signposted off Hwy 394. This takes you very close to the summit; at the time of research, the road was closed 6km before the summit. From there, it's a 20-minute walk to the peak.

makes for dramatic viewing from across Madain Saleh. The east face has two particularly well-preserved tombs. If you step back and look up near the northern end of the west face, you'll distinguish a tomb that was abandoned in the early stages of construction and would, if completed, have been the largest in Madain Saleh – only the step facade was cut. These tombs date to about AD 31.

Qasr Farid in the south is the largest tomb of Madain Saleh and perhaps the most stunning. It's carved from a free-standing rock monolith, in a location that gives it a rare beauty. Try to arrive for sunset, when the enigmatic tomb passes through shades of pink and gold until darkness falls: breathtaking.

Jebel Al Ahmar Area C is in the southeastern portion of Madain Saleh and features three tombs with drawings dating to between AD 16 and AD 61. The tombs are burial chambers without special adornments.

Tabuk تبوك

📄 014 / POP 455,450

Tabuk, a growing tourist destination, was a strategic stopping place for pre-20th-century hajj pilgrims trekking on foot from the Syrian capital of Damascus to Medina and onward to Mecca. The city's culture was deeply influenced by Egyptian travellers (one of the largest groups of land-travelling pilgrims)

from the west, and the Ottomans (who controlled pilgrimage routes for centuries) from the north, who left a physical reminder by way of the **Hejaz Railway** remnants near the centre of town.

Today Tabuk has bustling and extensive souqs, including **Souq Twaheen** (Windmill Souq; Al Imam Muhammad Ibn Abdul Wahhab Rd; 🌐 teaching.choice.trucks; ⊗ 8am-7pm Sat-Thu, 1-7pm Fri) for Bedouin goods and **Tabuk Souq** (Sharalom; btwn King Abdullah & Al Imam Abdullah Ibn Faisal Ibn Turki Rds; 🌐 sneezed.looked. stunts; ⊗ 9am-noon & 4-11pm Sat-Thu, 5-11pm Fri). Split into sections, this cluster of hundreds of shops offers every product imaginable, from *thobes* (men's shirt-dresses) to South Asian food.

Tabuk is also a good place to arrange visits to the surrounding region, home to pristine white beaches, virtually untouched islands and coral reefs, as well as the odd snowy mountain in winter.

History

Tabuk's historical identity is dominated by the Prophet Muhammad's visit to the area and the Battle of Tabuk, though the battle never actually came to pass. In AD 630 the Prophet organised an army of 30,000, then the most powerful force on the Arabian Peninsula. His men travelled to Tabuk to engage the Byzantines, who had planned an invasion to stamp out the Prophet's growing influence. When the Prophet's army arrived, the Byzantines were nowhere to be found.

Muslims worldwide make the journey to Tabuk because the Prophet visited Tabuk Castle and prayed where the **At Tawba Mosque** (Prophet's Mosque; off Al Imam Abdullah Ibn Faisal Ibn Turki St; 🌐 creeps.traps.tribal; ⊗ daylight hours; **P**) **FREE** now stands. The name of the mosque alludes to the fact that the ninth chapter of the Quran (Surah At Tawba) is said to have been revealed to the Prophet while he was here, and Tabuk is mentioned in numerous Hadiths (Prophetic traditions), giving the city special meaning for Muslims.

⊙ Sights

★ **Tabuk Castle** CASTLE
(📄 014 423 9696; Al Amir Fahd Bin Sultan Rd; 🌐 stops.slings.cloak; ⊗ 9am-5pm Sat-Thu, 3-5pm Fri) **FREE** Dating to 1559, Tabuk Castle is now a museum, with several rooms housing some interesting historical artefacts from the Ottoman period and lots of signage about the history of Tabuk, its connection to

Tabuk

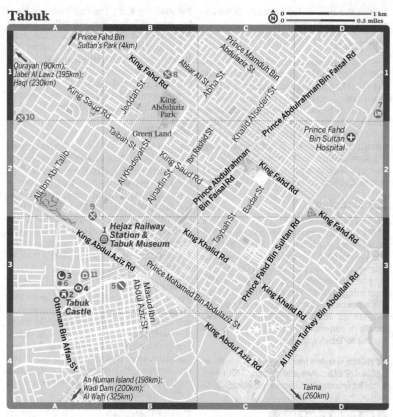

Map legend text:
- Prince Fahd Bin Sultan's Park (4km)
- Qurayah (90km); Jabel Al Lawz (195km); Haql (230km)
- Prince Mamduh Bin Abdulaziz St
- King Fahd Rd
- King Saud Rd
- King Abdulaziz Park
- Green Land
- Prince Abdulrahman Bin Faisal Rd
- Prince Fahd Bin Sultan Hospital
- King Fahd Rd
- Hejaz Railway Station & Tabuk Museum
- King Abdul Aziz Rd
- King Khalid Rd
- Tabuk Castle
- Prince Mohamed Bin Abdulaziz St
- King Abdul Aziz Rd
- Al Imam Turkey Bin Abdullah Rd
- An Numan Island (198km); Wadi Dam (200km); Al Wajh (325km)
- Taima (260km)

SAUDI ARABIA TABUK

the Prophet Muhammad and several famous travellers, including Ibn Battuta and Evliya Celebi. The castle features a ground-floor mosque, an open courtyard and a stairway to the castle's 2nd-floor mosque and watchtowers. Outside are cisterns that once captured water from a spring that the Prophet Muhammad reportedly drank from.

★ **Hejaz Railway Station & Tabuk Museum** MUSEUM

(📞014 421 6198; King Abdul Aziz Rd; 🌐valid.stuff. offhand; ⏰8am-3pm Sat-Thu; 🅿) FREE Tabuk's early-20th-century Hejaz Railway (p298) station is one of the best preserved in Saudi Arabia. There are 13 recently refurbished buildings spread over 80,000 sq metres and these include include a workshop, a handicrafts centre, and a building that houses a locomotive, a freight car and several Ottoman relics worth viewing. The site is also going to be the home of Tabuk's new state-of-the-art city museum, which was being built at the time of research and is scheduled to open in early 2020.

Tours

For the personal touch, **Tabuk Tourist Sights** (☑ 055 537 0555; tabuktourist@hotmail.com; Prince Fahd Bin Sultan Rd; 🔲 waiters.outdoors.handwriting; ⊙ hours vary) arranges history and activity-based trips, including hang-gliding. **Al Tayyar Travel & Tourism** (☑ 9200 12333; www.altayyaronline.com; 7507 Prince Abdulmajid Ibn Abdulaziz Rd; 🔲 halt.bronzed.hurray; ⊙ 8.30am-10.30pm Sat-Thu, from 1.30pm Fri), the country's biggest agency, also offers desert camping, hiking and farm tours.

🛏 Sleeping

Holiday Inn Tabuk   HOTEL $
(☑ 014 422 1212; www.holidayinn.com; Prince Sultan Rd; 🔲 shocks.paths.watch; r SR315; 🅿 🛜 🛣) The rooms here are comfortable and contemporary in style, plus there's a fitness centre and an outdoor pool, and the friendly, welcoming staff all speak English. The hotel's restaurant serves a decent buffet breakfast. It's an attractive option for business travellers, conveniently close to the highway leading to Tabuk's airport.

★ Hilton Garden Inn Tabuk   HOTEL $$
(☑ 014 422 6116; www.ar.hilton.com; 7701 Prince Sultan Rd; 🔲 incline.tuck.surface; r/ste/apt SR308/

OFF THE BEATEN TRACK

RED SEA BEACHES

Saudi Arabia's northern Red Sea coast currently has some of the country's least visited beaches, including **Bir Al Mashy** (Ras Suwayjil As Saghir; 🔲 fiesta.wifely.portal; 🅿), **Al Sharim** (Ras Al Hasha; 🔲 sandpit.intrusion.neutral; 🅿) and **Hawaz** (Prince Fahd Bin Sultan Beach; off Hwy 55; 🔲 dilating.agreeable.newsreel; 🅿) beaches. In fact, at the time of research, this was the least developed stretch of the Red Sea in the entire Kingdom, with much of it literally just desert meandering into the sea, complete with camels that can often be seen basking in the sun on the empty shore.

This situation is about to change, though, as stretches of this barren coastline are being developed into resorts. Fortunately, isolated spots are likely to remain for quite some time yet.

1080/1467; 🅿 🛜 🛣) The first high-end hotel to arrive in Tabuk, the Hilton has a brash glass building that makes quite the statement along the busy Prince Sultan Rd. Rooms are stylishly furnished and the customer service is impeccable. There's also an excellent cafe and restaurant with a children's menu, and a nice outdoor swimming pool. Excellent value at these prices.

Eating

★ Grill Alfi   MIDDLE EASTERN $
(☑ 014 424 6650; Umar Ibn Al Khattab; 🔲 progress.parks.ripe; grills SR20-198; ⊙ 1pm-1am) Serving the most popular no-frills local cuisine in town, Alfi comes highly recommended and you can see why. Fresh grilled meat is turned over rapidly as orders come thick and fast. Staff are friendly and one or two can speak English. At weekends you'll struggle to get a seat during the lunch and dinner rush, so get here early.

Falafel Restaurant   STREET FOOD $
(Hatim At Tai St; 🔲 drew.layover.nuns; wraps SR3; ⊙ 7am-midnight) Cheap eating options such as this are everywhere, but few do falafel wraps this well. Standard ingredients in Saudi falafel wraps are falafel, boiled egg, fries and hot sauce. Here they turn it up a notch and give you the option to stuff your wrap with a spicy omelette instead of a boring boiled egg – we recommend the omelette.

Qaryiat Therasiyah   MIDDLE EASTERN $$
(☑ 056 212 1111; King Khalid Rd; 🔲 insects.repair.rushed; mains SR14.50-976; ⊙ 11am-1am Sat-Thu, 1pm-1am Fri) Every town in Saudi has one, and this is Tabuk's version of a restaurant set within a beautiful mock fort. The Qaryiat has cosy rooms centred on an open courtyard, where a genuine black-and-white goat-hair tent has been erected for diners who want to sit Bedouin-style on the floor and enjoy the house favourite, *mandi* (chicken and rice). Located opposite the Hala Hotel.

ⓘ Getting There & Around

Tabuk has the regional **Prince Sultan Bin Abdulaziz Airport** (☑ 9200 11233; www.gaca.gov.sa; Tabuk Airport Rd; 🔲 majority.crunch.tonight) and a **Saptco bus station** (☑ 9200 00877; www.saptco.com.sa; Prince Sultan Rd), from where there are regular bus services to Hail, Yanbu, Medina and Riyadh.

There is no public transport in Tabuk – the easiest way to get around is by using Uber (www.

VISITING JUBBAH ROCK CARVINGS FROM HAIL

Arguably the Kingdom's premier pre-Islamic site, **Jubbah Rock Carvings** (☑016 533 8855; mokab@scth.gov.sa; 🌐honks.catastrophe.jostles; ⏰8am-3pm Sun-Thu, 3-6pm Fri & Sat; 🅿) 🆓 is an ancient open-air art gallery. Covering an area measuring 39 sq km are some of the most impressive petroglyphs (rock carvings) you are likely to ever see. The finest carvings date from around 5500 BC, when much of this area was an inland lake and inhabitants carved game animals that came to the waters. Elegant rock-cut ibex, oryx and camels abound, as well as significant Thamudic inscriptions dating to 1000 BC. The site is at the northwestern edge of the city of Jubbah and is signposted from the centre of town. Access is next to a new visitors centre. Phone or email ahead to ensure the site is open.

Jubbah is 100km northwest of Hail and can be visited as a day trip from this historic trading crossroads. Hail has one of the country's last remaining **flea markets** (off Al Udayra; 🌐lanes.escaping.revived; ⏰8am-8pm; 🅿) and a fun **Local Heritage Museum** (☑055 701 4441; off Al Amir Miqrin Ibn Abdul Aziz; 🌐emperor.serve.planting; SR20; ⏰9am-12.30pm & 3.30pm-midnight Sat-Thu, from 3.30pm Fri) set in a traditional Najd house. There is budget accommodation at the recommended **Golden Tulip** (☑016 541 9999; www.goldentuliphail.com; King Saud Rd; 🌐pavement.inserted.venue; d SR330; 🅿🛜❄) hotel and local Najd cuisine at **Al Turathi** (☑016 531 0000; King Abdul Aziz Rd; 🌐yoga.empires.strictly; mains from SR16; ⏰1pm-midnight); this part-museum, part-restaurant is stocked with vintage and antique items across its two storeys.

Hail is served by a regional **airport** (☑9200 11233; www.gaca.gov.sa; Hatim At Tai Rd; 🌐milkmaid.imagined.feudal), a **Saptco bus station** (☑9200 00877; www.saptco.com.sa; off King Abdul Aziz Rd; 🌐create.harder.inviting) and the **SAR Hail train station** (☑9200 00329, Whatsapp 053 310 4455; www.sar.com.sa; Station Rd; 🌐falsely.trustful.odds), 60km northeast of the city centre.

uber.com) and Careem (www.careem.com); fares start from SR10.

Al Wajh الوجح

☑014 / POP 26,600

The real attraction of Al Wajh is undoubtedly the town's remaining Hejazi architecture in the **Al Balad** (King Faisal Rd; 🌐intelligent.hoedown.longshore; 🅿). These are among the finest Red Sea coral buildings outside of Jeddah, and with the ghostly emptiness of the abandoned old town, they are easily the more atmospheric. Photographs of the town can be seen in **Al Wajh Castle** (Al Qalat St; 🌐calibrate.exalts.smear; 🅿) 🆓, the upper floor of which offers views of the town's port. These days, the town is virtually unknown despite unspoiled beaches stretching for 100km on either side. There is no hustle and bustle here, just the wind making its way through the empty shells as they stare silently out to sea.

Sleeping options are limited, with midrange **Wajeh Beach Hotel** (☑014 442 2020; King Abdullah Rd, An Nahdah; 🌐inspector.environments.apps; ste SR546; 🅿🛜) offering the best facilities. For food, wraps and salads are available from **Tawouk** (☑9200 20322; off King Abdullah Rd; 🌐revisions.cobwebs.pick; mains SR7-24; ⏰1pm-2am), a local fast-food chain.

Wajh Airport (☑9200 11233; www.gaca.gov.sa; Airport Rd; 🌐reinforce.unshaved.sustained) is served by domestic flights, and there is also a **Saptco bus station** (☑9200 00877; www.saptco.com.sa; Hwy 55; 🌐crickets.detectable.fling) south of the town centre that runs regular services to Tabuk, Al Ula and Medina.

CENTRAL NAJD نجد المركزي

The Najd region, which stretches deep into the desert north of Riyadh, presents the cultural foundation of modern Saudi Arabia and is traditionally considered the Kingdom's conservative heartland. Ironically, the Najdis, who see themselves as the purest of Bedouin Arabs and the most faithful inheritors of the strict orthodox Wahhabi legacy, are also the custodians of some of the finest and most sophisticated pre-Islamic rock art in the country, at Jubbah.

Buraydah

بريدة

⟁ 016 / POP 391,350

Home to the world's largest date market and festival, Buraydah has swathes of green neighbourhoods with forests of palms waiting to be explored on foot. One of the oldest, **As Sabbakh** (off As Sabbakh; ⓦ managed.caller. engaging; ⓢ daylight hours; ⓟ), close to the Dates City complex, offers a glimpse of what old Buraydah once looked like. Here you will find ruined mud houses and mosques peering out from beneath dense palm orchards.

There is good-value accommodation at the **Best Western Plus Buraidah** (⟁ 016 382 0606; www.bestwestern.com; Faisal Bin Misha'l Rd; ⓦ figs.believer.puns; r SR288; ⓟ 🛜) and delicious mezze on offer at the Lebanese restaurant, **Hashem** (⟁ 016 397 7701; King Salman Rd; ⓦ ventures.spelling.mirror; mains from SR10; ⓢ 5am-noon & 4pm-12.30am).

◉ Sights

★ **Al Mudaifar Mosque** MOSQUE
(off As Sabbakh; ⓦ displays.vented.starring; ⓢ daylight hours; ⓟ) Surrounded by a forest of palms, this quaint little Najd mud mosque, with its tall round minaret and engraved wood door, truly evokes the Saudi Arabia of yesteryear. It's respectfully restored, and inside storm lanterns hang from the ceiling of palm trunks and a red patterned carpet covers the floor. A simple white mihrab (niche indicating the direction of Mecca) is framed by wooden shutters and neat piles of green Qurans. Before leaving be sure to climb the roof and take in the wonderful views of the neighbourhood.

Dates City MARKET
(King Khalid Rd; ⓦ with.sporting.blows; ⓢ 3.30-9.30pm; ⓟ) Home of the world's biggest **date festival** (King Abdul Aziz Rd, Dates City; ⓦ with. sporting.blows; ⓢ Aug), this is the largest date market on earth, and the complex resembles a small airport. At the height of the harvest (July to September), loud auctions are held here almost daily. It's close to Buraydah's historic date forest area, and farmers from all over come here to sell their product. Wander around, tasting the delicious variety of dates, but beware – if you want to buy some, they're sold by the kilo here!

ⓘ Getting There & Away

Buraydah is served by the **Prince Nayef Bin Abdulaziz International Airport** (⟁ 9200 11233; www.gaca.gov.sa; off Hwy 419; ⓦ confines.exciting.costumes), and also has a **Saptco Bus Station** (⟁ 9200 00877; www.saptco.com. sa; King Abdulaziz Rd; ⓦ festivity.sock.teacher), from where buses regularly depart for Unayzah, Medina, Riyadh and Hail.

SAR Al Qassim Railway Station (⟁ 9200 00329; www.sar.com.sa; off Hwy 7011; ⓦ implements.toddlers.ownership) has trains to Hail, Jauf, Majmaah and Riyadh.

EASTERN PROVINCE

المنطقة الشرقية

The Eastern Province, with its large expat community, is home to some of the Kingdom's most liberal areas, especially around regional capital, Dammam. There is excellent international food here and many high-end hotels. It's home to Ithra, on the edge of Dammam, the first venue in Saudi Arabia for international performing arts. Much of this is down to the Saudi Arabian Oil Company (Saudi Aramco), which financed Ithra and employs most of the expats in a region that is the centre of the Kingdom's oil production.

Before the oil, the Eastern Province was known for being the heartland of the country's largest Shiite community and renowned for its ports along the Gulf coast that once connected Arabia to the rest of the world. It is also where the world's largest oasis can be found, near the town of Al Hofuf.

Al Hofuf

الهفوف

⟁ 011 / POP 293,200

Al Hofuf sits within the largest oasis in the world (there are reportedly more than 1.5 million palm trees), and was historically home to a fabulously vibrant market that attracted traders from all over the peninsula. Visitors come to enjoy the tastefully restored but still very local **Souq Al Qaisariah** (King Abdul Aziz Rd; ⓦ discouraged.guarding.paradise; ⓢ 8am-noon & 3pm-midnight) and the old town. Al Hofuf is also where the country's first **royal school** (⟁ 013 580 2639; off King Abdul Aziz Rd; ⓦ under. flock.polished; ⓢ 8am-4pm Sun-Thu, 4-8pm Fri, 9am-1pm Sat; ⓟ) can be found, complete with ink pots and the cane used on naughty royals.

The town's name means 'whistling of the wind', and it makes a lot of sense when you're atop its famous **Al Qarah Mountain** (⟁ 013 598 2888; Al Qarah; ⓦ situated.bravery.absolves; ⓟ), staring out across a sea of greenery with the wind whistling in your ear.

Al Hofuf was where the mischievous Qa-martians hid after stealing the Kaaba's Black Stone in the 10th century. The Ottomans ruled the area on two separate occasions between the 16th and 19th centuries before Abdul Aziz took it in 1913.

Sleeping & Eating

⭐**Al Koot Heritage Hotel**   BOUTIQUE HOTEL **$$**
(☑013 582 2279; www.alkootheritage.com; King Khalid Rd; �🖷crystals.page.foremost; s/d/ste SR400/550/1050; P🖭) Housed in a beautiful historic building that shares architectural features with the nearby royal school, Al Koot's comfortable rooms are tastefully decorated with traditional fabrics, rugs and artefacts. Works of art hang on the walls and residents sit on Najd patterned upholstery in the central courtyard, where breakfast and dinner is served.

Taj Family Restaurant   INDIAN **$**
(☑013 575 5334; King Khalid Rd; 🖷soft.notched. stiff; mains SR12-35; ⊙9.30am-12.30am; 🖉) Close to the historic centre, this restaurant has a comfortable and clean family area and a wide-ranging menu that includes an extensive vegetarian selection. Prices are very reasonable and the staff are attentive, even during busy periods. Try the *paneer masala* (the cheese makes a good alternative to meat), or for something lighter, their excellent *dosas* (stuffed Indian pancakes).

🛈 Getting There & Away

Hofuf has a **train station** (☑9200 08886; www. saudirailways.org; King Fahd Rd; 🖷journey.hairpin.crust) linking it to the capital and Dammam, and also has a **Saptco bus station** (☑9700 00877; www.saptco.com.sa; Ain Najm St; 🖷vocab.blend.fragment) with regular services to Dammam and Riyadh.

Dammam   الدمام

☑013 / POP 768,600

Dammam is the best place in the region for food and sleeping options. The city's cuisine has a truly international flavour to cater to its huge expat community, most of whom work for the Saudi Arabian Oil Company. It is also where the causeway to Bahrain is located, making it popular with those wanting to hop across to the Kingdom's more liberal neighbour.

Dammam is where Saudi Arabia's oil story began in the early part of the last century, when America discovered oil here and a partnership between the two nations began; one that has seen their economies intertwined ever since.

It is therefore no surprise that elements of modern Dammam have a distinctly American feel. The city is laid out in a typical American grid system, with streets identified by numbers, and it is home to the largest concentration of American fast-food outlets in Saudi Arabia. **Half-Moon Bay** (off King Fahd Rd, Dhahran; 🖷entertaining.agreeing. tribally; P) offers resort entertainment while the **Al Khobar Corniche** (Corniche Rd; 🖷fancy.fall.roosts; P) is popular with joggers.

⊙ Sights

⭐**Ithra**   CULTURAL CENTRE
(King Abdulaziz Center for World Culture; ☑800 122 1224; www.ithra.com; Ring Rd; 🖷twins.bats. deliver; museum adult/child SR35/15; ⊙9am-9pm Sat-Thu, 1-10pm Fri; P) Ithra is a world-class cultural venue like no other in Saudi Arabia. The building resembles a space station, and is home to a cinema, a museum, exhibition galleries, a library, and a theatre with world-class performing arts. Past performances have included Japans' Shizuoka Performing Arts Center and legendary oud player Naseer Shamma and his orchestra.

Taybeen Museum   MUSEUM
(☑5080 07333; www.altaybeen.com; Ash Sheraa; 🖷armchairs.utensil.putt; adult/child SR25/15; ⊙4-9pm; P) Relive your childhood at the privately owned Taybeen Museum. What started as the personal collection of Majid Al Ghamdi has now evolved into a 300-sq-metre museum that includes more than 10,000 toys, posters, cameras, electronics and food and drink containers. There's even a display showing the evolution of Coke bottles from the 1970s to the 1990s.

Sleeping

⭐**Park Inn by Radisson**   HOTEL **$**
(☑013 809 3311; www.parkinn.com; King Abdullah Bin Abdulaziz Rd; 🖷exclaim.arriving.doctors; d SR200; P🖭) This quirky budget option by a leading hotel chain is an excellent choice in Dammam. Rooms are decorated in a stylish, contemporary fashion and have ample space, though the design in one or two rooms can be a tad painfully hip. Staff are polite and speak excellent English, and the hotel is located close to the corniche.

ARABIAN DESERTS

The Empty Quarter

The 'Abode of Silence', the **Empty Quarter** (⊞ messily.supernatural.surer) covers almost 655,000 sq km and evokes all that was romantic and forbidden for European adventurers, such as British explorer Wilfred Thesiger, who famously crossed it. The Bedouin simply call it 'the sands', and its dunes, which can reach up to 300m high, form long chains of sculpted ridges that move up to 30m a year and are home to elusive Arabian wolf, sand cat, red fox, desert lynx, cape hare and spiny tailed lizard. It rains less than 35mm a year out here. One of the most unforgiving places on earth, it's not somewhere amateurs should explore alone. Instead, join an experienced guide or tour group such as Haya Tours (p277) from Riyadh. The edge of the Empty Quarter is usually accessed from the tiny agricultural town of Layla, three hours south of the capital.

Al Nafud Desert

While the Empty Quarter gets all the attention, it is actually far easier to visit the beautiful sands of **Al Nafud** (An Nafud; ⊞ loudspeaker.unrelated.hiker). Covering an area of 103,600 sq km, these sweeping red dunes sit in an oval-shaped depression towards the north of the country, just past Hail. A partially tarmacked road, south of Jubbah, heads several kilometres into the red dunes. Wild camping is possible but beware strong winds.

Red Sands

The **Red Sands** (off Route 5395; ⊞ birdbath.unifier.racks) are the most evocative desert dunes near Riyadh. These pristine, windswept mounds of deep, red sand are the closest the urban dwellers of Riyadh get to the Empty Quarter or Al Nafud Desert. Many head out at the weekends to hire a quad bike from one of the Bedouin stalls lining the highway, or to drive through the sea of dunes in their own off-road vehicle. Either option is great fun!

Kempinski Al Othman
Hotel Al Khobar   HOTEL **$$**

(☏ 013 829 4444; www.kempinski.com; King Saud Rd; ⊞ home.plastic.cloud; d/ste/apt SR860/1107/1620; P 🛜 🎱) This high-end hotel with midrange prices has stunning views over the city from almost every room. Each room is immaculately designed with much attention paid to detail. Staff are superfriendly and have excellent knowledge of the locality, and there's a nice indoor pool and gym. The hotel is very popular with business customers.

✖ Eating

★**Damascus**
Garden Pastries   BAKERY **$**

(☏ 013 894 2854; 7110 10th St; ⊞ jeering.cafe.national; pastries from SR3; ⊗ 9am-midnight Sat-Thu, from 12.30pm Fri) The best bakery in Dammam. The sweet and savoury pastries baked in brick kilns here are simply delicious, especially, the *pide* (a boat-shaped thick-crust pastry stuffed with lightly spiced minced meat). Place your order and patiently watch as each item is handmade and freshly baked before your very eyes. A great spot for a light lunch.

Samir Emis   MIDDLE EASTERN **$**

(☏ 013 864 8101; cnr 1st & Prince Talat Sts; ⊞ strays.notices.pasta; mains SR5-25; ⊗ 9-11.45am & 4pm-midnight Sat-Thu, from 4pm Fri) You can't leave Saudi Arabia without visiting at least one *boofiya* – an inexpensive cafeteria-style takeaway that serves up quick sandwiches of either chicken liver, egg and falafel, or shawarma. They also do sweet fresh juices such as *mushakkal* (a mixed-fruit mocktail made of strawberry, banana and vanilla ice cream).

★**Parkers**   INTERNATIONAL **$$**

(☏ 013 882 0260; Prince Faisal Bin Fahd Rd; ⊞ already.sensual.loyal; mains SR24-62; ⊗ 7am-1am; 🛜) After an elaborate social media campaign launched this trendy restaurant, it has become the place to be seen for young, hip Saudis. A nice open-air garden, with benches and a food truck, is more East London than Saudi Arabia, while the main restaurant serves up innovative comfort food like mac and Cheetos and corn on the cob with orange basil.

Al Marsah Seafood   SEAFOOD **$$**

(☏ 013 867 0976; cnr Prince Saad & 10th Sts; ⊞ fall.eats.modern; seafood per kg from SR45; ⊗ noon-midnight) You'll be greeted at the door at Al Marsah, the best seafood restaurant in Dammam, with a delicious range of fresh seafood for you to choose from. Sold by the kilo, the wide selection includes sea bream, hamra, huge crabs, lobsters and prawns. Take your seat while the seafood is freshly prepared and served with salad and bread.

Oah Yamal Restaurant   MIDDLE EASTERN $$
(☑ 013 802 2862; King Faisal Rd; ✉ flux.coolest.adopt; mains SR20-120; ☺ 7-10.30am & noon-midnight) Oah Yamal is a treat for the eyes as well as the palate. Reminiscent of Bahrain or Kuwait in the pre-oil era, when pearling and fishing were the main occupations, the restaurant is decorated with fishing nets and vintage knick-knacks. Seafood is a speciality; try the grilled fish or the shrimp biryani.

Heritage Village   MIDDLE EASTERN $$
(☑ 013 809 0000; www.heritage-village.com.sa; Prince Mohammad Bin Fahad Rd; ✉ hatter.using.librarian; mains SR15-100; ☺ noon-11.30pm Sun-Thu, to 12.30am Fri & Sat) Every city in Saudi Arabia boasts at least one of these restaurant-cum-museums, and Dammam's is among the better ones. Before dining on some excellent traditional Najd food, it's well worth perusing the top floor's various antique items, including muskets and regional attire (many labelled in English).

🍷 Drinking & Nightlife

★ Butlers Chocolate Cafe   CAFE
(☑ 013 840 7084; www.butlerschocolates.com; Prince Mohammad Bin Fahad Rd; ✉ disband.pumps. donation; ☺ 7am-midnight Sat-Wed, to 1.30am Thu & Fri; 🛜) A dangerous spot for chocolate lovers. Each gourmet cup of coffee here comes with a free chocolate truffle. The cafe is furnished in a classy, elegant and upmarket style that hints at the European (Irish) roots of the chain. There's an extensive breakfast menu but it's the exquisite Butlers artisan chocolate you'll be eyeing off.

Sky Lounge   TEAHOUSE
(☑ 013 829 4444; www.kempinski.com/en/al-khobar/hotel-al-othman; King Saud Rd, Kempinski Al Othman Hotel Al Khobar; ✉ home.plastic.cloud; ☺ 8am-midnight; 🛜) Enjoy a classic Saudi lemon and mint mocktail amid faux palm trees and glittering chandeliers, with views of the twinkling city below. If you'd rather something hot to drink, there's *gahwa* (coffee) and traditional pastries such as *kunafeh*

on the menu. The Sky Lounge also has a small sushi snack menu.

Vitamin Palace   JUICE BAR
(☑ 013 881 5222; 6546 King Abdulaziz Rd; ✉ popping.town.property; ☺ 10am-2am) Vitamin Palace is your one-stop shop for fresh fruit juices, mocktails and shakes. More than 200 kinds of juices are sold by the litre or the cup. Try the best-selling Jaffran juice, an Arab-inspired version of a mango shake, peppered with saffron and nuts, or the avocado and Bounty chocolate milkshake.

🛍 Shopping

Al Othaim Mall   SHOPPING CENTRE
(☑ 9200 08331; www.othaimmalls.com; Prince Mohammad Bin Fahad Branch Rd; ✉ amended. inches.parks; ☺ 9am-11.30pm Sat-Thu, from 1pm Fri) Al Othaim Mall is built to look like a gigantic ship – there's no way you can miss it. The four-storey shopping centre boasts 392 shops, ranging from high-end to affordable international brands, along with a floor dedicated to Arab-style apparel, wedding gowns and party dresses.

ⓘ Getting There & Away

Dammam is served by the **King Fahd International Airport** (Dammam Airport; ☑ 9200 11233; www.kfia.gov.sa; King Fahd Rd; ✉ couched.dairies.glittering; 🛜), a **train station** (☑ 9200 08886; www.saudirailways. org; Qais Ibn Alhaitham St; ✉ slippery.figs. credit) that links it to the capital, Riyadh, and a **Saptco bus station** (☑ 9200 00877; www. saptco.sa.com; Waqidi St; ✉ simply.grading. hinted) with daily services to Bahrain, Al Hofuf and Riyadh.

SOUTHERN SAUDI ARABIA

Asir is the jewel in the Kingdom's crown, with a beautifully distinct cultural heritage and spectacular natural wonders, but this is the Arabia you never hear about it: one where forest-covered mountains dramatically rise up a few kilometres from the desert, their peaks swirling in misty clouds, before plunging down to the Red Sea coast. Nestled within these rugged ridges are lush green valleys where centuries-old villages display the most innovative mud, stone and slate architecture you are likely to see anywhere in Saudi Arabia.

DHEE AIN VILLAGE

Named after the spring that waters its garden, Dhee Ain is the perfect image of traditional, mountainous Arabia. Sand coloured two- and four-storey houses of polished stone gently cascade down a marble hill to a lush green valley where the branches of banana, pepper and lemon trees are alive with birdsong. Dating back to the 8th century, 49 houses and a village mosque remain for visitors to wander around. Most are empty shells, though work is under way to develop the site further. Dhee Ain is 24km from the town of Al Baha, the road to which is a spectacular drive.

Abha   أبها

📕 017 / POP 210,886

Abha is the ideal base to explore the Asir National Park and its mysterious villages. This compact town, nestled in the green, mountainous interior, also boasts historic neighbourhoods of decaying mud houses with unique local architectural features. The best are in Al Nasb and Al Bastah, with the latter home to the country's only surviving pedestrian Ottoman Bridge, a reminder of the city's pre-Saudi life as capital of Ottoman-controlled Asir.

Abha is also at the heart of the Kingdom's artistic expression. Al Muftaha Village is centred around a beautiful mosque with calligraphy graffiti, and its museums and galleries have helped created one of the only places in Saudi Arabia with a bohemian air.

Sitting 2200m above sea level, Abha can be bathed in sunshine one minute and shrouded in mist and fog the next. This is a city contrary to everything you might expect of Saudi Arabia. There's a **Tourist Information Centre** (📕 017 231 1505; www.scth.gov.sa; off King Khalid Rd; ✍ honest.written.hugs; ⊘8am-3pm Sun-Thu) close to the Al Muftaha cultural complex.

◉ Sights

★ Al Nasb   AREA

(off King Faisal Rd; ✍ helm.rocky.bonds) Start at the eastern edge of this area for a wonderful vista of the old mud and slate houses backing onto a patchwork of greenery: this is what all of Abha once looked like. As you wander the neighbourhood admiring the dilapidated buildings, including a mosque built in 1862,

be sure to stop and converse with the South Asian migrants who now live here (some speak a little English), to get a fascinating perspective on one aspect of Saudi society.

★ Al Muftaha Village   CULTURAL CENTRE

(off King Khalid Rd; ✍ mailbox.movie.rockets; ⊘4-11pm; P) **FREE** This cultural village really embodies the artistic spirit of Asir. A mosque with stunning calligraphy graffiti sits surrounded by a series of small art galleries featuring beautiful work by local and regional artists and photographers. Either side of the mosque are two small museums and around the back is a grassy entertainment stage with a coffee shop. A platform for local creativity, the Al Muftaha Village is unlike any other space in the region and a great place to spend an afternoon.

Al Bastah   AREA

(off Al Imam Ali Bin Abi Talib Rd; ✍ lunges.copies.trend; P) Once a village on the outskirts of Abha, Al Bastah is now one of two neighbourhoods with a healthy number of old fort-like houses. These tall properties with tiny square windows were constructed using rocks, mud, slate and timber. Their distinctive features are the slate lines that helped against weather erosion. Many are in a sad state of decay, but a few have been repurposed – the two biggest are east of the mosque. The **Ottoman Bridge** (✍ cracking.gangway.passing) is also in this area.

🛏 Sleeping & Eating

Qasr Al Ertiqaa Apartments   APARTMENT $

(📕 017 225 3333; Al Imam Muhammad Ibn Saud Rd; ✍ assemble.abacus.beats; ste SR170; P 🛜) These mini apartments, a short walk northwest of the town centre, come equipped with small kitchenettes and laundry facilities. In a city not blessed with good accommodation options, here you get excellent value for your money. Qasr Al Ertiqaa has two entrances; the one with car parking is around the back, off Qatar St.

Abha Palace Hotel   HOTEL $$

(📕 017 229 4444; www.abhapalace.com.sa; off Nahraan Rd; ✍ troubles.punch.renews; r SR550; P 🛜 🏊) Resembling a space station from an '80s movie, this is Abha's only hotel claiming a questionable five stars. It overlooks the Abha Dam lake, has cool glass lifts and a nice terraced cafe. The rooms can be a tad small but have an understated elegance, and many come with lake views. There is also a good international restaurant on the 5th floor.

Almualem Yemeni Restaurant YEMENI $
(☎017 224 9885; Al Tabjiah; ⓦwarnings.slogans.barman; mains from SR5; ⊙6am-noon & 4.30-11pm; 🖉)
All the delicious Saudi staples that originate from Yemeni culture, such as *fuul, muthabbak* (omelette pancake) and *masoob* (a bread, banana and honey dish), are freshly prepared by Yemenis here, which might well explain why locals think there's no better place in Abha for these tasty vegetarian dishes.

❶ Getting There & Away

Abha Airport (☎9200 11233; www.gaca.gov.sa; Airport Rd; ⓦeschew.weaves.arrow) has regular flights to major Saudi cities. A taxi ride from the airport to the city centre starts from around SR40 and takes about 25 minutes. Abha's **Saptco bus station** (☎9200 00877; www.saptco.com.sa; King Faisal Rd; ⓦtable.fail.loose) has regular services to Jazan, Taif, Mecca and Jeddah. Abha is also well served by major highways connecting it to the north and south.

Jazan جازان

☎017 / POP 105,200

The regional capital for the tiny Saudi province of Jazan, this town was an anchorage for vessels travelling between the hinterland and the Hejaz, Yemen and the Indian Ocean. During the 18th century, the town was involved in the regional coffee trade, and in the early part of the 20th century it became something of a hub for the pearling industry.

For most visitors, this Red Sea port serves mostly as a gateway to the Farasan Islands, trips to which can be organised through Jazan Diver (p285) or **Farasan Tours** (☎056 594 5109; from SR250 per person). Jazan has an **Ottoman fort** (Dawsaria Fort; off Al Nastak St; ⓦcringe.pursuing.cursing; ℗) overlooking the town and a lively port area, both of which can be experienced in an hour or so, as well as budget accommodation at **Al Hayat Gizan Hotel** (☎017 322 1055; King Fahd Rd, Jazan Harbour; ⓦblunt.enabling.pulled; r SR250; ℗🖥🛜). Sudanese food, including *lahm madfun* (grilled strips of meat cooked in a spicy vegetable sauce and served with bread rolls), makes **Serei Uncle Idris** (☎055 765 9268; King Fahd Rd; ⓦriot.clues.listings; mains SR12-15; ⊙8am-noon & 1pm-midnight) a popular spot to eat. **Azam Najd** (☎053 554 5510; King Fahd Rd; ⓦroyally.desk.lend; mains from SR25; ⊙5am-midnight Sat-Thu, from 12.30pm Fri), with its reed shutters and cosy interior, serves tasty chicken and fish dishes.

❶ Getting There & Away

Jazan has the regional **King Abdullah Bin Abdulaziz Airport** (☎9200 11233; www.gaca.gov.sa; Airport Rd; ⓦpound.harp.threaten) and a **Saptco**

OFF THE BEATEN TRACK

ASIR NATIONAL PARK

The country's very first national park is home to spectacular scenery that encompasses **Mt Soudah** (Sawda; ⓦlettering.restyled.accuses; ℗), which towers some 3000m above Sarawat Valley, and is covered in juniper forests and accessible by a spectacular **cable car** (☎017 229 1500; www.syahya.com.sa; Al Souda Rd; ⓦmelodic.canals.primly; adult/child SR80/40; ⊙8am-9pm Apr-Sep) ride. The park covers an area measuring 4500 sq km, stretching from the desert in the east to the Red Sea coast, and is one of the last refuges of the critically endangered Arabian leopard and the home of plentiful Hamadryas baboons and majestic birds of prey.

Within the park are a number of remarkable villages, including the unique 'hanging village' of **Al Habala** (☎017 279 9160; www.syahya.com.sa; ⓦdeceives.trouser.translates; adult/child SR80/40; ⊙8am-9pm Apr-Sep; ℗), accessed by cable car from May to October or admired from the viewpoint. Comprising a series of sandstone houses on a ledge 400m down a sheer cliff, it was accessible only by *habal* (rope ladders). The Khatani tribe, who built it more than 370 years ago, chose this most inaccessible of spots to avoid the Ottomans. They lived here self-sufficiently on small livestock and terraced gardens up until the 1980s.

Of similar interest is **Al Yanfa** (ⓦpimples.dreadlocks.chewable; ℗) with a set of engineered tunnels that make the most of the limited, hill-top space. With their low timber ceilings and tiny wooden front doors, the houses here are best approached with a **local guide** (☎055 404 1828; www.waslcaravan.com). Built on the slopes of steep mountains that are enveloped by clouds in the winter, **Rija Alma** (off Route 211; ⓦscenting.decent.ailing; ⊙9am-9pm; ℗) village, dating back to the 8th century, contains some of the finest examples of the fort-like stone architecture of the Asir region.

bus station (☑ 9200 00877; www.saptco.com.
sa; King Faisal Rd; ⓦ websites.orchids.worth).
Jazan also has good road links from the north.

Farasan Islands   جزر فرسان

The waters around the stunning Farasan
Islands are rich in marine life, and diving is
growing in popularity here. The plankton-
rich waters are home to rays, dolphins, giant
whale sharks, many varieties of fish, including large numbers of parrotfish – subject
of a parrotfish festival from April to May
on **Hasees Beach** (off Hwy 1910; ⓦ emailing.
interns.plaiting; ℗) – and several endangered
species of turtle. The islands are also home
to some of the few remaining stretches of
coastal mangrove along the Red Sea, the
habitat of the endangered dugong.

Spare some time to visit the neighbourhood of the **pearl merchants** (Farasan Town;
ⓦ tablets.coexist.flipside). Staring at the mesmerising geometric and floral designs of the
carved patterns that adorn the houses and
arched gateways of Farasan's former pearl
merchants, or indeed the **Najd Mosque**
(Farasan Town; ⓦ swamped.liabilities.demote), you
could be forgiven for thinking you were in
the midst of Andalusian or Mughal ruins.
Also worth a visit is **Al Qessar** (ⓦ this.resistor.
excuses; ◷ 7.30am-noon & 4-9.30pm; ℗) **FREE**;
this collection of simple mud, coral and reed
structures, many with the names of the original owners etched over their facades, is a
heritage village with a cafe.

Farasan Park Hotel (☑ 017 316 0000; Ja-
naabah Beach; ⓦ brandishing.submitting.birthrate;
r/ste SR450/850; ℗ 🛜 🛝) is the only place
suitable for tourists to stay on the islands.
This resort is relatively close to Farasan
Town yet backs onto its own idyllic beach.
There's an outdoor pool, decent food in an
international restaurant and large, spacious
rooms with sea views.

❶ Getting There & Away

The only way to get to the main Island of Greater
Farasan is by the free passenger ferry, which
has two departures daily from the **ferry port**
(ⓦ submissions.operating.inaccurate; at 6am
and 3.30pm (returning 7am and 3.30pm). Tickets can be booked at the **Maritime Company
for Navigation ticket office** (Farasan Town;
ⓦ depicted.reclaims.simplifying; ◷ 5.15am-
7pm) in the town centre. Small private boat taxis
also ply the route, but their safety standards are
questionable so these are not recommended.
The only other way to get onto any of the islands
is by private boat hire.

UNDERSTAND SAUDI ARABIA

Saudi Arabia Today

Saudi Arabia is a country in transition.
Whether you arrive for pilgrimage, business
or something else, you won't be able to ignore the huge changes taking place across
the Kingdom. New roads, railways and
even cities are being built as Saudi Arabia
becomes more accessible and friendlier to
outsiders than ever before. Alongside this, a
wave of liberalisation is sweeping across the
country, eradicating many ancient traditions.

The Age of MBS

All over Saudi Arabia you will see two things:
the words 'Saudi Vision 2030' and a picture
of three men: King Abdul Aziz; his son, the
current monarch King Salman; and his son,
the Crown Prince and de facto ruler of the
Kingdom, Mohammed Bin Salman, or 'MBS'.

Saudi Arabia is living through what history will probably remember as the 'Age of
MBS': an era that, by the Kingdom's standards, is nothing short of a social and economic revolution, led by the young prince who
is overseeing sweeping changes. Since his
father took the throne and made him his key
adviser, it is MBS who has led a crackdown
on corruption within the government. He
also came up with the much-lauded Saudi
Vision 2030 road map and vowed to return
the country to a moderate Islam, already nul-
lifying the influence and power of the hitherto terrifying religious police, the *mutawwa*.

Despite international criticism for, among
other things, the ongoing war in neighbouring Yemen and his perceived role in the 2018
assassination of Saudi journalist and critic
Jamal Khashoggi, MBS remains a hero to
some Saudis, who hope he will continue to
move the country towards a new future.

Economic Reforms

Saudi Vision 2030 was launched by MBS in
April 2016, and lays out the country's plans
to completely reform the economy by wean-
ing it off oil revenue. This vision has seen the
introduction of taxes for Saudis for the first
time, as well as huge cuts in civic spending.

However, the key focus of the vision involves creating alternative revenue streams
via several major projects and the develop-

ment of a presently nonexistent tourism industry. One of the early flagship projects announced by the Saudi government was the US$500-billion development of Neom, a smart and tourist-friendly cross-border city to be built on marine land in northwestern Saudi Arabia, Egypt and Jordan. Another announcement was about the development of a 349-sq-km lagoon of 50 islands, for luxury tourism, off the Red Sea coast.

To prepare for mass tourism, e-visas allowing foreigners to attend specific Saudi festivals and events were trialled for the first time in 2018. Issued for 14 days, these visas came with no travel restrictions and have been widely seen as a precursor to the Kingdom eventually introducing tourism visas.

The Status of Women

Arguably the biggest strides, and the ones making the most headlines across the globe, have been made concerning the status of Saudi women.

In February 2017 a woman became the chair of the Saudi Stock Exchange for the first time, and later that year Lebanese singer Hiba Tawaji became the first female pop star to perform publicly in Saudi Arabia. However, more significant changes came in 2018. Firstly, in February it was declared that Saudi women no longer needed male permission to open their own business, and a month later divorced women were told they no longer had to appeal to the courts to gain custody of their children. Then in June, Saudi women were able to get behind the wheel of a car and drive legally for the first time in their own country. Each move is gradually chipping away at the country's male guardianship laws, which have historically dictated the lives of Saudi women.

International Criticism

In spite of all of this perceived progress, the Saudi government continues to come under fierce criticism from the rest of the world.

Human rights groups have heavily condemned its involvement in the war in Yemen and the increasing number of arrests of outspoken Saudi critics and women's rights activists. Then there is the continued blockade of Qatar, with whom Saudi Arabia cut diplomatic ties. The exact reasons for this are unclear, but among them is Saudi Arabia's claim that Qatar sponsors terrorism.

History

Saudi Arabia's history includes the distinct whiff of frankincense, the rise of a persistent and proud nomadic Bedouin heritage and the wealthy legacy of black gold. But all this pales into insignificance compared to the birth of Islam in the two holy cities of Mecca and Medina. For the 14 centuries since then, as the call to prayer has echoed out across the Kingdom, an intricate interplay of religion and politics has been taking place, and it continues to this day.

Ancient Arabia

The myriad kingdoms and empires that grew from the sands of Arabia before the Prophet Muhammad all had one commonality: frankincense. Ancient gods were placated with holy smoke and the peoples of Arabia got very rich providing frankincense to eager worshippers in ancient Egypt, Persia and Rome. One of the most intriguing groups from these trading states was the Nabataeans: Bedouin clans who gathered at the extraordinary rock-hewn twin cities of Madain Saleh (Saudi Arabia) and Petra (Jordan).

The phenomenal explosion of Islamic-inspired armies out of Arabia shattered the weary Byzantine and Sassanid Empires, but following the Prophet Muhammad's death in 632, Arabia slumped into torpor again and was economically insignificant to the sophisticated Umayyad and Abbasid caliphates, whose capitals were now elsewhere. Arabia was only saved from irrelevance by the spiritual significance of the holy cities of Mecca and Medina.

Trade caravans still crossed the desert, linking the cities and small towns of the Hejaz and the interior with the great cities of the wider Islamic world, but in 1517 the powerful Turkish Ottomans, under Salim I, invaded Arabia and took control of the two holy cities. The capture of the region by non-Arabs was a most unwelcome development in the eyes of those residing in the peninsula.

Wahhabi Islam & the Al Sauds

In 1703 a man was born in the insignificant oasis village of Al Uyaynah in Wadi Hanifa of central Arabia. The man, Mohammed Ibn Abd Al Wahhab, would ultimately transform the lives of all inhabitants of the Arabian Peninsula. After a period of itinerant religious scholarship, Al Wahhab returned to Al Uyaynah and preached his message, calling for the purification of Islam and a return to what he perceived as the original values proclaimed by the Prophet Muhammad.

Al Wahhab's reform agenda was initially successful, and he converted the local sheikh to his message. But the severe punishments Al Wahhab meted out to those he accused of sorcery, adultery and other crimes unnerved the local authorities and he was exiled. Al Wahhab sought refuge in Diraiyah, 65km from Al Uyaynah, where he was granted protection by Mohammed Ibn Al Saud, the local emir. Al Wahhab provided religious legitimacy to the Al Sauds, who in turn provided political protection for Al Wahhab. Together they built a power base that relied on the formidable combination of politics and religion.

With growing anger throughout Arabia that the holy cities of Mecca and Medina were under non-Arab Ottoman control, the Saudi-Wahhabi emirate began to expand rapidly. Upon his death, Al Saud was succeeded by his son Abdul Aziz, who captured Diraiyah's rival city in central Arabia – Riyadh – in 1765. In 1792 Al Wahhab died, but the inexorable expansion of the Saudi-Wahhabi emirate continued.

In 1803 the Saudi-Wahhabi army finally marched on the holy cities of the Hejaz and defeated Sherif Hussain of Mecca. The Saudi-Wahhabi emirate was recognised by the Mecca authorities, whereupon this first Saudi empire stretched from Al Hasa in the east to Hejaz in the west and Najran in the south.

The Birth of Saudi Arabia

The situation didn't last long. Ottoman sultan Mahmoud II ordered his powerful viceroy of Egypt, Mohammed Ali, to retake Hejaz in the sultan's name. Supported by many Arabian tribes who resented domination by the Saudi-Wahhabis, Mohammed Ali's armies successfully captured Mecca and Medina in 1814 and conquered the Saudi-Wahhabi stronghold of Diraiyah on 11 September 1818. Mohammed Ali topped off his triumph by executing Abdullah Ibn Al Saud (Abdul Aziz' successor).

The Al Sauds spent the rest of the 19th century fighting the Ottomans, rival tribes and themselves for no apparent gain. The decisive battle for the future of modern Arabia came in 1902, when a 21-year-old

Abdul Aziz Ibn Abdul Rahman Ibn Al Saud (Ibn Saud) and his small band of followers successfully stormed Riyadh under cover of night and daringly captured the fortress.

With deft diplomacy and the momentum of a successful military campaign, Ibn Saud orchestrated a conference at which Arabia's Islamic clergy condemned Sherif Hussain (ruler of Mecca) as a mere puppet of 'The Turk'. Sherif Hussain promptly responded by proclaiming himself king of the Arabs. In 1925 the Saudi-Wahhabis took Mecca and Medina; the following year Ibn Saud proclaimed himself king of the Hejaz and sultan of Najd, and on 22 September 1932, Ibn Saud announced the formation of the Kingdom of Saudi Arabia.

The Power of Oil

In 1933 Saudi Arabia signed its first oil concession. Four years later, the Arabian American Oil Company (Aramco) discovered commercial quantities of oil near Riyadh and Dammam. In 1943 US president Roosevelt established the Kingdom's political importance by telling the world that it was vital for the defence of the USA.

In 1964 King Faisal began to provide his subjects with a stake in the economic benefits of oil. He introduced a free health service for all Saudi citizens and began a building boom that would transform Saudi Arabia from an impoverished desert kingdom into a nation with a modern infrastructure.

In response to the USA's unconditional support for Israel, Saudi Arabia imposed an oil embargo in 1974, a move that quadrupled oil prices globally and reminded the world of the country's importance given the planet's dependence on oil.

While oil has made it one of the richest nations in the world, Saudi Arabia has always acknowledged that it is finite, and in April 2016, it did so formally when the country's Saudi Vision 2030 was announced. The primary objective: to divert Saudi Arabia's economy away from its current overreliance on oil revenue. It is the biggest admission by the Gulf nation that soon this source of riches will indeed run out.

A Kingdom of Contradictions

In 1975 King Faisal was assassinated by a nephew, and the throne formally passed to Faisal's brother, Khaled. In 1979 the Grand Mosque of Mecca was hijacked by 250 fanatical followers of Juhaiman Ibn Saif Al Otai, a militant Wahhabi leader, who claimed that the *Mahdi* (Islamic Messiah) would appear in the mosque that very day. During two bloody weeks of fighting 129 people were killed. In 1980 riots broke out in the town of Al Qatif (the heart of the Kingdom's 300,000 Shiites) – these were brutally repressed. Both events hinted at the simmering tensions lying beneath Saudi society.

When King Khaled died in 1982, his brother Fahd became king and made it a priority to prove himself a moderate and reliable friend of the West. In 1986 he proclaimed himself the 'Custodian of the Two Holy Mosques', a title that confirmed Saudi sovereignty over Islam's holiest cities, Mecca and Medina, in a bid to bestow legitimacy upon the Saudi royal family in the eyes of the wider Islamic world.

However, this legitimacy was undermined when Iraq invaded Kuwait in 1990 and Saudi Arabia allowed foreign military forces to operate from Saudi soil. In 1991 a petition calling for reforms and greater openness was sent to King Fahd by liberal intellectuals. It was quickly followed by a contrary petition from conservative Islamic scholars – this struggle within Saudi politics continues to this day.

In 1993 Fahd suffered a major stroke and the reigns of the Kingdom fell into the hands of then Crown Prince Abdullah, his half-brother. Abdullah had to negotiate the 9/11 terrorism events in the US, which saw several Saudis implicated, and he promised religious and educational reforms in their wake. After Fahd died in 2005 and he became king, Abdullah also oversaw the first major shift in Saudi attitudes towards women. Women were allowed to take part in the Olympics for the first time and he gave them the right to vote for municipal councils. Abdullah's half-brother, and current king, Salman, inherited the throne aged 79 following Abdullah's death in 2015.

Salman's reign has been notable for his crown princes. His half-brother Prince Muqrin Bin Abdulaziz Al Saud was appointed to the post, before swiftly being replacing by his nephew, Prince Mohammed Bin Nayef. Two years later, Prince Nayef was gone and replaced by King Salman's son, Mohammed Bin Salman, who is the driving force behind the country's current social and economic reforms, and widely regarded as the true power behind the throne.

People

Saudi Arabia's population has always been something of a paradox: the romantic Bedouin of the interior juxtaposed with the multicultural populace of coastal towns (the result of trade and pilgrimage traffic). This paradox has deepened further in the modern era as expat numbers, from the East and West, have continued to rise. Given the insular nature of the country and its peculiar gender segregation, understanding its people is essential to understanding the Kingdom.

Population

Around 80% of Saudi Arabia's population is concentrated in urban areas, with more than one-third of the country's people living in the megacities sprawling around Riyadh, Jeddah and Mecca.

Saudi Arabia's population is very young (almost 47% are aged under 25 years), with an annual population growth rate of 1.5% – meaning it doubles around every 30 years. Saudi authorities are confronted with the dilemma of providing for a disaffected, young, Islamicised demographic with not enough jobs to go around.

The Lives of Women

Until recently, a woman's life in Saudi Arabia was more controlled than in anywhere else in the industrialised world, particularly with regard to freedom of movement. This is now beginning to shift, and the tidal wave of these developments stands in contrast to the historically glacial pace of such changes here. Perhaps this is nothing short of a feminist revolution for Saudi women, but the picture is still not entirely rosy.

Huge barriers remain in place concerning matters such as travelling without a male chaperone and obtaining a passport. The plight of Rahaf Mohammed, the Saudi teenager who was detained in Thailand in January 2019 as she tried to flee from her family, was widely publicised on social media, as she tweeted her request for asylum that was eventually granted by Canada.

A number of women's rights activists who were campaigning for the right to drive and an end to the male guardianship system were arrested in May 2018 and remain in detention, even though some of their desired reforms have been passed. International rights groups claim that some of these

THE BEDOUIN

Bedouin represent 15% of the Saudi population and, although they're looked down upon by many city-dwelling Saudis, they still represent the essence of traditional Saudi identity. The traits historically associated with the Bedouin are legendary, and include a refusal to surrender to outside authority; a fierce loyalty to one's family and tribe; the primacy of courage and honour; the purity of language and dialect as preserved in poetry and desert legends; a belief in the desert codes of hospitality, blood feuds and mutual obligations; and the tradition of *razzia* (raiding travellers or members of other tribes).

Some 1.8 million Bedouin still claim to have a seminomadic lifestyle in Saudi Arabia, living for at least part of the year in movable encampments of black goat-hair tents, searching for water sources and fields for their livestock to graze on.

activists have been tortured and sexually harassed in prison.

Multiculturalism

Apparently one-third of all Saudi Arabia's inhabitants are expats (although even this is widely believed to be a gross underestimate), and the large cities can feel distinctly Asian rather than Arab because of the huge amount of cheap labour that has been brought in, from parts of the Indian subcontinent in particular.

Westerners often work in highly skilled and technical jobs for which Saudis do not yet have qualifications or experience – something the country's educational reforms are yet to fully address. Non-Western expats (primarily Pakistanis, Bangladeshis, Indians and Filipinos) work in mostly unskilled jobs, such as taxi-driving, construction work and domestic help. A substantial and growing cadre of medical professionals and information-technology specialists from the Indian subcontinent has begun to alter negative Saudi perceptions of workers from this part of the world. In the meantime, however, many unskilled labourers continue to complain about ill treatment, exploitation and abuse.

As the location of Islam's holiest sites, Saudi Arabia has always received millions of hajj and umrah (non-hajj) pilgrims from poor Islamic countries, and many of these stay on in the Kingdom to work illegally. The local media often attribute crime to illegal immigrants, which tends to stoke age-old racial prejudices.

Religion

Islam is not just the religion of Saudi citizens; it's the religion of Saudi society and the Saudi state, and it's all-encompassing. Officially, all Saudi citizens are Muslim; 15% are Shiites, who live mainly in the Eastern Province. The practice of other religions is strictly forbidden in Saudi Arabia. Non-Muslims cannot even be buried within the borders of the Kingdom.

Wahhabi Islam

Islamic orthodoxy in Saudi Arabia is Wahhabi Islam (an offshoot of Hanbali or the 'literalist' school of Islamic interpretation). Named after the 18th-century cleric Mohammed Ibn Abd Al Wahhab, Wahhabi doctrine calls for a return to the Arab purity of Islam and all rejection of Sufism, Turkish and especially Persian influences on Islamic thought and practice.

At the heart of Wahhabi Islam is a denunciation of all forms of mediation between Allah and believers, and a puritanical reassertion of *tawhid* (the oneness of God). Under the Wahhabis, only the Quran, the Sunnah (the words and deeds of Muhammad) and the Hadith (Muhammad's sayings) are acceptable sources of Islamic knowledge. Under Wahhabi doctrine, communal prayers are a religious duty and rulings on personal matters are interpreted according to Sharia law.

Environment

With at least half the country officially given over to desert, Saudi Arabia is often reduced to the image of sand dunes beneath an unforgiving sun. While this is clearly true for much of the Kingdom, it is also home to a wonderful array of natural features, including vast oases, stunning wildlife (both land and sea), and in the south, spectacular forest-covered mountain ranges that represent a completely different Saudi Arabia.

The Land

Saudi Arabia takes up 80% of the Arabian Peninsula. More than 95% of Saudi Arabia is desert or semidesert, and the country is home to some of the largest desert areas in the world, including Al Nafud Desert in the north and the Empty Quarter (Rub Al Khali) in the south. Just 1.5% of Saudi territory is considered suitable for agriculture and just 0.5% of the land is covered by forest.

Wildlife

Illegal hunting is still a major problem in Saudi Arabia, and according to the International Union for Conservation of Nature (IUCN), the list of endangered mammals in Saudi Arabia includes the rare dugong, Arabian oryx, Arabian leopard and Nubian ibex. Successful captive breeding and reintroduction programs for species including the Arabian oryx, Arabian leopard and houbara bustard are at the forefront of the government's work to arrest the threat to these animals.

The waters of Saudi's Red Sea are teeming with wildlife, and include five species of marine turtle. Whales, whale sharks and dolphins are also present in the Red Sea and the Gulf.

Environmental Issues

Saudi Arabia's environmental problems are legion and, in addition to hunting, include desertification, pollution, deforestation, critical depletion of underground water and lack of local education and awareness. The Kingdom's water shortages are especially worrying for the ruling family. Expensive seawater-desalination plants are all over the country, but the depletion of underground aquifers continues at an alarming rate.

SURVIVAL GUIDE

❶ Directory A-Z

ACCESSIBLE TRAVEL

The appearance of accessible parking spots is about the extent of assistance provided in most Saudi cities to those with disabilities. High-end hotels can prepare ramps and offer one-to-one assistance if they are notified in advance. Contact your airline if you need additional support.

SLEEPING PRICE RANGES

The following price ranges refer to a double room with bathroom in high season (November to March). Unless otherwise stated, breakfast is included in the price.

$ less than SR400
$$ SR400–SR1000
$$$ more than SR1000

ACCOMMODATION

The quality of accommodation drops dramatically outside of the big cities in Saudi Arabia, but the type remains the same: mainly uninspiring hotels and suites that you only go back to for sleep. In bigger cities, there are flash five-star hotel names, which prefer big-spending business clients, and some resorts around the coast can be fun for families. There are no accommodation options geared towards independent travellers at all.

CUSTOMS REGULATIONS

If you try to bring any of the following items into the country, the penalties range from confiscation for minor offences to imprisonment or deportation for more serious offences.
➡ Alcohol
➡ Artwork considered un-Islamic or items bearing non-Islamic religious symbols
➡ Many books, DVDs and videos
➡ Firearms and explosives

PRACTICALITIES

Post Post offices are situated in the centre of most small towns and in neighbourhoods of bigger cities. Allow more time if posting abroad as Saudi customs may need to inspect the parcel. Full details are on www.sp.com.sa.

Smoking Banned in most public spaces, including restaurants, coffee shops and shopping malls.

Time Saudi Arabia observes Arabia Standard Time (GMT/UTC plus three hours) all year; there are no daylight saving time changes.

Toilets Squat toilets are very common all over Saudi Arabia outside of the big cities. When booking accommodation in smaller towns, including places like Al Ula, it is worth asking what type of toilets the rooms have.

→ Illegal drugs, or medication without a doctor's prescription

→ Politically sensitive material and material overly critical of the government or royal family; this may include seemingly innocent newspaper articles

→ Pork products

→ Pornography or any publications containing pictorial representations of people (particularly women) in a less-than-conservative state of dress

→ Symbols or books of other religions (including the Bible)

EMERGENCY & IMPORTANT NUMBERS

Emergency	✔ 112
Ambulance	✔ 997
Fire	✔ 998
Police	✔ 999
Traffic Accidents (emergencies)	✔ 993
Najm (nonemergency traffic accident team)	✔ 9200 00560

HEALTH

→ No specific vaccinations are required ahead of travelling to Saudi Arabia. But during the period of hajj, pilgrims must have a valid certif-

icate of vaccination against the ACWY strains of meningitis.

→ Healthcare in major Saudi cities is of a high standard, and most towns have a health centre or basic hospital. A nonemergency visit to a hospital or clinic to see a doctor will cost around SR100.

→ Tap water is not safe to drink in Saudi Arabia. Consider buying a reusable bottle with a filter before you arrive.

INTERNET ACCESS

Most hotels and many restaurants and coffee houses have free wi-fi.

The internet is strictly policed, with more than 6000 sites blocked in Saudi Arabia at the time of research. Most are pornographic, but they also include sites discussing politics, health, women's rights and education.

LEGAL MATTERS

Saudi Arabia imposes strict Sharia (Islamic law), under which extremely harsh punishments can be imposed. For more information, consult your embassy.

If you're involved in a traffic accident, you must not call the police but an independent accident management team, called Najm, on 9200 00560, as they handle all nonemergency traffic accidents. Don't move your car and don't leave the scene until they have arrived. The Najm officer, who is authorised by law, will carry out an assessment based on the testimony of both parties and then issue you with a report that should be taken to your car-hire company.

LGBT+ TRAVELLERS

Homosexual acts and extra-marital sexual relations, including adultery, are illegal according to Saudi law and punishable by severe penalty. It is also illegal to be transgender in the Kingdom.

MAPS

The best maps of Saudi Arabia are produced by Farsi Maps. Costing SR25 each, they're available at branches of the Jarir Bookstore throughout the Kingdom. The series includes many general maps of most regions and excellent city maps for Riyadh, Jeddah, Yanbu, Taif, Mecca and Medina, among other locations.

MEDIA

The English-language dailies *Arab News* (www.arabnews.com) and *Saudi Gazette* (www.saudigazette.com.sa) are surprisingly frank, although they steer clear of any criticism of the royal family or Islam. Jeddah Radio (96.2FM) broadcasts in English and French, while the BBC World Service (www.bbc.co.uk/worldserviceradio) is available online and on short-wave frequency (11.760kHz or 15.575kHz).

ETIQUETTE

Dress Conservative dress is the rule of thumb in Saudi Arabia. Shorts in public are a big no-no (except for private beaches operated by some top-end hotels and expat compounds); if males wear shorts, they must reach over their knees, while women must cover themselves with the traditional *abaya* (robe-like dress).

Greetings Greetings are considered to be extremely important. The most common greeting is *salaam alaykum* ('may peace be upon you'), to which the reply is *wa alaykum as salaam* ('and peace upon you too').

Handshaking Shaking hands (between men) is an important gesture of mutual respect.

In public Almost every establishment, especially restaurants, have a male section and a 'family' section, which is essentially for women, and men can enter only with family. Sometimes there are also separate queues.

MONEY

Bargaining

Bargaining is expected in most souqs and casual shopping areas, where prices quoted are often double what a local might pay. It is therefore a good strategy to offer half of what is being asked, and use this as your starting position in any bargaining battles. In the modern malls, prices tend to be fixed, although asking for a discount is not out of the question.

Credit Cards & ATMs

Most establishments in big cities will accept credit cards, however, outside of these areas even hotels may demand cash. ATMs are widespread.

Currency

The unit of currency is the Saudi riyal (SR). One riyal (SR1) is divided into 100 halalas. Coins come in 25- and 50-halala denominations. Notes come in SR1, SR5, SR10, SR20, SR50, SR100, SR200 and SR500 denominations. The Saudi riyal is a stable, globally traded currency, and there are no restrictions on its import or export.

Changing Money

For the best rates, head to a money-exchange bureau, where all major currencies are exchanged and commission is not usually charged. Exchange desks at hotels offer poor rates.

Tipping

There is no tipping culture here; recipients may appear confused by the gesture. In cities with large expat communities, tipping is slowly spreading, and the following guidelines could be applied.

Airports SR5 to SR10 for baggage handlers.
Petrol Stations SR5 to SR10 for pump attendants.
Hotels SR10 to SR20 for porters; gratuity for cleaning staff is at your discretion.
Taxis 10% will be appreciated, as will rounding up to the nearest unit of SR10.
Restaurants 10% for good service.

OPENING HOURS

Saudi Arabia's weekend is Friday and Saturday. Note that during prayer times – five times a day – everything shuts. In general, opening hours are as follows:

Banks 8.30am–noon and 4.30pm–8pm Sunday to Thursday (at airports, banks are open 24 hours)

Offices 7.30am–2.30pm Sunday to Thursday

Post Offices 7.30am–10pm Sunday to Thursday and 4.30pm–10pm Friday

Restaurants 7am–noon and 3pm–midnight (from 3pm on Friday)

> ### EATING PRICE RANGES
>
> The following price ranges refer to a standard main course.
>
> **$** less than SR30
>
> **$$** SR30–120
>
> **$$$** more than SR120

Shopping Centres 9am–10pm (to midnight Friday and Saturday)

Shops and Souqs 8am–noon and 1pm–9pm Sunday to Thursday, from 1pm Friday

PHOTOGRAPHY

Due to security concerns, photography is off limits in certain areas – government buildings, embassies, airports, sea ports, desalination and electricity plants, oil rigs, royal palaces and police stations, or anything vaguely connected with the military or security services. Don't photograph people without their permission, and never photograph women (even in a general street scene).

PUBLIC HOLIDAYS

Saudi Arabia observes Eid Al Fitr (dates vary), Eid Al Adha (dates vary) and National Day (23 September) as public holidays. Although civic offices are closed, most commercial businesses will just shorten their hours, and transport services might just be reduced. This is to cater for the festive crowds who will eat out on Eid and who need to travel to visit family and friends. However, in more remote parts, places will shut down almost completely.

TELEPHONE

The main mobile phone providers are STC (www.stc.com.sa), Zain (www.zain.com) and Mobily (www.mobily.com.sa). SIM cards can be bought at airports and at any of the retail outlets for the main providers. To acquire a SIM you will need to provide your national ID. Mobile-phone signals are excellent in towns and cities, but can be weak away from built-up areas.

TOURIST INFORMATION

Saudi Arabia's Tourism website is www.saudi tourism.sa. There are no tourist offices in the country, except for one in the town of Abha (p310). However, Saudi Arabia has set up a tourism helpline (19988; +96611 261 4750 from abroad) to provide information about visiting sights and acquiring guides or agents to arrange tours. Other than this, concierges at high-end hotels and local guides are the best sources of tourist information.

VISAS

Alongside business and pilgrim visas, at the time of research, visitor visas were being issued for those attending festivals and events in the Kingdom (these had to be arranged via the festival organisers), though it was unclear if this was going to become a permanent method of entry to the country.

Hajj & Umrah Visas

For hajj visas, there's a quota system of one visa for every 1000 Muslims in a country's population. The system of administration varies from country to country but typically involves an application processed by a Saudi-authorised hajj and umrah travel agency. Every Saudi embassy has a list of authorised hajj and umrah travel agencies for that particular country (see www.haj.gov.sa).

Umrah (any pilgrimage to Mecca that is not hajj) visas are granted to any Muslim requesting one (in theory), although if you are not from a Muslim-majority country or don't have an obviously Muslim name, you'll be asked to provide an official document that lists Islam as your religion. Converts to Islam must provide a certificate from the mosque where they underwent their conversion ceremony.

Umrah and hajj visas are free but are valid only for travel to Jeddah, Mecca, Medina and the connecting roads.

Tourist Visas

The closest thing to a tourist visa being issued at the time of research were visit visas attached to specific festivals and events. These visas are being arranged through the organising body for the event. These visit visas suggest tourist visas for Saudi Arabia are not too far behind.

If you're planning to enter the country for a specific event or festival, it's best to allow the event organisers to arrange your visas. For a full list of possible visa types, see www.saudiembassy.net/visa-application.

Business Visas

Business visas are arranged via an employer and a sponsoring Saudi partner for a specific business purpose. Note that you must make your visa application in your country of nationality or permanent residency.

Residence (Work) Visas

Residence (work) visas are arranged via a Saudi employer who is also an individual's visa sponsor.

The visa restrictions and length of stay in Saudi Arabia granted to each family member will often differ depending on gender and age. These details should not be assumed to be the same for younger children, teenagers or spouses and should be carefully checked before arrival in the Kingdom.

Transit Visas

Anyone who is transiting through Saudi Arabia and will spend more than 12 hours in the country may require a transit visa. Check with your travel agent or airline if you are doing so: these companies should be able to apply for one on your behalf.

Visa Rules

When planning your Saudi visa, keep the following in mind:

➡ A Saudi sponsor is necessary for any visit to the Kingdom, and they are legally responsible for the conduct and behaviour of visitors while in the Kingdom.

➡ Passports must be valid for a minimum of six months.

➡ Check what methods of entry and exit are allowed on your visa, as some do not allow entry or exit by land.

➡ When applying for a visa, women under 25 years old must be accompanied by either their brother or their husband, who must also arrive in and leave Saudi Arabia at the same time.

➡ Women over 25 can travel without a male guardian, but only as part of a licensed tour group.

➡ Men and women are only allowed to travel together and granted a visa to do so if they are married (with an official marriage licence) or form part of a group.

➡ It's not permitted for an unmarried couple to travel alone together in Saudi Arabia and doing so runs the risk of arrest.

Israeli Passports & Stamps

At the top of the restricted list of travellers to Saudi Arabia remain citizens of Israel, but people of Jewish faith from other countries can also have trouble getting in. All visitors to Saudi Arabia must declare their religion – those declaring 'Jewish' or 'none' have been known to be refused a visa, though the changes sweeping the country suggest this will no longer be the case.

Any evidence of travel to and from Israel will result in refusal of entry into Saudi Arabia. If you have any evidence of travel to Israel in your passport and intend to travel to Saudi Arabia in the future, use a brand-new passport for your Saudi visa application.

WOMEN TRAVELLERS

Saudi Arabia is rightly considered one of the most difficult countries in which to travel if you're a woman by yourself. The strict segregation of the sexes and the need for a male chaperone leads to obvious limitations on freedom of movement. The fact that women can now drive has improved things, albeit marginally, but the reality is that a woman cannot move around Saudi Arabia alone without attracting unwanted

NON-MUSLIM TRAVELLERS

Non-Muslim travellers to Saudi Arabia should bear a few things in mind that are very peculiar to the Kingdom.

Prayer Time Businesses must close during the daily prayers. These are called five times a day, and last approximately 30 minutes. Prayer times are at sunrise, noon, mid-afternoon, sunset and a couple of hours after sunset. Don't be surprised to find yourself left alone eating in a restaurant while staff partially close the shutters and head to a mosque.

Women's Clothing It is law in Saudi Arabia that women wear a long gown (called an *abaya*) and headscarf in public, regardless of their faith. Men should ensure they do not wear shorts in public.

No Entry to Holy Cities Central Medina and the entire city of Mecca are off limits to non-Muslims. Sometimes checkpoints are put in place around these zones to check identification. The punishment for a non-Muslim entering these zones is at the discretion of the authorities, but is likely to involve deportation. Non-Muslims can use Medina's airport and travel to the outskirts of the city.

Mosque Entry Most mosques in Saudi Arabia's bigger cities stay open throughout the day, and can be visited by non-Muslims, although women are not allowed to enter the main prayer hall. Non-Muslims should avoid prayer times, remove shoes and refrain from photographing anyone. Sadly, some worshippers may take the position that non-Muslims should not enter a mosque at all. While this is not an Islamic position, to avoid a confrontation it may be best to walk away if this situation arises.

---

attention. Most restaurants outside of big towns are men-only affairs, and hotels can be reluctant to rent a room to an unaccompanied woman.

WORK

The only way for foreigners to work in the Kingdom is to arrange a residence (work) visa via a Saudi employer, who is also the employee's sponsor, before leaving their home nation.

Websites including www.gulftalent.com and www.edarabia.com have regular listings of jobs in the Kingdom.

🛈 Getting There & Away

ENTERING THE COUNTRY

During hajj and Ramadan expect long queues at immigration. Departure security is vigorous and time consuming. You're advised to arrive early – three hours before international flights. If you're arriving by land, procedures are similar, although expect long delays if you're bringing your own car into the Kingdom.

AIR

The national carrier is **Saudia** (www.saudia.com), which has an excellent safety record. The Kingdom has six international airports. The four busiest are Jeddah's King Abdul Aziz International Airport (p286), Riyadh's King Khalid International Airport (p281), Dammam's King Fahd International Airport (p309) and Medina's Prince Mohammad Bin Abdulaziz International Airport (p295).

LAND

At the time of research, the land borders with Iraq, Jordan and Yemen were closed to non-Arab travellers. In 2017, Saudi Arabia closed its land border to Qatar in a major diplomatic rift, and it remains shut.

Saptco (www.saptco.com.sa) offers the best international bus services; other companies from surrounding countries also cover the same routes for similar prices. Saptco fares are kept low by the government. International departures, primarily from Riyadh, Jeddah and Dammam, are to neighbouring countries Bahrain, the UAE and Jordan.

SEA

There are three ports to enter Saudi Arabia by sea: Duba, Yanbu and Jeddah. If you intend to enter or exit the country by sea, you must check that your visa allows you to do so.

At the time of research, ferries carrying foot passengers and cars were only travelling to the two Egyptian ports of Suez and Safaga. The service from Jeddah to Suez (25 hours) runs on Monday, Tuesday, Thursday and Friday. The service from Jeddah to Safaga (17 hours) is on Wednesday and Thursday. From Yanbu to Safaga (11 hours) there's a ferry on Tuesday and Wednesday, and there is one ferry from Duba to Safaga (four hours) on Sunday.

Tickets start from approximately SR300 and the ferries are run by Namma International Marine Services (www.nammashippinglines.com).

ⓘ Getting Around

AIR

The arrival of flynas (www.flynas.com) and flyadeal (www.flyadeal.com) has brought down the traditional cost of domestic flights, once only operated by Saudia (www.saudia.com). This means getting to almost every corner of the Kingdom by plane is a lot cheaper and quicker than driving. Where you can, you should fly: it will shave hours, if not days, off your journey.

BUS

The excellent **Saptco** (www.saptco.com.sa) national bus network is often the cheapest and easiest way to get around the Kingdom, especially to the more remote corners, as there always seems to be a Saptco station nearby, even if it's just a place the buses pull into.

Costs

The Saptco bus network is safe, reliable and very reasonably priced. Return tickets are 25% cheaper than two one-way fares, and tickets can be bought on machines or at booths inside Saptco bus stations. Alternatively bookings can be made online (www.saptco.com.sa).

Reservations

When purchasing bus tickets, you'll need to show your passport (for visitors) or *iqama* (residence permit; for expats). During hajj season, Ramadan or in summer (May to September), booking at least a week in advance is advisable.

CAR & MOTORCYCLE

Roads are generally sealed and well maintained. Motorcycles are rare.

Driving Licences

If you'll only be in the country for less than three months and want to hire a car, you will need an International Driving Permit (IDP).

If you're going to be in the Kingdom for more than three months, you'll need to get a local driving licence, which is arranged by your employer. You'll also have to do a driving test and purchase insurance.

Fuel

It seems miraculous to a foreigner, but it's only around 60 halalas per litre for unleaded petrol in Saudi Arabia. Petrol stations are ubiquitous throughout the country and all must charge the same price for petrol by law.

Car Hire

International and local car-hire agencies can be found in most airports, including some regional ones, and in all the larger towns across the King-dom. They will only rent cars to foreigners if an International Driving Permit is presented.

Rates at international companies start at around SR130 per day (including full insurance) for the smallest cars, and SR600 for 4WDs. Most cars come with a 150km-per-day cap (none come with unlimited mileage), and any distance beyond that is charged at a rate of between SR0.75 and SR2 per kilometre.

Insurance

If you are travelling with a car from another Gulf Cooperation Council (GCC) country, insurance and the Collision-Damage Waiver (CDW) are mandatory. With car hire it's usually included in the price, but it pays to check very carefully.

Road Rules

➡ Drive on the right side of the road.

➡ Right turns are allowed at red lights unless specifically forbidden.

➡ The speed limit in towns is between 60km/h and 80km/h.

➡ The speed limit on open highways is between 120km/h and 140km/h (but can drop to 90km/h or 100km/h).

➡ Leaving the scene of an accident is a serious offence and can result in fines of over SR1000, imprisonment and deportation.

➡ Not carrying a valid driving licence can result in a night in jail and a hefty fine.

TAXI

Taxis are found in most of the larger towns and are known as 'limousines'; they can be hailed anywhere. Note that it's much cheaper to negotiate the fare first (as locals do) rather than use the meter. Many major cities and towns also support the ride-hailing apps Uber (www.uber.com) and Careem (www.careem.com).

TRAIN

Trains in Saudi Arabia are safe, reliable, very comfortable and reasonably priced. There are three classes: 2nd, 1st and VIP class. The main difference between them is legroom (plus TV and a meal in the splendidly named 'Rehab' VIP class). Women can travel unaccompanied (with ID) and sit in any class. Reservations and bookings can be made at the stations, by phone or online for any of the three train routes:

Haramain (9200 04433; www.hhr.sa) Serves Mecca, Jeddah, Jeddah Airport, King Abdullah Economic City and Medina; it runs Thursday to Sunday only.

SAR (9200 00329; www.sar.com.sa) Serves Riyadh, Majmaah, Qassim, Hail and Jauf, and includes a sleeper service.

SRO (9200 08886; www.saudirailways.org) Serves Riyadh, Al Hofuf, Abqaiq and Dammam.

United Arab Emirates
الإمارات العربية المتحدة

POP 9.5 MILLION

Best Places to Eat

➜ Li Beirut (p381)
➜ Aroos Damascus (p340)
➜ Coya (p384)
➜ Pai Thai (p342)
➜ Shababeek (p360)
➜ Claypot (p341)

Best Places to Stay

➜ Al Sahel Villa Resort (p398)
➜ Grand Hyatt Abu Dhabi (p378)
➜ XVA Hotel (p336)
➜ Intercontinental Fujairah (p402)
➜ Southern Sun Abu Dhabi (p379)

Why Go?

For most people, the United Arab Emirates means just one place: Dubai, the sci-fi-esque city of iconic skyscrapers, palm-shaped islands, city-sized malls, indoor ski slopes and palatial beach resorts. But beyond the glitter awaits a diverse mosaic of six more emirates, each with its own character and allure.

Oil-rich Abu Dhabi, the UAE's capital, is positioning itself as a culture and leisure hub. Beyond looms the vast Al Dhafra region, home to the northern reaches of the Rub Al Khali (Empty Quarter) desert's rippling dunes. Its magical silence is interrupted only by the whisper of shifting sands rolling towards Saudi Arabia.

North of Dubai, Sharjah is the UAE's art and heritage centre while Ras Al Khaimah is all about the beach – with a dash of adventure-activities thrown in. Head east into the jagged embrace of the Hajar Mountains to experience a side of the UAE far removed from Dubai's gloss.

When to Go
UAE

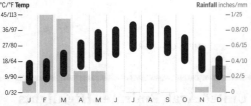

Nov–Mar Moderate temperatures, higher room rates, major festivals. Good for outdoor adventures.

Mar–May & Oct Hot days, balmy nights. Good for beach holidays, desert camping still OK.

Jun–Sep Hot and humid, hotel discounts. Life moves indoors.

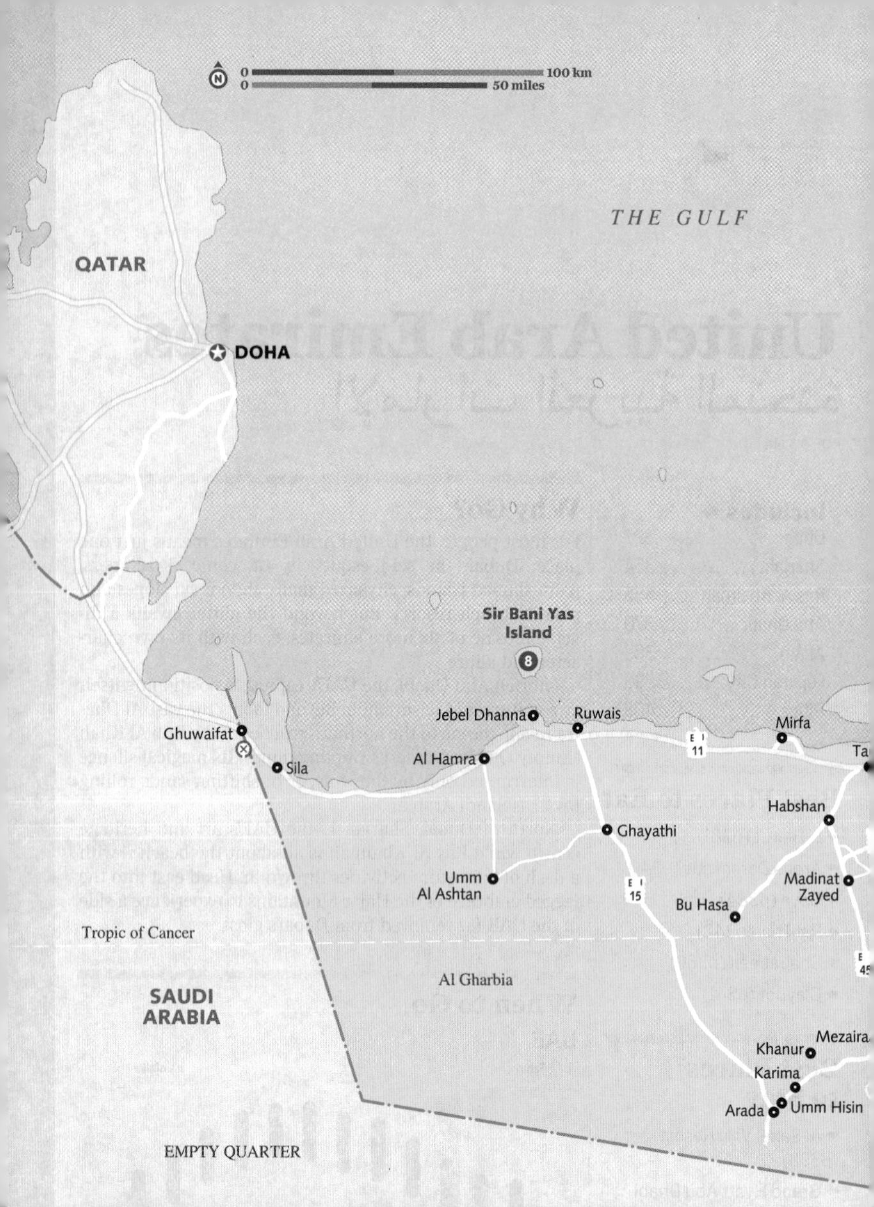

THE GULF

QATAR

⊕ DOHA

Sir Bani Yas
Island
⑧

Ghuwaifat ⊗

Sila

Jebel Dhanna

Ruwais

Mirfa

E
11

Ta

Al Hamra

Habshan

Ghayathi

Madinat
Zayed

E
15

Umm
Al Ashtan

Bu Hasa

E
45

Tropic of Cancer

SAUDI
ARABIA

Al Gharbia

Mezaira

Khanur

Karima

Arada

Umm Hisin

EMPTY QUARTER

United Arab Emirates Highlights

① **Dubai** (p327) Soaring up
Burj Khalifa before cocktails at
the Burj Al Arab.

② **Abu Dhabi** (p370) Gazing
at the magnificence of Sheikh
Zayed Mosque, then at the

collection under the Louvre
Abu Dhabi's dome.

③ **Liwa Oasis** (p394)
Soaking up the Empty
Quarter's rippling dune beauty.

④ **Sharjah** (p354) Delving

into art and heritage
museums.

⑤ **Dibba** (p403) Hiking
to abandoned villages
while exploring the barren
mountains.

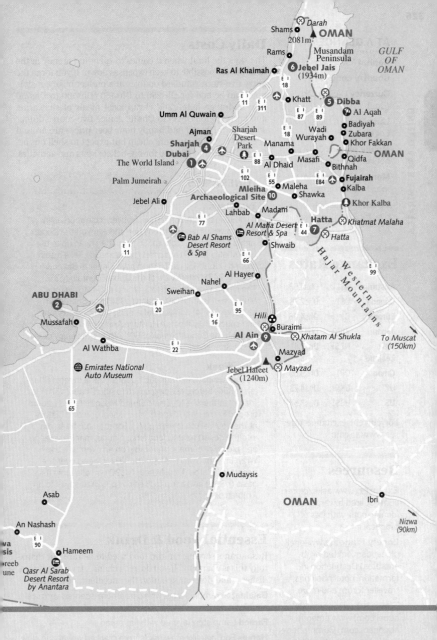

6 Jebel Jais (p365)
Zooming off the mountain on the world's longest zip line.

7 Hatta (p352) Kayaking on Hatta Dam, then hitting the mountain-bike trails.

8 Sir Bani Yas Island (p397) Spotting Arabian oryx on a safari.

9 Al Ain (p389) Losing your way amid the labyrinthine date-palm oasis.

10 Mleiha Archaeological Site (p359) Discovering this country's epic history – no, it didn't begin with the oil boom.

AT A GLANCE

Capital Abu Dhabi

Country code 971

Currency UAE dirham (Dhs)

Language Arabic, English

Mobile phones GSM network is widespread

Money ATMs are common in urban areas

Visas Free visas on arrival for 60 nationalities

Exchange Rates

Australia	A$1	Dhs2.63
Canada	C$1	Dhs2.78
Europe	€1	Dhs4.26
Japan	¥100	Dhs3.29
New Zealand	NZ$1	Dhs2.41
Oman	OR1	Dhs9.55
UK	UK£1	Dhs4.73
US	US$1	Dhs3.67

For current exchange rates see www.xe.com.

Resources

Explorer (www.askexplorer. com) Geared towards resident expats, with lots of practical info.

Lonely Planet (www.lonelyplanet.com/united-arab-emirates) Destination information, hotel bookings, traveller forum and more.

Time Out (www.timeoutdubai.com; www.timeoutabudhabi.com) Comprehensive listings of restaurants, bars, clubs and cultural events.

Zomato (www.zomato.com) User-generated restaurant reviews around the UAE.

Daily Costs

The sky's the limit when it comes to spending money in the UAE but it's possible to keep expenses down. If you forgo the glitzy five-stars, standard doubles at a budget business-style hotel can be had for Dhs250 to Dhs450 (Dhs500 to Dhs750 in a midrange hotel) and cheap local meals of shawarma and curry go for Dhs15 to Dhs30. A nice two-course dinner starts from Dhs150 and happy hour beer prices are around Dhs25. Most museums are cheap but expect to shell out between Dhs60 and Dhs400 for big-ticket sights and activities.

ITINERARIES

Two Days

If you're in the UAE on a short layover, base yourself in downtown Dubai. Spend day one checking off the iconic sights on a Big Bus tour (p335) and then head up to the Burj Khalifa (p330) at sunset (book ahead). Take a spin around Dubai Mall (p348) and have dinner in Baker & Spice (p342), with a view of the Dubai Fountain (p331). The next day, take a cab to Sharjah (p354) to visit the Museum of Islamic Civilization (p354), the Sharjah Art Museum (p354) and wander among the little museums and souqs (p360) of the Heritage Area before strolling through the Central Souq (p360). Afterwards enjoy dinner at Shababeek (p360).

One Week

Spend two days in futuristic Dubai and one in retro Sharjah (p354) before heading south to Abu Dhabi (p370) to marvel at the Sheikh Zayed Grand Mosque (p373), zoom around Ferrari World (p375) and discover world history at the Louvre Abu Dhabi (p371). For total contrast, dip into the desert next to face a huge dune, magical silence and plenty of camels, preferably on an overnight trip. Wrap up with a day in Al Ain (p389) for views over the desert from atop Jebel Hafeet (p390), strolls amid its oasis (p390) and a trip to the zoo (p392) to say hi to an Arabian oryx.

Essential Food & Drink

Restaurants serving Emirati food used to be rare but thankfully this is changing. If you do get a chance, try these typical dishes – and don't miss out on the succulent local dates.

Balaleet Scrambled eggs with cardamom-scented vermicelli noodles

Fareed Lamb stew layered with flat bread

Harees Porridge-like stew made from cracked wheat and slow-cooked chicken or lamb; sometimes called the 'national dish'

Khuzi Stuffed whole roasted lamb on a bed of spiced rice

Madrooba Salt-cured fish in gravy

Machboos Casserole of meat or fish, rice and onions cooked in a spicy sauce

DUBAI

دبي

♪ 04 / POP 3.1 MILLION

It's hard not to admire Dubai for its indefatigable verve, ambition and ability to dream up and realise projects that elsewhere would never get off the drawing board. This is a superlative-craving society that has birthed audaciously high buildings and palm-shaped islands. Sci-fi concepts such as flying taxis, a lightning-fast Hyperloop train and an army of robocops are all reflections of a mindset that fearlessly embraces the future. With many more grand projects in the pipeline for World Expo 2020, it's clear that Dubai is a city firmly in charge of writing its own narrative.

The first Middle Eastern city to make the Unesco list of creative cities of design, Dubai is a bustling microcosm peacefully shared by cultures from all corners of the world. This diversity expresses itself in the culinary landscape, fashion, music and performance. Although rooted in Islamic tradition, this is an open society where it's easy for newcomers and visitors to connect with myriad experiences, be it eating like a Bedouin, dancing on the beach, shopping for local art or riding a camel in the desert. Dubai is a fertile environment conducive to breaking down cultural barriers and preconceptions.

◉ Sights

Dubai may be vast and amorphous, but the areas of interest to visitors are actually fairly well defined. Bustling Deira and Bur Dubai are the city's oldest neighbourhoods, with mosques, markets and brimfuls of atmosphere. These areas are best explored on foot.

Dubai's main artery is skyscraper-flanked Sheikh Zayed Rd. Handily paralleled by the Dubai Metro, it links the Financial Centre and shiny Downtown Dubai with the Burj Khalifa and Dubai Mall, the Alserkal Avenue arts area and the Jebel Ali theme parks.

Along the coast, the newly carved Dubai Canal empties into the Gulf in villa-studded Jumeirah, which has shimmering sandy beaches that segue smoothly into those of Umm Suqeim, home to the landmark Burj Al Arab Hotel and Madinat Jumeirah Arab-style resort village. Just beyond is the turn-off to the artificially created Palm Jumeirah island before the coastal stretch culminates with the ritzy resorts and residential towers of Dubai Marina.

◉ Deira & Bur Dubai

ديرة و

Dubai Frame VIEWPOINT
(Map p330; www.thedubaiframe.com; Gate 3, Zabeel Park; adult/child Dhs50/20; ⊙9am-9pm; Ⓜ Al Jafiliya) Opened in January 2018, this 150m rectangular 'picture frame' sits in Zabeel Park (Map p330; ☑04 398 6888; Gate 1, off Sheikh Khalifa Bin Zayed Rd; Dhs5; ⊙8am-11pm Sat-Wed, to 11.30pm Thu-Fri; ⛲; Ⓜ Al Jafiliya), right between historic and modern Dubai, and provides grand views of both parts of

---

DUBAI IN...

One Day
Start with a Cultural Breakfast at the Sheikh Mohammed Centre for Cultural Understanding (p329) for a chance to meet locals and eat home-cooked Emirati food. Delve further into local culture and history with a spin around the Al Fahidi Historic District (p329) before finishing up at the nearby Dubai Museum (p329). Afterwards, lunch at the Arabian Tea House (p341). Enjoy the short stroll to the breezy Bur Dubai Souq (p328) via the atmospheric Hindi Lane, then catch an abra (traditional wooden boat) across the Dubai Creek to forage for bargains in the bustling Deira souqs (p330). Wrap up the day with a dinner cruise aboard Al Mansour Dhow (p341) then take a taxi to QDs (p344) and wind down with a drink or a shisha.

Two Days
Kick off day two with a tour of Jumeirah Mosque (p332) then cab it down the coast and explore charming Madinat Jumeirah (p333) village, taking an abra ride around its network of canals. Enjoy Burj Al Arab views and lunch at Souk Madinat Jumeirah (p348). After lunch beeline to Dubai Mall (p348) and visit the Aquarium (p331) before giving your credit cards a workout. Watch the sun set from the observation terrace of the Burj Khalifa (p330) (book way ahead) and then for dinner, pick any table with a view of the Dubai Fountain (p331). Wrap up the day with a nightcap at Bridgewater Tavern (p344) with views of the Dubai Canal.

Deira & Bur Dubai

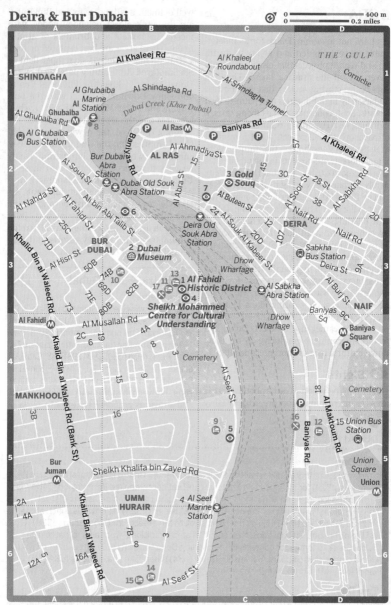

the city. Galleries on the ground floor tell the story of Dubai (the past) before visitors are whisked up to a viewing platform at roof level (the present). The final stop is another gallery depicting a vision of Dubai 50 years from now (the future).

Bur Dubai Souq　　　　　　　　　MARKET

(Map p328; btwn Bur Dubai waterfront & Ali Bin Abi Talib St; ⊙8am-1pm & 4-10pm Sat-Thu, 4-10pm Fri; ⓜAl Ghubaiba) Dubai's oldest souq flanks a central arcade canopied by an ornately carved wooden roof. Friday evenings here are especially lively, as it turns into a vir-

Deira & Bur Dubai

tual crawling carnival with expat workers loading up on socks, pashminas, T-shirts and knock-off Calvins on their day off. In a section known as the **Textile Souq** you can stock up on fabrics – silk, cotton, satin and velvet – at very reasonable prices. On the downside, although good humoured, the vendors here can be very pushy.

★ **Dubai Museum** MUSEUM
(Map p328; ☑ 04 353 1862; Al Fahidi St; adult/child Dhs3/1; ☺ 8.30am-8.30pm Sat-Thu, from 2.30pm Fri; Ⓜ Al Fahidi) The city's main historical museum charts Dubai's turbo-evolution from fishing and pearling village to global centre of commerce, finance and tourism. It has an atmospheric setting in the compact Al Fahidi Fort, built around 1800 and considered Dubai's oldest remaining structure. A walk-through mock souq, exhibits on Bedouin life in the desert and a room highlighting the importance of the sea illustrate the days before the discovery of oil. The last room showcases archaeological findings from nearby excavation sites.

★ **Al Fahidi Historic District** AREA
(Map p328; Al Fahidi St; Ⓜ Al Fahidi) Traffic fades to a quiet hum in the labyrinthine lanes of this nicely restored heritage area formerly known as the Bastakiya Quarter. Its narrow walking lanes are flanked by sand-coloured houses topped with wind towers, which provide natural air-conditioning. Today there are about 50 buildings containing museums, craft shops, cultural exhibits, courtyard cafes, art galleries and two boutique hotels.

★ **Sheikh Mohammed Centre
for Cultural Understanding** CULTURAL CENTRE
(Map p328; ☑ 04 353 6666; www.cultures.ae; House 26, Al Musallah Rd; heritage/Creekside tours Dhs80/275, meals Dhs90-120; ☺ 9am-5pm Sun-

Thu, to 1pm Sat; Ⓟ; Ⓜ Al Fahidi) Anyone keen on delving deeper into Emirati culture and history should take advantage of the activities, Emirati meals and tours offered through this nonprofit centre, based on the edge of Al Fahidi Historic District. Guided by the motto 'Open Doors, Open Minds', this unique institution was founded in 1995 by Dubai's current ruler, Sheikh Mohammed Bin Rashid, to build bridges between cultures and to help visitors and expats understand the traditions and customs of the UAE.

From mid-September to mid-July the centre runs highly informative 90-minute guided heritage **tours** of Al Fahidi Historic District several times weekly. For groups of 10 or more, staff can also organise more comprehensive 2½-hour 'Creekside' tours that include a peek inside a mosque, an abra ride and a spin around the textile, spice and gold souqs in Bur Dubai and Deira. All tours conclude with a Q&A session and Arabic coffee, tea and dates.

To experience the culinary side of Emirati life, join one of the centre's traditional Bedouin-style **meals**. Depending on when you come, you'll get to taste such local dishes as *balaleet* (sweetened crunchy vermicelli), *chabab* (cardamom-spiced pancakes), *saloona* (a stew) or *machboos* (a rice and meat or fish dish).

The centre also runs hugely popular tours of Jumeirah Mosque (p332). All tours and meals must be booked in advance. Check the website for the latest schedule.

Al Seef AREA
(Map p328; www.alseef.ae; Al Seef Rd; Ⓟ; Ⓜ Bur-Juman) In the early 1900s this historical area was Dubai's trading hub, during a period when the pearl diving industry was being developed. Stretching some 1.8km along

East Dubai

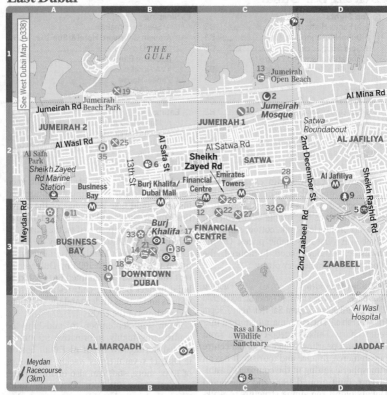

Dubai Creek, the developers have divided the area into two distinct areas: one sharply contemporary, with buildings that resemble piled-up shipping containers, and the other with an Old Dubai neighbourhood feel thanks to the rough-hewn facades, narrow alleyways and faux wind towers.

★ **Gold Souq**   MARKET

(Map p328; Sikkat Al Khail St; ⊙10am-1pm & 3-10pm; Ⓜ Al Ras) All that glitters is gold (and occasionally silver) along this covered arcade where dozens of shops overflow with every kind of jewellery imaginable, from delicate pearl earrings to lavish golden wedding necklaces. Simply watching the goings-on is a treat. Settle down on a bench and take in the lively street theatre of hard-working Afghan men dragging heavy carts of goods, African women in colourful kaftans and local women out on a shopping spree. It's liveliest in the evening.

Spice Souq   MARKET

(Map p328; btwn Baniyas Rd, Al Ras Rd & Al Abra St; ⊙roughly 9am-10pm Sat-Thu, from 4pm Fri; Ⓜ Al Ras) Steps from the Deira Old Souk abra station, the sound of Arabic chatter bounces around the lanes of this small covered market as vendors work hard to unload cardamom, saffron and other aromatic herbs photogenically stored in burlap sacks alongside nuts, incense burners, henna kits, shishas and dried limes, an essential ingredient in Middle Eastern cuisine. Away from the tourist-oriented main thoroughfare, the tiny shops also sell groceries, plastics and other household goods to locals and sailors from the dhows (traditional Arabian sailing craft).

◉ Downtown Dubai

★ **Burj Khalifa**   LANDMARK

(Map p330; ☎800 2884 3867; www.atthetop.ae; lower ground fl, Dubai Mall, 1 Mohammed Bin Rashid Blvd; At the Top prime hours adult/child 4-12yr

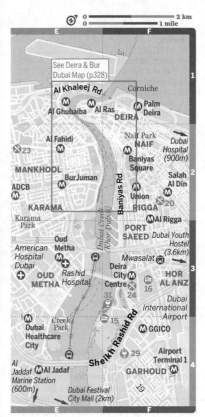

See Deira & Bur Dubai Map (p328)

drop a few dirhams into a high-powered telescope, which not only zeroes in on modern-day Dubai but also simulates the same view at night and in the 1980s.

The world's highest observation platform, though, is called At the Top Sky and is located at 555m on the 148th floor. You'll feel like a VIP upon being welcomed by a Guest Ambassador and treated to soft drinks, coffee and dates in a fancy lounge. Aside from the views, a highlight on this floor is an interactive screen where you 'fly' to different city landmarks by hovering your hands over high-tech sensors. This is followed by a trip down to the 125th floor where another VR experience awaits: A Falcon's Eye View, which lets you see Dubai from a bird's-eye perspective.

Note that prices go up during prime hours (around sunset) and that closing times may vary depending on demand and the season.

You can also expect some changes at the Burj from the summer of 2019, when renovations will be taking place as part of an ambitious US$1.7 billion Marsa Al Arab project that involves building two new manmade islands on either side of the hotel.

Dubai Fountain
FOUNTAIN

(Map p330; ☑04 362 7500; www.thedubaimall. com/en/entertain-detail/the-dubai-fountain-1; Burj Lake; ⊙shows 1pm & 1.30pm Sat-Thu, 1.30pm & 2pm Fri, every 30min 6pm-midnight daily; Ⓜ Burj Khalifa/Dubai Mall) **FREE** This dancing fountain is spectacularly set in the middle of a giant lake against the backdrop of the glittering Burj Khalifa. Water undulates as gracefully as a belly dancer, arcs like a dolphin and surges as high as 140m, all synced to stirring classical, Arabic and world music soundtracks played on speakers. There are plenty of great vantage points, including a 272m-long floating boardwalk (Dhs20), which takes you just 9m away from the fountain.

Dubai Aquarium & Underwater Zoo
AQUARIUM

(Map p330; ☑04 448 5200; www.thedubaiaquar ium.com; ground fl, Dubai Mall, Sheikh Mohammed Bin Rashid Blvd; packages Dhs120-315; ⊙10am-11pm Sun-Wed, to midnight Thu-Sat; Ⓟ⚓; Ⓜ Burj Khalifa/Dubai Mall) Dubai Mall's most mesmerising sight is this gargantuan aquarium where thousands of beasties flit and dart amid artificial coral. Sharks and rays are top attractions, along with sumo-sized groupers and massive schools of pelagic fish. You can see quite a lot for free from outside or pay for access to the walk-through tunnel. The

Dhs210/170, non-prime hours Dhs135/100, At the Top Sky prime/non-prime hours Dhs500/370, audio guide Dhs25; ⊙At the Top 8.30am-11pm, At the Top Sky 11am-10pm, last entry 45min before closing; Ⓜ Burj Khalifa/Dubai Mall) The Burj Khalifa is a stunning feat of architecture and engineering, with two observation decks on the 124th and 148th floors and a restaurant-bar on the 122nd. The world's tallest building pierces the sky at 828m and opened in January 2010, six years after excavations began. To avoid wait times or expensive fast-track admission, book tickets online as far as 30 days in advance. Note that high humidity often cloaks Dubai in a dense haze, making views less than breathtaking.

If you've bought tickets to the first observation deck (called At the Top), you'll walk past multimedia exhibits chronicling the construction of the Burj before squeezing into a lift that whisks you to the 124th floor (452m) at a speed of 10m per second. To intensify the viewing experience, you can

East Dubai

basic package also includes access to the Underwater Zoo upstairs, whose undisputed star is a 5.1m-long Australian saltwater crocodile named King Croc.

☉ Jumeirah

Nikki Beach Dubai
BEACH

(Map p330; ☑ 04 376 6162; www.nikkibeach.com/destinations/beach-clubs/dubai; Pearl Jumeirah Island, Jumeirah 1; sunloungers with reservation weekdays/weekends Dhs150/300; ⊙11am-9pm Sep-Jun; P; M Al Jafiliya) At this fashionable pleasure pit on the emerging Pearl Jumeirah residential peninsula, only the crisp all-white look is virginal. On weekends, the bronzed, beautiful and cashed-up descend on the Dubai branch of the famous Miami beach club to frolic in the vast pool, lounge on daybeds, load up on seafood and toast the sunset with bubbly. Weekdays are quieter.

★ Jumeirah Mosque
MOSQUE

(Map p330; ☑ 04 353 6666; www.cultures.ae; Jumeirah Rd, Jumeirah 1; tours Dhs20; ⊙tours 10am Sat-Thu; P; M Emirates Towers, World Trade Centre) Snowy white and intricately detailed, Jumeirah is Dubai's most beautiful mosque and one of only a handful in the UAE that are open to non-Muslims – one-hour guided tours are operated by the Sheikh Mohammed Centre for Cultural Understanding (p329). Tours conclude with pastries and a discussion session during which you're free to ask any question about Islam and Emirati culture. There's no need to book. Modest dress is preferred, but traditional clothing can be borrowed for free. Cameras are allowed.

Green Planet
ZOO

(Map p330; www.thegreenplanetdubai.com; City Walk, Al Madina St, Jumeirah 1; adult/child Dhs99/74; ⊙10am-10pm Sat-Wed, to midnight Thu & Fri; P ♿; M Burj Khalifa/Dubai Mall) ⬥ If you can build a ski slope in the desert, why not a rainforest too? The Green Planet is an indoor tropical paradise intended to 'edutain' about biodiversity, nature and sustainability. More than 3000 animals and plants live beneath its green canopy, including birds, butterflies, frogs, spiders and snakes. The latest addition is a bat cave on the 4th floor. The small fruit bats can be hard to spot; if possible visit at 2pm when they are fed.

★ Burj Al Arab
LANDMARK

(Map p338; ☑ 04 301 7777; www.burj-al-arab.com; off Jumeirah Rd, Umm Suqeim 3; M Mall of the Emirates) The Burj's graceful silhouette – meant to evoke the sail of a dhow – is to

Dubai what the Eiffel Tower is to Paris. Completed in 1999, this iconic landmark sits on an artificial island and comes with its own helipad and a fleet of chauffeur-driven Rolls Royce limousines. Beyond the striking lobby, with its gold-leaf opulence and attention-grabbing fountain, lie 202 suites with more trimmings than a Christmas turkey.

It's worth visiting if only to gawk at an interior that's every bit as garish as the exterior is gorgeous. The mood is set in the 180m-high lobby, which is decorated in a red, blue and green colour scheme and accented with pillars draped in gold leaf. The lobby atrium is tall enough to fit the Statue of Liberty within it.

If you're not staying in the hotel, you need a restaurant reservation to get past lobby security. Don't expect any bargains: there's a minimum spend of Dhs370 for cocktails in the **Skyview Bar** (Map p338; ☑04 301 7600; www. burjalarab.com; Burj Al Arab, off Jumeirah Rd, Umm Suqeim 3; ☺1pm-2am Sat-Thu, from 7pm Fri; M Mall of the Emirates), while afternoon tea will set you back Dhs590. Check the website for details and to make a (compulsory) reservation.

★ **Madinat Jumeirah** AREA
(Map p338; ☑04 366 8888; www.jumeirah.com; King Salman Bin Abdul Aziz Al Saud St, Umm Suqeim 3; M Mall of the Emirates) One of Dubai's most attractive developments, Madinat Jumeirah is a contemporary interpretation of a traditional Arab village, complete with a souq, palm-fringed waterways and desert-coloured hotels and villas festooned with wind towers. It's especially enchanting at night, when the gardens are romantically lit and the Burj Al Arab gleams in the background. There are exquisite details throughout, so if you see some stairs, take them – they might lead you to a hidden terrace with a mesmerising vista of the sprawling complex.

⦿ Dubai Marina & Palm Jumeirah

Cayan Tower ARCHITECTURE
(Map p338; Al Sharta St, Dubai Marina; M Damac, ⬚ Marina Towers) Stretching skyward for 307m, it may not be the tallest residential tower in the Dubai Marina, but it's certainly a building with twist: a 90-degree spiral over the course of its height, to be precise. Aside from looking cool, the design actually reduces wind forces on the building and reduces direct solar radiation. It was designed by the same firm as the Burj Khalifa.

Club Mina BEACH
(Map p338; ☑04 399 3333; www.clubminadubai. com; Le Meridien Mina Seyahi Beach Resort, King

---

DAY TRIPPING FROM DUBAI

The following well-established companies organise a vast range of city tours, activity bookings and desert safaris.

Desert tours with these big operators all use the desert near Dubai – usually the dunes near Maleha or the Dubai Desert Conservation Reserve. The desert camps are usually very big, organised, comfortable affairs.

If you prefer a more intimate overnight desert experience you're better off heading to Liwa Oasis and using the boutique firm Arabian Tours (p395).

Alpha Tours (☑04 701 9111; www.alphatoursdubai.com; 6hr desert safari adult/child Dhs305/255) Reliable Dubai operator with a full range of city tours, harbour cruises and deep-sea fishing trips as well as excursions in the desert.

Arabian Adventures (Map p330; ☑04 303 4888, 800 272 2426; www.arabian-adventures. com; Sheikh Zayed Rd, Emirates Holiday Bldg; Sundowner Dinner Safari Dhs250; ☺10am-10pm) As well as the usual city tours and desert trips, this big Dubai tour company also runs 4WD trips to the wadis and canyons of the Hajar Mountains on the east coast.

Desert Rangers (☑04 456 9944; www.desertrangers.net) Something for everyone from mountain safaris and desert trips to dhow dinner cruises.

Knight Tours (☑04 343 7725; www.knighttourism.com) This Dubai company sets itself apart with a couple of more culturally focused trips, including excursions to the camel races and to watch falconry breeding.

Orient Tours (☑04 282 8238; www.orient-tours-uae.com) A range of tours on offer, from dhow cruises and one-day city-highlights trips to desert excursions.

DON'T MISS

ART & DESIGN HUBS

Alserkal Avenue (Map p338; ☎050 556 9797; www.alserkalavenue.ae; 17th St, Al Quoz 1; Ⓜ Noor Bank, FGB) Edgy contemporary art from the Middle East and beyond has found a home in Dubai thanks to the vision of Abdelmonem Bin Eisa Alserkal. The local developer and arts patron has turned a sprawling warehouse complex in dusty Al Quoz into a buzzing gallery and cultural campus that also features a theatre, an indie cinema, cafes and a chocolate factory.

Dubai Design District (d3; Map p330; ☎04 433 3000; www.dubaidesigndistrict.com; off Al Khail Rd, Business Bay; Ⓟ; 🚌 Dubai Design District, Ⓜ Business Bay) Creative folks have a new HQ in Dubai. The fresh-off-the-drawing board Dubai Design District (d3) has drawn both regional and international talent and brands, including hot shots like Adidas and Foster + Partners. Visitors can tap into this laboratory of tastemakers by checking out the edgy architecture and public art, browsing showrooms and pop-ups, eavesdropping on bearded hipsters in sleek cafes, checking out art exhibits in building lobbies, or attending a free screening, workshop or other cultural event. The website has a schedule.

Salman Bin Abdul Aziz Al Saud St, Dubai Media City; day pass weekday/weekend adult Dhs220/310, child Dhs110/160; Ⓟ 🚻; Ⓜ Nahkeel) Set along 500m of private beach, this club is a family favourite thanks to its five pools (including a shaded one for kids), a children's club and a water-sports centre. Nice touch for grownups: cocktails in the swim-up bar. Children get free admission on Tuesdays.

The Beach at JBR
AREA

(Map p338; ☎04 317 3999; www.thebeach. ae; Jumeirah Beach Residence, Dubai Marina; ⊙10am-midnight Sun-Wed, to 1am Thu-Sat; Ⓟ🚻; Ⓜ DMCC, 🚌 Jumeirah Beach Residence 1, Jumeirah Beach Residence 2) Paralleling the beachfront for about 1km, The Beach at JBR is an open-plan cluster of low-lying, urban-style buildings wrapped around breezy plazas. Hugely popular with families on weekends, it mixes cafes and upmarket shops with a lively waterfront fun zone complete with a kiddie splash park, an outdoor gym, a crafts market and other diversions. A beach club rents out sunloungers, or you can spread your towel just about anywhere for free.

🏃 Activities

★ Aquaventure Waterpark
WATER PARK

(Map p338; ☎04 426 1169; www.atlantisthepalm. com; Atlantis The Palm, Palm Jumeirah; over/ under 120cm tall Dhs275/230; ⊙10am-sunset; 🚻; 🚌 Palm Jumeirah, 🚌 Atlantis Aquaventure) Adrenalin rushes are guaranteed at this water park at the Atlantis The Palm resort. A 1.6km-long 'river' with rapids, wave surges and waterfalls meanders through vast grounds that are anchored by two towers. A highlight is the ziggurat-shaped Tower of Neptune, with three slides, including the aptly named Leap of Faith, a near-vertical plunge into a shark-infested lagoon.

Aqua Fun
WATER PARK

(Map p338; www.aquafun.ae; Dubai Marina; Dhs120; ⊙9am-6pm; Ⓜ DMCC, 🚌 Jumeirah Beach Residence 1) Touted as the world's first inflatable water park, this small but challenging aqua park packs a punch. Don a lifejacket and get set to clamber, climb, slip and stumble over a network of floating obstacles. Popular with kids and adults alike, it's harder than it looks, and it's a great way to spend a few hours playing in the Gulf. Prepare to get wet. The minimum age is six years.

★ Al Boom Diving
DIVING

(Map p330; ☎04 342 2993; www.alboomdiving. com; Villa 254, cnr Al Wasl Rd & 33 St, Jumeirah 1; guided dives from Dhs250; ⊙10am-8pm Sun-Thu, to 6pm Fri & Sat; Ⓜ World Trade Centre) Al Boom is the largest and longest-established dive centre in the UAE and has an excellent reputation. It offers the gamut of PADI certification courses as well as guided dives and night dives around the World islands off the coast of Dubai, shark dives at the Dubai Aquarium and reef dives off the East Coast and the Musandam Peninsula in Oman.

Kitesurf School Dubai
KITESURFING

(Map p338; ☎050 254 7440; www.kitesurf.ae; 2D St, Umm Suqeim 1; private/group lessons per hour Dhs350/250, full rental per hour Dhs250; ⊙7am-7pm; Ⓜ Noor Bank) Appropriately located on hip and action-oriented Kite Beach, this licensed and professionally run outfit offers kitesurfing lessons and also rents out the necessary gear to get you up and out on the water. It also runs a shop selling all the equipment and accessories necessary for skimming the waves.

Skydive Dubai
SKYDIVING

(Map p338; ☑ 04 377 8888; www.skydivedubai.ae; Al Seyahi St, Dubai Marina; tandem jump, video & photos Dhs2199; ⊙ 8am-4pm Mon-Sat; Ⓜ Damac) Daredevils can experience the rush of jumping out of a plane and seeing Palm Jumeirah and the Dubai skyline from the air by signing up for these tandem parachute flights. The minimum age is 18; weight and height restrictions apply as well.

☞ Tours

★ Frying Pan Adventures
WALKING

(www.fryingpanadventures.com; tours Dhs350-395) The narrow lanes of Bur Dubai and Deira are a feast for foodies: a beehive of shoebox-size restaurants where global expats cook up comfort food from home. Sisters Arva and Farida Ahmed open the doors to the most exciting eateries to introduce you to delicious fare, from Moroccan to Nepalese to Indian, on their small-group walking tours.

★ Platinum Heritage Tours
TOURS

(Map p338; ☑ 04 388 4044; www.platinum-heritage. com; 3rd fl, Oasis Centre, Sheikh Zayed Rd, Al Quoz 1; ⊙ office hours 8am-6pm; Ⓜ Noor Bank, FGB) This is a top purveyor of year-round culturally sensitive and eco-minded desert safaris (ie no dune bashing), generally aboard vintage Range Rovers. A bestseller is the half-day

Bedouin Life, Falconry and Wildlife Drive (Dhs495) that visits a nomadic Bedouin camp where you have a traditional breakfast with locals, get a falconry demonstration and meet salukis, Arabian hunting dogs.

Absolute Adventure
OUTDOORS

(☑ 04 392 6463; www.adventure.ae; hiking/kayaking per person from Dh435/275; ⊙ Oct-Apr) This outdoor-adventure operator is a one-stop shop for exploring the raw beauty that lies beyond the UAE's high-rise cities. From kayaking to Hajar Mountains hiking, there's a range of activities at levels from beginner to advanced, with many suitable for families. As well as private excursions, the company organises regular group trips (usually on Fridays).

Big Bus Dubai
BUS

(☑ 04 340 7709; www.bigbustours.com; day pass adult/child Dhs273/174) These hop-on, hop-off city tours aboard open-topped double-decker buses are a good way for Dubai first-timers to get their bearings. Buses with recorded commentary in several languages run on three interlinking routes, making 35 stops at major malls, beaches and landmarks. Passes also include extras such as a dhow cruise, a night bus tour and museum admissions. Tickets are sold online (10% discount), on the bus or at hotels.

♣ Festivals & Events

Dubai Shopping Festival
SHOPPING

(DSF; www.mydsf.ae; ⊙ Jan) Held throughout January, Dubai's best-known shopping

---

THEME PARK THRILLS

MG Worlds of Adventure (☑ 04 403 8888, 600 500 962; www.imgworlds.com; Sheikh Mohammed Bin Zayed Rd (Hwy E311), City of Arabia; adult/child under 1.2m/child under 1.05m Dhs257/236/free; ⊙ 11am-10pm Sun-Wed, to 11pm Thu-Sat; Ⓟ 🚼) Housed in an air-conditioned hangar the size of 28 football fields, IMG Worlds of Adventure is the world's largest indoor theme park. The US$1 billion park is truly impressive, with more than 20 rides and attractions split across four themed zones – Marvel, Cartoon Network, Lost Valley Dinosaur Adventure and IMG Boulevard – and 28 dining outlets. Food is prepared on-site, and the quality is surprisingly high, with some healthy options. The theme park is located next to Global Village on the E311.

Motiongate (☑ 04 820 0000; www.motiongatedubai.com; Dubai Park & Resorts, Sheikh Zayed Rd (Hwy E11), Jebel Ali; adult/child under 3yr Dhs235/free; ⊙ 11am-8pm Sun-Wed, to 10pm Thu-Sat; Ⓟ 🚼 ; Ⓜ UAE Exchange) Whether you're seeking thrills or a family-friendly day out, this Hollywood-inspired theme park has something for everyone. The park is divided into four zones – DreamWorks, Lionsgate, Columbia Pictures and Smurfs Village – with 27 rides and attractions, including the world's first roller coaster inspired by *The Hunger Games*, river rapids, dark rides, 4D theatre rides, stage shows and kids' rides.

Motiongate Dubai is part of the larger Dubai Parks & Resorts theme park complex, which includes Bollywood Parks, Legoland Dubai and Legoland Water Park. Take the Red Line south to UAE Exchange station and then it's a 15-minute taxi ride to the park.

PICK YOUR PATCH OF SAND

Dubai residents love their beaches. Many who live in Jumeirah and the Dubai Marina, within splashing distance of the crystal-clear turquoise waters, make it a daily ritual to head down to the beach, while the rest of Dubai typically hits the sand on Fridays and Saturdays.

If you're not staying at a beachfront hotel fronted by its own sandy ribbon, you can either drop big dirham for a day guest pass, pay to chill at a snazzy beach club or go dipping for free at a public beach. All have undergone enormous infrastructure improvements in recent years and now come with changing rooms, toilets, showers, sunlounger and umbrella rentals, sports facilities, a jogging track, playgrounds and kiosks. Three of the best are:

Kite Beach (Sheikh Hamdan Beach; Map p338; 2c St, off Jumeirah Rd, behind Saga World mall, Umm Suqeim 1; ☉ sunrise-sunset; M Noor Bank) Long stretch of white sand with lots of activities on offer including kitesurfing and kayaking.

Jumeirah Public Beach (Umm Suqeim Beach; Map p338; Umm Suqeim 3; ☕; M FGB, Mall of the Emirates) Perfect for snapping that envy-inducing selfie with the Burj Al Arab as a backdrop.

JBR Beach (Map p338; Jumeirah Beach Residence, Dubai Marina; ☕; M DMCC, ☒ Jumeirah Beach Residence 1) Great facilities and plentiful food and drink outlets. Kids can keep cool in a splash zone.

---

festival lures bargain-hunters from around the world. There are huge discounts in the souqs and malls, and the city is abuzz with activities, ranging from live concerts to fashion shows and nightly fireworks.

Dubai Food Festival   FOOD & DRINK
(www.visitdubai.com/en/dff; ☉ Feb-Mar) Discover new trends, meet chefs, take a cooking class and, above all, sample fabulous fare during this month-long foodie festival held throughout the city.

Dubai World Cup   SPORTS
(☑ 04 327 2110; www.dubaiworldcup.com; Meydan Racecourse, Al Meydan Rd, Nad Al Sheba; tickets Dhs600-6750; ☉ Mar; M Burj Khalifa/Dubai Mall) Horse racing has a long and vaunted tradition in the Emirates. Racing season kicks off in November and culminates in March with the Dubai World Cup, the world's richest horse race until 2017 when it was surpassed by the Pegasus World Cup in Florida. While there's no betting, it's one of Dubai's biggest social events.

★ **Global Village**   FAIR
(☑ 04 362 4114; www.globalvillage.ae; Sheikh Mohammed Bin Zayed Rd (Hwy E311), exit 37; adult/child under 3yr Dhs15/free; ☉ 4pm-midnight Sat-Wed, to 1am Thu & Fri Nov-Mar; ☕; M Mall of the Emirates) The carnival-like Global Village is a bit like a 'world fair' for shoppers. Each of the 30-something pavilions showcases a specific nation's culture and – of course – products.

Aside from shopping, there's also lots of entertainment – from Chinese opera to Turkish whirling dervishes – as well as a fun fair with dozens of rides from tame to terrifying.

The grounds are about 20km southeast of the Mall of the Emirates; it's a 20-minute taxi ride from the Mall.

🛏 Sleeping

🛏 Deira & Bur Dubai

One of the cheapest areas to stay in Dubai, Bur Dubai is home to heritage B&Bs, the city's oldest hotel, modern budget and midrange chains and plenty of hotel apartments in the Mankhool area near the BurJuman mall; the latter are particularly ideal for longer stays and families with young children when self-catering can be a godsend.

Deira is close to the airport and therefore popular with visitors on stopovers. There are plenty of older, smaller, budget places in and around the souqs, although some can be quite – how shall we say? – shady. Nicer properties can be found along the Creek as far south as Dubai Festival City.

★ **XVA Hotel**   BOUTIQUE HOTEL $
(Map p328; ☑ 04 353 5383; www.xvahotel.com; s/d from Dhs320/470; ☕; M Al Fahidi) This riad-style boutique hotel occupies a century-old wind-tower house smack dab in the Al Fahidi Historic District, off Al Fahidi St. Its 15 compact rooms sport whitewashed

walls decorated with art that picks up on local themes like the Henna Room or the Dishdash Room. Most open onto a courtyard (making them rather dark) with a cafe where breakfast is served.

★**Rove City Centre** HOTEL $
(Map p330; ☎04 561 9100; www.rovehotels.com; 19B & 24B Sts; r from Dhs350; P 🛜 🏊; M Deira City Centre) This fast-growing budget chain offers superb value for money with a great Old Dubai location close to the souqs, Dubai Creek, great ethnic eats, public transport and the airport. Families will appreciate the adjoining rooms, the outdoor pool, free board games and 24-hour laundry. Crisp, contemporary rooms are good-sized, with floor-to-ceiling windows.

★**Zabeel Mini** HOTEL $
(Map p328; ☎04 707 7077; www.zabeelhouse.com/mini; Al Seef Rd, Dubai Creek; r from Dhs375; P 🛜 🏊; M BurJuman) As the name suggests, the rooms are smaller here than at the adjacent **Zabeel House** (Map p328; ☎04 707 7077; www.zabeelhouse.com; Al Seef Rd, Dubai Creek; r from Dhs800; P 🛜 🏊; M BurJuman), 23 sq metres to be exact. That said, they seriously pack a punch with bright red-and-black furnishings, a mural-style map of Dubai on the ceiling, espresso machine and classy eco-friendly bath products. There's an informal restaurant that specialises in street food and an interior courtyard with beanbags.

Orient Guest House HERITAGE HOTEL $
(Map p328; ☎04 351 9111; www.orientguesthouse.com; Al Fahidi Historical District, Al Fahidi St; r from Dhs444; P 🛜; M Al Fahidi) This romantic B&B in a former private home beautifully captures the feeling of Old Dubai. The 11 smallish rooms are entered via heavy wooden doors and surround a central courtyard that doubles as a cafe and breakfast spot. Furnishings exude traditional Middle Eastern flair and feature richly carved wooden armoires, four-poster beds with frilly drapes and tiled floors.

Dubai Youth Hostel HOSTEL $
(☎04 298 8151; www.uaeyha.com; 39 Al Nahda Rd, Al Qusais; dm/s/d HI members Dhs110/200/260, nonmembers Dhs120/230/270; P 🛜 🏊; M Stadium) Dubai's only Hostelling International–affiliated hostel is just north of the airport, far from most Dubai attractions but only 300m from a metro station and a mall. The range of facilities (pool, tennis court, coffee shop and laundry) is impressive. Private rooms in the newer wing (Hostel A) come with TV, fridge and bathroom.

Al Seef by Jumeirah HERITAGE HOTEL $$
(Map p328; ☎800 5863 4724; www.jumeirah.com/en/hotels-resorts/dubai/al-seef-by-jumeirah; Al Seef, Dubai Creek; r from Dhs850; P 🛜; M Al Fahidi) Located in the heart of Al Seef's meandering walkways, this gracious spot opened its first phase in September 2018 with 39 rooms; there will eventually be close to 200. Although new, they have been intuitively designed and built to emulate traditional Emirati dwellings with carved wood features, beams, warm earth colours and handwoven fabrics. There are courtyards, wind towers and Creek views.

Arabian Courtyard Hotel & Spa HOTEL $$
(Map p328; ☎04 351 9111; www.arabiancourtyard.com; Al Fahidi St; r from Dhs550; P 🛜 🏊; M Al Fahidi, Al Ghubaiba) Opposite the Dubai Museum, this hotel is an excellent hub for city explorers. The Arabian theme extends from the turbaned lobby staff to the design flourishes in the decent-sized rooms, some of which catch glimpses of the Creek across the souq. Facilities include a pub with live music, a much-lauded Indian restaurant, a swimming pool, a spa and a gym.

★**Park Hyatt Dubai** RESORT $$$
(Map p330; ☎04 602 1234; https://dubai.park.hyatt.com; Dubai Creek Club St, Dubai Creek Golf & Yacht Club; d from Dhs1100; P 🛜 🏊; M Deira City Centre) The mile-long driveway through a lush date-palm grove is the first hint that the Park Hyatt is no ordinary hotel – an impression quickly confirmed the moment you step into the domed and pillared lobby. Tiptoeing between hip and haute, it has oversized pastel rooms with subtle arabesque flourishes and balconies for counting the dhows plying the Creek. Close to the airport.

Downtown Dubai

Staying in Downtown Dubai puts you smack dab in the city's vortex of vibrancy. Aside from the big international chains, you'll also find a few home-grown players imbued with a local sense of place. With few exceptions, you'll need to shell out top dirham.

★**Rove Downtown** HOTEL $
(Map p330; ☎04 561 9999; www.rovehotels.com/hotel/rove-downtown; 312 Happiness St; r Dhs495; P 🛜 🏊; M Financial Centre, Burj Khalifa/Dubai Mall) Tailor-made for wallet-watching

West Dubai

globetrotters, Rove is a hip launch pad with sassy, contemporary decor and such millennial must-haves as an outdoor pool for chilling, a 24-hour gym, an industrial-styled cafe plus a hangover-friendly 2pm checkout. Pay a little extra for rooms with Burj Khalifa views.

Vida Downtown Dubai BOUTIQUE HOTEL $$
(Map p330; ☑04 428 6888; www.vida-hotels. com; Sheikh Mohammed Bin Rashid Blvd; r from Dhs900; P🛜🏊; ⓜBurj Khalifa/Dubai Mall) This crash pad for next-gen creatives and entrepreneurs has upbeat public areas with cool lamps and other urban accents that smoothly segue to white, bright rooms and huge open bathrooms with both a tub and walk-in shower. All electronics are controlled by the TV, there's a 24-hour gym to combat fat and fatigue, and a daybed-lined pool for chilling.

Carlton Downtown HOTEL $$
(Map p330; ☑04 506 9999; www.carltondowntown.com; Sheikh Zayed Rd, DIFC; r from Dhs520; P🛜🏊; ⓜFinancial Centre) Close to Dubai

International Finance Centre (DIFC) and the Dubai Metro, this hotel tower is a value-priced crash pad for urban explorers, with several restaurants and bars, Dubai's highest open-air rooftop pool with killer views, a spa and a well-equipped gym. Rooms are good-sized and modern, and even the smallest have a desk and a sofa for lounging.

★**Palace Downtown** HOTEL $$$
(Map p330; ☑04 428 7888; www.theaddress.com; Sheikh Mohammed Bin Rashid Blvd, Old Town Island; d from Dhs1600; P🛜🏊; ⓜBurj Khalifa/Dubai Mall) City explorers with a romantic streak will be utterly enchanted by this low-lying, luxe lakefront contender with its winning alchemy of old-world class and Middle Eastern aesthetics. Rooms are chic and understated, styled in easy-on-the-eye natural tones, and boast balconies overlooking Dubai Fountain. With the Burj Khalifa and Dubai Mall steps away, it's also a perfect launch pad for shopaholics.

🛏 Jumeirah

Luxury lovers should steer towards the Burj Al Arab or the hotels at Madinat Jumeirah. The cluster of midrange hotels and hotel-apartments next to the Mall of Emirates offer great value for money.

Dubai Marine Beach
Resort & Spa
RESORT **$$**

(Map p330; ☑ 04 346 1111; www.dxbmarine.com; Jumeirah Rd, Jumeirah 1; r from Dhs500; P 🛜 ⛱; Ⓜ World Trade Centre) You'll sleep well at this oldie-but-goodie beachside resort with villas set among pools and tropical gardens. The beach is rather small, but there's a water-sports centre and an entire village worth of restaurants, bars and nightclubs, including **Boudoir** (Map p330; ☑ 04 345 5995; www.clubboudoirdubai.com; ⊙10pm-3am; 🛜) and **Sho Cho** (Map p330; ☑ 04 346 1111; www.sho-cho.com; Dubai Marine Beach Resort & Spa,

Jumeirah Rd, Jumeirah 1; ⊙7pm-3am Sun-Fri; 🛜; Ⓜ World Trade Centre, Emirates Towers). Rooms vary considerably, especially in size, so check them out in advance, if possible.

★ Al Qasr Hotel
HOTEL **$$$**

(Map p338; ☑ 04 366 8888; www.jumeirah.com; Madinat Jumeirah, King Salman Bin Abdul Aziz Al Saud St, Umm Suqeim 3; r from Dhs1300; P 🛜 ⛱; Ⓜ Mall of the Emirates) If cookie-cutter hotels don't cut it, try this polished pad styled after a Middle Eastern summer palace. Details are extraordinary, from the lobby's Austrian-crystal chandeliers to mirror-polished inlaid-marble floors. Rooms sport arabesque flourishes, rich colours and cushy furnishings, while balconies overlook the waterways of Madinat Jumeirah. Top marks for the 2km-long private beach and one of the biggest pools in town.

West Dubai

🛏 Dubai Marina & Palm Jumeirah

Dubai Marina and Palm Jumeirah teem with five-star properties catering to the leisure brigade. Inland, along Sheikh Zayed Rd, and in Barsha Heights and Dubai Internet City, you'll also find midrange local properties and international chains.

Le Meridien Mina Seyahi Beach Resort & Marina RESORT $$
(Map p338; ☎04 399 3333; www.lemeridien-mina seyahi.com; King Salman Bin Abdul Aziz Al Saud St, Dubai Media City; r from Dhs825; P☏☂; MNak- heel, ⌂Mina Seyahi) This beachfront hotel is a sentimental favourite and nirvana for active types with water sports, tennis courts and an enormous state-of-the-art gym. The giant free-form pool is as lovely as the meandering palm-tree-lined gardens and calm beach, while rooms are dressed in cool white and have floor-to-ceiling windows with sea views.

FIVE Palm Jumeirah HOTEL $$$
(Map p338; ☎04 455 9988; www.fivehotelsand resorts.com; 1 Palm Jumeirah, Palm Jumeirah; r

from Dhs1100; P☏☂; MDamac, ⌂Palm Jumei- rah) One of Dubai's latest top-end hotels. The architecture is pure grandeur, with an entrance flanked by luminous glass cubes opening up to a sublime view of the palm- flanked infinity pool. Rooms are spacious and classy with a colour palette of soft yellows, creams and browns, and the bath- rooms have walk-in rainfall showers. There's a private beach and a fabulous rooftop bar.

🍴 Eating

🍴 Deira & Bur Dubai

Deira and Bur Dubai are heaven for eth- nic eats, with oodles of tiny, low-frills cafes catering to homesick expats from Kerala to Kathmandu with superb and authentic street food, especially around the Meena Bazaar area and the backstreets of Karama. For more upmarket authentic eats, head for the hotels.

★ Aroos Damascus SYRIAN $
(Map p330; ☎04 221 9825; cnr Al Muraqqabat Rd & Al Jazeira St; sandwiches Dhs4-20, mezze Dhs14-

35, mains Dhs15-50; ⌚7am-3am; Ⓜ Salah Al Din) A Dubai restaurant serving Syrian food to adoring crowds since 1980 must be doing something right. A perfect meal would start with hummus and a *fattoush* salad of toasted bread, tomatoes, onions and mint leaves before moving on to a plate of succulent grilled kebabs. There's a huge outdoor patio. This spot is busy until the wee hours.

★ XVA Café CAFE $

(Map p328; ☎04 353 5383; www.xvahotel.com/cafe; Al Fahidi Historic District, off Al Fahidi St; dishes Dhs25-55; ⌚7am-10pm; 📶🌿; Ⓜ Al Fahidi) Escape Dubai's bustle at this lovely courtyard cafe where the menu eschews meat in favour of a daily rotating menu of innovative vegetarian dishes, such as hummus made with broad beans or roasted carrots, aubergine burgers and *mojardara* (rice topped with lentils, sautéed veggies and yoghurt). The cheesecake and mint lemonade are both memorably delicious. Breakfast is served any time.

Indoor Food Market MARKET $

(Map p330; ☎04 295 1010; www.citycentredeira.com; level 2, Deira City Centre, Baniyas Rd; snacks from Dhs12; ⌚10am-10pm Sun-Wed, to midnight Thu-Sat; Ⓜ Deira City Centre) A winning idea, bringing street food under cover to escape the heat. There's around 16 different concepts to choose from, ranging from Lebanese to ice cream (sold from the driver's seat of a bright red Mini Cooper). There are communal tables and arcade games, and murals, exposed brick and a funky backing track complete the edgy urban look.

Arabian Tea House CAFE $$

(Map p328; ☎04 353 5071; www.arabianteahouse.co; Al Fahidi St; breakfast Dhs30-65, mains Dhs48-65; ⌚7.30am-10pm; 📶; Ⓜ Al Fahidi) A grand old tree, white wicker chairs, turquoise benches and crimson bougainvillea create a sun-dappled refuge in the courtyard of an old pearl merchant's house. The menu includes Emirati specialities, including *raqaq* (traditional bread), chicken *machboos* (spicy casserole with rice) and *saloona* chicken (in a tomato-based stew). Its traditional breakfast also comes highly recommended, but only if you are truly hungry.

★ Aseelah EMIRATI $$

(Map p328; ☎04 205 7033; www.radissonblu.com; Baniyas Rd, 2nd fl, Radisson Blu Hotel, Al Rigga; mains Dhs50-195; ⌚12.30-4pm & 6.30-11.15pm; 🅿📶; Ⓜ Union, Baniyas Square) With its mix of traditional and modern Emirati cuisine, this stylish restaurant ticks all the boxes. Many dishes feature a local spice mix called *bezar* (containing cumin, fennel, cinnamon and dried chillies), including the date-stuffed chicken leg and camel stew. To go the whole, well, goat, order *ouzi,* an entire animal filled with legumes and nuts, slow-cooked for 24 hours.

★ Claypot INDIAN $$

(Map p330; ☎050 100 7065; www.citymaxhotels.com; Citymax Hotel, cnr Mankhool & Kuwait Sts; mains Dhs45-75; ⌚noon-3pm & 7pm-midnight Sun-Thu, to 1am Fri & Sat; Ⓜ Al Fahidi, BurJuman) The chef here has Dorchester and Ritz cred, and studied under nouvelle cuisine guru Michel Guerard. Kickstart your menu with the *dahi puri* (stuffed crispy puris), a fabulous Indian street food. The saffron-infused biryanis are also fabled, along with the paneer dishes and smoked kebabs. There is live Indian music nightly from 9pm.

Al Mansour Dhow INTERNATIONAL $$$

(Map p328; ☎04 205 7033; www.radissonblu.com; Baniyas Rd, Radisson Blu Hotel; 2hr dinner cruise adult/child Dhs185/100; ⌚8pm; 🅿📶; Ⓜ Union, Baniyas Square) Take in the skyline on this moving feast aboard a traditional wooden dhow (cargo boat) decorated with bands of twinkling lights. Soulful Arabic song accompanies the lavish buffet spread that includes Middle Eastern and Western choices (including a live pasta station). There's a full bar and an upper-deck shisha lounge for chilling. Board outside the **Radisson Blu Hotel** (Map p328; Baniyas Rd; Ⓜ Union, Baniyas Square), which operates this dinner cruise.

Downtown Dubai

Downtown Dubai is the purview of high-roller restaurants, with most of them located in the five-star hotels and the Dubai International Financial Centre (DIFC). To take less of a bite out of your budget, head to the Dubai Mall food court or the funky cafes around Alserkal Avenue in Al Quoz.

Zaroob LEBANESE $

(Map p330; ☎04 327 6262; www.zaroob.com; Shop 1, Jumeirah Tower Bldg, Sheikh Zayed Rd; dishes Dhs12-32; ⌚24hr; 🅿📶🌿; Ⓜ Emirates Towers, Financial Centre) With its live cooking stations, open kitchens, fruit-filled baskets, colourful lanterns and graffiti-covered steel shutters, Zaroob radiates the urban integrity of a Beirut street-food alley. Feast on such delicious no-fuss food as falafel, shawarma (spit-roasted meat in pita bread), flat or wrapped *manoushe* (Levant-style pizza) or *alayet* (tomato stew), all typical of the Levant. Nice terrace too.

★ Baker & Spice INTERNATIONAL $$

(Map p330; ☑ 04 425 2240; www.bakerandspiceme.com; Souk Al Bahar; mains Dhs80-100; ⊘ 8am-11pm; ☎ ✐; Ⓜ Burj Khalifa/Dubai Mall) ✎ A pioneer of the local-organic-fresh maxim in Dubai, this London import offers a seasonal bounty of dishes, prepared in-house and served amid charming, country-style decor and on a Dubai Fountain–facing terrace. The salad bar brims with inspired creations, the breakfasts are tops, and the meat and fish dishes sustainably sourced.

Tom & Serg INTERNATIONAL $$

(Map p338; ☑ 056 474 6812; www.tomandserg.com; Al Joud Center, 15A St, Al Quoz 1; mains Dhs37-79; ⊘ 8am-4pm Sun-Thu, to 6pm Fri & Sat; ☎ ✐; Ⓜ Noor Bank, FGB) This always-bustling warehouse-style cafe with concrete floors, exposed pipes and an open kitchen would fit right into Madrid or Melbourne, which is exactly where its proprietors hail from. The menu teems with global feel-good food like Moroccan chicken, eggs benedict and a mean burger on a homemade bun. Great coffee too.

★ Zuma JAPANESE $$$

(Map p330; ☑ 04 425 5660; www.zumarestaurant.com; Bldg 06, Gate Village, Happiness St, DIFC; set lunches Dhs130, mains Dhs115-850; ⊘ noon-3.30pm Sun-Thu, 12.30-4pm Fri & Sat, plus 7pm-midnight Sat-Wed, to 1am Thu & Fri; ☎; Ⓜ Emirates Towers) Every dish speaks of refinement in this perennially popular bi-level restaurant that gives classic Japanese fare an up-to-the-minute workout. No matter if you go for the top-cut sushi morsels (the dynamite spider roll is a serious eye-catcher!), meat and seafood on the robata grill, or such signature dishes as miso-marinated black cod, you'll be keeping your taste buds happy.

Carnival by Tresind INDIAN $$$

(Map p330; ☑ 04 421 8665; www.carnivalbytresind.com; podium level, Burj Daman Tower, DIFC; mains from Dhs110; ⊘ noon-3.30pm & 5pm-2am; ✐; Ⓜ Financial Centre) Fun is firmly on the agenda at this wildly popular restaurant, which offers a playful take on Indian molecular gastronomy. Behind the smoke and mirrors, you'll find some seriously scrumptious food, with many dishes created at your table and equally clever offerings for vegetarians. Prices are sensible for this part of town; the Friday brunch is particularly good value (from Dhs250).

✗ Jumeirah

Jumeirah has some of the best eating in town, with a wonderful variety of restaurants, from ethnic street bites on 2nd December St and urban bistros at BoxPark or City Walk to humble fish shacks on the waterfront and top-dirham dining shrines at the Burj Al Arab and Madinat Jumeirah.

★ 3 Fils ASIAN $$

(Map p330; ☑ 056 273 0030; www.3fils.com; Jumeirah Fishing Harbour, Al Urouba St, Jumeirah 1; sharing plates Dhs38-75; ⊘ 1-11pm Mon-Wed, to midnight Thu-Sat; Ⓜ Burj Khalifa/Dubai Mall) Singaporean chef Akmal Anuar turns out innovative yet unpretentious Asian-influenced small plates at this tiny, unlicensed spot – a perfect foil to Dubai's expensive, overblown eateries. There are around 25 seats inside and a pint-sized kitchen in the corner, but try to nab one of the outside tables overlooking the bobbing yachts in the marina. Reservations are not taken.

★ Logma EMIRATI $$

(Map p330; ☑ 800 56462; www.logma.ae; BoxPark, Al Wasl Rd, Jumeirah 1; mains Dhs44-65; ⊘ 8am-1am; ☎ ✐; 🚌 12, 15, 93, Ⓜ Business Bay) This funky Emirati cafe is a great introduction to contemporary local cuisine. It's popular for breakfast dishes such as shakshuka (poached eggs in a spicy tomato sauce topped with feta), wholesome salads (try the pomegranate mozzarella) and sandwiches made with traditional *khameer* bread. Swap your usual latte for sweet *karak chai* (spiced tea) – a local obsession – or a date shake.

★ Bu Qtair SEAFOOD $$

(Map p338; ☑ 055 705 2130; off 2b St, Umm Suqeim Fishing Harbour, Umm Suqeim 1; meals Dhs40-125; ⊘ noon-11.30pm; Ⓟ; Ⓜ Noor Bank, FGB) Always packed to the gills, this simple eatery is a Dubai institution famous for its dock-fresh fish and shrimp, marinated in a 'secret' masala curry sauce and fried to order. Belly up to the window, point to what you'd like and wait (about 30 minutes) for your order to be delivered to your table. Meals are priced by weight.

★ Pai Thai THAI $$$

(Map p338; ☑ 04 432 3232; www.jumeirah.com; Madinat Jumeirah, King Salman Bin Abdul Aziz Al Saud St, Umm Suqeim 3; mains Dhs55-175; ⊘ 12.30-2.15pm & 6-11.15pm; ☎; Ⓜ Mall of the Emirates) An abra ride, a canalside table and candlelight are the hallmarks of a romantic night out, and this enchanting spot sparks on all cylinders. If your date doesn't make you swoon, then such expertly seasoned Thai dishes as wok-fried seafood and steamed sea bass should still ensure an unforgettable evening. Early reservations advised.

★**Pierchic** SEAFOOD $$$
(Map p338; ☑ 04 432 3232; www.jumeirah.com; Madinat Jumeirah, King Salman Bin Abdul Aziz Al Saud St, Umm Suqeim 3; mains Dhs125-450; ⊘12.30-3pm Sat-Thu plus 6-11pm Sat-Wed, to 11.30 Thu & Fri; 🗟; Ⓜ Mall of the Emirates) Looking for a place to drop an engagement ring into a glass of champagne? Make reservations (far in advance) at this impossibly romantic seafood house capping a historic wooden pier with front-row views of the Burj Al Arab and Madinat Jumeirah. The menu is a foodie's dream, with a plethora of beautifully prepared dishes, including grilled Canadian lobster, a sheer crustacean delight.

✗ Dubai Marina & Palm Jumeirah

Dubai Marina is dominated by sprawling beach resorts, each flaunting several top-end restaurants, bars and nightclubs. But you'll also find excellent eats away from the hotels, especially along the Marina Walk, The Walk at JBR and The Beach at JBR. Because of its compact nature, the area is conducive to hopping from one place to the next by foot.

Luchador MEXICAN $$
(Map p338; ☑ 04 247 5550; www.luchadordubai.com; 11th fl, Aloft Hotel, East Crescent, Palm Jumeirah; mains from Dhs55; ⊘5pm-2am Mon-Thu, from 1pm Fri & Sat; 🗟; 🚇 Palm Jumeirah) Vibrantly coloured murals, a wall of wrestling masks and a Mexican chef: Luchador feels like an authentic south-of-the-border cantina. The menu is reassuringly brief with an emphasis on inventive takes on traditional street food, such as fish tacos with roasted chilli mayo and ceviche with tuna, apricot and Serrano chilli. If you are not a coriander lover, let it be known.

★**Stay** FRENCH $$$
(Map p338; ☑ 04 440 1030; www.thepalm.oneandonlyresorts.com; One&Only The Palm, West Crescent, Palm Jumeirah; mains Dhs190-290; ⊘7-11pm Tue-Sun; 🅿🗟; Ⓜ Damac, 🚇 Palm Jumeirah) Three-Michelin-starred Yannick Alléno brings his culinary magic to Dubai in this subtly theatrical vaulted dining room ac-

WORTH A TRIP

FLAMINGO SPOTTING

Incongruously framed by highways, the surprising **Ras Al Khor Wildlife Sanctuary** (RAKWS; Map p330; ☑ 04 606 6822; http://wildlife-ae.herokuapp.com; Oud Metha Rd & Ras Al Khor St; ⊘9am-4pm Sat-Thu; Ⓜ Dubai Healthcare City, Al Jadaf) on Dubai Creek is an important stopover for migratory waterbirds on the east Africa–west Asian flyway. Gracious pink flamingos steal the show in winter, but avid birdwatchers can spot more than 170 species in this pastiche of salt flats, mudflats, mangroves and lagoons spread over an area of around 6.2 sq km.

cented with black crystal chandeliers. His creations seem deceptively simple (the beef tenderloin with fries and black pepper sauce is a bestseller), letting the superb ingredients shine brightly. An unexpected stunner is the Pastry Library, an entire wall of sweet treats.

★**Asia Asia** FUSION $$$
(Map p338; ☑ 04 276 5900; www.asia-asia.com; 6th fl, Pier 7, Dubai Marina; mains Dhs85-350; ⊘4pm-midnight; 🗟; Ⓜ Damac, 🚇 Dubai Marina Mall) Prepare for a culinary journey along the Spice Road at this theatrically decorated restaurant, which is entered via a candlelit corridor that spills into an exotic booth-lined lounge with dangling birdcage lamps. Dim sum to tuna tataki and crispy duck – dishes here are alive with flavours from Asia and the Middle East. Bonus: the grand marina views from the terrace. Full bar.

★**101 Lounge & Bar** SEAFOOD $$$
(Map p338; ☑ 04 440 1010; www.thepalm.oneandonlyresorts.com; One&Only The Palm, West Crescent, Palm Jumeirah; mains Dhs105-295; ⊘11.30am-2am Mon-Sat; 🗟; Ⓜ Damac, 🚇 Palm Jumeirah) It may be hard to concentrate on the food at this marina-adjacent al fresco pavilion, with its stunning skyline views. Come for nibbles and cocktails in the bar or go for the full dinner experience, with seafood the star attraction. Be sure to check out the ultraswish Champagne Bar. Note that there is a smart-casual dress code after 6.30pm.

The Croft BRITISH $$$
(Map p338; ☑ 04 319 4794; www.thecroftdubai.com; 5th fl, Dubai Marriott Harbour Hotel & Suites,

King Salman Bin Abdulaziz Al Saud St, Dubai Media City; mains Dhs90-165; ⊙ 5pm-1am Sun-Fri, 12.30-3.30pm Fri, 4pm-1am Sat; ☎⚑; Ⓜ Damac, ⛵ Marina Towers) Chef Darren Velvick flies the flag for modern British cooking at this relaxed restaurant with an open kitchen and spacious terrace overlooking the lights of Dubai Marina. There's an emphasis on locally grown and organic ingredients, along with craft beer, well-priced wine and a daily happy hour from 5pm to 8pm.

Drinking & Nightlife

Deira

★ **Irish Village** IRISH PUB

(Map p330; ☎ 04 282 4750; www.theirishvillage.com; 31A St, Garhoud; ⊙ 11am-1am Sat-Wed, to 2am Thu & Fri; ☎; Ⓜ GGICO) This always-buzzing pub, with its Irish-main-street facade (complete with post office) and made with materials imported straight from the Emerald Isle, has been a Dubai institution since 1996. There's Guinness and Kilkenny on tap, lovely gardens around a petite lake, the occasional live band and plenty of pub grub to keep those tummy rumblings at bay.

★ **QDs** BAR

(Map p330; ☎ 04 295 6000; www.dubaigolf.com; Dubai Creek Club St, Dubai Creek Golf & Yacht Club, Garhoud; shisha Dhs65; ⊙ 5pm-2am Sun-Wed, to 3am Thu & Sat, 1pm-3am Fri; ☎; Ⓜ Deira City Centre) Watch the ballet of lighted dhows floating by while sipping cocktails at this always-fun outdoor Creek-side lounge deck where carpets and cushions set an inviting mood. In summer, keep cool in an air-conditioned tent. Great for shisha-holics too.

Downtown Dubai

★ **Cirque Le Soir** CLUB

(Map p330; ☎ 050 995 5400; www.facebook.com/CirqueLeSoirDubai; Fairmont Hotel, Sheikh Zayed Rd; ⊙ 10.30pm-3am Mon, Tue, Thu & Fri; Ⓜ World Trade Centre) Is it a nightclub, a circus or a cabaret? One of Dubai's hottest after-dark spots – and London spin-off – is actually a trifecta of all three, a madhouse where you can let your freak out among clowns, stilt-walkers, sword swallowers and Dubai party A-listers. Music-wise it's mostly EDM, but hip-hop Mondays actually draw some of the biggest crowds.

★ **White Dubai** CLUB

(☎ 050 443 0933; www.whitedubai.com; Meydan Racecourse Grandstand Rooftop, Nad Al Sheba; ⊙ 11pm-3am Tue, Thu-Sat; ☎) The Dubai spawn of the Beirut original did not need long to lure local socialites with high-energy rooftop parties under the stars. International spinmeisters shower partygoers with an eclectic sound soup, from house and electro to bump-and-grind hip-hop and R&B, all fuelled by dazzling projections and light shows.

★ **Bridgewater Tavern** SPORTS BAR

(Map p330; ☎ 04 414 0000; www.jwmarriottmarquisdubailife.com/dining/bridgewatertavern; JW Marriott Marquis Hotel, Sheikh Zayed Rd; ⊙ 4pm-2am; ☎; Ⓜ Business Bay) This happening joint has ushered the sports bar into a new era. Sure, there are the requisite big screens to catch the action, but it's packaged into an industrial-flavoured space with (mostly) rock on the turntables, shisha on the canalside terrace, and an elevated gastropub menu whose signature 'black' burger is so messy it comes with a bib.

Poppy COCKTAIL BAR

(Map p330; ☎ 04 512 5555; www.poppy-dubai.com; Renaissance Downtown Hotel, Marasi Dr, Business Bay; ⊙ 6pm-3am; ☎; Ⓜ Burj Khalifa/Dubai Mall) Enquire with the concierge where Poppy is within the hotel and he (or she) will likely respond in a whisper. It's a venue of US Michelin-starred chef David Myers, and the idea is to keep this place secretive, but the word is out. Poppy is pure romance with candlelit lighting, plush seating and a vinyl-only vibe of blues and '60s music.

Jumeirah

★ **Bahri Bar** BAR

(Map p338; ☎ 04 432 3232; www.jumeirah.com; Mina A'Salam, Madinat Jumeirah, King Salman Bin Abdul Aziz Al Saud St, Umm Suqeim 3; ⊙ 4pm-2am Sat-Wed, to 3am Thu & Fri; ☎; Ⓜ Mall of the Emirates) This chic bar drips with sultry Middle Eastern decor and has a veranda laid with Persian rugs and comfy sofas perfect for taking in magical views of the Madinat waterways and the Burj Al Arab. Daily drink deals, elevated bar bites, and bands or DJs playing jazz and soul make the place a perennial fave among locals and visitors.

Dubai Marina & Palm Jumeirah

★ Lock, Stock & Barrel
BAR

(Map p338; ☑ 04 514 9195; www.lsbdubai.com; 8th fl, Grand Millennium Hotel, Barsha Heights; ⊘ 4pm-3am Mon-Thu, from 1pm Fri, from 2pm Sat & Sun) Since opening in 2016, LSB has been racking up the accolades as living proof that there's room in bling-blinded Dubai for keeping-it-real party hangouts. Dressed in industrial chic, this two-level joint is the place for mingling with unpretentious folk over cocktails and craft beer, twice-weekly live bands and fingerlickin' American soul food. Two-for-one happy hour daily from 4pm to 8pm.

★ Barasti
BAR

(Map p338; ☑ 04 318 1313; www.barastibeach.com; King Salman Bin Abdul Aziz Al Saud St, Dubai Media City; ⊘ 10am-1.30am Sat-Wed, 9am-3am Thu & Fri; ☏; Ⓜ Nakheel) Since 1995, Barasti has grown from basic beach shack to top beach club spot for lazy days in the sand, and is often jam-packed with shiny happy party people knocking back the brewskis. There's football and rugby on the big screen, plus pool tables (and pool parties), water-sports rentals, a daily happy hour, occasional bands and drink specials on most weeknights.

Tap House
PUB

(Map p338; ☑ 04 514 3778; www.thetaphouse.ae; Club Vista Mare, Palm Jumeirah; ⊘ noon-1am Sun-Wed, to 2am Thu-Sat; ☏; 🚡 Palm Jumeirah) This gastropub is as popular with the after-work crowd as it is with families on sunny Saturday afternoons. There are a dozen beers on tap, along with bottled European brews, tap-your-own 5L kegs and even beer-based cocktails (try the Leffe Fashioned: Jim Beam and bitters topped with Leffe Blonde). The breezy terrace boasts views of Burj Al Arab in the distance.

☆ Entertainment

★ Dubai Opera
PERFORMING ARTS

(Map p330; ☑ 04 440 8888; www.dubaiopera.com; Sheikh Mohammed Bin Rashid Blvd; Ⓜ Burj Khalifa/ Dubai Mall) Shaped like a traditional dhow Dubai Opera is the city's newest high-calibre performing-arts venue. Despite its name, it actually hosts a potpourri of shows, including musicals, ballet, comedy acts, rock bands and recitals. The 'bow' of the building contains a 2000-seat theatre and glass-fronted foyer overlooking Burj Lake.

★ Cinema Akil
CINEMA

(Map p338; www.cinemaakil.com; 68 Alserkal Ave, Al Quoz 1; Ⓜ Noor Bank, FGB) Treating cine buffs to smart indie flicks from around the world on a pop-up basis since 2014, this dynamic platform has now taken up permanent residence at Alserkal Avenue. Screenings generally take place from 4pm on Friday and Saturday and 7.30pm on weekdays and are often followed by Q&A sessions with directors.

La Perle by Dragone
PERFORMING ARTS

(Map p330; www.laperle.com; Al Habtoor City; tickets Dhs400-1600; ☏; Ⓜ Business Bay) A custom-designed theatre with a 270-degree angle makes for perfect sight lines even in the cheaper seats of this magical show centred on an aquatic stage where some 65 acrobats perform their stunning stunts. It is the brainchild of Franco Dragone, one of the original creators of Cirque du Soleil.

Junction
THEATRE

(Map p338; ☑ 04 338 8525; www.thejunctiondubai. com; 72 Alserkal Ave, Al Quoz 1; Ⓜ Noor Bank, FGB) Since 2015 this pint-sized indie performing-arts space has hosted some of Dubai's most exciting cultural programming, from plays to concerts and comedy to dance, showcasing mostly local talent. It also runs the annual Short & Sweet Poetry Festival in October showcasing local poets, rhymesters and storytellers aged from 12 years upwards.

Blue Bar
LIVE MUSIC

(Map p330; ☑ 04 310 8150; Novotel World Trade Centre Dubai, Happiness St; ⊘ noon-2am; ☏; Ⓜ World Trade Centre) Cool cats of all ages gather in this relaxed joint for some of the finest live jazz and blues in town, along with a full, reasonably priced bar line-up that includes signature cocktails named after jazz greats (try the Louis Armstrong–inspired Hello Dolly) ordered on an iPad's interactive menu. It's open daily with live concerts from 10pm Thursday to Saturday.

Fridge
LIVE MUSIC

(Map p338; ☑ 04 347 7793; www.thefridgedubai. com; 5 Alserkal Ave, Al Quoz 1; tickets from Dhs50; Ⓜ Noor Bank, FGB) Part of the Alserkal Avenue cultural campus, this talent-management agency runs a much beloved concert series (usually on Fridays) that shines the spotlight on local talent still operating below the radar. The line-up defines eclectic and may hopscotch from swing to opera, and jazz to pop, sometimes all in one night.

CHRISTIAN B./SHUTTERSTOCK ©

KAH LOONG LEE/SHUTTERSTOCK ©

Burj Khalifa
The Burj Khalifa (p330), the world's tallest building, pierces the sky at 828m and opened in January 2010.

Al Fahidi Historic District
Formerly known as the Bastakiya Quarter, this heritage area (p329) is home to museums, craft shops, cultural exhibits, cafes and boutique hotels.

Mall of the Emirates
One of the UAE's most popular shopping centres, Mall of the Emirates (p348) is home to Ski Dubai, a 14-screen cinema and 630 shops.

Global Village
'world fair' for shoppers, each of the pavilions the Global Village (p336) showcases a specific ation's culture and products. There's also lots of entertainment.

S-F/SHUTTERSTOCK ©

Meydan Racecourse HORSE RACING
(☑ 04 327 0077, tickets 04 327 2110; www.dubairac
ingclub.com; Al Meydan Rd, Nad Al Sheba; premium
seating Dhs50; ⊘ races Nov-Mar; 🛜🏃) Dubai
racing's home is the spectacular Meydan
Racecourse, about 5km southeast of downtown Dubai. Spanning 1.5km, its grandstand is bigger than most airport terminals
and lidded by a crescent-shaped solar-
panelled roof. It can accommodate up to
60,000 spectators and integrates a five-star
hotel, restaurants, an IMAX theatre and a
museum.

🛍 Shopping

Dubai is a top retail haunt that hosts not
one but two huge annual shopping festivals.
Shopping is a leisure activity here, and malls
are much more than just mere collections of
stores. Some look like an Italian palazzo or
a Persian palace and lure visitors with surreal attractions such as an indoor ski slope,
a giant aquarium or an open-air botanical
garden. Traditional souqs, too, are beehives
of activity humming with timeless bargaining banter. Meanwhile, a new crop of urban-style outdoor malls has expanded the
shopping spectrum yet again.

★**Dubai Mall** SHOPPING CENTRE
(Map p330; ☑ 800 382 246 255; www.thedubai
mall.com; Sheikh Mohammed Bin Rashid Blvd;
⊘ 10am-midnight; 🛜🏃; Ⓜ Burj Khalifa/Dubai
Mall) With around 1300 shops, this isn't
merely the world's largest shopping mall –
it's a small city, with a giant ice rink and
aquarium, a dinosaur skeleton, indoor
theme parks and 150 food outlets. There's
a strong European-label presence, along
with branches of the French Galeries Lafay-
ette department store, the British toy store
Hamley's and the first Bloomingdale's outside the US.

★**Mirzam Chocolate Makers** CHOCOLATE
(Map p338; ☑ 04 333 5888; www.mirzam.com;
Warehouse 70, Alserkal Ave, Al Quoz 1; tour & workshop Dhs37; ⊘ 10am-7pm Sat-Thu; 🏃; Ⓜ FGB,
Noor Bank) 🍫 The art of crafting fine chocolate is taken very seriously at this high-tech
'Willy Wonka' factory, where all stages from
roasting to handwrapping take place behind
glass walls. Only single origin beans from
such far-flung locales as Madagascar, Papua
New Guinea, Vietnam, India and Indonesia
are used. Sample the final product or sign
up for a tour and tasting workshop.

Souk Madinat Jumeirah SHOPPING CENTRE
(Map p338; ☑ 04 366 8888; www.jumeirah.com;
Madinat Jumeirah, King Salman Bin Abdul Aziz
Al Saud St, Umm Suqeim 3; ⊘ 10am-11pm; 🛜;
Ⓜ Mall of the Emirates) More tourist-geared
boutique mall than traditional Arab market, this handsomely designed souq is part
of the Arab-village-style Madinat Jumeirah
resort and not a bad spot for picking up
souvenirs. Options include camel toys at
Camel Company (☑ 04 368 6048; www.camel
company.ae), Bedouin daggers at **Lata's** (☑ 04
368 6216) and pashmina shawls at **Toshkha-
na** (☑ 04 368 6526). In some shops, bargaining is possible.

Mall of the Emirates SHOPPING CENTRE
(Map p338; ☑ 04 409 9000; www.malloftheemir
ates.com; Sheikh Zayed Rd, Al Barsha; ⊘ 10am-
10pm Sun-Wed, to midnight Thu-Sat; 🛜; Ⓜ Mall of
the Emirates) Home to **Ski Dubai** (☑ toll free
800 386; www.theplaymania.com/skidubai; Mall of
the Emirates, Sheikh Zayed Rd, Al Barsha; slope day
pass adult/child Dhs310/285, snow park Dhs210;
⊘ 10am-11pm Sun-Wed, to midnight Thu, 9am-mid-
night Fri, to 11pm Sat; 🏃; Ⓜ Mall of the Emirates),
a community theatre, a 24-screen multiplex
cinema and – let's not forget – 630 shops,
Mall of the Emirates is one of Dubai's most
popular shopping centres. With narrow
walkways and no daylight, it can feel a tad
claustrophobic at peak times (except in the
striking Fashion Dome, lidded by a vaulted
glass ceiling and home to luxury brands).

BoxPark SHOPPING CENTRE
(Map p330; ☑ 800 637 227; www.boxpark.ae; Al Wasl
Rd, Jumeirah 2; ⊘ 10am-midnight; 🛜; Ⓜ Business
Bay) Inspired by the London original, this
1.3km-long outdoor lifestyle mall was built
from upcycled shipping containers and has
injected a welcome dose of urban cool into the
Dubai shopping scene. The 220 units draw a
hip crowd, including lots of locals, with quirky
concept stores, eclectic cafes and restaurants,
and entertainment options including a cinema with on-demand screenings.

Dubai Festival City Mall SHOPPING CENTRE
(☑ 800 332; www.festivalcentre.com; Crescent
Dr; ⊘ 10am-10pm Sun-Wed, to midnight Thu-Sat;
Ⓜ Creek) Southeast of the airport, near Business Bay Bridge, this 350-store behemoth
has all the standard shops, plus Ikea –
a draw for locals and expats. Its main
plus is the picturesque location around
a semi-circular bay, which is lined with
bars and restaurants. All are great vantage
points from which to enjoy Imagine, a free

laser-light-water-pyrotechnics show presented nightly on the hour.

Ibn Battuta Mall SHOPPING CENTRE
(☑ 04 390 9999; www.ibnbattutamall.com; Sheikh Zayed Rd, btwn Interchanges No 5 & No 6, Jebel Ali; ☺ 10am-10pm Sun-Wed, to midnight Thu-Sat; 🛜; Ⓜ Ibn Battuta) The shopping is good if nothing extraordinary, but it's the lavish and exotic design and architecture of this 400-shop mall that steal the show, tracing the way stations of 14th-century Moroccan explorer Ibn Battuta in six themed courts (China, Persia, Egypt, India, Tunisia, Andalusia). Dubai's first IMAX cinema opened here in September 2018, promising cinema-goers an immersive cinematic experience.

🅘 Information

EMERGENCY

Ambulance	☑ 999
Fire Department	☑ 997
Police	☑ 999, 901 non-emergency

MEDICAL SERVICES

American Hospital Dubai (Map p330; ☑ 04 336 7777; www.ahdubai.com; Oud Metha Rd; Ⓜ Dubai Healthcare City) One of the top private hospitals in town with 24/7 emergency room.

Dubai Hospital (☑ 04 219 5000; www.dha. gov.ae/en/DubaiHospital; Al Khaleej Rd, Deira; ☺ 24hr; Ⓜ Abu Baker Al Siddique) One of the region's best government hospitals, with 24/7 emergency room.

Rashid Hospital (Map p330; ☑ 04 219 1000; www.dha.gov.ae/en/RashidHospital; off Oud Metha Rd, near Al Maktoum Bridge; Ⓜ Oud Metha) Public hospital for round-the-clock emergencies.

TOURIST INFORMATION

Dubai Department of Tourism & Commerce Marketing (☑ call centre 600 555 559; www.visitdubai.com; ☺ call centre 8am-8pm Sat-Thu) No brick-and-mortar office but a comprehensive website and a call centre for information on hotels, attractions, shopping and other topics.

🅘 Getting There & Away

AIR

Dubai International Airport (DXB; ☑ 04 224 5555; www.dubaiairports.ae; Ⓜ Airport Terminal 1, Airport Terminal 3) Located on the border with the Sharjah emirate, Dubai International Airport has three terminals. Terminal 1 is the main terminal used by major international airlines. Small and charter airlines are based at Terminal 2, and Terminal 3 is the sole domain of Emirates Airlines. There are duty-free shops in the arrival and departure halls and several excellent restaurants.

BUS

Dubai's Roads & Transport Authority (www.rta. ae) operates air-conditioned (often overcrowded) buses to other emirates between 6am and 11pm from three main terminals, as well as to Muscat, the capital of Oman. Maps, timetables and a journey planner are available at www. dubai-buses.com.

A shuttle bus runs between the airport and Ras Al Khaimah (www.rakshuttle.com; Dhs20); book your place online.

CAR

There are scores of car-rental agencies in Dubai, from major global companies to no-name local businesses. The former may charge more but give peace of mind with full insurance and 24/7 roadside assistance. You'll find the gamut at the airport and throughout the city. Most major hotels have desks in the lobby.

🅘 Getting Around

Dubai's local public transport is operated by the Roads & Transport Authority (www.rta.ae) and consists of the metro, buses, water buses and trams. For trip planning visit www.wojhati.rta.ae. For other information, call the 24-hour hotline (☑ 800 9090) or visit the website.

You can also download the local road and transport authority (RTA) app **S'hail**, which provides all local transport options on one platform, plus taxi bookings and real-time traffic conditions.

TO/FROM DUBAI INTERNATIONAL AIRPORT

Bus

The bus is only really useful at night when metro service stops. The handiest route is bus C1, which runs 24 hours to Deira, Bur Dubai and Satwa from terminals 1 and 3. Buy a Nol Card in the arrivals terminal. For route planning, see www.wojhati.rta.ae.

Dubai Metro

The Red Line stops at terminals 1 and 3 and is the most efficient way to get across town by public transport. Trains run roughly between 5.30am and midnight (until 1am on Thursdays and Fridays). On Fridays, train service starts at 10am. Up to two pieces of luggage are permitted. A Nol Card must be purchased at the station.

Taxi

Taxis wait outside each arrivals terminal 24/7. A surcharge of Dhs25 applies to rides originating at the airport, plus Dhs1.96 per kilometre.

Expect to pay about Dhs55 to Deira, Dhs60 to Bur Dubai, Dhs70 to Downtown Dubai, Dhs110 to Madinat Jumeirah and Dhs130 to Dubai Marina.

ABRA

Abras are motorised traditional wooden boats linking Bur Dubai and Deira across the Creek on two routes:

Route 1 Bur Dubai Abra Station (Map p328; Waterfront, Bur Dubai Souk, Meena Bazaar; Dhs1; M Al Ghubaiba) to **Deira Old Souk Abra Station** (Map p328; Baniyas Rd, near Spice Souk; Dhs1; ⊙ 6am-midnight; M Baniyas Square); operates daily between 6am and midnight; rides take five minutes.

Route 2 Dubai Old Souk Abra Station (Map p328; per ride Dhs1; M Al Ghubaiba) to **Al Sabkha Abra Station** (Map p328; Baniyas Rd; Dhs1; M Baniyas Square); operates around the clock; rides take about seven minutes.

Abras leave when full (around 20 passengers), which rarely takes more than a few minutes. The fare is Dhs1, and you pay the driver en route. Chartering your own abra costs Dhs120 per hour.

Air-conditioned abras also link **Al Jaddaf Marine Station** (Darwish Sulaiman; abra/ferry Dhs2/50; M Creek) with the **Dubai Festival City Abra Station** (Dubai Festival City; Dhs1) from 7am to midnight every 10 minutes, while petrol-operated abras operate from the new **Al Seef Marine Station** (Map p328; Al Seef St, Al Seef; Dhs2; M BurJuman) to **Al Ghubaiba Marine Station** (Map p328; Shindagha Waterfront; ferry from Dhs50, abra Dhs2; M Al Ghubaiba) between 7am and 10pm Saturday to Thursday

and 10am to midnight Friday; the fare for both is Dhs2 and both rides take less than 10 minutes.

In addition, pricey, tourist-geared sightseeing abras offer short rides around Burj Lake (Dhs65), Al Mamzar (Dhs60) and Global Village (Dhs50).

CAR

Driving in Dubai is not for nervous nellies given that local behind-the-wheel styles are rather quixotic, and negotiating seven- or eight-lane highways can be quite scary at first. Distances can be deceiving. Heavy traffic, detours and eternal red lights can quickly turn that 5km trip into an hour's journey.

However, well-maintained multilane highways, plentiful petrol stations and cheap petrol make car hire a worthwhile option for day trips from Dubai.

For navigating, Google Maps works reasonably well. A local alternative is the RTA Smart Drive app, downloadable free from Google Play and the Apple app store.

There are seven automated toll gates (Salik, www.salik.gov.ae/en), each costing Dhs4, set up along Dubai's highways, including two along Sheikh Zayed Rd: Al Barsha near the Mall of the Emirates and Al Safa near Burj Khalifa. All hire cars are equipped with sensors that record each time you pass a toll point. The cost is added to your final bill.

CITY BUSES

The RTA operates local buses on more than 120 routes primarily serving the needs of low-income commuters. Buses are clean, comfortable, air-conditioned and cheap, but they're slow. The first few rows of seats are generally reserved for

MAJOR BUS SERVICES FROM DUBAI

Several services depart from **Union Bus Station** (Map p328; www.dubai-buses.com; Union Sq, Al Rigga; M Union), next to the Union metro station.

DESTINATION	NUMBER	DURATION	FARE	FREQUENCY
Sharjah	E303	45min-1hr	Dhs10	every 15min
Ajman	E400	45min	Dhs12	hourly
Fujairah	E700	2hr	Dhs25	roughly hourly

Al Ghubaiba Bus Station (Map p328; www.rta.ae; Al Ghubaiba Rd; M Al Ghubaiba) sits handily within steps from the Al Ghubaiba metro station.

DESTINATION	NUMBER	DURATION	FARE	FREQUENCY
Abu Dhabi	E100	2hr	Dhs25	every 20min
Sharjah	E306	45min-1hr	Dhs10	every 30min

Sabkha Bus Station (Map p328; www.dubai-buses.com; cnr Al Sabkha Rd & Deira St; M Baniyas Square) is in the heart of the Deira souqs.

DESTINATION	NUMBER	DURATION	FARE	FREQUENCY
Hatta	E16	2½hr	Dhs10	hourly
Sharjah	E303A	45min-1hr	Dhs10	half-hourly

NOL CARDS: THE DUBAI TRANSPORT CARD

Before hopping aboard local transport, purchase a rechargeable pass (Nol Card; *nol* is Arabic for 'fare') from ticket offices or vending machines. The RTA network is divided into seven zones, with fares depending on the number of zones traversed. Cards must be tapped onto the card reader upon entering and exiting at which point the correct fare will be deducted.

Two types of tickets are relevant to visitors:

Nol Red Ticket (Dhs3, plus credit for at least one trip) Must be pre-loaded with the correct fare each time you travel; can be recharged up to 10 times; may only be used on a single mode of transport at a time. Fares: Dhs4 for one zone, Dhs6 for two zones, Dhs8.50 for three or more zones, Dhs20 for the day pass.

Nol Silver Card (Dhs25, including Dhs19 credit) With pre-loaded credit, this works on the pay-as-you go principle with fares deducted. Get this card if you're going to make more than 10 trips. Fares are Dhs3 for one zone, Dhs5 for two zones and Dhs7.50 for three or more zones.

For full details, see www.nol.ae.

women and children. Fares range from Dhs3 to Dhs8.50, and Nol Cards must be used.

For information, check www.dubai-buses.com; for trip planning, go to www.wojhati.rta.ae.

DUBAI FERRY

The Dubai Ferry (www.dubai-ferry.com) operates on various routes and provides a fun way for visitors to see the city from the water.

Dubai Marina to Al Ghubaiba (Bur Dubai) Route These 90-minute mini-cruises depart at 11am, 1pm and 6.30pm from the **Dubai Marina Ferry Station** (Map p338; Marina Walk, below Al Gharbi St Bridge, Dubai Marina; adult/child Dhs50/25; ⊙10am-7pm; Ⓜ Damac, 🚡 Dubai Marina Mall) and the **Al Ghubaiba Ferry Station** (Map p328; 🗐 800 9090; www.rta.ae; Shindagha Waterfront; adult/child Dhs50/25; ⊙10am-6pm). The route passes by Madinat Jumeirah, the Burj Al Arab and Port Rashid. Other options from either station include an afternoon-tea trip at 3pm and a sunset cruise at 5pm. Note that the ferries may cancel if they do not have sufficient passengers.

Dubai Canal Route Links Al Jaddaf Marine Station (near Creek metro station) with Dubai Canal station at 10am, noon and 5.30pm and at noon, 2pm and 7.30pm in the other direction. Stops include Dubai Design District, Al Wajeha, Marasi and **Sheikh Zayed Rd** (Map p330; 🗐 800 9090; www.dubai-ferry.com; Dhs25-50; ⊙11.30am-5.30pm; Ⓜ Business Bay). Fares depend on number of stations travelled; the entire one-way route is Dhs50.

Both routes connect at the Dubai Canal station. The fare from here to either Al Ghubaiba or Dubai Marina is Dhs25.

Dubai Mall to Dubai Marina Route A good service for shoppers, this route takes one hour and 20 minutes and connects two of the city's malls. It leaves from Dubai Marina at 3.15pm and 4.30pm and returns at 4.45pm and 6pm daily. Tickets cost Dhs68.25, and passengers are taken direct to Dubai Mall from nearby Al Wajeha Al Maeyah station by complimentary shuttle.

Fares and schedules change frequently; check www.dubai-ferry.com for the latest information.

DUBAI METRO

Dubai's metro (www.dubaimetro.eu) opened in 2010 and has proved a popular service.

Red Line Runs for 52km from near Dubai International Airport to Jebel Ali past Dubai Marina, mostly paralleling Sheikh Zayed Rd.

Green Line Runs for 22km, linking the Dubai Airport Free Zone with Dubai Healthcare City and Dubai Creek.

Intersection of Red & Green Lines At Union and BurJuman stations.

Onward Journey At each station, cabs and feeder buses stand by to take you to your final destination.

Frequency Red Line trains run roughly every 10 minutes from 5am to midnight Saturday to Wednesday, to 1am Thursday, and from 10am to 1am on Fridays. Green Line trains start slightly later at 5.30am from Saturday to Thursday.

Cars Each train consists of four standard cars and one car that's divided into a women-only section and a 'Gold Class' section, where a double fare buys carpets and leather seats. Women may of course travel in any of the other cars as well.

Tickets Nol cards can be purchased at the station and must be swiped before exit.

Fares These vary from Dhs3 for stops within a single zone to Dhs7.50 for stops within five zones.

Routes All metro stations stock leaflets, in English, clearly mapping the zones.

Penalties If you exit a station with insufficient credit, you will have to pay the equivalent of a day pass (Dhs14). Inspectors regularly check that cards have been swiped and will issue an on-the-spot Dhs200 fine for ticket evasion. Men should also be careful not to inadvertently step into the women-only section, for which there is a Dhs100 on-the-spot fine. Note that eating, drinking or chewing gum is not allowed on the metro and may also incur fines.

DUBAI TRAM

The Dubai Tram (www.alsufouhtram.com) makes 11 stops in and around the Dubai Marina area, including near the Marina Mall, The Beach at JBR and The Walk at JBR. It also connects with the Damac and DMCC metro stations and with the Palm Jumeirah Monorail at Palm Jumeirah station.

Trams run roughly every eight minutes from 6am to 1am Saturday to Thursday and from 9am to 1am on Friday. The entire loop takes 40 minutes. The fare depends on how many zones you travel through, starting with Dhs4 for one zone. Nol Cards must be used.

A second phase of the Dubai Tram has been announced, which will extend the track by 4km and link the tram network with the Mall of the Emirates. The estimated completion year is 2020.

PALM JUMEIRAH MONORAIL

The elevated, driverless Palm Jumeirah Monorail (www.palm-monorail.com) connects the Palm Jumeirah with Dubai Marina. There are three stations: Palm Gateway Station near the bottom of the 'trunk', Al Ittihad Park near the Galleria Mall and Atlantis Aquaventure at the Atlantis hotel. Two additional stations, The Pointe and Nakheel Mall, were expected to be up and running by the end of 2019 at the time of research. The 5.5km trip takes about 12 minutes and costs Dhs20 (Dhs30 return trip); cash only. Trains run every 15 minutes from 9am to 10pm. The monorail links to the Dubai Tram at Palm Gateway.

TAXI

Dubai is a taxi-centric city, and you're likely to find yourself in need of a cab at some point. Government-licensed vehicles are cream-coloured and operated by **Dubai Taxi Corporation** (☑ 04 208 0808; www.dubaitaxi.ae). They are metered, air-conditioned, relatively inexpensive and the fastest and most comfortable way to get around, except during rush-hour traffic. Taxis can be hailed in the street, picked up at taxi ranks or booked by phone. You'll also see private taxis with different-coloured roofs (eg Arabia Taxi has a green roof). These are licensed and fine to use.

Dubai's public transport authority RTA has introduced a free Smart Taxi App from which you can book the nearest taxi based on your location. It's available on Google Play and the Apple App Store.

As in other metropolises, taxis are facing stiff competition from mobile ride-hailing apps such as Uber (www.uber.com) and Dubai-based Careem (www.careem.com). Cost-wise, there's very little difference, but Uber and Careem tend to have much nicer cars that often come with free water, phone chargers and more clued-up drivers.

WATER BUSES

Air-conditioned water buses link four stops around the Dubai Marina every 15 to 20 minutes from 10am to 11pm Saturday to Thursday and from noon to midnight on Friday. Fares range from Dhs3 to Dhs5 per stop or Dhs25 for a day pass. Nol Cards are valid.

AROUND DUBAI

Dubai Desert Conservation Reserve
محمية صحراء دبي

On the outskirts of Sharjah, the 225 sq km **Dubai Desert Conservation Reserve** (www. ddcr.org; Ⓟ) accounts for 5% of the Emirate of Dubai's total land. The reserve was established in 1999 and has been involved in projects to reintroduce mountain gazelles, sand gazelles and Arabian oryx. It's possible to stay inside the reserve at Al Maha Desert Resort & Spa (p353), which was designed as a model for superluxe ecotourism.

The reserve is divided into four zones, the third of which is only open to resort guests and the fourth to a small number of desert tour operators, including Arabian Adventures (p333), offering a less costly admission than overnighting at the resort.

Hatta
حتا

Fresh-air fiends escaping the car-exhaust-clogged Dubai streets and sticky humidity of the coast have long made a beeline to this enclave of Dubai emirate on weekends. Scattered with palm trees and cradled by the jagged contours of the Hajar peaks, Hatta is a chilled-out mountain retreat within easy reach of the city. Kayaking on the highly photogenic green-blue waters of the Hatta dam is the main attraction for visitors,

WORTH A TRIP

DUBAI DESERT ESCAPES

Al Maha Desert Resort & Spa (☑04 832 9900; www.al-maha.com; Dubai Desert Conservation Reserve, Dubai–Al Ain Rd (Hwy E66); full board from Dhs6100; P ☎ ☒) It may only be 65km southeast of Dubai, but Al Maha feels like an entirely different universe. Gone are the skyscrapers, traffic and go-go attitude. At this remote desert eco-resort, it's all about getting back to some elemental discoveries about yourself and where you fit into nature's grand design.

Bab Al Shams Desert Resort & Spa (☑04 809 6498; www.babalshams.com; Al Qudra Rd; r from Dhs1400; P ☎ ☒) Resembling a fort and blending into the desertscape, Bab Al Shams is a tonic for escapists seeking to indulge their *Arabian Nights* fantasies. Its labyrinthine layout reflects both Arabian and Moorish influences; the 115 rooms are gorgeous, spacious and evocatively earthy, with pillars, lanterns, paintings of desert landscapes and prettily patterned Bedouin-style pillows.

---

though a recently opened series of interconnected mountain-bike trails in the surrounding hills is fast gaining in popularity.

Big plans are afoot to tap into Hatta's tourism potential with the creation of the Wadi Adventure Hub area, just east of town, which promises zip lines, a climbing wall and various other adrenaline-fuelled pursuits. Whether the development is built to harmonise with the majestic mountain environment or ends up having a jarring theme-park quality remains to be seen.

◎ Sights & Activities

★**Hatta Dam**   DAM
(Hatta Dam Rd; ⊙24hr) FREE Snuggled between craggy mountain peaks which tumble straight down to the shore, this reservoir, built in the 1990s, is the main reason for a Hatta trip. The vast expanse of motionless turquoise water set against such a barren, rocky environment evokes an eerie mirage quality that's only broken by the hoots and laughter of kayakers soaking up the Hajar Mountains scenery as they paddle.

On the road up to the main viewpoint and car park, the dam wall has been painted with a mammoth mural of Sheikh Zayed and Sheikh Rashid, founders of the nation. From the viewpoint, a short dirt track leads down to the shore where Hatta Kayak (☑056 616 2111; www.hattakayak.com; single/double kayak Dhs60/150, pedal boat Dhs120; ⊙6.30am-5.30pm) hires out kayaks. Free lockers, to store your bags while you take to the water, are provided at the kiosk. Swimming is not allowed.

Hatta Heritage Village   MUSEUM
(☑04 852 1374; www.dubaiculture.gov.ae; off Hatta main road; ⊙7.30am-8.30pm Sat-Thu, from

2.30pm Fri) FREE This sprawling village recreates the Hatta of yore. It's housed in the ruler's restored historic fort with a *majlis* (reception room), a traditional courtyard house and various *barasti* (palm-leaf) buildings. Displays on weaponry, local music, palm-tree products, handicrafts, weaving, traditional dress and old village society illustrate the past.

There are nice views from a restored defensive tower dating to 1880 whose doors are about 2.5m above the ground – guards had to use ropes to climb up there.

To get to the village, turn south at the main roundabout in Hatta, continue for about 3km and then turn left at the sign. If you're travelling by bus, it's about a 1.5km walk from the Hatta terminal.

Hatta Mountain Bike Trail   MOUNTAIN BIKING
(☑04 852 1002; http://hattamtb.ae; Wadi Adventure Hub) Explore the jagged hills of the Hatta region from the saddle of a bike using this series of excellent signposted mountain-biking trails. More than 50km of trails, ranging in difficulty from green (easy) to black (severe), have so far been waymarked. Maps can be downloaded from the website beforehand, and are also posted at every trailhead.

The starting point for the trails is in a wadi just east of town, where you'll also find a recently opened bike hire shop (Wadi Adventure Hub; hire per hr Dhs55-80; ⊙8am-5.30pm), toilets, car park and campground. This area is currently being developed as the 'Wadi Adventure Hub', and when we dropped in on our last trip in late 2018, a massive construction project was ongoing. If you're planning to pitch a tent while you enjoy a few days of biking, check the website beforehand as we can't be sure of the fate of the campground with all the new development.

🛏 Sleeping & Eating

The Hatta Fort Hotel used to be the only choice for lodging but two poshed-up mountain-hut developments were on the verge of opening when we were last in town: the Damani Lodge Huts on the hillside overlooking Wadi Adventure Hub and the Sedr Trailers (using a combined trailer-hut design) on the bank of Hatta Dam. Both will cost per Dhs250 per night. Book through www.visithatta.com.

The main road through Hatta town is scattered with simple canteens and cafes. Self-caterers and picnickers can grab supplies at the big **Emirates Co-op** (www. emcoop.ae; Main Roundabout; ⊙8am-11pm), opposite the Hatta Fort Hotel. For anything fancier (and a drink with your meal), head to Hatta Fort Hotel.

★ **Hatta Fort Hotel**   HOTEL **$$$**
(🖉 04 814 5400; www.jaresortshotels.com; Main Hatta Roundabout; d from Dhs1035; 🅿🛜⛱) It's the only hotel option in town, and it's a goodie. The stone-walled, red-tile-roofed chalets are surrounded by manicured lawns sprinkled with palm trees and tumbling bougainvillea. Inside the spacious chalets, lashings of white and natural stone exude a contemporary-countryside vibe while comfy loungers on the balconies offer up craggy Hajar Mountains views aplenty.

ℹ Getting There & Away

Bus E16 shuttles between Dubai's Al Sabkha station and **Hatta bus station** (Hatta main road), about 2.5km south of the main roundabout (Dhs10, 2¾ hours). From Dubai, the E16 leaves every two hours between 6.30am and 10.30pm. Making the return journey from Hatta, buses depart every two hours between 5.30am and 9.30pm.

The 135km drive from Dubai via Hwy E102 is a taster of the UAE's desert and mountain scenery. Once you pass through Maleha, the roadside views are punctuated by roaming camels, rippling sand dunes and goats scampering over rocky hillsides, all set against a backdrop of the mighty mountains. The alternative, more southerly E44 route between Dubai and Hatta cannot be used by non-GCC citizens further east of Al Madam, as stretches of that highway pass through Oman.

NORTHERN EMIRATES
الإمارات الشمالية

Sharjah   الشارقة

While Dubai is all about flashy tall buildings and shop-till-you-drop malls, neighbouring Sharjah takes a more subtle approach, forgoing glitz for culture and history. Some travellers are put off by its conservative reputation (the emirate is 'dry'; no alcohol is available anywhere), but if you can handle a day or two without a beer, Sharjah is home to some of the best museums and art galleries in the country: the restored Sharjah Heritage Area and the mind-bogglingly vast history of the Mleiha Archaeological Site. This emirate is doing more than anywhere else in the UAE to preserve its heritage – explaining why Unesco declared it Cultural Capital of the Arab World in 1998, recognition reaffirmed in 2014, when it became Capital of Islamic Culture.

⊙ Sights

★ **Sharjah Museum of Islamic Civilization**   MUSEUM
(🖉 06 565 5455; www.sharjahmuseums.ae; Corniche Rd; adult/child Dhs10/5; ⊙8am-8pm Thu, from 4pm Fri) Just about everything you'd want to know about Islam is addressed in this museum set in a stunningly converted souq on the waterfront. The ground-floor galleries zero in on different aspects of the Islamic faith, including the ritual and importance of the hajj (the pilgrimage to Mecca), and on Arab scientific accomplishments, especially in mathematics and astronomy, while the upper floor navigates 1400 years of Islamic art and artefacts. Don't miss the zodiac mosaic in the central dome.

The curation is decidedly old-fashioned and could do with a revamp, but there's no denying the beauty of the objects on display. In particular, in **gallery 1** look out for the 11th-century cat-shaped incense burner from Khurasan in eastern Iran and the gorgeous collection of lustreware ceramics. In **gallery 2**, don't miss the demon-headed and cow-headed iron maces.

Audio guides are available for free in six languages.

★ **Sharjah Art Museum**   MUSEUM
(🖉 06 568 8222; www.sharjahmuseums.ae; off Corniche Rd, Heart of Sharjah Art Area; ⊙8am-8pm Sun-Thu, from 4pm Fri) **FREE** Sharjah's heritage

and arts areas are anchored by one of the region's most dynamic art museums, a treat for committed art-lovers and casual visitors alike. Downstairs, two galleries present rotating temporary exhibits of international calibre. Upstairs, the permanent collection offers a comprehensive survey of art created in the Arab world from the late 19th century onward. Its importance, as one of the few spaces in the world where you can view such a vast collection of Arab art, is indisputable.

The permanent collection's most stunning pieces are found in the Barjeel Collection Wing – a long-term loan of some of the most pioneering and significant works by prominent Arab artists from the Barjeel Art Foundation. Some of the highlights include Lebanese artist Rafic Charuf's stark 'Palestinian Woman', influential Iraqi artist Kadhim Hayder's 'Fatigued Ten Horses Converse with Nothing', Egyptian artist Zeinab Abd El Hamid's chaotically colourful 'Quartier Populaire' and three works by post-Surrealist Syrian artist Marwan.

Bait Al Naboodah   HISTORIC SITE

(☑06 568 1738; www.sharjahmuseums.ae; Heart of Sharjah Heritage Area; adult/child Dhs10/5, joint ticket for 5 sights Dhs20/10; ☺8am-8pm Sat-Thu, from 4pm Fri) A fine example of early Emirati architecture, this 1845 house was once home to pearl merchant Obaid Al Naboodah. Note in particular the teak-wood ionic columns – an architectural feature unique to this building – and fine plasterwork decoration framing windows and niches. One salon holds exhibits on Sharjah's pearling and trading history while a couple more feature traditional interiors so you can better imagine daily life here in the mid-19th century.

Sharjah Heritage Museum   MUSEUM

(☑06 568 0006; www.sharjahmuseums.ae; Heart of Sharjah Heritage Area; adult/child Dhs10/5, joint ticket for 5 sights Dhs20/10; ☺8am-8pm Sat-Thu, from 4pm Fri) This museum goes a long way towards demystifying Emirati culture for visitors. Each of the five galleries examines different aspects of local life, from religious values and birth and burial rituals to wedding ceremonies, local fables and folk medicine. Excellent English-language information panels make a visit here an educational experience, and there are plenty of traditional implements on display; check out the mannequin showcasing the *al manyour* (a belt made from 307 dried goat hooves worn during the *noban* dance).

Sharjah Calligraphy Museum   MUSEUM

(www.sharjahmuseums.ae; Heart of Sharjah Heritage Area; adult/child Dhs10/5, joint ticket for 5 sights Dhs20/10; ☺8am-8pm Sat-Thu, from 4pm Fri) Don't think calligraphy is worthy of your time? Think again. The two galleries here showcase this swirling, beautiful art form at its best with works by some of the world's most famous masters including Egypt's Salah Abdul Khaliq and the UK's Sabah Al Arbili. Once you've finished admiring the work, sit on the cushions between the arches in the front gallery and help yourself to the complementary *gahwa* (Arabic coffee) and tea.

Sharjah Fort   HISTORIC BUILDING

(Al Hisn; ☑06 568 5500; www.sharjahmuseums. ae; Al Hisn Sq; adult/child Dhs10/5, joint ticket for 5 sights Dhs20/10; ☺8am-8pm Sat-Thu, from 4pm Fri) A row of cannons welcomes visitors to Sharjah's beautifully renovated 1823 fort *(hisn)*, which reopened as a museum in 2015. Once through its mighty teak gate, the series of rooms contain well-presented exhibits on Sharjah's ruling Qasimi family and the history of the building itself. Downstairs is the round prison tower, the old *medbasa* (a room used for making date molasses) and fascinating information panels on the destruction of the fort in 1969 and its restoration in the 1990s.

Sharjah Art Foundation
New Art Spaces   GALLERY

(www.sharjahart.org; off Corniche Rd, Al Mureijah Sq, Heart of Sharjah Heritage Area; ☺information centre 9am-9pm Thu-Sat, from 4pm Fri) Urban meets traditional in this cluster of white-cube galleries set within restored Emirati homes in the Heritage Area, behind Al Zahra Mosque. Inaugurated during the 2015 Sharjah Biennial, the six small galleries here present a programme of rotating cutting-edge exhibits by artists from across the Arab world and beyond. There's also occasional screenings of art-related movies in an outdoor cinema, and a cafe. The information centre here has a map of the complex.

Al Noor Mosque   MOSQUE

(www.shjculture.com; Corniche Rd, east Khalid Lagoon; ☺tours 10am Mon) FREE Among the most beautiful of Sharjah's 600 mosques, with its architecture based on traditional Ottoman design, Al Noor has a dream setting overlooking the Khalid Lagoon. It is the emirate's only mosque open to non-Muslims, on guided, free one-hour tours operated weekly by the nonprofit Sharjah

Sharjah

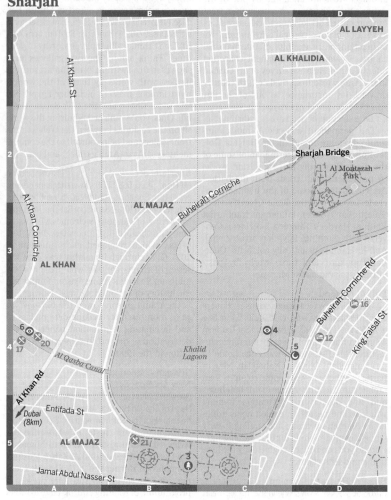

Centre for Cultural Communication. Tours take around 45 minutes and consist of a talk on the mosque's design, Islam and Emirati traditions and conclude with time to take photos and complimentary *gahwa*.

Al Noor Island ISLAND
(www.alnoorisland.ae; off Corniche Rd; adult/child Dhs35/20, butterfly house Dhs15/10; ⊗9am-11pm, butterfly house to 6pm) Paths meander past art sculptures amid landscaped gardens on this island across a bridge behind the Al Noor Mosque. The main draw is the wavy-roofed **butterfly house**, where you can spy 20 species including emerald swallowtails and

red lacewings flitting between plants. If butterflies aren't your thing, visit after sunset when the gardens are lit up like a magical fairyland with a 'glimmering meadow' of flickering neon flowers, pink cacti and glowing silk floss trees.

Al Majaz Waterfront PARK
(☑06 552 1552; www.almajaz.ae; Al Buheirah Corniche Rd) **FREE** This park at the bottom of the Khalid Lagoon fills with strolling families, roller-skaters and power-walkers after sunset. The main attraction are the stunning views of the neon-lit high rises and Al Noor Mosque (p355) across the lagoon

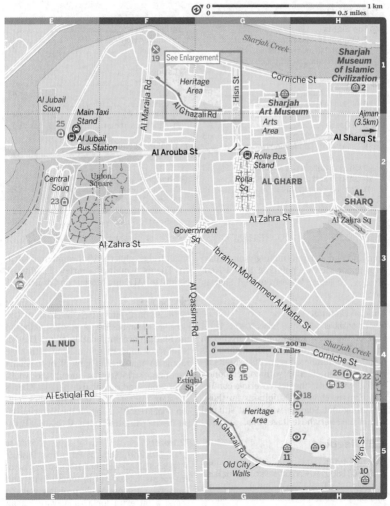

from the waterfront promenade, but kids are also kept busy with the after-dark Sharjah Fountain show, which combines lasers, lights and spurting water columns into five-minute shows. Other diversions include a playground, a camera obscura, boat rides and a mini-golf park.

Al Qasba AREA
(☏ 06 556 0777; www.alqasba.ae; Al Qasba Canal; 🐾) This canal-side pedestrian-zone development presents a mix of cafes and kid-friendly activities, including an outdoor amusement park and an inside soft-play area called Kids Fun House. Unsurpris-

ingly it's super popular with promenading families in the evening. Boat rides also launch out onto the lagoon if you want to see the city skyline from the water. Come in the evening, but avoid Friday and Saturday nights if you don't like crowds.

🎆 Festivals & Events

Sharjah Light Festival ART
(www.sharjahlightfestival.ae; ⊘ Feb) FREE For 10 nights in February, Sharjah's landmark buildings get the full-colour treatment, lit up with animated dazzling displays projected onto their facades. The free shows begin at

Sharjah

6pm and end at 11pm (midnight on Friday) with major viewing points at the Al Noor Mosque, Al Majaz Waterfront and Sharjah Heritage Area.

Sharjah Biennial ART
(www.sharjahbiennial.org; ⊙Mar-May) FREE One of the most important art events in the Arab world, the Sharjah Biennial is held in odd-numbered years. Its exhibits focus on art's interaction with contemporary topics, with past themes covering conflict and climate change. Exhibitions are hosted throughout Sharjah with most situated within the Sharjah Heritage Area.

🛏 Sleeping

★ Ibis Styles HOTEL $
(✆06 503 8800; www.accorhotels.com; King Faisal St; r from Dhs300; ❀) You definitely can't miss this purple building. Rooms may be smallish, but they're bright and modern with stencil drawings of Sharjah's cityscape on the walls, loads of power outlets for all your charging needs and crisp white bathrooms. It's in a great central position too, near the Central Souq. An all-round budget winner.

Sharjah Heritage Hostel HOSTEL $
(✆06 298 8151; www.uaeyha.com; off Corniche Rd, Sharjah Heritage Area; dm per person with shared bathroom Dhs70; ⊙reception 9am-11pm; ❀❀) This basic but super-clean hostel occupies a nicely restored historic courtyard building on the edge of the Heritage Area. Carved wooden doors lead to eight well-kept dorms with five or six single beds, air-con and a

small fridge, plus there's a communal kitchen. There's a midnight curfew. It's directly behind the Al Zahra Mosque on Corniche Rd.

★ The Act HOTEL $$
(✆06 598 0030; https://theacthotel.com; off Corniche Rd; r from Dhs660; ❀❀❀) Shaking up the Sharjah accommodation scene, The Act is all sleek modern minimalism with huge rooms in mauve and grey, floor-to-ceiling windows, strip-lighting along the walls, comfy sofas and ridiculously big TVs. There's a restaurant, cafe, spa and a very slick rooftop pool area. It's a hop off the corniche, opposite the palm-tree-laden Al Nakheel Park.

72 Hotel HOTEL $$
(✆06 507 9797; Corniche Rd; r from Dhs600; ❀❀❀) This 72-unit hotel has snazzy modern rooms decked out in tones of grey and lime-green accents. You'll probably want to spend a bit extra for a room with lagoon view so you can check out Sharjah's twinkling lights before you go to sleep. When you've finished sightseeing, there's an indoor pool, gym, sauna and steam room.

Al Bait Sharjah HOTEL $$$
(✆06 502 5555; www.ghmhotels.com/en/al-bait-sharjah; off Corniche Rd, Sharjah Heritage Area; r from Dhs2995; ❀) Nestled into the traditional architecture of the Heart of Sharjah heritage area, the low-rise luxury suites of Al Bait rest on the foundations of old houses, and are huddled around quiet courtyards for peak privacy. Low, cushioned seating welcomes guests into their romantically lit personal

DISCOVERING ANCIENT HISTORY AT MLEIHA

If you thought the UAE's history only really began when oil was struck, you'd be wrong. **Mleiha Archaeological Site** (☑ general enquiries 050 210 3780, visitor centre 06 802 1111; www.discovermleiha.ae; E55 Hwy, Maleha; archaeological centre museum adult/child/ family Dhs25/15/55; ⊙ 9am-7pm Sat-Wed, to 9pm Thu & Fri) is a fascinating introduction to a mind-boggling heritage. Archaeological excavations at Mleiha (pronounced '*maleha*') have unearthed evidence that early humans passed through here on their way to Asia during the Palaeolithic era; that a Neolithic community lived here in circa 8000 BC; and that this site was settled consecutively during the Bronze, Iron and pre-Islamic eras. An utterly riveting historic day-out.

The flash **visitors centre**, built around a massive tomb from the Bronze Age Umm An Nar culture, hosts a museum with plenty of multimedia displays and information panels that go a long way to explain Mleiha's historic importance, but as the various archaeological excavations from different eras are scattered across the surrounding desert, booking one of the centre's well-priced archaeological-site tours (per person Dhs150) is a great way to gain a deeper depth of understanding. You can also explore on a mountain bike (from Dhs90 per person) or hiking tour (from Dhs60 per person). All these tours will take you to the main sites. Highlights for history buffs are the **Faya Caves**, where archaeologists unearthed the earliest evidence of human occupation outside of Africa; the **wadi caves** and spring where remains of a Neolithic graveyard were uncovered; the circular Bronze Age **Umm An Nar tombs**; and the foundations of a **fort**, **palace** and **houses** from the settlement here in the pre-Islamic era.

Mleiha's position, right on the edge where the beige desert plains give way to yellow and orange dunes, is also prime for adventure activities and the Mleiha visitors centre can organise a full range of dune-driving 4WD excursions (from Dhs90 per person) as well as mountain biking, hiking, horse riding, stargazing and camping activities. If you're peckish after exploring there's a lovely cafe on-site (mains Dhs35 to Dhs80) that does the most delicious, thirst-quenching homemade ginger brew ever.

The visitor's centre is just off Hwy E55 in the scrappy town of Maleha, a one-hour drive down Hwy 102 from central Sharjah. If you don't have your own wheels, the centre can arrange transport from Sharjah (Dhs120 return) and Dubai (Dhs220 return).

reception room before they're inevitably drawn towards the plush teak four-poster bed and immaculate bathroom.

✖ Eating & Drinking

Cafe Arsah CAFE $
(Souq Al Arsah; mains Dhs15-20; ⊙ 8am-10pm) This brilliant little cafe inside Souq Al Arsah, its walls scattered with old photos and bric-a-brac, is as popular with local workers eating lunch as it is with tourists popping in for a tea. On the menu, there are just two biryanis, both served with a flourish of plastic-sheeting cast over your table and side dishes of salad and dates.

Beit Setti MIDDLE EASTERN $$
(☑ 06 525 9182; Al Qasba; mezze Dhs14-38, mains Dhs39-43; ⊙ 8am-midnight; 🛜 🖉) Grab some spicy hummus, *yalanji* (stuffed grape-leaves) and a *rocca* (rocket) salad and you've got a tasty lunch going on. This place is very popular with families who keep the kids

happy munching on a plethora of *manakeesh* (baked flatbread with toppings like cheese and minced meat) options. There's a nice canal-facing outdoor terrace for the cooler months.

Zahr El Laymoun LEBANESE $$
(☑ 06 552 1144; Al Majaz Waterfront; mezze Dhs24-42, mains Dhs38-81; ⊙ 8am-midnight; 🛜 🖉) Head here for a breakfast of shakshuka and *manakeesh* or a mezze feast of a dinner with lesser-seen Lebanese specialities of *hindbeh* (dandelion) salad and *makanek* (spicy Lebanese beef sausage doused in pomegranate molasses) on the menu as well as all the classics.

Sadaf IRANIAN $$
(☑ 06 569 3344; Al Mareija St; mains Dhs45-83; ⊙ noon-midnight; 🛜) The Sharjah branch of this popular mini-chain enjoys cult status among locals for its authentic Iranian cuisine. The spicy, tender kebabs are particularly good, and the *zereshk polo meat* (rice

with red barberries and chicken or meat) is another solid choice.

★ Shababeek
MIDDLE EASTERN **$$$**

(☑ 06 554 0444; www.shababeek.ae; Block B, Qanat Al Qasba; mezze Dhs25-38, mains Dhs62-145; ⊙noon-11.30pm; ☎ ☑) This chic space serves up contemporary Levantine dishes with creative flourishes. The mezze is what you want to focus on here, with beetroot and walnut *moutabel* (purée mixed with tahini, yoghurt and olive oil), green lentil *tabbouleh* (salad of tomatoes, parsley and onions) and vine leaves soaked in *hosrom* (sour grape molasses) all getting the thumbs up from us.

Ratios Coffee
COFFEE

(http://ratios.coffee; Al Shanasiyah Souq, Sharjah Heritage Area; ⊙8am-10pm; ☎) Caffeine nerds rejoice: this hipster coffee house digs deep with single-origin beans sourced from El Salvador, Ethiopia and Indonesia, among others, and offers all the usual barista-focused preparation methods such as V60, Chemex, Aeropress and also makes a mean cortado and flat white. In cooler months, there's a lovely back patio. In summer, go for the cold brew.

🛍 Shopping

Souq Al Jubail
FOOD

(Corniche Rd; ⊙7am-10.30pm Sat-Thu, 7-11.30am & 1-10.30pm Fri) Herb-infused honey, dates, nuts and dried figs make for great foodie gifts and treats, while the long lines of stalls piled high with fruit and vegetables are good for stocking up on all your produce needs. This mammoth market, with separate sections for meat, fish and fruit and veg, is housed in a domed building on the waterfront.

Head out the back entrance for views of the fishing dhows on the docks right outside. Get here after the *asr* (mid-afternoon) prayer to witness the daily fish auction held in the middle of the market building.

Souq Al Arsah
MARKET

(Courtyard Souq; Sharjah Heritage Area; ⊙9am-9pm Sat-Thu, from 4pm Fri) One of the oldest souqs in the UAE, Souq Al Arsah once crawled with traders from Iran and India and local Bedouin, their camels fastened to posts outside. Despite a facelift, it's still atmospheric, though vendors now vie for tourist dirham with pashminas, *dhallahs* (coffee pots), herbs and spices, old *khanjars* (daggers) and traditional jewellery in air-conditioned comfort.

Souq Al Shanisiyah
GIFTS & SOUVENIRS

(off Corniche Rd, Sharjah Heritage Area; ⊙10am-10pm Sat-Thu, from 4pm Fri) This new souq, shaded by *areesh* (palm fronds used to construct huts and houses) panels, is built over the site of an earlier souq discovered during archaeological excavations. As of late 2018, not all the shops had yet been opened, but there were a couple of boutiques selling contemporary handicrafts.

Central Souq
MARKET

(Blue Souq; King Faisal Rd; ⊙9.30am-10pm Sat-Thu, 4-11pm Fri) If you're in the market for glitzy gold jewellery studded with semi-precious stones, then this grand, tile-

MAJOR BUS SERVICES FROM SHARJAH

DESTINATION	FARE (DHS)	TIME	FREQUENCY	SERVICE
Abu Dhabi	30	3hr	every 30min	SRTA bus 117
Ajman	5	30min	every 10-15min	SRTA bus 112
Al Ain	30	2¾hr	hourly	SRTA bus 118
Dubai (DXB) Airport	10	50min	every 20-30min	SRTA bus 313
Dubai (Al Ghubaiba Station)	10	45min	every 30min	RTA bus E306
Dubai (Deira)	10	30min	every 30-45min	RTA bus E307
Dubai (Union Square)	10	50min	every 30min	RTA bus E303
Fujairah (via Musafi)	25	2hr	every 30min	SRTA bus 116 & 116E
Khor Fakkan	25	2½hr	hourly	SRTA bus 116
Ras Al Khaimah	25	1¼hr	every 45min	SRTA bus 115
Umm Al Quwain	15	45min	every 45min	SRTA bus 115

embellished market building, dating from 1978, is the place to be. Although much of what's on offer is seriously gaudy, the shop windows here are great for a browse. The Central Souq occupies two long domed buildings connected by indoor bridges.

🛈 Getting There & Away

AIR
Sharjah International Airport (☑ 06 558 1111; www.sharjahairport.ae; E88 Hwy), 15km east of the city centre, is the hub for budget airline Air Arabia (www.airarabia.com). There are regular flights to places around the Middle East including Amman (Jordan), Bahrain, Beirut (Lebanon), Cairo (Egypt), Istanbul (Turkey), Kuwait and Muscat (Oman), as well as many destinations further afield.

BUS
Sharjah's central **Al Jubail Bus Station** (☑ 06 052 5252; www.srta.gov.ae; Corniche St; 🛜) is opposite Souq Al Jubail. All buses, except for Dubai city-bound services – which are operated by Dubai Roads and Transport Authority (RTA; www.dubai-buses.com) – are run by SRTA (Sharjah Road and Transport Authority)

CAR
From Dubai, take Sheikh Rashid Rd across Garhoud Bridge and continue into Sharjah on Al Ittihad Rd. The drive should take 30 to 60 minutes, depending on traffic and where in Dubai you started from.

TAXI
Trips to other emirates come with a Dhs20 surcharge. Expect to pay about Dhs60 to Dubai International Airport, Dhs90 to Dubai Mall, Dhs200 to Fujairah, Dhs250 to Al Ain and Dhs350 to Abu Dhabi.

If possible, avoid travelling between Dubai and Sharjah during peak rush hour (weekdays 7am to 10am, 1pm to 2pm and 5pm to 9pm), as roads can get frustratingly clogged.

🛈 Getting Around

TO/FROM THE AIRPORT
Buses 99 and 15 link Sharjah airport to Sharjah city centre (Dhs7) with regular services between 5.30am and 11pm. Check www.mowasalat.ae for up-to-date schedules. A taxi ride into central Sharjah costs about Dhs60, including a Dhs20 airport surcharge.

BUS
Local buses nearly all start from **Rolla bus stand** (www.mowasalat.ae; Rolla Square, Al Arouba St) and travel on nine routes between 5.30am and 11.30pm at intervals ranging from

10 to 30 minutes with fewer services on Friday. Single-ride tickets cost Dhs7. Purchasing Sharjah's recently introduced Sayer Card (electronic top-up transport card) reduces single-ride tickets to Dhs5.50. As taxis are so well-priced, most visitors don't bother using the local buses.

TAXI
Taxis (☑ 600 525 252; www.shjtaxi.ae) can be flagged off the street or booked in advance. Flagfall is Dhs3 (Dhs4 from 11pm to 6am and Dhs5 if pre-booked) with a Dhs11.50 minimum fare. Nearly all short rides within the central city end up costing Dhs11.50.

Ajman   عجمان

Ajman is the smallest of the seven emirates. Most visitors are here for a beach-break and rarely move from their resort's slice of sand or the hotel pool. If you do feel like getting off your sun-lounger, the little museum and dhow-building yard provide a glimpse of Ajman's pearling past, while the corniche, where locals come to barbecue and picnic in cooler months, is a popular promenading spot at sunset.

On the north side of Ajman Creek the luxury Al Zorah development is slowly taking shape with marinas, more resorts, a golf club and exclusive residential neighbourhoods facing the shore front and mangroves.

◉ Sights

Ajman Museum   MUSEUM
(☑ 06 742 3824; Central Sq; adult/child Dhs5.25/2; ⊘8am-8pm Sat-Thu) This late-18th-century fort served as the ruler's residence until 1970 and also saw a stint as the police station. Now its rooms hold a higgledy-piggledy mix of exhibits on Ajman's past and Emirati culture. Check out the mock-up of a traditional souq with its highly detailed, mannequin-filled dioramas (our favourite is the barber display complete with a none-too-professional stylist, judging from the blood spurting from his customers' heads).

Ajman Beach   BEACH
(Sheikh Humaid Bin Rashid Al Nuaimi St/Corniche Rd) **FREE** The long strip of wide sandy public beach that trails along the Corniche Rd is decently clean and well maintained (though it can't compare to the manicured-sand expanses of the hotels' private beaches). The prettiest stretch, with soft white sand, is south of the Ramada Beach Hotel (☑ 06 742 9999; www.ramadabeachajman.com; r from

Ajman

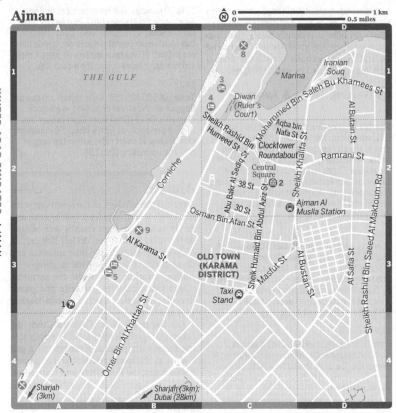

THE GULF

Corniche

Sharjah (3km)

Sharjah (3km); Dubai (28km)

Iranian Souq

Marina

Mohammed Bin Saleh Bu Khamees St

Sheikh Rashid Bin Humeed St

Diwan (Ruler's Court)

Aqba bin Nafa St

Clocktower Roundabout

Al Butain St

Ramrani St

Al Karama St

Abu Bakr Al Sedeeq St

38 St

30 St

Osman Bin Afan St

Central Square

Sheikh Khalifa St

Ajman Al Muslla Station

Sheikh Rashid Bin Saeed Al Maktoum Rd

OLD TOWN (KARAMA DISTRICT)

Sheikh Humaid Bin Abdul Aziz St

Masfut St

Al Bustan St

Al Safia St

Taxi Stand

Omer Bin Al Khattab St

Dhs340; P🛈📶🏊). There's usually a camel or two hanging out for camel rides along the beach as well. Note that you'll need to BYO shade.

Dhow Building Yard `AREA`

Ajman's dhow-building yard is one of the few left in the region, making both traditional wooden dhows and modern fibreglass versions. In the cooler months you can usually see craftsmen at work during the day here. It's on the north side of Ajman Creek.

🛏 Sleeping

⭐ Fairmont Ajman `RESORT $$`

(www.fairmont.com/ajman; Sheikh Humaid Bin Rashid Al Nuaimi St (Corniche Rd); r from Dhs900; P📶🏊) This is easygoing luxury, from the soaring foyer, with a striking net-sculpture (nodding to Ajman's fishing heritage) hung from the dome, to the rooms, all contemporary taupe tones and sea views. The big question each day is whether to loll beside the pool, with its shaded cabanas, or head out onto the wide stretch of white sand.

Ajman Saray `RESORT $$`

(📞 06 714 2222; www.marriott.com; Sheikh Humaid Bin Rashid Al Nuaimi St (Corniche Rd); r from Dhs850; P📶🏊) The manicured strip of white-sand beach framed by palms and the big pool area make the Saray a sand-in-the-toes getaway. Rooms, all with balconies, exude easygoing beach-chic with sea-green furnishings and silver lanterns adding a hint of Middle Eastern styling. You'll probably want to pay the extra for a beach-facing room; Ajman's cityscape is nothing to write home about.

Wyndham Garden `HOTEL $$`

(📞 06 701 4444; http://wyndhamgardenajman.com; Sheikh Humaid Bin Rashid Al Nuaimi St (Corniche Rd); r from Dhs500; P📶🏊) We love the modern vibes of this hotel with wall-length beachy pictures hung above beds, sea-green furnishings adding pops of colour, and slick,

Ajman

◎ Sights
1 Ajman Beach	A3
2 Ajman Museum	C2

🛏 Sleeping
3 Ajman Saray	C1
4 Fairmont Ajman	C1
5 Ramada Beach Hotel Ajman	B3
6 Wyndham Garden	B3

⊗ Eating
7 Al Roof	A4
8 Bukhara	C1
Mejhana	(see 3)
9 Themar Al Bahar	B3

curvy white workspaces. Even better, all rooms have good-sized balconies with sea views. If the inviting rooftop pool isn't good enough for your sunbathing, the white-sand private beach is just a hop across the road.

Eating

Al Roof   CAFE **$**

(Sheikh Humaid Bin Rashid Al Nuaimi St (Corniche Rd), Corniche Avenue Mall; mezze & manakeesh Dhs16-25, mains Dhs20-42) Al Roof is the place to be: always pumping with local families digging into mezze spreads, *manakeesh* or pizza, while couples and groups of women smoke shisha and sip juice. It's on the top floor, so there are sea views from its floor-to-ceiling glass windows and a narrow outdoor terrace.

Bukhara   INDIAN **$$**

(☑ 06 714 5555; Sheikh Humaid Bin Rashid Al Nuaimi St (Corniche Rd), Ajman Hotel; mains Dhs65-170; ⊙12.30-3pm & 6.30-11pm; 🅿🛜🍴) Rustic, homely Bukhara is a treat for Indian cuisine old-hands as well as those newer to India's flavours. The *dal bukhara* (slow-cooked black lentils in a creamy tomato sauce) is the meat-free signature dish while the *peshawri kebab* (succulent lamb, marinated in yo-

ghurt and then chargrilled) gets top marks on the meat menu.

Themar Al Bahar   SEAFOOD **$$**

(☑ 06 747 0550; Sheikh Humaid Bin Rashid Al Nuaimi St (Corniche Rd); fish per kilo Dhs73-178, mains Dhs28-70; ⊙noon-3am; 🍴) Locals love this place serving well-priced fresh seafood amid a very cheerful, and fish-thematic (fish mobiles hanging from the ceiling, plastic fish swimming across the walls) interior. Head to the back room first if you're choosing your own seafood, which is weighed and cooked according to your preference. Downstairs is smoking territory, so be seated upstairs if that bothers you.

Mejhana   MIDDLE EASTERN **$$$**

(☑ 06 714 2222; www.mejhanarestaurant.com; Sheikh Humaid Bin Rashid Al Nuaimi St (Corniche Rd), Ajman Saray; mezze Dhs32-44, mains Dhs63-148; ⊙noon-12.30am; 🅿🛜🍴) This is the place to get your mezze fix. Order up some *warak enab* (stuffed vine leaves), *batata harra* (roast potato cubes with coriander, chilli and garlic) and chicken livers doused in pomegranate molasses for starters before diving into the typical Middle Eastern chargrilled mains or Moroccan tajines (stews cooked in a traditional clay pot).

❶ Getting There & Away

Buses leave from **Ajman Al Muslla Station** (www. at.gov.ae; Sheikh Khalifa St) near Ajman Museum. Most buses are run by Ajman Bus, and its services often don't have displayed numbers, so ask at the ticket counter for the platform you need.

If you're heading to Ajman from Sharjah, take the Sharjah 112 bus. This bus doesn't take passengers on the way back. Instead, take the Ajman Bus service from platform one

❶ Getting Around

Taxis in Ajman are plentiful. Minimum fare is Dhs11, and meters start at Dhs3 (Dhs4 between 10pm and 6am), plus Dhs1 per 650m. There's

---

MAJOR BUSES FROM AJMAN

DESTINATION	FARE (DHS)	TIME	FREQUENCY	SERVICE
Abu Dhabi	35	3hr	6.30am & 8.30pm	Ajman Bus
Dubai (Union Sq Station)	15	1hr	every 20min 6am-11pm	E400
Ras Al Khaimah	20	1hr	every 90min 7am-9.30pm	Ajman Bus
Sharjah	5	30min	every 10min 6am-11pm	Ajman Bus
Umm Al Quwain	10	30min	every 90min 7am-9.30pm	Ajman Bus

a central **taxi stand** (Sheikh Humaid Bin Abdul Aziz St), but you can easily hail off the street.

Umm Al Quwain أم القيوين

The tiny emirate of Umm Al Quwain (pronounced '*oom-al-ku-wayn*'), wrapped around an island-dotted lagoon, is in many ways the 'anti-Dubai'. Its retro feel – without a flashy international resort or mega-mall to call its own – stands in sharp contrast to the glitz going on to the south. Much of the emirate's 12km-long narrow peninsula, accessed by the busy strip-mall-lined King Faisal Rd, feels a bit desolate, though the handful of resorts on the peninsula tip are all well-maintained. The complete lack of razzmatazz is because the emirate has no notable energy deposits to call its own. For an idea of how the entire UAE might have looked if oil hadn't been struck, head here.

Across the creek, uninhabited Al Sinniyah Island is noted for its mangroves and large colony of Socotra cormorants. It's also a stopover for migrating birds, including flamingos, gulls and terns.

◉ Sights & Activities

Umm Al Quwain Museum   MUSEUM
(☑ 06 765 0888; Al Lubna Rd; adult/child Dhs4/free; ⊙ 8am-2pm & 5-8pm Sat-Thu, 5-8pm Fri) Various rooms in this heavily restored 1768 fort have been decked out to demonstrate traditional furnishings and Emirati culture, though the diorama exhibits are sparse at best. Despite next-to-no information panels, the archaeological-finds room is a highlight: discoveries from the Ed Dour and Tell Abraq sites include two statues of headless falcons, a turtle-shaped stone plate and gorgeous, tiny human-shaped bone plaques.

Kite Beach Centre   WATER SPORTS
(☑ 055 507 3060; www.kitebeachcenter.ae; Sheikh Saud Bin Rachid Al Muella; adult/child Dhs25/free; kayak & SUP-board hire Dhs75, 1hr kite-surfing lesson Dhs350; ⊙ 8am-10pm Sat-Wed, to 11pm Thu & Fri) This water-sports centre sits on an inviting slice of soft white sand, strewn with hammocks and shaded seating. It offers kitesurfing and surfing lessons as well as rental of stand-up paddle boards, kayaks and kitesurfing gear. There's a great cafe onsite too.

Dreamland Aqua Park   WATER PARK
(☑ 06 768 1888; www.dreamlanduae.com; Hwy E11; adult/child under 1.2m Dhs160/100; ⊙ 10am-6pm, to 7pm Fri & Sat Mar-May & Sep-Oct, to 8pm Fri & Sat Jun-Aug) Packed with old-school charm, the UAE's first water park is well maintained and has attractions to please thrill-seeking young teens and gentle splash-about pools for tots as well. A pool bar serves cold beers (Dhs50) and snacks. Come Sunday to Thursday if you want to avoid the crowds.

🛏 Sleeping & Eating

Pearl Hotel   RESORT $
(☑ 06 766 6678; www.pearlhotel.ae; Sheikh Ahmed Bin Rachid Al Moalla; chalets from Dhs395; P ⏥ ☀ ⊇) The roomy chalets (both studios and suites) here have had a contemporary revamp in cool modernist style, with massive walk-in showers in the chic, grey-toned bathrooms. All have terraces overlooking the pool and wide strip of beige-sand beach. There are also cheaper 'apartment' rooms, but they've yet to be renovated. Ex-

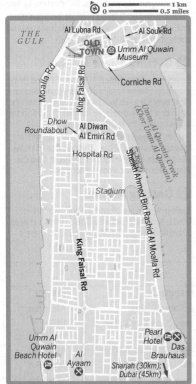

Umm Al Quwain

0 ____ 1 km
0 ____ 0.5 miles

THE GULF

Al Lubna Rd
Al Souk Rd
OLD TOWN
Umm Al Quwain Museum
Moalla Rd
King Faisal Rd
Corniche Rd
Umm Al Quwain Creek (Khor Umm Al Quwain)
Dhow Roundabout
Al Diwan
Al Emiri Rd
Hospital Rd
Sheikh Ahmed Bin Rachid Al Moalla Rd
Stadium
King Faisal Rd
Umm Al Quwain Beach Hotel
Al Ayaam
Pearl Hotel
Das Brauhaus
Sharjah (30km); Dubai (45km)

tra bonus, the friendly Das Brauhaus pub-restaurant is on-site.

Barracuda Beach Resort
RESORT $

(☑ 06 768 1555; www.barracuda.ae; Hwy E11; r from Dhs380; P ⬛ 🛜 🏊) Renowned for its off-license liquor store, this whitewashed Mediterranean-style resort has simple yet spacious tiled-floor studios and suites with balconies and views of the massive pool area. It's all fronted by a narrow strip of yellow-sand beach.

Al Ayaam
LEBANESE $

(☑ 06 766 6969; King Faisal Rd; mains Dhs15-75; ⊙ 8am-1am; 🍴) It won't win any design awards, but this family restaurant has some of the best Lebanese food in town. Start with some baba ganoush (smoked aubergine dip) and a watercress salad before tucking into big portions of mouthwatering grilled fish and meat, including camel and quail, all at very reasonable prices.

Das Brauhaus
PUB FOOD $$

(☑ 06 766 6678; www.brauhausuaq.com; Sheikh Ahmed Bin Rachid Al Moalla, Pearl Hotel; mains Dhs40-75; ⊙ noon-midnight; 🛜) This Bavarian restaurant-pub is just the ticket if you're looking for pub-grub comfort food with a German twist; think currywurst and goulash alongside steaks and schnitzel. There's a good range of beers and spirits and the bar has a relaxed, friendly feel. Happy hour is a very liberal noon to 8pm.

❶ Getting There & Away

Umm Al Quwain doesn't have a bus station. Buses en route to Ras Al Khaimah from Sharjah and Dubai stop to drop off passengers on the E11 highway, south of the peninsula. Buses are met by very enthusiastic taxi drivers who will take you the rest of the way. Buses do not pick up passengers the other direction, so you'll need to take a taxi.

Cab rides to Dubai or Ras Al Khaimah start at Dhs100; for Sharjah, budget Dhs60 and for Ajman Dhs50.

❶ Getting Around

The only way to get around Umm Al Quwain is by taxi, which you can flag down on the street. They don't have meters; most rides cost between Dhs5 and Dhs12.

Ras Al Khaimah   راس الخيمة

Surrounded by the fierce Hajar Mountains, Ras Al Khaimah (or simply 'RAK', pro-

nounced '*rass-al-kai-muh*') is the UAE's northernmost emirate. Both beach-sloths and outdoor enthusiasts love it here, thanks to sandy shores, sprawling oases and sun-baked desert, all on the emirate's doorstep.

While the call of the beach still laps up most visitors, who rarely move from the confines of their resort, RAK has been pulling out the stops in recent years to capitalise on its natural surroundings. Jebel Jais (the UAE's tallest mountain) is front-and-centre of the development, offering the world's longest zip line and a via ferrata route.

After the swish resort beaches and adrenaline-fuelled mountain vistas, RAK City itself can seem bland. To see the city looking its best, head here at sunset to join families and joggers for the evening promenade down Al Qawasim Corniche, fronting the creek and overlooked by the pearly white Sheikh Zayed Mosque.

◉ Sights

★ Jebel Jais
MOUNTAIN

(www.jebeljais.ae) **FREE** The highest peak in the UAE at 1934m, Jebel Jais is even occasionally dusted with snow. A switchback road snakes up the mountainside delivering vistas of barren, eroded cliffs, deep canyons and warped escarpments around every bend. There are pullouts for photograph-stops along the way, but for the ultimate panoramic mountain views, you'll want to head up to Viewing Deck Park (www.jebeljais.ae; adult/child Dhs5/free; ⊙ 8am-8pm Sun-Thu, to 11pm Fri & Sat) near the summit. For a more up-close-and-personal mountain experience, Jebel Jais has a zip line (p366) and via ferrata (p366).

The total drive is about 50km from the roundabout connecting Khuzam and Al Rams Rd in RAK City. Those without their own wheels can access the mountain using the Jebel Jais Shuttle (p370).

Dhayah Fort
FORTRESS

(off the E18 Hwy; ⊙ 24hr) **FREE** It's well worth climbing the zigzagging staircase (you'll need sturdy shoes – this is not flip-flops territory) to this twin-towered hilltop fortress to enjoy the sweeping 360-degree vistas of the RAK area, a vast date-palm oasis and the Hajar Mountains. Built in the early 19th century, the fort was the site of the last battle between British troops and local tribes in 1819. It's about 18km north of RAK City, off Al Rams Rd. Turn off at the sign for Dhayah Resthouse.

National Museum of Ras Al Khaimah
MUSEUM

(🖉07 233 3411; www.rakheritage.rak.ae; Al Hisn Rd; adult/child Dhs5/free; ⊘10am-6pm Wed-Thu & Sat-Sun, from 3pm Fri) This museum occupies a 19th-century fort – the residence of the Qawassim rulers until 1964. Behind the ornate wooden doors of its salons are a hodgepodge of tired ethnological displays, but there are also two small archaeological galleries that make the trip here well worth your while if you're interested in history. The exhibits, ranging from Neolithic up to the Islamic era, display artefacts unearthed from local digs, including at Julfar, an important port between the 14th and 17th centuries.

Mohammed Bin Salim Mosque
MOSQUE

(www.rakheritage.rak.ae; Old Town; ⊘open outside of prayer times) FREE This modest mosque dating to the late 19th century has recently been painstakingly restored using the traditional building method of plaster layered over coral-blocks and beach stones. Inside, a forest of squat columns with built-in niches holds up a palm-and-mangrove wood ceiling. Altogether, the effect is intimate and rather charming; a direct foil to the massive Ottoman-inspired mosques built in the UAE today. Non-Muslims are welcome to enter outside of prayer times. Dress modestly; women should don a headscarf.

Jazira Al Hamra Fishing Village
GHOST TOWN

(Al Hamra; ⊘24hr) With roots in the 16th century, this abandoned town is one of the oldest and best-preserved coastal villages in the UAE. Its people subsisted mostly on fishing and pearling until they picked up and left in 1968. Inside, the crumbled walls of coral-block houses, wind towers, schools and shops offer close-up views of this traditional building method. Beside the entrance gate, the old village mosque, with its squat, curvy minaret, was being finely restored on our last visit.

To get there, turn off Hwy E11 opposite Majan Printing and drive towards Al Hamra Village (also signposted for 'Al Jazirah Al Hamra Historic Site'). Turn right at the roundabout and right again, then take the road immediately on your left and drive for about 1km. If the gate in the metal fence by the mosque is shut, you can access the site by following the road around to the empty lot on the eastern side of the village and enter from there.

🏃 Activities & Tours

Jebel Jais Flight Zip Line
ADVENTURE SPORTS

(www.jebeljais.ae; Jebel Jais; from Dhs325; ⊘9am-5pm (last flight 4pm) Wed-Sun) If lolling on the beach becomes boring, you can always throw yourself off Jebel Jais. Launch from the transparent platform at 1680m and fly down the mountainside, reaching speeds of up to 150km/h, on the world's longest zip line – measuring 2.83km. You'll land on a platform completely suspended midair; from there it's another, shorter, zip-line trip back onto terra firma.

There's no age restriction, but participants must be taller than 122cm. Three slots are available hourly; booking is essential and must be made in advance on the website. The price can double (to Dhs650) at busy times such as weekends in the winter months, so it pays to time your trip for a weekday.

Jebel Jais Via Ferrata
CLIMBING

(www.jebeljais.ae; Bin Majid Rd, opp Tulip Inn Hotel, RAK City; Dhs325; ⊘9am & 1pm time slots Wed-Sun mid-Nov–mid-May) This via ferrata (a climbing route secured by steel cables) is a first for the Middle East. Climbers traverse a 1km course, including two short zip-line sections, around the base of Jebel Jais, reaching 120m at the highest point. Advance bookings are required. All participants are transferred to Jebel Jais by van from the meeting point in RAK City.

Challenging Adventure
OUTDOORS

(🖉07 244 8097; www.challengingadventure.com; Wadi Khdaa; kayaking tour adult/child Dhs295/185; ⊘8am-5pm) A good option if you're looking to get off the beach and experience the more natural side of RAK. This outdoor adventure company mostly organises trips for school groups and corporate events but also offers activities to families and individual travellers. In particular, it can arrange various trekking itineraries and also runs three-hour kayaking tours around Ras Al Khaimah's mangroves. It's based out of this centre on the road to Jebel Jais.

Bedouin Oasis Desert Camp
CULTURAL

(🖉04 266 6020, 055 228 4984; www.arabianincentive.com; Al Mazraa, Wadi Khadija; per person Dhs110; ⊘5-9pm) Dinner in a recreated Bedouin desert camp, lit by candles and lanterns, makes for a fun evening – just don't go thinking you're going to have an authentic experience. Rates include soft drinks, henna, camel rides, belly dancing and shisha. It's

Ras Al Khaimah

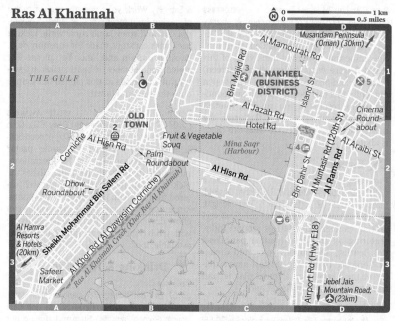

Ras Al Khaimah

also possible to spend the night 'glamping' in a comfortable tent.

🛏 Sleeping

Hilton Garden Inn HOTEL $
(📞 07 228 8888; www.hilton.com; Bin Dahir St; r from Dhs360; 🅿🛜🏊) Comfortable and good value, this is a great choice if you want to be in the central city rather than out along the coast in one of the resorts. Rooms are generously proportioned and have a smart, modern feel. Ask for one at the back overlooking the pool and harbour beyond.

★ Cove Rotana Resort RESORT $$
(📞 07 206 6000; www.rotana.com; Al Hamra Rd (Hwy E11); r from Dhs610; 🅿🛜🏊) Like a mirage of a Mediterranean village, this mega-resort's rooms and villas cascade down to a lagoon and a 600m stretch of white sand. Rooms, with brick-dome ceilings, are on the small side but have balconies for kicking back after a long, hot day. Bag a deluxe or premium room if you want to soak up those all-important water views.

Hilton Al Hamra Beach & Golf Resort RESORT $$
(📞 07 244 6666; www.hilton.com; Vienna St, Jazirat Al Hamra; r from Dhs550; 🅿🛜🏊) This sprawling resort keeps kids busy (and parents happy) with two pools, a 400m-long immaculately kept white-sand beach, tennis courts and water sports all on offer. Rooms are large and classically styled, if a bit sparsely furnished, and all come with terrace or balcony overlooking the sea or lush gardens of palms and bougainvillea. Great breakfast buffet and Friday brunch.

Ritz-Carlton Al Wadi Desert RESORT $$$

(07 206 7777; www.ritzcarlton.com; Al Mazraa, Wadi Khadija; villas from Dhs3000; P🐾🛜🛠) Desert life doesn't get more opulent than this. The arabesque-style mud-brick villas of this resort feature *mashrabiyya* (lattice-screen) detailing and private plunge-pools that open out onto the raw beauty of the surrounding nature reserve. If you can drag yourself away from your new desert flash-pad, the nature activities on offer are what this place is about.

Eating

Pure Veg Restaurant INDIAN $

(07 227 3266; Al Muntasir Rd; dishes Dhs8-14, thalis Dhs10-15; 7.30am-3pm & 5pm-midnight; 🛠) The extensive menu at this convivial vegetarian canteen hopscotches around India, featuring all the dosa (stuffed pancakes), dal (lentils), and curries you could dream of. Confused by the choice? Just have a thali (set meal served on a round platter) and sample lots of little dishes at once.

★**Madfoon Al Sada** EMIRATI $$

(Sheikh Mohammed Bin Salem Rd; mains Dhs20-65; 11am-midnight) Don't be put off by the humble looks of this hospitable haunt: its *mandi* (slow-roasted chicken or lamb served with rice and chilli sauce) is among the best in the country. Once you're through the front door, it's Arab-kitsch all the way so slide into your booth with its mocked-up Bedouin tent ceiling and start feasting. Locals love it here.

Trader Vic's Mai Tai Lounge INTERNATIONAL $$

(07 244 6666; www.hilton.com; Vienna St, Jazirat Al Hamra, Hilton Al Hamra Beach & Golf Resort; mains Dhs26-142; 5pm-1am, plus noon-3pm Fri & Sat; 🛜) Work your way through a menu of Asian-influenced mains like 'volcano prawns' and spicy lamb curry while kicking back with cocktails made for sunshiny days. Passionfruit, gin and lime? Yes, please. For added holiday vibes, a band strikes up sultry Cuban sounds at this chilled-out lounge once the sun goes down.

Basilico MEDITERRANEAN $$$

(07 206 6351; Al Hamra Rd (Hwy E11), Cove Rotana Resort; mains Dhs83-137; noon-3pm & 7-11pm; 🛜🛠) Pining for some pasta? This is RAK's top spot for Mediterranean-influenced dining with the Italian dishes the pick of the menu. Vegetarians are well catered for here with good choices like pumpkin and ricotta ravioli, while meat-eaters can chow down on seafood risotto or fettuccine with lamb ragu. There are gluten-free pastas available, too.

Drinking & Nightlife

Belgian Cafe PUB

(07 243 8489; http://belgianbeercafealhamra. com; Vienna St, Al Hamra, Al Hamra Golf Club House; noon-2am; 🛜) Sit amid the proper traditional bar set-up inside or head out onto the terrace for beers with views of players tee-ing off on the Al Hamra golf course. This is one of Ras Al Khaimah's most relaxed and friendly drinking spots with good draught beer choices including Leffe and Hoegaarden plus plenty more bottled brews. There's good pub-grub here too.

Coffee Club CAFE

(07 233 8986; Al Rams St, Manar Mall; 8am-11pm Sat-Wed, to midnight Thu & Fri; 🛜) Sure, you could head to one of the international coffee

---

ⓘ CROSSING INTO THE MUSANDAM PENINSULA

RAK is the jumping-off point for the magnificent Musandam Peninsula, an Omani enclave, via the Al Darah/Tibat border post about 35km north of RAK City. Beyond the border await a dramatic coastal drive and the town of Khasab, where you can catch dhow cruises and go snorkelling.

Officially, travellers must apply for an Omani visa (p417) in advance using the Royal Oman Police website (www.evisa.rop.gov.om), though some travellers report that visas are still available at the border for nationalities who qualify for a 30- or 90-day tourist visa to the UAE. A 10-day Omani visa is Dhs50 (OR5). The UAE exit fee is Dhs35.

Returning to the UAE, nationalities who receive 30-day tourist visas on arrival will simply get stamped in with a new 30-day visa. Those on the 90-day visa (which is multiple-entry) should make sure they still have days left on their visa for their return.

If you have a hire car, double-check with the firm beforehand that you are permitted to take it across the border and that you have insurance valid in Oman. Omani car insurance can usually be purchased at this border.

DON'T MISS

ROAD TRIPPING THROUGH THE UAE

Driving in the UAE means a fair amount on multi-lane highways rimmed by monotonous grey plains – but some routes offer a lot better scenery. All the routes below are along main arteries that can be driven in a normal 2WD.

Abu Dhabi to Hameem (mostly Hwy E65) When heading to Liwa Oasis, take the road to Hameem instead of the main route via Madinat Zayed; the turnoff is about 20km out of Abu Dhabi on the Mussafah–Tarif road. Once in the oasis, rolling dunes backdrop the date palms.

Liwa Oasis to Moreeb Dune (Tal Moreeb) From the old Liwa Resthouse to Moreeb Dune, both sides of the road are edged by the Empty Quarter's enormous rippling waves of dunes.

Sharjah to Hatta (Hwy E102) Count the camels, if you can! After you pass Maleha, the flat, beige plains fade away, replaced by orange dunes speckled with camels and then the craggy rust-coloured peaks of the Hajar Mountains.

Dubai to Al Ain (Hwy E66) Be amazed by the big tangerine dunes on the approach to Al Ain around Shabat. To truly appreciate them you'll have to pull over to get a look through the roadside greenery.

Sharjah to Dibba (Hwy E88 then Hwy E89) If heading to the East Coast, turn off Hwy E88 at Masafi and continue north on the E89 to drive through the jagged Hajar Mountains.

---

chains in RAK (they're all represented here), but why do that when the coffee is better at this local cafe that's often packed with Emirati women and families? The full gamut of flat whites, espresso and cappuccino are served up, and there's a good breakfast and bistro menu too.

Breakers on the Beach BAR
(☑ 07 206 6000; www.rotana.com; Al Hamra Rd (Hwy E11), Cove Rotana Hotel; ⊙ 10am-10pm Sat-Wed, to midnight Thu & Fri; 🐾) Chill with a coffee, cocktail or mocktail at this quintessential beach bar, where you can wriggle your toes in the sand and count the number of crashing waves as you sip. On Friday nights during the cooler months there are regular beach parties.

ℹ Getting There & Away

AIR
The grandly named but tiny **Ras Al Khaimah International Airport** (☑ 07 207 5200; www.rakairport.com; Hwy 118 (Airport Rd)) is about 18km south of RAK City via Hwy E18 (Airport Rd). It has a handful of flights with Air Arabia to destinations such as Cairo, Jeddah and Lahore, and charter flights from Russia and Germany.

BUS
Ras Al Khaimah bus station (E11 Hwy) is on the main highway opposite Cove Rotana Resort. Departing buses are operated by Al Hamrah bus company. There are hourly buses to

Dubai (Dhs25, two hours) via Umm Al Quwain (Dhs10, 30 minutes), Ajman (Dhs15, one hour) and Sharjah (Dhs25, 1½ hrs) between 8am and 9pm. There's also a direct Dubai bus at 6.30am.

Plenty of taxis wait at the bus station to whisk you into central RAK.

A shuttle bus between Dubai International Airport and Ras Al Khaimah launched in 2018 with drop-offs at all of RAK's major hotels. Tickets are Dhs30 one-way and are booked through the website www.rakshuttle.com.

CAR
RAK is linked to the other emirates via coastal Hwy E11, called Sheikh Mohammad Bin Salem Rd within city limits, and the much faster Hwy E311. E18 (Al Rams Rd) heads south to the airport before connecting to Hwy E87, which runs to Dibba on the east coast.

TAXI
The main taxi stand is on Hwy E11 opposite Cove Rotana Resort with other major taxi stands at the Al Hamra Mall and Manar Mall. For taxi travel to other emirates, approximate fares are Dhs200 to Dubai, Dhs150 to Sharjah and Dhs130 to Ajman or Dibba on the eastern coast.

ℹ Getting Around

RAK has no public transport system. Taxis are plentiful and can be flagged down on the street or booked by phone by calling 800 1700. Flagfall is Dhs3, plus Dhs1 for every 650m, with a Dhs5 minimum.

If you want to visit Jebel Jais and don't have a car, the Jebel Jais shuttle bus (www.jebeljais.ae) runs a regular daily schedule to and from the mountain for Dhs20 one way. It picks up from the major hotels (including the Hilton Garden Inn, Hilton Al Hamra, Marjan Island Resort and Cove Rotana Resort) and trundles up to Jebel Jais' viewing deck and Jebel Jais Flight platform three times daily and then runs a return route with drop-offs back at the hotels. Travel time depends on the pickup hotel but is approximately 90 minutes. Bookings can be made on the website in advance, or you can buy a ticket on the bus.

ABU DHABI أبو ظبي

📞 02 / POP 1.3 MILLION

Proudly modern and cosmopolitan, Abu Dhabi seems to have constant ants in its pants with its rate of flashy developments, but sit down for shisha at a Corniche park to watch the evening joggers puff past, or stroll downtown after dark as the skyscrapers peacock-battle for best rainbow neon, and you'll discover this thriving, multicultural city is more than flash-the-cash malls and roller-coaster screams. If you want glitz, sure Abu Dhabi can shovel it on, but this city is also the UAE's forward-thinking cultural heart. Paddle around the mangroves, gaze at the globe-trotting collection inside the Louvre and tour the no-expense-spared opulence of the Sheikh Zayed Grand Mosque – a triumph of Islamic architecture for the modern world – and you'll find there's more to this young capital than cocktails and Formula One.

◉ Sights

Sights are very spread out, so you'll need transport between them. Luckily, taxis are decently priced, which saves the annoyance of trying to find parking, and Abu Dhabi has a good, regular and cheap bus service that covers many destinations. If you only have one day, you want to hit the Sheikh Zayed Mosque and the Louvre Abu Dhabi. Otherwise, try to do sights by neighbourhood to save travelling time. There's a scatter of smaller sights, and some great city photo opportunities, around the Marina Breakwater area that can be easily walked if it's not too hot. Yas Island, with its beach and theme parks, is all about fun.

◉ Marina Breakwater

Abu Dhabi

Heritage Village MUSEUM

(Map p378; www.torath.ae; Breakwater Rd; ⊙9am-4pm Sat-Thu, 3.30-9pm Fri) FREE Although looking a bit worn and tired, this reconstructed village is one of the few places to get an insight into the pre-oil era of the United Arab Emirates. The walled complex includes all the main elements of traditional Gulf life: a fort to repel invaders from the sea, a souq to trade goats for dates with friendly neighbours and a mosque as a reminder of the central part that Islam plays in daily life.

★ **Founder's Memorial** MEMORIAL

(Map p378; 📞02 222 2235; www.thefoundersmemorial.ae; cnr Corniche & Breakwater Rds; ⊙9am-10pm) FREE After six years of planning and construction, this memorial celebrating the life and achievements of Sheikh Zayed, the founder of the United Arab Emirates, was inaugurated in April 2018. Set inside the landscaped garden is The Constellation, a giant avant-garde 3D art piece reflecting the portrait of the sheikh. By daylight, peruse the garden filled with native and medicinal plants, but to appreciate the full spectacle, return after dark when The Constellation comes alive with lights.

★ **Observation Deck at 300** VIEWPOINT

(Map p378; 📞02 811 5666; www.jumeirah.com; Corniche Rd (West), Tower 2, Jumeirah at Etihad Towers; entry Dhs95, high tea with/without champagne Dhs300/210; ⊙10am-7pm) Ride the lift to the 74th floor (your ears may pop along the way) for panoramic views looking down on the skyscrapers and coastline below. The '300' refers to metres above sea level. The coffee shop here serves the highest high tea in the city. Admission includes Dhs50 towards food and drink.

★ **Emirates Palace** NOTABLE BUILDING

(Map p378; 📞02 690 9000; www.emiratespalace.com; Corniche Rd (West)) FREE What the Burj Khalifa in Dubai is to the vertical, the Emirates Palace is to the horizontal, with audacious domed gatehouses and flying ramps to the foyer, 114 domes and a 1.3km private beach. Built for Dhs11 billion, this is the *big* hotel in the Gulf, with 1002 crystal chandeliers and 392 luxury rooms and suites. You don't have to check-in to check out the Emirates Palace, as it doubles as a cultural hub of the city.

⊙ Downtown

★ Corniche
WATERFRONT

(Map p378) The waterfront Corniche, with its white sandy beaches and generous promenade, stretches the entire length of the northwest shore of the city. Giving spectacular views of the iconic high-rise tower blocks assembled along the seafront, it also offers one of the city's main recreation opportunities with dedicated cycle paths along the promenade and weaving in and out of the Corniche's landscaped gardens. Refreshments are available from the public beaches that punctuate the western section of the road.

Qasr Al Hosn
FORT

(White Fort; Map p378; ☑ 02 697 6472; www.alhosn. ae; Sheikh Zayed the First St; ⊙ 9am-8pm) **FREE** Featured on the back of the Dhs1000 note, this fort started life in 1760 as a watchtower that safeguarded a precious freshwater well. After an expansion, it became the ancestral home of the ruling Al Nahyan family in 1793 and remained a royal residence until 1966 (its watchtower was Abu Dhabi's oldest surviving structure). An extensive years-long restoration ground to the finish line in late 2018, and it was reopened as a cultural hub with historic exhibits and gallery space.

⊙ Al Zahiyah & Al Maryah Island

Abu Dhabi Global Market Square
ARCHITECTURE

(Sowwah Sq; Map p378; www.almaryahisland.ae; Al Falah St, Al Maryah Island) If you're into modern architecture, this development's cluster of glass-and-steel office monoliths on Al Maryah Island is the heart of Abu Dhabi's new financial centre. At the back of the plaza, sitting snug against the waterfront, is the Galleria Mall (☑ 02 616 6999; www.thegalleria.ae; Al Falah St, Al Maryah Island; ⊙ 10am-10pm Sat-Wed, to midnight Thu, noon-midnight Fri; 🛜). Under its striking glass atrium is a bundle of restaurants, many fronting the waterfront promenade. The mall is bookended on its southern side by the aerofoil-shaped Rosewood hotel with mushroom-shaped exterior shading.

⊙ Al Mina & Saadiyat Island

Dhow Harbour
HARBOUR

(Map p378; Al Mina) There's something fascinating about sitting by the harbourside watching the dhows slip off to sea. At any time of day, there's work going on as fishers mend their nets, pile up lobster pots, hang out colourful sarongs to dry, unload fish and congregate for communal chats. As you survey the resting dhows strung together five abreast, you can almost forget Abu Dhabi's modern backdrop as its ancient past as a fishing village is revealed.

Al Mina Fish Market
MARKET

(Map p378; Dhow Harbour, Al Mina; ⊙ 7am-10pm) This large fish market bustles with traders selling row upon colourful row of the sea's bounty from the ice bars. It's busiest early in the day when wholesalers head here to buy up prawns, red snapper, blue-shelled crabs and pink Sultan Ibrahims.

★ Louvre Abu Dhabi
MUSEUM

(Map p372; www.louvreabudhabi.ae; Saadiyat Island; adult/aged 13-22yr/under 13yr Dhs63/31/ free; ⊙ 10am-8pm Sat & Sun, Tue & Wed, to 10am Thu & Fri) Designed by Pritzker Prize–winning architect Jean Nouvel, the highly anticipated Louvre Abu Dhabi finally arrived in late 2017. Through 12 galleries, the world-class collection traces humanity's artistic achievements from the Neolithic up to the present day, all the while breaking all norms of traditional museum curation. Here, artworks are grouped by theme and time-frame rather than country or specific civilisation. The result is a globe-trotting journey through human heritage that highlights the universal threads of all cultures.

From the First Villages (gallery 1) through Civilisations and Empires (gallery 3) and The Magnificence of the Court (gallery 8) all the way up to A Global Stage (gallery 12), where Ai Weiwei's 2016 'Fountain of Light' takes centre stage, the exhibits transcend geography and nationality. This means you encounter unexpectedly beautiful juxtapositions such as a bronze winged dragon from northern China sitting in front of a glazed-brick Persian archer from the Achaemenid Empire, and the bronze head of an Edo Culture king from Nigeria displayed amid a room lined with French and Italian 17th-century oil paintings of royalty.

Highlights include an eerily beautiful 7th-millennium-BC Ain Ghazal statue from Jordan; a 3rd-millennium-BC standing Bactrian princess; a black stone statue of Gudea, prince of Lagash from Iraq's neo-Summerian era; a c 2nd-century Buddhist stupa plaque from India; a 2nd-century bronze lion from

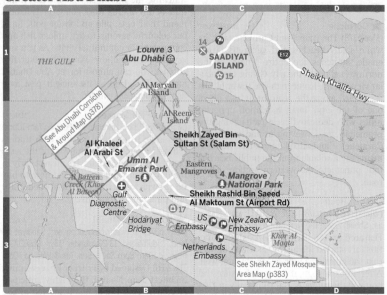

Spain; a 15th-century ceramic bust of St Peter of Verona; and paintings by Picasso, Rothko and Miró.

As well as the permanent collection, separate buildings house temporary exhibitions (four held annually), a children's museum and the excellent museum cafe (Map p372; ☑056 689 0019; www.louvreabudhabi.ae; Louvre Abu Dhabi, Saadiyat Island; mains Dhs71-139; ⊗10am-8pm Sat, Sun, Tue & Wed, to 10pm Thu & Fri; 🛜). These buildings are all grouped around a central plaza which juts straight out into the sea and is shaded by the museum's elaborate 7500-ton filigree dome, which seems to hover mid-air above. The dome pays homage to date-palm-leaf shading with its geometric star design dappling the plaza floor below in a 'rain of light' effect.

You'll need around two hours to explore the museum if you're just browsing, longer if you've got an interest in art or history. For a highlight snapshot of the collection, 90-minute tours (adult/child Dhs50/30) are offered at 11am and 2pm daily in English and at 5pm on Friday in Arabic and French.

⊙ Al Bateen & Al Mushrif

Zayed Heritage Centre   MUSEUM
(Map p378; ☑02 665 9555; www.torath.ae; Bainunah St, Al Bateen; ⊗8am-2.15pm Sun-Thu) FREE If you're into retro-tastic old muse-

ums, don't miss this eclectic, oddball collection of artefacts and personal memorabilia documenting the life of Sheikh Zayed, the founding father of the Emirates. Inside the main hall you'll find Zayed's favourite blue Mercedes, a beat-up Land Rover, his personal falcon clock, rifle and used cologne bottle and plenty of weird and wonderful gifts given to the Sheikh by visiting dignitaries including a stuffed leopard, an anaconda skin and a Guinness World Record–setting stamp mosaic.

★ **Umm Al Emarat Park**   PARK
(Mushrif Central Park; Map p372; www.ummalem aratpark.ae; 15th St; adult/child under 3yr Dhs5/ free; ⊗8am-midnight; 🚼) You almost walk away from this five-star urban park feeling like you've visited a museum. Manicured to perfection and full of design-forward and thoroughly interesting distractions, it more than justifies its admission fee. Highlights of the wonderful smoke-free space include a poignant memorial to the words of Sheikh Zayed; a three-floored shade-house with stupendous views; an animal barn with camels, goats, donkeys, llamas and the like for the kids to pet; a botanical garden; and an outdoor performing-arts venue.

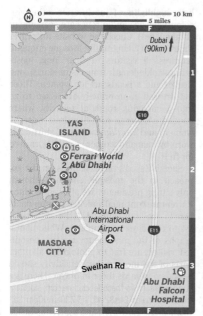

Greater Abu Dhabi

★ **Mangrove National Park** NATIONAL PARK
(Map p372; www.ead.ae; main access off Eastern Mangroves Promenade) FREE Abu Dhabi's Mangrove National Park covers 19 sq km of protected coastal mangrove forests. A critical link in the coastal ecosystem, mangroves protect against tidal surges and promote biodiversity by providing a home to fish, small coastal critters and birds. More than 60 bird species can be spotted here, including the greater flamingo and western reef heron. Both are easiest seen in the breeding season from April to July.

To experience the mangroves close up, you can head out by kayak, stand-up paddleboard or boat using one of the operators stationed at the marina on the Eastern Mangrove Promenade. Noukhada's (p376) kayak tours are particularly recommended.

◉ Sheikh Zayed Grand Mosque Area

★ **Sheikh Zayed Grand Mosque** MOSQUE
(Map p383; ☏ 02 419 1919; www.szgmc.ae; off Sheikh Rashid Bin Saeed St; ◷ 9am-10pm Sat-Thu, 4.30-10pm Fri, tours 10am, 11am & 5pm Sun-Thu, 5pm & 7pm Fri, 10am, 11am, 2pm, 5pm & 7pm Sat) FREE Rising majestically from manicured gardens and visible from the bridges joining Abu Dhabi Island to the mainland, the Sheikh Zayed Grand Mosque is an impressive welcome to the city. With more than 80 marble domes on a roof-line held aloft by 1000 pillars and punctuated by four 107m-high minarets, it's a masterpiece of modern Islamic architecture and design.

Conceived by Sheikh Zayed, and marking his final resting-place, the mosque is one of the few in the region open to non-Muslims.

More than 90,000 tonnes of pure white marble from the Republic of Macedonia were used in its construction. Delicate floral designs inlaid with semi-precious stones, such as lapis lazuli, red agate, amethyst, abalone, jasper and mother-of-pearl, decorate a variety of marbles and contrast with the more traditional geometric ceramic details.

While it includes references to Mamluk, Ottoman, Fatimid, Moorish and Indo-Islamic styles, the overwhelming impression is contemporary and innovative. In the interior, three steel, gold, brass and crystal chandeliers fill the main prayer hall with shafts of primary-coloured light. The chandeliers, the largest of which weighs approximately 11 tonnes, sparkle with Swarovski crystals and shine with 40kg of 24-karat galvanised gold.

One of the prayer hall's most impressive features is the world's largest loomed carpet fashioned from Iranian cotton and New Zealand wool and flown in from Mashad, Iran, on two aeroplanes. The medallion design with elaborate arabesque motifs took 1200 craftspeople two years to complete, half of which was spent on hand-knotting the 5700 sq metres of woollen thread on a cotton base. That translates as 2.268 billion knots!

Visitors are welcome to enter the mosque except during prayer times. A worthwhile free 45-minute guided tour (in English and Arabic) helps explain some fundamentals of Islam while pointing out some of the stylistic highlights of the interior (otherwise comprehensive audio tours are available in 11 languages). Check the website for prayer times, which change daily. Mosque etiquette requires all visitors to wear long, loose-fitting, ankle-length trousers or skirts, long sleeves and a headscarf for women. Those not dressed appropriately are asked to go into a changing room at security, where hooded *abayas* (a robe-like dress worn by women) and *kandouras* (casual shirt-dress worn by men and women) can be borrowed for free.

Sheikh Zayed's mausoleum is on the approach to the mosque entrance, though only sitting presidents are allowed to enter. Prayers are continually recited by attendants here in one-hour shifts 24/7 (the cycles takes 1½ to two days to complete). While photographs of the mausoleum are not permitted, visitors are free to photograph all other parts of the mosque, but sensitivity should be shown towards those in prayer. There is a good cafe (www.thecoffeeclubme.com; northern entrance; mains Dhs32-43; ⊙7.30am-10pm Sat-Thu, from 12.30pm Fri; 🐾) and a gift shop inside the complex on the mosque's northern side.

Wahat Al Karama
MEMORIAL

(Map p383; www.wahatalkarama.ae; 3rd St, Khor Al Maqta; ⊙9am-10pm, tours 11am & 5pm) **FREE** This memorial, opposite the eastern side of the Grand Mosque, was inaugurated in 2016 in memory of Emiratis who have given their lives in service to the nation. The main monument, a leaning stack of 31 mammoth aluminium-clad tablets inscribed with poems and quotations from prominent UAE figureheads, sits in front of a Memorial Plaza fashioned from Turkish travertine stone centred around a shallow, circular pool which reflects both the panels and the Grand Mosque just across the busy highway.

Khor Al Maqta
WATERFRONT

(Map p383; Bain Al Jessrain) This historic waterway separates Abu Dhabi from the mainland, guarded by the now somewhat hidden Al Maqta Fort (Al Maqta Bridge; ⊙24hr (interior closed)) **FREE** and a small watchtower, on a rocky promontory in the middle of the *khor* (creek). The mainland bank is home to a cluster of luxury resort-hotels and the Souk Qaryat Al Beri (p388) mall, all with restaurants and bars that have outdoor terraces with views of the snowy-white Sheikh Zayed Grand Mosque (p373) across the water.

LOCAL KNOWLEDGE

SIGHTSEEING TRANSPORT

To hop between the Grand Mosque and Wahat Al Karama, there are free shuttle buses (Map p383) every 30 minutes between 10am and 6pm daily. They leave from the mosque's north parking lot (car park D).

Traditional wooden abras (Map p383; 📱050 133 2060; www.captaintonys.ae; adult/child Dhs25/free; ⊙4-10pm Sun-Thu, 10am-11pm Fri & Sat) ferry passengers around the Khor Al Maqta, stopping at Shangri-La Hotel, Ritz-Carlton Hotel, Fairmont Hotel and Souk Qaryat Al Beri, on a hop-on, hop-off basis. Pay on the boat. Kids under six go free.

> **DON'T MISS**
>
> ## TOP THREE PUBLIC BEACHES
>
> **Saadiyat Public Beach** (Map p372; www.bakeuae.com; Saadiyat Island; adult/child Dhs25/15; ☺8am-8pm) By far Abu Dhabi's nicest public beach. A boardwalk leads through a protected zone of coastal vegetation, home to nesting turtles, to this prime slice of powdery white beach on the northwest coast of Saadiyat Island (neighbouring the Park Hyatt resort). There's a lifeguard until sunset and a cafe, though you're able to bring in your own picnic supplies (no alcohol allowed). Towel rental is Dhs10 and sunloungers with umbrella are Dhs25 weekdays and Dhs50 Friday and Saturday.
>
> **Yas Beach** (Map p372; ☎056 242 0435; www.yasbeach.ae; adult/child Sun-Thu Dhs60/ free, Fri & Sat Dhs120/free; ☺10am-sunset) A surprisingly low-key corner of this high-tech island, Yas Beach is a lovely place to relax and enjoy the sea views, dabble in some water sports or generally chill with a cool beer. The kitchen rustles up grilled local fish and other tasty light bites. A DJ plays soothing sounds during Friday pool parties.
>
> **Corniche Beach** (Map p378; Corniche Rd (West); family beaches adult/child Dhs10/5; ☺8am-8pm) There are several gates to this spotlessly maintained, Blue-Flagged public beach. The turquoise sea, view of Lulu Island, palm trees and gardens make it an unexpected pleasure in the heart of a capital city. A lifeguard is on duty until sunset.

◉ Yas Island & Around

Yas Marina Circuit   SPORTS GROUND
(Map p372; ☎02 659 9800; www.yasmarinacir cuit.ae; off Yas Leisure Dr; 2hr venue tours Dhs130; ☺tours 10am & 2pm Tue-Sat) Even if you're not in town in November for the Formula One Grand Prix, it's possible to experience Abu Dhabi's Yas Marina track year-round. For a behind the scenes look at the circuit, tours (book beforehand) take you into the grandstand, the race-control centre and the media centre.

★Ferrari World Abu Dhabi AMUSEMENT PARK
(Map p372; ☎02 496 8000; www.ferrariworld abudhabi.com; Yas Leisure Dr; adult/child under 1.3m from Dhs295/230, with Yas Waterworld from Dhs295/230; ☺11am-8pm) If you want bragging rights to having 'done' **Formula Rossa**, the world's fastest roller coaster, visit this indoor (perfect in summer) temple of torque and celebration of all things Ferrari in a spectacular building. Accelerating from 0km/h to 240km/h in 4.9 seconds, this is as close to an F1 experience as most of us are likely to get.

**Warner Bros World
Abu Dhabi**   AMUSEMENT PARK
(Map p372; www.wbworldabudhabi.com; Yas Leisure Drive; adult/child under 1.1m Dhs295/230; ☺11am-8pm) The world's first Warner Bros–branded theme park is a hit with kids and adults alike (DC Comics fans, we're talking to you). Spread among six 'Lands' – Warner Bros Pla-za, Metropolis, Gotham City, Cartoon Junction, Bedrock and Dynamite Gulch – are 29 rides, entertaining shows and interactive attractions, all indoors and air-conditioned.

Masdar City   AREA
(Map p372; ☎800 627 327; www.masdar.ae; btwn Hwys E10 & E20; ☺9am-5pm Sun-Thu) FREE For architecture with a sci-fi vibe make the trip to Masdar City, near Abu Dhabi Airport, touted as the world's first zero-carbon, zero-waste city powered entirely by renewable energy when plans for it were first unveiled. Although those goals haven't worked out, the city core (the only portion yet finished), where the teflon-coated wind tower, domed knowledge hall and sharp-edged incubator building rub up against wavy terracotta-coloured walls of residential blocks, is a futuristic vision of city-planning.

🏃 Activities

Kayaks and SUP-boards can be hired at many of the beaches and the Eastern Mangroves Promenade is the main point for kayaking trips amid the mangroves and boating trips around them. For harbour cruises, Marina Breakwater is where dhow cruises depart. PADI-certified diving operators (usually based in the resorts) can arrange dive trips from beginner to advanced in the surrounding area.

DriveYas   ADVENTURE SPORTS
(Map p372; ☎02 659 9800; www.yasmarina circuit.com; Yas Marina Circuit; driver/passenger

ABU DHABI FALCON HOSPITAL

Standing outside **Abu Dhabi Falcon Hospital** (Map p372; ☑02 575 5155; www.falcon hospital.com; Sweihan Rd; 2hr tour adult/child Dhs170/60; ☺tours 2pm Sat, 10am & 2pm Sun-Thu), watching anxious owners from across the region delivering their hooded 'patients' in person, you will quickly realise that this is a much-needed and much-loved facility. Falcons are an integral part of traditional Gulf culture, and no expense is spared in restoring these magnificent birds to full health. Tours include visits to the falcon museum, the examination room – including intimate glimpses into coping procedures – and the free-flight aviary. Tour reservations (bookable online) are mandatory. If you're willing to brave an arm, the well-behaved raptors will even perch for a photograph.

The hospital is about 6km southeast of Abu Dhabi airport. Coming from central Abu Dhabi, follow Airport Rd (E20) to Sweihan Rd in the direction of Falah City; about 3km past the junction with Hwy E11, turn right after the water tank (before exit 30A) and follow the signs to the hospital.

rides from Dhs690/350; ☺9am-11pm) Outside the racing calendar, DriveYas offers several opportunities on Tuesdays (winter only), Thursdays and Saturdays to experience the Yas Marina Circuit up close – so close, in fact, that there seems to be only a friction burn between you and the racetrack. Opt to drive a racing car on your own or book three laps in the passenger seat.

Yas Waterworld   WATER PARK
(Map p372; ☑02 414 2000; www.yaswaterworld. com; Yas Leisure Dr; adult/child under 1.1m from Dhs250/210; ☺10am-6pm Nov-Mar, to 7pm Apr, May, Sep & Oct, to 8pm Jun-Aug) The UAE's most elaborate water park offers opportunities to get soaked on 45 rides, slides and other liquid attractions as you follow Emirati cartoon character Dana on her quest for a magical pearl. A wave pool, two lazy rivers and the region's first water-cinema offer more relaxing alternatives to the rides if you're just looking to beat the Gulf heat.

Dhow Cruises Abu Dhabi   CRUISE
(Map p378; ☑050 966 0720; www.dhowcruiseabu dhabi.ae; Marina Breakwater; adult/child Dhs95/55; ☺cruises 10.30am, 11.30am, 3.30pm & 4.30pm) These dhow cruises head out from Breakwater's marina and do a one-hour cruise with good views of Abu Dhabi along the way.

Murjan Splash Park   WATER PARK
(Map p383; ☑050 878 1009; www.murjansplash park.weebly.com; Al Salam St, Khalifa Park; over/under 1m Dhs50/free; ☺10am-7pm) Offers a range of water-based children's activities including bumper boats, a 'lazy river ride' and a couple of small water slides. Good for tots though older kids won't be too impressed. There's

also a 'surf wrangler' for learning surfing with an instructor present.

☞ Tours

Noukhada Adventure Company   KAYAKING
(Map p372; ☑02 558 1889; www.noukhada.ae; Eastern Mangroves Promenade; 90min kayaking tour adult/child Dhs160/130, eco-tour Dhs220/170; ☺office 8.30am-5.30pm) Specialising in local exploration by paddle, this local tour operator runs kayaking trips through the mangrove forests, allowing you to experience Abu Dhabi's mangrove habitat up close. If you're interested in the ecology of this unique environment, opt for the two-hour eco-tour. There are also night tours and a monthly full-moon tour; both are great during the hotter summer months.

Abu Dhabi Pearl Journey   BOATING
(Map p372; ☑02 656 1000; www.adpearljour ney.com; Eastern Mangroves Promenade; 1hr tour Dhs300; ☺cruises 9am-7pm) Ply the mangrove channels while laying back on the cushions aboard this traditional wooden dhow. Cruises include presentations and information on Abu Dhabi's pearling culture past plus Arabic coffee and dates. You're welcome to bring along picnic supplies to munch while you enjoy the scenery. The price is for the boat, not per person. No pre-booking necessary.

Emirati Experiences   TOURS
(www.visitabudhabi.ae; tours per person Dhs50-1000) Organised by Abu Dhabi's Department of Culture and Tourism (DCT), these tours allow an insight into Emirati culture and traditions. The tours range from a visit to the Al Dana factory, where traditional Emirati sandals are produced (Dhs50 per person) and a food tour munching your way

through the city's traditional restaurants, to a trip to a local home.

Captain Tony's
CRUISE

(Map p372; ☑ 02 650 7175; www.captaintonys.ae; Yas Marina; 90min daylight or sunset cruise adult/child Dhs250/150; ☺ 8.30am-6pm) Offering a wide range of cruises with an ecofriendly approach, this company runs a relaxing and popular sunset tour, ecotours to the mangroves, and a four-hour escape to a natural sandbar with sandwiches, umbrellas, deckchairs, buckets and spades. Stand-up paddleboarding and fishing is also on offer. Most departures are from Yas Marina. Book beforehand through the website.

Big Bus Abu Dhabi
BUS

(Map p378; ☑ 02 449 0026; www.bigbustours.com; 24hr adult/child Dhs260/166; ☺ 9am-5pm) This hop-on, hop-off bus tour with recorded commentary is an easy way to get the lie of the land. The main route loops past all the major sights, including Etihad Towers (p370), Sheikh Zayed Grand Mosque (p373) and the Louvre Abu Dhabi (p371). A second connecting route covers Yas Island.

You can board the bus at any stop, but the nominal starting point is the **Marina Mall** (Map p378; www.marinamall.ae; ☺ 10am-10pm Sat-Wed, to midnight Thu & Fri; ☎), with buses on the main route operating from here every 30 minutes between 9am and 5pm.

🎉 Festivals & Events

Mother of the Nation Festival
CULTURAL

(www.motn.ae; Al Bahar Corniche Beach; adult/child Dhs25/15; ☺ Mar) For 10 days in March, cultural exhibitions sit alongside zip lines, play areas, cooking demonstrations, concerts, food trucks, arts and crafts workshops, a handicraft market, wandering musicians and artistic acts. The festival opens mid-afternoon and rolls on to midnight every night. It's best visited after dark when the temperature cools but the action heats up.

Abu Dhabi Grand Prix
SPORTS

(☑ 02 659 9800; www.yasmarinacircuit.com; Yas Marina Circuit; 2-day ticket from Dhs1970; ☺ Nov) The Formula 1 Abu Dhabi Grand Prix is one of the city's top annual events, attracting visitors from across the region as well as international racing fans. This annual day-night race has one of the most impressive circuits on the race calendar, including a marina setting and a section of track that passes through the Yas Viceroy Abu Dhabi hotel.

Mubadala World Tennis Championship
SPORTS

(www.mubadalawtc.com; International Tennis Centre, Zayed Sports City, Al Khaleel Al Arabi St; 3-day package from Dhs550; ☺ Dec) This three-day event kicks off the tennis season and is a chance to see six of the world's best players in action. In 2017 stars of the women's game joined in the championship for the first time. Serena Williams, Rafael Nadal, Andy Murray and Novak Djokovic have all graced the courts here.

🛏 Sleeping

Five-star luxury hotels and beach resorts or business-trade-focused city hotels are what Abu Dhabi does. Whatever the budget, most are big multi-floor hotels. There aren't any boutique-style places here. Swimming pools are the norm, as are onsite bars, restaurants and gyms. Prices bounce around throughout the year, especially May to September.

DESERT TOURS FROM ABU DHABI

Abu Dhabi Desert Safari (☑ 055 484 2001; www.abudhabi-desert-safari.com; evening desert safari per person Dhs300; ☺ 7am-11.30pm) This company has friendly on-the-ball staff and specialises in overnight trips to the desert rimming Liwa Oasis, home to some of the largest sand dunes in the Empty Quarter. Prices include transport from Abu Dhabi, breakfast, barbecue dinner with various entertainments and shisha as well as sandboarding. Most of its other desert offerings are private trips.

Emirates Tours & Safari (☑ 02 491 2929, 24hr 050 532 6837; www.eatours.ae; city tour half-/full day Dhs160/360; ☺ 8am-7pm Sun-Thu) This professional operator runs half- and full-day city bus tours of Abu Dhabi as well as overnight camping 4WD tours into the desert including dune rides, a visit to a camel farm, sandboarding and a barbecue supper with belly dancing or other traditional entertainment in a Middle Eastern tent setting (per person Dhs480)

Abu Dhabi Corniche & Around

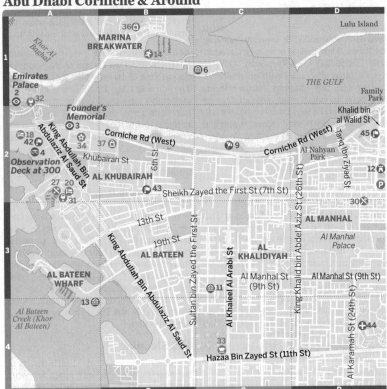

🛏 Marina Breakwater

⭐ **Grand Hyatt Abu Dhabi**   HOTEL $$
(Map p378; ☎ 02 510 1234; www.hyatt.com; Corniche Rd (west); r from Dhs800; P🛜🏊) Now, *that's* a view. The Grand Hyatt swaggered onto the Abu Dhabi hotel scene in 2018, and its rooms, all with floor-to-ceiling glass doors and wrap-around balconies with panoramas either looking across the sea or to the city skyscrapers, are its calling card. Take our advice and book a city-facing room for the full-on Abu Dhabi by night experience.

Jumeirah at Etihad Towers   HOTEL $$
(Map p378; ☎ 02 811 5555; www.jumeirah.com; Corniche Rd (West); r from Dhs847; P🛜🏊) The lobby's show-stopping glass wall ushers you into this exclusive cocoon where guests float from spa treatment to private beach before choosing between some of the city's top-class restaurants and bars once the sun goes down. In the rooms, with their floor-to-ceiling windows, beds are positioned so you can watch the twinkling city lights as you drift off to sleep.

🛏 Downtown

Novel Hotel   HOTEL $
(Map p378; ☎ 02 633 3555; www.novel-danathotels.com; Sheikh Hamdan Bin Mohammed St; r from Dhs420; P🛜🏊) Always popular, this big tower has a cracking central position in Downtown and friendly staff, making it a solid option. Rooms are spacious, comfortable and well kitted-out if a tad old-fashioned, and there's a pool for chilling out after a long day's sightseeing. Room rates are often energetically slashed.

Courtyard by Marriott   HOTEL $$
(Map p378; ☎ 02 698 2222; www.marriott.com; Sheikh Hamdan Bin Mohammed St, World Trade Center Mall; r from Dhs694; P🛜🏊) Slapped onto

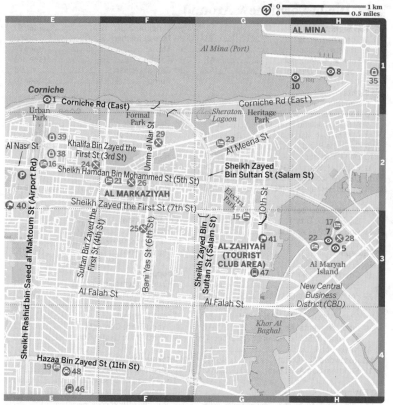

the side of the World Trade Center (p387), this Marriott is a midrange winner. Shots of orange and wood add fresh vibes to the light-filled rooms while super-comfortable beds guarantee a good sleep. Away from the room, head up for the pool and cocktails at **Up & Below** (Map p378; Sheikh Hamdan Bin Mohammed St, Courtyard by Marriott World Trade Center; ⊘11am-2am; 🛜) or down for a flat white in **Fifth Street Cafe** (Map p378; ☑02 698 2222; Sheikh Hamdan bin Mohammed St, Courtyard by Marriott World Trade Center; mains Dhs35-105; ⊘7am-11pm; 🛜).

⌘ Al Zahiyah & Al Maryah Island

★**Southern Sun Abu Dhabi**   HOTEL **$**
(Map p378; ☑02 818 4888; www.tsogosun.com; Al Meena St; r from Dhs340; **P**🛜🏊) This shiny high-rise packs in the flair of a hotel twice the price from the moment you walk into the triple-height lobby hung with swooping

contemporary lamps. A fresh, modern vibe runs through the rooms with a sprinkle of Middle Eastern design touches thrown in, and there's a buzzing social vibe throughout thanks to a bundle of popular bars and cafes.

Al Manzel   APARTMENT **$**
(Map p378; ☑02 406 7009; www.almanzel-hotel apartments.com; Sheikh Zayed the First St; studio/1-bedroom apt Dhs250/350; **P**🛜🏊) Sure, the furnishings are a bit ho-hum beige but you get a lot of bang for your buck in these spacious hotel studios and apartments, all with well-kitted-out kitchenettes including microwave, two-hob cooker and (glory-be!) a washing machine. Staff here are ultra-helpful and there's a tiny kidney-shaped pool on the roof to top it all off.

★**Rosewood Abu Dhabi**   HOTEL **$$**
(Map p378; ☑02 813 5592; www.rosewoodhotels. com; Al Maryah Island; r from Dhs600; **P**🛜🏊)

Abu Dhabi Corniche & Around

From Glo, its rooftop pool-bar, at the tip to snug wine-haunt La Cava (Map p378; ☑02 813 5550; www.rosewoodhotels.com/en/abudhabi/dining/la-cava; Rosewood Hotel, Al Maryah Island; ⊙5pm-1am; 🕾) secreted in its toe, the Rosewood is one sophisticated customer. Rooms exude contemporary, non-stuffy style with lashings of white, and baths overlooking the waterway. There's so much here – including D (p383)ai Pai Dong, one of Abu Dhabi's most beloved restaurants – that you may decide to never step outside.

Four Seasons Abu Dhabi　　　HOTEL $$$
(Map p378; ☑02 333 2222; www.fourseasons.com/abudhabi; Al Maryah Island; r from Dhs900; P🕾🏊) From the wavy articulated lobby wall hat-tipping Abu Dhabi's pearling heritage to the oblong banquettes layering the facade, which look like desert-evoking copper from a distance, there are milestone-level nods to local culture everywhere you look in this art-inspired hotel (2000 pieces dot the property, 90% sourced locally). Rooms themselves are classically styled with outstanding water and city views.

🛏 Al Mina & Saadiyat Island

★Park Hyatt Abu Dhabi
Hotel & Villas   RESORT $$$
(Map p372; ☑ 02 407 1234; www.hyatt.com; r from Dhs1400; P🌊❄) 🏊 From the expansive bronze-toned foyer with its silver sand-rose sculptures to the 50-sq-metre rooms with daybed-strewn balconies and bathtubs made for long soaking sessions, this is a subtly elegant retreat still within easy reach of the city. The infinity pool is flanked by over-water cabanas, while the white-sand beach is reached by an elevated boardwalk protecting the turtle nesting sites.

🛏 Al Bateen & Al Mushrif

**Grand Millennium
Al Wahda Hotel**   HOTEL $$
(Map p378; ☑ 02 443 9999; www.millenniumhotels.com; Hazza bin Zayed the First St, Al Wahda; r from Dhs550; 🌊❄) Popular with the business crowd, this always-busy big hotel has large, modern rooms in beige and navy blue. Porters Pub is downstairs, there's a pool, gym and spa and Al Wahda Mall is right next door. It's a good-value choice with on-the-ball staff.

★Eastern Mangroves
Hotel & Spa   HOTEL $$
(Map p372; ☑ 02 656 1000; www.abu-dhabi.anantara.com; Sheikh Zayed Bin Sultan St, Eastern Mangroves; r from Dhs750; P🌊❄) Stepping into the lobby with its *mashrabiyya* patterns and *oud* (lute-like traditional stringed instrument) player beside the infinity pool, it's clear that Arab hospitality is taken seriously here. Rooms, all with balconies, either overlook the eponymous mangroves or the highway – spend the extra on the mangrove view – and are soothingly furnished in matching nature tones.

🛏 Sheikh Zayed Grand Mosque Area

★Ritz Carlton Abu Dhabi
Grand Canal   RESORT $$$
(Map p383; ☑ 02 818 8888; www.ritzcarlton.com; Khor Al Maqta; r from Dhs1470; P🌊❄) This mammoth hotel, with one of the biggest pools we've seen in the UAE, a slice of private beach and rooms which come with big balconies and marble-clad bathrooms, is just the ticket for city breaks with lashings of sumptuous resort styling. With the ca-

boodle of drinking and dining choices here, many struggle to even leave the leafy hotel grounds.

🛏 Yas Island

Yas Hotel   HOTEL $$
(☑ 02 656 0000; www.marriott.com; Yas Marina Circuit; r from Dhs750; P🌊❄) This bright, airy and entirely contemporary hotel sits in pole position on Yas Island, literally straddling the Yas Marina Circuit. Its avant-garde, steel-and-glass roof with its corrugated mantle flung over the racetrack is dramatically studded with lights at night, while inside, starkly minimalist rooms in white and grey are a haven of cool in the Gulf heat.

Taken over by Marriott in mid-2018, the hotel was on the verge of undergoing a rebranding to become a W Hotel when we visited in late 2018, though no one could give us an exact date. Expect the hotel name to have changed by the time you blow into town. The hotel's key USP though will still be the same – during the F1 race the cars literally speed right under your balcony.

🍴 Eating

Abu Dhabi's top fine-dining restaurants tend to be found in the five-star hotels and newer shopping malls. Al Maryah Island is fast becoming one of the major destinations for dining in style. In contrast, the streets one block south of Zayed the First St present a geography of regional cuisine from Syria to Yemen.

🍴 Marina Breakwater

Cho Gao Marina Walk   ASIAN $$
(Map p378; ☑ 02 666 6888; www.abudhabi.intercontinental.com/cho-gao-marina-walk; Marina Walk, Intercontinental Hotel; mains Dhs50-180; ⊗noon-1am Sat-Wed, to 2am Fri & Sat; P🌊) The second branch of this much-loved restaurant – the **original** (Map p378; ☑ 02 616 6149; www.facebook.com/chogaoasianexperience; Sheikh Hamdan Bin Mohammed St, ground fl, Crowne Plaza Abu Dhabi; mains Dhs50-130; ⊗noon-1am; 🌊) is downtown – has a desirable waterfront location with marina views, making it a standout option. The pan-Asian menu draws on classic cooking from across the continent while the atmosphere is sociable and upbeat.

★Li Beirut   LEBANESE $$$
(Map p378; ☑ 02 811 5666; www.jumeirah.com; Corniche Rd (West), Jumeirah at Etihad Towers;

mezze Dhs40-50, mains Dhs80-210, set menus from Dhs295; ☺noon-3pm & 7pm-midnight Sep-May, dinner only Jul & Aug; ☏) A fine-dining Levantine feast awaits. Scoop up Lebanese mezze classics of *moutabel* (purée of aubergine mixed with tahini, yoghurt and olive oil) and *muhammara* (red chilli and walnut dip) before moving on to rack of lamb encrusted with *zaatar* (a blend of spices that includes hyssop, sumac and sesame) or quail stuffed with *freekeh* (roasted green wheat).

★ **Mezlai**   EMIRATI $$$
(Map p378; ☑02 690 7999; www.kempinski.com; Corniche Rd (West), Emirates Palace; mains Dhs128-318; ☺1-10.30pm; ☏) ✐ Meaning 'old door lock', Mezlai delivers a rare chance to enjoy traditional Emirati cuisine in an upmarket and airy Bedouin-tent-inspired atmosphere. The food is prepared from organic and locally sourced ingredients with favourites including *medfoun* (shoulder of lamb, cooked underground, wrapped in a banana leaf) and slow-cooked camel delicately flavoured with rose water and served with raisins and cashews.

✕ Downtown

★ **Cafeteria Al Liwan**   SYRIAN $
(Map p378; ☑02 622 1250; www.facebook.com/liwanabudhabi; off Sheikh Hamdan Bin Mohammed St; mezze Dhs12-19, mains Dhs20-40; ☺8.30am-11.30pm Sun-Thu, noon-1am Fri; ☏✐) This budget canteen will exceed your expectations every chance it gets. This is Middle Eastern flavours Syrian-style, with some of Abu Dhabi's best hummus and *fuul* (mashed fava beans), falafel fried to crispy perfection and *kawaj* (tomato and mincemeat casserole) that would make a Damascene mamma proud. It's all served in a slightly beaten but welcoming environment with graffitied walls.

★ **Zahrat Lebnan**   LEBANESE $
(Lebanese Flower; Map p378; ☑02 667 5924; near Zayed the First St, Al Manhal; mezze & sandwiches Dhs8-36, mains Dhs18-55; ☺8am-3am; ☏) Amid a cluster of Middle Eastern snack and grill outlets, a short walk from the Qasr Al Hosn, the Lebanese Flower is a local legend, attracting a multinational clientele of city residents who come here for mezze feasts of stuffed vine leaves, falafel, hummus, and *fatayer* (stuffed mini-pastries), generously portioned kebab and shawarma plates, and cheap sandwiches. You can't go wrong.

Bait El Khetyar   MIDDLE EASTERN $
(Map p378; Sheikh Hamdan Bin Mohammed St; sandwiches & shawarma Dhs6-27, mains Dhs24-37; ☺8am-1am; ✐) This place buzzes after dark when families pack the street-side tables, eating big shawarma plates with salad and hummus, while takeaway customers wait inside as their falafel and shawarma sandwiches are getting made. It's busy, cheap and always solidly good. Its other **branch** (Map p378; ☑02 633 3200; Fatima Bint Mubarak St; sandwiches & shawarma Dhs6-27, mains Dhs24-37; ☺8am-midnight Sun-Thu, 8am-noon & 1pm-midnight Fri; ✐) is just as popular.

Hanôi Naturally   VIETNAMESE $
(Map p378; ☑02 626 1112; www.hanoinaturally.com; 1st fl, World Trade Center Mall; mains Dhs32-52; ☺noon-11pm; ☏✐) If you're missing your *pho* (Vietnamese noodle soup), head here. Sure the broth isn't as complex and full-bodied as you'd get in a Hanôi canteen but it's still good. We like the main dishes of tamarind-spiked shrimp and tofu doused in a fragrant lemongrass and chilli sauce, and could munch on its green mango and prawn salad all day.

Tamba   INDIAN $$
(Map p378; ☑02 672 8888; www.tambarestaurant.com; 6th fl, The Hub, World Trade Center Mall; mains Dhs42-232; ☺noon-1am Sun-Thu, to 2am Fri & Sat; Ⓟ☏✐) Despite the mall location this is a classy, dim-lit joint that takes the flavours of the subcontinent and adds contemporary tweaks. Get stuck into masala-rubbed Wagyu beef or Mangalorean-style chicken. If vegetarian is more your thing, order up small plates of *paneer makhani* (paneer in a creamy tomato and cashew sauce) and sweet and sour pumpkin.

Market Kitchen   INTERNATIONAL $$$
(Map p378; www.marketkitchenabudhabi.com; Khalifa Bin Zayed the First St, Le Royal Méridien; mains Dhs76-195; ☺noon-4pm & 7-11pm Sat-Wed, to midnight Thu & Fri; ☏) Cosy dining, complete with tree sprouting in the middle of the restaurant and a mezzanine-level bar area. Concentrating on bistro-style cooking, dishes like Parmesan-crusted chicken, roasted beetroot salad sprinkled with crystallised ginger, and soy-glazed beef short ribs with apple and jalapeno puree head up a menu filled with creative flair. Market Kitchen is one cool, contemporary customer.

Sheikh Zayed Mosque Area

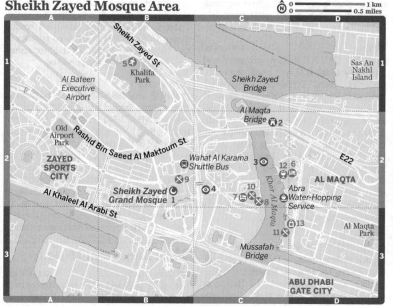

Sheikh Zayed Mosque Area

Bu! LATIN AMERICAN $$$

(Map p378; ☑ 02 666 8066; www.butrinity.com; 4th fl, The Hub, World Trade Center Mall; mains Dhs95-285; ⊙5pm-1am Sat-Wed, to 3am Thu, 12.30-4.30pm & 5pm-1am Fri; 🕿) Book ahead for a table at this trendy pan-Latin restaurant-bar, an anchor of the dining and nightlife tower inside the World Trade Center Mall known as the Hub. It has excellent ceviche, fish and lobster tacos and other festive Latin staples (Brazilian fish stews, Peruvian fried rices, Argentine beef cuts); the salsa and merengue music ensure the mood is merry.

✖ Al Zahiyah & Al Maryah Island

★**Dai Pai Dong** CHINESE $$

(Map p378; ☑ 02 813 5552; www.rosewoodhotels.com; Rosewood Hotel, Al Maryah Island; mains Dhs48-194, dim sum Dhs30-55; ⊙noon-3pm & 6-11pm Sun-Wed, to midnight Thu & Fri; 🕿☑) All cosy alcoves surrounding an open kitchen, Dai Pai Dong's award-winning Chinese is where Asian foodies chase Cantonese roasted duck, spicy braised chicken and wok-fried beef tenderloin with green tea and kumquat mojitos. Once you've chowed down on its roasted pork buns or truffle and vegetable stuffed dumplings, you'll understand why Dai Pai Dong is known for its dim sum.

★ Coya
PERUVIAN $$$

(Map p378; ☑ 02 306 7000; www.coyarestaurant. com; Galleria Mall, Al Maryah Island; small plates Dhs50-124, mains Dhs98-980; ⏰ noon-5pm Sun-Thu, 12.30-4pm Fri, to 5.30pm Sat, plus 7pm-12.30am daily) The contemporary Peruvian cuisine with its flavour-fusion of Latin American and Asian is a tastebud sensation. Dig into the menu of sharing plates featuring traditional ceviche, Peruvian sashimi and tacos (we recommend the *cangrejo* stuffed with crab and wasabi) and you'll see what the fuss is about. Impressive waterfront views add a luxurious feel: perfect for a romantic night out.

Butcher & Still
STEAK $$$

(Map p378; ☑ 02 333 2444; www.fourseasons.com/ abudhabi/dining/restaurants/butcher_and_still; Four Seasons Abu Dhabi, Al Maryah Island; steak Dhs280-490; ⏰ 6pm-midnight; 🕾) How good is this 1920s Chicago–inspired steakhouse at Four Seasons Abu Dhabi? We don't have enough space to tell you. American chef Marshall Roth sources his meat from the Temple Grandin–designed Creekstone Farms in Kansas (USA); when paired with his from-scratch béchamel-creamed spinach, you have a perfectly executed classic combination.

Zuma
JAPANESE $$$

(Map p378; ☑ 02 401 5900; www.zumarestaurant. com; Galleria at Maryah Island, Al Maryah Island; mains Dhs120-358; ⏰ noon-3.30pm & 7pm-midnight Sat-Wed, to 1am Thu & Fri; 🕾) The summit of Japanese cuisine in Abu Dhabi. Book ahead to enjoy the superb sushi and sashimi, the signature miso-marinated black cod or a hunk of meat cooked to perfection on the robata grill. Alcohol served (sake, finely curated cocktails and Hitachino, one of Japan's best craft beers). The beautiful bar, fashioned from striking Indonesian teak, is buzzy to boot.

✖ Al Mina & Saadiyat Island

★ Beach House
MEDITERRANEAN $$$

(Map p372; ☑ 02 407 1138; www.hyatt.com/en-US/ hotel/united-arab-emirates/park-hyatt-abu-dhabi-hotel-and-villas/abuph/dining; Saadiyat Island, Park Hyatt Abu Dhabi; mains Dhs115-205; ⏰ 12.30-11.30pm Sun-Thu, 9am-11pm Fri & Sat) Open for breakfast on weekends and lunch and dinner otherwise, this restaurant, with its emphasis on sunny Mediterranean flavours

(think slow-cooked brisket with olives and tzatkiki, and seafood cassolette) has an enviable location fronting Saadiyat's coastal dunes. In the cooler months, go upstairs to the Beach House Rooftop (p386) for arguably Abu Dhabi's best sunset views.

★ Sontaya
ASIAN $$$

(Map p372; ☑ 02 498 8443; www.sontayaabudhabi. com; St Regis Saadiyat Island Resort, Saadiyat Island; mains Dhs70-340; ⏰ noon-3pm & 6pm-midnight; ⛗🕾⟋) You can't beat the beachy atmosphere of this restaurant, surrounded by narrow water-feature canals and looking out towards the sand. The pan-Asian flavours, and twists on traditional dishes, are spot on, from its prawn and banana blossom salad to confit duck in a red curry laced with lychee and aubergine. Bonus points for an extensive, and varied, separate vegetarian menu.

✖ Al Bateen & Al Mushrif

★ Café Arabia
MIDDLE EASTERN $

(Map p372; ☑ 02 643 9699; www.facebook.com/ cafearabia; Villa No 224/1, 15th St, Al Mushrif, opposite Umm Al Emarat Park entrance; mains Dhs25-90; ⏰ 8am-11pm Mon-Thu, from 9am Fri-Sun; ⛗🕾⟋) Housed in a three-floor villa, this cafe is run by a Lebanese arts enthusiast, Aida Mansour. Vast breakfast choices from avocado toast to shakshuka (poached eggs in a spicy tomato sauce) and a mains menu that waltzes from sweet potato and feta salad to *harira* (Moroccan lentil soup), falafel platters and a camel burger keep the crowds of regulars happy.

Home Bakery
CAFE $

(Map p372; www.homebakery.ae; Umm Al Emarat Park, Al Mushrif; mains Dhs32-48; ⏰ 8am-midnight; ⛗🕾) The United Arab Emirates is made up of a mere 10% Emiratis, and we'll be damned if you don't find nearly all of them sipping tea and savouring the decadent cakes at this trendy bakery-cafe inside Umm Al Emarat Park. For something less sweet to eat there are gourmet breakfasts and sandwiches.

Cafe Blanc
MIDDLE EASTERN $$

(Map p372; Eastern Mangroves Promenade; mezze Dhs28-45, mains Dhs68-75; ⏰ 10.30am-11.30pm; ⛗⟋) We can think of few places more pleasant to sit in the early evening than the outdoor terrace here looking over the water while puffing on a shisha. Chuck a few mezze dishes into the equation – its house *moutabel* is delicious – and you have a perfect light dinner.

Pepper Mill INDIAN $$
(Map p372; ☑02 441 3582; www.peppermill.ae; Eastern Mangroves Promenade; mains Dhs38-84; ⊙noon-11.30pm; P☎🖥️) Where you come to tuck into rich classic curries and *tandoor* (clay-oven) dishes. The Pondicherry seafood curry of fish and shrimp is delicious. Top marks also for its creative vegetarian options, which go beyond the typical *dals*, with *tandoor* choices of *paneer* cubes stuffed with mango pickle, and yogurt-marinated soy kebabs.

✕ Sheikh Zayed Grand Mosque Area

★ Li Jiang ASIAN $$
(Map p383; ☑02 818 8282; www.ritzcarlton.com; Khor Al Maqta, Ritz-Carlton Abu Dhabi Grand Canal; mains Dhs60-260; ⊙6pm-midnight) Asia's multi-layered, spice-tinged flavours are presented amid a red-toned dining room replete with gorgeous Thai textile detailing. Malaysian, Thai and Chinese flavours dominate the menu. Graze on crispy taro cakes, chicken satay and dim sum, sup up a spicy laksa or dig into mains of ginger lotus sea bass or massaman curry. Head here Monday for unlimited dim sum night.

Al Fanar EMIRATI $$
(Map p383; ☑02 448 1144; Venetian Village, Ritz-Carlton Abu Dhabi Crand Canal; mains Dhs52-83; ⊙8.30am-10pm; ☎) The faux 'Emirati house' set-up and fake camel plonked outside the front door may get your tour-group radar buzzing, but this place is actually a favoured haunt of Emirati families and regional tourists, who come here for traditional mutton, seafood and chicken stews, *jasheed* (minced baby shark with onions and spices) and grilled seafood dishes spiced with tamarind and date-syrup.

★ Ushna INDIAN $$
(Map p383; ☑02 558 1769; Khor Al Maqta, ground fl, Souk Qaryat Al Beri; mains Dhs56-201; ⊙12.30-11.30pm; ☎🖥️) 🍴 Romantic and elegant, this place hums with appreciation for the complex cuisine of India, brought to the United Arab Emirates by a large expat community. There are many curry houses across town, but this restaurant offers some of the most luscious variations, alongside beautiful views across the canal to the Grand Mosque, with a sustainable seafood commitment to boot.

✕ Yas Island & Around

★ Felini Garden ITALIAN $$
(Map p372; ☑02 656 2000; Golf Plaza, Radisson Blu Hotel; mains Dhs68-160; ⊙4.30pm-1am Sun-Wed, to 2am Thu, 12.30pm-2am Fri, to 1am Sat; ☎🖥️) This restaurant-bar with its terrace opening out onto the reed-covered coastal dunes is one of the most pumping places on Yas Island. Order up a pumpkin gnocchi or a prosciutto pizza and soak up the knockout indoor-outdoor setting. It's renowned for its epic all-Italian Friday brunch (from Dhs170), which features a wandering saxophonist (jazzy!) and a sunset after-party.

★ Nolu's Café CAFE $$
(Map p372; ☑02 557 9500; www.nolusrestaurants.com; Al Bandar Marina, Al Raha Beach; mains Dhs50-120; ⊙9am-11pm; ☎🖥️) California meets Afghanistan at this cafe charmer where almond butter and chia pancakes are offered alongside *borani banjon* (oven-baked aubergines with mint-flecked garlic yoghurt) and hearty fodder like lamb shank with brown rice pilau. The Afghan menu-spin comes from the secret recipes of the owner's Afghan mother. Wash it all down with fresh juices or an activated charcoal matcha latte.

🍷 Drinking & Nightlife

🍸 Marina Breakwater

★ Ray's Bar BAR
(Map p378; ☑02 811 5666; www.jumeirah.com; Corniche Rd (West), Jumeirah at Etihad Towers; ⊙5pm-2am; ☎) For a prime perspective on Abu Dhabi's audacious architectural vision, let the lift whisk you up to this 62nd-floor bar at Jumeirah at Etihad Towers, which is all about cocktails and mocktails and skyscraper views – arrive at sunset to be dazzled by the light bouncing off all the steel and glass.

Hakkasan COCKTAIL BAR
(Map p378; ☑02 690 7749; www.hakkasan.com; Corniche Rd (West), Emirates Palace; ⊙3.30pm-1am; ☎) All other cocktail bars may be dead to you once you've sipped a Pearl Sky (gin, rhubarb liqueur, yuzu, blackberry and lemon) or Sake Samurai (vodka, sake, mango, pineapple, cumin syrup and Prosecco) cocktail (Dhs62) on Hakkasan's bar terrace while soaking up the views overlooking the vast, manicured grounds of the **Emirates Palace**

(Map p378; ☑02 690 9000; www.kempinski.com; Corniche Rd (West); r from Dhs1900; ⓟ🛜🏊).

Belgian Café
BAR

(Map p378; ☑02 666 6888; www.belgianbeercafe.com; King Abdullah Bin Abdulaziz Al Saud St, InterContinental Hotel; beers Dhs28-65; ⊗4pm-1am Sat-Tue, to 2am Wed; 🛜) The Arabian Peninsula is dire territory for hopheads, but the Belgian Café at the InterContinental (Map p378; www.intercontinental.com/abudhabi) boasts a satisfying suds selection, featuring five Belgian offers on draught and another 20 or so by the bottle.

🍺 Al Zahiyah & Al Maryah Island

★ Dragon's Tooth
COCKTAIL BAR

(Map p378; www.rosewoodhotels.com; Dai Pai Dong restaurant, Rosewood Hotel, Al Maryah Island; ⊗6pm-1am Sat-Wed, to 2am Thu & Fri) Just the coolest speakeasy-style bar in town. Walk through the front door of Dai Pai Dong (p383) and head left to stumble into this secret drinking den, all leather and brass, which seems to have fallen out of the 1920s. Cocktails are super creative. Our favourite is the Black Panda with rum, amaretto, activated charcoal, and blackberry and rosemary syrup.

Glo
ROOFTOP BAR

(Map p378; ☑02 813 5550; www.rosewood hotels.com; Rosewood Hotel, Al Maryah Island; ⊗noon-1am Oct-May; 🛜) The rooftop bar at the Rosewood hotel (p379) is one of our top choices for a chilled-out night. Lounge with friends while drinking wine and taking in Abu Dhabi's skyline. Tuesday is Ladies' night, with free Prosecco between 6pm and 9pm.

🍺 Al Mina & Saadiyat Island

Beach House Rooftop
ROOFTOP BAR

(Map p372; ☑02 407 1138; www.hyattrestaurants.com; Park Hyatt Abu Dhabi Hotel & Villas; ⊗5pm-1am Mon-Sun) Don't be deceived by the unassuming back staircase entrance. Climb to the top, and you'll be dazzled by incredible turquoise waters and panoramic ocean vistas. Atmospheric music at just the right volume and low, emotive lighting set the tone, though it's Mother Nature's stunning sunsets and gentle sound of waves lapping that really steal the show.

🍺 Al Bateen & Al Mushrif

Joud Cafe
CAFE

(Map p378; ☑056 525 8235; www.joudcafe.com; cnr Al Khajeel Al Arabi & Hazaa bin Zayed the First Sts, Al Bateen; ⊗8am-10pm; 🛜) Although earnest artisan-coffee guff generally gets on our nerves – when ordering you'll be asked the origin you want and whether you'd like it served hot or their standard warm – there's no denying this place serves some of the best coffee in town. This is a much-loved neighbourhood hang-out with its mid-century-meets-minimalism interior usually packed with young Emiratis.

Art House Cafe
CAFE

(Map p378; www.facebook.com/arthousecafead; Villa 15, Al Huwelat St, Al Bateen; ⊗9am-11.30pm Sun-Thu, 10am-midnight Fri & Sat; 🛜) Beside, and connected to, Etihad Modern Art Gallery (☑02 621 0145; www.etihadmodernart.com; ⊗10am-10pm Sat-Thu) FREE, this artsy cafe, with its shaded patio scattered with tables and seating made from recycled oil-barrels and fuel canisters, is a colourful bohemian hangout. There's good coffee, excellent smoothies and breakfast plates as well as wraps, salads and burgers if you're peckish.

🍺 Sheikh Zayed Grand Mosque Area

Chameleon Terrace
BAR

(Map p383; ☑02 654 3238; www.fairmont.com; Khor Al Maqta, Fairmont Bab Al Bahr; ⊗6pm-1am Nov-Apr; 🛜) In the cooler months, this is the place to be. Cool cucumber mojitos, passion-fruit Collins, and kiwi gin and tonics are just some of the signature cocktails (Dhs55 to Dhs95) you can enjoy on this outdoor terrace with Grand Mosque views in the distance on the ground floor of the Fairmont Bab Al Bahr (Map p383; ☑02 654 3000; r from Dhs1154; ⓟ🛜🏊).

🍺 Yas Island & Around

Stars 'N' Bars
SPORTS BAR

(Map p372; ☑02 565 0101; www.starsnbars.ae; Yas Marina; cocktails Dhs55-75; ⊗noon-3am; 🛜) Voted Abu Dhabi's best sports bar, this wildly popular and rowdy bar and grill is unapologetically American. With 24 taps, including craft selections from Brewdog, Anchor Steam and Brooklyn Brewery, it's certainly a beer destination, but it draws hordes for food, live music and shisha too. Throw in nearly 80 TVs and there's something – and something on – for everyone.

Iris
BAR

(Map p372; ☑ 055 160 5636; www.yasmarina.com; Yas Marina; ☺ 6pm-3am Wed-Sun; ☎) Late at night, this place gets packed with trendy young things sipping signature cocktails (Dhs55 to Dhs75). DJs spin progressive deep house on Thursdays and '80s classics on Sundays. From October to April the partying spills out onto the outdoor deck with the twinkling lights of the Yas Hotel across the water creating a suitably dramatic background.

☆ Entertainment

NYUAD The Arts Center
ARTS CENTRE

(Map p372; www.nyuad-artscenter.org; East Plaza, NYU Abu Dhabi Campus) This multi-venue arts centre, inside the New York University's Abu Dhabi campus, hosts a regular, eclectic program of dance performances, music concerts, poetry open-mic events and film screenings. Tickets for events, usually announced a couple of weeks in advance, can be booked through the website.

Heroes
LIVE MUSIC

(Map p378; ☑ 02 418 2474; Sheikh Hamdan bin Mohammed St, Crowne Plaza Abu Dhabi; ☺ noon-4am; ☎) This old-timer doesn't need chi-chi designer interiors or a fancy-pants cocktail list put together by a world-famous mixologist to pull punters in. Heroes has a rocking house band that gets the party started most nights of the week. And it can get packed in here. A fun, down-to-earth, no-posing kind of place.

Porters Pub
LIVE MUSIC

(Map p378; ☑ 02 495 3936; Hazza bin Zayed the First St, Grand Millennium Al Wahda Hotel; ☺ noon-3am; ☎) This cavernous British-style pub gets crammed on Thursday and Friday nights when the house band takes to the floor. There's a swag of weekly events and plenty of beer choice. This is a good place to pull up a bar stool and check out Abu Dhabi's after-work drinking scene.

Jazz Bar & Dining
LIVE MUSIC

(Map p378; ☑ 02 681 1900; Corniche Rd (West), Radisson Blu Hotel & Resort Abu Dhabi; mains Dhs105-155; ☺ 7pm-2am Sat-Wed, to 3am Thu & Fri; ☎) Cool cats flock to this sophisticated supper club at the Radisson Blu that serves international cuisine in a modern art deco-inspired setting. But the venue is less about food and drink and more about music – a four-piece jazz band plays from 9.30pm to an audience of sagely nodding aficionados. It's ladies' night Monday and Wednesday.

🛍 Shopping

★ Wafi Gourmet
FOOD

(Map p378; www.wafigourmet.com; Corniche Rd (West), Nation Galleria; ☺ 9am-midnight Mon-Sat, from 8.30am Sun) Offering beautiful Medjool dates stuffed with pistachios, cashews, almonds or oranges; gorgeous marzipan, baklava and other Middle Eastern sweets; take-home bottles of rose water; and a full-service deli, bakery and restaurant, Wafi Gourmet is one-stop shopping for foodies looking to take home the taste of Arabia.

FBMI
TEXTILES

(Fatima Bint Mohammed Bin Zayed Initiative; Map p372; ☑ 02 566 9600; www.fbmi.ae; ground fl, Yas Mall; ☺ 10am-10pm Sat-Wed, to midnight Thu & Fri) 🌿 The beautiful handmade carpets on sale here are the backbone of Sheikha Fatima Bint Mohammed Bin Zayed's NGO, which aims to support and enhance the economic opportunities of Afghan women; 70% of the weaving artisans it hires are women. All the textiles are made from wool and cotton sourced in Afghanistan and then dyed using traditional natural colours.

Yas Mall
MALL

(Map p372; www.yasmall.ae; Yas West; ☺ 10am-10pm Sat-Wed, to midnight Thu & Fri; ☎) Bright, spacious and hosting 370 shops, Yas Mall is the star of Abu Dhabi's shopping scene. Look out for the growing plant wall and the two 12m-high tree-themed sculptures by acclaimed South African artist Marco Cianfanelli, with leaves inspired by Arabic calligraphy. There's access to Ferrari World (p375), cinemas, a **fun park** (☑ 02 565 1242; www.funworks.ae; wizz works/mini works Dhs60/30; ☺ 10am-10pm Sat-Wed, to midnight Thu & Fri) for wee ones and a Carrefour hypermarket.

World Trade Center Souk
MALL

(Map p378; www.wtcad.ae; Khalifa Bin Zayed the First St; ☺ 10am-10pm Sat-Wed, to 11pm Thu & Fri; ☎) British architect Norman Foster's immensely pleasant reinterpretation of the traditional souq is a stylish composition of warm lattice woodwork, stained glass, walkways and balconies. On the site of the old central market, it connects with the modern **World Trade Center Mall** (Map p378; ☑ 02 508 2400; www.wtcad.ae; Hamdan St; ☺ 10am-10pm Sat-Wed, to 11pm Thu & Fri).

Beautiful Henna Centre
BODY ART

(Map p372; ☑ 02 634 3963; www.beautifulhenna centre.com; Villa 141, Salama bint Butti St, Al Mushrif; ⊙ 9.30am-9pm Sat-Thu, from 10am Fri) Henna application (on hands and feet) is a traditional ritual of local bridal preparation, though these days it's not limited to weddings and is appreciated as an art form in itself. With 20 years of experience, this henna bar offers both traditional and modern artistic henna applications in a luxurious salon setting.

Souk Qaryat Al Beri
MALL

(Map p383; ☑ 02 558 1670; www.soukqaryatalberi. com; Khor Al Maqta; ⊙ 10am-10pm Sun-Wed, to 11pm Thu, 3-11pm Fri) This small mall's 21st-century take on the classic souq gets a thumbs-up for its appealing Middle Eastern architecture and waterfront location. The shops here stock items with roots in Arabia including oil-based perfumes and chocolate-covered dates. There's also a couple of art stores that sell original, contemporary crafts a step above what you'll find in most gift-type shops in Abu Dhabi.

Fruit & Vegetable Market
MARKET

(Map p378; Al Mina; ⊙ 7am-midnight) This vast wholesale market, partly open-air, is the exchange point for melons from Jordan, potatoes from Turkey and onions from just about everywhere. A highlight is cruising along 'date alley', where shops sell around 45 varieties (from Dhs25 per kilogram). Giant Medjool dates from Saudi Arabia cost Dhs70 to Dhs120 per kilogram, while medicinal Ajwa dates fetch Dhs120 per kilogram.

ℹ Information

MEDICAL SERVICES

The standard of health care in Abu Dhabi is generally high, and emergency treatment is free. For locations of 24-hour pharmacies, call 777 929.

Gulf Diagnostic Centre (Map p372; ☑ 02 417 7222, appointments 800 4324; www.gdc-hospital.com; Al Khaleej Al Arabi St; ⊙ 8am-8.30pm Sat-Wed, to 1pm Thu) Well-regarded private health centre.

Sheikh Khalifa Medical City (Map p378; ☑ 02 819 0000, appointments 80 050; www.seha.ae; cnr Al Karama St & Hazza Bin Zayed the First St; ⊙ 24hr) One of numerous well-equipped hospitals in the city with 24-hour emergency service.

TOURIST INFORMATION

Visit Abu Dhabi (www.visitabudhabi.ae) The city's main tourist-oriented website.

Yas Island Information (www.yasisland.ae) A good online overview of what's on, when and where on Yas Island.

ℹ Getting There & Away

AIR

Abu Dhabi International Airport (☑ 02 505 5555; www.abudhabiairport.ae; Airport Rd) About 30km southeast of the city centre, this ever-expanding airport has three terminals, including Etihad's exclusive base, Terminal 3. The airport is compact and efficient, meaning that you can sometimes get from the plane to the street in under half an hour.

BUS

Al Wahda Bus Station (Map p378; www.dot. abudhabi.ae; Rashid Bin Saeed Al Maktoum St) is about 4km south of the Corniche. Buses within the emirate of Abu Dhabi are run by the Abu Dhabi Department of Transportation (DOT). Buses to Dubai are run by the Dubai Roads and Transport Authority (RTA; www. dubai-buses.com). Services to Sharjah are operated by the Sharjah Roads and Transport Authority (SRTA; www.srta.gov.ae).

To use bus transport within the emirate of Abu Dhabi, you need to purchase a Hafilat card.

MAJOR BUSES FROM ABU DHABI

DESTINATION	FARE (DHS)	TIME (HR)	FREQUENCY	SERVICE
Al Ain	25	2½	every 30-45min	DOT bus X90
Dubai (Al Ghubaiba Station)	25	2	every 15min	RTA bus E100
Jebel Dhanna & Ruwais	35	4	4.40am, 5.40am, 8.50am & 1.30pm	DOT bus X87
Madinat Zayed	25	2½	9am & 7.30pm	DOT bus X60
Mezairaa	30	3¼	9am & 7.30pm	DOT bus X60
Sharjah	30	3	every 30min	SRTA bus 117

CAR

Abu Dhabi is 150km south of Dubai via Hwy E11. All the international car-hire agencies have branches at the airport and within the city.

TAXI

A taxi ride to Dubai or Al Ain costs around Dhs300 and can be booked in advance through **Abu Dhabi Taxi** (☑ 600 535 353; www.itc.abud habi.ae/en), or you can simply hail off the street or from a **taxi stand** (Map p378).

ⓘ Getting Around

TO/FROM THE AIRPORT
Bus

Air-conditioned airport bus A1 picks up from outside the arrivals area of Terminals 1, 2 and 3 every 40 minutes around the clock (Dhs4, one hour) and travels via Zayed Sports City and Al Wahda bus station into town, terminating at the **City Terminal** (Map p378; ☑ 02 644 8434; www.abudhabiairport.ae; 10th St; check-in fee adult/child Dhs30/20; ⊙24hr, buses every 40min) opposite Abu Dhabi Mall in Al Zahiyah. To the airport, it takes the same route in reverse.

To use the airport bus, purchase a Hafilat card (p389) from the vending machine at the airport terminal bus stop.

Taxi

Taxis cost Dhs75 to Dhs85 for the half-hour trip to the city centre, including flagfall of Dhs25. Only official airport taxis are allowed to pickup from the airport. Any Abu Dhabi taxi can drop-off.

CITY BUS

Abu Dhabi City Bus (www.dot.abudhabi.ae) operates on 14 routes around the clock. Between 6am and 11pm buses operate every 10 to 20 minutes (less frequent services 11pm to 6am). There is an excellent route map on the website.

Most fares are Dhs2 per ride within the city.

Useful bus lines include:

Bus 5 Marina Mall–Al Zahiyah–Al Maryah Island

Bus 54 Al Mina Fish Market–Al Zahiya–Sheikh Zayed Grand Mosque

Bus 94 Sheikh Zayed Grand Mosque–Al Wahda bus station–Al Zahiyah–Louvre Abu Dhabi

Bus 180 Al Wahda bus station–Downtown–Yas Mall and Ferrari World

TAXI

Taxis are metered and charge Dhs5 at flagfall (Dhs25 at the airport) plus Dhs1.82 per kilometre. Between 10pm and 6am the flagfall climbs to Dhs5.50. A Dhs12 minimum fare is in effect at all times. Cabs can be flagged down or ordered through the call centre (Dhs4 to Dhs5 fee).

Government-monitored Abu Dhabi Taxi runs metered taxis and also operates a ladies' cab

---

ABU DHABI TRANSPORT CARD

You need to purchase a Hafilat card (re-loadable transport card, Dhs5 plus money for fares) before using any bus. These are available from vending machines at bus stops and at Al Wahda bus station. Hold up your Hafilat card to the validator upon boarding and exiting the bus.

---

service. You can book either over the phone or, if you have a UAE phone number, by downloading the Abu Dhabi Taxi app. Taxis are available for wheelchair users.

Ride-hailing service Careem (www.careem. com) matches customers to private drivers closest to them. Cars can be booked online or via the app. It operates more or less like Uber (which was banned in Abu Dhabi in mid-2016) but follows strict guidelines on ride pricing and regularity fees.

EASTERN ABU DHABI EMIRATE إمارة أبو ظبي الشرقية

Al Ain العين

☑ 03 / POP 519,000

Fed by natural springs and set amid date-palm plantations, Al Ain was once a vital pit-stop on the caravan route between Oman and the Gulf and is the birthplace of the United Arab Emirates' founding father, Sheikh Zayed. This sprawling city, radiating out from the green heart of its central oasis, is a laid-back place. Its lack of ultramodern skyscrapers, preserved fort and smattering of Unesco World Heritage sites has given it a reputation as a cultural hub, while the zoo and Wadi Adventure water park are popular family destinations on the weekend. It's all loomed over by the craggy contours of Jebel Hafeet just south of town. Drive up the snaking road to the summit for sweeping views of the arid splendour of the Empty Quarter along the way.

⊙ Sights

Al Ain is confusing to navigate because of its many roundabouts. Brown signs directing visitors to the major tourist attractions are helpful, but a few more wouldn't hurt. Be on the lookout for His Highness Sheikh Khalifa

Bin Zayed Al Nahyan Masjid – this impressive new mosque, one of the UAE's largest, will hold some 20,000 worshippers when it is completed (pegged for 2019).

★ Al Ain Oasis
OASIS

(⌨ 03 712 8429; West (main) Gate; ⊘ 8am-5pm) **FREE** This tranquil world of wide paths meandering past walled date-palm gardens, right in the centre of Al Ain, is a welcome respite from the city hubbub. The UAE's first Unesco World Heritage site, the date plantations here contain around 150,000 trees of around 100 varieties. The oasis is still watered using the 3000-year-old *falaj* (irrigation channel) system; you can easily spot the channels as you're wandering around.

There are eight gates, but enter through the West Gate (just north of Al Ain Palace Museum, off Sultan Bin Zayed the First St), which acts as the main information centre for the oasis and gives out a decent free map of the plantation area. Beside the entrance is a small **eco-centre** containing multimedia exhibits (including a very flashy, multiscreen documentary that will keep the kids interested), which provide a historical grounding on Al Ain oasis as well as botanical information on date palms in general. The West Gate is also where you can **hire a bike** or organise a short **buggy tour**. In winter, there's also the option of horse and pony rides.

Al Jahili Fort
HISTORIC SITE

(Mohammed Bin Khalifa St; ⊘ 9am-7pm Tue-Thu & Sun, from 3pm Fri) **FREE** Surrounded by a lush park, this squat fort was constructed in the 1890s as the summer residence of Sheikh Zayed I (1836–1909) and expanded by the British in the 1950s. The original parts are the square fort in the far-left corner of the courtyard and the wedding-cake-tiered tower opposite. It won the prestigious Terra Award for the best earthen architecture in the world in 2016.

Al Ain Palace Museum
MUSEUM

(⌨ 03 751 7755; Al Ain St; ⊘ 8.30am-7.30pm Tue-Thu & Sat-Sun, from 3pm Fri) **FREE** This nicely restored, rambling palace was the residence of Sheikh Zayed, the UAE's founding father, from 1937 to 1966. There's frankly little to see inside, but the low-rise cinnamon-coloured compound, divided into private, guest and official quarters by courtyards and landscaped with cacti, magnolia trees and palms, is pleasant to wander around. You can step inside the *majlis* (reception room) where Zayed

received guests and snap a photo of the Land Rover he used to visit the desert Bedouin.

Qasr Al Muwaiji
HISTORIC BUILDING

(⌨ 03 767 4444; www.qasralmuwaiji.ae; Sheikh Khalifa Bin Zayed St; ⊘ 9am-7pm Tue-Thu & Sat-Sun, from 3pm Fri) **FREE** This carefully restored fort was the birthplace of Sheikh Khalifa Bin Zayed Al Nahyan, current president of the UAE. A stylised *falaj* marks the entrance while inside the thick mud-brick walls, a glass-walled display hall contains exhibits on the lives and leadership of both Sheikh Khalifa and his father, Sheikh Zayed, as well as the history of the fort itself. The hall leads to the northwest tower, Sheikh Khalifa's childhood home, which you can explore.

★ Jebel Hafeet
MOUNTAIN

This jagged 1240m-high limestone mountain rears out of the plain south of Al Ain. Its arid crags are home to red foxes, feral cats and the rock hyrax, which resembles a large rabbit but is, improbably, related to the elephant, as well as 5000-year-old single-chamber domed **tombs**, which are part of Al Ain's Unesco World Heritage sites. A 12km-long paved road – completely lit after dark – corkscrews to the **Mercure Grand Jebel Hafeet** (⌨ 03 704 6888; www.mercure. com; r from Dhs400; P ⊕ ⊛) hotel and a couple of coffeehouses at the summit.

There are several pullouts to admire the views along the way. The virulently green slopes at the bottom of the mountain are fed by **natural hot springs** emanating from the mountainside. A small resort with a lake and giant fountain has grown up around the springs, with segregated bathing, camping and picnicking opportunities.

The top of Jebel Hafeet is about 30km from central Al Ain, including the 12km stretch of mountain road. From the town centre, head west on Khalifa Bin Zayed St towards the airport, then follow the brown signs.

Hili Archaeological Park
ARCHAEOLOGICAL SITE

(Mohammed Bin Khalifa St, Hili; ⊘ 4-11pm) **FREE** These remarkable vestiges of a settlement and tombs dating back some 5000 years to the Umm Al Nar period open up a window on early life in the region. On the edge of town, they've been integrated into a peaceful park, and were designated as a Unesco World Heritage site in 2011. A highlight is the **Great Hili Tomb**, whose two entrances are decorated with carvings of humans and antelopes.

Al Ain & Buraimi

Al Ain Camel Market

MARKET

(Zayed Bin Sultan St; ⏱7am-sunset) **FREE** Dusty, noisy, pungent and chaotic: Al Ain's famous camel market is a full immersion in traditional Arab culture. All sorts of camels are holed up in pens, from wobbly legged babies that might grow up to be racers to imposing studs kept for breeding. The intense haggling is fun to watch. Trading takes place in the morning, but it's usually possible to see the corralled animals all day long.

🛏 Sleeping

City-dwellers decamp en masse for Al Ain on Thursday evenings for a weekend break at one of its big and slightly old-fashioned resorts. Room rates drop during the rest of the week.

Aloft Hotel

HOTEL **$**

(📞03 713 8888; www.marriott.com/hotels/travel/aanlo-aloft-al-ain; Al Ain Sq; r from Dhs380; 🛜) The cornerstone of the new Al Ain Square

AL AIN FOR KIDS

Al Ain Zoo (📞 03 799 2000; www.alainzoo.ae; off Zayed Al Awwal & Nahyan Al Awwal Sts; adult/child Dhs30/10; ⊘ 9am-8pm, longer in winter) Al Ain's remarkable zoo is the region's largest and most acclaimed; its spacious enclosures, inhabited by indigenous and exotic species, are impressively authentic. Observe grazing Arabian oryx, big-horned Barbary sheep, rhinos, hippos, tigers and lions and more. Some were born at the zoo, which has a well-respected conservation and breeding programme. Highlights include giraffe feedings, a fascinating walk-through lemur experience and the world's largest human-made safari, a 217-hectare landscape housing more than 250 African and Arabian animals.

Wadi Adventure (📞 03 781 8422; www.wadiadventure.ae; Jebel Al Hafeet St; admission adult/child/family Dhs65/45/150, attractions Dhs25-150; ⊘ 11am-7pm) Unleash your inner daredevil at this water park, which features the region's first human-made white-water kayaking facility (Dhs150) as well as surfing (from Dhs160) and wakeboarding (Dhs55). Admission buys access to pools, restaurants and a low-ropes course only.

Reserve online to book time slots for add-on activities and to check for the regular combo entry-and-activities special deals.

development, Aloft has quickly become the buzziest place to stay in town with its on-site bars, two of the city's most popular drinking holes. Staff are great and the contemporary rooms have funky retro features and huge walk-in showers, though cleaning standards aren't as vigorous as elsewhere in town.

Danat Al Ain Resort RESORT $$
(📞 03 704 6000; http://alain.danathotels.com; Al Salam St; r from Dhs760; 🅿 🛜 ❄ 🏊) Set within flowery gardens, this resort has a kid-focused pool area set up with slides and a separate one for swimming laps. Although furniture and facilities in the rooms are a tad bland, that won't matter much when you step out on your balcony and take in the view of Jebel Hafeet (request a front-facing room).

Al Ain Rotana Hotel RESORT $$
(📞 03 754 5111; www.rotana.com; Zayed Bin Sultan St; d from Dhs580; 🅿 🛜 ❄ 🏊) This behemoth of a hotel is Al Ain's most central lodging, with a big outdoor pool area and soaring atrium complete with fake palm trees. Spacious rooms all have balconies but rather dated beige furniture. Slightly more modern rooms are in the newer Falaj wing, set around five circular pools.

🍴 Eating & Drinking

Restaurants are scattered throughout the city. Al Ain Sq, west of the centre, is a new, up-and-coming cafe hub.

Cafeteria Al Mallah MIDDLE EASTERN $
(📞 03 755 6616; Mohammed Bin Khalifa St; sandwiches Dhs5-22, mains Dhs22-67; ⊘ 8.30am-midnight) This simple, spotless canteen serves reliable Lebanese staples, including succulent chicken shawarmas (meat sliced off a spit and stuffed in a pocket of pita-type bread with chopped tomatoes and garnish) and a kick-ass hummus with pine nuts.

★ Tanjore INDIAN $$
(📞 03 704 6000; Al Salam St, Danat Al Ain Resort; mains Dhs35-115; ⊘ 12.30-3pm & 7-11pm Tue-Sun; 🛜 🅿) This restaurant at the Danat Al Ain Resort will have your taste buds doing cartwheels. Tandoori (clay oven) specialities like tandoori fish tikka and favourites like fiery *chicken chettinad* (yoghurt-and-chilli-marinated chicken) rival any curry in India, but the menu's standout stars are vegetarian dishes such as *mirch baigan kasalan* (chillies and aubergines in a peanut and coconut sauce).

Jones The Grocer INTERNATIONAL $$
(📞 03 766 0115; www.jonesthegrocer.com; Hamdan Bin Mohd St, Al Ain Sq; mains Dhs58-85; ⊘ 8am-11pm Sun-Thu, from 9am Fri & Sat; 🛜 🅿) Come to this comfort-food haven for poshed-up fish and chips or Australian striploin steak, which feature on a menu that jumps from the Antipodes to Italy and onto Morocco. There are interesting salads as well for lighter bites – we like the goat's cheese and *freekeh* (roasted green wheat) salad with roasted pumpkin and beetroot.

Al Fanar EMIRATI $$
(📞 03 766 5200; www.alfanarrestaurant.com; Souq Al Zafarana; mains Dhs52-83; ⊘ 9am-10pm Sat-Wed, to midnight Thu, 9am-noon & 1-11pm Fri; 🛜) Part of a mini UAE chain, this is a good place to start if you're looking to dig into Emirati cuisine. Locals go for dishes such as *robyan*

biryani (shrimp with rice, onions and coriander), *samek mashwi* sea bream (grilled spiced whole fish), *jasheed* (minced baby shark with onions and spices) and various lamb-shank biryanis.

McGettigan's   IRISH PUB

(☑ 03 704 6174; www.mcgettigans.com; Al Salam St, Danat Al Ain Resort; ⊙ noon-2am Sat-Wed, to 4am Thu & Fri; ☏) Al Ain's most fun place to hang out for a few drinks, McGettigan's is the prime spot to catch sports on the big screen. It's also known for its bevy of regular events: Monday quiz night, Thursday live band and DJ and Friday brunch party (Dhs175 with unlimited drinks). There's good pub-grub too.

Rooftop   ROOFTOP BAR

(☑ 03 713 8888; www.therooftopalain.com; Al Ain Sq, Aloft Hotel; ⊙ 9am-2am; ☏) Al Ain's biggest party spot, Rooftop sits – you guessed it! – on top of the Aloft Hotel (p391) with views that stretch all the way to Jebel Hafeet. Happy hour between 5pm and 7pm has half-price drinks while Friday is party night with blasting house music once the sun sets.

ⓘ Information

The little **information centre** (☑ 03 711 8311; www.visitabudhabi.ae; Al Jahili Fort; ⊙ 9am-5pm Sat-Thu, from 3pm Fri) inside Al Jahili Fort has a good city map, a couple of glossy brochures and free *gahwa*.

ⓘ Getting There & Away

BUS

Al Ain's shiny central **bus station** (http://dot. abudhabi.ae; off Zayed Bin Sultan St) – shaped like a tent – sits near Al Ain Oasis opposite the market. Bus X90 shuttles back and forth to Abu Dhabi (Dhs30, 2¾ hours, every 45 minutes between 5.30am and 2am); Al Ghazal Transport runs buses between Al Ain and Dubai's Al Ghubaiba bus station (Dhs30, 2¼ hours, hourly between 5.40am and 11.40pm); and to get to Sharjah's Al Jubail bus station, take bus 118 (Dhs30, 2¾ hours, hourly between 6am and 11pm).

To use the X90, you need a Hafilat card (Dhs5), which can be purchased and topped-up at the ticket machines in the bus station. Tickets for Dubai and Sharjah are bought at the ticket counter.

CAR

From Dubai, it's 150km south to Al Ain via Hwy E66. Coming from Abu Dhabi, head east on Hwy E22 for about 160km. Europcar, Avis and Hertz are among the car-hire agencies with branches in Al Ain.

TAXI

Taxis, easily caught from the main taxi stand at the bus station, cost Dhs270 to Dubai or Dhs300 to Abu Dhabi. Shared taxis leave across the street from the bus station and are considerably cheaper (Dhs35 to Dubai or Sharjah, Dhs30 to Abu Dhabi).

ⓘ Getting Around

Al Ain has an extensive network of public buses that run roughly every 30 minutes from 5am to midnight at Dhs2 per trip. Check https://dot. gov.abudhabi/en (click through Public Transport to Bus Transportation and then Eastern Region Bus Services) for routes and schedules.

Taxis are metered; most in-town rides cost between Dhs12 and Dhs20 (minimum fare is Dhs12).

ⓘ CROSSING INTO OMAN

Al Ain rubs up against the town of Buraimi across the Omani border. Rules for which of the borders here can be used by foreign travellers change frequently. Check locally for the latest status; car-hire firms are usually good sources of information.

Travellers who are not citizens of countries in the Gulf Cooperation Council (GCC) must use either the Khatam Al Shukla border post 24km east of central Al Ain or the Mayzad border post, 25km south. The Mayzad border is the most efficient.

GCC citizens can use the Al Hili border, 7km north of downtown Al Ain and the more central Al Mudeef crossing.

Officially you need to apply online for your Oman visa beforehand through the Royal Oman Police website (www.evisa.rop.gov.om). A 10-day Oman visa costs Dhs50 (OR5) and confirmation by email usually takes 24 hours. There have been reports of Oman visas still being available to purchase at the Khatam Al Shukla border, though this could change at any time. For peace of mind, if you don't have time for a travel schedule muck-up, applying for the e-visa is a good idea.

There's a Dhs35 exit fee when leaving the UAE.

AL DHAFRA الظفرة

If you really want to get away from it all, steer your pony south and west of Abu Dhabi into this region, which is all desert, all the time. The desert is a land of contradictions: vast yet intimate, barren yet beautiful, searing yet restorative. In short, it's a special, spiritual, almost mystical place that's often so whisper-quiet that it feels as though someone has pushed the mute button. While the monotonous flat, grey plains you have to travel through for hours may not be much of an introduction, both Liwa Oasis, hemming the Empty Quarter, and Sir Bani Yas Island's wildlife reserve, off the far western coast, are worth the mind-numbing drive.

Madinat Zayed مدينة زايد

✏ 02 / POP 30,000

The scruffy town of Madinat Zayed, with its town centre a hotchpotch of dusty old buildings clashing with a handful of blocky modern developments, is not the most inspiring desert introduction. But this is the biggest town of the Al Dhafra region, en route to the Liwa Oasis, just past the Shams 1 Solar Plant (one of the largest in the world). There are good facilities along the main commercial strip with ATMs, shops, cafes and supermarkets, while one step removed from the hubbub, out in the desert itself, is the Tilal Liwa Hotel.

✦✦ Festivals & Events

Al Dhafra Festival   CULTURAL
(https://aldhafrafestival.ae; off Hwy E45; ⊙ late Dec) For 11 days, up to 25,000 long-legged dromedaries descend upon Madinat Zayed to take part in this hugely popular festival. Aside from camel races and the famous Mazayna (a camel beauty contest), there are other competitions involving falcons, classic cars, Arabian horses and salukis (dogs), along with heritage activities, auctions, a traditional souq and merriment of all sorts.

⌂ Sleeping & Eating

Tilal Liwa Hotel   RESORT $$
(✏ 02 894 6111; http://tilalliwa.danathotels.com; Million St; r from Dhs770; ℗ 🛜 🏊) Overlooking the dunes, this modern and comfortable fort-style retreat lets you count the colours of the desert through a giant arch spanning the infinity pool. Rooms are subtly accented with Middle Eastern touches, such as

Persian-style rugs and Moroccan metal lamps. Most have a balcony or terrace. Rates include free bike hire and sandboarding.

Il Cafe de Roma   CAFE $$
(Salama Bint Butti Rd (Hwy E45); mains Dhs30-56; ⊙ 8am-midnight; 🛜 🍴) This cafe with loungey chairs on the terrace, good espresso-based coffee and a short menu of pastries, sandwiches and pasta is the nicest place to stop for miles around if you need a break from the road on the drive between Abu Dhabi and Liwa Oasis. It's in the strip mall alongside the highway on the southern edge of town.

☆ Entertainment

Camel Race Track   SPECTATOR SPORT
(off Hwy E45) The camel races are the place to head to if you want to immerse yourself in local culture. Madinat Zayed's camel race track is just south of town and hosts regular races on Fridays between October and March.

ⓘ Getting There & Away

Madinat Zayed is about 180km southwest of Abu Dhabi via Hwy E11 west and E45 south. From here, it's another 45km to Mezairaa, the main town in the Liwa Oasis.

Bus X60 from Abu Dhabi to Mezairaa stops at Madinat Zayed twice a day each way as it runs through town. From Abu Dhabi (Dhs25, 2½ hours) it comes through at 11.30am and 10pm. From Mezairaa (Dhs15, one hour) it picks up at 6am and 4pm. Coming from Abu Dhabi, it stops directly opposite the **bus station** (http://dot.abudhabi.ae; Salama Bint Butti Rd (Hwy E45)) on the other side of the road.

To Mezairaa, there's also the more regular Bus 660 (Dhs15, one hour), which leaves roughly every two hours between 8am and 10pm from the bus station.

Liwa Oasis ليوا

A 150km arc of villages and farms, the Liwa Oasis hugs the edge of the Rub Al Khali (Empty Quarter) desert – an endless landscape of undulating sand dunes shimmering in shades of gold, apricot and pink.

This is the Arabia described by British explorer Sir Wilfred Thesiger, but it's also the birthplace of the Al Maktoum and Al Nahyan families, now the rulers of Dubai and Abu Dhabi respectively. Once you visit, you'll understand why the Liwa Oasis has a special place in the hearts of nationals, who come here to get back to their roots, relax and just take in the arid splendour of this glorious landscape.

The commercial heart of the oasis is Mezairaa, with activity centred on the junction of Hwy E43 from Madinat Zayed and Hwy E90, the main road through the oasis. Here you'll find a gas station, an ATM, a supermarket and a hospital.

◉ Sights

The Liwa Oasis is best visited in your own vehicle, as the joy of travelling here is to be able to drive through the villages and stop spontaneously to photograph a lone camel, a proud fort or a beautiful 'desert rose' (flower-like crystallised gypsum).

Along the main road (Hwy E90), the most spectacular stretch is between Hameem and Mezairaa. The dunes here are like shifting mountain ranges of sand, with green farms creating an occasional and unexpected patchwork effect. The landscape west of Mezairaa, towards Karima, is flatter and more open.

Moreeb Dune   DUNES
(Tal Moreeb; Moreeb Rd) The paved road out to the Moreeb Dune (Tal Moreeb) is a decent taster of desert scenery if you don't have a 4WD. This is the edge of the beautiful but fearsome Rub Al Khali and undulating, orange sand-dune fields rim both sides of the road along the route. The bitumen runs out at the foot of Tal Moreeb (the name translates as 'scary mountain'), one of the world's tallest dunes, soaring almost 300m high.

The area directly under the dune is unfortunately rather built up, with a camel race track and various buildings and porta-cabins that are used in the annual Liwa Sports Festival (p396), which spoils any romantic ideal of desert panoramas you may have had. Still, the dune scenery along the way out here makes the visit more than worthwhile. If you want more than this tantalising glimpse of desert majesty, you're going to need a 4WD.

To get to Moreeb Dune, turn left at the second roundabout, about 5km west of central Mezairaa, and keep right when you reach the old Liwa Resthouse building. Continue along this well-signposted, paved road for about 20 minutes; signs will say 'Moreeb Dune' or 'Tal Mireb'. The dune is where the road ends – you can't miss it!

LIWA ROAD TRIP STOP-OFF

Like a kooky mirage, a pyramid-shaped structure rises from the desert sands some 45km south of Abu Dhabi on the lonely highway that leads to the Liwa Oasis. The **Emirates National Auto Museum** (☑ 055 749 2155; www.enam.ae; Hwy E65; adult/child Dhs50/free; ⊗ 10am-6pm) holds the private car collection of Sheikh Hamad Bin Hamdan Al Nahyan, aka the 'Rainbow Sheikh': some 200 vehicles – from prototypes to concept cars to American classics – the oldest being a steam-powered 1885 Mercedes.

Dhafeer Fort   FORT
(E90 Hwy; ⊗ 24hr) **FREE** This modest fort is one of a handful of strongholds scattered throughout the oasis that once helped guard the area from attack by rival tribes. There's nothing to see inside, but it's worth a quick stop to climb the stairs to the roof for views of the surrounding dunes and to get an idea of the region's 19th-century mud-brick architecture.

☞ Tours

Arabian Tours   TOURS
(http://arabiantours.com; Mezairaa, Liwa Hotel; Liwa Adventure tour per person (min 2 ppl) Dhs300) The only specialist Liwa tour operator, this boutique firm offers a range of 4WD tours in the area. The 2½-hour 'Liwa Adventure' ventures into the vast dune fields past Tal Moreeb, offering up panoramas of sculpted red, orange and blush pink dunes at every turn. It's a brilliant snapshot of desert vistas if you're short on time.

With more time up your sleeve, opt for the overnight desert-camping tour, which explores the dune fields before settling down for the night at a simple but comfortable camp set up snug atop a dune surrounded by fantastic desert views.

Although most of this outfit's offerings are private tours, those on Friday and Saturday are usually run as group tours. For solo travellers, this is a godsend monetarily.

✷✷ Festivals & Events

Liwa Date Festival   FOOD & DRINK
(Liwa Oasis; ⊗ Jul) The quest for the best date is on at this weeklong festival, which also features cooking contests, a souq and a kids tent. These are accompanied by various

HEADING INTO THE RUB AL KHALI

The Rub Al Khali (Empty Quarter) is the world's longest uninterrupted sweep of sand dunes, traversing Saudi Arabia all the way down to Yemen, but its northern tip creeps into the United Arab Emirates, brushing against Liwa Oasis. Although you can get close-up views of the dune fields from the oasis – with the best vistas along the road to Moreeb Dune (p395) – you're not going to appreciate the sheer scope of this harsh, dramatic landscape unless you get out there among the dunes yourself.

Once the road runs out, the scale of the desert is revealed with mammoth rolling dunes, tinged delicate rose-pink to near-neon orange, swooping down to white-streaked salt pans and rippling out to the horizon.

Unless you've been properly trained in 4WD off-road driving and are fully equipped for desert safety measures, you're going to need to take a tour. For those who want to head away from the typical tour itineraries and have off-road driving skills, Arabian Tours (p395) offers a tag-along service, which gives you the peace of mind of an experienced desert driver leading you in convoy. Itineraries from half-day to weeks-long can be arranged. The firm also runs normal 4WD desert tours, rents 4WDs and runs desert-driving half-day courses.

competitions, including one for the most beautiful date (the fruit, that is).

Liwa Sports Festival SPORTS
(www.lsc.ae; Moreeb Dune area; ☺usually Jan) The large, flat area at the base of the Moreeb Dune (p395) is the staging ground of the Liwa Sports Festival, featuring car and bike races alongside shooting competitions, falcon and camel racing and a classic car show.

🛏 Sleeping

With the old Liwa Resthouse sadly closing its doors, there's no cheap digs left in Liwa Oasis.

Camping is hugely popular in the Liwa Oasis, although there are no designated campgrounds. If you do decide to camp, make sure to take out all your trash. Discarded rubbish, especially anything made of plastic, is highly dangerous when ingested by camels and other local wildlife.

Liwa Hotel HOTEL **$**
(☏ 02 882 2000; www.almarfapearlhotels.com/liwa; Mezairaa; r from Dhs445; 🅿🛇🗗) This comfortable hilltop contender set amid gardens offers dust-free respite after a day in the desert. Enjoy a sunset beer on your balcony facing a palace of the late Sheikh Zayed (itself on a green sand dune!). Big rooms have plenty of retro charm and the lobby restaurant dishes up a tasty menu of international favourites.

Qasr Al Sarab Desert Resort RESORT **$$$**
(☏ 02 886 2088; http://qasralsarab.anantara.com; 1 Qasr Al Sarab Rd; r from Dhs2500; 🅿🛇🗗) This

discreet retreat captures the desert vibe and blends seamlessly into its surroundings. Earth-toned rooms are decorated with original Bedouin artefacts – as is the resort throughout – and have balconies looking out over the dunes. There are three restaurants, two bars, a relaxing spa, a library, a huge free-form swimming pool with canopied day beds and various outdoor activities.

It's near Hameem, with nothing at all around it, but as the resort organises its own batch of desert experiences – including desert walks, 4WD tours and horse rides, fat-biking on the dunes and falcon shows – you're at no risk of getting bored.

🍴 Eating

There's (unsurprisingly) little choice here in terms of dining options. The main E45 Hwy as you enter Mezairaa has a scattering of small canteens along its length.

Green Liwa Oasis INTERNATIONAL **$$**
(☏ 02 882 2000; Mezairaa, Liwa Hotel; mains Dhs63-115; ☺24hr; 🖢) It may look like a rather bland hotel-lobby restaurant – sit outside on the terrace overlooking the garden and pool if the weather's cool enough – but the Liwa Hotel's sole eating option serves up a tasty menu of generously portioned global favourites. The chicken curry and the mezze platter are both good choices. Beers cost from Dhs33.

★ Suhail STEAK **$$$**
(☏ 02 886 2088; www.qasralsarab.anantara.com; near Hameem, off E90 (Liwa Rd), Qasr Al Sarab Desert Resort; mains Dhs120-500; ☺dinner

7-10.30pm, cocktails from 4pm; ☎) You really don't get more romantic than sitting on Su-hail's terrace with the rolling dunes as your backdrop. The Qasr Al Sarab Desert Resort's fine-dining restaurant serves up an international menu of steaks and more modern-creative mains like duck with yuzu and passionfruit gel. There's an excellent wine list to pair with your meal.

If you're not a guest at the resort, booking beforehand is essential. It's well worthwhile getting here for pre-dinner cocktails to watch the sun set over the desert.

ⓘ Getting There & Away

BUS

Bus X60 travels to **Mezairaa bus station** (http://dot.abudhabi.ae; main roundabout, Hwy E45 & E90) from Abu Dhabi (Dhs30, 3¼ hours) via Madinat Zayed at 9am and 7.30pm daily. It makes the return trip from Mezairaa bus station at 5.10am and 3.10pm. Bus 660 shuttles between Mezairaa and Madinat Zayed bus stations (Dhs15, one hour) roughly every two hours between 8am and 9pm.

Taxis (no meter or taxi signage) wait at the bus station for passengers.

CAR

All the main roads are fit for 2WD vehicles, but you'll need a 4WD to go off-road.

Coming from Abu Dhabi, head west on Hwy E11 and turn south on Hwy E65 to Hameem or E45 to go via Madinat Zayed. The total trip is 250km either way. There are petrol stations on Hwy E65 at the Emirates National Auto Museum, in Tarif on Hwy E11 and in Madinat Zayed. In the Liwa Oasis, you'll find gas in Hameem, in Mezairaa, near the Khanur turnoff, and in Umm Hisin.

From Jebel Dhanna/Ruwais, the long and lonely Hwy E15 also goes to the oasis; petrol is available in Ghayathi.

ⓘ Getting Around

From Mezairaa, local bus 640 travels west along Hwy 90 as far as Arrada Farms, while bus 650 goes east to Hammeem Farms. There is no public transport to Moreeb Dune.

Jebel Dhanna   جبل الظنة

The jumping-off point for wildlife-watching on Sir Bani Yas Island, Jebel Dhanna is also home to white-sand beaches and shallow azure water, great for the kids to splash about.

Getting here, however, means driving on the relentlessly tedious, 350km-long dual-carriage E11 highway that links Abu

Dhabi with Sila on the Saudi Arabia border. It's a forlorn, unchanging panorama of flat plains the entire way with the road flanked by stunted-looking palm trees and fences, beyond which lie the emirate's rich oil and gas fields.

If you need to break the journey, the low-key town of Mirfa with its tidy waterfront promenade is the best place to stop. The industrial town of Ruwais, an hour past Mirfa, exists only to service the massive refineries in the area and its blocky march of apartment buildings provides little inspiration.

ⓘ Getting There & Away

As remote as it is, there are buses going out here from Abu Dhabi's central bus station. Bus X87 makes the trip all the way to the Muhurraq ferry terminal to Delma Island in Jebel Dhanna, going via Mirfa and Ruwais bus station (Dhs35, four hours, four daily).

From Ruwais bus station, local bus 881 trundles past the Dhafra Beach Hotel in Jebel Dhanna on its route (Dhs2, 15 minutes, seven daily); and local bus 882 runs to and from the Sir Bani Yas Island ferry terminal in Jebel Dhanna (Dhs4, 30 minutes, every one to two hours).

If you're driving, note that, even though the region is surrounded by oil fields, there's a dearth of petrol stations, so take every opportunity to refuel – Hwy E11 is not a good place to run out of gas.

Sir Bani Yas Island   جزيرة صير بنى ياس

In the country's remote far west, this 87-sq-km desert island with its craggy interior swooping down to acacia-studded plains was originally the private retreat of UAE founding father Sheikh Zayed. His love of animals inspired him to turn it into a wildlife reserve and bring many native species back from the brink of extinction. Today, 60% of the island is home to 13,000 free-roaming indigenous and introduced animals, including the world's largest herd of the endangered Arabian oryx, sand gazelles, Barbary sheep, Indian blackbuck and even giraffes and cheetahs.

Abu Dhabi's royal family maintains two palaces on the island, but if they forgot your invitation, you can visit by staying (or booking an activity-and-lunch package) at one of the island's three resorts. The unique wildlife-viewing opportunities combined with lunar-scape vistas are a highlight of the UAE. If you're going to splash out just once on your trip, make it here.

 Activities & Tours

The wildlife drive and wildlife walks are the most popular activities here, but there's also mountain biking, horse riding, kayaking and short wadi hikes exploring the harshly beautiful island interior.

Without staying overnight, you can also visit if you pre-book one activity plus lunch at one of the island's restaurants.

Nature & Wildlife Drive   DRIVING
(📞 02 801 5266; adult/child Dhs315/125; ⊙tours 6.30am, 8.30am, 10.30am, 3pm & 5pm) If you only do one thing while on Sir Bani Yas, make it this 90-minute 4WD safari around the wildlife park that makes up the interior of the island. You'll get great viewing of the park's free-roaming animals, including the flourishing population of Arabian oryx, sand and mountain gazelles, Barbary sheep, cheetahs and giraffes.

Guides are very knowledgeable about the fauna and flora and go out of their way to find the best viewing spots. Book an early-morning or late-afternoon tour, when the animals are at their most active.

Wadi Walk   HIKING
(adult/child Dhs185/95; ⊙6.30am, 8.30am & 5pm) One of the best ways to get up close to the visceral beauty of Sir Bani Yas' landscapes are these 90-minute walks, with highly knowledgeable guides. They'll take you on a trail through the island's mountain wadis (valley or river bed, often dry except after heavy rainfall) where the rock faces are streaked crimson, yellow and mauve from mineral deposits.

Sir Bani Yas Stables   HORSE RIDING
(rides Dhs315-625; ⊙rides 6am, 6.30am, 8.30am, 5pm & 7pm) For an intimate nature encounter, confident riders can tour the wildlife park on horseback while beginners can take a scenic ride along the beach. At the state-of-the-art Sir Bani Yas stables, guides will match the horse to your level of experience and kit you out with shoes, chaps and a helmet before taking you out to explore.

Anantara Spa   SPA
(📞02 801 5400; www.anantara.com; Desert Islands Resort & Spa; massages from Dhs565; ⊙10am-10pm) Choose from an extensive massage and treatment menu to work out the kinks and turn you into a glowing centre of tranquillity. Options include a Thai herbal compress massage, 45-minute body scrubs and a two-hour detoxifying and cleansing experience.

🛏️ Sleeping

The three Anantara-run resorts are the only lodging options on Sir Bani Yas Island. Each has its own ambience. Al Sahel is fantastic for wildlife and nature fans, beach bums can't beat Al Yamm and the bigger Desert Islands is best for families. Check online for deals. Room rates drop hugely outside of November to April.

⭐**Al Sahel Villa Resort**   RESORT $$$
(📞02 801 4300; www.anantara.com; r from Dhs1800; 🛜❄️) Offering laid-back luxury with gazelles and peacocks grazing on the lawn out front, Al Sahel resort sits on the island's west, surrounded by the scrubland of the reserve, with fantastic wildlife-spotting at your doorstep. Each of the 30 safari-chic airy villas comes with thatched African-style roof, open-beam cathedral ceiling, four-poster bed and a wide, canvas-shaded terrace (many with private plunge-pool).

Al Yamm Villa Resort   RESORT $$$
(📞02 801 4200; www.anantara.com; villas from Dhs1800; 🛜❄️) With *barasti* (palm-leaf) detailing and private terraces opening onto the sand (many with private plunge-pool), this cluster of villas overlooking the sea and mangroves is imbued with easygoing beach glamour at every turn. Bonus points for the chic bathrooms with freestanding oval tubs and opulent shower-rooms. Wriggle your toes in the soft sand and count the flamingos flapping over sea.

Desert Islands Resort & Spa   RESORT $$$
(📞02 801 5400; www.anantara.com; r from Dhs1350; 🛜❄️) Sheikh Zayed's old guest house – an atmospheric mix of art deco and mid-20th-century glamour with common areas home to much of the original furnishings – forms the central hub of Sir Bani Yas' main resort. You'll sleep sweetly in elegant, oversized rooms with tasteful regional art and big balconies overlooking the flower-filled garden, free-form infinity pool and the sea.

Eating

Each of the resorts has its own restaurant, and resort staff will arrange complimentary transport to any of them.

Savannah Grill & Lounge
AFRICAN $$$

(☑ 02 801 5400; www.anantara.com; Al Sahel Villa Resort; mains Dhs160-310; ⊘ noon-11pm; 🐾)
Bringing a fine-dining touch to the flavours of Africa, the restaurant of Al Sahel Villa Resort is a treat for even the most well-travelled palates. Dig into giant South African mushrooms on a bed of cornbread and strawberry chilli jam, braai-grilled (barbecued) Mozambique tiger prawns and venison loin or a Nigerian snack-platter with sweet potatoes and guinea-fowl 'lollipops'.

Olio
ITALIAN $$$

(☑ 02 801 5400; www.anantara.com; Al Yamm Villa Resort; mains Dhs65-250; ⊘ 7am-10.30pm; 🐾🖰)
It's all about seaside views and breezy Mediterranean style at Al Yamm Villa Resort's restaurant, where the Italian menu runs from porcini pizza drizzled with white truffle oil to salmon doused in mustard sauce. There are good pasta and sandwich options, too, for something lighter.

🛈 Getting There & Away

BOAT

Boats make the 20-minute trip to Sir Bani Yas Island from the plush ferry terminal in Jebel Dhanna at noon, 3pm, 6pm and 11pm with an extra 10.30am trip on Fridays. A car or minivan then whisks you to the resorts (another 15 to 20 minutes). You book your boat time after your hotel reservation has been confirmed.

BUS

Bus X87 from Abu Dhabi doesn't make it as far along the Jebel Dhanna peninsula as the Sir Bani Yas ferry, but you can get off the bus in Ruwais (Dhs35, 3½ hours, four daily) and then catch local bus 882, which runs through Ruwais bus station, all the way to the ferry terminal at Jebel Dhanna's tip (Dhs4, 30 minutes, every one to two hours).

CAR

The Jebel Dhanna ferry jetty is about a 250km drive west of Abu Dhabi and 370km southwest of Dubai via Hwy E11. Past Ruwais, follow the signs to the jetty.

If you want someone else to do the driving, ask the resort where you're staying to arrange a limo service, which starts at Dhs650 from Abu Dhabi and Dhs1000 from Dubai.

FUJAIRAH & THE EASTERN COAST
الفجيرة والساحل الشرقي

Time has always seemed to move more slowly in the UAE's east, where the narrow coastline quickly gives way to the Hajar Mountains' rocky contours. Today, this low-key vibe is changing with a handful of new resorts in the Al Aqah area and more tourism development on the way – including a plan to create the longest coral garden in the world.

Away from the beach, this region remains one of the best places to dust off your hiking shoes and explore. Dibba's hikes and climbs remain well below most travellers' radars but offer vistas of craggy, barren beauty at every turn while kayaking amid Kalba's protected mangrove forests is a tranquil, wildlife-filled respite from city razzmatazz.

Facing the Indian Ocean, the east coast belongs mostly to Fujairah emirate, interrupted by the Sharjah enclaves of Kalba, Khor Fakkan and Dibba Al Hisn with Omani Dibba Al Baya only accessible from here.

Fujairah City
الفجيرة

🗹 09 / POP 97,226

As the bare, rugged foothills of the Hajar Mountains give way to the coast, Fujairah City's line of mid-rises and office blocks rises up from the arid plain. The commercial hub for Fujairah emirate, its busy main street, Hamad Bin Abdullah Rd, is a muddle of worn strip-malls and semi-flashier glass and steel running down to the sea while the northern waterfront is hemmed in by vast fields of circular oil-storage containers. It's not the prettiest place in the world, but it's worth a look as you pass through for the archaeological collection housed in its old-fashioned museum and the tiny fort, looking decidedly out of place on the edge of the city sprawl.

👁 Sights

Fujairah Fort
HISTORIC SITE

(cnr Al Nakheel & Al Salam Rds; ⊘ approx 9am-5pm Sat-Thu, from 2.30pm Fri) **FREE** Enter the double-turret gate of the fort compound with its vestiges of Fujairah's old village and spy this dollhouse of a fort, draped over a rocky mound. Built from mud, gravel, wood and gypsum in the 16th century, it's a compact composition of circular and square towers that aided in the town's defence.

Fujairah

Fujairah

◎ Sights

🛏 Sleeping

✕ Eating

🛍 Shopping

Fujairah Museum MUSEUM

(📞 09 222 9085; cnr Al Nakheel & Al Salam Rds; adult/child Dhs5/1; ⊕ 8am-6.30pm Sat-Thu, from 2.30pm Fri) This old-school local-history museum holds a wealth of significant archaeological finds from local sites at Badiyah, Dibba and Qidfa inside its two ornate halls, with baroque-style ceilings and dangling chandeliers. The examples of Bronze Age soft-stone vessels and pot lids, all intricately decorated with geometric designs, are particularly impressive. The ethnographic section, crammed into two smaller rooms, is ho-hum with some pretty Bedouin jewellery and various dioramas depicting traditional market stalls and scenes from Fujairah's fishing industry.

Sheikh Zayed Mosque MOSQUE

(cnr Al Ittihad & Al Salam Sts) Fujairah's grand mosque is the second largest in the UAE, after the one in Abu Dhabi. Festooned with six 100m-high minarets, the white granite and marble edifice can accommodate up to 28,000 worshippers. It's not open to non-Muslims, but the impressive exterior alone warrants a look, especially when it's lit up at night.

Al Hayl Fort HISTORIC SITE

(⊕ 8.30am-1pm & 4.30-6.30pm Sat-Thu, from 2.30pm Fri) FREE Built around 1830, this small, well-preserved fort is tucked deep into the jagged Hajar Mountains near the village of Al Hayl, about 13km southwest of Fujairah. Constructed from mud-brick and plaster, it's a good example of traditional architecture. There's not much inside, but the surrounding views of the palm-speckled valley backed by mountains – best seen when the sun is low – make it worth a visit. There's usually a caretaker to show you around (tip appreciated).

🛏 Sleeping

Novotel Fujairah　　　　　　　　HOTEL **$**
(☑ 09 203 4851; Hamad Bin Abdullah Rd; r from
Dhs350; P 🛜 ≋) Central and well run, the
Novotel is your best bet if you're planning
to bed down in Fujairah City. The bright,
comfortable rooms have a funky teal-and-
grey theme and come with good-sized bathrooms, plus there's a modern gym, swimming pool and a kids club.

Ibis Fujairah　　　　　　　　　　HOTEL **$**
(☑ 09 223 9997; www.accorhotels.com; Hamad
Bin Abdullah Rd; r from Dhs250; P 🛜 ≋) The
Ibis provides small, well-maintained rooms
with bright red tile details in the bathroom.
Guests have access to all the facilities at the
adjoining Novotel (with its entrance just
around the corner).

🍴 Eating & Drinking

Nalukettu　　　　　　　　SOUTH INDIAN **$**
(☑ 09 222 3070; Hamad Bin Abdullah Rd, City
Plaza Hotel; mains Dhs18-45; ⊗ noon-3pm &
6.30pm-midnight; 🛜) The decor is a bit worn,
but the pungently flavoured dishes from the
South Indian province of Kerala are fresh
and authentic in this licensed restaurant
at the City Plaza Hotel. Menu stars include
the prawns masala and the *meen moily*
(Kerala-style fish curry in a coconut sauce).
During busy times, the staff can be a bit
overwhelmed.

Al Meshwar　　　　　MIDDLE EASTERN **$$**
(☑ 09 222 1113; Hamad Bin Abdullah Rd; mezze
Dhs15-35, mains Dhs35-75; ⊗ 9am-1am; 🛜 ☑)
It's easy to spot this popular local joint, with
its weird crazy-brick exterior and arched
upstairs windows – and you'll be glad of
it, for the Middle Eastern staples here are
finger-licking good. Make a meal out of a
few mezze plates or go for one of the grills.
There's a shisha lounge downstairs, and a
family dining area upstairs.

McGettigan's FJR　　　　　　　IRISH PUB
(☑ 09 224 4880; www.mcgettigans.com; Tennis
& Country Club; ⊗ noon-1am; 🛜) McGettigan's
has injected some much-needed pizzazz into
Fujairah's nightlife. Events such as happy
hour, quiz night and open-mic night bring
in the punters, as does the pub fare, from
burgers to fish and chips.

🔒 Shopping

Fujairah City Centre　　　　　　　MALL
(www.citycentrefujairah.com; Sheikh Khalifa Bin
Zayed Hwy; ⊗ 10am-11pm Sun-Wed, to midnight
Thu & Fri; 🛜) Fujairah's biggest and most
modern mall has a Carrefour supermarket
for all your road-trip snacking needs, the
usual international-chain restaurants, a
multiplex 3D cinema and Magic Planet in-
door amusement park.

Central Souq　　　　　　　　　MARKET
(⊗ 8am-9pm) Foodies looking for dates to
bring home should pop into this market
hall, with its spice, produce, meat and fish
stalls, at the bottom of Fujairah's main strip,
Hamad Bin Abdullah Rd.

ℹ Getting There & Away

BUS

From Dubai, bus E700 (www.dubai-buses.com,
Dhs25, two hours) runs between Dubai's Union
Square station to central Fujairah roughly every

LOCAL KNOWLEDGE

BULL BUTTING

Every Friday evening in the cooler months, the unusual spectacle of **Bull Butting** (Fujairah
Corniche; ⊗ approx 5pm Fri Nov-Apr) takes place in a muddy patch off the Fujairah corniche:
the ancient sport of bull butting. In the arena, two sumo-sized, humpbacked animals lock
horns and pit their strength against each other as hundreds of locals cheer them on.

　　The first animal to back away loses, which usually takes a couple of minutes. If neither
does, handlers will separate the beasts with ropes. Little harm comes to the bulls beyond
a sore head and dented pride. There is no prize money, but a win increases the value of
the bull and brings honour to its owner.

　　The origin of the sport, which is even more popular in Oman, is disputed, with one
theory saying that it was introduced by the Portuguese, although it's possible that the
tradition goes back a lot further. Today it is upheld by two local clubs, who take turns to
host the fights.

　　The ground is just south of the 'Hand Roundabout' (look for the huge fleet of parked
SUVs). The action starts from about 5pm.

WORTH A TRIP

SHOPPING AT MASAFI

Despite the name, **Masafi Friday Market** (Masafi; ⊙8am-10pm), a strip of nearly identical stalls, is actually a daily affair, though it's at its bustling best on its namesake day. Rugs, pottery, household goods and knick-knacks are for sale, but it's best for stocking up on local produce and also makes a nice photo-op. The market is on Hwy E88 from Dubai towards the eastern coast.

90 minutes. For the return journey, it departs from a **bus stand** (Hamad Bin Abdullah Rd) just east of Choithrams Supermarket.

From Sharjah's Al Jubail station, buses 116 and 116E depart for Fujairah (Dhs25, two hours) via Dhaid (Dhs15) and Masafi (Dhs20) every 30 minutes. Bus 116 carries on to Khor Fakkan while the 116E finishes at Kalba.

All these services drop off passengers on Hamad Bin Abdullah Rd in Fujairah.

CAR

The scenic Sheikh Khalifa Hwy (Hwy E84) cuts through the Hajar Mountains and reaches Dubai in just over an hour. It meets the old Hwy E89 (via Masafi) near Al Hayl on the western outskirts of Fujairah.

TAXI

It's around Dhs180 to Dhs200 for a taxi from Sharjah city to Fujairah and Dhs250 from Dubai.

🛈 Getting Around

Taxis have a minimum Dhs10 fare. Most rides within Fujairah City cost between Dhs10 and Dhs14.

Khor Fakkan   خورفكان

☑09 / POP 33,500

Khor Fakkan is not without its charms, especially along its well-maintained corniche, which runs the full length of the waterfront. It's good for a stop to stretch your legs if you're driving up the coast. The city, though, is dominated by its super-busy container port. At times, an entire armada of ships can be seen on the horizon, queuing to dock, unload or refuel.

🛏 Sleeping & Eating

Oceanic Khorfakkan
Resort & Spa   HOTEL **$$**
(☑09 238 5111; www.sharjahnationalhotel.com/oceanic-khorfakkan-resort; Al Mufidi St; r from

Dhs550; P🅿🛜🏊) This Khor Fakkan landmark, with its distinctive rooftop rotunda, is still going strong thanks to package-tour deals. Yes, it's a bit (well, a lot) dated, but the good-sized rooms all have sea views, and the well-maintained pool area and sickle-shaped private beach are sun-slouching bliss.

Rebou Lebanon   MIDDLE EASTERN **$**
(☑09 238 2522; Corniche Rd; mezze Dhs12-25, mains Dhs25-45; ⊙11am-midnight; 🛜🅿) Right on the corniche, this little place is a winner for its mezze menu and hearty biryanis with chicken or fish. Despite the name (and the prominent cedar tree on the sign above the door), Rebou also serves up pasta and a variety of steaks on a menu page titled 'West Food'. We'd suggest sticking to the Middle Eastern dishes.

🛈 Getting There & Away

The 116 bus leaves for Sharjah (Dhs25, 2½ hours) via Fujairah (Dhs5, 20 minutes) hourly between 8.45am and 1.45am from a signposted **bus stand** on the edge of Khor Fakkan.

Al Aqah   العقة

Al Aqah is the sun-worshipper haven of Fujairah emirate, with its golden-sand beaches flanked by a smattering of high-end resorts devoted to seaside relaxation. Waters are generally calm and temperatures pleasant even in winter, making this prime swimming and snorkelling territory. The area is pegged for plenty of further development with construction on 'The Address', a luxury resort and villa complex, already in the works at the southern end of town.

Just offshore is Snoopy Island, named by some clever soul who thought the shape of this rocky outcrop about 100m off the coast resembled the *Peanuts* cartoon character sleeping atop his doghouse (it doesn't).

🛏 Sleeping

⭐**Intercontinental Fujairah**   RESORT **$$**
(☑09 209 9999; www.ihg.com; Dibba Rd, Hwy E99; r from Dhs700; P🅿🛜🏊) The Intercontinental swaggered onto the Al Aqah scene in 2017 and has been wowing beachgoers ever since. Fujairah hasn't seen sophistication like this before: it's lavish yet subtle and completely contemporary, from its airy marble-clad foyer to the guest rooms, each with spacious balcony, modern art and a big brass lamp dangling over the bed.

BADIYAH بادية

Considered the oldest mosque in the UAE, **Al Badiyah Mosque** (Dibba Rd, Hwy E99; ⊙9am-5pm), a curvaceous, squat mud-brick structure, dates to 1446. It's adorned with four pointed domes and rests on a single internal pillar. Badiyah (also spelt Bidyah and Bidiya), 8km north of Khor Fakkan, is famous for its bijou structure. Non-Muslims are free to enter but must be modestly dressed and remove their shoes; women must also cover their hair. Headscarves and *abayas* (a robe-like dress worn by women) can be borrowed from the attendant.

The inside prayer hall, with colourful rugs laid out on palm-leaf plaited matting and Qurans stacked into the niches of its smooth plastered walls, has a tranquil, contemplative feel. Note the simple geometric designs on the domes and the minbar (mosque pulpit) made from stones and coral-block. The mosque is built into a low hillside along the coastal road just north of Badiyah village and guarded by two ruined watchtowers. It's well worth walking up here for the sweeping views of the Hajar Mountains and the Gulf.

Fujairah Rotana Resort & Spa RESORT **$$**
(☑09 244 9888; www.rotana.com; Dibba Rd, Hwy E99; r from Dhs850; 🅿 🛜 🌊) This sprawling, low-slung resort, with its palm-tree gardens and well-maintained beach, has a tranquil, family-friendly vibe. Classically furnished rooms, nearly all with spacious balconies, look out towards the sea, while poolside there's a wealth of shaded seating plus a water slide, children's pool and kids club to keep wee ones busy.

ⓘ Getting There & Away

Al Aqah has no public transport to or from town. A taxi from Fujairah costs around Dhs90.

Dibba دبا

Sitting snugly between orange-tinged, rugged mountains and the sea, Dibba town is a geopolitical oddity straddling not only two different emirates but also across the border into Oman's Musandam Peninsula.

At its southern end, Dibba Al Fujairah has a resort-speckled coastline that meanders into a slightly shabby town centre inland. Sharjah-owned Dibba Al Hisn, squeezed in the middle, is shipshape and orderly thanks to major government investment in recent years. Directly across the border, Oman's Dibba Al Baya is a ragtag collection of buildings running parallel to a gorgeous sweep of beach with a bijou fishing port plonked in the middle.

This dusty Omani outpost is a launching-pad for exploring the Musandam's stark mountain scenery or taking to the water to admire it all while chilling out aboard a dhow. To experience this dramatic landscape, book activities with an operator based in Dibba Al Baya; independent travel is not allowed.

🏃 Activities

Absolute Adventure OUTDOORS
(☑Dubai office 04 392 6463; www.adventure.ae; Dibba Al Baya, Oman; Secret Staircases hike/Aqaba–Lima hike per person Dhs435/875; ⊙Sep-May) This Dubai-based outdoor adventure company offers assorted activities exploring the jagged contours of the coastal mountains on Dibba's Omani side. There's hiking, biking and rock climbing as well as deep-water soloing (sea-cliff rock climbing) and camping on Dibba beach. Along with private trips, the company organises regular group excursions (usually on Fridays). Check the Facebook page (https://www.facebook.com/absoluteadventureuae) for trip announcements.

The popular **Secret Staircases** and **Aqaba–Lima** hikes are great introductions to the Musandam Peninsula's stark, beguiling beauty; both are suitable for kids. The Secret Staircases trail heads inland to the mountains, traversing rock-cut stairs to abandoned ridgetop villages with terraced fields once used by farmers, plus ancient petroglyphs. The Aqaba–Lima trail starts with a boat ride to the trailhead before following a series of ledges and rock-cut stairs up to another abandoned mountain village with craggy coastal scenery the entire way.

All activities should be booked two days beforehand so that the required Dibba entry permits can be organised.

Al Marsa DIVING
(☑in Oman +968 26 836 550; www.almarsamusandam.com; Dibba Port, Dibba Al Baya, Oman;

2-night dhow trip per person Dhs1600; ⏲8am-1pm & 3-6pm) Based at Dibba Port in the Omani section of town, this reliable local dhow and diving operator offers a wide range of PADI courses, dive excursions and private dhow trips. It also organises a two-night group dhow excursion that departs on Thursdays.

Sheesa Beach CRUISE
(☎in Oman +968 26 836551; www.sheesabeach.com; Dibba Port, Dibba Al Baya, Oman; shared dhow trip per person Dhs150; ⏲8am-5pm) If you don't have the dirhams for a private dhow excursion, this outfit, based in the Omani section of Dibba, runs a weekly group dhow cruise on Fridays along the coastline of the Musandam Peninsula. It sails at 11.45am and comes back into dock at 5.30pm.

Sheesa Beach also organises private dhow trips and dive excursions.

Sleeping

Most visitors come here on day trips but if you want to stay overnight, Dibba Al Fujairah has a handful of resorts along the coast. Absolute Adventure (p403) can organise camping on Dibba Al Baya beach (from Dhs275 per person), complete with campbeds in the tent, separate tent with chemical toilet and cooking equipment if you want to cook for yourself.

Royal Beach Hotel RESORT $$
(☎09 244 9444; www.royalbeach.ae; Dibba Rd (Hwy E99), Dibba Al Fujairah; d from Dhs820; 🛜🏊) This old-fashioned, salmon-pink resort sits on a stretch of sand facing Dibba Rock, a popular diving and snorkelling site thanks to its shallow coral gardens. On-site outfitter **Freestyle Divers** rents gear, and offers dive trips and PADI courses. All rooms have a private terrace facing a manicured lawn and the hotel's private beach, strewn with palm-leaf umbrellas.

The hotel is 8km south of Dibba.

Radisson Blu Resort, Fujairah RESORT $$
(☎09 244 9700; www.radissonblu.com; Dibba Rd (Hwy E99), Dibba Al Fujairah; d from Dhs640; P🛜🏊) With its modest entrance and generic lobby, the Radisson may not wow instantly, but it's an immaculately kept, full-service resort with five swimming pools, a super-long private beach and several good restaurants. Even the standard rooms are large, and all have sea-facing balconies.

It's 7km south of Dibba.

Eating

There are simple restaurants along the corniche in Dibba Al Hisn (Sharjah) and clustered along Hwy E89 in Dibba Al Fujairah. For something fancier, head to the resort restaurants on Hwy E99.

Across the border in Dibba Al Baya, it's more slim-pickings on the food front. With advance booking, Absolute Adventure (p403) can arrange lunch or dinner, often using fish fresh from the market at Dibba Al Baya's port.

Omani Foods Restaurant & Kitchen OMANI $
(Corniche Rd, Dibba Al Baya, Oman; dishes Dhs8-35) You wouldn't know it from its ramshackle appearance – or its exceedingly snappy name

TRAVELLING INTO OMANI DIBBA AL BAYA

The Dibba border post is not an official crossing into Oman, and there is no border checkpoint on the Oman side, so there are special rules for entering Omani territory here.

You cannot enter the Omani side of Dibba (Dibba Al Baya) as an independent traveller. All people entering here need to have a free permit, which is provided by any of Dibba Al Baya's tour operators when you make a booking. The process is exceedingly easy for those on UAE tourist visas. When booking your activities, email a copy of your passport photo page and UAE entry stamp page to the tour operator; they will then organise the permit and meet you at the border with it in hand.

Dibba Al Baya's operators typically ask for 48 hours' notice but can usually rustle up a permit within 24 hours for last-minute bookings. Note that for UAE foreign residents, the process is slightly more complicated and does require 48 hours.

When exiting Dibba Al Hisn on the UAE side of town, your passport and permit will be checked at the UAE border checkpoint but will not be exit-stamped.

As you have not been stamped out of the UAE or stamped into Oman, the only way to exit is back through the same border point.

– but this is the best joint on the Omani side of town for a meal. There are absolutely no frills, but the kitchen serves up simple, tasty grilled meat and seafood dishes.

ℹ️ Getting There & Away

There's no public transport to Dibba, so you'll need to either rent a car or hire a taxi. If you're renting a car and heading to Dibba Al Baya on the Omani side, you will not be allowed to drive it across the border unless you have already purchased Omani car insurance from the car-hire firm, as you cannot buy it on the border. Most people simply park the hire car at the car park next to the border crossing on the UAE side and head through the checkpoint in their Dibba Al Baya tour operator's vehicle.

Kalba كلباء

The Sharjah enclave of Kalba, about 15km south of Fujairah City on the Omani border, is famous for its creek (Khor Kalba), a pastiche of mangroves, tidal creeks and sandy beaches that are a birders' paradise. A key breeding ground for rare bird species, including the white-collared kingfisher and the Sykes's warbler, the area is also a wintering spot for the Indian pond heron.

In 2012, the Sharjah government closed access to Khor Kalba, whose fragile habitat had become threatened by a growing influx of off-road drivers and dune bikers, with plans to develop the area into an ecotourism destination with a visitor centre, sea turtle rehabilitation centre, campground and sustainable outdoor adventures. The opening of the exclusive Kingfisher Lodge in 2018 is the first completed phase of the plan. For a less expensive way of experiencing the mangrove environment and its wildlife, take a kayaking trip with Absolute Adventure.

👁 Sights & Activities

Absolute Adventure (p335) runs sunset kayaking trips (Dhs275 per person) amid the Khor Kalba mangroves with excellent opportunities to spot both birdlife and turtles. Groups of four or more can book a private trip. Otherwise, check the website and Facebook page for announcements of group trips (usually on Fridays).

Al Hefaiyah Mountain Conservation Centre ZOO
(www.epaashj.ae; adult/child Dhs25/free; ⊙10am-6pm Sat-Thu, from 2pm Fri) Thirty mountain species, including Arabian leopards and gazelles, can be seen at this small wildlife centre, which opened in 2016. A shuttle whizzes around the various outdoor enclosures for easy viewing, and excellent information panels help explain the biodiversity of mountain environments and the fauna and flora of these regions.

🛏 Sleeping

Kingfisher Lodge BOUTIQUE HOTEL **$$$**
(📞054 701 9356; https://sharjahcollection.ae; tents Dhs1700; 🕏) The height of glamping luxury, these safari-style tents, all with patio and private plunge pool, sit in glorious isolation upon the skinny Khor Kalba peninsula. It's a chic get-away-from-it-all for nature lovers with views of the beach from your bed and opportunities to explore the surrounding mangroves for birdwatching and turtle-spotting.

Remember that as Kalba is in the emirate of Sharjah, this is a 'dry' hotel so alcohol is not allowed.

ℹ️ Getting There & Away

The 116E bus connects Sharjah with Kalba (Dhs25, 2½ hours), leaving Al Jubail station in Sharjah hourly between 5.30am and 10.30pm and making the return trip from Kalba every hour between 8.15am and 1.15am.

UNDERSTAND THE UNITED ARAB EMIRATES

UAE Today

Best known as a financial centre and an oil and gas exporter, in recent years the United Arab Emirates has moved to take on a bigger role internationally. In particular, as a leading player in both the Qatar blockade and in the coalition forces fighting in Yemen, it is emerging as a regional power. Back at home, the UAE continues to plough ahead with efforts to diversify its traditionally oil-dependent economy, investing heavily in tourism and trade.

Diversifying the Economy

The UAE is best known for its oil: it has the world's seventh-largest oil reserves (after Venezuela, Saudi Arabia, Canada, Iran, Iraq and Kuwait), with the vast majority concentrated in the emirate of Abu Dhabi. Reserves are predicted to last for another century at current levels of extraction, but – as the dramatic drop in oil prices in 2015 showed – the country has realised that it cannot afford to be complacent about preserving its wealth.

In common with Gulf neighbours, therefore, the UAE is looking at alternative sources of energy and ways of diversifying its economy. Dubai has been especially successful in this, largely thanks to the vision and ambition of its ruler, Sheikh Mohammed Bin Rashid Al Maktoum. Dubai's reserves of oil and gas were never that large to begin with, but the resources were used wisely to finance a modern and efficient infrastructure for trade, manufacturing and tourism. Today, Dubai is a business and tourism hub, and revenues for oil and gas account for less than 2% of Dubai's GDP.

Abu Dhabi has realised the power of this strategy and is catching up on non-oil enterprises. The Saadiyat Island cultural district development and the building of the new central business district on Maryah Island are two of the major ongoing projects that Abu Dhabi is investing in as part of a strategy to help it weather future storms.

A Bigger Player on the World Stage?

Since the Arab Spring in 2011, the UAE's military operations and expenditure have expanded significantly to make it one of the Middle East's rising military powers.

Since the government of President Hadi in Yemen was ousted by the Houthi rebel group in 2015, the UAE has taken a leading role in the coalition military campaign to unseat the Houthis from the capital Sanaa and restore President Hadi's rule across the country. The UAE has, however, also backed south Yemen secessionist groups in Aden and established a military base on the Yemeni island of Socotra, drawing accusations that the UAE is more focused on expanding its influence in Yemen for the long term than restoring the Hadi government to power. The campaign has also taken its toll on the UAE's military forces. In 2015, the UAE suffered its highest-ever combat casualties when 45 soldiers were killed in a missile strike.

As well as rapidly expanding military pursuits, the UAE is one of the major players in the Qatar blockade – ongoing since June 2017 – which began when quotes supporting Iran appeared to have been posted by the Qatar News Agency. The UAE (and its blockade partners) accused Qatar of sponsoring terrorism as well as allying itself with Iran. Qatar, in turn, claimed the posts were the work of hackers, and blamed the UAE, which denies responsibility for the incident. Within the first month of the crisis, all ties with Qatar were severed, all Qataris were expelled from UAE territory, and transport links halted. Public expressions of sympathy towards Qatar were made illegal, and access to Doha's Al Jazeera news network was blocked.

Aside from regional disputes, the UAE is making a bid to become an international player in space research, exploration and technology, creating the UAE National Space Programme in 2014. It plans to send an unmanned probe (named the Hope Spacecraft) to Mars in 2020, which would make it the first Arab nation to launch such a mission. The mission's scientific aims are to provide the first comprehensive study of Martian atmosphere while the longer-term goal is to establish space technology as one of the UAE's key industries.

History

Early History

The earliest significant settlements in the UAE date back to the Bronze Age. In the 3rd millennium BC, a culture known as Umm Al Nar arose near modern Abu Dhabi. Its influence extended well into the interior and down the coast to today's Oman. There were also settlements at Badiyah (near Fujairah) and at Rams (near Ras Al Khaimah) during the same period.

The Persians and, to a lesser extent, the Greeks were the next major cultural influences in the area. The Persian Sassanid empire held sway until the arrival of Islam in AD 636, and Christianity made a brief appearance in the form of the Nestorian Church, which had a monastery on Sir Bani Yas Island, west of Abu Dhabi, in the 5th century.

During the Middle Ages, the Kingdom of Ormus controlled much of the area, including the entrance to the Gulf, as well as most of the regional trade. The Portuguese arrived in 1498 and by 1515 they occupied Julfar (near Ras Al Khaimah). They built a customs house and taxed the Gulf's flourishing trade with India and the Far East, but they ended up staying only until 1633.

CAMEL RACING IN THE UAE

Camel racing is deeply rooted in the Emirati soul and attending a race is hugely popular with locals and visitors alike. It's quite an exhilarating sight when hundreds of one-humped dromedaries fly out of their pens and onto the dirt track, jostling for position in a lumbering gallop with legs splayed out in all directions, scrambling towards the finish line at top speeds of 40km/h.

More than 100 animals participate in a typical race. Each camel is outfitted with 'robot jockeys', which have remote-controlled whips operated by the owners while driving their white SUVs on a separate track alongside the animals.

Racing season runs between October and early April. There's no fixed schedule, although two- or three-hour meets usually take place from around 7am on Friday, sometimes with a second race around 2.30pm. Training sessions can sometimes be observed at other times. For exact times, check the local newspapers or call the numbers below. Admission is free.

The main tracks where you can see these great desert athletes go nose to nose are **Al Wathba** (☑ 02 885 8888; Al Wathba; ☉ 7.30am & 2.30pm Thu-Sat Oct-Apr) FREE in Abu Dhabi, **Al Marmoum** (☑ 04 832 6526; www.dcrc.ae; off Dubai–Al Ain Rd (Hwy E66); ☉ Nov-Apr) in Dubai and **Al Sawan** (Hwy E18; ☉ usually 6.30-9.30am Fri & Sat Nov-Mar) in Ras Al Khaimah.

British Rule

The rise of British naval power in the Gulf in the mid-18th century coincided with the consolidation of two tribal factions along the coast of the lower Gulf: the Qawassim and the Bani Yas, the ancestors of the rulers of four of the seven emirates that today make up the UAE.

The Qawassim, whose descendants now rule Sharjah and Ras Al Khaimah, were a seafaring clan based in Ras Al Khaimah whose influence extended at times to the Persian side of the Gulf. This brought them into conflict with the British, who had forged an alliance with the Al Busaid tribe, the ancestors of today's rulers of Oman, to prevent the French from taking over their all-important sea routes to India.

The Qawassim felt that Al Busaid had betrayed the region, and they launched attacks on British ships to show that they weren't going to be as compliant. As a result, the British dubbed the area the 'Pirate Coast' and launched raids against the Qawassim in 1805, 1809 and 1811. In 1820, a British fleet destroyed or captured every Qawassim ship it could find, imposed a peace treaty on nine Arab sheikhdoms in the area and installed a garrison.

This was the forerunner of another treaty, the 1835 Maritime Truce, which greatly increased British influence in the region. In 1853, the treaty was modified yet again and renamed the Treaty of Peace in Perpetuity.

It was at this time that the region became known as the Trucial States. In subsequent decades, the sheikhs of each tribal confederation signed agreements with the British under which they accepted formal British protection.

Throughout this period, the main power among the Bedouin tribes of the interior was the Bani Yas tribal confederation, made up of the ancestors of the ruling families of modern Abu Dhabi and Dubai. The Bani Yas were originally based in Liwa, an oasis deep in the desert, but moved their base to Abu Dhabi in 1793. In the early 19th century, the Bani Yas divided into two main branches when around 800 of its members moved north and took charge of a tiny fishing settlement along the Dubai Creek. This laid the foundation for the Al Maktoum dynasty that rules Dubai to this day.

Black Gold

Until the discovery of oil in the first half of the 20th century, the region remained a backwater, with the sheikhdoms nothing more than tiny enclaves of fishers and pearl divers. Rivalries between the various rulers occasionally erupted into conflict, which the British tried to thwart. During this time the British also protected the federation from being annexed by Saudi Arabia.

After the collapse of the world pearl market following the 1930 Japanese discovery of artificial pearl cultivation, the Gulf coast sank into poverty. While Abu Dhabi threw in its lot with the exploration for oil, Dubai embraced the concept of re-export. This exporting involved the importing of goods (particularly gold), which entered and exited Dubai legally but which were sold on to other ports abroad tax free.

The wealth generated from trade in yellow gold in Dubai was quickly trumped by the riches earned from black gold in Abu Dhabi. The first commercial oil field was discovered at Babi in Abu Dhabi in 1960 and, six years later, Dubai struck it lucky, too. The discovery of oil greatly accelerated the modernisation of the region and was a major factor in the formation of the UAE.

The Road to Unification

In 1951, the British set up the Trucial States Council, for the first time bringing together the rulers of the sheikhdoms of what would eventually become a federation. When Britain announced its departure from the region in 1968, Sheikh Zayed Bin Sultan Al Nahyan took the lead in forming alliances among the seven emirates that made up the Trucial States.

On 2 December 1971, thanks to Sheikh Zayed's persistence, the United Arab Emirates was created. It consisted of the emirates of Dubai, Abu Dhabi, Ajman, Fujairah, Sharjah and Umm Al Quwain; Ras Al Khaimah joined in 1972. Impressively, given the volatility in the region, the UAE remains to this day the only federation of Arab states in the Middle East. In fact, if anything, the financial bailouts by oil-rich Abu Dhabi of Dubai during the 2009 economic crisis tightened the bond and demonstrated the emirates' commitment to – and interdependence on – one another.

Government & Politics

The UAE is a federation of seven autonomous states – Dubai, Abu Dhabi, Sharjah, Ras Al Khaimah, Fujairah, Umm Al Quwain and Ajman – each governed by a hereditary absolute monarch called a sheikh. Among the emirates, Dubai has the highest profile abroad, but Abu Dhabi is the indisputable capital, with the greatest wealth and the largest territory. A certain tribal rivalry between them has helped spur the union on.

The seven rulers of the UAE form the Supreme Council, the highest body in the land. The council ratifies federal laws and sets general policy. New laws can be passed with the consent of five of the seven rulers. The Supreme Council also elects one of the emirs to a five-year term as the country's president. After the death in late 2004 of Sheikh Zayed, the founder and first president of the country, power passed peacefully to his son, Sheikh Khalifa Bin Zayed Al Nahyan.

There is also a Council of Ministers, or cabinet, headed by the prime minister (the ruler of Dubai) who appoints ministers from across the emirates. The more populous and wealthier emirates such as Abu Dhabi and Dubai have greater representation.

The cabinet and Supreme Council are advised, but can't be overruled, by a parliamentary body called the Federal National Council (FNC). It has 40 members, apportioned among the seven emirates. Since 2006, 20 members are elected, while the other 20 are directly appointed by the ruler of each emirate. The FNC debates proposed legislation and the federal budget. During the most recent elections in 2015, voter turnout came to 35%, a rise of 7% over the 2011 elections. Of the nine female FNC members, only one was elected, the other eight were appointed.

People & Society

The UAE population is one of the most diverse, multicultural and male (three-quarters of the population) in the world. It is, overall, a tolerant and easygoing society. Most religions are tolerated (Judaism being an exception), and places of worship exist for Christians, Hindus and Sikhs. Notwithstanding, traditional culture and social life are firmly rooted in Islam, and day-to-day activities, relationships, diet and dress are very much dictated by religion.

Islamic Values

Islam is not just the official religion in the UAE; it is the cultural lifeblood. Religion is more than something performed on a Friday and put aside during the week; it is part of everyday life. It guides the choices an individual makes and frames the general context in which family life, work, leisure, care of the elderly and responsibility towards others take place. As such, Islam has played a socially cohesive role in the rapidly evolving UAE, providing support where old structures (both physical and social) have been dismantled to make way for a new urban experience.

For the visitor, understanding this link between religion and daily life can help make better sense of often misunderstood practices. Take dress, for example. Islam prescribes modest dress in public places for both men and women. The origin of the custom of covering the body is unclear – it certainly pre-dates Islam and to a large degree makes excellent sense under the ravaging desert sun. Similarly, Muslims are forbidden to consume anything containing pork or alcohol. These strictures traditionally made good sense in a region where tapeworm was a common problem with pork meat and where the effects of alcohol are exaggerated by the extreme climate.

Role of Women

Modern life has provided new opportunities for women beyond care of the family, largely thanks to the equitable nature of education in the UAE. More women than men graduate from the region's universities, and many go on to work in a variety of roles, including as doctors, engineers, government ministers, innovators and corporate executives. Several initiatives have further elevated women's participation in the nation's development. In 2012 the UAE cabinet made it compulsory for corporations and government entities to appoint women to their boards of directors. The region's first military college for women opened in 2014. Nearly one quarter of cabinet posts are currently filled by women, and in 2016 the Federal National Council became the region's first to be led by a woman.

Despite such advances, women still have to contend with social and legal constraints, a situation the Gender Balance Council, founded by Sheikh Mohammed in 2015, is tasked with remedying. It strives to bring the UAE into the world's top 25 countries on the UN's gender equality index by 2021 (it currently ranks 46 out of 159 countries).

The Workplace

Most Emiratis work in the public sector, as the short hours, good pay, benefits and early pensions make for an attractive lifestyle. The UAE government is actively pursuing a policy of 'Emiratisation', however, which involves encouraging Emiratis to work as entrepreneurs and employees in the private sector.

Until more locals take up the baton of small and medium enterprise, it will be hard for the government to decrease the depend-

ency on an imported labour force, but equally it is hard for this to happen while Emiratis are employed only in a token capacity in the private sector. At some point, a leap in the dark will be inevitable to allow for local people to assume the roles for which they are being trained.

Multicultural Population

You can't talk about the identity of the Emirates without factoring in the multinational composition of the population. Across the UAE expats comprise around 80% of the population. Therefore, the visitor experience is largely defined by interaction with the myriad nationalities that have been attracted to the Gulf in search of a better (or at least more lucrative) life.

Different nationalities have tended to dominate specific sectors of the workforce: people from the Philippines are employed in health care, construction workers are predominantly from Pakistan, financial advisers are from India, while Western countries have traditionally supplied technical know-how. Discussion prevails as to who benefits most from the contract between employer and employee, with serious concerns about the welfare particularly of construction and domestic workers. Some steps have been taken to right the wrongs of those in low-paid work, but it's fair to say that conditions for many remain far from ideal.

On the positive side, the international composition of the resident population has resulted in a vibrant multiculturalism. This is expressed in different religious festivals (including Diwali and Christmas), and gives the opportunity to experience the food and customs of each community in restaurants and shops. A visit here is likely to involve memorable conversations that allow the visitor to travel the world in an afternoon.

Dissent

Although society as a whole in the UAE is tolerant, to a point, of different cultural norms and practises, it does not allow dissent. All local media is government controlled, and a variety of laws are in place to crack down harshly on anyone stepping out of line. Both the legislation put in place after the beginning of the Qatar blockade, which made showing sympathy for Qatar a crime (punishable by a jail term of up to 15 years) and the jailing of prominent Emirati human rights activist and blogger Ahmed Mansoor in May 2018 for remarks he made on social media, show that the UAE has not softened its stance on dissent.

Arts

Owing to its Bedouin heritage, the most popular art forms in the UAE are traditional dance, music and poetry, although of late other forms of artistic expression have seen a surge in popularity. Sizeable art communities have sprouted in Dubai and Sharjah alongside world-class galleries and international art festivals.

Abu Dhabi is especially ambitious when it comes to positioning itself as an art-world leader, with plans to turn a corner of Saadiyat Island into the world's biggest cultural district. In 2017, the Louvre Abu Dhabi (p371) became the first of the three planned anchor museums to open here.

Poetry

In Bedouin culture, a facility with poetry and language is greatly prized. Traditionally, a poet who could eloquently praise his own people while pointing out the failures of other tribes was considered a great asset. One of the most important poets in the region was Mubarak Al Oqaili (1880–1954). There's an entire museum dedicated to him in a traditional building in the Deira Spice Souq in Dubai. Modern UAE poets of note include Sultan Al Owais (1925–2000) and Dr Ahmed Al Madani (1931–95).

Nabati (vernacular poetry) is especially popular and has traditionally been in spoken form. Sheikh Mohammed Bin Rashid Al Maktoum, Dubai's ruler, is a well-respected poet in this tradition, as is the award-winning contemporary female poet Ousha Bint Khalifa. The Women's Museum in Dubai's Deira district devotes an entire room to her work.

There are scores of well-known male poets in the UAE who still use the forms of classical Arab poetry, though they often experiment by combining it with other styles. Well-known female poets writing in the modern *tafila* (prose) styles include Rua Salem and her sister Sarah Hareb, as well as Sheikha Maisoon Al Qasimi.

Music & Dance

Emiratis have always acknowledged the importance of music in daily life. Songs were traditionally composed to accompany different tasks, from hauling water to diving for pearls. The Arabic music you're most likely to hear on the radio, though, is *khaleeji*, the traditional Gulf style of pop music. Alongside this, an underground rock and metal music scene is increasingly taking shape, especially in Dubai.

The UAE's contact with East and North African cultures through trade, both seafaring and by camel caravan, has brought many musical and dance influences to the country. One of the most popular dances is the *ayyalah*, a typical Bedouin dance performed throughout the Gulf. The UAE has its own variation, performed to a simple drumbeat, with anywhere between 25 and 200 men standing with their arms linked in two rows facing each other. They wave walking sticks or swords in front of themselves and sway back and forth, the two rows taking it in turn to sing. It's a war dance, and the words expound the virtues of courage and bravery in battle.

A traditional dance performed by women is the *al naashat*, where the dancers roll their heads from side to side to show off their long, jet-black hair to songs that pay tribute to the love, honour or bravery of the men of the tribe.

Environment

Environmental awareness is increasing at the macro level in the UAE, due in no small part to the efforts of the late Sheikh Zayed, who was posthumously named a 'Champion of the Earth' by the UN Environment Programme (UNEP) in 2005. With his efforts in wildlife preservation, such as Sir Bani Yas Island, which operates a breeding programme for endangered Arabian wildlife species, as well as the ban on hunting with guns put in place decades ago, Sheikh Zayed foresaw the acute threats to the region's endangered native species.

In Dubai, the Dubai Desert Conservation Reserve (DDCR) comprises 225 sq km (5% of the area of the Dubai emirate) and integrates both a national park and the super-luxe Al Maha Desert Resort & Spa. One of the DDCR's most notable achievements is the successful breeding of the endangered scimitar-horned oryx. Migrating birds and flamingos are the darlings of the Ras Al Khor Wildlife Sanctuary, at the head of Dubai Creek within view of the Burj Khalifa and the high-rises on Sheikh Zayed Road. Sharjah has a successful breeding centre at Sharjah Desert Park, as does Al Ain Zoo.

In terms of going green at the micro level, however, much work needs to be done in the UAE. Single-use plastic consumption is atrociously high, and water and energy wastage (nearly all water comes from desalination plants) and littering are major issues. Resources are consumed at a much faster rate than they can be replaced, which is why the ecological footprint of the Gulf cities is so high. It is no easy feat to reverse the trend and achieve environmental sustainability when the UAE relies so heavily on imported goods and urban dwelling has become the norm.

There are a few projects aimed at reducing the impact, such as the Shams 1 solar plant south of Madinat Zayed. Other projects such as Abu Dhabi's Masdar City – which was touted to be the world's first carbon-neutral, zero-waste community powered entirely by renewable energy – have so far turned out to be more useful as greentech experiments, having failed to meet the aimed-for carbon-neutral goals.

For more information, check the website of the UAE's leading environmental organisation, the nonprofit, nongovernmental Emirates Environmental Group (www.eeg-uae.org).

SURVIVAL GUIDE

ℹ️ Directory A–Z

ACCESSIBLE TRAVEL
Compared to many other Middle Eastern countries, the UAE has come forward leaps and bounds in making facilities more accessibility friendly.

Access All malls, most restaurants (except for budget places), public buildings and most sights and attractions have access ramps and fitted-out toilet facilities.

Airports Both Abu Dhabi International and Dubai International offer separate check-in gates and meet-and-assist services for travellers with accessibility needs.

Hotels Many budget, most midrange and all top-end and international-name hotels have rooms fitted out for wheelchair users. Nearly all hotels have elevators.

Transport Dubai Taxi (p352), Abu Dhabi Taxi (p389) and Sharjah Taxi (p361) all have a limited number of vehicles for wheelchair users. Book in advance.

Download Lonely Planet's free Accessible Travel guides from http://lptravel.to/AccessibleTravel.

ACCOMMODATION
The UAE deals mostly in luxury beach resorts, swish city hotels and more business-minded budget and midrange hotels. The only boutique-hotel scene is in Dubai, which has a handful of heritage hotels in Bur Dubai and downtown.

Camping
Although the UAE has no official public campgrounds, pitching a tent on a beach or in the desert is very popular with locals and is a free and safe way to spend the night. Be prepared to take everything in (and out), don't litter and bring a shovel to bury your 'business'.

For camping destinations, consult the locally published specialist guides widely available in bookstores. Because of the coastal resorts gobbling up a lot of the beaches, many of the remaining seashores used for camping are very popular on weekends. For a 'glamping' option with no other campers around, check out the Dibba camping organised by Absolute Adventure (p335).

Hostels
There are three hostels affiliated with Hostelling International in the UAE: one each in Dubai, Fujairah and Sharjah. Of all of them, the Sharjah option is the nicest. All are open to men and women, although solo women are a rare sight. Facilities are basic and shared, and smoking and alcohol are prohibited. Accommodation is in dorms or family rooms, which may be booked by small groups and couples depending on availability and the manager's mood.

Hotels
Hotels in the UAE are to a good standard, though their star system can be a bit laughable at times; five-star ratings seem to be given out like

SLEEPING PRICE RANGES

The following price ranges refer to a double room with private bathroom in high season (November to March). Unless otherwise stated, breakfast is included in the price.

$ less than Dhs500

$$ Dhs500–1000

$$$ more than Dhs1000

lollipops with a huge disparity in maintenance and service levels between top-rated hotels.

Budget hotels are completely safe for solo female travellers. Most are made for business travellers, and although the older (cheaper) ones can be a little worn in places, they're still perfectly comfortable. More interesting at this level are the heritage hotels in Dubai.

Midrange hotels usually offer good value for money, and many are international-name chains. At the top end, it's all the bells and whistles you can think of – plus more.

Rates

Room rates fluctuate enormously, spiking during festivals, holidays and big events and dropping in the summer months (May to September). The best beds often sell out fast, so make reservations as early as possible if you've got your eye on a particular place. Most properties can be booked online with a best-price guarantee.

Rates are subject to a municipality fee and a service charge, which vary by emirate but are usually around 10% each. Dubai, Abu Dhabi and Ras Al Khaimah also tack on a tourism tax ranging from Dhs7 to Dhs20 per room per night, depending on the property's star rating.

INTERNET ACCESS

Places in the UAE are well-wired, and you should not have a problem getting online. Hotels, cafes and restaurants nearly all offer free wi-fi.

Most shopping malls offer free public wi-fi, if you're using a UAE SIM card, as part of the WiFi UAE initiative (www.wifiuae.ae/en). Check the website for a map of all public wi-fi locations.

Pornography, LGBT-interest sites, websites considered critical of Islam or the UAE's leaders, dating and gambling sites, drug-related material, Qatar's Al Jazeera news network and the entire Israeli domain are blocked in the UAE.

VoIP call services such as Skype, FaceTime and WhatsApp's call function continue to be officially blocked (WhatsApp chat is unaffected).

Note that although VPN (Virtual Private Network) usage is rampant in the UAE, using a VPN remains illegal.

LEGAL MATTERS

Locals are tolerant of cultural differences – to a point. Go beyond that point and you could find yourself subject to some of the harshest penalties in the region.

Penalties for breaching the code of conduct or breaking the law include warnings or fines (for littering, for example), or jail and deportation (for drug possession and criticism of Islam, for example). Ignorance is no defence.

If arrested, you have the right to a phone call, which you should make as soon as possible (ie before you are detained in a police cell or prison pending investigation, where making contact with anyone could be difficult). Call your embassy or consulate first so they can get in touch with your family and possibly recommend a lawyer.

Detained in Dubai (www.detainedindubai.org) is a leading NGO specialising in UAE law and can provide legal representation.

The UAE police have established a Department of Tourist Security (www.dubaipolice.gov.ae) to field any complaints from visitors.

Drugs

Attempting to use illegal drugs in the UAE is simply a bad idea. The minimum penalty for possession of even trace amounts is four years in prison, and the death penalty is still on the books for importing or dealing in drugs (although in practice the sentence usually ends up being a very long jail term). Just being in a room where drugs are used, even if you are not partaking, could land you in trouble. The secret police are pervasive, and they include officers of many nationalities.

Prescription Medications

There are import bans on many prescription medications that are legal in most countries, such as diazepam (Valium), dextromethorphan (Robitussin), fluoxetine (Prozac) and anything containing codeine. The full up-to-date list

---

PRACTICALITIES

Electricity Electrical current 220V. British-style three-pin wall sockets are standard.

News & Magazines Widely read English-language dailies are *The National*, *Gulf News*, *Gulf Today* and *Khaleej Times*. Content is government controlled. *Time Out* produces the most popular weekly listings magazine.

Radio Dubai Eye (103.8) for news and talk, and Dubai FM (92), Channel 4 FM (104.8) and Emirates Radio 1 (104.1) and 2 (99.3) for music.

Smoking A comprehensive smoking ban is in place in public areas, with the exception of nightclubs and enclosed bars.

Weights & Measures The UAE uses the metric system.

of banned medications can be found at www.mohap.gov.ae/en/AwarenessCenter/Pages/UnauthorizedMedicines.aspx. To bring any other prescription medication into the country, you must carry no more than a three-month supply in its original packaging and with the original prescription. Failure to do this has resulted in visitors being prosecuted.

In 2018, the UAE introduced a pre-approval entry form for importing controlled, but not banned, medications for personal use. It can be found at www.mohap.gov.ae/en/services/Pages/361.aspx. Approval generally takes around five days.

LGBT+ TRAVELLERS

Homosexual acts are illegal under UAE law, and those accused can incur deportation, fines or a jail term. Discretion here is key.

You cannot access many LGBT+ websites and dating apps such as Grindr from inside the UAE.

Note that all public displays of affection (cuddling, kissing and hand-holding) between opposite-sex couples are also illegal in the UAE as is sex outside of marriage. A same-sex couple sharing a room is likely to be construed as companionable or cost-cutting, but unless you're staying at a five-star resort, where staff are likely to look the other way, it's advisable to book two single beds rather than a double bed.

Despite this, there is an active but very underground LGBT+ scene in Dubai and Abu Dhabi because of the large number of young international residents, though tapping into it can be difficult as a visitor on a short stay.

A useful read is *Gay Travels in the Muslim World* by Michael Luongo.

MONEY

ATMs are widely available. Credit cards are accepted in most hotels and restaurants.

Currency

The UAE dirham (Dhs) is fully convertible and pegged to the US dollar. One dirham is divided into 100 fils. Notes come in denominations of five, 10, 20, 50, 100, 200, 500 and 1000 dirham. Coins are Dhs1, 50 fils, 25 fils, 10 fils and five fils.

Tipping

Tipping is common practice but at your discretion.
Hotels Tip porters Dhs5 to Dhs10.
Restaurants If a 10% service charge is already included, a small tip to your server is greatly appreciated, as that service charge rarely reaches their pocket.
Spas Tip therapists 5% to 10% of the fee for expensive treatments. Add an extra Dh5 to Dh10 onto the fee for smaller treatments.
Taxis Round fares to nearest Dhs5.

EATING PRICE RANGES

The following price ranges refer to an average main course. Prices may or may not include VAT and a service charge, as this varies by emirate. Details are almost always spelled out (in fine print) on restaurant menus.

$ less than Dhs30

$$ Dhs30–90

$$$ more than Dhs90

OPENING HOURS

The UAE weekend is on Friday and Saturday. Hours are more limited during Ramadan and in summer.

Banks 8am to 1pm (some until 3pm) Sunday to Thursday, 8am to noon Saturday

Government offices 7.30am to 2pm (or 3pm) Sunday to Thursday

Restaurants noon to 3pm and 7.30pm to midnight

Shopping malls 10am to 10pm Sunday to Wednesday, 10am to midnight Thursday and Friday

Souqs 9am to 1.30pm and 4pm to 9pm (often later in Dubai and Abu Dhabi), closed Friday morning

Supermarkets 9am to midnight daily, some open 24 hours

PHOTOGRAPHY

Taking video or photographs of airports, government offices, or military and industrial installations may result in arrest and/or prosecution. Taking photos of people without first asking permission is also officially illegal.

POST

The postal system, operated by Emirates Post (www.emiratespost.com), is reliable. Standard postcards and letters to Europe cost Dhs6 and to Asia, Australasia, and North and South America Dhs7. Post offices are found in every city or town.

PUBLIC HOLIDAYS

As well as the major Islamic holidays (p478), the UAE observes the following public holidays:
New Year's Day 1 January
Commemoration Day 30 November
National Day 2 December

A mourning period of up to one week usually follows the death of a royal-family member, a government minister or a head of a neighbouring state. Government offices, some businesses and state-run tourist attractions (such as museums)

may be closed on these days, and events may be cancelled.

SAFE TRAVEL
➡ The UAE has a low incidence of crime; even pickpocketing and bag snatching are rare.

➡ If you're swimming at an unpatrolled (ie public) beach, be very careful. Despite the small surf, there may be dangerous rip tides and drownings are not uncommon.

➡ Dissent is not permitted. Don't strike up conversations about sensitive matters such as the Qatar blockade or the UAE's involvement in Yemen.

TELEPHONE
When calling the UAE from another country, dial that country's international access code, then the UAE country code, followed by the area code (dropping the zero) and then the seven-digit local number. When calling abroad from the UAE, dial the international access code 🗗 00 then the relevant country code.

To make a call within the UAE using a landline, dial the seven-digit local number if already in the city. If dialling a number in another city – or using a mobile phone – dial the two-digit area code first.

UAE's country code	🗗 971
International access code	🗗 00
Directory enquiries	🗗 181
International directory assistance	🗗 151

Mobile Phones
The UAE's mobile phone network uses the GSM 900 MHz and 1800 MHz standard. Mobile numbers begin with either 050 or 055. If your phone is unlocked, consider buying a prepaid SIM card, available at the airport or city shops.

The three mobile phone service providers are Etisalat (www.etisalat.ae/en), Du Mobile (www.du.ae) and Virgin Mobile (www.virginmobile.ae).

Etisalat and Du Mobile both offer rechargeable pre-paid plans specifically targeted at tourists.

Etisalat's 14-day 'tourist plan' costs Dhs100 (rechargeable at Dh75) with three minute-and-data choices, including one with 700MB of data, 40 minutes of local and international calls plus 40 local and international SMS.

Du Mobile's 7-day 'tourist plan' costs Dhs65 (rechargeable at Dh55) with 500MB of data, 20 minutes of local calls and 20 local SMS.

You'll need to bring your passport to purchase a local SIM card.

Recharge cards in various denominations are sold at grocery stores, supermarkets and petrol stations.

TOILETS
➡ Public toilets in shopping centres, museums, restaurants and hotels are sit-down affairs and are generally very clean and well maintained.

➡ Bus stations have toilet facilities for both men and women. These can be less maintained. It's a good idea to bring tissues as they're often out of paper.

➡ Outside of the cities, you might have to contend with hole-in-the-ground toilets at the back of restaurants or petrol stations, although these are increasingly rare.

➡ You'll always find a hose and nozzle next to the toilet, which is used for rinsing (left hand only if you want to go native); toilet paper is used for drying only.

VISAS
➡ Free 30-day single-entry tourist visas are available on arrival for 20 countries including Australia, Canada, China, Ireland, Japan, Malaysia, New Zealand, Singapore, South Korea, UK and USA. These visas have a further nine-day grace period (making 39 days in total) before you are charged for overstaying, though rumours abound that the grace period will soon be removed.

➡ Free 90-day multiple-entry tourist visas are available on arrival for an additional 40 nationalities including passport-holders from nearly all European countries, Barbados, Brazil, Chile, Costa Rica, Honduras and Uruguay.

➡ Israeli passport-holders and Qatari passport-holders are not currently granted visas to enter the UAE.

➡ Citizens of Bahrain, Kuwait, Oman and Saudi Arabia only need a valid passport to enter the UAE and stay indefinitely.

➡ Overstaying a tourist visa costs Dhs340 for the first day and Dhs100 for each additional day, payable at immigration on exiting the country.

Sponsored Tourist Visas
➡ If you are a citizen of a country that does not receive a visa on arrival, you must arrange a tourist visa through a sponsor before you arrive.

➡ Sponsors could include your UAE hotel or tour operator, but by far the easiest way to arrange a sponsored tourist visa is to fly into the country using either Emirates Airlines, Etihad Airways or Fly Dubai, which will all arrange visas for their passengers (see their websites for details and the application process).

➡ A four-day transit visa costs Dhs50, a 30-day single-entry sponsored tourist visa costs Dhs350 and a 60-day multiple-entry sponsored tourist visa costs Dhs650.

➡ No sponsored tourist visa is extendable.

ALCOHOL IN THE UAE

Buying When arriving by air, you may, as a non-Muslim visitor over the age of 18, buy 4L of spirits, wine or beer in the airport duty-free shop. With the exception of the 'dry' emirate of Sharjah, where alcohol and even shisha (water pipe) smoking are banned, you can also purchase alcohol in licensed restaurants, bars and clubs (many generally attached to hotels); alcohol purchased in these places is for on-site consumption.

Non-Muslim UAE residents may obtain an alcohol licence, which entitles them to a fixed monthly limit of alcohol sold in such places as the African & Eastern liquor stores and some branches of Spinneys. Visitors are not permitted to legally purchase alcohol in these places, and staff members are supposed to ask to see the licence. The only stores where visitors can legally buy alcohol are at the Barracuda Beach Resort (p365) and the Umm Al Quwain Beach Hotel, both in Umm Al Quwain. Note that you are not officially allowed to transport alcohol through Sharjah.

Driving There is zero tolerance in the UAE when it comes to drinking and driving. And we mean zero: under no circumstances should you get behind the wheel of a car if you've had even one sip of alcohol. Getting caught could get you a one-month stint in jail, a fine and deportation.

Public drunkenness Being drunk in public is illegal and may also result in jail time and a fine of several thousand dirham.

Also note that even if you are the victim of a crime (eg sexual assault or robbery), police protection may be limited if you are found to have been under the influence.

Visa Extensions

Thirty-day tourist visa extensions are possible for 20 nationalities through the local immigration office of the emirate you arrived in, but applying for an extension can be an expensive and convoluted process. Most visitors from nationalities permitted to extend their visa simply do a visa-run to Oman instead; exiting the country and then turning around to re-enter the UAE on a new free on-arrival tourist visa. There is no limit to the number of times you can do this.

The 20 nationalities permitted to do this are citizens of Argentina, Australia, Brazil, Brunei, Canada, Chile, China, Hong Kong, Ireland, Japan, Malaysia, New Zealand, Russia, Seychelles, Singapore, South Korea, UK, Ukraine, Uruguay and USA.

For those who don't want to drive themselves to and from the border, **Go Tours** (☑ 055 410 5611; www.gotoursdubai.com; per person Dhs150) offers daily, year-round visa-run trips from Dubai. The trip takes around five hours with comfortable minivan transport and an experienced English-speaking driver. As well as the trip cost, each passenger must bring Dhs85 to pay for the UAE exit fee and Oman visa fee. Go Tours' website is also the most up-to-date source on Emirati visa-extension information.

WOMEN TRAVELLERS

Women will encounter few problems travelling around the UAE by themselves. Harassment (both vocal and physical) is rare, though not nonexistent. It's safe to walk around late at night by yourself in most areas, take taxis and public transport and to stay in budget hotels as a solo woman. You will often be asked about why you're travelling by yourself and where your family is. If you're single and childless and don't feel like fielding a barrage of questions about why this is, you can always make up an imaginary husband to satisfy the questioner.

Dispelling the Myths

Many women imagine that travel to the Gulf cities and within the UAE is much more difficult than it is. Some key facts:
➡ You don't have to wear a burka, headscarf or veil.
➡ You won't be constantly harassed.
➡ In taxis, it's normal for a woman to sit in the back of the taxi. On public buses, solo females usually sit towards the front. Also on buses, it's not normal for an unrelated man to take a free seat next to a woman.
➡ Public beaches are one of the few places where you are likely to receive unwanted male attention – generally just long, lewd stares.

Attitudes Towards Women

Some of the biggest misunderstandings between Middle Easterners and people from other parts of the world occur over the issue of women. Half-truths and stereotypes exist on both sides: foreigners sometimes assume that all Middle Eastern women are veiled, repressed victims, while some locals see foreign women, particularly Western ones, as sex-obsessed and immoral.

Traditionally the role of a woman in this region is to be a mother and matron of the household, while the man is the financial provider. However, as with any society, the reality is far more nuanced. There are thousands of middle- and upper-middle-class professional women in the UAE, who, like their counterparts elsewhere in the world, juggle work and family responsibilities.

The issue of sex is where the differences between cultures can be particularly apparent. Premarital sex (or indeed any sex outside marriage) is taboo, although, as with anything forbidden, it still happens. Emirati women are expected to be virgins when they marry, and a family's reputation can rest upon this point. The presence of foreign women provides, in the eyes of some Arab men, a chance to get around these norms with ease and without consequences – hence the occasional hassle foreign women experience.

What to Wear

Even though you'll see plenty of female tourists wearing skimpy shorts and tank tops in shopping malls and other public places (especially in Dubai), you should not assume that it's acceptable to do so. While as hosts they're too polite to say anything, most Emiratis find this disrespectful. Despite the UAE's relative liberalism, you are in a country that holds its traditions dear and it's prudent not to parade a different set of values. A bit of common sense (such as covering up to and from a beach party or when taking a taxi to a nightclub) helps keep the peace.

Generally speaking, dressing 'modestly' has the following advantages: it attracts less attention to you; you will get a warmer welcome from locals (who greatly appreciate your willingness to respect their customs); and it'll prove more comfortable in the heat. Dressing modestly means covering your shoulders, knees and neckline. Baggy shirts and loose cotton trousers or below-the-knee skirts will not only keep you cool but will also protect your skin from the sun. Areas outside Dubai and Abu Dhabi are often more conservative, though that's not always the case.

❶ Getting There & Away

ENTERING THE UAE

If you are a passport-holder of any of the 60 countries granted tourist visas on arrival, simply proceed straight to the immigration desk or border post and get your passport stamped.

Otherwise, if you are entering on a sponsored visa (p414), you'll need to go to the clearly marked visa-collection counter at the airport when you arrive

Passport

All travellers' passports must be valid for at least six months from the date of arrival.

Although you cannot enter the UAE with an Israeli or Qatari passport, an Israeli or Qatari entry stamp in any other nationality's passport shouldn't cause problems.

AIR

Airports & Airlines

Abu Dhabi International Airport (p388) The second-busiest airport in the UAE and Etihad Airways' hub.

Al Maktoum International Airport (DWC; ☑ 04 224 5555; www.dubaiairports.ae; off Sheikh Mohammed Bin Rashid Al Maktoum Rd (E611); ☎ ; Ⓜ UAE Exchange) Dubai's second airport is used by some FlyDubai services to and from Amman, Beirut and Kuwait. A few low-cost carriers flying from Eastern European destinations such as Bucharest also use this airport.

Dubai International Airport (p349) The UAE's major entry point and the hub for Emirates Airlines.

Ras Al Khaimah International Airport (p369) Mostly used by Air Arabia flights operating from Middle Eastern and South Asian destinations.

Sharjah International Airport (p361) Most flights operate to/from regional destinations such as Istanbul and Cairo and cities in south Asia. Air Arabia's hub, it is also used by some Egypt Air flights as well as a small number of Eastern European low-cost carriers.

Air Arabia (www.airarabia.com) Sharjah-based low-cost carrier flying to African, Middle Eastern, Turkish, Central and South Asian, and a couple of Eastern European destinations.

Emirates Airlines (www.emirates.com) Dubai-based; has an extensive route network, excellent service and good safety record.

Etihad Airways (www.etihad.com) Based in Abu Dhabi; like Emirates, it's known for its good safety record and service and has a comprehensive route network.

FlyDubai (www.flydubai.com) Discount carrier with around 50 destinations, mostly within the Middle East, Africa, Eastern Europe and Central and South Asia.

LAND

Border Crossings

The UAE shares borders with Oman and Saudi Arabia, but only Gulf Cooperation Council (GCC) citizens are permitted to cross into Saudi Arabia at the Ghuwaifat/Sila border post in the far west of the UAE.

To/From Oman

UAE–Oman border crossing procedures change frequently. It's vital to get up-to-date information on which borders travellers can currently use once on the ground.

The handiest border crossings for non-GCC citizens headed for mainland Oman are the Mayzad and Khatam Al Shukla checkpoints in Al Ain, the Hatta checkpoint east of Dubai and the tiny coastal Khatmat Malaha crossing south of Fujairah.

Despite local media, and the Omani government itself, reporting that Oman tourist visas would only be available as e-visas, 10-day tourist visas for Oman (OR5) could still be purchased at the Hatta and Khatam Al Shukla border crossings at the time of research. This could change at any time though and depends on the whim of the border guards on the day. To make sure your travels are not delayed, purchase the e-visa beforehand. Ten-day and one-month (OR20) Oman tourist visas can be purchased online in advance at www.evisa.rop.gov.om. Approval by email usually takes 24 hours.

If you're headed for Khasab on the Musandam Peninsula, use the Al Darah border north of Ras Al Khaimah. It's best to purchase the 10-day Oman tourist visa online in advance if using this border, though several travellers have reported that visas are available on arrival.

There's a Dhs35 exit fee when leaving the UAE.

The other crossing into the Musandam, at Dibba on the east coast north of Fujairah, is not an official border as there is no checkpoint on the Omani side. To enter here, you must have a booking through a tour operator in Dibba. The tour operator needs a copy of your passport for your free entry permit. The process is simple and quick (for tourists it can be completed in less than 24 hours, though most tour companies ask for two days' notice) and the operator then applies for an entry permit. Note that as you are not being stamped into Oman here, the only way to exit after your tour is back through the Dibba crossing.

Bus

Mwasalat (Map p330; ☑ 04 252 5909; http:// mwasalat.om/en-us/Services/Intercity; 10A St; one-way Dhs55) runs comfortable buses with televisions and toilets on board between Muscat (Oman) and Dubai. Bus 201 leaves Azaiba station in Muscat at 6.20am, 3.20pm and 11.20pm and takes about 6½ hours for the trip to the Mwasalat bus office near the Deira City Centre. From Dubai, Bus 201 leaves for Muscat at 7.30am, 3.30pm and 11pm.

Car & Motorcycle

To cross into Oman in a hire car, you will need to have insurance that covers Oman. This can usually be purchased from the car hire company or can be bought at most border crossings.

❶ Getting Around

BICYCLE

Cycling is one of the UAE's fastest-growing sports with the Hatta Mountain Bike Trail (p353) in Hatta, the **Al Wathba cycling track** (Al Wathba; bike rental Dhs30-60; ⊙24hr) in Abu Dhabi and the 85km loop of the **Al Qudra Cycle Course** in Dubai (which offers plentiful desert scenery) being three of the best new additions to the cycle scene.

Using a bike as your sole form of transport to travel through the UAE remains unusual, however. If you're planning a cycle trip, make sure to choose your season wisely – October to March are the best months to avoid the worst of the heat. Plan to carry as much water as possible. Be prepared for plenty of long, flat monotonous stretches of road, strong crosswinds and the possibility of sandstorms. Note that drivers in the UAE aren't used to sharing the road with cyclists so keep alert, particularly on city roads, and fit lights to your bike for extra visibility.

If you don't want to bring your bike with you, there are several places that hire out good-quality road and mountain bikes.

Adventure HQ (Map p372; ☑ 02 565 0996; www.adventurehq.ae; 1st fl, Yas Mall; ⊙10am-10pm Sat-Wed, to midnight Thu & Fri) Outdoor equipment store with branches in Dubai and Abu Dhabi that rent and sell bikes.

Trek Bikes (www.trekbikes.ae) Has a bike-hire facility at the Al Qudra Cycle Course as well as a shop and bike service centre on Sheikh Zayed Rd in Dubai.

Wolfies Bike Shop (www.wbs.ae) The central hub for cycling in Dubai with bike servicing and rentals as well as the full gamut of bike accessories for sale. Also home to the Dubai Roadsters cycling club which runs weekly group rides open to all.

BUS

The following companies provide travel between the major cities.

Abu Dhabi Department of Transportation (www.dot.abudhabi.ae) Service within the emirate of Abu Dhabi including to Al Ain and Mezairaa.

Ajman Bus (www.at.gov.ae) Services from Ajman to Abu Dhabi, Al Ain, Ras Al Khaimah, Sharjah and Umm Al Quwain.

Al Hamrah bus company Services to and from Ras Al Khaimah and Dubai (via Umm Al Quwain, Ajman and Sharjah).

Dubai Roads & Transport Authority (www. dubai-buses.com) Services to and from Abu

Dhabi, Ajman, Fujairah, Hatta and Sharjah from several bus stations throughout Dubai.

Sharjah Roads & Transport Authority (www.st.gov.ae) Services from Sharjah to Ajman, Fujairah, Ras Al Khaimah and Umm Al Quwain; and to and from Abu Dhabi, Al Ain, Kalba and Khor Fakkan.

CAR & MOTORCYCLE

Having your own wheels is a great way to see the UAE, allowing you to get off the major highways and to stop as you please. Well-maintained multi-lane highways link the cities, often lit along their entire length. For off-road driving, you need a 4WD. If you have a breakdown, call the Arabian Automobile Association (http://aaaemirates.com).

Car Hire

To hire a car, you'll need a passport, a credit card and a valid driving licence. International driving licences are not usually compulsory, but it's better to have one.

Daily rates start at about Dhs200 for a small manual car such as a Toyota Yaris, including comprehensive insurance and unlimited miles.

Expect surcharges for airport rentals, additional drivers, one-way hire and drivers under 25. Most companies have child and infant safety seats for a fee, but these must be reserved well in advance.

GPS devices are also available for hire for about Dhs35 per day. Although somewhat useful, their data (especially outside of Dubai) is not usually current and should not be relied upon entirely.

Local agencies may be cheaper, but the major international ones have the advantage of larger fleets and better emergency backup.

For longer rentals, pre-booked and prepaid packages, arranged in your home country, may work out cheaper than on-the-spot rentals. Check for deals with online travel agencies, travel agents or brokers such as Auto Europe (www.autoeurope.com) or Holiday Autos (www.holidayautos.com).

If you plan on taking the car to Oman, bring written permission from the car-rental company in case you're asked for it at the border. You'll also need car insurance that's valid in Oman. Omani insurance is available at most border crossings.

Road Rules

➡ Drive on the right.

➡ Seat belts are compulsory for all car occupants.

➡ The alcohol limit is zero.

➡ Speed limits are between 40km/h and 80km/h in urban areas and up to 140km/h on freeways.

➡ If you have an accident, even a small one, you must call the police (☑ 999) and wait at the scene. If it's a minor accident, move your car to the side of the road. You cannot file an insurance claim without a police report.

Driving Conditions

Driving in the United Arab Emirates is not for the faint of heart. Although it's not as chaotic as in other parts of the Middle East, drivers tend to cut in front of you, turn without indicating and view roundabouts as a lane-less free-for-all. Out on the freeway, driving in the lane closest to the centre of the road at speeds of less than 160km/h will invoke some serious headlight flashing from the latest-model Mercedes trying to break the Dubai–Abu Dhabi land-speed record.

So it's no surprise that the UAE has one of the world's highest rates of road deaths per capita. Inappropriate speed and reckless driving are the major causes, as well as pedestrians crossing against the lights or not at crossings. Thankfully public-awareness campaigns are beginning to make an impact.

Things to keep in mind:

➡ Headlight-flashing from the car behind you is UAE driver-speak for you're driving too slow and they want to overtake. Avoid these confrontations by driving in the far-right lane on freeways.

➡ Keep a cool head when faced with aggressive or dangerous driving. Being reported for obscene hand gestures or language can land you with a fine, a prison sentence or deportation.

➡ Be alert for camels wandering onto the road and for encroaching sand when driving outside of the cities.

TAXI

Taxis are decently priced, metered, ubiquitous and within emirates like Umm Al Quwain often the only way of getting around.

Most drivers can also be hired by the hour. In that case, rates should be negotiated unless fixed fees are set in place. In Dubai, for instance, the fee for six hours is Dhs300, for 12 hours Dhs500.

Most cabs can also be engaged for long-distance travel to other emirates, in which case you should negotiate the fee at the beginning of the trip.

Few drivers are fluent English speakers, but the vast majority have a good grasp on the language. Many are more familiar with landmarks than street names. It helps if you mention parks, shopping malls or hotel names when giving directions for your desired destination. Tip about 10% for good service.

Yemen

At a Glance

Currency Yemeni riyal (YER)

Language Arabic

Population 28 million

Time Arabia Standard Time
(GMT/UTC plus three hours)

Best in Music

Music from Yemen Arabia
(Kawkabani Brothers; 2017)
Traditional poetry accompanied by oud and percussion.

**Qat, Coffee & Qambus:
Raw 45s from Yemen** (various artists; 2012) Trippy
compilation of vinyl recordings of Yemeni music from
the 1960s and '70s.

Ghanni Habibi (Ahmad
Fathi; 2015) Yemen's internationally recognised classical
oud player.

Country in Crisis

Yemen is in crisis. Mired in a civil war, its infrastructure and economy have been destroyed, and the violence is taking a desperate toll on most of the population, with famine conditions in the worst-hit regions and a cholera epidemic sweeping through the country. Needless to say, it is not safe to travel here. Off the coast, the island of Socotra has escaped the mainland's turmoil, although the UAE and Saudi Arabia have stationed troops there. Travel is now again possible but you'll have to carefully weigh up safety considerations as the only current flight does stop on the mainland.

In days past, the sons of Noah knew Yemen as the land of milk and honey, Gilgamesh came to this land to search for the secret of eternal life, wise men gathered frankincense and myrrh from its mountains and, most famously, the Queen of Sheba called Yemen her home.

Further Reading

Yemen: Travels in Dictionary Land (Tim Mackintosh-Smith; 1997) Witty, erudite portrait of Yemen and its people.

They Die Strangers (Muhammad Abdul-Wali; 2001) Novella and short-story collection, threaded together by themes of poverty and exile.

The Last Refuge (Gregory D Johnsen; 2012) Well-researched account of Al Qaeda's rise in Yemen and its impact on the nation.

Hurma (Ali Al Muqri; 2012) Sex and religion are the themes of this Sanaa-set, controversial, coming-of-age novel.

Yemen: Dancing on the Heads of Snakes (Victoria Clark; 2010) Highly readable rundown on Yemen's history and culture.

UNDERSTAND YEMEN

Yemen Today

Yemen's 2011 Arab Spring protests lit the fuse that blew the country's ongoing conflicts into full-scale violence. Since 2014, when the Houthi rebel group captured Sanaa, Yemen has descended into civil war. A coalition force led by Saudi Arabia began a campaign of aerial bombardments while Al Qaeda took advantage of the chaos to gain control of some eastern areas. Meanwhile, a vast humanitarian crisis is unfolding, and a widespread cholera epidemic is gripping the country.

The Players Battling for Control

The 2011 Arab Spring ended Ali Abdullah Saleh's two-decade reign as Yemen's president, paving the way for his long-term vice president Abdrabbuh Mansour Hadi to assume office in the 2012 elections. However, the transition of power failed to provide political stability or improvements in everyday life. Exploiting President Hadi's weak grip on power, the Houthis (a rebel group that backs Yemen's Zaydi Shia minority) gained control of the far northern provinces, and Al Qaeda advanced their influence in the central highlands and the east.

In 2014 the Houthis – aided by their old foe, ex-president Saleh, who threw his backing behind them – advanced into Sanaa taking over the capital. A power-sharing agreement between the Houthi-Saleh alliance and President Hadi's government was signed but then overturned. Hadi fled to the port city of Aden, which he proclaimed the new capital of Yemen, and factions of the South Yemen Movement (which believe in autonomous rule for southern Yemen) joined forces with Hadi to fight against the Houthis. Meanwhile, Al Qaeda and other jihadist groups took advantage of the power vacuum to launch a series of attacks across the country.

The Houthi-Saleh alliance then began a southern advance, successfully taking Aden in March 2015, leading to Hadi fleeing again, this time to Saudi Arabia. Saudi Arabia (leading a coalition of regional allies including the United Arab Emirates and backed by the US, the UK and France) launched a combined bombing campaign and maritime blockade on Yemen to restore President Ha-

di's rule. The Houthis replied by firing missiles into Saudi Arabia. At the same time, the US began airstrikes on Al Qaeda positions in the east. By July 2015 Aden had been fully re-captured by pro-Hadi factions, but the country was mired in a full-scale civil war.

The civil war (and its several wars within the war) continues to rumble on, with three failed UN-initiated peace proposals so far. The Houthi-Saleh alliance broke down in late 2017, and ex-president Saleh was assassinated. Meanwhile, in January 2018, Aden fell again, this time to the Southern Transitional Council (STC; a faction of South Yemen Movement who had once been allied with Hadi). Confusingly, the STC are backed by the UAE, but the UAE are also part of the pro-Hadi Saudi-led coalition. This splintering of all factions has done nothing to stem the violence. An estimated two million Yemenis have so far been displaced by the war, and the UN has stated that Yemen is the worst humanitarian crisis in the world.

Humanitarian Crisis

The UN states that more than 22 million Yemenis are in need of aid, with 16 million lacking basic access to sanitation and clean water. Malnutrition is affecting more than seven million.

With the health system collapsing (more than 50% of Yemen's medical facilities are now not functioning), a cholera outbreak in October 2016 quickly spread, its speed aided by the destruction of much of the country's sanitation and water systems by the Saudi coalition airstrikes. In December 2017 the World Health Organization (WHO) announced that the number of infected cholera cases in country was estimated at more than one million people, making Yemen's cholera epidemic the worst in modern history.

UN-sponsored talks in December 2018 aimed to demilitarise the Red Sea port of Hodeidah (under Houthi control) to allow access to humanitarian supplies. Negotiations were still ongoing in early 2019.

History

Yemen has a rich history that stretches back to the Palaeolithic era and is one of the oldest centres of civilisation in the Middle East. With its strategically placed ports, Yemen has been coveted through the ages by both

---

ℹ SAFETY & TRAVEL
....

Yemen is teetering on the brink of collapse. Travelling anywhere in the country is not advised. Not only is the risk of kidnapping or getting caught up in conflict-related violence extremely high, but there is an acute shortage of food, clean water and medicine.

In late 2018 Yemenia Airways resumed flights to the island of Socotra. This flight has a one-hour stop at Seiyan on the Yemen mainland, so travellers need to consider the safety risks and check whether their travel insurance coverage will be valid if taking the flight.

---

empire builders and regional players, a role that continues to fuel the bloodshed and instability of today.

Ottoman & British Occupation

From the 15th century onwards, foreign powers vied for control of the Red Sea coast. But it was the Ottomans who made the greatest impact. Occupying parts of Yemen from 1535 to 1638 and again from 1872 to 1918, they ignored, or failed to capture, the remote inland areas ruled by local imams (prayer leaders).

From 1839 to 1967, the British occupied and controlled parts of southern Yemen, including the port of Aden, which was declared a British protectorate.

Meanwhile in the north, after WWI and the defeat of Germany (with whom the Ottomans were allied), a new royal Zaydi dynasty, the Hamid Al Din, rose up to take the place of the former occupiers.

Civil War

Until 1962, central and northern Yemen had been ruled by a series of local imams. However, on the death of the influential imam Ahmad, a dispute over succession broke out, embroiling the whole region in a war that dragged on for the next eight years.

On the one side, army officers supported by Egypt proclaimed the Yemen Arab Republic (YAR), while on the other, the royalists based in the north, and backed by Britain and Saudi Arabia, were loyal to Ahmad's son and successor. The YAR forces eventually won.

Following the National Liberation Front's victories in the guerrilla campaign against the British, the colonialists were forced to withdraw from southern Yemen in 1967. Three years later the People's Democratic Republic of Yemen (PDRY) was born. It became the first and only Marxist state in the Arab world.

In the north of the country, meanwhile, Field Marshall Ali Abdullah Saleh had instituted a progressive rule of the YAR with his General People's Congress (GPC).

In the PDRY, however, there was turmoil. Power struggles within the Yemen Socialist Party (YSP) had led to rising tension. Finally, in Aden in January 1986, a two-week civil war broke out. The situation was aggravated by the collapse of the Soviet Union, previously the major benefactor of the PDRY. As a result, the south was thrown into a state of bankruptcy.

Reunification

On 22 May 1990 a reunified Republic of Yemen was declared, and the country became the first multi-party parliamentary democracy on the Arabian Peninsula. Saleh took the position of president and Ali Salim Al Bidh (the leader of YSP, the ruling party of the former PDRY) became vice president.

Things didn't get off to a good start for the new nation. During the 1990–91 Gulf War, Yemen appeared to side with Iraq and in doing so managed to alienate not only the US but also its Gulf neighbours. This led to the expulsion of more than one million Yemeni emigrant workers from Saudi Arabia and devastated the economy.

On the home front, things also began to sour, and the YSP and its members started to feel increasingly marginalised by the GPC.

Eventually tensions came to a head, and in 1994, civil war again broke out between the north and the south. Bidh's attempts to secede from the north were quashed, and he fled the country.The country was reunified shortly afterwards, and the GPC again swept to power in elections held in 1997.

In September 1999 the country held its first-ever presidential election, and Saleh was re-elected as the country's president.

ⓘ TRAVELLING TO SOCOTRA

Although the Yemeni island of Socotra has seen none of the violence of the mainland, it suffered two devastating cyclones in 2015 and another in early 2018. All commercial flights to the island were suspended in 2015, cutting off the island completely for travellers. In mid-2018 UAE troops took over the island's ports and airport. Most of the troops, though, were later withdrawn after local protests. Not long afterwards Yemenia Airways once again began advertising a scheduled weekly flight, which at the time of writing remained the only way to reach the island. It flies between Cairo and Socotra every Wednesday, via a one-hour stop at Seiyun on Yemen's mainland. Note that at the time of writing the flight was unable to be booked online, meaning to book independently you had to physically visit Yemenia Airways' offices (in Cairo or Dubai) to procure a ticket.

Yemen tourist visas are now only issued with a letter from a tour operator. The very few specialist Socotra tour companies can arrange your visa for you (about US$150) as part of a tour package. If you want to visit, and have carefully weighed up the safety considerations, local company www.socotra-eco-tours.com is run by Socotri nature guides who have all received training by the UNDP-Socotra Conservation and Development Program. They arrange custom-made itineraries for both individuals and groups.

Brewing Social Unrest

Following the attacks of 11 September 2001, Yemen was viewed with suspicion by the US. With its remote, unruly and little-policed interior, Yemen was suspected of providing – even unwittingly – a refuge for Al Qaeda.

In the 2006 presidential elections, Saleh was re-elected by a large margin in elections that international monitors declared largely free and fair. The general consensus among the populace, however, was that after so many years under his rule it was a case of better the devil you know.

Following the elections, the country appeared to be on the rise and was the most stable it had been in years. However, the good times weren't to last. In Sada province a bloody uprising that had rumbled on between the army and the Houthis since 2004 flared up, and a stop-start civil war engulfed the far north. Trouble was also brewing in the south, where secessionists started calling for independence of the former South Yemen.

As these two events threatened to tear the country apart, Al Qaeda's influence started to grow, unemployment rose and levels of corruption grew.

The Arab Spring

When the Arab Spring protests erupted across the wider region it didn't take long for the people of Yemen to come out onto the streets to call for change.

The first big demonstration took place in Sanaa on 27 January 2011. Within three weeks tens of thousands of Yemenis were protesting across the country. By the start of March the protests were becoming more violent, and on 18th March 52 protesters were killed in Sanaa after they were fired on by government security agents.

By April a Gulf Cooperation Council-brokered plan allowing Saleh to cede power in exchange for immunity was put forward. Three times Saleh agreed to sign only to back down at the last moment. When, towards the end of May 2011, Saleh refused to sign the deal for the third time, Sheikh Sadiq Al Ahmar, the head of the Hashid tribal federation, one of the most powerful tribes in the country, declared his support for the opposition and brought his armed supporters to Sanaa. Almost immediately fighting erupted between them and loyalist security forces, with the result that Sanaa was turned into a battleground. Things culminated on 3 June when Saleh was seriously injured in an attack on a mosque he was praying in. The next day he was flown to Saudi Arabia for medical treatment, and Yemenis celebrated the fall of Saleh. Or so they thought.

Saleh's vice president, Abd Al Rab Mansur Al Hadi, was made acting president, but from his hospital bed, Saleh kept indicating that he would return to Yemen. For three months Yemen was trapped in limbo and, taking advantage of the chaos, Al Qaeda in the Arabian Peninsula started taking control of huge swaths of the east and south of the country. Finally, in September 2011, Saleh suddenly reappeared in Yemen, but his time was up, and on 23 November he finally signed a Saudi-brokered agreement to resign.

Understand Arabian Peninsula

Arabian Peninsula Today

With the exception of Yemen, the Arabian Peninsula is enjoying what is termed in Oman as a 'renaissance' – a rebirth of former confidence and strength, marked by investment in culture, education, health care and infrastructure, and a gentle relaxation of the strictly autocratic regimes of the mid-20th century. Guided by the Islamic faith, each country on the Peninsula is feeling its way towards a modern society, sharing many of the aims of the wider world while endeavouring to maintain an Arab identity.

Best in Print

Seven Pillars of Wisdom (TE Lawrence; 1935) Evocative desert descriptions during the Arab Campaign of 1915 to 1918.

Arabian Sands (Wilfred Thesiger; 1959) Captures the Bedouin way of life before it is lost forever.

Orientalism (Edward Said; 1978) The book that redefined the Western love affair with the Middle East.

The Travels of Ibn Battutah (ed Tim Mackintosh-Smith; 2002) Includes illuminating commentary on the great Arab traveller's lifework.

Nine Parts of Desire: The Hidden World of Islamic Women (Geraldine Brooks; 1994) Probing account by an Australian journalist of what it means to be a woman living in an Islamic country.

Best on Film

Lawrence of Arabia (1962) David Lean's classic desert epic.

A Dangerous Man: Lawrence after Arabia (1991) An unofficial sequel to *Lawrence of Arabia*.

Lessons of Darkness (1992) Herzog's exploration of apocalypse in Kuwait's oil fields after the Gulf War.

The Kingdom (2007) Action film examining Saudi Arabia's relationship with USA.

Rapid Change

It is hard to think of another region where the pace of change has been so phenomenal. Grandparents across Arabia remember travelling by donkey, studying under a tree and sleeping in hot and inadequate housing. Infant mortality rates were high, and life expectancy low. Within the space of 50 years, the Peninsula has changed beyond recognition. Icons of the region's success are visible from the superhighways of Saudi Arabia to the soaring towers of Gulf cities. This rapid growth is, of course, largely because of the discovery of oil, but it is also thanks to a willingness to embrace modernity and the complex technologies it involves.

Political Sensibilities

Rapid growth inevitably has social and political repercussions, and in 2011 the Arabian Peninsula witnessed its own Arab Spring. Mostly propelled by students who sympathised with the democratic aspirations of their Arab neighbours, there were minor protests in Oman and Kuwait and more pronounced problems in Bahrain.

Despite the unrest, many Peninsula Arabs glanced at the chaos in Yemen (the Peninsula's only democracy) and questioned the desirability of democratic governance. They looked to their own regimes and saw other ways of effecting positive change, for example strong leadership and a mandate to govern, which lie behind the phenomenal growth and modernisation of Gulf countries. The promise of higher education and jobs further helped quell the unrest, while a groundswell of interest in canvassing for local elections has laid the groundwork for greater participation in government across the region. Today political disenchantment, where it exists, is less about ideology and more about friction between the urge to modernise and the desire to honour Arab heritage.

Diversification & Cooperation

The Arabian Peninsula has some of the highest youth unemployment rates in the world. This issue has contributed to the placement of Kuwait at 55 and Oman at 47 on the UN's Human Development Index (global standard-of-living benchmark).

Providing more employment opportunities is difficult when all countries across the region have been hit by falling oil prices prompted by new methods of extraction and a resulting oversupply. This has placed greater emphasis on economic diversification through trade, commerce and tourism. Dubai is the obvious success story in this regard, with only 5% of the emirate's GDP based on oil revenue.

Hindering local employment is the continued reliance on a largely expatriate workforce. It takes time for the benefits of a modern education system to produce home-grown expertise, and there is resistance from some immigrant communities to train local replacements. Without progress in the human-resource development of the region, however, there is concern that a two-tier society will inevitably lead to further resentment and instability.

Qatar & Yemen

Despite the cooperative spirit of the region, there are still tensions between the members of the GCC. Qatar is currently isolated by all countries in the region, except Oman and Kuwait, as a result of its alleged interactions with Iran. This has resulted in a blockade on air travel between some Gulf cities and Doha.

The biggest challenge facing the region today, however, is Yemen. The complex conflict in Yemen is fuelled by a sectarian dimension in the form of a Shiite insurgency, carried out by Houthi rebels against government forces. In 2015 this provoked Saudi Arabia and its allies to launch air strikes aimed at restoring the internationally recognised regime. Fears that Saudi Arabia's offensive, involving the UAE, may spill across the wider region as competing ideologies battle for a foothold in the only impoverished corner of the Peninsula, have not been realised, but the conflict remains a source of hand-wringing in the region.

Balancing the Future

Peninsula Arabs have braved the shock of the new, but now each country is weighing up to what extent they should honour their heritage while giving a greater sense of inclusion to citizens. The establishment of *majlis ashura* (advisory councils) in public policy signalled a slight shift in approach, and the inclusion of women as they join the ranks of government ministers has been viewed favourably. In 2018 Saudi Arabia made history by permitting women to drive. Propelled ahead of male colleagues by a proven propensity for education and with less commitment to *wasta* (nepotism), Arabia's women are seen as the change agents of the future.

AREA: **3,097,988 SQ KM**

POPULATION: **78 MILLION**

LANGUAGES SPOKEN:
ARABIC, ENGLISH

if the Arabian Peninsula were 100 people

36 would be Arab
64 would be expatriate

belief systems
(% of population)

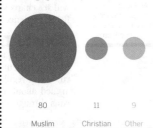

| 80 | 11 | 9 |
| Muslim | Christian | Other |

population per sq km

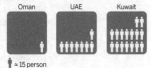

Oman   UAE   Kuwait

👤 ≈ 15 person

History

In the 1950s, the countries of the Arabian Peninsula were a collection of impoverished, disparate states, more easily defined by tribe than by nation. Any sense of the former glory days of incense routes and East African empires was lost in the sands of time. So how did the region suddenly reinvent itself as a major economic powerhouse with a strong sense of identity? The answer lies in Arabia's inheritance of trading excellence and social coherence, two subjects worth further investigation within the context of the region's history.

Tropical Roots (66 million–10,000 BC)

Stand in the middle of Wadi Fanja on the outskirts of Muscat and you may just uncover more than the toads and grasshoppers of today's arid vista. This was where archaeologists discovered the remains of a herbivorous dinosaur, not unlike Zalmoxes or Rhabdodon dinosaurs from France and Romania. What is interesting about this discovery is that it shows the climate of eastern Arabia some 66 million years ago was far more verdant than it is today, with savannah-like grasslands and abundant rainfall. Crocodiles also inhabited places such as Wadi Fanja, suggesting that permanent rivers helped to cut the deeply incised mountain ranges of today's Peninsula.

Homo erectus was attracted to the rich hunting and gathering grounds of southern Arabia more than a million years ago. Homo sapiens arrived on the scene around 100,000 BC and began more organised settlement. Visitors to museums across the region, particularly the Mleiha Archaeological Site and national museums in Bahrain and Muscat, will see charcoal burners, flint axes and spearheads, dating from 10,000 BC, as evidence of the earliest forms of social cohesion.

Born to Trade (10,000 BC–AD 500)

Visit any souq across the Peninsula, or attend a meeting between doctor and patient, teacher and pupil, and you will realise instantly that rules and regulations are fluid, negotiable entities to be haggled over, argued about and artfully manipulated. Perhaps this is because trade runs through the blood of Peninsula people, shaping modern daily in-

Staying in religious schools to avoid expensive hostelries, 14th-century Muslim pilgrim Ibn Battuta set the standard for budget travel. Intending to perform hajj at the age of 20, his 'gap year' lasted 24 years. He clocked up an impressive 120,000km in Arabia and Asia, far out-travelling his contemporary, Marco Polo.

TIMELINE	c 66 million BC	c 100,000 BC	c 5000 BC
	Unlike the deserts of modern Arabia, the Peninsula is covered in savannah-like grasslands, rainfall is abundant and permanent rivers are home to crocodiles and herbivorous dinosaurs.	Homo sapiens live a hunter-gatherer life across the Peninsula, burning fires and rearing their own livestock. They form the first organised communities in the region.	Loose groups of Stone Age and Bronze Age individuals occupy the Peninsula, setting up intricate trade routes between Arabia and Mesopotamia (Iraq) and the Indus Valley.

teractions as it has shaped each country's ancient heritage. Indeed, trade informed the very earliest aspects of the region's history.

Early Commodities

Copper was where it all began. It was mined in Majan (the ancient name of Oman) and traded through the mighty Dilmun Empire (focused on modern-day Bahrain). It's easy to simplify the lives of the ancients, but the early seafaring traders of Dilmun were no barbarians. They spent their mineral wealth on fine glass, ate too many dates and suffered bad teeth, took the time to thread beads of carnelian to hang round their beloveds' necks, enjoyed complex legends and expressed their interest in life through their administrations of death – much like their contemporaries in Egypt.

The Peninsula's early wealth wasn't founded on ore alone, however. It was due in large part to a tree, and a particularly ugly one at that. Frankincense, the aromatic resin of the *Boswellia sacra* tree, was the

The Incense Route

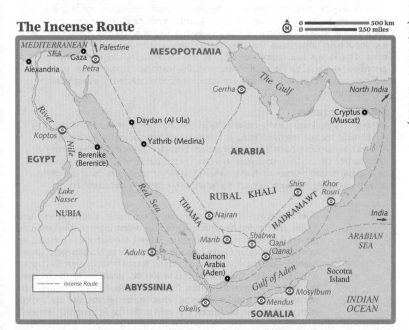

c 3000 BC	c 2000 BC	323 BC	c AD 100
Dilmun, the first great civilisation on the Peninsula, is founded off the coast of Bahrain; it extends from Failaka Island (near present-day Kuwait) towards the mountains of Oman.	In Oman, tombs at Bat and Jaylah are erected along mountain ridges by the Hafit and the Umm An Nar cultures – people belonging to the low-lying territories of the Gulf.	Alexander the Great is attracted to Arabia's wealth but dies before he can mount an expedition. His admiral, Nearchus, establishes an important trading colony on Failaka Island.	The Nabataean Empire controls northwestern Arabia and grows rich by taxing frankincense caravans travelling between southern Arabia and Damascus. The Gulf comes under the influence of Persian dynasties.

THE FRANKINCENSE TREE

Drive along the road from Salalah to the Yemeni border and you may be forgiven for missing one of the most important aspects of the Arabian Peninsula's history. Sprouting from the limestone rock as if mindless of the lack of nutrition, leafless and (for much of the year) pretty much lifeless, *Boswellia sacra* must be one of the least spectacular 'monuments' on a traveller's itinerary. Indeed, with its peeling bark and stumped branches, the frankincense tree looks more like something out of *The Day of the Triffids* than a tree that established the early fortunes of the region.

Aromatic Sap

What makes the tree so special, of course, is its aromatic sap, known as *luban* in Arabic or frankincense in English. The sap oozes in white- or amber-coloured beads from incisions made in the bark and is left to harden in the sun. Frankincense has a natural oil content, allowing it to burn well, and the vapour is released by dropping a bead of the sap onto hot embers.

To this day the pungent aroma is used locally with great enthusiasm, wafted at the entrance of a house to ward away evil spirits, guard against the evil eye or perfume garments. It has other traditional uses, too. The sap has medicinal qualities and was used in just about every prescription dispensed by the Greeks and the Romans. It is still used in parts of the Peninsula to treat a wide range of illnesses, including coughs and psychotic disorders believed to be the result of witchcraft. Internationally, frankincense remains a part of many (particularly Christian) religious rites and is included as an ingredient in exotic perfumes.

Finest Fragrance

Although the frankincense tree grows in Wadi Hadramawt in Yemen, as well as in northern Somalia, the specimens of Dhofar in southern Oman (including the ancient trees of Wadi Dawkah) have been famed since ancient times for producing the finest-quality sap. The tree favours the unique weather system of this corner of southern Arabia, just beyond the moisture-laden winds of the *khareef* (summer season), but near enough to enjoy their cooling influence. As such it is notoriously difficult to root elsewhere.

chief export and economic mainstay of the region. Grown in southern Arabia and carried by caravan across the desert interior, it helped fund powerful civilisations for 500 years. Indeed, the Nabataeans, famed for carving spectacular tombs into the desert cliffs at Madain Saleh (Saudi Arabia), similar to those of their capital Petra (Jordan), controlled much of northwestern Arabia from 200 to 100 BC, sustained by the precious sap. Along ancient trade routes, frankincense found its way into the inner sanctum of temples in Egypt, Jerusalem and Rome, and was recorded in the Bible and the Quran. It is used to this day in many of the world's

c 300	570	610	622–632
Central and western Arabia develop into a patchwork of independent city states, sustained by the frankincense trade or by farming, while the Gulf is subsumed into the Sassanian Empire from Persia.	The Marib dam, upon which the livelihoods of 50,000 people depend, bursts its banks, scattering the people of Adz in the Peninsula's most significant migration. Prophet Muhammad is born.	Muhammad receives his first revelation. Considered by Muslims as the word of God, the Quran subsequently lays the foundations of a new, monotheistic religion that condemns the worship of idols.	Muhammad and his followers flee Mecca for Medina in 622, marking the beginning of the first Islamic state. The new religion spreads across the Peninsula, despite Muhammad's death in 632.

most sacred ceremonies. According to Pliny, writing in the 1st century AD, it was thanks to the frankincense trade that the people of southern Arabia became the richest on Earth.

The Frankincense Trade

Tradition dictated that the frankincense tree was a gift from Allah and was thus not to be propagated, bought or sold, and only harvested if it happened to be within your plot of land. That didn't stop people, however, from trying their luck. In an attempt to protect their precious resources, the Jeballi, the caretakers of Omani frankincense groves, honed the art of misinformation. Flying red serpents and toxic mists were just some of the mythical tribulations rumoured to protect trees from evil eye and thieving hand. Gathering the aromatic gum was fraught with danger because of deadly indigenous infections and the harsh environment beyond the monsoon catchment. Little wonder the collectors were often slaves, or those banished to the area as punishment.

The frankincense trade was centred on Sumhuram, which the Greeks called Moscha and which is now known as Khor Rori. Today the ruins of this once-great port are a short drive from Salalah, the capital of Dhofar and the second-largest city in Oman. Looking out to sea on a wet and windy July day, when the grazing camels and flamingos shelter in the upper reaches of the lagoon, leaving the violent shore to the ghost crabs, it's no surprise that easier ports would eventually be found for readier cargo, and Khor Rori left to slip back to nature.

The Birth & Growth of Islam (570–1498)

Given that today one out of every four people worldwide are Muslim, there can be no greater moment of historical importance on the Arabian Peninsula than the birth of the Prophet Muhammad in AD 570.

As one of the world's most influential spiritual leaders, it is easy to focus on Muhammad's teachings and forget his historical context, but in many ways the limited descriptions of his childhood give a good indication of life in the desert at that time. As his father died before he was born, Muhammad became the poor ward of his grandfather. Although his family were settled Arabs, he was given to a Bedouin foster mother, as was the custom at the time, to be raised in the desert. Perhaps it was this experience that gave him a sense of moderation and the preciousness of resources. In the desert, too, there were no intermediaries, no priests and no prescribed places of worship – nothing separating the people from the things they believed in.

Muhammad went on caravans and became a trusted trader before returning to Mecca, which at that time was a large and prosperous city that profited from being the centre of pilgrimage. Mecca was the home of the

The Queen of Sheba is fabled to have laid frankincense at the feet of King Solomon and the wise men took it to Bethlehem. According to Pliny, only 3000 families had the right to harvest frankincense, and there were restrictions even then - men were forbidden to cut trees after contact with women.

632–850	850–1300	1498	1507
The Muslim capital moves to Damascus, heading an empire that extends from Spain to India. Mecca and Medina lose their earlier political importance, but grow as the spiritual homes of Islam.	Arabia's old trade routes collapse and the Peninsula declines in wealth and importance. Petty sheikhdoms bicker over resources, under the control of Tartar moguls, Persians and Ottoman Turks.	In a generous but ominous gesture, a celebrated sailor from Oman, Ahmed Bin Majid, helps Vasco da Gama navigate the Cape of Good Hope, leading a decade later to occupation.	Portugal annexes the Yemeni island of Socotra. It uses this vantage point to complete an occupation of Oman and goes on to colonise the island of Bahrain.

Kaaba, a sanctuary founded by Abraham but occupied by the images and idols of many other tribes and nations.

The worship of 'the one true god' and the condemnation of idols was at the heart of Muhammad's teaching and inevitably the Meccans took fright, forcing Muhammad to flee to Medina in 622. Muhammad's mighty legacy, however, transcended his personal history, and the new religion of Islam quickly spread across the Peninsula and to the world beyond. Ironically, as Islam expanded, the fortunes of Arabia waned, but to this day the Peninsula holds a special place in history as the birthplace of one of the world's great monotheistic religions.

LAWRENCE OF ARABIA

If there is one name in Arab history that most Western people will recognise, it's surely that of British archaeologist and explorer TE Lawrence, better known as Lawrence of Arabia – the same Lawrence, in fact, who wrote to his sceptical biographer that 'history isn't made up of the truth anyhow, so why worry'. This is an interesting question when it comes to the history of the Arabian Peninsula, as there appears to be no definitive version of events. The story assumes a different shape, particularly since the beginning of the 20th century, according to whose account you read.

Lawrence's own account of Arabian history, so eloquently described in *The Seven Pillars of Wisdom*, is a case in point. You might imagine, from what he writes, that Lawrence and General Allenby, the senior British officer responsible for the Arab Campaign, single-handedly brought the modern Arabian Peninsula into being during the Arab Revolt from 1915 to 1918. 'On my plan, by my effort,' he states triumphantly on the taking of Aqaba.

But where are the Arabs in Lawrence's account? What did they make of the pale-skinned, blue-eyed eccentric? Read Suleiman Mousa's account of the campaign in *TE Lawrence: An Arab View*, and you barely recognise the same moment in history. While Lawrence is busy taking credit for little skirmishes, larger battles led by the Arabs are only briefly mentioned, and Lawrence arrives triumphant in cities where Arab leaders Feisal and Auda have been waiting for days. Far from the great white hunter, he is remembered in many Arab accounts as a sickly individual with boils who, like a spoof in a Western, mistakenly shot his own camel.

We'll never know whether Lawrence was centre stage or sideshow. What the example illustrates, however, is the caution with which you need to approach the history of the Peninsula. In the early 21st century this must surely sound familiar to anyone following current events in the region in local and Western media. It's tempting to agree with Lawrence that history can at times be more about fiction than fact.

1902	1912	1916	1932
Abdul Aziz Bin Abdul Rahman Al Saud, known as Ibn Saud, begins a series of conquests that eventually lead to the formation of the state of Saudi Arabia.	The Saudis pose a serious threat to the Gulf sheikhdoms. British protection prevents Kuwait, Qatar and the UAE from being subsumed into Saudi Arabia.	Hussein Bin Ali Al Hashimi leads an Arab revolt against the Ottomans in anticipation of being crowned 'King of the Arabs'. The British sign the Balfour Declaration instead, favouring the establishment of Israel.	Ibn Saud combines the two crowns of Hejaz and Najd, renaming his country the 'Kingdom of Saudi Arabia'. In the same year, oil is struck in commercial quantities in Bahrain.

Europeans Arrive (1498–1650)

There is something satisfying about standing under the Tomb of Bibi Miriam in Qalhat, Oman, knowing that two of the world's great medieval travellers, Marco Polo and Ibn Battuta, also stood there. Their travels prefigured a revival in Western trading interests in Arabia, and it wasn't long before the pilgrim caravans of Mecca were once again transporting spices and drugs from the Orient to Europe via the ports of Istanbul and Venice.

Meanwhile, a great Omani seafarer, Ahmed Bin Majid, helped Vasco da Gama navigate the Cape of Good Hope in 1498 and, in good faith, told him of his own wondrous country on the Straits of Hormuz. The Portuguese quickly understood the strategic significance of their 'discovery', and by 1507 Portugal had annexed the Yemeni island of Socotra, occupied Oman and colonised Bahrain. Travel along the coast of the Gulf today and Portuguese forts appear with regularity – cut inland and there's no trace of them. The Portuguese were only interested in protecting their trade routes and made no impact on the interior of these countries at all – a suitable metaphor for the negligible cultural exchange that took place. When they were eventually ousted by the mid-17th century, they left little more than a legacy of military architecture – and the Maria Theresa dollar.

> Travel to museums in Pakistan and around the Mediterranean and you'll be sure to find the small round seals that were the hallmark of Dilmun traders. These seals represented their personal signatures and their wide distribution is evidence of the extent of their trading influence, far beyond the Arabian Peninsula.

British 'Protection' (1650–1914)

Respect and civility towards outsiders, wrote English diplomat James Silk Buckingham in his 1816 book, *Travels*, are two values that impressed him during his interactions in Muscat. It is an interesting comment because it appears to show that the intimate British involvement with Oman and the 'Trucial States' (the countries along the southern rim of the Gulf) over the next two centuries was founded on mutual benefit rather than solely on colonisation and exploitation. On the one hand, the various treaties and 'exclusive agreements' that Britain signed with the sultan and emirs of the region kept the French at bay and thereby safeguarded British trading routes with India. On the other hand, the British helped maintain the claims to sovereignty of the emerging Gulf emirates against marauding Turkish and Persian interests and from the powerful ambitions of the eventual founder of Saudi Arabia, Ibn Saud.

During WWI British interests in the Gulf were threatened by the Ottomans. The sultan, siding with the Germans, declared jihad (holy war), calling on Muslims everywhere to rise up against the Allied powers of Britain, France and Russia. In response, the British persuaded Hussein Bin Ali, the Grand Sherif of Mecca, to lead an Arab revolt against the Ottomans in exchange for a promise to make him 'King of the Arabs' once the conflict was over. To the famous disgust of British army officer

1948	1960	1961–71	1973
The Gulf rupee replaces the Indian rupee as the common currency of all Gulf States, reflecting a shift away from the jurisdiction of the British Raj after India's independence.	The Middle East produces 25% of the non-Communist world's oil. The 1960s bring the winds of change and hand-in-hand with independence comes a sense of national and regional identity.	In 1961 Kuwait gains independence from Britain. In late 1971 Bahrain and Qatar follow suit, followed by the sheikhdoms of the lower Gulf, which combine to form the United Arab Emirates.	The Gulf States' embargo of oil to the West – the 'oil weapon' – is first used to powerful effect during the Arab-Israeli War to protest against the West's support for Israel.

TE Lawrence, the British negotiated with the French on the carving up of the Ottoman Empire instead, and assisted the Zionist movement in the formation of Israel.

Despite this monumental sell-out, visit any corner of the Arabian Peninsula today and you are bound to meet a pink-faced Brit, basking in the desert sun. Equally, talk to leaders across the region and chances are they were educated in part in the UK. The relationship between the British and the Arabs of the Peninsula has endured the trials and tribulations of history.

The Pearling Industry (1914–1930)

One of the mixed pleasures of visiting a Gulf jewellery shop is to hold a natural pearl in the palm of one's hand and see reflected in its gorgeous lustre the not-so-illustrious history of the region.

Although pearls have come to be associated with Bahrain, they were harvested throughout the Gulf, and each region gave rise to a specific type of pearl. Pteria shells, or winged oysters, were extensively collected for their bluish mother-of-pearl off the coast of Ras Al Khaimah. The large shells known in the trade as 'Bombay Shells' were found in Omani waters and chiefly exported to London for pearl inlay and decorative cutlery. With an annual export of 2000 tonnes, worth UK£750,000, the most common pearl oyster of the Gulf was *Pinctada radiata,* collected off the coasts of Kuwait, Bahrain and the UAE.

Given the volume of the trade, it is not surprising that it supported the local economies of much of the Gulf. Trading in pearls has existed since the 3rd millennium BC, but it was only in the 19th century, with the collapse of other trade routes in the region, that pearls assumed their economic value. In the 1920s, with what seemed like an insatiable international appetite for pearls, the trade reached its apex.

Pearling was brutally hard work. Workers were divided into divers (who descended for the shells with a weight between their feet) and pullers (who would hoist the divers to the surface by rope). Neither were paid wages. Instead they would receive a share of the total profits for the season. A puller's share was half to two-thirds of a diver's. Boat owners would usually advance money to their workers at the beginning of the season. But the divers were often unable to pay back these loans and became further indebted each year. As a result they were often bound to a particular boat owner for life, and it was not unusual to see quite elderly men still working as divers. If a diver died, his sons were obliged to work off his debts.

Suddenly, around 1930, the unthinkable happened. The Japanese invented a method of culturing pearls. This, combined with the Great Depression, caused the bottom to drop out of the international pearl market. The Peninsula's great pearling industry petered out almost over-

Nicknamed 'Ruffian Dick' by his contemporaries, famed 19th-century traveller Richard Burton learned Arabic and entered Mecca disguised as a *hajji* (pilgrim), an adventure he recorded in a vast tome entitled *Personal Narrative of a Pilgrimage to Al Madinah and Meccah.*

1981	1990	1991	2006
In May Saudi Arabia, Kuwait, Bahrain, Qatar, UAE and Oman form the Gulf Cooperation Council (GCC) to increase economic cooperation and in response to the perceived threat from Iran.	Iraq invades Kuwait in August and annexes the state. King Fahd of Saudi Arabia appeals to the US for help, and the US and Allied forces launch Operation Desert Storm.	The Gulf States eye up developments in Yemen as it makes regional history by becoming the first multiparty democracy on the Arabian Peninsula.	The Asian Games are hosted in Doha – a coup for Qatar and the region as a whole. Oman pulls out of a proposed single currency, a setback for greater GCC integration.

night. Although the collapse brought great hardship to the Gulf in the decades before the discovery of oil, few had the heart to regret it.

Impact of Oil & Modernisation (1930–Today)

Early in the 20th century, a rare resource was discovered on the Peninsula that was to change the face of the region forever. It is upon this resource that the super-modern cities of the Gulf have been crafted out of the sea on reclaimed land, and upon which the nations of Arabia have been pulled by the sandal straps into the 21st century.

Within a few years almost every ruler in the Gulf had given some kind of oil concession in an attempt to bolster their finances. The region's nascent industry was suspended temporarily during WWII but resumed soon after, increasing output to rival that of Iran, the world's biggest producer, by 1960.

In the 1960s and '70s the new wealth, and the threat of cutting off oil supplies to Europe and the US, gave Middle Eastern countries an international influence they hadn't enjoyed for centuries. After each embargo, a surge in oil prices increased both their wealth and their power, triggering the first wave of an enormous building boom in the Gulf that has continued almost unabated for half a century. Western expatriates flocked to the region, providing engineering and financial expertise while hundreds of thousands of Asian expatriates were brought in as manual labour. This change in demographics has left a legacy that continues to have profound effects on the indigenous populations. On the one hand, it has resulted in tolerant, multicultural societies and greatly enhanced infrastructure; on the other hand, it has led to an outnumbering in some countries of the indigenous Arab population and a difficulty in all countries of ensuring work opportunities for locals.

Each time the bottom falls out of the oil market (through global recession or the threat of new technologies such as renewable energy or fracking), Gulf countries have trouble maintaining their building programmes and the generous welfare support their people have come to expect. Each crisis has had hidden benefits, however, forcing the countries of the Gulf Cooperation Council (GCC) to diversify their economies.

But the days of black gold are not over yet. Exploration continues across the region, together with investment in research into ever-more-sophisticated ways of extraction. Despite the hunt for renewable energies such as solar, wind, wave and waste-to-energy power, it's unlikely that any of these green technologies will replace oil in the collective memory of the region. Oil, after all, has given Arabia its place in the modern world.

Books: Early History

Arabia & the Arabs: From the Bronze Age to the Coming of Islam (Robert Hoyland)

Frankincense & Myrrh (Nigel Groom)

HISTORY IMPACT OF OIL & MODERNISATION (1930–TODAY)

2007	2011	2015	2017
The building boom across the Peninsula reaches its peak as high value projects attract investment in all Peninsula countries except Yemen; many, however, become casualties of the 2008 global recession.	The Arab Spring erupts across the region, leaving Bahrain in particular in turmoil. Peninsula governments crack down on corruption and review their policies to quell local restiveness.	Conflict between elected government forces and Houthi rebels plunges Yemen into civil war and attracts air strikes from neighbouring Saudi Arabian–led coalition, threatening to destabilise the region.	Sectarian in nature, a spat between former allies leaves Qatar out in the cold as Saudi Arabia, UAE and Kuwait impose a blockade on the country restricting trade and travel.

People & Society

Although Peninsula countries cover a large area and vary considerably in terms of geography, history and recent fortunes, they nonetheless share a strong continuity of culture quite distinct from neighbouring Arab regions. Whether this arises out of a shared desert experience, from being at the crossroads of East–West trade, or from proximity to the birthplace of Islam, it makes for a coherent experience for visitors, who are likely to sense Bedouin roots as equally in a mall as a souq.

People

The Arabs: Myth and Reality by Gerald Butt, the ex-BBC Middle East correspondent, traces the geopolitical history of the region and examines its complex relationship with the West, including the stereotypical images of the Peninsula Arab.

Although national and tribal allegiances are fiercely maintained, a greater distinction among Peninsula peoples is whether they are resident for work or are native to the region. That may sound obvious, but given that expatriates outnumber the indigenous population in many quarters, this takes on a particular significance, fuelling the social debates in the coffeehouses and affecting policy in and between Gulf states. Distinctions are also drawn between city dwellers who have made their fortunes in the era of oil, and those who have either chosen or been obliged to continue living the harsh desert life of their forebears. All indigenous Arabs share, and are proud of, the Peninsula's Bedouin roots, but only a very few would welcome living a life of such hardships today.

Lifestyle

Drive through the suburbs of Peninsula cities and you'll see domed villas with spangled concrete that glistens in the sun. Walk through the gold souqs and you'll see women with Gucci handbags, buying diamonds and pearls. Park outside the Ritz-Carlton in Manama, or the Burj Al Arab in Dubai, and you'll be embarrassed to be driving a Toyota Echo. Undoubtedly, huge private fortunes have been made in the oil rush and building expansion.

But that isn't the whole picture. Universal education and the mass media have increased expectations, and people who were content with little now want more. Cement and steel prices have doubled over two decades and the burgeoning Arab middle class frets over securing loans to finish the house or pay college fees. If shopping just before payday is anything to go by, most families are left with little at the end of the month.

Minority Population Statistics

Pastoral nomads: less than 5% of Arabia's Bedouin population

Emiratis in UAE: 12% of population

Qataris in Qatar: 12% of population

The rest of the picture is completed by stepping out of the city altogether. Lives in mountain villages, in desert oases, on the dunes or in coastal fishing villages may seem to have been little impacted by city incomes, but then you spot the satellite dish attached to the *barasti* (palm frond) homes, the electricity poles marching up the wadis, the communally owned truck that has allowed settlement to replace nomadic existence. Water, electricity, roads, education and healthcare: this is the real wealth of the region today, and it is remarkably evenly spread given the challenges of geography and topography.

Health & Life Expectancy

A more modern lifestyle, be it in the city or the interior, together with immunisation and improved healthcare systems, has brought radical benefits to the health of much of the Peninsula's population. Life expectancy has risen, child mortality has reduced and diseases such as malaria have been eradicated. On the terraces of southern Arabia 20 years ago, women were bent double in the fields, baked by the sun, arthritic in the mud, or weighed down with herbage, trudging back to their homes, pausing to

A COSMOPOLITAN POPULATION

Although officially treated equally, expatriates who work on the Peninsula are often discriminated against, either positively or negatively, depending on their ethnicity. Middle-income workers from other Middle Eastern countries, for example, are given a friendly reception as brother Arabs and fellow Muslims, but are viewed somewhat condescendingly as poor relations and it is partially true that these expats often stay only long enough to build a house back home and send their children to college. Indeed, in some countries, such as Egypt, Jordan and Yemen, remittances from nationals working abroad constitute the backbone of the home economy.

The number of Europeans and Americans in the region has declined over the past few decades, now that the military and much of the oil and gas industry has been transferred into local hands. Often viewed as a necessary, but not altogether welcome, route to rapid modernisation, employment of these expats focuses on those with advanced educational qualifications, specific skills, or teaching and training abilities. This group, with its larger disposable income, is now somewhat making way for the rise of professionals from India and China, who often command smaller salaries for similar experience and accomplishment.

Expats from India (and to a lesser extent, Pakistan and Bangladesh) have traditionally formed the middle management of the region, particularly in trade, commerce and industry, and the new generations of indigenous graduates look to them for inspiration as entrepreneurs and small business owners. The majority of expats from these countries, however, tend to be employed as manual labourers, for whom life is unremittingly hard. Long hours, poor conditions, unsafe working practices, daily exposure to 45°C heat, visa restrictions and lengthy periods without permission to return home all contribute to often-miserable lives. Most of these migrant workers are on bachelor-status visas and their plight has been the subject of much media coverage, especially in the wake of the decision to host the FIFA World Cup in Qatar in 2022. Despite their treatment being condemned by some human rights organisations, many of these expats find that the benefits outweigh the hardships of a life without work back home and they continue to be recruited in ever-larger numbers. Many return home to a hero's welcome, their meagre remittances capable of transforming the lives of their families due to the strength of regional currencies.

Women expats, largely from the Philippines, India and Sri Lanka, play an important role in the education sector and the healthcare industry. Many of the region's domestic workers are from Muslim countries such as Malaysia and Indonesia. Often required to work long hours for wages much lower than those paid to other expats, and with the risk of sexually related abuse, many nonetheless manage to support an entire extended family from their wages.

It is fair to say that, despite the negative media coverage, not all low-income expats are unhappy with their lot, with many remaining on the Peninsula for 20 years or more, bonding with the families they help to bring up, or attaining satisfaction in the infrastructure they helped build. Equally, their employers are not uniformly callous in their regard for workers' rights, and progress is being made to safeguard the rights of migrant workers across the region. Gulf Cooperation Council labour ministers agreed to a standardised employment contract for domestic workers in 2014 that, for example, discards the controversial sponsorship system. Legally, employees now do not have to surrender their passports, have the freedom to change employment and their working hours are regulated by law. Welcomed by the expat community as a step in the right direction, these rights are not always respected by less scrupulous employers.

THE BEDOUIN – SURVIVAL OF THE MOST GENEROUS

Meaning 'nomadic', the name Bedouin is today a bit of a misnomer. Though thought to number several hundred thousand, very few Bedouin are still truly nomadic, despite retaining some traditional practices such as rearing livestock and living under the stars.

Traditionally, after pitching their distinct black, goat-hair tents – the *beit ash shaar* (literally 'house of hair') – they graze their goats, sheep or camels in one area for several months. When the sparse desert fodder runs out, it's time to move on again, allowing the land to regenerate naturally.

The hospitality of the Bedouin is legendary, even in a region known for its generosity. Part of the ancient and sacrosanct Bedouin creed is that no traveller in need of rest or food should be turned away. A traveller, in turn, assumes the assured protection of his hosts for a period of three days and is guaranteed a safe passage through tribal territory.

The philosophy is simple: you scratch my back, I'll scratch yours – only in the desert, it's a matter of survival. Such a code of conduct ensures the survival of all in a difficult environment with scant resources. It allows the maintenance of a nomadic lifestyle and the continuation of trade. It's a kind of survival, in other words, of the most generous.

stack stones in the crumbling terrace walls. For many Peninsula inhabitants, it's pointless being nostalgic about the demise of hard manual labour, even if a modern lifestyle comes at the price of 'modern' diseases such as diabetes, hypertension and stroke.

Population & Ethnic Diversity

In the Gulf, names are all important. Names say a lot about who is from where, and each country is acutely mindful of such distinctions: 'with a name like that, he must be a Baluchi (not real Emirati)'; 'he speaks Swahili so he must be Zanzibari (not real Omani)'; 'he's from the coast (not real Saudi)'. And so it goes on until you wonder if there's any such thing as a 'real' anybody. Such comments on ethnicity make you realise that Arab allegiances are linked to tribe before nation. Centuries of trading and pilgrimage have resulted in an extraordinarily mixed population and only a few pockets of people, such as the Jebbalis of southern Oman, can claim ethnic 'purity'.

For the visitor, Arabs are often less in evidence anyway. The indigenous population of the entire Peninsula numbers less than 50 million out of a total population of 78 million. In Saudi and Oman, non-nationals account for 37% and 45% respectively of the population, but this figure rises to 48% in Bahrain, 69% in Kuwait, and 88% in the UAE and Qatar.

The large presence of other nationals on the Peninsula came about after the discovery of oil. Hundreds of thousands of expatriate workers were brought in to help develop the region's industries and provide skills and knowledge in creating a modern infrastructure. Although none of these nationals were originally permitted citizenship, many have stayed a lifetime, raising families and setting up businesses under local sponsorship, changing the demographics of the entire Peninsula.

The issue now is how to reduce the dependence on expatriate labour and train the local population to fill their place. Inevitably, few expats willingly train locals to take over their jobs. Equally, in some of the wealthier Gulf countries, there is a reluctance from locals to take on manual labour and a traditional distaste for jobs in the service industry.

Bedouin Roots

It's easy to underestimate the Bedouin heritage of Arab society if your visit is concentrated on the big cities of the Gulf. Yet even here there are weekend escapes to the desert in Oman, an enormous falcon souq in Doha and tents set up outside houses in Kuwait. These are all indicative

Less exercise, more stress and a fast-food diet high in fats, sugar and salt have led to an increase of diabetes in Arabia. Alarmingly, five of the 15 countries with the world's highest rates of diabetes are on the Peninsula, namely the United Arab Emirates, Qatar, Bahrain, Kuwait and Saudi Arabia.

of a strong attachment to an ancient culture that runs through all the countries of the Peninsula.

The attitude towards the camel is an interesting case in point. The donkey played just as important a role in transport in the mountains of the Peninsula, but no one breeds donkeys for fun. Camels, on the other hand, are as prevalent as ever and in some corners of Arabia (such as Dhofar in Oman) are proliferating at such a speed, because of their leisurely modern lifestyle, they are threatening the fragile ecology of their habitat. Of course, racing has something to do with the obsession with camel ownership, but the animal is more deeply involved in the Arab psyche than mere racing. Camels, commonly involved in beauty pageants, evoke ancient nomadic lifestyles, the symbol of community through hardship and endurance – the inheritance, in short, of Bedouin roots.

The term 'Bedouin' refers not so much to an ethnic group as to a lifestyle. City Arabs today, stressed by familiar modern anxieties regarding wealth and how to keep it, are wistful about a bygone era to which they claim lineage, even if they are more likely to be the descendants of townspeople and seafarers.

Bedouin: Nomads of the Desert, by Alain Keohane, is a beautiful photographic and textual testimony to the Arabian Bedouin.

PEOPLE & SOCIETY SOCIETY

Society
Marriage & the Role of Women

Although polygamy is legal, and the marrying of two wives is reasonably common, few Peninsula Arabs exercise their Islamic right to four wives, unable or unwilling to afford the emotional, physical and financial cost of multiple households. This is particularly burdensome given that according to the Quran, each wife must be treated equally, in as much as this is possible.

Divorce is easily enacted and is becoming less of a taboo, especially in Oman and the Gulf countries. Modern Peninsula women are educated, usually study far harder at university than men and therefore are often more successful in the workplace. They are entitled to earn and keep their own income (unlike the man, who surrenders his salary to the household) and as such have an independence unthinkable to their grandmothers.

On the one hand, discussion in the region focuses on fundamental women's rights – in Saudi Arabia, for example, women only earned the right to vote and to drive in 2015 and 2018 respectively, and they are still unable to travel unescorted by male relatives. On the other hand, in

THE MODERN BEDOUIN

Most Bedouin have modernised their existence with 4WD trucks (it's not unusual to find the camel travelling by truck these days), fodder from town (limiting the need to keep moving) and purified water from bowsers. Most have mobile phones and satellite TV and everyone listens to the radio. Many no longer move at all. Bedouin customs, dating from the earliest days of Islam, remain pretty much unchanged, however, especially their legendary hospitality towards strangers.

Living arrangements tend to stay the same too, with tents generally divided into a *haram* (forbidden area) for women and an area reserved for the men. The men's section also serves as the public part of the house, where guests are treated to coffee and dates, or meals. It's here that all the news and gossip – a crucial part of successful survival in a hostile environment – is passed along the grapevine.

The Bedouin family is a close-knit unit. The women do most of the domestic work, including fetching water (sometimes requiring walks of many kilometres), baking bread and weaving. They are also often the first to come to a tourist's rescue by pulling, digging and driving a stuck 4WD out of soft sand. The men are traditionally the providers in times of peace, and fierce warriors in times of war.

Why the Low Crime Rate?

Strict codes of moral conduct expounded by Islam

A legal system rigorously enforced

Traditional Arab values

Ancient concepts of honour

the UAE and Oman, where equality of education has led to an equality of expectation, the discussion focuses more on issues such as breaking through the glass ceiling and how to train in traditionally male-oriented disciplines such as engineering, while respecting cultural norms regarding shift hours or working on site.

With more women than men graduating from some of the top universities across the region, inevitably questions are being asked about primary carers in the family. There's also concerns about the psychological fallout on men, whose once-unquestioned authority is being undermined by poor performance relative to their female counterparts.

Family Size & Welfare

The family, guided by Muslim principles, is still at the centre of the Arab way of life. The family is an extended unit often comprising whole villages, united around a common tribal name. Avoiding actions that may bring shame to the family is of paramount importance. Saving face is therefore more than a reluctance to admit a mistake; it's an expression of unwillingness to make a family vulnerable to criticism. Equally, promotion or success is not calculated in individual terms, but in the benefits it bestows on the family. Of course, everyone knows someone who can help in the collective good, and accruing *wasta* (influence) is a Peninsula pastime.

The efforts of one generation are reflected in the provision of education and opportunity for the next. This comes at a cost and few Arabs these days can afford the large families of a dozen children common a decade ago; indeed the average in the Gulf States has now dropped to around two children.

The governments of each country have made generous provision for families across the region in terms of free education and healthcare, but the resources won't last forever and the younger generations are beginning to see that they have to work hard to secure the same opportunities for their own children.

Guests are usually seen to the door, or even to the end of the corridor or garden. Traditionally this represents the safe passage of guests across your tribal territory. If you have Arab visitors, make sure you do the same!

Dress & Fashion

Men take huge pride in their costume, which, in its simplicity and uniformity, is intended to transcend wealth and origin. A loose headscarf, known as *gutra,* is worn by many Peninsula males. In the Gulf States it is of white cloth, while in western Kuwait and Saudi Arabia it is checked. The black head rope used to secure the *gutra* is called *agal*. It's said to originate in the rope the Bedouin used to tie up their camels at night. Omani men usually wear a pastel-hued turban decorated with intricate and brightly coloured embroidery, wrapped deftly about a cap.

Most Peninsula men also wear the floor-length shirt-dress, which in Saudi Arabia, Bahrain and Qatar is known as a *thobe,* and in Kuwait, the UAE and Oman as a *dishdasha*. These are officially white (but unofficially come in various colours) and some have collars and cuffs, while others are edged with tassels and white-thread embroidery at the neck.

TEA & TALK

A *diwaniya* (gathering), usually conducted at someone's home – in a tent or on cushions just outside it, to be precise – is an important aspect of Gulf life, and any visitor who has the chance to partake in one will find it the best opportunity to observe Arab social life first-hand. The object of the gathering, which has its origin in Bedouin traditions of hospitality, is to drink endless cups of hot, sweet tea – oh, and to chew the political cud, of course. It is usually a 'man thing'. As one Kuwaiti woman explained, the women of the house are usually too busy living life to waste time discussing it.

Men drinking coffee

On ceremonial occasions the dress is completed with a finely wrought belt and ceremonial dagger and a transparent silk outer garment known as a *bisht*.

Women's dress is more varied. Traditionally, it often comprises a colourful long dress or an embroidered tunic with trousers and heavily decorated ankle cuffs. In the cities, modern clothing is common. Over the top, women usually wear a black gown known as an *abaya*. This can either be worn loose and cover the head (as in Saudi Arabia) or it can be worn as a fashion item, tailored to the body and spangled with diamante (as in Oman).

Almost all women on the Arabian Peninsula cover their hair, but they don't all wear the burka (veil) – in Oman and the UAE, they mostly do not cover the face. Veils can be of a thin gauze; a cloth that covers the face but not the eyes, or a mask concealing the nose, cheeks and part of the mouth. Women often choose such coverings in order to pass more comfortably through male company, or to protect prized pale skin and glossy hair from the harsh penalties of sun and sand – a custom that predates Islam.

Nine Parts of Desire, by journalist Geraldine Brooks, was a ground-breaking investigation into the lives of women under Islam in the 1990s, covering various countries of the Middle East and exposing some of the many myths regarding the treatment of women in the Arab world.

Religious Zeal

Only a tiny minority of people on the Peninsula are involved in religious fundamentalism, and most of those channel their zeal into peaceful attempts to reconcile the liberties of modern life with the traditional values of Islam. Those who resort to violence to accomplish largely political aims are mistrusted by their own communities and considered misguided by most religious leaders in the region. It is unfortunate that this small minority gain maximum media coverage abroad and are the people upon whom the entire culture of the mostly peaceful, amiable, adaptable and tolerant Arabian Peninsula is judged.

Arts, Sports & Leisure

If you chose one feature that distinguishes art on the Arabian Peninsula (and Arab art generally) from other traditions, it is the close integration of function with form. In other words, most Arab art has evolved with a purpose. That purpose could be as practical as embellishing the prow of a boat with a cowrie shell to ward off 'evil eye', or as nebulous as creating intricate and beautiful patterns to intimate the presence of God and invite spiritual contemplation. By this definition the Arabian passion for falconry, camel rearing and horse racing can be described as an art form, arising out of a need to hunt and celebrated for the aesthetic beauty of form in motion.

Arts

Poetry

The Son of a Duck is a Floater, by Arnander and Skipworth, is a fun collection of Arab sayings with English equivalents. It's worth buying just to see how wisdom is universal – not to mention the thoroughly enjoyable illustrations.

Poetry is part and parcel of the great oral tradition of storytelling that informs the literature of all Peninsula countries, the roots of which lie with the Bedouin. Stories told by nomadic elders to the wide-eyed wonder of the young serve not just as after-dinner entertainment, but as a way of binding generations together in a collective oral history. As such, storytelling disseminates the principles of Islam and of tribal and national identity. It extols the virtues of allegiance, valour, endurance and hospitality – virtues that make life in a harsh environment tolerable.

All the best-known figures of classical Arabic and Persian literature are poets, including the famed Omar Khayyam, the 11th-century composer of *rubai* (quatrains), and the 8th-century Baghdadi poet, Abu Nuwas. The great Arab poets were regarded as possessing knowledge forbidden to ordinary people and, as such, they served the purpose of bridging the human and spirit worlds. To this day, poetry recitals play an important part in all national celebrations, and even the TV-watching young are captivated by a skilfully intoned piece of verse.

Music

Arabian song and dance have evolved for a purpose. Generally, music was employed to distract from hardship – like the songs of the seafarers marooned on stagnant Gulf waters or the chanting of fishermen hauling in their nets. There are also harvest songs and love ballads, all of which are either sung unaccompanied or to syncopated clapping or drum beats. East African rhythms, introduced into local music from Arab colonies, lend much Peninsula music a highly hypnotic quality, and songs can last for more than an hour.

While the austere Wahhabi and Ibadi sects discourage singing and dancing, no wedding or national celebration on the Peninsula would be the same without them. Men dance in circles, flexing their swords or ceremonial daggers while jumping or swaying. If they get really carried away, volleys of gunfire are exchanged above the heads of the crowd. Women have a tradition of dancing for the bride at weddings (which are generally gender-segregated, with the women gaining the better part of the bargain in feasting and dancing). Unobserved by men, they gyrate suggestively in their revealing dresses as if encouraging the bride towards the marital bed.

While traditional music plays a big part in contemporary Arab life, it is not the only form of music. Arab pop, especially of the Amr Diab type, is ubiquitous, while radio stations and nightclubs featuring DJs showcasing the latest international trends are also popular, particularly in the UAE, Qatar and Bahrain. A classical orchestra in Oman and military drum and pipe (bagpipes) bands have won international acclaim.

Crafts

Function and form are most noticeably linked in the rich craft heritage of the Peninsula, encompassing jewellery, silversmithing, weaving, embroidery and basket making. Take jewellery, for example – the heavy silver jewellery, so distinctively worn by Bedouin women, was designed not just as a personal adornment, but as a form of portable wealth. Silver amulets, containing rolled pieces of parchment or paper, bear protective inscriptions from the Quran, to guarantee the safety of the wearer. Jewellery is traditionally melted down rather than handed on – the ultimate pragmatic gesture.

The sad fact of practical craft is that once the need for it has passed, there is little incentive to maintain the skills. What is the point of potters in Al Hofuf and Bahla making clay ewers when everyone drinks water from branded plastic bottles? Many regional governments encourage local craft associations in the hope of keeping the craft heritage alive, resulting in successful ventures such as the Bedouin weaving project at Sadu House in Kuwait City and the women's centres in Manama and Abu Dhabi. The Omani Heritage Documentation Project is another worthwhile enterprise. Launched in 1996 to document Oman's great craft heritage, it resulted after eight years of study in a two-volume definitive guide, *The Craft Heritage of Oman*.

Architecture

In common with other arts, Peninsula architecture is also steered by purpose. The local climate plays an important role: the wind towers of the Gulf, for example, not only look attractive, but also function as channels

The Thousand and One Nights, translated by Richard Burton, is a collection of tales (including Ali Baba and Aladdin) that originate from Arabia, India and Persia. They are told, night by night, by the beautiful, beguiling narrator, Sheherazade, to save herself from beheading by a vengeful king.

ORAL TRADITION

For the nomadic Bedouin, life is lived on the move. Permanence, beyond a month or two, is virtually unknown – even the footsteps that mark their passing shift with the sands. The artistic expression of their culture has evolved to be similarly portable – weaving that can be rolled up and stowed on a camel, beadwork that can be tucked in a pocket, stories unfurled around the campfire.

Bedouin tales, with their endless digressions, allegories and parables, are used to clarify a situation, to offer tactful advice to a friend, or to alert someone diplomatically to trouble or wrongdoing. More often, they lampoon corrupt leaders and offer a satirical commentary on current affairs, particularly those of the mistrusted 'townspeople'. They can be very funny, highly bawdy and verging on the libellous, depending on the persuasions of the teller.

There is said to be a tale for every situation. Travellers may be surprised at how often the Bedouin resort to proverbs, maxims or stories during the course of normal conversation. It is said that the first proverb of all is: 'While a man may tell fibs, he may never tell false proverbs'!

Sadly, the modern world has encroached on storytelling. The advent of TV and other forms of entertainment has led some to fear that this valuable oral patrimony is in danger of disappearing forever, but look at any national-day gathering and it's clear that it still has the power to touch Arab hearts.

In the souqs of eastern Arabia, silver jewellery was often sold according to weight, measured in *tolahs* (11.75g). *Tolahs* are sometimes called *thallers* after the Maria Theresa dollar, an 18th-century Austrian coin used in much of Arabia's currency in the 19th and early 20th centuries.

of cooler air; gaily painted adobe walls and window frames help water-proof homes in the Asir. Positioning forts around rocky outcrops gives them solid foundations. And then there's the question of space: in the mountains whole villages appear to be suspended in air, storeys piled high to save from building on precious arable land.

The love of the tower block in modern architecture stems perhaps from this common heritage, but the use of materials such as glass and concrete, inappropriate to the desert heat, have corrupted the balance between function and form. It will take more than traditional Arab motifs, such as a pointed window or a wooden screen, to bring back a harmony between architecture and its environment, but this is a challenge taken up across the region, resulting in energy-efficient urban projects such as Masdar City in Abu Dhabi.

Islamic Art

There is no greater example of the marriage of function and form than Islamic art. For a Muslim, Islamic art remains first and foremost an expression of faith, and many Peninsula Arabs are cautious of art for art's sake, or art as an expression of the self without reference to community.

The prime example of instructive, inspirational art is calligraphy. Arabic is not just a language for Arabs – for Muslims throughout the world it is the language of the Quran and, as such, plays a cohesive, unifying role. Islamic calligraphy, the copying of God's own words, is seen by many as a pious act and remains to this day the highest aesthetic practised in the Arab world. In Arabia's museums there are magnificent examples of this highly refined art with its repetition of forms and symmetry of design.

The most visible expression of Islamic art, however, is surely the mosque. It too is built on mostly functional principles. In fact, the first mosques were modelled on the Prophet Muhammad's house. To this day the basic plan (with courtyard, domed prayer hall and vaulted niche indicating the direction of Mecca) provides a safe, cool and peaceful haven for worship and has changed little, although the first minarets appeared long after Muhammad's death. Before that time, the *muezzin* (prayer caller) often stood on a rooftop or some other elevation so that he could be heard by as many townsfolk as possible. Traditionally mosques had an ablution fountain at the centre of the courtyard, often fashioned from marble. Today most modern mosques have a more practical row of taps and drains alongside.

The mosque in Arabian Peninsula countries serves the community in many ways. Young children run on a hand-loomed carpet, their siblings receive Quranic lessons beneath tiled domes, parents sit in quiet contemplation of carved panels and elders enjoy a peaceful nap in the cool of flowering gardens. Art, in other words, remains at the service of people.

Contemporary Art

Not all artistic expression on the Peninsula shares the same Islamic roots, and increasingly there is a trend across the region to explore international lines of aesthetic enquiry through challenging contemporary exhibitions and the opening of museums that showcase a broader tradition. The most obvious example of this is the cluster of contemporary buildings taking shape on Saadiyat Island in the UAE, which include French architect Jean Nouvel's Abu Dhabi Louvre (p371). Opened in late 2017, this magnificent gallery, with a canopy issuing a rain of light inspired by palm fronds, exhibits work from the Paris Louvre and other museums in France.

Books on Arab Arts

....

Arab Contemporary: Architecture & Identity (Kallehauge, Tøjner & Holm, 2014)

....

Islamic Art (Luca Mozatti, 2010)

....

Craft Heritage of Oman (Richardson & Dorr, 2004)

Cinema

Recently, Arab cinema has attracted world attention, largely thanks to the growing popularity of international film festivals held in Dubai, Abu Dhabi and Doha. Around 75% of all Arab films are made in Egypt, the unchallenged Hollywood of Arab film, but with the encouragement of well-funded initiatives such as the Doha Film Institute, Gulf film-makers are starting to make a name for themselves.

Sports & Leisure

The people of the Arabian Peninsula love sport, and Qatar and the UAE in particular have become major hosts and patrons of international events. An interest in sport is no new phenomenon. For centuries Arab men have been demonstrating their prowess in agility, speed and courage. Most of these traditional games, which involve barefoot running, ball games, wrestling and even rifle throwing, are hard for a visitor to fathom, but since 2007 the Gulf Cooperation Council (GCC) countries have been trying to encourage greater participation in these kinds of sports, and they may well receive more popular promotion in future.

> Betting is against Islamic principles, but at camel races, vast sums of money change hands in the form of prize money, sponsorship and ownership. In UAE, a beauty-pageant-winning camel fetched more than US$2 million.

Camel Racing

Camel racing is a grumbling affair of camels (who'd really rather not run) and owners (who make sure they do). The rider, traditionally, is almost immaterial. Racing usually involves a long, straight track (camels are not very good at cornering) with very wide turns. Camel fanciers race alongside in their 4WDs to give their favourite camel encouragement.

Camel racing can be seen throughout the region from October to May. Authorities, sensitive about the bad press associated with the traditional recruitment of young jockeys, outlawed child riders nearly a decade ago, obliging owners to replace child jockeys with lightweight adults, or even robots (see p444). Visitors can see races in Al Shahaniya in Qatar and Al Marmoum Camel Racecourse en route to Al Ain from Dubai in the UAE.

Horse Racing

The breeding of horses, shipped from ports such as Sur in Oman, has been a source of income in Arabia for centuries. Now, partly thanks to the efforts of Lady Anne Blunt, a 19th-century British horse breeder, the fleet-footed, agile Arabian horse is raced all over the world.

Horse racing is a major spectator event for Peninsula people, and the event is at its most expensive and glamorous at the Dubai World Cup (p336). Heads of states, royalty, celebrities and top international jockeys gather for the occasion. Like Ascot in the UK, it's *the* place to be seen. The Meydan Racecourse (p348) in Dubai holds regular events.

CAMEL ON COMMAND

Traditionally, camels were raced by child jockeys, who were often 'bought' from impoverished families in Pakistan and Bangladesh, trained in miserable conditions, kept deliberately underweight and then exposed to the dangers of regular racing. The plight of these young boys attracted international condemnation, with the result that the practice has now died out.

In finding something similarly lightweight to replace child jockeys, inventors came up with the 'robo-rider'. These robotic jockeys are remote controlled, look vaguely humanoid and can crack an electronic whip. The camels appear to respond just as well (or just as badly) to their new mounts, and some versions of this gadget now sport robotic eyes through which the owner can take virtual strides at 60km/h around the racetrack.

LEISURE & THE CORNICHE

Until very recently there was no time in the lives of the indigenous population, beyond the demands of work and family, to devote to other pursuits. With the wealth that oil brought to the region, however, the concept of leisure has become a reality.

Alas, it's fair to say that the infrastructure to support the new-found leisure time has been slow to catch up. Take the seaside as an example. Two decades ago the coast was considered a place of work for fishermen; now it is teeming with walkers and joggers, swimmers and footballers, but still few facilities exist to cater for these activities.

This is beginning to change, however, and most capital cities now sport a corniche – a road with a wide footpath running along the coast, giving access to sandy beaches, cafes, water sports and toilets. For the visitor, one of the best ways to watch each nation at play is to walk or cycle along these attractive thoroughfares. Sit nearby long enough and you're bound to be seconded to the local volleyball team.

Falconry

The ancient art of falconry is still practised across the Peninsula. It dates back at least to the 7th century BC, when tradition has it that a Persian ruler caught a falcon to learn from its speed, tactics and focus. Modern owners continue to admire, respect and love their birds.

Many raptors are bred for falconry on the Asir escarpment in Saudi Arabia, but the easiest place to see a peregrine up close is in the Falcon Souq (p239) in Doha. The magical spectacle of birds being flown can be seen in Dubai and at most festivals, such as the Jenadriyah National Festival (p277) in Riyadh.

Bull-Butting

A curiosity of the east coast of Arabia, bull-butting is the pitching of one Brahman bull against another in a contest of strength. Much effort is taken to ensure the animals are not harmed, but occasional injuries occur to ears or necks. Bull-butting takes place in a dusty arena where the animals are nudged into a head-down position, and push and shove from one side of the arena to the other. The bulls are precious to their owners and much beloved so the minute the going gets tough, thankfully the tough get going.

During the flying season (October to February), 10,000 birds are tended at Doha's Falcon Hospital, a measure of how popular the sport remains. Top falcons can cost US$1 million.

Modern Sports

A range of modern sports are popular in the region, including rally driving, quad biking, volleyball and even ice skating. At Ski Dubai (p348) there are even five ski runs with real snow. You can't possibly talk about sports in the area, however, and not mention football. At 4pm on a Friday, the men of just about every village in Arabia trickle onto the local waste ground to play, all hopeful of joining international European clubs one day like some of their compatriots. Football is usually a shoeless business, on a desert pitch, played in *wizza* (cotton underskirt) and nylon strip, but it is taken just as seriously as if it were played in a multi-million-dollar stadium...which of course at least one Gulf country owns in another part of the world!

Islam in Arabia

On the Arabian Peninsula, as distinct from other countries with mainly Muslim populations, such as Turkey, there's little distinction between politics, culture and religion: each flows seamlessly through the other. Recognising the religious integrity of Peninsula people makes sense of certain customs and manners. In turn it guides the traveller in appropriate conduct and minimises the chance of giving offence, whatever one's own beliefs.

The Islamic Legacy

Social Cohesion

You don't have to stay on the Arabian Peninsula for long to notice the presence of a 'third party' in all human interaction. Every official occasion begins with a reading from the Holy Quran. A task at work begins with an entreaty for God's help. The words *alhamdulillah* (thanks be to God) frequently lace sentences in which good things are related. Equally, the words *inshallah* (God willing) mark all sentences that anticipate the future. The concept of *mashallah,* said when giving a compliment or celebrating good news, is a reminder that all good things extend from the will of God.

These common expressions, ubiquitous throughout the region, are not merely linguistic decoration. They evidence a deep connection between society and faith, a shared lexicon of social experience that extends beyond the common language. In other words, for most Muslims on the Peninsula, Islam is not just a religion, it's a way of life. It suggests what an Arab should wear and what an Arab should eat. It directs how income should be spent, who should inherit and by what amount. It guides behaviour and social intercourse and defines punishment for transgression.

Shades of Difference: Sunnis & Shiites

The Peninsula's social cohesion, built on the Islamic faith, stems not just from the religion itself but from the particular sect of Islam followed by most Peninsula Arabs. Most Arab people across the region are Sunnis; only Bahrain has a majority Shiite population.

Islam split into the two main sects shortly after its foundation in the early 7th century. The division was based not so much on theological interpretation, but

ISLAM'S PENINSULA ORIGINS

AD 570
Prophet Muhammad, founder of Islam, is born in Mecca in modern-day Saudi Arabia.

610
Muhammad receives his first revelation. Considered by Muslims as the word of God, the revelations gathered in the Quran lay the foundations of a new, monotheistic religion.

622
Muhammad and his followers flee Mecca for Medina, marking the beginning of the first Islamic state.

632
Muhammad dies. The Muslim capital moves to Damascus. Mecca and Medina grow as the spiritual homes of Islam.

656
Ali Bin Abi Taleb, Muhammad's cousin and son-in-law, becomes caliph as the fourth of Muhammad's successors. His followers are known as Shiites ('partisans' of Ali).

661
Ali is assassinated by troops loyal to a distant relative of Muhammad. From this point on, the Muslim community separates into two competing factions, Sunnis and Shiites.

680
Ali's son Hussein is murdered at Karbala (in today's southern Iraq), an event that further widens the gap between the two sects. Today, only Bahrain has a Shiite majority among Peninsula nations.

on historical events. When Prophet Muhammad died in 632, he left no instructions as to who should be his successor, or the manner in which future Islamic leaders (known as caliphs) should be chosen. The community initially chose Abu Bakr, the Prophet's closest companion and father-in-law, as the new leader of the Muslim faith, but not everyone agreed with this approach, preferring the claim of Ali Bin Abi Taleb, Muhammad's cousin and son-in-law. Ali's supporters became known as Shiites ('partisans' of Ali). Ali eventually became the fourth of Muhammad's successors but was assassinated after five years as caliph.

From that point the Muslim community separated into two competing factions, the Sunnis and the Shiites, who believed that only a descendant of Muhammad should lead the Muslims. As with any religion approaching one billion adherents, Islam has produced many sects within the traditional Sunni–Shiite division. The two most important Sunni sects in the Gulf States are the Wahhabis, whose austere doctrines are the official form of Islam in Saudi Arabia, and the Ibadis, who also espouse a strict interpretation of Islam and are the dominant sect in Oman.

A scholar or judge learned in Sharia law has to determine the proper 'Islamic' position or approach to a problem using his own discretion. This partly explains the wide divergence in Muslim opinion on some issues – such as with regard to jihad today.

The Five Pillars of Islam in Arabia

With its emphasis on direct relationship with God, Islam historically appealed to the scattered people of the Peninsula, who were given access to a rich spiritual life without having to submit to incomprehensible rituals administered by hierarchical intermediaries. Believers needed only to observe the transportable Five Pillars of Islam in order to fulfil their religious duty.

Shahada

In a region where almost the entire population espouses a single religion, there is a tangible sense of *shahada,* or the profession of faith. In many secular countries the declaration 'There is no God but Allah, and Muhammad is his Prophet' represents a private or even internalised act, but in Arabia it is a lived daily experience that is knitted into the fabric of society.

Salat

No one can miss *salat,* or the five-times-daily call to prayer. It is an audible part of the Arabian soundscape, hovering above the noise of daily lives, even in the Gulf cities where one eye is kept on Mammon. Whole communities across the Peninsula stop work or study at these times or pause by the side of the road with an unfurled prayer mat facing Mecca in Saudi Arabia and let their prayers stream across the desert wind.

DISTRIBUTION OF SUNNIS & SHIITES

This table shows the approximate distribution of Sunni and Shiite Muslims across the Arabian Peninsula. For updates of this information, consult www.populstat.info.

COUNTRY	SUNNI MUSLIMS	SHIITE MUSLIMS	OTHER RELIGIONS
Bahrain	26%	57%	17%
Kuwait	45%	30%	25%
Oman	83% (Ibadi)	5%	12%
Qatar	92%	0%	8%
Saudi Arabia	90%	9%	1%
UAE	80%	16%	4%

AND YOUR RELIGION IS ...?

After exchanging pleasantries with acquaintances on the Peninsula, the conversation inevitably tends towards three subjects from which many people around the world shy away: sex, politics and religion. The level of frankness involved in some of these discussions can come as a surprise. Forewarned is forearmed, however, and there's no better way of getting under the skin of a nation than talking about the things that matter most.

While all three subjects may seem like potential minefields (don't talk about sex with the opposite gender, especially if you're male; if you're talking politics, avoid saying 'you' when you mean 'your government'), religion is the one topic of conversation that takes a bit of practice.

For most Muslims, tolerating Christians, Jews (both 'People of the Book'), Buddhists or Hindus is easy – knowing what to do with a heretic is the problem. Stating you don't believe in God is as good as saying you doubt the very foundation of a Muslim's life. So how do you say you're an atheist in Arabia without causing offence? Try saying 'I'm not religious'. This will likely lead to understanding nods and then, on subsequent meetings, a very earnest attempt at conversion. Phrases such as 'You'll find God soon, God willing' should be seen as a measure of someone's like for you and not as a rejection of your 'position'. A reasonable response would be 'shukran' ('thank you').

Zakat

On the Peninsula the duty of alms giving, where Muslims must give a portion of their salaries to those in greater need, is carried out through formal schemes. One-fortieth of each individual's annual income is deducted for this purpose.

Ramadan

Perhaps it is because of the proximity to the Prophet Muhammad's birthplace, perhaps it is because of the shared experience of hardship in the heat of a desert climate, but Ramadan has a particular resonance across the Peninsula. This holy month, with its dawn-to-dusk fasting, marking the time when Muhammad received his first revelation in AD 610, isn't a lifestyle choice: for most people across the region it is a fervent act of communal worship, as evidenced by joyous *iftar* (fast-breaking) suppers in tents across the region.

Hajj

Although many Peninsula people have a greater opportunity to visit Mecca at other times of the year (in a journey known as umrah, the 'lesser pilgrimage' or 'visitation'), the undertaking of a 'true' hajj (p31), performed during a few specific days of the Muslim year, is considered a crowning achievement. During the *eid* (holiday) that follows hajj, towns across the Arabian Peninsula come alive with convoys of pilgrims, their car horns hooting, cheered on by those welcoming the *hajjis'* return. Of course, hajj is richly rewarded: all past sins are forgiven and the addition of Al Haj(a) to a pilgrim's name evokes much respect.

Islam's Peninsula Context

The Quran

For many Muslims the Quran, believed to be the literal word of God, is not just the principal source of doctrine in Islam, but also a source of spiritual rapture in its own right. It is recited often with emotional elation, as a blessing to the reciter and the listener. For Arabs on the Peninsula, there is the added connection that the 'sacred' language of the holy book is their mother tongue.

Muslims comprise 24.1% of world population. Over the centuries Sunnism has developed into the 'orthodox' strain of Islam, and today comprises about 90% of the world's 1.8 billion Muslims. There are large Shiite minorities, however, spread across the Middle East. Bahrain is notable for its Shiite majority.

Arabic, with its unique rhythms, gives the recitation a sacramental quality that eludes translation, and many Muslims around the world still learn large portions of the Quran in its original form (*fus-ha*, or formal Arabic) to feel closer to the words of Allah. Those who can recite the Quran well are highly respected across the region, and many formal occasions, including conferences, government meetings and graduations, commence with a reading from the Holy Quran.

Sharia Law

The Arabian Peninsula has a reputation, not wholly deserved, for extreme forms of punishment meted out to transgressors in the strict interpretation of Sharia law: amputation of limbs for repeat-offending thieves, flogging of those caught committing adultery, public beheading for murderers. In fact, these punishments are associated mostly with the austere Hanbali school of jurisprudence practised in Saudi Arabia and are intended as a deterrent first and foremost. As such, they are only occasionally enforced.

Across all Peninsula countries, Sharia is quite specific in areas of inheritance law and the punishments for certain offences, but in many other cases it provides only guidelines.

Jihad

In Arabia most Arabs are inclined to associate the word 'jihad' with its literal meaning of 'striving' or 'struggle'. Far from 'holy war', it more often means 'striving in the way of the faith' – struggling against one's own bad intentions, or rooting out evil, indecency or oppression in society. Islam dictates that this struggle should occur not through anger and aggression but through peaceful, just means so that wisdom prevails.

If the local papers are anything to go by, the rise of militancy in neighbouring countries is viewed mostly with fear and consternation. Much has been gained in terms of peace and prosperity over the past 50 years (with the exception of Yemen), and the common sentiment expressed on social media within the region shows a fear of losing these gains through sectarian violence fuelled by religious intolerance.

Keeping the Faith Today

Modern life requires daily compromises with religion, but then it always has. As such, there's not much that separates a Peninsula life from any other life, except perhaps in the degrees of temptation and opportunity. But even that is changing as access to foreign cultures becomes more prevalent in the region.

Except in Saudi Arabia and Kuwait, alcohol is widely available and has become a source of curiosity and experimentation for many youngsters and a way of life for some Arabs who have studied and worked abroad. Drugs, largely smuggled in from across the Gulf, have led to addiction (together with the familiar misery, shame in the community and family disruption) in a small but growing number of youths who seek to emulate the kind of rock-star lifestyles they see celebrated on satellite TV.

All of these temptations and opportunities are causing a new generation, educated to think and research the truth for themselves, to question the knowledge handed down from their elders. The uprisings of the Arab Spring of 2011 were partly symptomatic of the pull in two directions between a traditional life, governed by Islamic principles and concern for society, and the realities of a modern life, where the individual and his or her own personal needs and satisfactions take priority.

Books on Islam

Muhammed: A Biography of the Prophet (Karen Armstrong)

The Concise Encyclopedia of Islam (Cyril Glasse)

Websites on Islam

Al Bab (www. al-bab.com) Comprehensive site providing links to information on and discussions of Islam.

Islamicity (www. islamicity.com) Good reference for non-Muslims interested in Islam.

Omani man at prayer in the Grand Mosque (p140), Muscat.

Other Religions on the Peninsula

All the indigenous people of the Peninsula today are Muslim. One or two Muslim converts to Christianity wander in a state of miserable purgatory on the periphery of society, barred from all social interaction with family and friends by a decision that most Muslims would consider not just heretical but also a rejection of common sense, history and culture.

This is not the case with expatriate Christians, whose religion is respected and provision for worship catered for in church services across the region. There are also Hindu and Buddhist temples tucked away in small suburbs of the region's big cities and travelling missions visit expat camps in rural areas to bring comfort to those separated from the familiar props of their home communities. Small enclaves of Jewish people have lived on the Peninsula for centuries. Saudi Arabia, as keeper of Islam's holiest shrines, is the exception: no religious observance is formally permitted other than Islam.

Flavours of Arabia

Bedouin feasts – of lavish meats stuffed with rice and sultanas, served with chilled sherbets defying the desert heat – may be largely the product of a hunger-ravished imagination, but eating is nonetheless a central part of Peninsula life. Few social interactions take place without sharing 'bread and salt', or at least Arabic coffee (*gahwa*) and dates. The staple dishes may not immediately appeal to Western palates, but with knowledge of the customs informing their preparation, they assume a whole new flavour.

The Basics

Above Chicken *kabsa* rice dish

Cuisine across the Arabian Peninsula shares much similarity with Middle Eastern food in general: boiled rice and unleavened bread form the staples of the diet, served with barbecued meats or fish and vegetable stews. Mezze, small dishes of hummus, chopped salads and local cheese, accompany the main meals. Visitors will also find Indian food (such as curry and dal) widely available, even in the smallest towns, due to the large expatriate communities across the region. International food is becoming more widespread in the cities, and fast food has exploded in popularity in big city malls.

Staples & Specialities

Arabian

Breakfast

For most Arab people on the Peninsula, breakfast means eggs in some shape or form and locally produced salty white cheese with a glass of buttermilk or *labneh* (thick yoghurt) and tahini sweetened with date syrup. It might come with *fuul medamas,* a bean dish lubricated with olive oil, garnished on high days and holidays with pickles and eased along with olives. There may be lentils, heavily laced with garlic, to the chagrin of coworkers, and, of course, bread.

Known generically as *khobz,* bread (in up to 40 different varieties) is eaten in copious quantities with every meal. Most often it's unleavened and comes in flat discs about the size of a dinner plate (not unlike an Indian chapatti). It's traditionally torn into pieces, in lieu of knives and forks, and used to pinch up a morsel of meat, a scoop of dip and a nip of garnish.

Lunch

Lunch means one word only: rice. It is often flavoured with a few whole cardamom pods and, during feasts and festivals, with saffron and sultanas. Buried in or sitting on top of the rice will be some kind of delicious spiced stew with okra or grilled and seasoned chicken, lamb, goat or even camel – but of course never pork, which is *haram* (forbidden) for Muslims. Popular seasoning includes some or even all of the following: cardamom, coriander, cumin, cinnamon, nutmeg, chilli, ginger, pepper and the all-important, health-giving and almost-flavourless turmeric. Chillies are not often used, although they sometimes add a punch to a minimal broth or bean dish when least expected.

Unsurprisingly for a Peninsula with such a rich coastline, fish (fresh or dried) is an equally important lunchtime staple. Hamour (a species of grouper), *beya* (mullet), kingfish, Sultan Ibrahim and tuna are grilled, fried or barbecued and served with rice and chopped raw cabbage with the essential half lime or lemon. Sardines, piles of which spangle the shore in season and are raked into malodorous heaps between houses, are seldom eaten: they're usually dried for animal fodder.

Dinner

The evening meal is a ragged affair of competing interests – children clamouring for hot dogs or burgers, maids slipping them 'keep-quiet food', mothers going for a sandwich in Starbucks and grandmothers making sweetmeats and aubergine dips, nibbling on dates and trying to persuade fathers to enjoy the company of the family instead of going out for a kebab.

City dwellers on the Peninsula enjoy a diversity of international dishes (including sushi, Mongolian lamb chops, crab rangoon and spaghetti bolognese); these are readily available not just in hotel restaurants, but in local-style eateries too, albeit prepared by Indian chefs. Lebanese food, with its copious selection of hot and cold appetisers known as mezze, is a particular regional favourite, lending itself to lengthy chats over selective grazing. The peeled carrots, buffed radishes, whole lettuces and

The world's oldest cultivated fruit has been the staple of Arabs for centuries. Of the world's 90 million date palms, 64 million are in Arab countries.

FLAVOURS OF ARABIA STAPLES & SPECIALITIES

In Lebanese restaurants the number of mezze can run to 50 or more dishes and include delicacies such as chopped liver, devilled kidney, sheep brain and other offal.

bunches of peppery spinach leaves, provided complimentary, are a meal in themselves.

Arab families invariably entertain guests at home and go out to eat something different. For travellers to the region, it can therefore be difficult to find indigenous food, although this is currently enjoying something of a renaissance. Ask locally where to sample 'real' Peninsula food, and you may find you're taken home for supper.

Snacks & Sweets

Fast food has caught on among Peninsula people, with the consumption of burgers and fries verging on epidemic proportions. The concept has translated easily from traditional practices of visiting small eateries that sell kebabs, falafel and other types of sandwiches. Shawarma (meat sliced off a spit and stuffed in a pocket of pita-type bread with chopped tomatoes and garnish), usually served with some form of salad, is the snack of choice across the whole region. Outings to the coffeeshops that sell these traditional fast foods are more about sharing time with friends than eating, and men in particular may spend all night on the same plastic chair, puffing on shisha tobacco and sipping tea.

Peninsula residents are not big on 'puddings', preferring fruit after (or often before) the meal, and thick fruit juices. On holidays, however, baklava (made of filo and honey) or puddings, including *mahallabiye* (milk based) and *umm ali* (bread based), might put in an appearance after lunch or supper.

> Pork is *haram* (forbidden) to Muslims, but it's sometimes available in Gulf supermarkets. Pork sections are clearly marked and often obscured with a curtain: customers slink out with wrapped sausages as if they're top-shelf items.

Asian

All across Arabia large populations of expatriates have brought their own cuisine to the Peninsula, with the result that it dominates the menus of the region. For many Asian expats – often men on 'bachelor' contracts – breakfast, lunch and dinner consists of the same thing: rice and dal, or rice and vegetables, or so-called 'non-veg' curry, separated into three round, metal lunchboxes, stacked one on top of the other, and including a bag of rolled-up chapati.

Providing a cheap and cheerful alternative to the 'lunchbox', and serving samosas, biryani or spicy mutton curry, a string of Indian and Pakistani restaurants have sprung up across the region, catering for hungry workers who would normally be looked after by wives and daughters. Those who do have their families with them enjoy as varied a cuisine as their nationality and local supermarket allow. Filipino restaurants make chicken *adobo* (coconut-flavoured stew), while Sri Lankan maids win over their adoptive families with fish curries. In many of the big cities, travellers can sample all of these delights too, often in world-class restaurants.

Bedouin

Historical descriptions of Bedouin delicacies, elaborated with sherbets and dainties, sound enticing, but the reality is far more prosaic. British archaeologist TE Lawrence memorably describes a feast with the Arab Sheikh Sherif Nasir of Medina, in which he dips his fingers into a mess of boiling-hot lamb fat while ripping the meat from the carcass. This was probably *kebsa,* a whole lamb stuffed with rice and pine nuts. The most prized pieces of this dish are the sheep's eyeballs, which irreverent hosts delight to this day in waving towards horrified non-native guests.

Bedouin food mostly consists of whatever is available at a particular time, and hunger and thirst are far more attendant on a day's travelling in the desert than sumptuous feasting. Camel's milk and goat's cheese are staple parts of the diet, as are dried dates and, of course, water. Water takes on a particularly precious quality when it is rationed and the

> There are more than 600 species of date. The best come from Al Hasa in Saudi Arabia, where a variety called *khlas* is pre-sold to regular customers before it's even harvested.

Omani *halwa*

Bedouin are renowned for consuming very little, particularly during the day when only small sips are taken, mostly to rinse the mouth.

The legendary hospitality of the Bedouin means that travellers in the Empty Quarter (in Saudi Arabia) or the Sharqiya Sands (Oman) who bump into a Bedouin camp are bound to be invited to share 'bread and salt'. At the least this will involve Arabic coffee, camel's milk and a thatch of dried meat, usually with a host of flies dancing in the bowl. The flies don't harm the Bedouin, and it's unlikely they'll bother the traveller much either, but the milk can upset a sensitive stomach.

Every town has a baklava or pastry shop selling syrupy sweets made from pastry, nuts, honey and sometimes rose water. Sweets are ordered by a minimum weight of 250g.

Habits & Customs

The main meal for most Peninsula residents is usually a home-cooked family affair involving rice at lunchtime – but there the region's similarities end. There is huge diversity in the kinds of food prepared and the habits practiced across the Peninsula. Learning about regional customs associated with shopping for food, as well as cooking and preparing it, provides insight into the important place that dining has within the Arab community as a whole.

Shopping

Catering for food is largely a man's job, and men are often dispatched to Thursday wholesale markets to find fresh produce. Giant shopping malls, such as Carrefour, have met with instant success among city locals, perhaps because they resemble an air-conditioned version of the wholesale market. For many, however, buying meat from the livestock market is a matter of male pride, and the animal will be taken home live, ready for dispatch under specific Islamic guidelines.

Cooking

Dining is essentially a communal affair, and it's traditional at weekends for many families who work in the city to travel long distances back to their villages to enjoy 'mum's cooking'. Women almost exclusively prepare food outside the big cities: grinding spices, peeling vegetables and plucking chickens is seen as an opportunity to chat with female relatives and catch up on the news. That said, a few 'modern men' are taking pride in trying their hand in the kitchen, egged on by imported cooking programs on television.

Eating

As an extravagant gesture in a Bedouin emir's tent, a camel is stuffed with a sheep, which is stuffed with a goat, which is stuffed with a chicken.

In more traditional towns and villages, men and women will eat separately, with the eldest son helping to serve the men first while the women await their turn in another room. It's considered good manners for men to reserve the best parts of the meal for the women. Arab people assert that eating is enjoyed best, even by city dwellers with Western-style furniture, on the floor from shared dishes using bread and the right hand as utensils. This makes eating very easily transferable to an outdoor setting and indeed picnics are the number-one regional pastime.

Relaxing

A dish of rose water, the petals harvested from Arabian mountains, marks the traditional end of a meal. Diners rinse their hands in the scented water, and guests make a quick exit immediately after, as sleep is generally enjoyed by all after the midday meal.

Ramadan

The holy month is a time of great conviviality and, perhaps somewhat surprisingly given that the month is about fasting and abstinence, many Arab people put on weight at this time. The reason for this is the long Ramadan nights, which are generally marked by bonhomie and socialising and the sharing of seasonal delicacies and sweetmeats. The fast (between dawn and dusk) is broken each day with a communal 'breakfast' comprising something light (such as dates and *laban*, an unsweetened yoghurt drink) before prayers. Then comes *iftar*, at which enough food is usually consumed to compensate for the previous hours of abstinence, with socialising that continues well into the early hours. The venue for this communal meal is often the *wali*'s office (equivalent to a town hall), the mosque precinct or a specially erected Ramadan tent. People then rise again before dawn to prepare a meal to support them through the day.

Where to Eat & Drink

For an exquisite tang on the palate, dates should be eaten half ripe, biting the fruit lengthwise and savouring the bitter zest with the mellow ripe part. Don't forget to discard the pip discreetly in a napkin – Sinbad spat his out and blinded a genie's son, who claimed mischievous revenge.

One of the undoubted pleasures of the Peninsula's modern cities is the variety and quality of the restaurants. In the Gulf in particular, world-class dining in magnificent surroundings is a highlight.

On the whole, restaurants are open (mostly for expats) during lunch. They're closed in the afternoon and open from about 6pm to the early hours of the morning to cater for the late-night eating habits of most people across the region. In Saudi Arabia, restaurants must comply with certain strict regulations (regarding segregation of men and women and the observation of prayer hours, for example).

Expatriate & Local Cuisine

Lebanese and Indian restaurants are the most prevalent throughout the region, followed by Chinese and Thai in bigger towns. Food from all over the world is available in the Gulf cities.

Top Lemon mint juice

Bottom Shisha cafe

The venue of preference for 'that special meal' for many Peninsula families is a well-lit grassy verge on a highway with kebabs brought in by the kilo.

Kebabs with roast vegetables

The hardest food to find in a restaurant is local, traditional fare, but chains such as Bin Ateeq (p177) in Nizwa, and restaurants in Souq Waqif (p239) in Doha or the Heritage Village (p370) in Abu Dhabi, have helped to redress that imbalance. Every year a few more venues open specialising in indigenous cuisine.

In very local restaurants, seating is sometimes on the floor on mats and food is served from a communal plate placed on a tray. Shoes should be left outside the perimeters of the mats.

Friday Brunch

One of the best ways to experience local dishes and regional delicacies on the Peninsula is to skip breakfast on a Friday and visit the nearest five-star hotel for brunch – a regional speciality much beloved by locals and expats alike. Buffets offering a spectacular array of local, Middle Eastern and international dishes will be on display, decorated with ice carvings and garnished extravagantly, for a relatively modest price.

Surrounded by the Red Sea, the Gulf and the Arabian Sea, it's little surprise that fish is such a staple of the Peninsula diet. Kingfish, pomfrey and hamour are local favourites. Lobsters and prawns, now widely eaten, used to be discarded as bottom feeders, not fit for human consumption!

Seafood Nights

Seafood is a highlight of the region, and many hotels arrange weekly seafood nights, often with belly dancing or local entertainment. This is often a more economical way of sampling the Peninsula's famous oysters, lobsters, squid and prawns than reserving a table at an exclusive seafood restaurant. The latter, however, usually offer the opportunity to select your own fish from the specimens swimming in the restaurant's tanks, a way of guaranteeing its freshness in the often-intense heat.

A visit to the local fish market (in every seaboard town) is a good way of becoming acquainted with the bewilderingly large variety of seafood available. Don't shy away from the dried-fish counters: the dried crustaceans and sardines make a tasty, if pungent, equivalent of biltong or jerky.

Mezze, including hummus and olives

Quick Bites

Traditional snacks (such as shawarma and kebabs) are quick, cheap and usually safe to eat, as the food is prepared and cooked in front of you. There's also a good range of well-stocked supermarkets (selling many international foods) in the large cities and extensive food halls are found in all the malls.

Ramadan Tents

During Ramadan, most hotels set up elaborate buffets of Ramadan specialities that non-Muslims are welcome to join. These buffets are generally in air-conditioned tents, which helps evoke the sense of community in breaking the fast under one roof. Alcohol is generally not available in non-dry countries during Ramadan, except as room service at hotels.

Vegetarians & Vegans

While Arab people are traditionally thought of as full-blooded, red-meat eaters, the reality is that for many of modest income across the region, meat is a treat for holidays. This fact, coupled with the influence of southern Indian cuisine introduced by large expat communities of vegetarian Hindus, means that vegetable dishes appear more often than might be expected on a restaurant menu.

Vegetarian staples include many bean and pulse dishes such as soup, *fuul* (fava bean paste) and dal, or lentil stews. Chickpeas, either fried into falafel or ground into a paste with oil and garlic (hummus), are a common supplement. Aubergines and okra are used in many delicious stews, and salad vegetables are usually locally grown and organic.

In most Peninsula countries, mixed dining is common in more expensive or modern city restaurants. In smaller establishments, men eat on the ground floor, while women and families eat upstairs in a section reserved for them.

Eating with Kids

Eating out as a family is a popular pastime on the Peninsula for Arabs and expats. Whole minibuses of relatives arrive at the outdoor, seaboard city venues, particularly in the winter months when huddling round a mobile stove is part of the fun. Equally, many parents join their children for a halal 'MacArabia' chicken roll-up, or a beef pepperoni pizza in the spreading rash of fast-food outlets.

Children are welcome in restaurants across the Peninsula, except in the more exclusive, chic establishments of the Gulf, and many midrange restaurants provide children's menus. High chairs are not commonly available.

Fresh or powdered milk is widely available, except in remote areas. *Labneh* is generally considered safe for children.

> Although much Arab cuisine is vegetarian in nature, this is more to do with the availability of meat than a conceptual dedication to vegetarianism. To avoid uncomfortable conversations about soup ingredients, stick to Indian restaurants.

Drinking

Sipping *gahwa* (local-style coffee) under the stars is an ancient tradition in Arabia and every family has its own treasured coffee pot, or *dhallah*, or, more usually today, a *dhallah*-shaped thermos. Visitors are bound to be invited to partake in the custom if they stray beyond the city for any length of time or attend official functions, as this is the beverage of social cohesion. Tea with mint and spiced *karak* tea, fresh juices and *laban* (thin yoghurt) are also widespread drinks across the region, with alcohol

EATING ETIQUETTE

Sharing a meal with Arab friends is a great way of cementing a newly formed friendship. But Peninsula eating etiquette is refined and complex. Note that food is traditionally shared by all from the same serving dishes, spread on a cloth on the floor, without the use of cutlery.

Pre-Meal

➡ If you're eating in someone's house, bring a small gift of flowers, chocolates or pastries, fruit or honey.

➡ Carry out your ablutions – it's polite to be seen to wash your hands before a meal.

➡ Avoid sitting with your legs stretched out – it's considered rude during a meal.

During the Meal

➡ Use only your right hand for eating or accepting food; the left is reserved for ablutions.

➡ Don't take the best part of the meal, such as the meat, until offered; it is usually saved until last.

➡ Your host will often lay the tastiest morsels in front of you; it's polite to accept them.

➡ Don't put unwanted food back on the plate. Discard it in a napkin.

Post-Meal

➡ It's traditional to lavish food upon a guest – if you're full, pat your stomach contentedly.

➡ Leave a little food on your plate. Traditionally, a clean plate was thought to invite famine.

➡ Feel free to pick your teeth after a meal – it is quite acceptable, and toothpicks are often provided.

➡ Stay for coffee – it's polite to accept a cup of coffee after a meal and impolite to leave before it's served.

➡ Know when to go. The chatting is usually done before the meal, so once the meal is over it's time to leave – but don't go before the chief guest.

Umm ali, a bread-based pudding with sultanas and nuts

When it comes to customs and manners, there's one thing most Peninsula people agree upon: after you eat, you go. Talking is conducted over mezze. During the main course, focus is on the food. After eating, once coffee has been served, all anyone wants to think about is sleeping.

confined to major hotels in Oman, parts of United Arab Emirates, Bahrain and Qatar.

Coffeehouses & Coffeeshops

Across the Arabian Peninsula, there are bastions of old-world Arab hospitality that go by the name of 'coffeehouses'. These relics of an era when people had more time to sit and chat are places of male camaraderie and tend often to be no more than a mere hole-in-the-wall, a bench up against a souq alleyway, or even a favourite perch under a tree. These coffeehouses dispense coffee from copper pots, or tea in disposable paper cups, while *sheibas* (old men) with beards dish out dates, advice and opinions in equal measure to anyone who'll listen. For a male visitor, they offer a unique engagement with Arab society. Women are politely tolerated, but it is more sensitive to leave the men to their bonding.

'Coffeeshops', on the other hand, welcome all comers. These ubiquitous cafes, with their plastic chairs and compulsory string of fairy lights, are dotted across Arabia. They are usually run by expatriates from the subcontinent, and they form the social hub of many small villages, selling kebabs, roasted chickens or omelettes rolled up in flatbread. Most are simple shopfronts with seating on the pavement, but the more upmarket coffeeshops stretch to a plate and a napkin and are scented with the regional passion for shisha.

Saudi 'champagne' is less exciting than it sounds: it's a mixture of apple juice and Perrier water, but that doesn't stop it being used to anoint sporting winners.

Alcoholic Drinks

Despite its reputation as a dry region, alcohol is available in all Peninsula countries, except Saudi Arabia, Kuwait and some of the Emirates (where both possession and consumption for locals and foreigners is strictly forbidden).

FOOD & DRINK GLOSSARY

Note that because of the imprecise nature of transliterating Arabic into English, spellings will vary. For example, what we give as *kibbeh* may appear variously as *kibba, kibby* or even *gibeh*.

Middle Eastern Mezze

baba ganoush	smoky-flavoured dip of baked, mashed aubergine, typically mixed with tomato and onion and sometimes pomegranate
batata hara	hot, diced potatoes fried with coriander, garlic and capsicum
börek	pastry pockets stuffed with salty white cheese or spicy minced meat with pine nuts; also known as *sambousek*
fatayer	small pastry triangles filled with spinach
fattoush	fresh salad of onions, tomatoes, cucumbers, lettuce and shards of crispy, thin, deep-fried bread
fuul	paste made from beans, tomatoes, onions, and chilli; also spelled foul, fool, ful
hummus	chickpeas ground into a paste and mixed with tahini, garlic and lemon
kibbeh	minced lamb, bulgur wheat and pine nuts mixed into a lemon-shaped patty and deep fried
kibbeh nayye	minced lamb and cracked wheat served raw
kibda	liver, often chicken liver *(kibda firekh* or *kibda farouj)*, usually sautéed in lemon or garlic
labneh	yoghurt usually flavoured with garlic or mint
lahma bi ajeen	small lamb pies
loubieh	French bean salad with tomatoes, onions and garlic
mashi	baked vegetables such as courgettes, vine leaves, peppers or aubergines stuffed with minced meat, rice, onions, parsley and herbs
mujadarreh	traditional 'poor person's' dish of lentils and rice garnished with caramel-ised onions
muttabal	similar to baba ganoush, but the blended aubergine is mixed with tahini, yogurt and olive oil to achieve a creamier consistency
shanklish	salad of small pieces of crumbled, tangy, eye-wateringly strong cheese mixed with chopped onion and tomato
soojuk	fried, spicy lamb sausage
tabbouleh	bulgur wheat, parsley and tomato–based salad, with a sprinkling of sesame seeds, lemon and garlic
tahini	thin sesame-seed paste
waraq aynab	vine leaves stuffed with rice and meat

In the more liberal countries, such as Bahrain and some parts of the UAE, bars, cocktail bars and even pubs can be found. In others, such as Qatar and Oman, usually only certain mid- or upper-range hotels are permitted to serve alcohol. Wine is served in most licensed restaurants in Bahrain, Oman, Qatar and the UAE.

Officially, no Peninsula country produces its own alcoholic drinks, though rumours abound where grapes and dates ferment. The high pric-es of imported alcohol are intended to keep consumption low – not very successfully (alcoholism is a small but growing social problem). The legal age to be served alcohol is usually 18 years old. You can't buy alcohol

Middle Eastern & Arabian Main Courses

bamiya	okra-based stew
fasoolyeh	green-bean stew
falafel	deep-fried balls of mashed chickpeas, often rolled in Arabic bread with salad and hummus, also called *taamiyya*
harees	slow-cooked wheat and lamb
kabbza	lamb or chicken cooked with onion, tomato, cucumber, grated carrot and fruit
kebab	skewered, flame-grilled chunks of meat, usually lamb, but also chicken, goat, camel, fish or squid; also known as *sheesh* or shish kebab
kebab mashwi	meat paste moulded onto flat skewers and grilled
kebsa	whole stuffed lamb served on a bed of spiced rice and pine nuts; also known as *khuzi*
kofta	ground meat peppered with spices, shaped into small sausages, skewered and grilled
machboos	casserole of meat or fish with rice
mashkul	rice served with onions
mihammar	lamb cooked in yogurt sauce and stuffed with nuts, raisins and other dried fruit
muaddas	rice served with lentils
mushkak game	seasoned camel meat grilled on a skewer – usually tough as old boots!
samak mashwi	fish barbecued over hot coals after basting in a date puree
shish tawooq	kebab with pieces of marinated, spiced chicken
shuwa	lamb cooked slowly in an underground oven
shawarma	Middle Eastern equivalent of Greek gyros or Turkish döner kebab; strips are sliced from a vertical spit of compressed lamb or chicken, sizzled on a hot plate with chopped tomatoes and garnish and then stuffed or rolled in bread

Middle Eastern Pastries & Desserts

asabeeh	rolled filo pastry filled with pistachio, pine and cashew nuts and honey; otherwise known as 'ladies' fingers'
baklava	a generic term for any kind of layered flaky pastry with nuts, drenched in honey
barazak	flat, circular cookies sprinkled with sesame seeds
isfinjiyya	coconut slice
kunafeh	shredded wheat over a creamy, sweet cheese base baked in syrup
labneh makbus	sweet yogurt cheese balls, sometimes made into a frittata-like creation or rolled in paprika; sometimes eaten for breakfast
mahallabiye	milk-based pudding
mushabbak	lacework-shaped pastry drenched in syrup
umm ali	bread-based pudding made with sultanas and nuts, flavoured with nutmeg
zalabiyya	pastries dipped in rose water

to take off the premises unless you are a resident and are eligible for a monthly quota.

Nonalcoholic Drinks

Camel's milk makes an interesting drink but it can upset sensitive stomachs; if you want to try it without the stomachache, look for it in supermarkets, rather than trying it direct from the leather bowls offered by the Bedouin. It's often found next to the *labneh*.

One of the best culinary experiences in the region is sampling the fresh juices of pomegranate, hibiscus, avocado, sugar cane, mango, melon or carrot – or a combination of all sorts – served at juice stalls

THE SHISHA EXPERIENCE

In any city across the Peninsula, two sensations mark the hot and humid air of an Arabian summer's evening: the wreaths of scented, peach-flavoured smoke that spiral above the corner coffeehouse and the low gurgle of water, like a grumbling camel, in the base of the water pipe. Periodically banned by governments concerned for public health (very high nicotine content) and morality (the pipes are not narcotic, only time-wasting), and inevitably returned to the street corners by the will of the people, these shisha establishments are an indispensable part of Arabian social life.

In the region's traditional coffeehouses, shisha is an entirely male affair. Men sprawl on cushions in Jeddah, Saudi Arabia, or lounge on benches in the souqs of Doha, Qatar. They indolently watch the football on TV, occasionally breaking off from the sucking and puffing to pass a word of lazy complaint to their neighbour, snack on pieces of kebab, or hail the waiter for hot coals to awaken the drowsy embers of the shisha bottle.

In Dubai, Manama and Muscat, shisha has long since spread to the more family-oriented coffeeshop. It has even become a fashionable occupation in international-style cafes. Here, women in *abayas* (full-length robes) and sparkling diamante cuffs drag demurely on velvet-clad mouthpieces, their smoking punctuating a far more animated dialogue as they actively define the new shape of society.

known as *aseer*. Mint and lemon or fresh lime is a refreshing alternative to soda.

Tea, known as *chai* or *chai libton,* could be tea *min nana* (with mint, especially in Saudi Arabia), tea with condensed milk (in the Gulf) or plain black tea (in Oman), but whatever the flavour of the day, it will contain enough sugar to make a dentist's fortune. The teabag is left dangling in the cup and water is poured from maximum height as proof of a host's tea-making skills. *Karak* tea, where the tea and sweetened condensed milk is boiled with cardamom and other spices, is another popular drink.

Coffee, known locally as *gahwa,* is consumed in copious quantities on the Peninsula and is usually strong. Arabia has a distinguished connection with coffee. Though no longer involved in the coffee trade, Al Makha in Yemen gave its name to the blend of chocolate and coffee popularly known as 'mocha' that spread across the region. The traditional Arabic or Bedouin coffee is heavily laced with cardamom and drunk in small cups. Turkish coffee, which floats on top of thick sediment, is popular in the Gulf region.

Nonalcoholic beer is widely available. Incidentally, travellers shouldn't think that cans of fizzy drink will suffice for hydration in the desert: they often induce more thirst than they satisfy.

> If as a traveller you try to opt out of the fifth spoonful of sugar in your tea or coffee, you will inevitably be assumed to have diabetes.

The Natural Environment

Spend time in Arabia after rain and it becomes immediately apparent that the Peninsula is far from a barren wasteland of undulating sands. On the contrary, the diverse desert landscapes support uniquely adapted plants and animals, particularly in the region's wadis (valleys) and oases. This extraordinary environment forms the backdrop for dramas of survival and endurance by the hardiest of inhabitants, and is a revelation and a joy to visitors.

The Land

Geology

The Arabian Peninsula is a treasure trove for geologists. Though not particularly rich in metals, minerals or gems (except the copper that is found in northern Oman), the Peninsula reveals the Earth's earliest history, supporting theories of plate tectonics and continental drift. Indeed, geologists believe the Peninsula originally formed part of the larger landmass of Africa. A split in the continent created Africa's Great Rift Valley (which extends from Mozambique up through Djibouti, into western Yemen, Saudi Arabia and Jordan) and the Red Sea.

As Arabia slipped away from Africa, the Peninsula began to tilt, with the western side rising and the eastern edge dropping, a process that led to the formation of the Gulf.

Extensive flooding millions of years ago led to the remains of marine life being deposited in layers of sediment across the tilted landmass, as indicated by the rich fossil remains found across Arabia. When sufficient dead organic matter is laid down and trapped under the surface, where a lack of oxygen prevents it from decaying to water and carbon dioxide, the raw material of hydrocarbons is produced – the origin, in other words, of oil and gas. The conversion from dead organic matter to hydrocarbons is subject to many other conditions such as depth and temperature. Arabia's geology is uniquely supportive of these conditions, and 'nodding donkeys' (drilling apparatus, capable of boring holes up to 5km deep) can be seen throughout the interior.

Governments across the region speculate endlessly on the quantity of reserves remaining. Given that the economies of all the Peninsula countries rely to a lesser or greater extent on oil and gas, this is one issue that can't be left to *inshallah* (God's will). As such, Peninsula countries are busy diversifying their economic interests in case their reserves run out sooner rather than later.

The Al Hasa Oasis, near the town of Al Hofuf in eastern Saudi Arabia, is the largest oasis in the world. Covering 2500 sq km, it's home to more than three million palm trees.

Geography

Stand on top of Kuwait Towers and the eye roams unhindered along flat country. The low-lying coastal plains and salt flats stretch along the limp waters of the northern Gulf until the Mussandam Peninsula brings the plain to an abrupt close. This is the environment of mudhoppers, wading birds and long stretches of dazzling-white sands.

DESERT, YES – DESERTED, NO

Visiting any wilderness area carries a responsibility and no more so than in a desert, where the slightest interference with the environment can wreak havoc with fragile ecosystems. The rocky plains of the interior may seem like an expanse of nothing, but that is not the case. Red markers along a road, improbable as they may seem on a cloudless summer day, indicate the height of water possible during a flash flood. A month or so after such floods, a flush of tapering grasses marks the spot, temporary home to wasp oil beetles, elevated stalkers and myriad other life forms.

Car tracks scar a rock desert forever, crushing plants and insects not immediately apparent from the driver's seat. Rubbish doesn't biodegrade as it would in a tropical or temperate climate. The flower unwittingly picked in its moment of glory may miss its first and only opportunity for propagation in seven years of drought.

With a bit of common sense, however, and by taking care to stick to existing tracks, it's possible to enjoy the desert without damaging the unseen communities it harbours. It also pays to turn off the engine and just sit. At dusk, dramas unfold: a fennec fox chases a hedgehog, a wild dog trots out of the wadi without seeing the snake slithering in the other direction, tightly closed leaves relax in the brief respite of evening and a dung beetle rolls its reward homewards.

Much of the interior is flat too, but some major mountain ranges, such as the Hajar Mountains of Oman and the Asir Mountains of Saudi Arabia, bring an entirely different climate and way of life to the high ground.

There are no permanent river systems on the Peninsula. Water-laden clouds from the sea break across the mountains, causing rainfall to slide along wadis with dramatic speed. Smaller tributaries of water collect in the wadis from natural springs and create oases in the desert. On much of the Peninsula, the water table is close enough to the surface to hand dig a well, a fact not wasted on the Bedouin who, until very recently, survived on a system of wells and springs discovered or made by their ancestors. Irrigation, in the form of elaborate ducts and pipes (called *aflaj* in Oman), helps channel water through plantations, allowing more extensive farming in the region than might be supposed.

Ecosystems

Desert

Geologists speak of the Peninsula in terms of the Arabian shield and Arabian shelf. The shield, which consists of volcanic sedimentary rock, comprises the western third of the landmass. The shelf comprises the lower-lying areas that slope away from the shield, from central Arabia to the waters of the Gulf.

The harsh lands of Arabia have for centuries attracted travellers, from the 14th-century Moroccan Ibn Battuta, to a host of Europeans from the 18th century onward. According to Sir Richard Burton in *Personal Narrative of a Pilgrimage to El Medinah and Meccah*, the desert was a region that excited the imagination because it was assumed to be populated by wild beasts and wilder people. The very words 'Empty Quarter' (a sea of dunes that lies at the heart of the Peninsula, straddling Saudi Arabia, Oman and the UAE) invite speculation, exploration and discovery to this day.

Visitors often come to the desert expecting it to be entirely comprised of sand, even if, like British travel writer Alexander William Kinglake, in *Eothen*, their physical experience of largely gravel plains has contradicted this assumption. So strong is the connection between the words 'desert' and 'sand', Kinglake felt obliged to comment on what he thought he should see, rather than on what was there.

The Empty Quarter, or Rub Al Khali as it is known locally, may be the most famous geographical feature, but it is not the only desert of interest. Much of the Peninsula is made up of flat gravel plains dotted with outcrops of weather-eroded sandstone in the shape of pillars, mushrooms and ledges. Fine examples of these desert forms can be seen near Al Ula in Saudi Arabia, Bir Zekreet in Qatar and Duqm and the Huqf Escarpment in Oman. There are many other kinds of desert too, including flat coastal plains and the infamous volcanic black Harra of northern Arabia.

Nowadays, camels (few of which are wild) and feral donkeys dominate the landscape of thorny acacia (low, funnel-shaped bushes) and life-supporting *ghaf* trees. Sheltering under these trees, sustained by dew from the leaflets in the morning, are gazelle, protected colonies of oryx and a host of smaller mammals – hares, foxes and hedgehogs – that provide a food source for the land's many raptors. Easier to spot are the lizards, snakes and insects that provide the building blocks of the desert ecosystem.

Mountains

They may not be the mightiest mountains in the world, but the ranges of the Peninsula are nonetheless striking. This is partly because they rise without preamble from flat coastal plains.

The Peninsula has two main mountain ranges. The Hejaz range runs the length of Saudi Arabia's west coast, generally increasing in height as it tends southwards. The term 'mountain' may seem a misnomer for much of the range. Saudi Arabia's landmass is often likened to a series of half-toppled books, with flat plains ending in dramatic escarpments that give way to the next plain. The last escarpment drops spectacularly to the sea. If you follow the baboons over the escarpment rim, from the cool, misty, green reaches of Abha to Jizan on the humid, baking Red Sea coastal plains of the Tihama, the effect of this range is immediately felt. The settlers of the fertile mountains in their stone dwellings live such a different life to the goat herders in their mud houses on the plains, they may as well belong to different countries – and indeed the Tihama shares much in common with Eritrea and Ethiopia's Tigré region on the opposite side of the Red Sea.

Arabia's other principal mountain range is found in the east of the Peninsula. Here, Oman's Hajar Mountains protect the communities around the Gulf of Oman from the encroachment of deserts from the interior. Terracing similar to that of southern Saudi Arabia and Yemen can be seen on Jebel Akhdar and on pocket-handkerchief scraps of land in the Musandam. The hills of Dhofar, in the south of Oman, catch the edge of the monsoon from India, bringing light rains that cause the arid hills to burst into life during the summer when most of the rest of the Peninsula is desiccated by heat.

Dhofar is home to the elusive leopard, one of Arabia's most magnificent animals. It is the largest, but not the only, predatory mammal of the Peninsula. Caracals, wolves, striped hyenas and sand cats are all resident (though in small and diminishing numbers) in the mountains and wadis of Oman in particular, where they prey on snakes and the plentiful rodents.

The mountains are the best (though far from the only) place to see wildflowers. After rains they bloom in abundance. In the wadis,

The stoic early-20th-century traveller Charles Doughty described the utter desolation of the volcanic Harra in his epic book *Arabia Deserta*. Even camels have trouble crossing this type of desert as the small black rocks heat in the sun and catch in their feet.

It may look immutable, but the desert changes shape regularly: dunes driven by wind, sandstone eroded by flood and a pebbly beach transformed overnight into sand. Shaping forces also include the dung beetle and ghost crab, responsible for moving A to B with astonishing industry.

DESERT ADAPTATIONS

One of the remarkable aspects of life in the desert is the very existence of life here. Some species go to enormous lengths to cope with the searing heat of the summer sun and the minimal presence of water. Officially, a desert refers to land that receives less than 250mm of rain per year. In these conditions, animals have had to evolve remarkable adaptations to drought conditions to survive. These include nocturnal living (foxes and hedgehogs), hairy paws and big ears that provide protection against hot surfaces (jerboas), the ability to survive on dew (gazelle) and remaining dormant in the ground for years in a state of semi-hibernation (toads).

THE NATURAL ENVIRONMENT THE LAND

pink-flowering oleander and tall stands of Sodom's apples flower year-round. On the mountainsides, juniper trees, wild olives, lavenders and many plants with medicinal properties flourish.

Seas

The Peninsula is bordered by three distinct seas, each of which has its own character.

The Red Sea, with its world-renowned underwater landscape and great diversity of tropical fish, is mostly calm and its shores are flat and sandy. Groupers, wrasse, parrotfish and snapper inhabit the colourful gardens of coral, sea cucumbers and sponge, while sharks and barracuda swim beyond the shallows, only venturing into the reefs to feed or breed.

The Arabian Sea, home to dolphins and whales and five species of turtle, many of which nest along the eastern Arabian shore, has a split personality. Calm for much of the year, it becomes violently rough in the *khareef* (summer monsoon), casting up shells on some of the most pristine, uninterrupted beaches in the world. Rimmed by cliffs for much of its length, this sea is punctuated with fishing villages that continue a way of life little changed for centuries, supported by seas rich in sardine and tuna.

The Gulf has a completely different character to the other two seas. Flat, calm, so smooth that at times it looks solid, like a piece of shiny coal, it tends to be shallow for up to 1km from the shore. With lagoons edged with valuable mangroves, this is an important habitat for birds. It is also conducive to human development and much of the rim of the Gulf has been paved over or 'reclaimed' for the improbable new cities at its edge.

National Parks & Protected Areas

The idea of setting aside areas for wildlife runs contrary to the nature of traditional life on the Peninsula, which was, and to some extent still is, all about maintaining a balance with nature, rather than walling it off. The Bedouin flew their hunting falcons only at certain times of the year and moved their camels on to allow pasture to regrow. Fishermen selected only what they wanted from a seasonal catch and threw the rest back. Goat and sheep herders of the mountains moved up and down the hillside at certain times of the year to allow for regrowth. Farmers let lands lie fallow so as not to exhaust the soil.

Modern practices, including settlement of nomadic tribes, sport hunting, trawler fishing and the use of pesticides in modern farming, have had such an impact on the natural environment over the past 50 years, however, that all governments in the region have recognised the need

Books on Arabian Plants
....
Handbook of Arabian Medicinal Plants (SA Ghazanfar)
....
Vegetation of the Arabian Peninsula (SA Ghazanfar)

GO LIGHT ON THE LITTER

There's a wonderful tale in *The Thousand and One Nights* that describes the inadvertent chain of devastation caused by a merchant spitting out his date pip and unknowingly blinding the son of a genie.

It may not be immediately apparent to a visitor watching pink and blue plastic bags sailing in the breeze, but Peninsula authorities are making concerted efforts to clean up the countryside. They have a stiff task: according to some estimates, the average person uses 300 plastic bags a year, prompting Friends of the Earth Middle East to run a 'Say No to Plastic Bags' campaign. It's immensely difficult to avoid adding to the rubbish, especially when local attitude still maintains that every soft-drink can thrown on the ground represents one more job for the needy.

Attitudes are beginning to change, however, thanks in part to educational schemes that target children and the adoption of environment days in Oman, the UAE and Bahrain. 'Bag it' and 'out it' is a pretty good maxim as, hardy as it seems, the desert has a surprisingly fragile ecosystem that, once damaged, is as difficult to mend as the eye of a genie's son.

to actively protect the fragile ecosystems of their countries. This has resulted in the creation of protected areas (10% of the regional landmass), but with tourism on the increase, there is a strong incentive to do more.

Most countries have established conservation schemes, with the UAE leading the way. Five percent of the emirate of Dubai is a protected area, thanks to the example set by the late Sheikh Zayed, posthumously named 'Champion of the Earth' by the UN Environment Programme (UNEP) in 2005. Sir Bani Yas Island has an important and growing collection of Arabian wildlife, and Al Ain Zoo has been transformed into a sustainable wildlife centre. Saudi Arabia's Asir National Park is the largest on the Peninsula, comprising 4500 sq km of Red Sea coast, escarpment and desert. In addition, Saudi authorities have designated 13 wildlife reserves (amounting to more than 5000 sq km) as part of a plan for more than 100 protected areas. The Hawar Islands, home to epic colonies of cormorants and other migrant birds, are protected by the Bahrain government.

Although it has no national parks as such, Oman has a reasonable record with regard to protection of the environment, a subject in which the sultan has a passionate interest. His efforts have repeatedly been acknowledged by the International Union for the Conservation of Nature. A reserve protects the internationally important turtle nesting grounds of Ras Al Jinz, while *tahr* (a mountain-dwelling, goat-like mammal) and leopard sanctuaries provide protection for these endangered species.

Environmental Issues

Water

The major concern for all Peninsula countries, particularly those of the Gulf, is water – or rather, the lack of it. Sustained periods of drought and dramatically increased water consumption over the past two decades have led to a depleted water table. Saudi Arabia is predicted to run out of groundwater long before it runs out of oil.

Bahrain's freshwater underground springs have already dried up, leaving the country reliant on expensive desalinated water. Higher demand for residential use is another factor forcing countries to rethink ways of managing water. Desalination and modernisation of irrigation systems appears to be the way forward, though public awareness also has a role to play. At present, it would be unthinkable to impose a hose-pipe ban on municipal and private gardens, as flowering borders are considered the ultimate symbol of a modern, civilised lifestyle.

That said, mostly gone are the days when you could cross parts of Saudi Arabia and see great green circular fields dotted across the desert. There was much to regret in the attempt to make the desert bloom. While Saudi Arabia became an exporter of grain, it used up precious mineral deposits and lowered the water table, and to no great useful purpose – the country can easily afford to import grain at the moment. There may be times to come when it cannot, and many experts are of the opinion it's better to retain precious resources, if not for the proverbial rainy day, then at least for the expected prolonged drought.

Pollution & Rubbish

In a region where oil is the major industry, there is always a concern about spillage and leakage, and the illegal dumping of oil from offshore tankers is a constant irritation to the countries of the Gulf. The oil spillage, following the deliberate release of oil by Iraq during the Gulf War, resulted in an environmental catastrophe that, though not quite as bad as initially predicted, caused significant damage that is still being addressed today.

Books on Seashells

....

Collectable Eastern Arabian Seashells (Donald Bosch)

....

Seashells of Eastern Arabia (Donald Bosch et al)

Books on the Desert

....

In the Deserts of the Earth, Uwe George (1977)

....

Desert: Nature and Culture, Roslynn Haynes (2013)

THE NATURAL ENVIRONMENT ENVIRONMENTAL ISSUES

Gazelle in the desert near Dubai

The oil industry isn't the only sector responsible for environmental degradation. As one of the Peninsula's fastest-growing industries, tourism is becoming a major environmental issue – as seen at the turtle beaches of Ras Al Jinz, where many tourists show a dismal lack of respect for both the turtles and their environment. The irresponsible use of 4WD vehicles in 'dune bashing' is another lamentable problem.

By far the biggest concern created by larger numbers of visitors to the desert is the discarding of rubbish. Indeed, for several decades the Arabian Peninsula has been afflicted by the scourge of plastic bags and tin cans. These are unceremoniously dumped out of car windows or discarded at picnic sites where they can be seen drifting across the desert, tangled in trees or floating in the sea. Expatriates and many Peninsula Arabs don't feel it is their responsibility to 'bag it and bin it' – that would be stealing the job, so the argument goes, of the road cleaner. You can see these individuals on a scooter, or even walking in the middle of summer, with a dustpan and brush and a black bin liner, 100km from the nearest village. The idea that Arabs have inherited the throwaway culture from the Bedouin and can't distinguish between organic and non-biodegradable is often cited, but lacks credibility. The Bedouin know very well that an orange peel, let alone a Coke can, does not decompose in a hurry in the dry heat of the Peninsula.

The Arab response to litter, like the Arab response to conservation in general, probably has more to do with a lack of interest in the great outdoors for its own sake. But times are changing, and school trips to wild places may just be the answer. In the UAE, recycling was made mandatory in 2010, and Masdar City in Abu Dhabi is taking the lead on carbon-neutral living.

The Breeding Centre for Endangered Arabian Wildlife is dedicated to programs preserving the endangered species of the Peninsula. Some of the animals can be seen in Arabia's Wildlife Centre in Sharjah's Desert Park, the largest of its kind.

Survival Guide

Safe Travel

Rightly or wrongly, the Arabian Peninsula has historically earned a reputation as a high-risk destination, marked by hardline political regimes, Islamic fundamentalism and home-grown terrorism. Added to that, the uprisings of 2011 left a legacy of unrest that increased the negative impression of security in the region.

This is a reputation, however, that is not wholly deserved and today the threats to safety are largely confined to one or two trouble spots in Bahrain and some sensitive areas in Kuwait and Saudi Arabia. With a war raging across the border with Saudi Arabia, and entrenched internal conflicts, Yemen is currently the only country on the Peninsula that poses a high risk, and for this reason it should be entirely off-limits for visitors.

Politics aside, the Peninsula overall represents a very safe destination, boasting one of the lowest average crime rates in the world. That doesn't mean you should take unnecessary risks, but it does mean you can largely travel without worrying about theft, mugging and scams.

COUNTRY BY COUNTRY

Safety is a subjective topic. As far as security on the Peninsula is concerned, most people's perceptions are shaped by media stories of Islamic fundamentalism. It's a picture that bears little relation to reality. Interestingly, Arabs travelling abroad share similar safety fears, bearing in mind Al Jazeera reports of violent gun crime, car-jacking and theft that appear to plague many cities around the world. Needless to say, day-to-day life on the Peninsula revolves around violence about as much as it does in Kentucky, Kent or Kerala.

Fortunately, the people of the Middle East are ready and willing to distinguish between foreign travellers and the policies of their governments. You might receive the occasional question about politics, but you'll never be held personally accountable. Keep abreast of current events, and visit your embassy for travel advice if you're feeling cautious, but otherwise (with the current exception of Yemen) just go.

Bahrain

The areas of tourist interest in Bahrain are safe to visit. Although a few areas remain restricted due to political tensions following the Arab Spring uprisings of 2011 and 2012, the visitor is unlikely to be much affected by these. As a precaution, however, it is worth keeping an eye on international news for unrest and checking with your consulate before booking a visit. A ban on public demonstrations is in place, and there are no-go areas in and around the capital city. Sporadic violent outbursts, fuelled by frustration from opposition groups at what is regarded as a lack of government reform, remain an issue. While visiting in the country, therefore, remain vigilant, keep abreast of local news and avoid large gatherings, especially after dark.

Kuwait

Crime of any sort against visitors is rare, but this a conservative country, and it is wise to avoid provoking prob-

AVOIDING TROUBLE

Do...

➡ Carry some form of identification with you at all times, including some or all of the following: passport, labour card, residence card, driving licence and travel permit (Saudi Arabia).

➡ It's helpful to carry something with the contact details of your next of kin and your blood type.

➡ Be vigilant in the cities, keeping clear of large public gatherings.

➡ Cooperate politely with security checks in hotel foyers and at road checkpoints.

➡ Keep abreast of the news in English-language newspapers published locally.

➡ Check the latest travel warnings online through your country's state department or ministry.

➡ Consult your embassy/consulate in the region for specific concerns.

➡ Register with your embassy/consulate on arrival if there have been recent issues around public order.

➡ Trust the police, military and security services. They are overwhelmingly friendly, honest and hospitable, in common with their compatriots.

Don't...

➡ Be paranoid – the chances of running into trouble are no greater than at home.

➡ Get involved if you witness political protests or civil unrest.

➡ Strike up conversations of a stridently political nature with casual acquaintances.

➡ Touch any unidentified objects in the wilds – ordnance from earlier conflicts is still an occasional issue in Dhofar in Oman and Kuwait.

---

lems by, for example, dressing immodestly. Landmines continue to be a problem, so refrain from going off-road except on clear, well-travelled tracks, and do not pick up objects in the desert.

Oman

Oman is one of the safest countries in the entire Middle East to visit. The main danger is from the weather: flash floods, particularly in the mountains, often catch visitors unaware. Wadis should be avoided during and immediately after rain. Visitors also sometimes underestimate the strength of the current in the Gulf and the Arabian Sea, so local guidelines should be observed.

In the desert, getting a vehicle stuck in soft sand in remote areas can be life-threatening, but if you have plenty of water with

you, remain with the vehicle and keep calm; there is a strong likelihood of being noticed within a few days. In popular tourist spots, getting stuck is more an inconvenience than a hazard.

Qatar

Despite some Arab states cutting diplomatic ties with Qatar and the land border with Saudi Arabia being closed, Qatar remains a safe destination for visitors.

Saudi Arabia

Despite the pivotal role Saudi Arabia has played in engendering Al Qaeda, the government in Riyadh has made a concerted effort to stamp out terrorism in the kingdom. This has not eradicated it entirely, however, and sectarian violence sometimes flares

up, most recently targeting mosques.

Tourism (almost exclusively in groups, as independent travel remains difficult) has increased in recent years and the security of these visitors is taken very seriously as the authorities seek to grow this nascent industry.

Stay away from the border with Yemen (up to 80km). In the north, stick to corridors approaching land borders as a 20km 'out-of-bound zone' is in place with prison sentences for violations.

United Arab Emirates

This country is safe to visit, but beware of expressing open sympathy with Qatar, either verbally or through social media, as this has been declared an imprisonable offence. There's little violent crime, even in the big cities.

Yemen

Yemen, which continues in a state of civil war, is completely off-limits to visitors. The security situation is exacerbated by air strikes by a Saudi-led coalition, terrorist attacks, kidnapping and the targeting of foreigners by a number of dangerous factions, including local militia and armed tribespeople.

DANGERS & ANNOYANCES

Road Accidents

Traffic accidents are the largest threat to safety on the Peninsula, with a high incidence of fatalities on the road and heavy congestion in cities. A decade of campaigning for safe driving has helped stamp out the worst abuses but problems remain in the form of tailgating, queue jumping, pushing in, lack of indication, not using mirrors, jumping red lights and turning right across the traffic when sitting in the left lane. Car horns, used at the slightest provocation in some cities, take the place of caution and courtesy and almost no one likes to give way, slow down or wait. During Ramadan, drivers are often tired, thirsty, hungry and irritable (due to the day's fasting) and everyone is in that much more of a hurry – generally to get home for a nap.

The one good-news story of the region is Oman, where (on the whole) drivers stick to the speed limits, let people into their lane and thank others for the same courtesy. Use of the horn is forbidden, except in an emergency, and you can be fined for having a dirty car.

Hazards to look out for while driving in the region include the following:

➜ animals on the road (particularly camels and goats)

➜ dust storms that loom out of nowhere and obscure the road ahead

➜ cars travelling without lights on

➜ heavy rain washing out sections of road

➜ sudden flash floods that sweep away vehicles

➜ corrugated surfaces (like a rumble strip) on graded roads that damage tyres

➜ batteries that run out of juice without warning as they are quickly exhausted in high temperatures

Extreme Temperatures

Visitors should be aware that most of the Arabian Peninsula comprises desert, and this extreme environment can bring its own hazards, especially in temperatures that exceed 50°C in summer. With common sense and a few precautions, however, encountering this unique environment is one of the highlights of a Peninsula visit.

The major hazard of the region is undoubtedly the heat. At any time of year, the high midday temperatures, combined with high humidity, can quickly lead to heat exhaustion, sunstroke and serious sunburn. If you are travelling in summer, breaking down on an isolated road without water can be life-threatening. You should bear this in mind when planning a trip outside urban areas and think twice about travelling alone unless you are highly resourceful.

Avoiding problems is largely a matter of common sense: always carry more water than you think you'll need; cover your head and neck; wear sunglasses; cover up, especially between 11am and 3pm; and avoid too much activity in the summer months – in other words, do as the locals do!

Hazards at Sea

The waters of the Red Sea and the northern part of the Arabian Sea are usually calm and safe for swimming, but there are a few hazards to avoid.

STRONG CURRENTS

During summer (July to September), huge swells occur, making swimming very dangerous. Every year there are casualties associated with the strong tides and powerful undercurrents. On some stretches of the normally quieter Gulf and Red Sea coasts, lifeguards using internationally recognised flags patrol the beach at weekends. Make sure you obey the red-flag directives: in Dubai there have been casualties, with tourists being swept out to sea in unexpected currents.

POLLUTION

Plastic has become a problem affecting many public beaches despite the best efforts of local authorities, and tar, released from irresponsible tankers, can be a nuisance on a few wild beaches. The practice is illegal but hard to police.

DANGEROUS MARINE LIFE

Most problems can be avoided by wearing shoes and a t-shirt when swimming (also useful against sunburn). Common hazards of the sea include the following:

➜ Stonefish have a highly venomous sting.

➜ Jellyfish deliver a fairly innocuous but persistent sting.

➜ Most urchins are not toxic, but spines break off easily if brushed against and can embed in the skin for months.

➜ Sea snakes are highly toxic but thankfully shy.

➜ Some species of cones deliver a paralysing sting if handled.

➜ Coral can inflict cuts that can easily lead to infection.

➡ While sharks are common, only very rare incidents of aggressive behaviour have been reported and generally in predictable circumstances (such as in waters where fishermen are gutting fish).

➡ The bloom of blood-coloured algae known as red tide can affect the waters of the Gulf and Arabian Sea for months at a time, making swimming unappealing. It is not fully understood whether these tides are harmful.

Hazards on Land

Most of the hazards of the desert are related to over-exposure to the sun and the danger of getting caught in flash floods. These walls of water roll quickly across land too hard-baked to absorb it, sweeping away everything that gets in its path. The key strategies to staying safe are to avoid camping in wadis, don't approach the mountains during rains, don't travel alone and never cross roads where water is flowing over the red marker signs, however shallow that appears to be.

There are a few other land hazards to watch out for, such as poisonous plants (eg pink oleander in the wadis and the Sodom's apples that strew the desert floor), camel spiders, scorpions that deliver a nasty but nonfatal bite, large ants with painful bites, and annoying clusters of mosquitoes and wasps at certain times of the year. Snakes are also common in the region. Most problems can be avoided by wearing shoes and resisting the temptation to prod holes and overturn rocks.

WOMEN TRAVELLERS

Many women imagine that travel on the Peninsula is a lot more difficult than it actually is. Unaccompanied women will certainly attract curious stares and glances, and occasionally comments too, but they will receive hospitable treatment almost universally.

Harassment

Sometimes women may be followed (particularly on beaches) or find unwanted visitors in a hotel, but this is far less prevalent than in other parts of the Middle East where there is more exposure to tourists. Sexual harassment in some Peninsula countries is considered a serious crime, but women are more likely to encounter harassment and sexual innuendo.

Modesty

Modesty is one of those culturally defined concepts that is hard to define, but it is highly prized by men and women in all Peninsula societies. A lack of this so-called virtue is likely to bring trouble to women travellers, especially those travelling alone.

Tight clothing that reveals shoulders, knees and cleavage is the quickest way to earn the opprobrium of local women. It will also send conflicting messages to men who, especially in rural areas, often confuse attractive dress with sexual invitation.

Modesty includes, but isn't restricted to, clothing, drinking and smoking copiously in public, talking in a loud voice in mixed company, partying and dancing suggestively with male friends, engaging in conversations of innuendo, flirtatiousness of any kind – all these modes of conduct may well be harmlessly intended, but they often give offence and may result in disdain from men and women and/or unwanted male advances.

Modesty should not be confused with attempting to dress and behave like local women. Wearing an *abaya* (full-length robe) is only expected in Saudi Arabia, and it is not necessary to cover hair in any of the Peninsula countries. Similarly, foreign women are welcome to mingle publicly in mixed company, providing they remain sensitive to the cultural environment.

Repelling Suitors

Engaging with locals is always a highlight of travel in the Middle East, and it's easy for women to strike up conversation if travelling alone. The key when interacting with local men is to realise that initiating conversation can be misinterpreted. Report serious harassment to the local police, who are likely to take the matter very seriously. Here are some tips to deter would-be suitors:

➡ Master the art of detachment by remaining aloof in a conversation rather than being animated; local women are good role models in this.

➡ Keep eye contact to a minimum – unless delivering the killer cold stare if someone oversteps the mark.

➡ Approach a woman for help first (for directions and so forth) rather than a man.

➡ Ask to be seated in the 'family' section if dining alone.

➡ Avoid sitting in the front seat of taxis and the back seat of buses.

➡ Invent a husband if the situation feels alarming, but beware that this may lead to uncomfortable questions about abandoning the home and kids.

➡ Retain your self-confidence and keep a sense of humour in compromising situations. This is far more effective than losing your temper or showing vulnerability.

➡ Insist on being told the family name of pestering individuals and their place of work – the threat of shame is often enough to dampen their ardour.

Directory A–Z

Accessible Travel

Generally speaking, scant regard is paid to the needs of travellers with disabilities on the Peninsula. Steps, high kerbs and other assorted obstacles are everywhere. Roads are made virtually uncrossable by heavy traffic, while some doorways are narrow and many buildings have steep staircases and no lifts.

In top-end hotels, facilities are usually better (with lifts, ramps and more accommo- dating bathrooms) but still leave much to be desired. Trips have to be planned carefully and may be restrict- ed to luxury-level hotels and private, hired transport.

Before setting off, travel- lers with disabilities can get in touch with their national support organisation (pref- erably with the travel officer, if there is one). In the UK, try www.disabledtravelers. com or Tourism For All (www. tourismforall.org.uk).

Download Lonely Planet's free Accessible Travel guides from http://lptravel.to/ AccessibleTravel.

Accommodation

Travellers should book well in advance during local holiday periods (particularly over *eid*), popular festivals (such as the shopping festivals in Dubai and Kuwait), Western holidays (Christmas and New Year) and major fixtures (such as the Dubai Rugby Sevens). Discounts in sum- mer (except in Salalah in Oman) are common.

Outside the big cities, accommodation is scarce and choice limited. Rooms in all categories generally have air-conditioning, hot water, telephone, fridge, some form of internet connection and TV (usually with satellite channels, including BBC and CNN).

Budget Hotels

Accommodation prices on the whole are much higher than international norms, and the region lacks an established network of backpacker hotels. A few dormitory-style hostels are available in the UAE and Qatar, but these are men only, and women will struggle to find any suitable cheap rooms as budget hotels in cities often double as broth- els. Finding a bit of extra cash to upgrade usually pays dividends.

PRACTICALITIES

Discount Cards Student, youth and senior-citizens cards are of little use anywhere on the Peninsula.

Smoking Banned in indoor public spaces (including malls, restaurants, educational premises and offices). With the exception of Qatar, these bans are mostly well enforced, especially in cities. Nonsmoking rooms in hotels are available in all top-end and some midrange hotels. Smoking is off limits in some taxis, too.

Telephone International calls cost around US$1 for two minutes for most destinations. Rates don't usually vary during the day or night, but in some countries there are reductions at weekends. Local SIM cards are widely available in all cities and most airports across the region.

Time Saudi Arabia, Kuwait, Bahrain and Qatar are three hours ahead of GMT/UTC. The UAE and Oman are four hours ahead of GMT/UTC. Daylight-saving time is not observed in any of the Gulf countries (in other words, the time remains constant throughout the year).

Weights & Measures The metric system is in use through- out the Peninsula. However, there are some local variations where petrol is sold by the imperial gallon, not litre.

Midrange Hotels

Where there is a choice of accommodation, it is generally worth choosing a midrange hotel over a budget hotel. These tend to offer the best value for money, are often family-run and may well have more character than the glossy five-star alternatives.

Top-end Hotels

Ranked as some of the best in the world, Arabia's luxury hotels come with spas, personal fitness and shopping services, infinity pools, fine dining, world-class architecture and palatial interior designs. With their sociable bars and/or coffeeshops, they generally double as entertainment venues for residents.

Resorts

Over the past few years, the resort concept has burgeoned across the region. Generally occupying superb locations, they are often destinations in their own right, offering magical, landscaped retreats from the city. Given the nature of the Peninsula's geography, they can be marooned in splendid isolation with few surrounding amenities, but this is compensated for by the sumptuous architecture and the well-resourced activity centres.

Camping

Camping is a major highlight of a trip to Arabia, and the good news is that, with a 4WD, your own supplies and a sense of adventure, there are endless opportunities. It's easy to find your own piece of wilderness – just avoid camping in wadis, Bedouin areas and turtle beaches (ones with large pits at the top of the tide line) and remember to remove all rubbish.

Glamping

While wild camping is the norm, it is not the only way to overnight in beauty spots in Arabia, and organised desert camps can be found in the Asir National Park in Saudi

---

Arabia, Khor Al Adaid in Qatar, the Sharqiya Sands and Jebel Shams in Oman. Even a basic camp in these areas generally offers fixed tents, showers and cooked food. Some come with private showers, air-con, a bar and pools!

Customs Regulations

Customs regulations vary from country to country, but in most cases they don't differ significantly. All luggage is X-rayed and sometimes also opened. That said, with greater numbers of tourists arriving, and in the drive to appear more tourist friendly, many of the old customs nightmares (such as long queues while officials check the contents of your soap box) are things of the past.

Alcohol It is strictly forbidden to take alcohol into dry or semi-dry regions (Kuwait, Qatar, Sharjah, Abu Dhabi and Saudi Arabia). If you're caught attempting to smuggle in even small quantities of alcohol, punishments range from deportation and fines to imprisonment. In most other countries, foreigners (but not Muslims) are permitted a small duty-free allowance but only if entering the country by air (empty the cool box if crossing into or out of Oman by car).

Drugs Syringes, needles and some medicinal drugs (such as tranquillisers and even some antidepressants and sleeping pills) are banned, unless you have a doctor's prescription to prove you need them.

Israeli and 'incendiary' material Books critical of Islam, Peninsula governments or their countries, or pro-Israeli books, may be confiscated.

Money There are no restrictions on the import and export of money (in any currency) in and out of Peninsula countries.

Pork products Some countries make allowances for foreigners, but it's better not to get stopped with a pork chop in your pocket.

Pornography Officials may construe images in style magazines, or of women in swimwear, as pornographic and remove the offending page from the magazine.

Video material and DVDs Censors sometimes examine these and then allow you to collect them after a few days.

Electricity

All countries in the region have an electrical supply of 220 to 240V. Saudi Arabia and UAE use other plugs in addition to those shown here.

**Type C
220V/50Hz**

**Type G
240V/50Hz**

Embassies & Consulates

Embassies are a fairly good, if somewhat cautious and at times alarmist, source of information on current hot spots and dangers. Many embassies advise travellers to register with them upon arrival, especially if you're staying in the country for an extended period: if you should disappear, have a serious accident or suddenly need to be evacuated from the country, you will at least be in a better position to receive help. If you break the law, you're on your own.

Insurance

Travel insurance covering accidents and medical problems is strongly advised, particularly as traffic accidents are a major hazard of the region and problems can easily occur if visiting the desert (particularly on off-road excursions). Although some regional hospitals do not charge for emergency treatment, you cannot rely on this. The cost of complicated surgery (for a fracture, for example) is comparable with international rates.

A policy that pays doctors or hospitals directly rather than you having to pay on the spot and claim later is a better option for the region. If you have to claim later, make sure you keep all documentation.

Note that some policies specifically exclude 'dangerous activities', which can include activities you may want to engage in on the Peninsula, such as scuba diving, rock climbing, motorcycling and even trekking. Car insurance does not usually include automatic off-road coverage. Specify that you need this if hiring a 4WD for off-road adventure.

Internet Access

Internet access is offered free in hotels and in many coffeeshops. Unless you are off-road in the desert or camping in the mountains, use of all connectivity devices (smartphones, tablets and so forth) is virtually guaranteed.

Be aware that internet usage and browsing is monitored in Gulf countries and can attract severe penalties. In 2019 a woman was arrested in Dubai for insulting another woman on Facebook.

Legal Matters

Although the law varies in specifics from country to country, it does share certain similarities. The legal system in all Peninsula countries is based wholly or partly on Sharia law, derived mainly from the Quran.

Sharia law is often perceived as notoriously harsh and inflexible, but in reality it shares many commonly held legal values, such as the presumption of innocence until proven guilty. The severest punishment for a crime is in practice rarely exacted (even in Saudi Arabia).

Visitors should remember that they are subject to the laws of the country they find themselves in and that ignorance of the law does not constitute a defence. In Saudi Arabia, in particular, it is vital that travellers (particularly women) acquaint themselves with the local laws.

If you are arrested and detained, call your embassy or consulate and wait until a representative arrives before you sign anything. In a car accident you should not move the car, even if you're causing a traffic jam, until the police arrive.

Those caught in possession of drugs (including ecstasy, amphetamines, cannabis and cocaine) can face the death penalty. In Saudi Arabia, with its policy of zero tolerance, this means what it says.

LGBT+ Travellers

Homosexual practices are illegal in all of the Peninsula countries. Under Sharia (Islamic) law, homosexuality incurs the death penalty in some countries, though punishment usually ranges from flogging to imprisonment or deportation. In other countries infractions are punished by fines and/or imprisonment.

Visitors are unlikely to encounter outright prejudice or harassment so long as they remain discreet. However, this may well change if you become involved with a local. Room sharing is generally not a problem (it will be assumed you're economising). Condoms are fairly widely available, though there may be a limited selection.

Useful Resources

Global Gayz (www.globalgayz. com/middle-east) Country-by-country guide to gay and lesbian activity.

Barra (www.facebook.com/bar-ramagazine) A news-and-views forum for the LBGT community based in the Middle East.

BARGAINING

Bargaining over prices (except in malls) is still very much a way of life on the Peninsula, although to a lesser extent than in some other Middle Eastern countries. Oman is perhaps the exception, where aggressive bargaining can offend. Prices rarely come down below half the original quote; 25% to 30% discount is around the norm.

Arabs are committed shoppers, and they make an art form out of it, promenading the main street and popping into shops to vex the owners without any intention of buying. Buying, meanwhile, is a whole separate entertainment, focused on the business of bartering and bargaining.

Bartering implies that items do not have a value per se – their value is governed by what you are willing to pay balanced against the sum for which the vendor is happy to sell. This subtle exchange, often viewed with suspicion by those from a fixed-price culture, is dependent on many factors, such as how many other sales the vendor has made that day, whether the buyer looks like a person who can afford an extra rial or two, and even whether the vendor is in a good mood or not.

As with all social interaction, there's an unwritten code of conduct that keeps negotiations sweet:

➡ Bartering is your chance to decide what you are willing to pay for an item, so use your interpersonal skills to see if you can persuade the vendor to match it.

➡ Haggling is a sociable activity, often conducted over refreshments, so avoid causing offence by refusing hospitality.

➡ Don't pay the first price quoted. This is often considered arrogant.

➡ Start below the price you wish to buy at so you have room to compromise – but don't quote too low or the vendor may be insulted.

➡ If negotiations aren't going to plan, simply smile and say goodbye – you'll be surprised how often the word *maa salaama* (goodbye) brings the price down.

➡ Resist comparing prices with other travellers. If they were happy with what they paid, they certainly won't be if you tell them you bought the same thing for less. Besides, you can't put a price on the thrill of the deal.

Money

ATMs are widely available; credit cards are accepted by most hotels and city restaurants.

ATMs

Virtually all banks in the region, from big cities to small villages, have ATMs from which you can withdraw funds from an overseas bank or gain a cash advance with a credit card. ATMs are also widespread in shopping malls and petrol stations.

Cash

Cash in US dollars, pounds sterling or euros is easily exchanged anywhere in the region. Other currencies, such as Indian rupees, less so. In small businesses, in-cluding cheap restaurants, bus stations and budget hotels, and in rural areas, you will need cash for most transactions. Change money before leaving one Peninsula country for another as neighbouring currency is not often accepted across borders (with the possible exception of Emirati dirhams in northern Oman).

Credit Cards

Credit cards are widely accepted on the Peninsula, and almost everything can be paid for by plastic, including your morning cup of coffee. Visa and MasterCard are the most popular credit cards; American Express is less widely accepted. It's possible to get cash advances on credit cards.

Moneychangers

Moneychangers are easy to find in all Peninsula cities, but the rates do not differ much from banks.

Tipping

Tips are not generally expected in the Gulf and the concept of *baksheesh*, common throughout the rest of the Middle East, is little known on the Peninsula. That said, those who have contact with tourists (such as guides and hotel porters) have grown to expect tips.

Note that the service charge added to most hotel and restaurant bills is not an automatic gratuity that goes to the waiters. It usually goes into the till and is often the restaurant's way of making the prices on the menu look 10% to 15% cheaper than they really are. Waiters in the Gulf tend to be paid derisory wages, so a small tip discreetly left on the table, while not required, is greatly appreciated if the service is good. The practice of automatic, lavish tip giving, however, can backfire as many establishments simply reduce the wages of their employees if they know that tips are expected.

Coffeehouses Not required.

Hotels Equivalent of a couple of dollars for carrying bags; entirely discretionary for cleaning staff.

Restaurants Discreet tipping for exceptional service only.

Taxis Not expected but appreciated (not required on short, metered city hops).

Guides Ask the tour operator before engaging a guide as rates vary in each country.

Photography

Restricted areas Do not photograph anything vaguely military in nature (including the police), or anything construed as strategic (including airports, bridges and ports). In general terms, Bahrain and the UAE are the most relaxed countries on the Peninsula when it comes to photography, while Kuwait and Oman seem to have the broadest definitions of what constitutes a strategic site. In Saudi Arabia it

often seems that the authorities just don't like cameras.

Photographing people Do not photograph anyone without their permission, especially women. In the more conservative countries, such as Saudi Arabia and Kuwait, you can cause real offence in this way and may risk having stones thrown at you.

Photographing poverty People on the Peninsula are often offended when you take photographs of run-down houses or anything that resembles poverty, as the tendency is to emphasise what their country has achieved in the last few decades.

Religious sites Photography is usually allowed inside religious and archaeological sites (when entry is permitted), unless there are signs indicating otherwise. Avoid taking photos of religious observance.

Post

Although most postal systems in the Gulf are reasonably efficient, they can be on the slow side. Post offices are found in all the larger towns and cities of the Peninsula.

In some countries incoming packages, even fairly small ones, are still sometimes sent to customs for lengthy searches, during which books, magazines or videos will probably have been vetted for 'inappropri-

ate material'. Note that you may be held responsible for the contents of the parcels sent to you, and sometimes prosecuted (particularly in Saudi Arabia).

Public Holidays

All Peninsula countries observe the main Islamic holidays. Some of the Peninsula countries also observe the Gregorian New Year (1 January). Every country has its own national days and other public holidays. Most share the following holidays:

Islamic New Year Also known as Ras As Sana, it literally means 'the head of the year'.

Ashura The anniversary of the martyrdom of Hussein, the third imam (religious teacher) of the Shiites (not observed in all countries).

Prophet's Birthday Known as Moulid An Nabi, it's 'the feast of the Prophet'.

Ramadan The ninth month of the Muslim calendar, this is when Muslims fast during daylight hours. How strictly the fast is observed depends on the country, but most Muslims conform to some extent. Foreigners are not expected to follow suit, but visitors should not smoke, drink or eat (including gum chewing) in public during Ramadan. Hotels make provision for non-Muslim guests by erecting screens for

ISLAMIC HOLIDAYS

Dates of Islamic holidays are dependent on moon sightings and consequently may occur a day later, but not generally earlier, than listed. Not all countries spot the moon on the same day (cloud cover doesn't count), so regional differences between countries occur each year. In fact, speculation regarding whether tomorrow will bring *eid* is the subject of great public debate and private expat exasperation. Treat the following table as a guide only.

YEAR HEJIRA	NEW YEAR	ASHURA	PROPHET'S BIRTHDAY	RAMADAN BEGINS	EID AL FITR	EID AL ADHA
1441	1 Sep 2019	10 Sep 2019	10 Nov 2019	24 Apr 2020	24 May 2020	31 Jul 2020
1442	21 Aug 2020	1 Sep 2020	1 Nov 2020	14 Apr 2021	14 May 2021	21 Jul 2021
1443	11 Aug 2021	21 Aug 2021	21 Oct 2021	4 Apr 2022	4 May 2022	11 Jul 2022
1444	1 Aug 2022	11 Aug 2022	11 Oct 2022	24 Mar 2023	24 Apr 2023	1 Jul 2023
1445	22 Jul 2023	1 Aug 2023	1 Oct 2023	14 Mar 2024	14 Apr 2024	21 Jun 2024

discreet dining. Opening hours tend to become more erratic and usually shorter and many restaurants close for the whole period. Alcohol is not available during Ramadan, except as room service. Once the sun has set each day, the fast is broken with something light, such as dates, before prayers. Then comes *iftar* (the meal that breaks the evening fast), at which enough food is usually consumed to compensate for the previous hours of abstinence. People then rise again before dawn to prepare a meal to support them through the day.

Eid Al Fitr The festivities mark the end of Ramadan fasting; the celebrations last for three days and are a time of family feasting and visiting.

Eid Al Adha This feast marks the time that Muslims make the pilgrimage to Mecca.

Islamic Calendar

Although most secular activities and day-to-day life are planned on the Peninsula according to the Gregorian calendar (the most commonly used system internationally), all Islamic holidays are calculated according to the Islamic calendar. For visitors this can cause confusion, such as when trying to decipher official documents, including the date of expiry of travel permits and visas. Calendars showing parallel systems are available.

The Muslim year is based on the lunar cycle and is divided into 12 lunar months, each with 29 or 30 days. Consequently, the Muslim year is 10 or 11 days shorter than the Christian solar year, and Muslim festivals gradually move around the common year, completing the cycle in roughly 33 years.

Year zero in the Muslim calendar was when Muhammad and his followers fled from Mecca to Medina (AD 622 in the Christian calendar). This Hejira, or migration, is taken to mark the start of the new Muslim era, much as Christ's birth

marks year zero in the Christian calendar. Just as BC denotes 'Before Christ', so AH denotes 'After Hejira'.

Solo Travellers

Travel for Arab people and Asian expats entails large convoys of family groups and great gatherings at the airport. As such, solo male travellers are often regarded either with sympathy or with suspicion, as it is inconceivable to most Arabian Peninsula people that someone might choose to travel alone.

A woman travelling on her own is an even hotter topic of discussion. Women will want to adopt you, men will either ignore you (out of respect) or treat you as a token man. Either way, you will inevitably be showered with well-meaning solicitations for your safe keeping, extra help on public

transport and even offers of accommodation.

Without knowing Arabic, travelling on the Arabian Peninsula can be quite lonely at times – the roads are long and the deserts wide. Without an established network of tourism facilities, you may spend days without seeing another traveller.

Single rooms are available in most hotels, though they're often just a few dollars cheaper than double rooms. Walking around alone seldom presents a safety problem.

One word of caution: if you drive away from urban areas by car alone, you need to be quite resourceful. Many roads see very little traffic and you could wait hours before help arrives. It is not recommended that you go off-road alone.

MOSQUE ETIQUETTE

The impressive grand mosques that grace each Peninsula capital city are often open to non-Muslims. A mosque tour can be inspirational in terms of cultural insights. The following advice will help ensure no offence is unwittingly caused during visits.

Do...

➡ Dress modestly in loose clothing, covering shoulders, arms and legs (plus cleavage and hair for women); some mosques require women to wear an *abaya* (full-length robe).

➡ Remove shoes before stepping into the prayer hall.

➡ Sit on the carpet, enjoy the ambience and marvel at the usually exquisite interior design.

➡ Take photographs unless otherwise directed.

Don't ...

➡ Enter a mosque during prayer times if you're not a Muslim.

➡ Wear frayed denim jeans or any clothing that may be deemed disrespectful.

➡ Enter the women's prayer hall if you're a man (women may enter the men's prayer hall in most mosques open to the public).

➡ Use the ablution area – it's reserved for the preparation of worship.

➡ Touch the Holy Quran.

➡ Extend your feet out front while sitting; tuck them underneath in a slouched kneeling position.

➡ Speak in a loud voice, sing or whistle.

➡ Take inappropriate selfies or photographs of people praying.

Taxes & Refunds

The Peninsula used to be famous as a low-tax area. Nowadays, however, a mixture of taxes, often reaching 17%, is added to hotel and restaurant prices.

VAT of 5% went into effect in the UAE in January 2018. The Federal Tax Authority of the UAE is currently implementing a digital system at Abu Dhabi, Dubai and Sharjah International Airports to facilitate the refund of VAT for departing visitors. Some 4000 shops and retail outlets across the country will be connected electronically to the system, making the process of claiming the refund (against a validated receipt) relatively straightforward. Look for a poster indicating eligibility in participating shops and outlets.

Toilets

Outside the midrange and top-end hotels and restaurants of the Peninsula, where Western-style toilets are found, visitors will encounter the Arab-style squat toilet (which according to physiologists, encourages a far more natural position than the toilet-seat invention!). Beyond the towns you're unlikely to find public toilets, except poorly maintained ones at petrol stations.

It's a good idea to carry a roll of toilet paper with you on your travels if you normally use this. Most toilets only provide water, and the use of paper is considered barbaric for anything except drying hands.

Tourist Information

Despite the fact that tourism is a growing industry on the Peninsula, there are surprisingly few tourist offices. Staff training and office facilities are equally minimal. Sometimes the most you'll find is a free map (often very outdated) or an aged brochure.

There are two good, unofficial sources of information on the Peninsula: your hotel and local travel agents, many of whom generously offer information without necessarily expecting you to engage their services in return.

Visas

Visas, required by all visitors in all Peninsula countries except Qatar, are available for many nationalities on arrival at airports and most land borders (except Saudi Arabia and Oman).

Saudi Arabia is currently hosting festivals and cultural events open to foreigners, which allows tourists to visit the kingdom on a visitor visa as part of their attendance of the organised events. This development is in line with the country's Vision 2030, which plans to open up the country for mainstream tourism. This is expected to include tourist visas with fewer restrictions on travel within the country. Check the latest with a Saudi consulate.

Entry to Qatar (www.visitqatar.qa/plan/visas-requirements.html) is visa-free for citizens of 83 countries, including Australia, many EU nations, New Zealand, the UK and the US. Visa waivers are issued on arrival and are single entry. Visitors are granted either a 30-day or a 90-day visa depending on nationality.

Note that passports need to be valid for at least six months beyond your expected departure date from the region. Note also that most Peninsula countries require you to carry your passport with you at all times. Spot checks occasionally occur.

Collecting Visas

If you've arranged your visa in advance of arrival, make sure you have some proof of it with you before setting off (such as an email with the visa number), or you may not be allowed to board your plane, let alone enter the country of your destination.

Transit Visas

Saudi Arabia issues transit visas for people travelling overland between Jordan and Bahrain, Kuwait, Oman and the UAE. The border between Saudi Arabia and Qatar is currently closed. Transit visas can be sought from Saudi Arabian embassies in any of these countries with proof of onward connections beyond Saudi borders. They are not easy to obtain, however, as you often have to show you can't reach your destination by other means.

Visa Sponsorship

Sponsorship is no longer required for tourist visas; for work visas, the employer takes care of this formality.

Israeli Passport Stamp

On the Arabian Peninsula, all countries may refuse to admit anyone whose passport has evidence of a visit to Israel, even though a relaxation of this rule is officially in place in all Gulf countries except Saudi Arabia. Israeli immigration officials do not stamp your passport, but if you are crossing into Jordan or Egypt overland, the entry/exit stamps into those countries (marked, for example, 'Taba' or 'Aqaba') are considered proof of a visit.

It remains best to arrange your itinerary so that any visit to Israel is the final stop on your tour of the Middle East.

Women Travellers

It is important to be aware that there are 'men areas' and 'women areas' and that this is something that is enforced mainly by women, not by men. As such, it can be quite uncomfortable for both sexes if a woman sits in a male area. In some instances, it could compromise a woman's safety.

Traditional coffeehouses, cheaper restaurants, budget hotels, the front seat of taxis and the back seats of buses all tend to be men-only areas, and it's culturally sensitive to avoid them. At some budget Gulf hotels, unaccompanied women may be refused a room and insisting on one will likely attract the wrong kind of attention in the middle of the night. Women areas include family rooms in better restaurants, public beaches on certain days of the week and the front rows of buses.

Rather than seeing segregation as being excluded from male company, it is regarded locally as providing a safe haven for women to relax and enjoy their own company with or without the kids and without worrying about harassment or unwanted attention. For the female visitor, it presents a great opportunity to see into the lives of Arab women, an opportunity rarely, if ever, afforded to a male visitor.

Be aware that some religiously devout men prefer not to shake hands with a woman, so be ready to put your hand on your heart instead.

Transport

GETTING THERE & AWAY

Entering the Region

Passports need to be valid for at least six months beyond your expected departure date from the region. Note also that most Peninsula countries require you to carry your passport with you at all times. Spot checks occasionally occur.

Air

The cities of the Gulf have developed into major international air hubs with some of the world's best airlines and most modern and impressive airports.

All major European, Asian and Middle Eastern airlines (with the obvious exception of El Al, the Israeli airline) serve the principal cities of the Arabian Peninsula, and

---

DEPARTURE TAX

Departure tax is almost invariably included in the cost of an airline ticket. It's still applicable, however, at some land borders (for example, between the UAE and Musandam).

---

routes to the Americas and Australasia are increasing.

The national carriers of almost all Peninsula countries link one country to another, with regular flights at reasonable prices. In June 2017, Bahrain, Saudi Arabia and the United Arab Emirates closed off travel to Qatar in a major diplomatic rift that is still ongoing.

Land

Border Crossings

Travelling overland from Jordan or Egypt and travelling between the countries of the Arabian Peninsula is hampered by the fact that it is very difficult to get a transit visa through Saudi Arabia. In addition, many border crossings are closed to non-nationals.

The only really feasible overland route is between Oman and the UAE. There are several border checkpoints between these countries, and crossings may take anything from 30 minutes to more than two hours. Showing patience, politeness and good humour is likely to speed up the process, and it also helps to have prepaid insurance if you're driving, or to have a pen ready for form-filling if you're travelling by bus!

Bus

At present the border crossings between Saudi Arabia and Jordan are closed to

non-Arab travellers. If the situation changes, then Jordan Express Tourist Transport (www.jett.com.jo), the Jordanian national bus company, has a reliable website and operates air-conditioned, modern coaches for any travellers lucky enough to obtain a Saudi visa or transit visa.

Car & Motorcycle

The following documents are required if you are hoping to enter the region with your own transport.

Green Card Issued by insurers. Insurance for some countries is only obtainable at the border.

International Driving Permit (IDP) Compulsory for foreign drivers and motorcyclists in Bahrain and Saudi Arabia. Most foreign licences are acceptable in the other Peninsula countries, but even in these places an IDP is recommended.

Vehicle Registration Documents Check with your insurer whether you're covered for the countries you intend to visit and whether third-party cover is included.

The Arabian Automobile Association (www.aaauae.com) can provide up-to-date advice on documentation and border crossings open to travellers with their own transport as this information changes frequently.

Bringing your own car is not recommended for short-stay visitors, given the administrative hurdles involved (see p486).

Sea

Cargo boats call erratically at Muscat and Jeddah on their way to Europe and Asia. Getting aboard is mostly a question of luck and being in the right place at the right time. Your passage may well be dependent on the whim of the captain. Ask at the port of departure to see what boats are headed where. Some offer comfortable passenger cabins (intended for family members of the crew); for others you may need to come equipped with food, drink and bedding and be prepared for a miserable, hot and uncomfortable journey.

Some cruise ships call at Salalah, Muscat, Khasab, Dubai and Doha, and these ports offer passengers the opportunity to go ashore.

Several ferry services operate between the Peninsula and Egypt and Iran, but they are not geared up for tourists. If you're in for an adventure then bear the following in mind.

➡ In summer, conditions may be impossibly hot for many people, especially in deck class.

➡ Many passengers prefer to take their own food rather than rely on that served on board.

➡ Vehicles can be shipped on ferry services, but advance arrangements should be made.

➡ Ferry destinations and their timetables change frequently, but most ferry companies have good websites where you can check current fares, routes and contact details.

➡ Be aware of migrant routes and avoid paying a third party for your fare in case you find yourself dealing with people traffickers.

EGYPT

The Alexandria-based Misr Edco Shipping Company (www.acs.org.eg/members/misr-edco-shipping-co-s-a-e) and four Saudi companies sail between Jeddah and Suez. The journey takes about 36 hours direct, and about 72 hours via Aqaba (Jordan). Misr Edco also sails about twice weekly between Port Safaga (Egypt) and Jeddah.

IRAN

If you're travelling to/from the east and want to avoid Iraq and Saudi Arabia, you can cross the Gulf Sea from Iran into Kuwait, Dubai or Sharjah (UAE).

Ferries only have 1st-class (cabin) accommodation, but are much cheaper than the equivalent airfare, and most are overnight journeys. They are operated by Valfajr Shipping Company (www.valfajr.ir) in Tehran, which has a good online booking service.

QATAR BLOCKADE

A diplomatic row that broke out in 2017 between the Saudi-led coalition and Qatar has resulted in the latter being left out in the cold by some neighbouring countries through the imposition of a travel blockade. The dispute is over alleged support of terrorism, which some translate as referring to Qatar's friendly relationship with Iran.

For the visitor, the blockade means that it's not presently possible to fly, travel overland or go by boat between Qatar and Saudi Arabia, Bahrain or the UAE. It's also not possible to travel between Qatar and some other Arab countries, such as Jordan and Egypt.

Kuwait is taking a neutral stand in the spat, while Oman has maintained ties with Qatar and has even opened up a new air route between Doha and Sohar. This offers an opportunity to explore the north of Oman on a weekend break from the Gulf.

Tours

Tours to the Peninsula have become a popular way to reduce the logistic issues of travelling independently in the region. Some offer two-country trips between the UAE and Oman.

On the Peninsula itself there are a host of reputable tour agencies offering good trips at competitive prices. Many of these are tailor-made around a key activity (eg history tours, biking, hiking etc). Additionally, most regional airlines usually offer short tours of Peninsula cities for a reasonable supplement to an airfare.

For most would-be visitors, unless they are undertaking hajj, tours are often the only way of visiting Saudi Arabia.

THE ART OF THE STOPOVER

All major Gulf airlines periodically promote free or discounted stopovers in their capital cities, especially during off-peak travel periods. These sometimes include short breaks in major hotels, such as the **Atlantis The Palm** (☑04 426 2000; www.atlantisthepalm.com; Crescent Rd, Palm Jumeirah; r from Dhs1200; ℗🖲🏊; 🚇Palm Jumeirah, 🎢Atlantis Aquaventure) in Dubai, which has a tie-up with Emirates.

CLIMATE CHANGE & TRAVEL

Every form of transport that relies on carbon-based fuel generates CO_2, the main cause of human-induced climate change. Modern travel is dependent on aeroplanes, which might use less fuel per kilometre per person than most cars but travel much greater distances. The altitude at which aircraft emit gases (including CO_2) and particles also contributes to their climate change impact. Many websites offer 'carbon calculators' that allow people to estimate the carbon emissions generated by their journey and, for those who wish to do so, to offset the impact of the greenhouse gases emitted with contributions to portfolios of climate-friendly initiatives throughout the world. Lonely Planet offsets the carbon footprint of all staff and author travel.

Adventure World (www.adventureworld.com.au) Has Australian branches in Adelaide, Brisbane, Melbourne and Perth, and is the agent for the UK's Explore Worldwide.

Kuoni (www.kuoni.co.uk) Offers comprehensive tours of the UAE and Oman; UK-based.

Original World (www.original-world.com) Offers multidestination tours of the UAE and Oman.

Passport Travel (www.travelcentre.com.au) Australia-based Middle East specialist, assisting in tailor-made itineraries for individuals and groups.

Reiseservice Graw (www.first-classtravel.de) Germany-based, offering comprehensive tours to the Peninsula. Its website is in English and the service is available across Europe.

GETTING AROUND

Air

Reputable travel agencies in all major Peninsula cities can advise you about the best intercity deals, and it's better to use their services than go directly to the airlines. Note that prices fluctuate considerably according to the season, or if there's a public holiday (such as *eid*).

Airlines on the Arabian Peninsula

The Peninsula boasts some world-class airlines with good safety records, modern aircraft and well-trained crew. Dubai offers a famously slick international airport with good facilities, including hotels, business centres and extensive duty-free sections. Abu Dhabi, Doha and Muscat have excellent modern airports, too. Some other key information:

➡ For detailed information on safety records, visit www.airsafe.com. Award-winning Gulf Air, Emirates, Qatar Airways, Etihad and Oman Air increase their direct-flight networks regularly.

➡ Saudi Arabia, Oman and the UAE have reasonably priced domestic flight networks.

➡ Smaller regional airports are adequate, and many are in the process of being modernised and expanded.

➡ Arrival procedures are straightforward, quick and efficient. Note, however, the prohibition on various items at customs, particularly in Saudi Arabia.

BUDGET AIRLINES

The arrival of budget airlines in the region revolutionised intercity transport on the Peninsula. As elsewhere, the airlines tend to use less-frequented cities as their hubs to avoid the high taxes of major airports. This minor inconvenience is worth considering for the cheap travel they offer.

Air Arabia (www.airarabia.com)

Al Jazeera Airways (www.jazeeraairways.com)

Fly Dubai (www.flydubai.com)

Salam Air (www.salamair.com)

Bicycle

The Peninsula offers good cycling opportunities, cyclists are made welcome (the annual Tour of Oman attracts international cyclists, including celebrities such as Tour de France winner Bradley Wiggins) and police are helpful and friendly to all road users. Repair shops are easy to come by, and local expats are able bush mechanics. Post any queries on the Thorn Tree on www.lonelyplanet.com, under the Activities branch. Some difficulties to consider:

➡ In most cities, especially in the Gulf, it is very hazardous to cycle as car drivers are not used to anticipating cyclists.

➡ Most bicycles on the Peninsula are simple machines, so spare parts for mountain or touring bikes are only available in major cities.

➡ The heat is a major challenge and cycling is not recommended from June to August, or during the middle of the day at other times of the year.

Cyclists Touring Club (www.ctc.org.uk) is a UK-based organisation offering good tips, a helpful website, and useful information sheets on cycling in different parts of the world.

Boat

A ferry service is offered in Oman between Khasab in

Musandam and Shinas in northern Oman; there are also water taxis between Muscat and Al Seifa and car ferries between the mainland and Masirah Island. In the UAE, water taxis are available in Dubai and Abu Dhabi. Ferries connect Bahrain with the Hawar Islands.

Bus

With oil cheap across the Peninsula, car ownership levels have historically been so high that there was little demand for public bus services. Where services existed, they were often primarily intended for expat workers getting to and from their place of work. That has begun to change now with comprehensive public bus routes offered in Oman, Qatar and the UAE.

Of the major regional routes, there are four principal ones currently open to foreigners: Saudi Arabia to Bahrain, Saudi Arabia and Bahrain to Kuwait, and the UAE to Oman.

Bus travel is usually comfortable, cheap and on schedule, roads are good, and air-conditioned buses are the norm. Take a warm layer as the air-conditioning systems can be brutal. Women accompanied by men can usually sit anywhere, but women travelling alone are expected to sit in the front seats.

Minibus, Big Bus & Hotel Transfer

Muscat, Doha, Abu Dhabi and Dubai have modern, air-conditioned bus networks that run on time and extend across the city;

some networks even boast air-conditioned bus stops. Such networks are presently the exception rather than the rule. More usually, minibus or local bus services tend to connect residential or commercial areas. An alternative to public bus routes are the Big Bus routes that operate in some cities, offering a hop-on, hop-off service linking the main sites of interest, accompanied by an audio tour.

Some cities have a bus service connecting the airport with town, and top-end hotels and travel agents (if you're taking a tour) usually provide a complimentary transfer in many cities. Some hotels also provide bus services to city centres, and limousines organised by the airline (in some classes of travel) are a popular feature of the region.

TRAVELLING OVERLAND THROUGH THE ARABIAN PENINSULA

Travelling between the countries of the Arabian Peninsula is challenging, but not impossible.

BETWEEN	BORDER CROSSING NOTES	VISA AT BORDER?
Oman & Saudi Arabia	No border crossing open.	N/A
Oman (mainland) & UAE	The Wajaja/Hatta border crossing is the most commonly used.	Yes
Oman (Musandam) & UAE	The Tibat/Al Darah border crossing was the only one open at the time of writing.	Yes
Saudi Arabia & Bahrain	The border crossing is on King Fahd Causeway.	To Saudi Arabia, no; to Bahrain, yes.
Saudi Arabia & Kuwait	The border crossing at Al Khafji/Al Nuwaiseeb is usually only used by those on public transport.	To Saudi Arabia, no; to Kuwait, yes.
Saudi Arabia & Qatar	Saudi Arabia closed the land border to Qatar in June 2017.	N/A
Saudi Arabia & UAE	The border crossing is at Al Bat'ha/Guwaifat on the Salwa Rd.	To Saudi Arabia, no; to UAE, yes.
Bahrain, Kuwait and UAE	A Saudi transit visa must be obtained before travelling overland between any of these countries. Application forms can be obtained from a Saudi embassy. Travellers must have a ticket with confirmed reservations and a visa for the country of final destination. Transit times cannot exceed 72 hours. Women can only apply for a transit visa if accompanied by a male relative – proof of kinship (eg marriage certificate) is required. Children need a copy of their birth certificate. If travelling by your own vehicle you are required to register your *carnet* at the embassy. In June 2017 Bahrain and the UAE suspended air and sea travel to Qatar.	No but you need to show your visa for your final destination at the Saudi border to transit through the country.

Reservations

It's always advisable to book bus seats in advance at bus stations, and it's a must over the Muslim weekend (especially Friday), as well as during public holidays such as *eid*.

Car & Motorcycle

Until very recently car was pretty much the only way of getting around Peninsula countries, and car ownership remains a virtual must for expats. Motorcycles remain an uncommon form of transport, largely on account of the punishingly hot summer months.

Bringing Your Own Vehicle

Unless you're coming to the Peninsula for an extended duration, bringing your own vehicle may prove more trouble than it's worth. Obtaining a *carnet de passage* is expensive, and progressing through the Peninsula (because of visa regulations and paperwork) is challenging. For most short-term visitors, it makes more sense to hire a car locally. For long-term residents, it is cheaper and more straightforward to buy a car in the country and sell it before leaving.

Carnets

For those determined to arrive or leave with their own vehicle, a *carnet de passage* is a must. This booklet is stamped on arrival and at departure to ensure that the vehicle has not been misappropriated. It's usually issued by a motoring organisation in the country where the vehicle is registered. Contact your local automobile association for details about required documentation at least three months in advance and bear the following in mind.

➜ You have to lodge a deposit to secure a *carnet*.

➜ If you default (ie you don't have an import and export stamp that match) then the country in question can claim your deposit, which can be up to 300% of the new value of the vehicle.

➜ If your vehicle is irretrievably damaged or stolen, you may be suspected by customs officials of having sold the vehicle, so insist on police reports.

➜ The *carnet* may need to specify any expensive spare parts, such as a gearbox, you bring with you. This is designed to prevent spare-part importation rackets. Despite the above challenges, bank guarantees or *carnet* insurance are available and every year a few people make it in or out of the region with their own vehicle.

Driver's Licence

Travellers from many countries can use their own national driver's licences for a limited period in most Peninsula countries but an International Driving Permit (IDP) is essential for Saudi Arabia.

For longer stays an International Driving Permit (IDP), obtainable from your own country, is recommended (and required by some countries). Check individual countries rules before travelling.

Car Hire

Availability & Cost Car hire is possible in all Peninsula countries, with international as well as local companies represented at international airports and five-star hotels. Costs are comparable to international rates. Reservations are necessary in some countries during peak tourism times, particularly during hajj, or major national or religious holidays.

Vehicle Type For off-road driving in the desert, a 4WD is essential; these are available from all hire companies. Don't cut costs by hiring a 2WD for off-road driving – for one thing, your insurance will be null and void as soon as you leave the sealed road and secondly, you won't know whether the previous person who hired your saloon car similarly abused the vehicle ... if you break down, the hire company won't help you. Motorcycle hire is near unheard of.

Documentation To hire a vehicle you'll need your driver's licence and, for some Peninsula countries, an IDP and copies of both your passport and visa. The minimum age varies between 21 to 25. Invariably, credit cards are now a prerequisite.

Insurance

Insurance is compulsory. Given the large number of traffic accidents, fully comprehensive insurance (as opposed to third-party) is strongly advised. This covers the ancient law of paying blood money in the event of the injury or death of a person (and sometimes livestock). Car-hire companies automatically supply insurance, but check carefully the cover and conditions.

Make certain you're covered for off-road travel, as well as travel between Peninsula countries if you're planning cross-border excursions. If you are taking the car outside Gulf Cooperation Council (GCC) borders, you'll need separate insurance.

In the event of an accident, don't move the vehicle until the police arrive and make sure you submit the accident report as soon as possible to the insurance or car-hire company.

Road Conditions & Driving Amenities

Road Quality The Peninsula's road system is one of the best in the world, with high-quality multi-lane highways. Few roads are unsealed (except in Oman) and 4WDs are, on the whole, only necessary for driving off-road in the desert.

Off-road Routes The term 'off-road' refers to unsealed roads that have been graded, or levelled, with a roller, or tracks that have simply been made by

DESERT DRIVING

Driving Tips

➡ In all desert areas follow prior tracks.

➡ Keep the acceleration up through areas of soft sand. Don't stop or you'll start sinking.

➡ Never camp at the bottom of a wadi, even on a clear day. Be wary of wadis when rain threatens. Flash flooding rips through the narrow channels of a wadi with huge force. Each year many people lose their lives this way.

➡ Engage low gear on extended mountain descents, even if it slows your progress to walking speed: many people run into trouble by burning out their brakes.

Getting Stuck in Sand

➡ In sand the minute you feel the wheels are digging in, stop driving. The more you accelerate, the deeper you'll sink.

➡ If your wheels are deeply entrenched, don't dig; the car will just sink deeper.

➡ Partially deflate the tyres (for greater traction), clearing the sand away from the wheel in the direction you want to go (ie behind if you're going to try to reverse out).

➡ Collect brushwood (you'll wish you brought the sand ladders!) and anything else available, and pack under the tyres, creating as firm a launch pad as possible.

➡ Plan your escape route or you'll flip out of the sand only to land in the next dune. In most dune areas, there are compacted platforms of sand. Try to find one of these on foot so that you have somewhere safe to aim for.

➡ Engage low ratio and remember that going backwards can be as effective as going forwards, especially if you stalled going uphill – gravity is a great help.

➡ Keep your eye on the petrol gauge: low ratio consumes a lot of fuel. Reinflate your tyres before rejoining a sealed road.

What to Do if You're Lost

➡ Stay with your vehicle, which offers shade and water. The Bedouin or local villagers will find you before you find them. It's easier for a search party to spot a vehicle than people wandering in the desert.

➡ Use mirrors, horns or fires to attract attention, and construct a large sign on the ground that can easily be seen from the air as most search and rescue in remote regions is carried out by helicopter.

---

cars driving along old camel or donkey tracks. To drive on any of these roads you need a 4WD. Responsible drivers stick to prior tracks and never cut new routes.

Fuel Petrol stations are widespread along major roads and in cities. On desert roads they can be few and far between. Away from the main towns it's advisable to fill up whenever you get the chance, as remote stations sometimes run out of fuel. Fuel remains cheap throughout the region. Most cars run on unleaded petrol.

Garages Found even in the smallest towns and villages in most countries, these rough and ready garages sell spare parts and carry out puncture repair and other servicing. The most popular car models (Toyota and Land Rover, especially) are usually well catered for – getting spare parts for less represented brands can take weeks.

Signposting Good bilingual signposts mark the roads throughout the region using international symbols. English spelling of place names, however, is erratic and seldom matches the maps. Most countries indicate places of interest to a visitor on dedicated brown or green road signs, but street names are almost universally lacking.

Parking A lack of parking space is a challenge for motorists in all city centres in the region. Traffic inspectors and parking meters are becoming more prevalent.

Road Rules

Noncompliance with the following common road rules can lead to a hefty fine – although this may come as a surprise considering the generally poor standard of driving in some parts of the Peninsula.

➡ Driving is on the right side of the road in all Peninsula countries.

➡ Speed limits range between 100km/h and 120km/h on highways and 40km/h and 60km/h in towns and built-up areas. Speed cameras are in operation in most city areas and on highways.

➡ Wearing a seat belt is a legal requirement.

➡ The use of handheld mobile phones for talking or texting while driving is an offence.

➡ Use of the horn is discouraged except in an emergency.

➡ Running a red light often carries a jail sentence.

➡ You should keep your licence with you at all times.

➡ Carrying a first-aid kit, fire extinguisher and warning triangle is required in some Peninsula countries.

➡ Driving under the influence of either alcohol (of any quantity) or drugs is not only considered a grave offence with serious consequences, but also automatically invalidates your insurance and makes you liable for any costs in the event of an accident, regardless of fault.

➡ Swearing or rude gesturing is punishable by law in some countries, so keeping your temper despite provocation is a must.

If You Have an Accident...

➡ Don't move the car until the police arrive.

➡ Don't sign anything you don't understand in the accident report (as you may be accepting responsibility for an accident that wasn't your fault).

➡ Call your insurance or car-hire company immediately.

➡ Try at all costs to remain calm. Aggression may be held against you and will only worsen the situation.

➡ The traffic police are generally helpful and friendly, and it's customary for men to shake hands with policemen before commencing discussions.

➡ In Saudi Arabia, call the accident management company Najm, rather than the police; they will deal with the administration and recording of the accident before issuing you a report to take to your rental company. It is worth having someone who speaks fluent Arabic on hand to ensure the report you sign accurately reflects what you believe to have happened.

Taxi

In many countries taxis are an avoidable luxury, but on the Peninsula they are often the best way for travellers to get about town. Many cities have no other form of urban public transport, and there are also many rural routes that are only feasible in a taxi or private vehicle.

The way in which taxis operate varies widely from country to country, and often even from place to place within a country. So does the price. As a general rule, it's best to establish the price in advance.

Regular Taxi

The regular taxi (also known as 'contract', 'agency', 'telephone', 'private', 'engaged' or 'special taxi') is found in all the main Peninsula towns or cities, coexisting alongside less expensive means of transport (such as shared taxis or minibuses).

Ask for the price in advance of a journey in a regular taxi or request the meter to be used (if it has one!). Regular taxis are often the only way of reaching airports or seaports outside capital cities and are generally considered safe for women travellers, who should always sit in the back.

Shared Taxi

Known also as 'collect', 'collective' or 'service taxi' in English, and *servees* in Arabic, most shared taxis can take up to four or five passengers, but some seat up to 12 and are indistinguishable from minibuses.

Shared taxis are far cheaper than private taxis and, once you get the hang of them, can be just as convenient. They're usually a little dearer than buses, but run more frequently and are usually faster (they don't stop as often or for as long). They also tend to operate for longer hours than buses. Shared taxis used to function as urban, intercity and rural transport but have been superceded in countries that have developed a public transport system.

Fixed-route taxis wait at the point of departure until full or nearly full. Usually they pick up or drop off passengers anywhere en route, but in some places they have fixed stops or stations. Generally a flat fare applies for each route, but sometimes it's possible to pay a partial fare. On 'routeless' taxis, fares depend largely on time and distance and the number of passengers on board.

Beware of boarding an empty shared taxi. The driver may assume you want to hire the vehicle as a 'regular taxi' and charge accordingly (in other words, you'll pay for the empty seats). You may have to wait a long time (sometimes several hours) for a shared taxi to leave, particularly if it's destined for a remote place.

Passengers are expected to know where they are getting off. 'Shukran' means 'thank you' in Arabic and is the usual cue for the driver to stop. Make it clear to the driver or other passengers if you want to be told when you reach your destination.

Train

The only train services in the region at present are in Saudi Arabia, connecting the capital with the east of the kingdom (running from Riyadh to Dammam, via Hofuf and Dhahran, among other places), and a metro service in Dubai. Decisions have been made to build a railway from Kuwait to Salalah in Oman, but this is currently on hold.

Health

While prevention is better than cure, medical facilities in Peninsula countries are of a high standard. Ambulance services are available in capital cities, but emergency and specialised treatment is less readily or extensively so.

Problems particular to the Peninsula include respiratory complaints (because of the arid climate and high levels of dust), sunburn and sunstroke, heat exhaustion and prickly heat, eye problems and injuries resulting from the exceptionally high incidence of traffic accidents – it pays to be extra vigilant on the roads, especially as a pedestrian.

BEFORE YOU GO

Medical Checklist

Consider packing the following items:

☐ acetaminophen/ paracetamol or aspirin

☐ antibacterial ointment for cuts and abrasions

☐ antibiotics (if travelling off the beaten track)

☐ anti-diarrhoeal drugs

☐ antihistamines (for allergic reactions)

☐ anti-inflammatory drugs

☐ bandages, gauze and gauze rolls

☐ DEET-containing insect repellent for the skin

☐ iodine tablets (for water purification if hiking or staying in remote areas)

☐ oral rehydration salts

☐ permethrin-containing insect spray for clothing, tents and bed nets

☐ steroid cream or cortisone (for allergic rashes)

☐ sunscreen

Insurance

You are strongly advised to have insurance before travelling to the region. Check it covers the following:

➡ direct payments to health providers (or reimbursement later)

➡ emergency dental treatment

➡ evacuation or repatriation, or access to better medical facilities elsewhere

Travelling with Medication

Bring medications in their original, clearly labelled containers with a signed and dated letter from your physician describing your medical condition and the medications (including generic names).

If carrying syringes or needles, carry a physician's letter documenting their medical necessity.

In the UAE, travellers are advised that the amount of controlled medicines should not exceed that required for 30 days of treatment.

ON THE ARABIAN PENINSULA

Availability & Cost of Healthcare

Though some Peninsula countries allow travellers access to free state medical treatment in emergencies, you should not rely on this and are strongly advised to have insurance cover. The availability of healthcare in Arabia can be summarised as follows:

CALL A CAB!

If you find you suddenly require urgent medical treatment outside major Peninsula cities, calling a cab may be the best bet. The ambulance services – where they exist – are usually reserved for road accidents when the victim is unconscious or immobile. It's common (and often quicker) to take a taxi.

→ High ratio of doctors to patients.

→ Modern, well-equipped hospitals with well-qualified, English-speaking staff in all cities and most of the larger towns throughout the Peninsula.

→ Emergency units in most hospitals.

→ Limited and less well-equipped clinics in rural areas.

→ Pharmacies (signposted with green crosses) able to dispense advice by well-trained, English-speaking staff who may assist in place of doctors in very remote areas.

→ High standards of dental care in the larger towns and cities.

Infectious Diseases

Dengue Fever

→ Known as break-bone fever.

→ Spread through mosquito bites.

→ Causes a feverish illness, with a headache and muscle pains, that's like a bad, prolonged attack of influenza. There may also be a rash.

→ Take precautions to avoid being bitten by mosquitoes.

Diphtheria

→ Spread through close respiratory contact.

→ Causes a high temperature and a severe sore throat. Sometimes a membrane forms across the throat, requiring a tracheotomy to prevent suffocation.

→ Vaccination is recommended for those likely to be in close contact with the local population in infected areas. The vaccine is given as an injection by itself, or with tetanus, and lasts 10 years.

RECOMMENDED VACCINATIONS

The World Health Organization (WHO) recommends that all travellers, regardless of the region in which they are travelling, should be covered for diphtheria, tetanus, measles, mumps, rubella, polio and hepatitis B.

Many vaccines take four to eight weeks to provide immunity. Ask your doctor for an International Certificate of Vaccination, listing all the vaccinations you've received.

Peninsula countries require proof of yellow-fever vaccination upon entry for travellers who have recently visited a country where yellow fever is found.

Hepatitis A

→ Spread through contaminated food (particularly shellfish) and water.

→ Causes jaundice; rarely fatal but can cause prolonged lethargy and delayed recovery. Symptoms include dark urine, a yellow colour to the whites of the eyes, fever and abdominal pain.

→ Hepatitis-A vaccine (Avaxim, VAQTA, Havrix) is given as an injection. A single dose will give protection for up to a year, while a booster 12 months later will provide protection for a subsequent period of 10 years. Hepatitis-A and typhoid vaccines can also be given as a single-dose vaccine in the form of Hepatyrix or Viatim.

Hepatitis B

→ Transmitted by infected blood, contaminated needles and sexual intercourse.

→ Causes jaundice and affects the liver, occasionally causing liver failure.

→ All travellers should make this a routine vaccination – many countries now give hepatitis-B vaccination as part of routine childhood vaccination. The vaccine is given by itself, or at the same time as the hepatitis-A vaccine. A course protects for at least five years and can be given over four weeks or six months.

HIV

→ Spread via infected blood and blood products, sexual intercourse with an infected partner, and from an infected mother to her newborn child. It can also be spread through blood-to-blood contacts such as contaminated instruments used during medical, dental, acupuncture and other body-piercing procedures, as well as from sharing intravenous needles.

AIDS ON THE PENINSULA

Though it's strictly illegal for AIDS or HIV sufferers to visit or to live on the Peninsula (and detection of the disease usually results in instant deportation), the region is not the AIDS-free place you might imagine. In recent years prostitutes have flowed into the area under the guise of tourism. Locals have also returned infected after sexual adventures abroad. Additionally, there is something of a cultural taboo about condom use among many Arab men. Travellers who form new relationships should also note that fornication, adultery and homosexuality are considered grave crimes in some Peninsula states.

➡ All Peninsula countries except Bahrain require a negative HIV test as a requirement for some categories of visas (particularly employment visas).

Malaria

➡ Spread by bite from infected mosquito.

➡ Causes shivering, fever and sweating. Muscle pains, headache and vomiting are also common. Symptoms may occur any time from a few days up to three weeks or more after being bitten. Symptoms can occur even if taking preventative tablets.

➡ The prevalence of malaria varies throughout the Peninsula. The risk is considered minimal in most cities, but may be more substantial in rural areas. Check with your doctor or local travel-health clinic for the latest information.

➡ Antimalarial tablets are essential if the risk is significant.

Meningitis

➡ Spread through close respiratory contact.

➡ A meningococcal vaccination certificate covering the A and W135 strains is required as a condition of entry if embarking on a hajj pilgrimage to Mecca and Medina in Saudi Arabia, and for all travellers arriving from the meningitis belt of sub-Saharan Africa.

➡ Visas for pilgrimages are not issued unless proof of vaccination is submitted with the visa application.

Rabies

➡ Spread through bites or licks (on broken skin) from any warm-blooded, furry animal.

➡ Rabies can be fatal. Seek immediate medical assistance if bitten by an animal suspected of being infected with rabies. Clean skin immediately and thoroughly. A course of five injections starting within 24 hours, or as soon as possible after the injury, is needed. Vaccination does not provide immunity; it buys more time to seek appropriate medical help.

➡ Animal handlers and those travelling to remote areas where a reliable source of post-bite vaccine is not available within 24 hours should be vaccinated. Three injections are needed over a month.

Tuberculosis (TB)

➡ Spread through close respiratory contact and occasionally through infected milk or milk products.

➡ Can be asymptomatic or can include a cough, weight loss or fever, months or even years after exposure. An X-ray establishes the presence of TB.

➡ BCG vaccine is recommended for those likely to be mixing closely with the local population. BCG gives a moderate degree of protection against TB. It's usually only given in specialised chest clinics and is not available in all countries. As it's a live vaccine, it should not be given to pregnant women

or immunocompromised individuals.

Typhoid

➡ Spread through food or water contaminated by infected human faeces.

➡ Causes fever or a pink rash on the abdomen. Septicaemia (blood poisoning) may also occur.

➡ Typhoid vaccine (Typhim Vi, Typherix) gives protection for three years. In some countries, the oral vaccine Vivotif is also available.

Yellow Fever

➡ Does not occur on the Peninsula, but any traveller coming from a country where yellow fever is found will need to show a vaccination certificate at immigration.

➡ Vaccination must be given at an approved clinic, and is valid for 10 years. It is a live vaccine and must not be given to immunocompromised or pregnant travellers.

Environmental Hazards

Diarrhea

PREVENTION

➡ Clean, filtered mains water (as opposed to water delivered by tanker) is available in all Peninsula cities except in Yemen, but avoid tap water in rural areas.

➡ Eat fresh fruit or vegetables you have peeled yourself, or eat cooked produce.

➡ Avoid dairy products that might contain unpasteurised milk (especially camel milk), or have been refrozen after defrosting.

TREATMENT

➡ Drink plenty of fluids.

➡ Take an oral rehydration solution containing salt and sugar.

➡ If you start having more than four or five loose stools

TAP WATER

Tap water is safe to drink in all Peninsula cities except in Yemen. In rural areas or those supplied by tanker, boil water for 10 minutes, use water-purification tablets or a filter. Never drink from wadis (valleys or riverbeds) or streams, as animals are invariably watered nearby.

IF BITTEN BY A SNAKE...

Snakes are some of the most remarkable creatures of the desert and deserve considerable respect for their survival skills. Most are non-venomous, or only mildly toxic, but a few are a bit more challenging. The only time you're likely to encounter them is camping in the sands or walking up wadis, where they will make every attempt to avoid a confrontation – and you should do the same. If you are unlucky enough to get bitten, follow this advice:

➡ Don't panic: half the people bitten by venomous snakes are not actually injected with poison (envenomed).

➡ Immobilise the bitten limb with a splint (eg a stick).

➡ Apply a bandage over the site, with firm pressure, similar to bandaging a sprain.

➡ Do not apply a tourniquet, or cut or suck the bite.

➡ Seek medical help as soon as possible so that antivenin can be given if necessary.

➡ If you have the presence of mind, take a photo of the snake for identification to aid doctors in giving the appropriate antivenin.

a day, take an anti-diarrhoeal agent (such as loperamide).

➡ Seek medical attention if the diarrhoea is bloody, persists for more than 72 hours, or is accompanied by fever, shaking, chills or severe abdominal pain.

Heat-Related Illness

Heat exhaustion Occurs following heavy sweating and excessive fluid loss. In summer, temperatures can reach 50°C, making even a short walk dangerous without drinking. Symptoms include headache, dizziness and tiredness. Drink sufficient water to produce pale, diluted urine. To treat heat exhaustion, drink lots of water, cool down in an air-conditioned room and add a little more salt to foods than usual.

Heatstroke A serious condition that occurs when the body's heat-regulating mechanism breaks down. An excessive rise in body temperature leads to the cessation of sweating, irrational and hyperactive behaviour and, eventually, loss of consciousness

and death. Rapid cooling of the body by spraying with water or fanning is an effective treatment. Emergency fluid and electrolyte replacement (by intravenous drip) is also usually required.

Insect Bites & Stings

➡ Using DEET-based insect repellents helps prevent mosquito bites.

➡ Bed bugs, causing very itchy lumpy bites, and sometimes scabies are occasionally found in cheap hotels and desert camps. Spray the mattress, lay a thick cotton sheet over the offending camel blanket or find new lodgings!

➡ Scorpions and snakes are common in the desert, though not often seen. This is because they usually lie under the sand, or lurk beneath rocks, but occasionally you may come across a specimen sunning itself in the open. Although bites can be painful, they are rarely life threatening. Avoid

walking on sand dunes in bare feet, don't prod holes in wadis, don't overturn large rocks and check shoes for unwanted wildlife.

Women's Health

Some health considerations for women travelling in the region:

➡ The International Planned Parent Federation (www.ippf.org) can advise about the availability of contraception in each Peninsula country. Condoms should be checked before use as they crack in the hot climate.

➡ Tampons are not always available outside the major cities; sanitary pads are more widespread.

➡ High standards of obstetric and antenatal facilities are offered throughout the Peninsula, particularly in Gulf cities.

Language

Arabic is the official language on the Arabian Peninsula, but English is widely understood. Note that there are significant differences between the MSA (Modern Standard Arabic) – the official lingua franca of the Arab world, used in schools, administration and the media – and the colloquial language, ie the everyday spoken version. The Arabic variety spoken throughout the Arabian Peninsula (and provided in this chapter) is known as Gulf Arabic.

Read our coloured pronunciation guides as if they were English and you'll be understood. Note that a is pronounced as in 'act', aa as in the 'a' in 'father', ai as in 'aisle', aw as in 'law', ay as in 'say', ee as in 'see', i as in 'hit', oo as in 'zoo', u as in 'put', gh is a throaty sound (like the French 'r'), r is rolled, dh is pronounced as the 'th' in 'that', th as in 'thin', ch as in 'cheat' and kh as the 'ch' in the Scottish *loch*. The apostrophe (') indicates the glottal stop (like the pause in the middle of 'uh-oh'). The stressed syllables are indicated with italics and (m) and (f) refer to the masculine and feminine word forms respectively.

BASICS

Hello.	اهلا و سهلا.	*ah*·lan was *ah*·lan
Goodbye.	مع السلامة.	ma' sa·*laa*·ma
Yes.	نعم.	na·'am
No.	لا.	la
Please.	من فضلك.	min *fad*·lak (m)
	من فضلِك.	min *fad*·lik (f)
Thank you.	شكران.	*shuk*·ran
Excuse me.	اسمح.	is·*mah* (m)
	اسمحي لي.	is·mah·*ee* lee (f)

WANT MORE?

For in-depth language information and handy phrases, check out Lonely Planet's *Middle East Phrasebook*. You'll find it at **shop.lonelyplanet.com**, or you can buy Lonely Planet's iPhone phrasebooks at the Apple App Store.

| Sorry. | مع الأسف. | ma' al·*as*·af |

| How are you? | كيف حالك/حالِك؟ | kayf *haa*·lak/*haa*·lik (m/f) |

| Fine, thanks. And you? | بخير الحمد الله. | bi·*khayr* il·*ham*·du·li·laa |
| | و انت/و انتِ؟ | *win*·ta/*win*·ti (m/f) |

| What's your name? | اش اسمك/اسمِك؟ | aash is·mak/is·mik (m/f) |

| My name is ... | ... اسمي | is·mee ... |

| Do you speak English? | تتكلم انجليزية؟ | tit·*kal*·am in·glee·*zee*·ya (m) |
| | تتكلمي انجليزية؟ | tit·*ka*·la·mee in·glee·*zee*·ya (f) |

| I don't understand. | مو فاهم. | moo *faa*·him |

| Can I take a photo? | ممكن اتصور؟ | *mum*·kin at·*saw*·ar |

ACCOMMODATION

Where's a ...?	وين ...؟	wayn ...
campsite	مخيم	moo·*khay*·am
hotel	فندق	*fun*·dug

Do you have a ... room?	عندك/عندِك	'and·ak/'and·ik
	غرفة ...؟	ghur·fa ... (m/f)
single	لشخص واحد	li·shakhs waa·hid
double	لشخصين	li·shakh·*sayn*
twin	مع سريرين	ma' sa·ree·*rayn*

How much is it per ...?	بكم كل ...؟	bi·*kam* kul ...
night	ليلة	*lay*·la
person	شخص	shakhs

| Can I get another (blanket)? | احتاج الى (برنوس) | ah·*taaj* i·la (bar·*noos*) |
| | الثاني من فضلك؟ | i·*thaa*·nee min *fad*·lak |

SIGNS

Entrance	مدخل
Exit	خروج
Open	مفتوح
Closed	مقفول
Toilets	المرحاض
Men	رجال
Women	نساء

The (air conditioning) doesn't work.

(الكنديشان) (il·kan·*day*·shan)
ما يشتغل. ma yish·*ta*·ghil

DIRECTIONS

Where's the ...? من وين ...؟ min wayn ...

bank	البنك	il·*bank*
market	السوق	i·*soog*
post office	مكتب البريد	*mak*·tab il·ba·*reed*

Can you show me (on the map)?

لو سمحت وريني law sa·*maht* wa·*ree*·nee
(علخريطة)؟ ('al·kha·*ree*·ta)

What's the address?

ما العنوان؟ ma il·'un·*waan*

Could you please write it down?

لو سمحت اكتبه لي؟ law sa·*maht* ik·ti·*boo* lee (m)
لو سمحت اكتبيه لي؟ law sa·*maht* ik·ti·*bee* lee (f)

How far is it?

كم بعيد؟ kam ba·'*eed*

How do I get there?

كيف ممكن اوصل kayf *mum*·kin aw·sil
هناك؟ hoo·*naak*

EATING & DRINKING

Can you recommend a ...?

ممكن تنصح/ *mum*·kin tan·sah/
تنصحي ...؟ tan·sa·*hee* ... (m/f)

| cafe | قهوة | *gah*·wa |
| restaurant | مطعم | *ma*·ta'm |

I'd like a/the ..., please.

اريد... a·*reed* ...
من فضلك. min *fad*·lak

| nonsmoking section | المكان ممنوع تدخين | il·ma·*kaan* mam·*noo*·a' tad·*kheen* |
| table for (four) | طاولة (اربعة) اشخاص | *taa*·wi·lat (ar·*ba*') ash·*khaas* |

What would you recommend?

اش تنصح؟ aash tan·*sah* (m)
اش تنصحي؟ aash tan·sa·*hee* (f)

What's the local speciality?

اش الطبق المحلي؟ aash i·*ta*·bak il·*ma*·ha·lee

Do you have vegetarian food?

عندك طعم نباتي؟ '*an*·dak ta·'am na·*baa*·tee

I'd like (the) ..., please.	عطني/ عطيني الـ ... من فضلك.	'*a*·ti·nee/ '*a*·tee·nee il ... min *fad*·lak (m/f)
bill	قائمة	*kaa*·'i·ma
drink list	قائمة المشروبات	*kaa*·'i·mat il·mash·roo·*baat*
menu	قائمة الطعام	*kaa*·'i·mat i·ta·'*aam*
that dish	الطبق هاذاك	i·*tab*·ak *haa*·dhaa·ka

Could you prepare a meal without ...?	ممكن تطبخها/ تطبخيها بدون ...؟	*mum*·kin tat·bakh·*ha*/ tat·bakh·ee·*ha* bi·*doon* ... (m/f)
butter	زبدة	*zib*·da
eggs	بيض	bayd
meat stock	مرق لهم	ma·*rak* la·ham

I'm allergic to ...	عندي حساسية لـ ...	'*an*·dee ha·saa·*see*·ya li ...
dairy produce	الألبان	il·al·*baan*
gluten	قمح	*ka*·mah
nuts	كرزات	ka·ra·*zaat*
seafood	السمك و المحارات	i·*sa*·mak wa al·ma·haa·*raat*

Drinks

coffee ...	نقهوة ...	*kah*·wa ...
tea ...	شاي ...	shay ...
with milk	بالحليب	bil·ha·*leeb*
without sugar	بدون شكر	bi·*doon* shi·ker

bottle of beer	بوتل بيرة	*boo*·til *bee*·ra
glass of beer	قلاس بيرة	glaas *bee*·ra
(orange) juice	عصير (برتقال)	'a·seer (bor·too·*gaal*)
(mineral) water	ماي (معدني)	may (ma'a·da·*nee*)

... wine	خمر ...	... *kha*·mar
red	احمر	*ah*·mer
sparkling	فوار	fa·*waar*
white	ابيض	*ab*·yad

EMERGENCIES

Help!
مساعد! moo·*saa*·id (m)
مساعدة! moo·*saa*·id·a (f)

Go away!
ابعد! ib·'ad (m)
ابعدي! ib·'ad·ee (f)

I'm lost. انا ضعت. a·na duht

Call ...!
تصل على ...! ti·*sil* 'a·la ... (m)
تصلي على ...! ti·si·*lee* 'a·la ... (f)

a doctor طبيب ta·*beeb*

the police الشرطة i·*shur*·ta

Where are the toilets?
وين المرحاض؟ wayn il·mir·*haad*

I'm sick.
انا مريض. a·na ma·*reed* (m)
انا مريضة. a·na ma·*ree*·da (f)

SHOPPING & SERVICES

Where's a ...? من وين ...؟ min wayn ...

department محل ضخم ma·*hal dukh*·um
store

NUMBERS

1	١	واحد	*waa*·hid
2	٢	اثنين	ith·*nayn*
3	٣	ثلاثة	tha·*laa*·tha
4	٤	اربع	ar·*ba*'
5	٥	خمسة	*kham*·sa
6	٦	ستة	*si*·ta
7	٧	سبعة	*sa*·ba'
8	٨	ثمانية	tha·*maan*·ya
9	٩	تسعة	*tis*·a'
10	١٠	عشرة	'*ash*·ar·a
20	٢٠	عشرين	'*ash*·reen
30	٣٠	ثلاثين	tha·la·*theen*
40	٤٠	اربعين	ar·ba'·*een*
50	٥٠	خمسين	kham·*seen*
60	٦٠	ستين	sit·*een*
70	٧٠	سبعين	sa·ba'·*een*
80	٨٠	ثمانين	tha·ma·*neen*
90	٩٠	تسعين	ti·sa'·*een*
100	١٠٠	مية	*mee*·ya
1000	١٠٠٠	الف	alf

Note that Arabic numerals (in the second column), unlike letters, are read from left to right.

grocery محل ma·*hal*
store ابقالية ib·gaa·*lee*·ya

newsagency محل ma·*hal*
يبيع جرائد yi·*bee*·a' ja·*raa*·id

souvenir محل سياحي ma·hal say·*aa*·hee
shop

supermarket سوبرمركت soo·ber·mar·ket

I'm looking for ...
مدور على ... moo·*daw*·ir 'a·la ... (m)
مدورة على ... moo·*daw*·i·ra 'a·la ... (f)

Can I look at it?
ممكن اشوف؟ *mum*·kin a·*shoof*

Do you have any others?
عندك اخرين؟ 'and·ak ukh·*reen* (m)
عندك اخرين؟ 'and·ik ukh·*reen* (f)

It's faulty. فيه خلل. fee *kha*·lal

How much is it? بكم؟ bi·*kam*

Can you write down the price?
ممكن تكتبلي/ *mum*·kin tik·*tib*·lee/
تكتبيلي السعر؟ tik·*tib*·ee·lee i·*si'r* (m/f)

That's too expensive.
غالي جدا. *ghaa*·lee *jid*·an

What's your lowest price?
اش السعر الاخر؟ aash i·*si'r* il·*aa*·khir

There's a mistake in the bill.
فيه غلط في الفطورة. fee *gha*·lat fil fa·*too*·ra

Where's ...? من وين ...؟ min wayn ...

a foreign صراف si·*raaf*
exchange office

an ATM مكينة صرف ma·*kee*·nat sarf

What's the exchange rate?
ما هو السعر؟ maa *hoo*·wa i·*sa'r*

Where's the local internet cafe?
من وين انترنيت كفي؟ min wayn *in*·ter·net ka·*fay*

How much is it per hour?
بكم كل ساعة؟ bi·*kam* kul *saa*·a'

I'd like to buy a phonecard.
اريد اشري كرت a·*reed ish*·ree kart
لتلفون. li·til·*foon*

TIME & DATES

What time is it?
الساعة كم؟ i·*saa*·a' kam

It's (two) o'clock.
الساعة (ثنتين). i·*saa*·a' (thin·*tayn*)

Half past (two).
الساعة (ثنتين) و نس. i·*saa*·a' (thin·*tayn*) wa nus

QUESTION WORDS

When?	متى؟	ma·ta
Where?	وين؟	wayn
Who?	من؟	man
Why?	لاش؟	laysh

At what time ...?
الساعة كم ...؟ i·saa·a' kam ...

At ...
الساعة ... i·saa·a'...

yesterday ...	البارح ...	il·baa·rih ...
tomorrow ...	باكر ...	baa·chir ...
morning	صباح	sa·baah
afternoon	بعد الظهر	ba'd a·thuhr
evening	مساء	mi·saa

Monday	يوم الاثنين	yawm al·ith·nayn
Tuesday	يوم الثلاثة	yawm a·tha·laa·tha
Wednesday	يوم الاربعة	yawm al·ar·ba'
Thursday	يوم الخميس	yawm al·kha·mees
Friday	يوم الجمعة	yawm al·jum·a'
Saturday	يوم السبت	yawm a·sibt
Sunday	يوم الاحد	yawm al·aa·had

TRANSPORT

Is this the ... (to Riyadh)?	هاذا ال ... يروح (لرياض)؟	haa·dha al ... yi·roh (li·ree·yaad)
boat	سفينة	sa·fee·na
bus	باص	baas
plane	طيارة	tay·aa·ra
train	قطار	gi·taar
What time's the ... bus?	الساعة كم الباص ...؟	a·saa·a' kam il·baas ...
first	الاول	il·aw·al
last	الاخر	il·aa·khir
next	القادم	il·gaa·dim

One ... ticket (to Doha), please.	تذكرة ... (الدوحة) من فضلك.	tadh·ka·ra ... (a·do·ha) min fad·lak
one-way	ذهاب بص	dhee·haab bas
return	ذهاب و اياب	dhee·haab wa ai·yaab

How long does the trip take?
كم الرحلة تستغرق؟ kam i·rah·la tis·tagh·rik

Is it a direct route?
الرحلة متواصلة؟ i·rah·la moo·ta·waa·si·la

What station/stop is this?
ما هي المحطة هاذي؟ maa hee·ya il·ma·ha·ta haa·dhee

Please tell me when we get to (Al-Ain).
لو سمحت خبرني/خبريني وقت ما نوصل الى (العين). law sa·maht kha·bir·nee/kha·bir·ee·nee wokt ma noo·sil i·la (al·'ain) (m/f)

How much is it to (Sharjah)?
بكم الى (شارقة)؟ bi·kam i·la (shaa·ri·ka)

Please take me to (this address).
من فضلك خذني (علعنوان هاذا). min fad·lak khudh·nee ('al·'un·waan haa·dha)

Turn left/right.
لف يسار/يمين. lif yee·saar/yee·meen (m)
لفي يسار/يمين. li·fee yee·saar/yee·meen (f)

Please stop here.
لو سمحت وقف هنا. law sa·maht wa·gif hi·na

Please wait here.
لو سمحت استنا هنا. law sa·maht is·ta·na hi·na

Driving

I'd like to hire a ...	اريد استأجر ...	a·reed ist·'aj·ir ...
4WD	سيارة فيها دبل	say·aa·ra fee·ha da·bal
car	سيارة	say·aa·ra

with ...	مع ...	ma' ...
a driver	دريول	dray·wil
air conditioning	كنديشان	kan·day·shan

How much for ... hire?	كم الإيجار ...؟	kam il·ee·jaar ...
daily	كل يوم	kul yawm
weekly	كل اسبوع	kul us·boo·a'

Is this the road to (Abu Dhabi)?
هاذا الطريق الى (ابو ظبي)؟ haa·dha i·ta·reeg i·la (a·boo da·bee)

I need a mechanic.
احتاج ميكانيك ah·taaj mee·kaa·neek

I've run out of petrol.
ينضب البنزين. yan·dab al·ban·zeen

GLOSSARY

Following is a list of some unfamiliar words you might meet in the text. For a list of common foods you may encounter, see p460.

abaya – woman's full-length black robe; also *abeyya*

abra – water taxi

agal – black head-rope used to hold a *gutra* in place; also *igal*

ardha – traditional Bedouin dance

attar – rosewater

badghir – wind tower

barasti – palm-frond material used in building the traditional coastal houses of the Gulf region, especially along the coast of Oman

barjeel – wind tower

Bedouin – (pl Bedu) a nomadic desert dweller

beit ash-sha'ar – Bedouin goat-hair tent

bijou – service taxi

bukhnoq – girl's head covering

burda – traditional Qatari cloak

burj – tower

burka – *see* hijab

compound – residential area of expats, usually with high security (Gulf States)

corniche – seaside road

dalla – traditional copper coffeepot

dhow – traditional Arab boat rigged with a *lateen* (triangular) sail; also *sambuq* or *sambuk*

dishdasha – man's floor-length shirt-dress, usually of white cotton cloth, worn in Oman

diwan – Muslim meeting room or reception room

diwaniya – gatherings, usually at someone's home

eid – Islamic feast

Eid al-Adha – Feast of Sacrifice marking the pilgrimage to Mecca

Eid al-Fitr – Festival of Breaking the Fast, celebrated at the end of Ramadan

emir – literally 'prince'; Islamic ruler, military commander or governor

falaj – traditional irrigation channel

GCC – Gulf Cooperation Council; members are Saudi Arabia, Kuwait, Bahrain, Qatar, Oman and the UAE

gutra – white head-cloth worn by men in Saudi Arabia and the Gulf States; also *shemaag*

hajj – annual Muslim pilgrimage to Mecca; one of the Five Pillars of Islam

halal – literally 'permitted'; describes food permitted to Muslims including animals slaughtered according to the prescribed Islamic customs; also *halaal*

hammam – bathhouse

haram – literally 'forbidden'; anything forbidden by Islamic law; also prayer hall

hijab – woman's head scarf or veil, worn for modesty

Hejira – Islamic calendar; Mohammed's flight from Mecca to Medina in AD 622

iftar – the breaking of the day's fast during Ramadan

imam – preacher or prayer leader; Muslim cleric

insha'allah – 'If Allah wills it'; 'God willing'

iqama – residence permit and identity document (Saudi Arabia)

jambiya – tribesman's ceremonial dagger (Yemen and southern Saudi Arabia)

jamrah – pillars

jebel – hill, mountain; also *jabal*, *gebel*

jihad – literally 'striving in the way of the faith'; holy war

jizari – people of the Gulf

Kaaba – the rectangular structure at the centre of the Grand Mosque in Mecca (containing the Black Stone) around which hajj pilgrims circumambulate; also *Kabaa* and *Qaaba*

khanjar – tribal curved dagger; also *khanja* (Oman and southern Saudi Arabia)

khareef – southeast monsoon, from mid-June to mid-August in Oman

khor – rocky inlet or creek

kilim – flat, woven mat

kohl – eyeliner

Kufic – type of highly stylised old Arabic script

kuma – Omani cap

madrassa – Muslim theological seminary; also modern Arabic word for school

mafraj – (pl mafarej) 'room with a view'; top room of a tower house (Yemen)

majlis – formal meeting room; also parliament

mandoos – Omani wooden chest

manzar – attic; room on top of a tower house (Yemen)

mashrabiyya – ornate carved wooden panel or screen; feature of Islamic architecture

masjid – mosque

medina – city, town, especially the old quarter

midan – city or town square

mihrab – niche in a mosque indicating the direction of Mecca

mina – port

minaret – mosque tower

minbar – pulpit used for sermons in a mosque

misbah – prayer beads

muezzin – cantor who sings the call to prayer

mutawwa – religious police charged with upholding Islamic orthodoxy (Saudi Arabia)

Nabataeans – ancient trading civilisation based around Petra in Jordan

qat – mildly narcotic plant, the leaves of which are chewed

Ramadan – Muslim month of fasting; one of the Five Pillars of Islam

ras – cape or headland; also head

sabkha – soft sand with a salty crust

sadu – Bedouin-style weaving

salat – prayer; one of the Five Pillars of Islam

sambuq – see *dhow*; also *sambuk*

shahada – the profession of faith that Muslims publicly declare in every mosque, five times a day; one of the Five Pillars of Islam

shai – tea

sharia – street

Sharia'a – Islamic law

sheesha – water pipe used to smoke tobacco; also *nargileh* or hubble-bubble

sheikh – head of a tribe; religious leader; also *shaikh*

Shiite – one of the two main branches of Islam

souq – market

stele – (pl stelae) stone or wooden commemorative slab or column decorated with inscriptions or figures

sultan – absolute ruler of a Muslim state

Sunni – one of the two main branches of Islam

suras – chapters of the Quran

tawaf – circling required during the pilgrimage to Mecca

thobe – men's floor-length shirt-dress similar to a *dish-dasha*, but more fitting, worn in the Gulf; also *thawb*

umrah – Islamic ritual performed outside of hajj; literally 'little pilgrimage'

wadi – valley or river bed, often dry except after heavy rainfall

Wahhabi – conservative and literalist 18th-century Sunni orthodoxy prevailing throughout Saudi Arabia and Qatar

wali – regional head in Oman, similar to mayor

wusta – influence gained by way of connections in high places

yashmak – veil

zakat – the giving of alms; one of the Five Pillars of Islam

Behind the Scenes

SEND US YOUR FEEDBACK

We love to hear from travellers – your comments keep us on our toes and help make our books better. Our well-travelled team reads every word on what you loved or loathed about this book. Although we cannot reply individually to your submissions, we always guarantee that your feedback goes straight to the appropriate authors, in time for the next edition. Each person who sends us information is thanked in the next edition – the most useful submissions are rewarded with a selection of digital PDF chapters.

Visit **lonelyplanet.com/contact** to submit your updates and suggestions or to ask for help. Our award-winning website also features inspirational travel stories, news and discussions.

Note: We may edit, reproduce and incorporate your comments in Lonely Planet products such as guidebooks, websites and digital products, so let us know if you don't want your comments reproduced or your name acknowledged. For a copy of our privacy policy visit lonelyplanet.com/privacy.

WRITER THANKS

Jenny Walker

I owe the Arabian Peninsula two decades of happy residence, exciting career and wonderful friendships. I even met my beloved husband, Sam Owen, here. Together, we have explored every corner of Oman, our home for 20 years, and I would like to dedicate the acknowledgement this time solely to him, as co-researcher, joint author of an off-road book on Oman, and fellow traveller. His insights have enriched my own perception and enjoyment of the region and hopefully shine through in the text.

Jessica Lee

Huge thanks to everyone along the way who shared tips, advice, ideas and information on what's new. In particular, I'd like to say a huge thanks to Prabhakaran Andiappan, Corrine Roucou and Mike Camp who went out of their way to help out.

Jade Bremner

Thanks to knowledgeable destination editor Lauren Keith for all her quick support on the road. Plus the hardworking Middle East chefs for preparing all that creamy *moutabal,* tangy fresh fattoush and fresh barbecued lamb, which fuelled my entire trip around the desert. Thanks to the welcoming Kuwait locals, who offered me tea at every meet, and showed me true Arabic hospitality. Last, but definitely not least, thanks to everyone working hard behind the scenes – Cheree Broughton, Dianne and Jane, Helen Elfer and Neill Coen.

Tharik Hussain

Thanks to my wonderful friends Rob Wagner, Tawfeeq Sleett, Dawoud Sliat, Toufiq Chawdhury and Omar Hamid for their hospitality, support, and expertise. A huge thanks to my mentor, Jenny Walker, and editor, Lauren Keith, for their guidance. Finally, thank you Tamara, my beloved wife, for your endless support and patience.

Josephine Quintero

Firstly I would like to thank Dubai residents and friends Mike and Linda Gillam for their invaluable advice. Also the many helpful people I met on the research journey, including Ahmed Abadi and Sara Batille in Bur Dubai, Fatima Kouri for her invaluable insight into the clubbing scene, and longtime resident Joan Phillips for her eagle expat knowledge of what is new.

ACKNOWLEDGEMENTS

Climate map data adapted from Peel MC, Finlayson BL & McMahon TA (2007) 'Updated World Map of the Köppen-Geiger Climate Classification', *Hydrology and Earth System Sciences*, 11, 1633–44.

Cover photograph: Nakhal Fort, Oman, Justin Foulkes/Lonely Planet ©

THIS BOOK

This 6th edition of Lonely Planet's *Oman, UAE & Arabian Peninsula* guidebook was curated by Jenny Walker, Jessica Lee and Lauren Keith, and researched and written by Jenny Walker, Jessica Lee, Jade Bremner, Tharik Hussain and Josephine Quintero. The previous edition was written by Jenny Walker, Anthony Ham and Andrea Schulte-Peevers, with contributions from Rob Wagner and Mariam Nihal.

This guidebook was produced by the following:

Destination Editor
Lauren Keith

Senior Product Editor
Elizabeth Jones

Regional Senior Cartographer Valentina Kremenchutskaya

Product Editor Kate Kiely

Book Designer Aomi Ito

Assisting Editors Imogen Bannister, Nigel Chin, Andrea Dobbin, Bruce Evans, Jennifer Hattam, Gabrielle Innes, Kate James, Jodie Martire, Lauren O'Connell, Sarah Reid

Assisting Cartographer
Michael Garrett

Cover Researcher
Naomi Parker

Thanks to Elizabeth Branca, Polly Byles, Hannah Cartmel, Megan Eaves, Ilana Myers, Catherine Naghten, Claire Naylor, Karyn Noble, Lindsey Parry, Albert Pincis, Kathryn Rowan, Hayley Skirka, Victoria Smith, Ross Taylor

Index

Map Legend

Sights

- Beach
- Bird Sanctuary
- Buddhist
- Castle/Palace
- Christian
- Confucian
- Hindu
- Islamic
- Jain
- Jewish
- Monument
- Museum/Gallery/Historic Building
- Ruin
- Shinto
- Sikh
- Taoist
- Winery/Vineyard
- Zoo/Wildlife Sanctuary
- Other Sight

Activities, Courses & Tours

- Bodysurfing
- Diving
- Canoeing/Kayaking
- Course/Tour
- Sento Hot Baths/Onsen
- Skiing
- Snorkelling
- Surfing
- Swimming/Pool
- Walking
- Windsurfing
- Other Activity

Sleeping

- Sleeping
- Camping
- Hut/Shelter

Eating

- Eating

Drinking & Nightlife

- Drinking & Nightlife
- Cafe

Entertainment

- Entertainment

Shopping

- Shopping

Information

- Bank
- Embassy/Consulate
- Hospital/Medical
- Internet
- Police
- Post Office
- Telephone
- Toilet
- Tourist Information
- Other Information

Geographic

- Beach
- Gate
- Hut/Shelter
- Lighthouse
- Lookout
- Mountain/Volcano
- Oasis
- Park
- Pass
- Picnic Area
- Waterfall

Population

- Capital (National)
- Capital (State/Province)
- City/Large Town
- Town/Village

Transport

- Airport
- Border crossing
- Bus
- Cable car/Funicular
- Cycling
- Ferry
- Metro/MTR/MRT station
- Monorail
- Parking
- Petrol station
- Skytrain/Subway station
- Taxi
- Train station/Railway
- Tram
- Underground station
- Other Transport

Routes

- Tollway
- Freeway
- Primary
- Secondary
- Tertiary
- Lane
- Unsealed road
- Road under construction
- Plaza/Mall
- Steps
- Tunnel
- Pedestrian overpass
- Walking Tour
- Walking Tour detour
- Path/Walking Trail

Boundaries

- International
- State/Province
- Disputed
- Regional/Suburb
- Marine Park
- Cliff
- Wall

Hydrography

- River, Creek
- Intermittent River
- Canal
- Water
- Dry/Salt/Intermittent Lake
- Reef

Areas

- Airport/Runway
- Beach/Desert
- Cemetery (Christian)
- Cemetery (Other)
- Glacier
- Mudflat
- Park/Forest
- Sight (Building)
- Sportsground
- Swamp/Mangrove

Note: Not all symbols displayed above appear on the maps in this book

OUR STORY

A beat-up old car, a few dollars in the pocket and a sense of adventure. In 1972 that's all Tony and Maureen Wheeler needed for the trip of a lifetime – across Europe and Asia overland to Australia. It took several months, and at the end – broke but inspired – they sat at their kitchen table writing and stapling together their first travel guide, *Across Asia on the Cheap*. Within a week they'd sold 1500 copies. Lonely Planet was born.

Today, Lonely Planet has offices in Franklin, London, Melbourne, Oakland, Dublin, Beijing and Delhi, with more than 600 staff and writers. We share Tony's belief that 'a great guidebook should do three things: inform, educate and amuse'.

OUR WRITERS

Jenny Walker
Plan, Understand and Survival chapters, Oman A member of the British Guild of Travel Writers, Jenny has travelled to over 125 countries and has been writing for Lonely Planet for more than 20 years. Currently working in Oman as Deputy CEO of Oman Academic Accreditation Authority, her MPhil thesis focused on the Arabic Orient in British Literature (Oxford University) and her PhD (nearing completion) is on the Arabian desert as trope.

Jessica Lee
UAE, Yemen In 2011 Jessica swapped a career as an adventure-tour leader for travel writing, and since then her travels for Lonely Planet have taken her across Africa, the Middle East and Asia. She has lived in the Middle East since 2007 and tweets @jessofarabia. Jess has contributed to Lonely Planet's *Egypt, Turkey, Cyprus, Morocco, Marrakesh, Middle East, Europe, Africa, Cambodia* and *Vietnam* guidebooks and her travel writing has appeared in *Wanderlust* magazine, the *Daily Telegraph*, the *Independent*, BBC Travel and Lonelyplanet.com.

Jade Bremner
Kuwait, Qatar Jade has been a journalist for more than a decade. She has lived in and reported on four different regions. Wherever she goes she finds action sports to try, the weirder the better, and it's no coincidence many of her favourite places have some of the best waves in the world. Jade has edited travel magazines and sections for Time Out and Radio Times and has contributed to the *Times*, CNN and the *Independent*.

Tharik Hussain
Bahrain, Saudi Arabia Born in Sylhet, Bangladesh and raised in London, Tharik is a freelance travel writer and occasional broadcaster/journalist who specialises in Islamic culture. He loves writing about forgotten Muslim heritage on his travels across the globe, often accompanied by his family. Tharik's work has been published by the BBC, Lonely Planet, Aljazeera and Arab News amongst others. He has a Masters in Islamic Studies and has previously lived in Jeddah, Saudi Arabia.

Josephine Quintero
Dubai Josephine launched her journalism degree at a wine and lifestyle magazine followed, ironically, with a move to 'dry' Kuwait where she worked as the Editor of the *Kuwaiti Digest* until the day Iraq invaded. After six weeks as a hostage, Josephine moved to the relaxed shores of Andalucía in southern Spain. She has worked as a ghostwriter for crooks and minor celebrities, while also writing for in-flight magazines and Lonely Planet. She primarily covers Spain and Italy; other titles include *Mexico City, Australia, Portugal* and *Mediterranean Europe*.

Published by Lonely Planet Global Limited
CRN 554153
6th edition – Sept 2019
ISBN 978 1 78657 486 2
© Lonely Planet 2019   Photographs © as indicated 2019
10 9 8 7 6 5 4 3 2 1
Printed in Singapore